C000144451

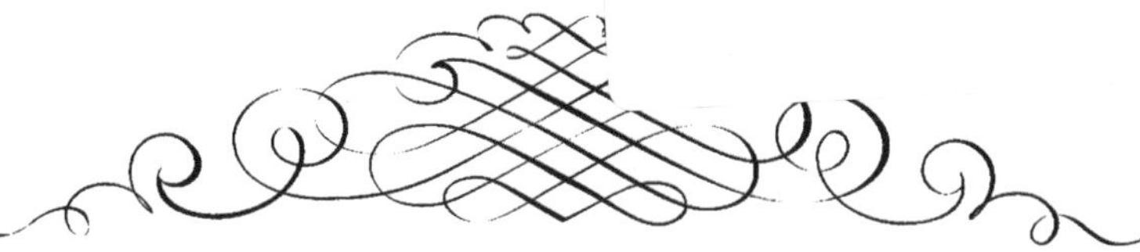

ISBN 978-1-5281-3174-2
PIBN 10925920

Loose Leaf

DIGEST OF SHORT BALLOT CHARTERS

A DOCUMENTARY HISTORY OF THE COMMISSION FORM OF MUNICIPAL GOVERNMENT

Edited by

CHARLES A. BEARD, Ph. D.

Associate Professor of Politics, in Columbia University

FIRST EDITION—FIVE HUNDRED COPIES

No.

Published by

THE SHORT BALLOT ORGANIZATION

383 Fourth Avenue, New York

Definition of

The "City Manager Plan"

Unification of Powers:

All corporate powers to be vested in a single group of elective officers, constituting a Council or Commission.

[The unification of powers is essential in order to avoid confusion of responsibility. There should be no other elected officers in the city government. Every power of the city should be possessed by the council. This makes it impossible for the council to lay the blame on any other officer if things go wrong. If there is no one who can hinder the council in its work the council is robbed of every possible excuse and is obliged to "face the music" in times of public criticism.

Unification of powers is a basic merit of the commission plan and must not be departed from in the city manager plan.]

The Short Ballot:

The Council to be elected in one of the following ways:

(a) at large (if the number of members to be chosen at any one time is five or less).

(b) by wards.

(c) by proportional representation.

[The need for the Short Ballot is based on the familiar psychological difficulty which the average voter will have in remembering more than a short list of candidates. Experience with non-partisan ballots and party primary elections has demonstrated that when the number of offices is five or less, each voter will pick out his own ticket to suit himself and thus express a genuine personal opinion with every mark of his pencil. On the other hand, if the number to be chosen exceeds five, the average voter will accept some ready made ticket devised for him by a civic club or a party machine, which has been promoted and advertised *en bloc*. The real selection and control of public officers then shifts from the voters to the makers of the tickets, who thus

representation, elect a board of four Republicans, two Democrats, two Progressives and one Socialist, each party securing the election of its favorite candidates in the order of their strength with their party voters, each party having just the proportion of members that it is entitled to.

The advantage of proportional representation is its fairness to all hands and the stability which it gives to the city government by preventing sharp changes in control due to mere fluctuating majorities. Proportional representation is impracticable in the commission plan, but the city manager plan which makes the council a representative body opens the way for it in America. It is a favorite proposal of the Socialists, who see that under this system they would poll their fullest strength without losing the support of those sympathizers who now hate to waste their vote on a party that now has no immediate chance of victory.]

3. *Executive Organization:*

Non-political executive functions delegated to an official appointed by the Commission to serve during their pleasure, to be known as the "City Manager" or by other appropriate title; position of city manager to be open to non-residents; salary of city manager to be determined by the Council and variable from time to time; the city manager's executive powers to include appointment and removal and general control of all subordinates, subject to such restrictions (*e.g.*, civil service regulation and audit) as may be necessary to prevent abuses of power without diffusing responsibility.

[The general advantages of creating the new office of city manager are treated at length elsewhere in this pamphlet.

The city manager must be strictly the servant of the council, with no independence. The council must have absolute control of him and not be able to say "it is the city manager's fault and we can't overrule him." The city manager must not have any fixed tenure or any protection against swift removal, save possibly the right to an explanation of the reasons for his discharge and an opportunity to present his defense.

While the manager will be expected to make all the subordinate appointments, there is no safe way of preventing the council from having and exercising an opinion regarding appointments. On the other hand, in the hope of keeping questions of patronage away from the council, it would be advisable not to require confirmation of appointments by the council, or in fact demand in the charter any specific action by the council in such matters. The feature of the Dayton plan which provides that the manager may be recalled by the people is of dubious value, since it interferes with the accountability of the council and gives opportunity for public hostility to be directed at the manager rather than at the elected board. The council should not be given this opportunity to let the manager be the scapegoat. Neither should the council be given this opportunity to justify their retention of an unsatisfactory manager by saying that the people must have approved this attitude, since they did not recall the manager.] *R. S. C.*

Table of Contents

Chapters on Commission Government

Outlines of Short Ballot Charters

Tabulations

Texts of Short Ballot Charters

(*In order of adoption.*)

Texts of Proposed Charters

Reports from Short Ballot Cities

Bibliography

Miscellaneous Documents

ERRATA.

Page 21303. In sixth line from bottom of page, second column, read "represented" instead of "elected." In lines 13 and 15, first column, read "principle" for "principal."

Page 21501. Last line, second column, read "rule 5" instead of "rule 6."

Page 34503, the words "*Commissioner-Departments*" should be followed by the words: (1) Fire, Police and Health, (2) Streets and Public Utilities, (3) Education, Finance and Revenue.

Page 35401. In the last line, the words in bold face type should be **"Bismarck, Mandan, Minot."**

Preface.

It was originally the hope of the editor that the Digest of Short Ballot Charters would be one of the first contributions to political science from a new bureau of research to be established by the Department of Politics in Columbia University. The deferring of the foundation of this bureau, however, made this for the time impossible. The Short Ballot Organization which had for a year been accumulating a mass of information regarding the operation of the Commission Plan of Government, deploring the prospect of a postponement of the work, voluntarily placed its facilities at the disposal of the editor and supplied the necessary funds and clerical force.

The work has proven unexpectedly laborious and complex. It deals entirely with living history, and the evidence must of necessity be based on the information of observers, who in many cases are not trained political scientists. The kaleidoscopic progress of the movement has necessitated the getting of evidence at first hand without the help of the compilations of earlier writers which usually eases the historian's burdens.

The Digest is presented to the public with the frank statement that it is not and never will be complete. We have already in mind a number of additions which we expect to make to it in the near future. We expect to allow critics of the present compilation to submit additional data, and we shall keep our columns open to contributions from those who disagree with our interpretations.

It is our belief and hope that this volume will grow in size and value year by year. The publisher has now a reasonably complete system of obtaining authoritative information. Current news is constantly being filed in a manner that will make it instantly available at any time in the future, and these files of information kept from day to day will soon become invaluable. It is intended to make the office a national clearing house for information on the subject and it is hoped that the Digest will accurately reflect the changes of the movement from year to year.

Neither the publisher nor the editor is pleading for the commission plan, or any feature of it, except to the extent outlined by the definition of "A Short Ballot Charter" on page 10,201. The purpose of the book is to present the cogent facts relating to the Commission Government movement, without undertaking to warp the judgment of students and readers in any direction.

The *List of Short Ballot Cities* will be kept as nearly up to date as the difficulties of securing accurate information will permit. Notice will be given from time to time of developments which are indirectly related to the Commission movement in the sense of our definition, under the title of *Quasi-Short Ballot Cities.* In the division entitled *Chapters on Commission Government,* we shall endeavor to cover as far as possible all the phases of the Commission plan, including the features thereof which are only incidentally related to the movement. The *Outlines of Short Ballot Charters* present the essentials of the structure of government established by legislation throughout the country. The *Tabulations* are intended to present the variations of structure in the several cities in a graphic way. In the *Texts of Short Ballot Charters* are included a number of the most significant and typical instruments. The division entitled *Texts of Proposed Charters* will help to indicate the directions in which the Commission movement is developing. The *Reports from Short Ballot Cities* constitute a department which we trust will develop in the future into a comprehensive and adequate statement of the operation of the Commission plan in the various localities. The *Bibliography* will be as nearly complete a list of published material on the subject of Commission Government as it is possible to make it. The fact that the book is in loose-leaf form, makes it possible to invite criticisms, suggestions, corrections and contributions at any time, inasmuch as they can be added to the publication as soon as available.

In the preparation of this volume we have been aided by many friends, and we take this opportunity publicly to extend our thanks to them for their interest and co-operation. In particular we acknowledge the contributions of the following men: Dr. Charles W. Eliot, President Emeritus of Harvard University; Robert Tyson, former Secretary of the Proportional Representation League; Elliot H. Goodwin, Secretary of the National Civil Service Reform League; John MacVicar, member of the Des Moines City Council, and Richard S. Childs, Secretary of The Short Ballot Organization. For the contributions which will be made in the future, we extend our appreciation herewith in advance.

CHARLES A. BEARD.

NEW YORK CITY, Feb. 5, 1911.

Definition of the term

"Short Ballot Charter"

The phrase "Commission Government" has, of course, been a misnomer ever since the Galveston Commission ceased to be appointive by the Governor and became elective. The word "commission" implies appointment, and in the strict sense of the word there have been no cities in the country "governed by Commission" except Washington, D. C. and Chelsea, Mass. The phrase, however, has been applied in the popular mind to all the new city charters that have been modelled on Galveston and Des Moines. These charters vary from almost exact copies through a twilight zone to charters that are essentially unlike the Galveston plan in all but name. One city changed the title of its Council to "Commission," and proceeded to call itself "Commission Governed" and is still included in most lists on that slender basis!

"Commission Plan" to the average American means a new plan of city government that seems to be bringing about a substantial and permanent reform in cities where it has been tried. There exists in the popular mind, however, no little confusion as to the precise nature of this new plan, and a variety of definitions are given. Nevertheless, when all incidental features are eliminated, the essential element which accounts for the success thus far achieved is simply this: conspicuous responsibility—and hence accountability-of all elected officials to the people.

Another way of expressing it is to say that a true Commission Plan is one whicq conforms to the Short Ballot principle which is defined by the Short Ballot Organization as follows:

First: That only those offices should be elective which are important enough to attract (and deserve) public examination.

Second: That very few offices should be filled by election at one time, so as to permit adequate and unconfused public examination of the candidates.

This excludes Boston for instance. Under its recent amended charter, Boston has only six names on the ballot, but all except the mayor are of insignificant authority and uninteresting character so that they are dangerously obscure. Waco, Texas, is likewise excluded, for although it has the "Commission" of five members, there are a number of obscure, independently-elected officials to get in their way. In neither city should complete popular control be expected to ensue.

Accordingly a Commission Governed City means to us one that has a "Short Ballot" according to the Short Ballot principle which results in popular supremacy with efficient government as a probable by-product—*Ed.*

List of Short Ballot Cities†

(Destrov previous lists)

Corrected to September 15, 1915

Population, over 100,000	Population, 25,000 to 100,000	Population, 10,000 to 25,000	Population, 2,500 to 10,000
	ALABAMA		
Birmingham, 1911.. 132,685	Mobile, 1911....... 51,521		Florence, 1914...... 6,689
	Montgomery, 1911.. 38,136		Huntsville, 1911.... 7,611
			Sheffield 4,865
			Talladega, 1911..... 5,854
			Tuscaloosa, 1911.... 8,407
	ARIZONA		
		★Phoenix, 1913..... 11,134	
	ARKANSAS		
		Fort Smith, 1913... 23,975	
	CALIFORNIA		
Oakland, 1910...... 150,174	Berkeley, 1909..... 40,434	★Bakersfield, 1915... 12,727	Modesto, 1910...... 7,258
	Pasadena, 1912..... 30,291	Santa Cruz, 1911... 11,146	Monterey, 1911..... 4,923
	Sacramento, 1911... 44,696	Stockton, 1911...... 23,256	Napa, 1915......... 5,791
	San Diego, 1909.... 39,578	Vallejo, 1911....... 11,340	San Luis Obispo, 1911 5,157
	★San Jose, 1915.... 28,946		San Mateo 4,384
			Santa Monica, 1915. 7,847
	COLORADO		
Denver, 1913....... 213,381	Colo. Springs, 1909.. 29,178		Colorado City, 1913. 4,333
			Durango, 1912...... 4,686
			Fort Collins, 1913.. 8,210
			Grand Junction, 1909 7,754
			★Montrose, 1914.... 3,252
	FLORIDA		
	Pensacola, 1913..... 22,982		★Lakeland, 1914.... 3,719
			Orlando, 1913...... 3,894
			★St. Augustine, 1915 5,495
			St. Petersburg, 1913 4,127
	GEORGIA		
			Cartersville, 1911... 4,067
	IDAHO		
		Boise, 1912......... 17,358	Lewiston, 1909...... 6,043
	ILLINOIS		
	Bloomington, 1914.. 25,768	Cairo, 1913......... 14,548	Carbondale, 1911.... 5,411
	Decatur, 1911...... 31,140	Jacksonville, 1911.. 15,326	Clinton, 1911....... 5,165
	Elgin, 1911......... 25,976	Lincoln, 1915....... 10,892	Coal City, 1915..... 2,667
	Joliet, 1915........ 34,670	Moline, 1911....... 24,199	Dixon, 1911........ 7,216
	Springfield, 1911.... 51,617	Ottawa, 1911....... 11,121	Effingham, 1915.... 3,898
		Rock Island, 1911.. 24,335	Flora, 1914......... 2,704
		Waukegon, 1911.... 16,069	Forest Park, 1911... 6,594
			Highland Park, 1915 4,209
			Harvey, 1912....... 7,227
			Harrisburg, 1913.... 5,309
			Hillsboro, 1911..... 3,424
			Kewanee, 1911..... 9,307
			Marseilles, 1913..... 3,291
			Murphysboro, 1913.. 7,485
			Pekin, 1911....... 9,897
			Princeton, 1915..... 4,131
			Rochelle, 1911...... 2,732
			Spring Valley, 1911. 7,035
			Sterling, 1915...... 7,467

† The numerals after the name of the city (e. g., 1911) indicate the year in which plan was adopted.
★ City Manager Form.

10301

Population, over 100,000	Population, 25,000 to 100,000	Population, 10,000 to 25,000	Population, 2,500 to 10,000
		IOWA	
	Burlington, 1909.... 34,324	Fort Dodge, 1910... 15,543	★Webster City, 1915. 5,208
	Cedar Rapids, 1907. 33,811	Keokuk, 1910...... 14,008	
	Des Moines, 1907... 86,368	Marshalltown, 1910. 13,374	
	Sioux City, 1910.... 47,828	Mason City, 1913... 11,230	
		Ottumwa, 1913..... 22,012	
		KANSAS	
	Kansas City, 1909... 82,331	Coffeyville, 1909.... 12,687	Abilene, 1910....... 4,118
	Topeka, 1909....... 43,684	Fort Scott, 1914.... 10,463	Anthony, 1909...... 2,669
	Wichita, 1909...... 42,450	Hutchinson, 1909... 16,364	Arkansas City, 1912. 7,508
		Independence, 1908. 10,480	Caldwell, 1911...... 2,205
		Lawrence, 1913..... 12,374	Chanute, 1911...... 9,272
		Leavenworth, 1908.. 19,363	Cherryvale, 1910.... 4,304
		Parsons, 1909...... 12,463	Council Grove, 1911. 2,545
		Pittsburgh, 1910.... 14,755	Dodge City, 1910... 3,214
			Emporia, 1910...... 9,058
			Eureka, 1911....... 2,333
			Garden City, 1913.. 3,171
			Garnett, 1913....... 2,334
			Girard, 1911....... 2,446
			Great Bend, 1912... 4,622
			Hiawatha, 1913..... 2,974
			Holton, 1912....... 2,842
			Iola, 1910.......... 9,032
			Junction City, 1912. 5,598
			Kingman, 1912..... 2,570
			Manhattan, 1911.... 2,872
			McPherson, 1914.... 3,546
			Neodesha, 1910...... 2,872
			Newton, 1910....... 7,862
			Olathe, 1912....... 3,272
			Ossawatomie, 1914.. 4,046
			Ottawa, 1913....... 7,650
			Pratt, 1911......... 3,302
			Wellington, 1910.... 7,034
		KENTUCKY	
	Covington, 1912..... 53,270	Paducah, 1914...... 22,760	Harrodsburg, 1915.. 3,147
	Lexington, 1911..... 34,099		Hopkinsville, 1915.. 9,419
	Newport, 1910...... 30,309		Middlesboro, 1915... 7,306
		LOUISIANA	
†New Orleans, 1912. 339,075	Shreveport, 1910.... 28,015	Alexandria, 1913.... 11,213	Donaldsville, 1913.. 4,090
		Baton Rogue, 1913.. 14,897	Natchitoches, 1913.. 2,532
		Lake Charles, 1913.. 11,449	Hammond, 1913.... 2,942
			Jennings, 1913...... 3,925
			La Fayette, 1914.... 6,392
			New Iberia, 1912... 7,499
		MAINE	
			Gardiner, 1911...... 5,311
		MARYLAND	
		Cumberland, 1910... 21,839	
		MASSACHUSETTS	
Lowell, 1911........ 106,294	Haverhill, 1908..... 44,115	Gloucester, 1908.... 24,398	
	Lawrence, 1911..... 85,892		
	Lynn, 1910......... 89,336		
	Salem, 1912........ 43,697		
	Taunton, 1909...... 34,259		

★ City Manager Form.

†The ballot contains the names of a variety of state and county officers to be voted for along with the candidates for commissioners of the city.

Population, over 100,000		Population, 25,000 to 100,000		Population, 10,000 to 25,000		Population, 2,500 to 10,000	
MICHIGAN							
		Battle Creek, 1913..	25,267	Adrian, 1914.......	10,763	★Cadillac, 1914.....	8,375
		★Jackson, 1914.....	31,433	★Manistee, 1914.....	12,381	Eaton Rapids, 1915.	2,094
		Saginaw, 1914......	50,510	Marquette, 1914....	11,503	Fremont, 1912......	2,009
				Pontiac, 1914.......	14,532	Grand Haven, 1915.	5,856
				Port Huron, 1910...	18,863	Monroe, 1914.......	6,893
				Traverse City, 1913.	12,115	Owosso, 1914.......	9,639
MISSISSIPPI							
				Hattiesburg, 1910...	11,733	Clarksdale, 1910....	4,079
				Jackson, 1912......	21,262	Greenwood, 1914....	5,836
				Meridian, 1912.....	23,285	Gulfport, 1911......	6,386
				Vicksburg, 1912....	20,814	Laurel, 1911........	8,465
MINNESOTA							
St. Paul, 1912......	214,744	Duluth, 1913.......	78,466	Faribault, 1911.....	19,001	Eveleth, 1913.......	7,036
				Mankato, 1910......	10,365		
MISSOURI							
		Joplin, 1913........	32,073			Aurora, 1915.......	4,148
						Kirksville, 1914.....	6,347
						Monette, 1914......	4,177
						West Plains, 1914...	2,914
MONTANA							
				Helena, 1915.......	12,515		
				Missoula, 1911......	12,869		
NEBRASKA							
Omaha, 1911.......	151,388	Lincoln, 1912.......	43,973			Beatrice, 1911......	9,356
						Nebraska City, 1912.	5,488
NEW JERSEY							
Jersey City, 1913...	267,779	Atlantic City, 1912..	46,150	Asbury Park, 1915..	10,150	Beverly, 1913.......	2,140
		Bayonne, 1915......	55,545	New Brunswick, 1915	23,388	Bordentown, 1913...	4,250
		Hoboken, 1915......	70,324	Phillipsburg, 1914..	13,903	Haddonfield	4,142
		Orange, 1914.......	26,630	Irvington, 1914.....	11,877	Hawthorne	3,400
		Passaic, 1911.......	54,773	Long Branch, 1912..	13,298	Nutley, 1912........	6,009
		Trenton, 1911......	96,815	Millville, 1913......	12,541	Ridgewood, 1912...	5,416
						Vineland, 1913......	5,282
						Wallington, 1913....	3,448
NEW YORK							
Buffalo, 1914.......	423,715	★Newburgh, 1915...	27,805	Beacon, 1913.......	10,629	Mechanicville, 1915..	6,634
		★Niagara Falls, 1914	30,445	Saratoga Spgs., 1915	12,693		
NORTH CAROLINA							
		Wilmington, 1911...	25,748	Asheville, 1915.....	18,762	★Elizabeth City, 1915	8,412
				Greensboro, 1911...	15,895	★Hickory, 1913.....	3,716
				Raleigh, 1913.......	19,218	High Point, 1909....	9,529
						★Morganton, 1913...	2,712
NEW MEXICO							
						Las Vegas, 1913....	3,719

★ City Manager Form.

Population, over 100,000	Population, 25,000 to 100,000	Population, 10,000 to 25,000	Population, 2,500 to 10,000
	NORTH DAKOTA		
		Fargo, 1913........ 14,331	Bismark, 1909...... 5,443
			Devil's Lake, 1912.. 5,157
			Mandan, 1907...... 3,873
			Minot, 1909........ 6,188
			Williston, 1913..... 3,124
	OHIO		
★Dayton, 1913...... 116,577	★Springfield, 1913... 46,921	★Ashtabula, 1914... 18,266	
		Middletown, 1913... 13,152	
		★Sandusky, 1914.... 19,989	
	OKLAHOMA		
	Muskogee, 1910..... 25,278	Enid, 1909......... 13,799	Ada, 1912.......... 4,309
	Oklahoma City, 1911 64,205	Guthrie, 1911....... 11,654	Ardmore, 1908...... 8,618
		MacAlester, 1910.... 12,954	Bartlesville, 1910... 6,181
		Tulsa, 1908........ 18,182	Duncan, 1911....... 2,477
			El Reno, 1911...... 7,872
			Lawton, 1911....... 7,788
			Miami, 1910........ 2,907
			Okmulgee, 1912..... 4,176
			Purcell, 1910....... 2,740
			Sapulpa, 1910...... 8,283
			Wagoner, 1910...... 4,018
			Weatherford, 1914.. 2,118
	OREGON		
Portland, 1913...... 207,214			Baker, 1910........ 6,680
			★La Grande 4,843
	PENNSYLVANIA		
	Allentown, 1913.... 51,913	Beaver Falls, 1913.. 12,191	Corry, 1913......... 5,991
	Altoona, 1913....... 52,127	Bradford, 1913..... 14,454	Franklin, 1913...... 9,767
	Chester, 1913....... 31,537	Carbondale, 1913... 17,040	Lock Haven, 1914.. 7,772
	Easton, 1913....... 28,532	Connellsville, 1914... 12,845	Titusville, 1913..... 8,533
	Erie, 1913.......... 66,525	Lebanon, 1913...... 19,240	
	Harrisburg, 1913.... 64,186	Meadville, 1913..... 12,780	
	Hazleton, 1913...... 25,452	Oil City, 1913...... 15,657	
	Johnstown, 1913.... 55,482	Pittston, 1913....... 16,267	
	McKeesport, 1913... 42,604	Pottsville, 1914..... 20,236	
	New Castle, 1913... 36,280	S. Bethlehem, 1913.. 19,973	
	Reading, 1913...... 96,071		
	Wilkes Barre, 1913. 67,105		
	Williamsport, 1913.. 31,860		
	York, 1913......... 44,750		
	SOUTH CAROLINA		
	Columbia, 1910..... 26,311	Spartanburg, 1913.. 17,517	Florence, 1912...... 7,057
			Orangeburg, 1913... 5,906
			★Sumter, 1912...... 8,109
	SOUTH DAKOTA		
		Aberdeen, 1911..... 10,753	Canton, 1911....... 2,103
		Sioux Falls, 1908.... 14,094	Huron, 1910........ 5,791
			Lead, 1911......... 8,392
			Madison, 1912...... 3,137
			Pierre, 1910........ 3,656
			Rapid City, 1910.... 3,854
			Vermillion, 1911.... 2,187
			Watertown, 1912.... 7,010
			Yankton, 1910...... 3,787

★ City Manager Form.

Population, over 100,000		Population, 25,000 to 100,000		Population, 10,000 to 25,000		Population, 2,500 to 10,000	
		TENNESSEE					
Memphis, 1909	131,105	Chattanooga, 1911	44,604	Jackson, 1915	15,779	Bristol, 1913	7,148
Nashville, 1913	110,364	Knoxville, 1911	36,346			Lebanon, 1912	3,659
						La Follette, 1914	2,816
						Murfreesboro, 1914	4,679
						Springfield, 1913	2,085
		TEXAS					
		Austin, 1909	29,860	Denison, 1907	15,632	★Amarillo, 1913	9,957
		Dallas, 1907	92,104	Marshall, 1909	11,452	Coleman, 1914	3,046
		Fort Worth, 1907	73,302	Palestine, 1909	10,297	Corpus Christi, 1909	8,222
		Galveston, 1901	36,981	★San Angelo, 1915	10,321	★Denton, 1914	4,732
		Houston, 1905	78,800	★Sherman, 1915	12,412	Greenville, 1907	8,850
		San Antonio, 1914	96,614			McKinney, 1913	4,714
						Port Arthur, 1911	7,663
						★Taylor, 1914	5,314
						★Tyler, 1915	10,400
		UTAH					
		Salt Lake City, 1911	92,777			Logan, 1911	7,522
		Ogden, 1911	25,580			Murray, 1911	4,057
						Provo, 1911	8,929
		WASHINGTON					
Spokane, 1910	104,402	Tacoma, 1909	83,743	Everett, 1912	24,814	Centralia, 1911	7,311
				North Yakima, 1911	14,082	Chehalis, 1911	4,507
				Walla Walla, 1911	19,364	Hoquiam, 1911	8,171
		WEST VIRGINIA					
		Huntington	31,161	Bluefield	11,188	Fairmount, 1913	9,711
		★Wheeling, 1915	41,614	Parkersburg, 1911	17,842	Grafton, 1913	7,563
		WISCONSIN					
		Oshkosh, 1911	33,062	Appleton, 1911	16,773	Antigo, 1914	7,196
		Superior, 1911	40,384	Ashland, 1913	11,594	Ladysmith, 1913	2,352
				Eau Claire, 1909	18,310	Menominee, 1911	5,036
				Fond du Lac, 1914	18,797	Portage, 1911	5,440
				Janesville, 1911	13,894	Rice Lake, 1911	3,968
		WYOMING					
				Cheyenne, 1913	11,320	Sheridan, 1911	8,408

The following is an incomplete list of cities, towns and villages under the commission form, having a population of less than 2,000 (1910 census):

ALABAMA: Cordova, 1,747; Hartselle, 1,374. FLORIDA: Passe-a-Grille. ILLINOIS: Hamilton, 1,627. KANSAS: Marion, 1,841. MICHIGAN: Harbor Beach, 1,556; Fremont. NEW JERSEY: Deal Borough, 273; Margate City, 129; Wildwood, 898. OHIO: ★Westerville, 1,903. OKLAHOMA: Holdenville. SOUTH DAKOTA: Chamberlain, 1,275; Dell Rapids, 1,637. TEXAS: Aransas Pass, 1,197; Kennedy, 1,147; Marble Falls, 1,061; Nixon; Port Lavaca, 1,699; Robstown WISÇONSIN: Ladysmith.

★ City Manager Form.

Quasi-Short Ballot Cities

(Replacing page of original edition.)

The cities in the following list have been more or less frequently reported as belonging to the group of so-called "Commission Governed Cities." An examination of their charters, however, reveals a lack of one or more elements which this publication lays down as the essentials of the Short Ballot Form of City Government in the Definition given herein.

WACO, TEX.

In addition to the City Council, there are several elective officers. The Council apparently has no adequate control over the administrative functions of the City. The Charter provides for the Initiative, Referendum and Recall.

EL PASO, TEX.

The municipal government consists of a Mayor and four aldermen and the following elective officers: Judge of the Corporation Court, Treasurer, City Assessor and Collector of Taxes.

The selection of appointive City officers is divided between the Mayor and the City Council, the former selecting the Chief of Police, Clerk of the CorporationCourt, City Physician, members of the Board of Health and other specially designated agents of the City. The City Attorney and City Clerk are elected by the City Council. The Mayor has the veto power over the ordinances of the Council.

BOSTON, MASS.

The government of Boston consists of a Mayor and a City Council of nine members elected at large. The term of the Mayor is four years, subject to recall after two years. The members of the City Council hold office for three years. Three members of the City Council are elected annually. There is also a school committee of five members, elected at large. There is no primary election and the ballots are non-partisan. Names are placed upon the election ballot by petition bearing 5,000 names. The Mayor may make recommendations in the form of ordinances or loan orders, except in matters relating to schools, which the Council must either adopt or reject in ten days after their filing. If not rejected, the ordinance or loan order goes into effect, unless previously withdrawn by the Mayor. The Council may originate ordinances or loan orders and may reduce or reject items in any loan, and, subject to the approval of the Mayor, may amend an ordinance.

All appropriations for current expenses must originate with the Mayor who must submit an annual budget, items of which the Common Council may reduce, but may not increase. The heads of departments submit estimates of necessary expenditures to the Mayor.

The Mayor and Council may reorganize the administrative departments, but the appointing power is in the hands of the Mayor, without the confirmation of the Council. The Mayor approves contracts. He is required to attend meetings of the Council.

The Finance Commission is appointed by the Governor of the State with the advice and consent of the Council. It is their duty to investigate appropriations, loans, expenditures and accounts and the methods of administration.

The Charter thus provides for a system of checks and balances which materially reduces the power of the Council.

CHELSEA, MASS.

Under an emergency measure of 1908, the Governor, with the advice and consent of the Council, was authorized to appoint a commission of five persons to be known as the Chelsea Board of Control. In like manner the Governor fixed the compensation of the commissioners, which was paid by the city. He could remove any commissioner and fill vacancies in the commission. At the state elections held in 1909 and 1910, successors to these commissioners were nominated and elected by direct vote in the manner prescribed for the election and nomination of the Mayor of the city. Upon the appointment of the Board of Control, the Mayor, aldermen and members of the school committee under the old law, ceased to hold office, and their powers were devolved upon the new board, which is authorized to establish departments and appoint officers and to give them such powers and duties as it should deem proper. They were especially authorized to appoint a school committee to hold until November, 1911, at which time members of the school committee will be elected by the people.

The Legislature of 1911 passed an act whereby were submitted to the people in November, 1911, two options. One was a commission plan charter; the other provided for a modified Boston plan. The latter was adopted.

PUEBLO, COLO.

This city adopted a charter in 1911 embodying most of the features of the commission plan, but providing for an elective Civil Service Commission, thus departing from the principle laid down in the definition given in this volume of a Short Ballot Charter.

ST. CLOUD, MINN.

A charter was adopted here in 1912, in some respects like the commission plan. In addition to the council, however, there are three "commissioners" charged with administrative duties. Constitutional difficulties are said to be responsible for this peculiar form.

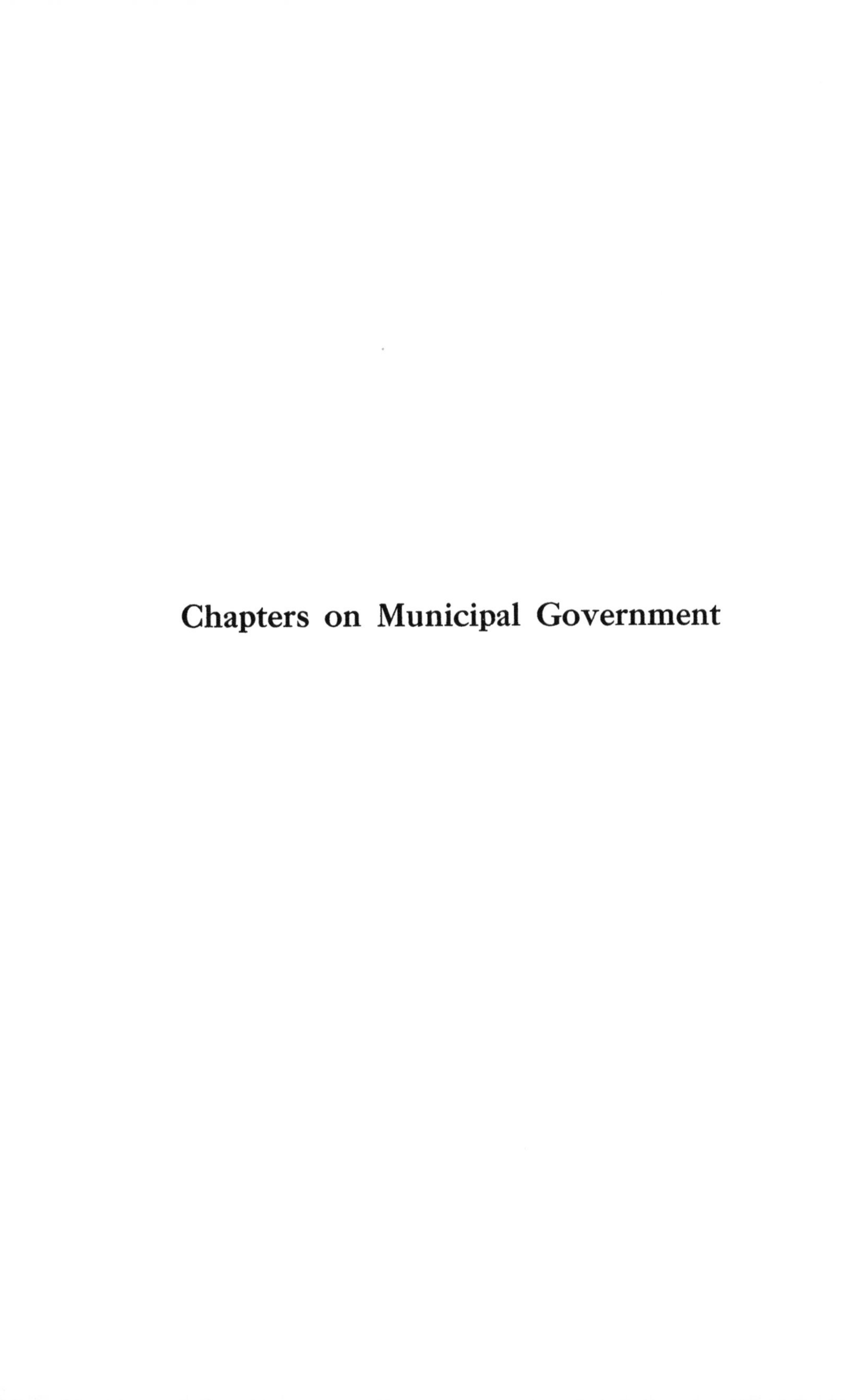

Chapters on Municipal Government

Introduction

Better Municipal Government.*

By Charles W. Eliot, President Emeritus of Harvard University.

The subject of better municipal government is attracting a great deal of attention in all parts of the country. This new interest seems to have started from the great disaster which overtook the city of Galveston in 1900, when a fearful storm drove a series of great waves over the low island and destroyed about three-fifths of the city. Nearly 7,000 people were killed, and immediately as many more fled from the city and did not return. The city had about 30,000 inhabitants when the storm came, and you readily see what a small number of people remained, a considerable proportion of them being colored people. Now Galveston had an old fashioned city government with two chambers and a mayor elected by the people; and this government had been both inefficient and dishonest, so that the credit of Galveston had been completely destroyed before the storm struck the island. Galveston, before that disaster, was unable to borrow a dollar. It had no credit. Under these circumstances, three Galveston lawyers agreed that they would meet in the house of one of them, which had not been severely damaged, every evening, after a hard day spent in relief work, to devise if possible a new government for the crippled city. They met for two months in that way, and in that short time those three men devised a new charter for Galveston, abandoning completely the former form of government, and really making an original invention. One of them told me how little guidance they had. They procured from Boston the amended charter which was then about fifteen years old; they got some information about the evil condition of things in New York; they learned how the school committee of St. Louis had been reorganized successfully, being greatly reduced in number, made independent of the city council as regards its resources, and composed of twelve citizens elected at large—three at a time—to serve four years. That was about all the guidance they had. They were of the opinion that it would be impossible to redeem Galveston under the old form of government and that it was indispensable to get a much simpler form, and one that would offer to the votes of the people only a small number of elective officers. Having elaborated their charter, they went, practically alone, to the legislature of Texas, and got their bill introduced. Having got the bill referred to a committee, they then brought from Galveston a considerable number of citizens to urge the adoption of the new statute by the legislature. The result was promptly reached, and the act passed by heavy majorities in both branches of the legislature.

Now, that is the start of what is called commission government in this country. It arose in consequence of a catastrophe. It was devised for a small city with a population not much exceeding 30,000. It was carried with very little opposition through a southern legislature, sympathizing profoundly with the sufferings of the stricken city.

What were the fundamental ideas in this charter? In the first place, these lawyers had a considerable distrust of the capacity of universal suffrage in Galveston to elect wisely any large number of city officials. It had been the custom to elect various city officers besides the members of the two boards, the aldermen and the councilmen. These men said: "Our voting body, almost exclusively composed of whites though it is, is incompetent to select wisely the men who are to have charge of the actual departmental work of our city, and to carry to successful completion great public works." In the next place, they wanted to simplify to the utmost the structure of the city government—they would have no two chambers, no separate mayor, and no elective officers at all except the one commission of five. Those were their fundamental ideas, and these ideas have traveled over this country with extraordinary speed. Diminution in the number of officers to be elected —that is a primary consideration in all municipal re-

* An address before the Good Government Club of Williams College, December 17, 1909. Reprinted by permission.

form. Did you ever see the ballot used in the last election in the city of New York? It was four feet long, and had upon it an extraordinary number of names for an extraordinary number of offices. No voter can make any intelligent use of such a ballot as that. A long ballot of that description, offered to a voter who is asked to elect a dozen, twenty, even thirty officers, is the main support of the machine and the boss. Such ballots almost necessitate the boss and the machine. The voter cannot discriminate among this mass of candidates. At the last election in this Commonwealth I was wholly unable to cast a discriminating vote, although the Massachusetts ballot is by no means so bad as that of New York. What I did was to vote for all the persons who had been suggested by the Republican machine—I who in general call myself a Democrat.

Now it is not an exaggeration to say that a long ballot of that nature is what has given power to the machine and the boss in our country. Such a ballot must be cut and dried beforehand; and primary or preliminary party elections, I regret to say, only shift to a previous election the determination of the candidates by the boss and the machine. We have not yet devised in our country a wholly satisfactory method of selecting candidates; but the nearest approach to a good method that I have seen is the method by petition, followed by a preliminary non-partisan election which several of the commission governments have adopted—or rather, I should say, ments have embodied. Boston is trying an interesting experiment on that nomination by petition. It is clearly not a perfect success in a large city, but equally clearly it is an improvement on nominations by party conventions or party primaries.

The Galveston Charter, then, led off in reducing to five the number of persons to be elected. Des Moines has followed suit—or rather I should say Iowa has followed suit; because Iowa has adopted a general law applicable to any city having at least 25,000 inhabitants, under which a commission form of government may be established by popular vote, and the commission is to consist of five persons. Boston is to have a short ballot. When the new charter gets to work, there will ordinarily be three members of a council of nine, and either one or two members of the school committee, to be elected each year, and then once in four years a mayor will be elected. The ordinary ballot would be for four or five men, but once in four years there will be a fifth or sixth man, the mayor, and the mayor's tenure will be one year longer than the tenure of the others. The Boston charter is in many respects a new departure—of course it remains to be seen whether it is a wise departure—but it has the merit, at any rate, of setting before the citizens of Boston each year—not in the initial year—a very short ballot. I cannot but think that this short ballot is the most important feature in all the municipal reforms which have been attempted in our country during the last ten years. The short ballot offers to the voter a chance to exercise a discriminating choice. That is, of course, what the voter ought to do. Now our voters in the cities, the large cities particularly, have not had that chance for many a long year.

Another thing those Galveston inventors did—they made the mayor just a slightly superior member of the commission of five. He was to have the direction of the most important departments of the city and he was to represent the city on public occasions. When Galveston was to have a spokesman, it was the mayor who was to speak. But he was only slightly elevated above his comrades of the commission. Boston has gravely departed in its new charter from this feature of the Galveston charter; great power is given to the mayor, and but little to the council.

In the numerous discussions in which I have taken part in public and in private on this general subject, I have heard it said by experienced politicians, and by theorists too, and by good and independent observers of public affairs, that the question underlying all municipal reform is the very serious question:—can universal suffrage contrive an intelligent and honest municipal government and put it in power? The question has often been put as if it were universal suffrage that were on trial—not the officials elected to serve a city, but universal suffrage itself. Can a democracy elect, by popular vote, an intelligent and honest set of officials to conduct the business of a large city? I have heard very experienced politicians openly declare that they believed that it was impossible under universal suffrage. My answer has always been that universal suffrage has never had the chance to try. We know from the history of New England, that the town meeting, a pure democracy, did succeed in electing once a year three men to whom the conduct of the entire business of the town was thereupon committed. It used to be very unusual to have more than one town meeting in a year. See what a short ballot that was—only three men to be chosen, and the whole business of the town committed to those three men for a year. Of late years we now and then find that a fourth officer is elected, a treasurer, or a treasurer and collector of taxes. There are good precedents for that; but even then the voters were called upon to choose only four men. As the town business has increased in complexity and in scientific quality some towns have found it necessary to elect still another agent. They have elected an officer who is often called a road commissioner. A road commissioner would make a fifth man to be elected at a town meeting.

It is noticeable that town government in New England is not so sound and effective today as it was sixty years ago. The reason for this decline is that town business now includes some matters which can only be sensibly conducted by experts, by men who know a good deal about applied science. For instance, the New England towns do not always succeed in electing a competent road commissioner. A road commissioner in these days needs to possess a good deal of knowledge as to the materials for road building, as to the best shape of roads, and as to the means of preventing rushing waters from destroying roads. The road commissioner has to know enough to make permanent inprovements in the roads instead of just making temporary repairs for a single season. Now the democracy of a town meeting has trouble in selecting that kind of a man.

The recent changes in the nature of city business go far to explain the failure of the American democracy to provide capable and honest city government. The business of a modern city is almost all new in kind. I have personally seen during my lifetime the coming in of everything which we now regard as proper city business. There is hardly a single department of city business today which existed at all when I was a boy in Boston. Indeed, there is nothing now done by the city of Boston which was done in the same way, or in any approach to the same way, when I was a boy in that old town. In its early days Boston was as well managed as any American city, and it had a series of highly respected and competent citizens at the head of its government. One cannot say that of Boston now. What cities need now is to apply to public work science of all sorts—chemistry, physics, medicine, bacteriology, and engineering. Fifty years ago there was no such need and no such knowledge. For example, when I was a boy in Boston, there was no public water supply—none whatever—there was no sewer in the entire town, and no pavement except a cobble-stone pavement in a few streets, a rough pavement made of rounded beach stones. There were no lights to speak of in the city streets,—only a few widely scattered whale oil lamps. There wasn't such a thing in the world as a street railway—therefore no question about granting franchises for street railways. No use of electricity was known—no electric lights, no electric transmission of power, no telephone and hardly any telegraphic communication. Consider how absolutely different the business of a city was then from what it is now. Water works, gas and electric light works, paved streets, clean streets, sewers, garbage removal, preventive medicine, and schools carefully organized, well heated and lighted, thoroughly equipped, and inspected by medical officers—all these things we regard as everyday work for a city. None of these things existed sixty years ago. I have seen pigs running freely through the streets of Albany, the capital of a great state, the only scavengers known to the city.

Now, it is this newness of a city's business, and this absolute necessity for experts to superintend all this business—an expert for each department indeed—which makes so difficult the work of municipal reform. It is this same newness combined with the too common secrecy of city administration which has given opportunity for vicious men to rob cities, to rob the whole people of a city.

Let us next consider the way out from this mortifying condition of things. The first remedy is a short ballot—very few agents to be elected by popular vote. It is impossible for the popular vote to select from many candidates the right man, the best man, to be chief engineer of a city. It is impossible for popular suffrage to select from a dozen candidates the best health officer. It is impossible for popular suffrage to elect the right superintendent of schools, although in that selection the people will take more interest than in the selection of any other city officer. That stronger interest has been repeatedly demonstrated in our country. Propose to the city voters a task which is possible for them, not a task which is manifestly impossible. If then universal suffrage does not succeed, it will be time to consider other measures. When, therefore, I hear the politicians say that universal suffrage cannot provide an honest and intelligent government for a city, I venture to postpone in my own mind the discussion of that question. Let us first see what universal suffrage can do when it has a fair chance.

Government by commission has now been in operation some years in cities of widely different character, and situated in different parts of our country. There are eight Texan cities which have tried it, including Burlington, which has just voted to have a charter of this sort. There are six Massachusetts cities which have obtained commission charters, one of these charters, to be sure, being like that of Galveston, a catastrophe charter. The city of Chelsea in Massachusetts lost a large part of its real estate valuation in a great fire which swept a large fraction of its total territory. Thereupon the legislature upon the petition of some of its citizens provided a commission government of five members, appointed by the governor,—with this provision, however, that one of these appointed commissioners should retire each year, his place to be filled by a member elected for five years. Therefore this catastrophe government will in time become an elective commission of five members.

I am often asked what is the best way to study the commission form of government. I always answer now:—get the annual reports of some of the commission governments, selecting two from Texas, for example, one from Iowa, and two from Massachusetts, and see what has been accomplished. Every commission government illustrates the advantages of the short ballot.

There are two or three directions in which we may make very instructive inquiries as to these experiments in municipal reform. One direction is the financial result to the experimenting cities. I lately sat two hours with the commission which had been governing Houston for two years, and was just about to encounter another election. Our conversation turned chiefly on the financial results of commission government. The mayor of Houston had driven me over many miles of new streets which the commission government had laid out in the outskirts of Houston, making ready for the building of houses along these streets. There were many miles of these new streets—the roadways well formed and well surfaced, the curbstones set, the sewers and gas pipes put in, the lamp posts set—everything ready. He astonished me very much by telling me that all that had been done (and it was a very extensive work) out of the receipts of the year,—not by the issue of bonds, but out of the taxes of the year. We passed on that drive four large new brick schoolhouses. I asked how those schoolhouses were paid for;—"Out of the receipts of the year; no bonds issued." In the meeting with the commission later I pursued this subject, and inquired first what the assessment was on the abutters on all those new streets. What did they pay or contribute towards the cost of those new streets? "Nothing." "Didn't you require anything of the abutters?" "Yes, when a house was built on the lot of an abutter, we required him to build a granolithic sidewalk along his premises." This was the only requirement made of the abutters. I never heard before of any such transaction as that in any American city. In meeting with the commission I asked:—"To build those four large brick schoolhouses in one year did you raise the valuation of property in Houston?" "Not at all." "Did you raise the tax rate in Houston?" "No, we lowered it a little." "How then did you get the money for these very large public expenditures without borrowing anything, and without taxing anybody any more—not even the abutters on the new streets?" They looked at each other and smiled; and finally one of them said that he thought the explanation was that the commission had secured for the city a dollar's worth of work or materials for a dollar. That seemed a desirable business result; but still I did not see clearly how these extraordinary expenditures had been met. On pursuing the subject a little farther, one of the commissioners said: "We think that our predecessors did not get more than fifty cents' worth of work for a dollar." That meant, you see, that well-nigh half the entire income of the city under the former administration was available for the commisison government towards new expenditures; towards new welfare work for the community in general. Now, in some degree, I think, that has been the result in all the cities governed by commission. They have succeeded in getting for the city some approach to a dollar's worth of work for a dollar paid. That is the line of inquiry which I hope all you gentlemen who are interested in this subject will follow up; because if that sort of result turns out to be obtainable, not in the first two years only of a particular commission government, but in general and in the long run, you will find just there the demonstration of the success of the commission form of government. It is notorious that the American city in general does not get a dollar's worth of work for a dollar. It is notorious that employment by the city is regarded by many politicians, first, as charitable aid for infirm and incapable people, and, secondly, as affording the means of paying off political obligations. The procuring of a day's work for a day's pay from the city employee is the last thing the low politician thinks of. I have read many of the reports of the commission governments, and I have never failed to find that they have been measurably successful in this very direction. You see how important that sort of success is. There is no more demoralizing schooling for adults in our country than employment under city governments, when those governments are administered by incapable or dishonest people. Very much the larger part of the losses and corruptions in American cities in the last fifty years has been due not so much to actual dishonesty as to inefficiency and neglect of duty on the part of careless citizens who have acted on a false theory of what municipal government should be.

The next question which arises with regard to the success of the commission-form of government is this:—Are American citizens of the right sort willing to serve in a government by commission? Are they willing to be members of a commission of five, with only a slight superiority for the mayor? Are they willing to work in and for such a group,—for the success of the group will be the thing they have to seek, not the success of any individual in the group? We already have got some light on that question. Until this very year only one change had been made in the commission of Galveston, and that change was caused by the death of the first mayor. The citizens were obliged to elect another mayor. I understand that there have been two changes in the commission at an election which occurred this year, and that the commission has not been impaired in value by these changes. That is an unheard of continuity in city offices. I find in all the commission governments which I have thus far personally examined, that good American citizens have proved to be willing to take office, and to hold it continuously when the public so willed. Most of these commissions are paid, but the salaries are low, much less than any man competent for the work would earn in his own business. It already appears distinctly from the experience of more than a dozen American cities that public-spirited citizens, who are competent business or professional men, will serve their cities under the commission form.

Now, under the new charter of Boston we are having trouble at this moment in the very first election on just this point. The new charter provides for a very powerful mayor who is to hold office for four years. He is, some people would say, encumbered, others would say, supported by a council of nine with very moderate, not to say slender powers, serving each one year less than the mayor serves. It has been difficult in this very election, notwithstanding the gravity of the situation, to get the kind of man that is needed to stand for the council. Indeed, it has proved impossible with the utmost exertion to induce really leading business men of the largest experience to agree to serve on this new council, although it has but nine members, and although the regular term of service is three years. What is the cause of this difficulty? Too much power in the mayor's hands, and too little in the council's to make it probable, in the view of the competent business man, that as a member of the council he shall have a real opportunity to serve his city greatly. My conviction is, and I have often expressed it, that what the right kind of American citizen needs in order to feel encouraged to put all his intelligence, experience, and uprightness at the service of the community in which he lives—that what he needs is to see that he has a fair chance of rendering some considerable public service. Commission government gives that chance to five men; because it is manifest that every member of one of these commissions is going to have a fair chance to serve liberally and largely the community in which he dwells.

A related question which all men should study who are interested in municipal reform is this:—Is it a fact that these commissions, so far, have been well-manned? I believe it to be a fact that they have been well-manned; but we must have a liberal definition of well-manned. At the very first election in Des Moines under the new charter the leaders who had induced Des Moines to adopt the commission form of government prepared a "slate" of five candidates. Now these men all belonged to the class known in that region as "silk-stockings;" and when it came to the election those five men were defeated. I was looking anxiously at the result of this first election under the commission form of government and I felt it necessary at once to inquire carefully what the five successful candidates represented. I found not one of them could be correctly described as a "silk-stocking." Nevertheless when I had had the advantage of talking with them and of hearing three of them state what their purposes were, what they thought of the new charter, and how they meant to use it, I became entirely satisfied that the voters had not made a mistake in selecting those five men. It is possible that the other five men would have been better; but the voters had selected five proper men, although they had gone against the advice of the intelligent and public-spirited citizens who had procured for Des Moines the new charter. This is an all-important point with regard to the working of government by commission.

There is another feature of commission government which should be carefully watched by all who are interested in municipal reform,—the degree in which the policy of a city is made continuous under this form of government. It has been very common, you know, for American cities to change their mayors every two years—sometimes every year. It has been very common for aldermen and councilmen to be rapidly replaced in the annual or biennial elections. City administration, therefore, has often lacked continuity. Now since the whole of a city's administration needs to be conducted on the exact principles of applied science, continuity is an important object, in order to get the best results for the people. So far, the governments by commission have been decidedly more stable or continuous than any of the forms which government by commission has replaced; but this is a point which needs to be watched for ten or twenty years, before we shall be able to make up our minds as to whether we have found a satisfactory form of municipal government. The experiment at Boston is going to be very interesting indeed in respect to continuity as well as in respect to the selection by the voters of discreet men of good character.

In most of the experiments on government by commission there appears one item of a character which is very encouraging, although this item does not always appear with the same completeness or definiteness. Under the Iowa law the charter for a city of over 25,000 inhabitants expressly declares that all the employees of the city shall be appointed under civil service rules; but the civil service commission is appointed by the governing body itself. There has already been some trouble with that arrangement in Des Moines. A civil service commission should not be dependent on the government under which the appointees are to serve. A civil service commission should be itself an independent body; else, as one may easily see, the appointing or governing power may make the civil service commission its creature, subservient to its will, and the selective power will therefore be practically exercised by the government itself. In Massachusetts we have a satisfactory system, which we have enjoyed now for a good many years; and the rest of the country is at liberty to learn from Massachusetts what a good system really is. We have a state civil service commission, and that commission examines and recommends candidates for municipal positions. When a city is put, therefore, under civil service rules, it is put under the civil service commission of the commonwealth. A corrupt city government cannot make its own civil service commission, and so practically appoint its own servants. Every appointee in the city must have passed through the inspection and examination of the state civil service commission. However, although the arrangement for civil service examinations and appointments by the civil service commission are not perfect in the governments by commission as a whole, it is by far the most general approach to that only right method of appointment which has been made in our country outside the national service. It is a most interesting and delightful phenomenon, that the general agitation for the reform of municipal government is pledged, with more or less ardor, to the selection of appointees under civil service rules, that is, by impartial examination, close inspections and careful inquiry into antecedents and character—in short, to the merit system. That is a very hopeful feature of the commission form of government; but the administration of the civil service rules is on some of the commission charters intrusted to an inadequate authority, and particularly to an authority which is not sufficiently independent.

There is another feature in most of the commission charters, including those of two Massachusetts cities that have adopted the commission form of government, which has awakened a great deal of criticism, and which the Finance Commission which contrived the new charter for the city of Boston was willing to adopt only in part and in a highly modified form. Under the general law of Iowa, every city with a charter of the commission form is empowered to use the initiative, the referendum, and the recall. Those are three democratic powers of a strenuous character, which the Iowa law commits to the voters of any newly chartered city. Let us look for a moment at the cause of the introduction of these tremendous democratic powers. I think the real cause was the feeling that in adopting the commission form of government, the people as a whole, or the body of voters as a whole, were parting with powers formerly possessed. They used to have the power of electing, for example, a large council by wards, and the councilmen were supposed to represent each his own ward's interests, and the council was supposed to be a legislative body making laws for the city. In the first place it is an entire delusion that election by wards yields better local representatives. On the contrary, they are ordinarily inferior men that are elected under the ward system or the district system. Election at large we have learned by broad experience produces as a rule better aldermen, a better mayor, and a better school committee, than election by wards or districts. This is one of the results of experience which may be said to be admitted. Now, the election of five men only, instead of the election of a board of aldermen, a board called the common council, a mayor, and perhaps a school committee, is imagined to be an abandonment of power. It has never seemed so to me, because I see no reality in a power which cannot be independently exercised—no reality and no usefulness. Nevertheless, to meet this objection the Iowa law put in—and the Massachusetts charters have followed the example of Iowa twice out of three times—the initiative, referendum, and recall. The initiative means that a majority of voters of a city shall have the right to say whether such and such a law, which the city government has refused to pass, shall nevertheless be put into force. The referendum means that on the demand of a moderate number of voters the city government shall be compelled to put to the vote of the people a law or ordinance which the government has passed; and the people, if they do not like it, shall thus have a chance to declare that the enacted ordinance shall not continue in effect or shall not go into effect. The recall is an even more strenuous power—a moderate number of voters may compel the electors to vote on this question: Shall John Jones, now a member of the commission, be discharged from further service, or be "recalled" from his function? The law is fair in that it gives an opportunity to John Jones to go before the people in his own defense —and he need not be nominated again in order to use that opportunity. He may go to the people without any preliminary process, and if he succeeds in defending himself, he gets from his fellow citizens the valuable affirmation that he has done no wrong. Nevertheless, this power of recall is a formidable one. In Massachusetts we have as yet no experience of its working. The Iowa law limits, I think, the use of the recall to once in six months. The new charter of Boston provides a possible recall for the mayor, but not for the councilmen. At the end of two years of the Mayor's service, that is, at the end of the first half of his term, a moderate number of voters can compel the putting of the question to the people:—Shall this mayor serve two years longer or not?—and if the popular vote goes against him, he is thereby out of office. That is a modified recall. Surely with such powers put into the hands of the people, there can be no question about the people's having abandoned any useful or valuable power in adopting the commission form of government. They will have much more control over the new city government than they ever had over the older ones.

I have made a rapid sketch of the condition of this great agitation for municipal reform. What is the source of the interest in it on the part of hundreds of thousands of American citizens? In the first place, many of us are profoundly ashamed of American municipal governments. It is many years ago now that James Bryce, the author of the *American Commonwealth,* pointed out that American city government was the point of greatest weakness and greatest danger in American institutions. He has since had occasion to testify to the same effect with even more force; and innumerable American citizens, some educated, many uneducated, many of the plainest sort of American citizens, believe that the safe future of free institutions in this country will depend on the democracy's discovering some way to make city government efficient and honest. You know there is a continuous rush from the country into cities and large towns. We are doing something to prevent the exaggeration of that rush, and in some small measure we see signs of improvement in that respect; but still this congestion in cities continues, and still there come to us from foreign lands immense additions to our population every year, ignorant of our institutions, having no experience of liberty, and difficult to assimilate with promptness; and a large part of these annual additions abides in the cities. Under such conditions, there are hundreds of thousands of American citizens who believe that this is the point at which the united efforts of all good and true men should be applied; that in this matter of the reform of municipal government we should all combine to bring new and indefinitely better things to pass.

You perceive that, like all great popular movements, this is a moral movement. It is difficult to interest millions of our people in any public question that is not a moral one. We are accused of being a materialistic people, and in a limited sense we are; but in a far truer sense we are an idealistic people, and particularly we are idealistic with regard to the effects and objects of public liberty. We see our governments, far from winning for us the real fruit of public liberty,—a steady gain in public welfare,—moving in the wrong direction physically, intellectually, and morally. We band together to set out city governments in the right way; but to do that we must make sure what the right way is. Commission forms of government are not already demonstrated successes. They cannot be, for they have existed too short a time. But this is true of them, that they are the most promising experiments which the last ten years have seen in the direction in which good citizens want to advance. Therefore, I commend the study of this form of government. Many other devices will doubtless appear,—perhaps better ones. It is an admirable experiment which is now in progress in Staunton, a little Virginia city of about 12,000 inhabitants. Staunton had an archaic form of city government, mayor, aldermen, and common council, which had been thoroughly inefficient for years, though not dishonest. The people could not get the things done they wanted to have done. Some wrong men were elected to the government,—incapable men, inefficient, and neglectful of duty. About a year and a half ago, this very city government decided to try an experiment. They elected an engineer of some local reputation as general manager, like the general manager of a railroad, and into his hands they put all the business of the city. They were so much pleased with the first year's results, during which he is said to have saved his entire salary on coal purchases and coal consumption alone, that they appointed him again and raised his salary by $500 to $2,500 a year. This example is likely to be followed in Virginia.

We shall not lack for various experiments on this subject. Let us study them all, push forward every experiment which promises to be successful, and bring to bear on this vital question the best force of public opinion. Take up this cause; by so doing you will greatly serve your country, and through your country, we hope, mankind.

The Short Ballot—The Secret of the Success of the Commission Plan.*

By Richard S. Childs, Secretary of The Short Ballot Organization.

The following analysis of the Commission plan of city government may be fairly said to represent the scientific view of the subject and accords with the interpretation generally accepted by teachers of political science throughout the country.

It reflects also the spirit of the conference on the subject held by the American Political Science Association in New York, December, 1909.—Ed.

Our American cities under the old style of government simply were not democracies! For democracy means government controlled solely by the people, whereas in our cities the government was controlled jointly by the people and by political machines. It was absolutely necessary for the people to share their power with these machines. To beat one machine it was necessary to create another. The form of government was not adapted to be operated without machine help.

A political machine and a party are two very different things. A party is a group of individuals united by opinion on public policies. Parties cannot be abolished and should not be.

A political machine was an unofficial arm of the government, doing work which could not be done by the people and was not attended to by the government. Machines can be abolished by abolishing their functions.

The function of the political machine in the old style government was (1) to nominate candidates for petty offices in which the people took no interest. If the machines had not stepped in to do this work, the absence of public interest would have resulted in a much reduced and very careless scattered vote for minor offices. There would have been a disorderly scramble for offices and the winner would not have behind him any majority. The machines brought order out of chaos and instituted a certain degree of responsibility. The voter recognizes this responsibility when he votes the straight ticket for petty offices without knowing the names of the candidates or anything worth knowing about them. Among these petty officers are coroners, city clerks, and the weak, powerless aldermen, characteristic of the old regime.

The second function of the machines was to bring order out of chaos when the number of candidates to be selected was greater than the voter would remember. When a great number of offices are filled at one time by election, the voter cannot be relied upon to compile his own ticket without aid and is certain to resort to ready-made tickets supplied to him by interested friends or vote seekers.

The political machine organized this ticket-making business, combined the strength of the candidates for various offices, and with the aid of the voters' natural tendency to avail themselves of the convenience, became so impregnable that it was more important for a candidate to be on a certain party ticket than it was to deserve the office.

In consequence of the two foregoing considerations, candidates who won office owed their election partly to the people and partly to the political machines. Likewise, voters in casting their long ballots were voting in some cases for officers whom they knew about and knew they wanted, and in other cases for meaningless names put forward by the machines, thus conferring power upon the machines to use their discretion.

The Commission plan is a democracy. Moreover it is the first instance of democracy which we have had in our cities for fifty years. It puts the powers into the hands of five conspicuous men. No petty officers are elected and the ballot is short enough so that each voter can make up his own ticket in his head on the basis of his own personal preference. The voter has no need for machine help and is complete master of his ballot. He does not need to become a politician or to "go into politics" to become master of his ballot. The issues are so simple, the burden on the memory is so slight, the limelight on the candidates is so ample, that every voter is a complete politician. Accordingly, ready-made tickets have actually been unpopular in some of these cities and their promotion has been a boomerang upon the promoters. Non-partisan ballots have become possible since the voter no longer needed a guide in the shape of a party label.

The candidates likewise have been under no obligations to get on any particular ticket since there was no advantage in so doing. Each candidate has simply represented himself and his respective constituents. This frees office holders from all obligations to party machines and leaves them solely under obligation to the people.

These fundamental differences are the distinctive characteristic of the Commission plan and are sufficient

*This article has been accepted for publication in the *Twentieth Century Magazine*. The publishers and editor of the *Digest* are indebted to this magazine for permission to use the material here.

of government. *All these differences trace back to that Short Ballot.*

There is another way of looking at it: The word "conspicuous" is the key note of the whole plan. Conspicuous candidates, conspicuous officers after election, conspicuous responsibility! Under the old form of government the people were constantly delegating power to public servants who were but dimly seen in the gloom on account of the naturally obscure and insignificant character of their offices. After election those public servants passed almost completely out of sight of their masters, the people, and found themselves in a gloomy environment which permitted almost any kind of misbehavior without detection. Invisible officials are the only ones who can long misuse their power.

In politics *in*conspicuous accountability to the people is not accountability at all!

Under the Commission plan all the public servants are visible or are responsible to those who are. Each of the five Commissioners stands in the spot-light. His power is great enough to make him worthy of the interest of the whole city.

One of the Commissioners of Des Moines is reported to have said during one of the tense public discussions which have become a feature of life under the Commission plan, that he felt as if he had been indicted by the grand jury. A public servant who is conspicuous is under the strongest inducements to good behavior. He gets credit for good acts and gets condemned for bad ones. Even a wicked man would be apt to make a good public servant under those conditions.

The people oversee the government under the Commission plan. It is conducted in the light right under their eyes. Interest is not dissipated to extinction but is sufficiently concentrated to be effective.

In every Commission-governed city there has been observed the phenomenon of a sudden increase in civic interest. Discussion of city policies has suddenly become popular. The newspapers have given much increased space to the doings at city hall, and every time the Commission makes a move it is the subject for street corner chats and for talks at the home dinner table. Civic pride is not a cause of responsible government but a result of it. The fact that governmental authorities will feel public pressure instantly makes it worth while to bring public pressure to bear upon them whenever the people desire anything. When mass meetings, newspaper scare-heads and public indignation are all in vain, such ebullitions on the part of the public are scarce. When there is a chance to get something done, it is easy to start about it. Under the old form of government a citizen went to a mass meeting to protest and then went to the polls and unwittingly supported the opposition. Under the new plan he protests, and the public servant who ventures to disobey him stands out to be hit plain as day on the ballot.

Various reasons aside from the above have been alleged as causes for the success of the Commission plan.

1. The initiative, referendum and recall. Galveston and Houston, however, the first and perhaps the best examples of the success of the Commission plan, did not have these features.

2. The abolition of wards is cited as another reason for the success of the plan. Election at large does away with the log-rolling to some extent to be sure, but Galveston had no wards for some years before the flood and the unanimous report is that the change to election at large without the short ballot feature did little good. There are other cities in the United States without wards and the government of none of them has been strikingly superior to other cities.

3. Another reason frequently quoted is that the Commission plan is a "business plan." No such plan, however, was ever seen in business practice. In no corporation do the stockholders elect the departmental managers, or, to express it in another way, in no business do the directors act as department chiefs. It would be better indeed if the Commission plan were more like a business. Several Commission-governed cities have had trouble because the Commissioners were not particularly adapted to the executive and technical work which fell to their lot. There has also been unnecessary confusion of responsibility because the Commission as a whole was responsible for all departments and each department head also was responsible for his own department. Let the Commissioners have simply the function of representing the people at city hall. Let them create the office of city manager, who in turn will appoint the department heads. Let it be a permanent single-headed business organization subject to review, direction, criticism and control by the five population, without being limited to candidates who are fit to assume direct charge of technical city departments as chief administrators.

Proportional Representation Through the Single Transferable Vote.

BY ROBERT TYSON, OF THE AMERICAN PROPORTIONAL REPRESENTATION LEAGUE.

I purpose to show that the principle of "wieldiness" can be better put in operation by using a "Wieldly Quota" instead of a "Wieldy District," besides gaining those advantages of real representation which can never be got by a Single Member District, be it wieldy or unwieldy.

I also agree with Mr. Childs that the Commission plan of government is not suited to large cities. I submit that for large cities the solution of the problem of popular government is to be found in the election of a really representative City Council; that such a Council can only be elected by some form of proportional representation; that to such a Council all powers of city government may safely be entrusted; and that with such a Council the popular election of a Mayor is needless. It is not the custom in Europe for the Mayor to be elected by the people. A realy representative Council can elect its own presiding officer; and no checks or balances or vetoes are needed. Primary elections may also disappear.

In our larger cities, the best form of proportional representation is the Single Transferable Vote. For this, the essential factors are three, and three only, namely:

1. *The Multiple District.* This means that several members shall be elected from one district; not less than seven, and not more than will allow the ballot to conveniently hold all candidates.

2. *The Single Vote.* Each elector shall have but *one vote* that finally counts, although he may mark several candidates as alternates; that is, he may mark a first choice, a second choice, etc.; but as soon as one of these choices counts, the others go for nothing.

3. *Transfer of Votes.* That is, some plan by which votes shall be transferred, from candidates who cannot use them, to candidates who can.

I purpose now to deal with the practical working out of these three factors or principles of the Single Transferable Vote. There are four ways of doing it; on the Hare system, on the Proxy plan, on the Schedule system, and on the List plan. Of these, the Hare system is by far the most complete and scientific; it has been well tried; and the only objection against it is that it involves a certain amount of elaboration in the counting of votes. All four plans are easy enough for the voter. Objections of considerable weight lie against the Schedule system and the List plan; so I will deal with them very briefly near the end of this article.

CONSTITUTION OF THE COUNCIL.

It is neither desirable nor necessary to have a very large Council. All that we require is to have it large enough to include all the real leaders of those substantial bodies of public opinion who are sure to be brought to the front by the operation of proportional voting. I should place the maximum at about twenty members, and the minimum at about twelve—for large cities. These could either be elected at large, or in two electoral districts, according to convenience.

For the purposes of illustration, I will assume a district from which ten members are to be elected. I will further assume sixteen candidates; and I will take small numbers, for the sake of simplicity of description. By adding one or two cyphers to the figures they may be made to look large enough for as big an election as you choose. Throughout, I will use a set of figures taken from an excellent article of Mr. William Hoag in the issue of *Equity Series* for April, 1910. On every transfer plan, the "first choices" alone are dealt with on the first count, and, at that stage, those first choices are the Single Vote of the elector. Take letters for the names of the candidates, and assume the first count of the votes to be as follows:

A	175
B	90
C	85
D	80
E	75
F	70
G	65
H	60
I	55
J	50
K	45
L	40
M	35
N	30
O	25
P	20
Total	1,000

The first thing to bear in mind is that here are sixteen separate and distinct groups of electors represented, and that the units or individuals of each group come from all over the electoral district. That is a necessary and most desirable result of the Single Vote in a Multiple District. The 175 voters who have marked A as their first choice are a different lot of voters entirely from the 90 who marked B as first choice; and so on all down the list until it ends with P.

Now, we have sixteen separate groups of electors; and in an actual election of ten members there might be eighteen or twenty or more groups. But we only want ten groups; and the purpose of the Single Transferable Vote is to reduce these sixteen or more groups to ten groups, each group being the supporters of one elected candidate.

Here I may remark that there is so much virtue in those two simple principles of the Single Vote with the Multiple District that you might dispense with transfers, declare the ten highest candidates elected and you might get precisely the same result as you get after all the electoral machinery of transfer has operated. It is really so in perhaps four or five cases out of six. But it is not always so, and we must not take too many chances. So I will go on to explain transfer methods.

The Proxy Plan.

You will ask at once, Why do I begin with a plan or system which I have already indicated that I do not believe to be the best? For good reasons. The Proxy plan is very simple, and the processes used in it are the same as those used in the Hare system; the latter adding more processes and more elaboration. Therefore I am advancing towards the Hare system without the necessity of repeating descriptions. And you may perhaps prefer the Proxy plan, as does Mr. Charles Frederick Adams, Mr. John M. Berry, and others. Here it is:

1. Each voter marks his ballot with as many candidates as he chooses in the order of his choice, with the figures 1, 2, 3, etc., etc.; understanding that his vote will ultimately count for one candidate only.

2. At the close of the poll, the precinct officers count and tally the ballots according to the first choice votes only, sorting them into a bundle for each candidate, and giving the results at once to the press. The newspapers can therefore immediately publish the result of the first count, such as I have tabulated above. The bundles of sorted ballots are then securely and separately tied up, put back into the ballot boxes, along with tally sheets, spoiled ballots, etc., etc., and taken to the central office at the City Hall.

3. At the central office the bundles of ballots without being untied, are sorted into compartments in such a manner that the first-choice votes for each candidate are together in his special compartment.

4. The precinct tallies are added up, and the total number of first choices for each candidate is officially ascertained. This has probably already been done informally in the newspaper offices.

5. The candidate having the lowest number of first-choice votes is declared "out of the count." His bundles of ballots are untied, and all his ballots are transferred to such other candidates as are second choice thereon. Thus the wishes of his supporters are given effect to. No voter need fear to mark any comparatively weak candidate as his first choice, because he knows that his vote will go to a stronger candidate if the first choice is defeated.

6. This process of excluding the lowest candidate is continued until only enough candidates remain to fill the seats in the Council, and these are the elected ones. In our illustration, the ten candidates having the highest number of votes, at the conclusion of the transfers, would be those elected. At the beginning of the transfer operation, J stood to be elected; but the result of the transfers might be to give K so many more votes than J that K would be put above J, and would be elected.

7. The desirability of marking several choices is shown in this way. "P" having been counted out, we will suppose that "O" is the next one to be excluded. A ballot marked "P, 1; O, 2; B, 3," etc., would go to B on third choice, because, O being counted out, the second choice could not be used. But if that voter had marked his ballot "P, 1; O, 2," and there stopped, his ballot could go no further and would become "null"; he would lose his vote, through his own fault.

8. At the close of the transfer there would remain ten elected candidates, with varying numbers of votes; perhaps two or three popular men having many more than their seven or eight colleagues. To equalize this, each member would be entitled to cast, on a division in the Council, as many votes as he received at his election; the theory being that each Councillor acts as proxy for those who voted for him.

Objections. (*a*) This plan has nowhere been tried for municipal or legislative elections. (*b*) As electors have to vote without knowing how the great body of their fellow-electors are voting, a popular candidate might receive many more votes than he required, just because those voting for him wanted to make sure of his being on the Council, not that they wanted him especially as their proxy. A minority of such candidates would then be in a position to outvote the majority of the elected Councillors, on questions which were not before the voters at the time of election. (c) Influence and *personnel* count as well as mere votes on a division, and it would be a very distasteful thing to the average man to see a minority of the elected members having the controlling power in the Council.

Advantages. (a) Great simplicity. (b) More groups of voters could be represented than under other forms of the Single Transferable Vote. (c) Exact proportionality, so far as voting in Council is concerned.

The Hare System.

The first operations are identical with paragraphs 1, 2, 3, and 4 of the Proxy Plan, which please read again. Here the systems diverge.

The Quota Principal. Instead of beginning to transfer the votes at the foot of the poll, a "quota" is got, on the principal that if a thousand votes are cast to fill ten seats, each one-tenth of the voters is entitled to fill one seat. On this principle, the 1,000 votes of our illustration would be divided by ten; any candidate getting his quota of a hundred votes would be elected; and any votes that he had over and above his quota would be regarded as a surplus, and would be distributed to second choices. In our illustration, A heads the poll with 175 votes. He would have a surplus of 75, which would be taken away from him as not being needed by him—100 being all he wanted—and this surplus of 75 would be distributed to second choices according to the wishes of the electors as expressed on their ballots.

Here is an illustration of the way the quota idea works: All the candidates are in the running when any surpluses are distributed, because that is the first operation in the Hare transfer. Suppose A and O are running in the same general interest, supported by the same voters, but that A is so much more popular personally that the greater part of the first choices go to him. This is, of course, an extreme case, but it illustrates the principle all the better for that reason. A's supporters all take especial care to mark O as their second choice. Then all A's surplus votes go to O; O gets the quota of 100; and O is at once elected, and is saved from being knocked out by the excluding process, of which we shall presently speak. Then two hundred like-minded voters, being two quotas, are proportionally elected by two elected members.

Whilst on the quota question, I will describe another method of getting the quota, which is becoming largely used in practice. It is said nowadays that a candidate ought not to receive, by way of quota, any more votes than are required to elect him, and that, taking our illustration, 100 votes are more than he needs; in fact, that if a candidate gets 91 votes nothing can prevent his election. We are dealing with a total of a thousand votes, and electing ten candidates. Now, if ten candidates get 91 votes each, there are only ninety votes left; not enough to put anyone above the ten who have got 91 each. Hence this simple formula:

Divide the total number of votes by one more than the number of seats to be filled, and add one to the quotient. Applying the figures to our illustration, we get this:

```
Divide by 11 ) 1,000
               -----
                  90
         Add       1
               -----
                  91
```

The "remainder" of 10 is disregarded, because it does not affect the result.

This latter plan is called the "Droop" quota, from the name of its inventor. Or you may call it the "small quota" and the other the "large quota." Another advantage of the small quota is that it leaves more votes available for transfer.

Now comes the question, On what principle shall the surplus be transferred? Which 75 of the 175 ballots shall be transferred, if we use the large quota; or which 84 of the 175 shall be transferred if we use the small quota of 91?

It is in the distribution of surplus ballots that all the elaboration of the Hare plan comes in. A rough and ready way of doing it is to turn the ballots face down, shuffle or cut them several times, and then count the surplus off the top. That system is not used in municipal or legislative elections. Instead, there is a set of rules by which the surplus can be distributed with mathematical exactness by anyone conversant with ordinary school arithmetic. I will not take up space to describe this, because a complete set of working rules can be obtained from me at 10 Harbord Street, Toronto, Canada; from Mr. William Hoag, 19 Milk Street, Boston, Mass., or from Mr. John H. Humphreys, 179 St. Stephen's House, Westminster Bridge, S. W., London, England.

We will make short work of the remainder of the Hare process. After all the surplus votes have been distributed, candidates are excluded exactly as set forth in paragraphs 5, 6 and 7 of the Proxy plan. This closes the election. Of course, on the Hare system, each elected Councillor has equal powers, and has only one vote on a division.

Objections. The elaboration and care required in distribution of surplus votes, and consequent difficulty of explaining the process to minds unfamiliar with it, are really the only objections to the Hare system.

Advantages. Great practical success in Legislative elections in Tasmania, in the city elections of Johannesburg and Pretoria, and in the election of the South African Senate. Adopted for propaganda purposes by the powerful and influential Proportional Representation Society of Great Britain, which has held three great illustrative elections to prove the practicability of the system. In these three elections ballots by the thousand were counted in a single evening and the results published next morning in the newspapers.

Ballots to Central Office.

It may be urged as an objection to both Hare and Proxy plans that the ballots have to be taken to the City Hall before transfers are made. This strikes me as rather an advantage, because the brightest supporters of each candidate can attend and conduct such a scrutiny of the process as to make fraud or blundering impossible. If the Hare system be used, an expert and impartial mathematician may be engaged to conduct the transfer operations, whilst at the same time these are simple enough to permit of any ordinarily bright person checking the expert's operations.

As to quick publication of election returns, the first choice count at the precincts gives that. The operation of the transfers will, at most, make a difference of one or two candidates out of the ten; sometimes no difference at all.

Schedule and List Plans.

If local circumstances render the taking of ballots to the Central Office an insuperable objection, then either the Schedule or the List plan may be used. Neither of them is as desirable as either the Hare or Proxy plan, although both are simple. I therefore attempt no description, but refer interested readers to the addresses already given, if information as to these two systems is desired.

The City Manager Plan with Proportional Representation

Otherwise Called

The Representative Council Plan

By C. G. Hoag, Secretary for the U. S. American Proportional Representation League

The City Manager Plan itself and its advantages over the ordinary Commission Plan have been set forth by Mr. Childs and Mr. Gilbertson. Proportional representation has been briefly explained by Mr. Tyson. What I have to say is on the combination of the two into what, in my work for the P. R. League, I have been calling, for short, the Representative Council Plan.

It will help, perhaps, to clear up the confusion in many people's minds to admit at the outset that under the Commission Plan in its original form, that is, where the commissioners are the actual heads of administrative departments, instead of the responsible supervisors of a manager to whom all purely administrative work is delegated, the "block vote"—that is, the present system, under whch every voter votes for all the commissioners—is actually preferable to the proportional system. For under the Commission Plan the administrative functions of the commissioners are more important than their deliberative functions; and to make five *administrative* officials representative of the various interests and opinions of the community would be an absurdity. Under the City Manager Plan, however, which provides for the delegation of administrative work by the commission or council to the city manager, there is not only no objection to electing the council so as to make it reflect truly the community's various interests and opinions but every advantage in doing so. The City Manager Plan with proportional representation, then, seems to be just what we have been looking for so long in this country, the plan that combines with the highest efficiency genuine democracy.

For the highest efficiency we must put the chief administrative official, as well as subordinate officials of the same sort, on a professional basis, which means simply that we must leave his selection and his indefinite retention to some person or body that is in a position to examine his work closely and therefore judge of it intelligently, and that we must also take the matter out of politics not by incessantly harping on the desirability of doing so but by *relieving him of all except purely administrative duties.* That is not saying, you will notice, or even implying, that "the people cannot be trusted to choose" the chief administrator: it is implying merely that they are *not in a position* to do so to advantage, and that if the official in question is given the veto and other policy-determining functions, neither the people nor anybody else can be expected, no matter how well they realize the advantage of experience in administrative work, to do anything but oust him as often as his *opinions* are not in conformity with those of the majority. We can have the highest efficiency in city government as soon as we are ready to take the steps obviously necessary to get it.

It may be asked why, if the city manager is to be appointed, he should not be appointed by the mayor? Well, if what is mean by the term "mayor" here is a chief official having both deliberative and executive powers, and elected at the polls, it may be answered that he should not exist. In so far as such a mayor is a mere administrator, he should be supplanted, as Mr. Childs has shown, by the city manager himself. And in so far as he is a deliberative or policy-determining official, he should be supplanted by the council as soon as that body has been made, by the application of proportional representation to its election, truly representative of all the voters.

Moreover, quite aside from the fact that there should be no mayor of the old-fashioned sort to whom the appointment of the city manager could be entrusted, there is every advantage in giving the responsibility for his appointment and his retention to the council. Instead of changing completely with the turn-over of a few votes at any election, as would frequently happen in the case of a mayor elected at the polls, the council will change in complexion only as fast as, and to the degree that, the whole body of voters changes. Thus the council is the most stable basis for the managership to rest on. Moreover, if the manager is not to be elected by all the voters, and if he is to be kept in office indefinitely so long as he is satisfactory to those who appoint him, as is required in the interest of efficiency, it is obviously important, in the interest of democracy, to entrust his appointment and his retention to the one body in the government that can be made truly representative of the whole electorate.

Efficiency and democracy, then—the two fundamental requirements of the ideal city government—are satisfied by the City Manager Plan with proportional representation, provided only that proportional representation itself can accomplish all that its advocates maintain. In undertaking now to settle that question I shall assume that the particular system of proportional representation in question is the Hare. That is the system successfully in use for the election of the Parliament of Tasmania and the Senate of South Africa; it has recently been approved by the British Parliament for the Senate and the House proposed for Ireland; and it is now receiving powerful support for the election of the councils of British municipalities. I shall assume also that in our cities that system would be carried out under the provisions recommended in the publications of the American P. R. League, which are printed in full at the end of this article.

That the Hare system focuses the voters of a community into a representative body almost as perfectly as a burning-glass focuses the rays of a sunbeam into a point is pretty clear to anybody who fully grasps the fundamental difference between the Hare or any other proportional system and our present one. That difference concerns simply the nature of a "constituency." Under our present system a member's constituency is defined arbitrarily as all the voters who happen to live within a certain district—in spite of the fact that from thirty to seventy per cent. of them may actually have voted against him either in the final election or in the primaries. Under a proportional system a member's constituency is defined as *enough voters, unanimous in his support, to deserve to send him in.* This fundamental difference is like the difference between the two sides of a barn the ridge-pole of which happens to form the continental divide. Turn a pailful of water down one side of the barn, and it flows into the Pacific; turn it down the other, and it flows into the Gulf of Mexico. Define the constituency of a member of a deliberative body as all the voters who happen to live inside of a certain line, and you have no choice but to give the entire representation of the district to one person in spite of the fact that he may, and often does, more or less flagrantly misrepresent from thirty to seventy per cent. of the voters in the constituency thus defined; and the aggregate of such misrepresentation in all the districts may well be sufficient, in the absence of unusual good luck, to confound the very basis of the government. Define a constituency, on the other hand, in terms of *unanimity of will* instead of in those of mere *proximity of home*, and the result, provided only that the means of attaining it are adequate, is the elimination of misrepresentation and the consequent establishment of a basis of government that inspired John Stuart Mill "with new and more sanguine hopes respecting the future of human society."*

The Hare system—or any other good system of proportional representation—is nothing but a form of ballot, and a set of rules for counting ballots, that make it easy for the voters to build up at a single election—without any primaries whatever—approximately equal constituencies each of which is unanimous, under the actual circumstances existing, in the desire to support a certain candidate. The specific means employed—under the Hare system—are covered by the provisions following this article. How effectively they work out can be realized best by seeing an actual election carried out and the ballots counted. It is interesting, when the results of such an election have been reached, to take up and go over, one by one, the pile of ballots that elects any member. Such an examination shows that every ballot in the pile is that of a voter who preferred, under the actual circumstances existing, and considering how all the other electors had voted, to have his vote go to the support of the member it has actually helped to elect.

This is "effective voting" as applied to the election of representative bodies, and it is utterly different from our present system of voting for such bodies by arbitrarily defined single-member districts. It provides a basis for government as scientific, stable, and democratic as our present representative system—so called—is crude, unstable, and conducive to political trickery and corruption. To make a specific comparison, at the municipal election of 1909 in Cape Town, South Africa, where our present system was used, only 42 per cent. of the votes cast were effective in electing members of the council, whereas at the elections of the same year in Johannesburg and Pretoria, where the Hare system was used, 96 per cent. and 99 per cent. respectively of the ballots cast were effective in electing members.

---

*Autobiography, London, 1873. A more extended passage on the Hare system will be found in Mill's book on "Representative Government."

CORRUPTION*

To elect a councilman corruptly under the single-member district or ward system it is necessary to corrupt only the few voters necessary to turn the scale in a close ward. To elect one corruptly under the Hare system it is necessary to corrupt approximately as many voters as there would be in a whole ward.

JUSTICE

The ward system may be very unjust, for under it the seats in the council are often won not by force of voting power but by the tricks of politics: experienced politicians can often make of no avail thousands of votes cast by their opponents simply by pitting faction against faction in close wards and then swinging the small vote necessary to control each. It is only under a system by which each voter's ballot is insured its full weight of one when marked in accordance with the real will of the voter that we can expect the council to reflect the will of the voters truly. Under the ward system a small minority of the voters of the city may control a majority of the council. Under the Hare system a majority of the people is sure to elect a majority of the council, and yet at the same time every minority group large enough to deserve representation gets it.

CONTINUITY OF POLICY

Under the ward system the personnel of the council may be changed considerably by the change of a few voters in a few close wards. Under that system, therefore, there is no assurance that the complexion of the council will not change abruptly when there is no marked change of opinion on the part of the voters of the city generally. Under the Hare system each councilman is sure of his seat so long as he remains the candidate really preferred by one of the full constituencies of the city. If a councilman is not re-elected, it is only because those who elected him formerly now really prefer some one else. The complexion of the council changes, in other words, only as fast as the interests and opinions of the community change, or as fast as councilmen are found to be other than they were thought to be when formerly elected. The Hare system makes possible, therefore, that continuity of policy which is absolutely essential to consistent and orderly progress, for it insures the retention in the council of experienced leaders until leaders more truly representative of the community are discovered.

*The next few paragraphs are reproduced, slightly changed, from an article by the present writer which appeared in "The American City" for April, 1913.

POLITICAL APATHY

Under the ward system political apathy is fostered in a ward where one party or fraction is almost sure to win with many votes to spare. For in such a ward a voter of the leading party knows that his vote will probably have no effect on the result; and a voter of any other party knows in respect to his vote the same thing. A system that causes thousands of votes to be thus "thrown away" at every election is sure to breed apathy among large classes of voters. The cure for political apathy is not continual exhortation to "do your duty as a citizen and go to the polls," but *making each ballot count one towards the make-up of the council, even when the voter has dared to record on it his real will.*

CRANKS

It may be asked whether the Hare system would not permit any crank who could muster more than a tenth of the voters to his support to get a seat in council of nine? Certainly. But that means neither more nor less than that it is fair. The implication of those who ask this question, namely that the system would fill the council with cranks, is absurd. Clearly the number of cranks in the council would correspond to the number of crank-supporters in the city. It is only in a city full of crank-supporters, therefore, that the council would be full of cranks. Moreover, the thing works both ways: besides insuring a seat to any candidate having the necessary support whom you might consider a crank or "undesirable," it would insure a seat there also to any person of exceptional intelligence, education, or equipment who could get the same support.

PARTY LINES

Would the Hare system divide the voters into solid factions and interests? It would do just the opposite. The ward system has kept the voters divided into factions and parties meaningless in municipal elections. The Hare system would set the voter free to cross all factional lines, including national party lines, if he wanted to; but it would make him free also to vote according to any lines, whether those of the most temporary sort or those of national party divisions, which he wanted to follow at the particular election in question. It is the cramping restrictions of the present plan of electing representatives by plurality (or majority) vote in single geographical constituencies that maintain parties and factions rigidly where they would disappear at once or change as municipal issues changed under a system that allowed the voters to form their groups freely by means of the ballots themselves, *each one of which would be insured full effectiveness under whatever circumstances of grouping might arise.* Under the Hare system national party lines would not persist in city elections except in so far as the voters really wanted them to.

DISTRICT REPRESENTATION

Have not geographical districts a right to representation as such? Certainly—*to precisely the extent that the voters want such representation.* Any system of election, therefore, that prevented a voter from giving as much weight to the geographical proximity of a candidate as he wanted to would be unreasonable. But the Hare system does not do that, and it has the advantage also of not forcing voters by the thousand to be "represented" by men they are utterly opposed to simply because a constituency has been defined as all the voters, no matter how diverse in interests and opinions, who happen to live within a certain line.

SUPPOSED DIFFICULTY IN VOTING

Is it hard for uneducated voters to vote a Hare ballot? It is not. On this point there is conclusive evidence in official documents, notably the testimony of the Agent General of Tasmania in the Blue Book of the British Government designated "Miscellaneous No. 3, 1907."

THE TITLE OF MAYOR

Is a city to have no mayor if it adopts the City Manager Plan with proportional representation? By all means let it have a mayor—if there is no danger that the retention of the title will mean the retention of the official we now call by that name. Give the title of mayor, if you wish, to the person selected by the council as its president or chairman, for that is the person who should represent the dignity and the hospitality of the city. And let that person also, as the Lockport bill puts it, "be recognized as the official head of the city by the courts for the purpose of the advice of civil process and by the Governor for the purposes of the military law.'

THE RECALL

Should the Recall be made applicable to the city manager under this plan of government? Preferably not, for there is nothing to be gained by giving the council the least loophole for excuses in case the manager whom it is keeping in office is inefficient or otherwise unsatisfactory. There is no objection, however, to making the Recall applicable to the council itself. It must not be made applicable to members of the council *separately,* of course, for that would be utterly inconsistent with the principle on which the body is made up—the principle that any man deserves a seat who has a whole constituency behind him, even if every other voter in the city is against him: it must be made applicable to the council *as a whole.* There need be no fear that any member who ought to remain in the council will lose his seat at such a recall election: the system of election itself will take care of that: the only members dropped will be those who ought to be dropped because they no longer have the support of constituency of voters. In this connection it may be added that as there is no objection, under the Hare system, to frequent elections—that system itself assuring stability to the council—a simple solution of the problem of the Recall in respect to a council elected by that system is to provide that the regular elections for the council shall be at intervals as short as one would think of making the interval required between a regular election and a recall election. With regular elections for the council annually, say, provisions for recall elections applying to that body might be considered unnecessary. If longer intervals between the regular elections were preferred, provisions for recall elections applying to all the seats at once should be included in the city's charter.

A SLIGHT PRACTICAL OBJECTION

Under the Hare system is it not necessary to have all the ballots, after the counting of first choices at the precincts, brought together to a central place for the completion of the count? It is, and one must admit that this is a slight practical objection to the system. Wherever the system is thoroughly understood, of course, an appreciation of its advantages will make this slight objection seem not worth considering. Wherever, however, the public cannot be educated sufficiently, and the objection mentioned seems an insuperable obstacle to the introduction of the Hare system, a simple list system of proportional representation, such as that explained on pages 14-17 of the American P. R. League's Pamphlet No. 3, is to be recommended.

"PREFERENTIAL VOTING" AND PROPORTIONAL REPRESENTATION

Just what is the advantage of proportional representation for the election of the council over what is usually called "preferential voting?" Preferential voting, as the term is commonly used, means preferential *majority* voting, that is, the use of a ballot on which the

stead of very limitedly
ıe majority against the
ot that allows such a
ll, that is, of a "pre-
ject does all that both
ler the old system, and
question but that the
feature of any rational
ect in view. But when
t all, but the building
as it unquestionably
body is being elected,
l ballot *in connection*
make unanimous con-
from being rational or
he object in view, the
be used, but the rules
ıimous-constituency or
najority rules.
ious to everybody that
t should be used in all
n it is used, officially
useless; but it will be
wo objects of voting,

quite distinct from each other, the making of decision in which majority voting is in order, and the making u of a body fit to make them on behalf of all the peopl in which majority voting is quite out of order.

COMPARISON WITH THE ORDINARY COMMISSION PLAN

This brings us back to the comparison of the ordinar Commission Plan with the City Manager Plan with prc portional representation. Under the former, since th commissioners are primarily administrators—being sort of executive committee of the majority—they shoul be elected at large by the majority system of votin as in fact they are. But when they are elected thus, th city is left without the services of any body that eve pretends to be representative of all the voters. Th ordinary Commission Plan, therefore, is weaker than th City Manager Plan with proportional representatio not only in having its chief administrators on a non professional basis, which must make the highest efficienc in administration impossible, but in depriving the cit altogether of the services of a truly representative bod composed of more or less experienced leaders of publi opinion.

ONAL REPRESENTATION, NOMINATION AND ELECTION PROVISION

Revised July, 1913.

ates for the council shall
ho have signed no other
the council at the same
alities of not more than
per cent of the number
ceding regular municipal
alities of more than ten
ive thousand inhabitants
ectors who voted at the
tion; and to the number,
ty-five thousand inhabit-
the number of electors
ular municipal election;
ıall the number required

In printing the first series of ballots the names of cand dates for the council shall be arranged in alphabetical orde After printing the first series the first name in the list candidates shall be placed last in such list and the next seri printed, and the process shall be so repeated until each nam in the list of candidates shall have been printed first an equ number of times. The ballots so printed shall then be com bined in tablets, so as to have the fewest possible ballots ha ing the same order of names printed thereon together in th same tablet. The ballots shall in all other respects confor as nearly as may be to the ballots prescribed by the gener election laws of the state.

The form of the ballot shall be as follows:

[See next page]

Section 3. The numerals thus marked on the ballot sha

marked on the outside, and the two for each candidate shall then be tied up in one bundle which shall also be properly marked on the outside. All the bundles thus made up at a precinct, together with the invalid ballots and a record of all the ballots cast at the precinct, showing the number of invalid ballots, the number of valid ballots, the total number of first-choice ballots for each candidate, and the number of ballots in each of the two groups of first-choice ballots received by each candidate, shall be forwarded to the Board of Deputy State Supervisors of Elections or the Board of Deputy State Supervisors and Inspectors of Elections,* as directed by that Board, and the counting of the ballots shall proceed under its direction.

Section 5. First-choice votes for all candidates shall be added and tabulated as the first count.

Section 6. The whole number of valid ballots shall then be divided by a number greater by one than the number of seats to be filled. The next whole number larger than the quotient thus obtained shall be the quota or constituency.

Section 7. All candidates the number of whose votes on the first count is equal to or greater than the quota shall then be declared elected.

Section 8. All votes obtained by any candidate in excess of the quota shall be termed the surplus of that candidate.

Section 9. The surpluses of those candidates who have a surplus shall be successively transferred, beginning with the largest surplus and proceeding to the smallest, each ballot of the surplus being transferred to and added to the votes of that continuing candidate for whom a preference is indicated on the ballot.

Section 10. "Ballots capable of transfer" means ballots from which the preference of the voter for some continuing candidate can be clearly ascertained. "Continuing candidates" means candidates who have not been declared elected or defeated.

Section 11. The particular ballots to be transferred as the surplus of any candidate shall be taken as they happen to come, without selection, from such of his ballots as are capable of transfer, and the order in which those ballots shall be transferred shall be that in which they happen to come, without selection. All the ballots not so transferred as surplus shall be set aside as effective in the election of such candidate.

Section 12. After the transfer of all surpluses, the votes standing to the credit of all the candidates shall be counted and tabulated as the second count.

Section 13. After the tabulation of the second count (or after that of the first count if no candidate received a surplus on the first) the candidate lowest on the poll as it then stands shall be declared defeated and all his ballots capable of transfer shall be transferred to the continuing candidates, each ballot being transferred to and added to the votes of that continuing candidate preferred by the voter. After the transfer of these ballots a fresh count and tabulation shall be made. In this manner candidates shall be successively declared defeated and their ballots capable of transfer transferred to continuing candidates and a fresh count and tabulation made. Each time the candidate to be declared defeated shall be the one lowest on the poll at the last preceding count.

Section 14. Whenever in the transfer of a surplus or of the ballots of a defeated candidate the votes of any candidate shall equal the quota, he shall immediately be declared elected and no further transfer to him shall be made.

Section 15. When candidates to the number of the seats to be filled have been declared elected, all other candidates shall be declared defeated and the count shall be at an end; and when the number of continuing candidates shall be reduced to the number of seats to be filled, those candidates

* In some states the proper officials would have some other title. The alternative title given is intended to be correct for all municipalities in Ohio.

shall be declared elected and the count shall be
and in this case the ballots of the last candida
need not be transferred.

Section 16. If at any count two or more candid
bottom of the poll have the same number of vote
didate shall first be declared defeated who was lo
next preceding count at which their votes wer
Should it happen that the votes of these can
equal to each other on all counts, they shall be d
feated successively from the younger to the older

Section 17. No ballot shall be counted in such
to make it effective in the election of more than one

Section 18. Upon each tabulation a count sh
of those ballots which have not been used in the
some candidate and which are not capable of tran
the designation "Non-Transferable Ballots."

Section 19. Upon each tabulation a count sh
of the invalid ballots; but no ballot shall be decla
except one on which the first choice of the voter
clearly ascertained. A ballot marked with a cro
one name but with no other mark shall be treated
if it had been marked with the figure 1 opposit
name but with no other mark.

Section 20. So far as may be consistent with
and with convenience in the counting and transfer
ballots, the public, representatives of the press, an
the candidates themselves, shall be afforded every
being present and witnessing these operations.

** For the last twelve words may be substituted the
they are preferred: "lots shall be drawn to decide whi
shall next be declared defeated."

[Form of Ballot]*

FOR REPRESENTATIVES IN THE COUNCIL

Directions to Voters: Put the figure 1 opposite the na
first choice for the council. If you want to express s
third, and other preferences, do so by putting the figure
the name of your second choice, the figure 3 opposite th
your third choice, and so on. You may express thu
preferences as you please. A ballot is spoilt if the figu
opposite more than one name.

If you spoil this ballot, tear it across once, return it to
officer in charge of the ballots, and get another from hin

CANDIDATES FOR THE COUNCIL

	A	(Domicile Address.)
	B	
	C	
	D	
	E	
	F	
	G	
	H	
	I	
	J	
	K	
	L	

* The squares for the voter's marks should be at the
names instead of at the left in states where custom would
a change.

Will Commission Government Succeed in Large Cities? *

Yes, but not so well as in Small Cities.

RICHARD S. CHILDS.

"Yes, there is graft in Galveston," remarked a prominent citizen of that town not long ago. "We shall have to get rid of Commissioner Blank at the next election, and perhaps one other man.

"Over in Houston, too, there is one man on the Commission who is out for himself instead of the people. They will clear him out at the next election with a bounce."

The promoters of the Commission Plan are apt to believe that efficiency is its primary object. Efficiency, on the contrary, is only a by-product. The main idea of the new plan of city government is to give the people control,—a control that is not shared by any self-established group of politicians or bosses. In the ordinary American city, the prominent citizen remarks, "Yes, there is graft here, and we can't help it, although we are fighting bitterly for reform all the time." In Galveston and in Houston the people say, "Yes, there is graft, but we will get rid of Commissioner Blank at the next election." Furthermore, the chances are excellent that they will do so. Commissioner Blank with his large powers attracts a limelight that floods his every act, and is a clear target for public criticism. Everybody in town knows him and knows what he is responsible for. He is a visible public servant and is therefore under much more effective public scrutiny than the obscure Aldermen and other petty elected officers of the old regime.

The Commission Plan has not yet been tried in any large city except New York, which, with its Board of Estimate, is a close parallel. Boston has been influenced by the movement and has adopted the non-partisan ballot, but otherwise its whole plan is unique. Baltimore, Indianapolis, Pittsburgh, Buffalo, Cincinnati and other large cities are now debating the adoption of the Commission plan, following the Des Moines model, and the time is ripe to discuss the philosophy underlying the whole scheme and ascertain whether this plan of government will achieve in large cities the same responsiveness to public sentiment which is its fundamental merit in the smaller places.

In small cities there can be no doubt that the Commission plan abolishes the professional politician. There is no obscurity or confusion for the politician to be expert in. There is nothing in a local political situation which the average citizen does not easily master. The citizen assumes the functions of the boss and the result is true democracy, of which an efficient and economical government is the by-product, because that happens to be a kind of government which finds favor with the people. In a large city the duties of the citizen would be equally simple. He would still have only five names to choose. He could and would make up his own ticket and select, as well as elect, his public servants.

The candidates, however, face an entirely different situation. In a small city any man who deserved success would be reasonably certain to be known by personal reputation to a considerable percentage of the electorate. In a city of 60,000 population he would have to reach an audience of approximately 10,000 voters. To woo his plurality is not a task calculated to stagger a candidate of reasonable ability. Out of his private purse he could print enough pamphlets to furnish one for every voter in the city and the postage on them would be only $100. If he chooses advertising in the newspapers as a means of propaganda, the newspaper rates in a small city will not be so high as to prevent his making an adequate representation of his claims. He can hire the Opera House, plant some red fire in front and speak to all who will come to hear, and since there are only 10,000 voters to hear him, he will not have to hire the Opera House many nights before he will have reached all the voters who are likely to attend such meetings. If an office and headquarters are likely to help him, the expense of this is comparatively small. An impromptu organization built up of personal acquaintances working for him as a matter of personal loyalty and interest, will be adequate to conduct the campaign. Time and again business men who had never been in politics before, have gone after the votes on their own responsibility in just this fashion in the little Commission governed cities and have found it possible to get the votes and get elected. After election they had no one to thank but the voters. Among their supporters no one man or organized clique had been essential to success. The candidate could at any time during the campaign have dispensed with any one of his supporters without feeling that his campaign had been ruined by the defection. After election his gratitude was to the people alone, whereas under the old plan of government he would have been grateful partly to the people and partly to that indispensable machine.

*This article has been accepted for publication in *The American City*. The publishers are indebted to that magazine for permission to print the material in the *Digest*.

In a large city, however, all this is changed. If the population be 600,000, there will be 100,000 voters to be reached with his arguments. His postage bill is now $1,000. He must hire not merely one Opera House for a few meetings, but must conduct a continuous whirlwind campaign, hiring several houses a night, while the task of advertising himself sufficiently to attract the necessary audiences becomes stupendous. Mr. Storrow, in Boston, for example, spent $95,000 in such efforts. No organization adequate to carry on so vast a campaign with any hope of success can be improvised by a single candidate. Organizations that are permanent and in working order at the beginning of the campaign, will have an overwhelming advantage. Their attitude will be the first thing that is inquired about when a candidate announces himself. Any man whom they support will immediately leap into prominence, while their failure to support a candidate immediately relegates him to the rear. In the first non-partisan election in Boston, Mr. Hibbard, the Mayor of the previous administration, well known as he was, and with an excellent reputation for efficiency, was unable to secure the support of the Republican machine which had elected him under the previous charter, and immediately dropped out of sight as a serious possibility in the contest. On election day, out of the 100,000 votes he got only 1,800. The people did not settle his fate that way. A few leaders having at their finger tips a great ready-made and efficient machinery for conducting a campaign and for reaching the people, were able to determine at a single stroke the fate of the candidate. Per contra, it was certain that Fitzgerald would be a prominent candidate, for as soon as he appeared in the field it was recognized that the Democratic machine would support him. Had the Democratic machine seen fit to decide otherwise, Fitzgerald would have ceased to be a factor in the contest at the very beginning.

No ordinary candidate can hopefully campaign for election to an office in so large a district against candidates who have the support of a standing political organization. It is the old story of the amateur against the expert, the amateur organization against the expert organization. In such circumstances the amateur can only hope for some huge stroke of luck that will bring about a public paroxysm. In all ordinary times the controlling forces of the principal political organizations, whether they are acting formally or informally, will hold a virtual monopoly over the business of nomination, and candidates, when elected, will owe gratitude partly to the people and partly to the machine, whose support they found essential. Just as in Boston, with its non-partisan ballot, Mr. Fitzgerald must acknowledge that the support of a certain coterie of politicians was essential to his success, so in a large city under the Commission plan a candidate would find that he could not succeed except by catering to the good graces of certain political groups.

In New York City we have an example of the Commission form of government in a great city. The Board of Estimate holds practically all the power. It consists of eight men, three of whom are elected at large and one from each of the five boroughs. An independent candidacy for membership in this Board is practically out of the question. Hearst tried it, but he had to build for years to get even a fighting chance. He had the support of four newspapers printed in three languages, with an enormous circulation. He had also a huge private fortune. His campaign demonstrated how enormous are the proportions of the machinery required to conduct so huge a canvass. Practically speaking, whether the ballot be non-partisan or partisan, no man could hope for election in New York City unless he had the support of either the Republican machine or the Democratic machine or the organized Independents. To beat the old machine it is necessary to build a new one.

To give to the few men who guide these machines the power to decide who the candidates shall be is highly oligarchical. It may result in barring out the man whom the people really want. It is not the condition of free competition such as is seen in a wieldy district. It is incomplete democracy and cannot be considered the ultimate plan of government.

One exception must be noted in New York City, namely, the Borough of Richmond, with 100,000 population. This borough is much smaller than any of the others. It is the only one in which the machines are weak, the only one in which there is any hope or opportunity for an independent candidate. It is significant that among all the boroughs it is the only one whose administration has not been a scandal. It has been well governed and the same Borough President has held office for three successive terms to the great satisfaction of the people of the borough. His position is unique, for he can say at the end of his term: "If you politicians do not renominate me, I will run independently and beat you." They need him more than he needs them. If their machine will not support him, he can improvise a machine of his own from among his personal friends and go after the votes with reasonable hope of success. If all the elective officers of New York City were chosen from districts small enough to bring about the same political conditions in each, there would be no powerful machines and perhaps no reformers in New York City.

There are two solutions for the government of large cities. One is the plan known as proportional representation by which offices are filled by election at large, but the voters, instead of each voting for the entire list, vote only for a first choice, a second choice, etc. Thus, if twenty men were to be elected, each of the twenty would have to capture only one-twentieth of the voters instead of a plurality. This simplifies the task of the candidate and the method of counting can be such as to bring about a fair and accurate analysis of public opinion.

The other method is to divide the city into wards and elect one candidate from each ward. This is the English

The City Manager Plan to Date*

BY H. S. GILBERTSON, EXECUTIVE SECRETARY, THE NATIONAL SHORT BALLOT ORGANIZATION.

In December, 1910, the Board of Trade at Lockport, N. Y., began to grow weary of the way municipal affairs had been run in their town under the familiar and complicated mayor and council plan of organization. Like hundreds of other such bodies, they turned instinctively to commission government. But there was no optional law on the statute books which they could adopt, as is now the case in many states, by which the only proceeding necessary to put the law into effect is to secure a local referendum.

Unexpectedly there was presented to the board a bill whose purpose was to put a form of commission government within the reach of every third-class city in the state. The Board of Trade accepted this as their own and had it introduced in the legislature of 1911; hence the term "the Lockport bill."

The form of government set forth in this measure has now come to be widely known as the "city manager plan." It is built upon certain conspicuous essentials of the simple type now in use in Galveston, Des Moines and nearly three hundred American cities: the unification of all the local powers of government in the hands of a single elective body, and the Short Ballot. But here the similarity ends. It is true that in most of the applications of the city manager plan thus far, other features of commission government have been borrowed —election at large, non-partisan elections and the Initiative, Referendum and Recall. But none of these things is in itself essential to the definition of this new form of city government.

It is on the administrative and executive side that the city manager plan introduces a radical change. The more familiar type of commission government makes each member of the council (usually five in all) the head of an operating department, either in an active or a supervisory capacity. Every member of the council or commission is expected to devote all, or at least a large part, of his time to the service of the city, and is paid a substantial salary. No single member of the commission, under most of the charters, could be called its executive head. The Mayor is such, in theory, but the other commissioners, as a rule, do not take him seriously as their superior, as well might be inferred from the fact that they stand with him on an equal basis of popular election.

Commission government in the old sense, then, is a five-headed affair. It is not always intended to be such, but it is so regarded by the average citizen, and so it works out so in practice.

A SINGLE-HEADED ADMINISTRATION.

The city manager plan does away with this five-headedness of municipal administration and substitutes a single head, not with advisory powers merely, but, with certain safeguards, with the powers of administrative "life and death," through actual control of appointments and removals.

The chief executive or city manager is not an elective officer, but is appointed by the council; he therefore does not divide responsibility with the council, but is subordinate to it; he need not be, at the time of his appointment, a resident of the city, but may be chosen from anywhere in the country; he is not chosen for a definite term, but holds office so long as he gives satisfaction to his superiors.

There are, however, certain exceptions to the executive powers to be exercised by the city manager. A city is not altogether a business affair; it is, in certain respects, a political agency, and there are some occasions on which it has been thought suitable that the official head of the city should be an elective one. There come in the history of many cities times of great public danger, when it is necessary that the ordinary machinery of government be set aside in favor of a single person who can get quickly on his own initiative—occasions, for example, such as those which beset the Ohio cities in the floods of March, 1913.

To meet such contingencies the Lockport bill, and most of its successors, have provided that the Mayor should be the head of the city for the purposes of the military law, under which he has power, when necessity arises, to govern the city by proclamation. Also, it was thought fitting that on ceremonial occasions, as when the President is to be welcomed to the town, that the "head of the city" should be its first citizen. And so for such purposes and for the service of legal process in civil actions to which the city is a party, the Lockport bill provided that the Mayor should be the head of the city; not that

*October 15, 1913

he should be elected as such, but should be "that member of the city council who at the regular election of city officers shall have received the highest number of votes cast." By not diverting the attention to the Mayor, the bill aimed to focus the whole scrutiny of the voters on the council, to the end that the highest possible type of citizens would be chosen for that body.

SUMTER, S. C.

Lockport never came under the influence of such a charter, much as the people of that city are desirous of coming out from under boss rule and putting their public affairs on the business basis. The legislature of 1911 did not see Lockport conditions in quite the same light. It remained for the little city of Sumter, S. C. (population 8,109), to pick up the general idea, influenced partly by the example of Staunton, Va., which had a general manager with functions somewhat different from those of the proposed city manager of Lockport. Sumter voted, on June 12, 1912, on an option between an old-line commission form and a new city manager plan, which carried out the Lockport idea in every essential. The latter was adopted by a majority of three to one. Early in the fall the first commission was elected, and there appeared at once one of the advantages of the new system over the old: The commission of three men which was elected was, according to all reports, composed of the strongest and ablest of men that could be brought together. They were not attracted to public office by the salary, which was only $200 a year. Nor, on the other hand, were they deterred from seeking the office by the prospect of having to perform detailed administrative duties, which, under the regular commission plan, would have been imposed upon them. They accepted the responsibility of running the government as a Board of Directors, knowing that under the charter it was not only possible, but required of them, to delegate the details of administration to a competent, trained man who would spend all his time on the job. They set out to secure such a man by sending this advertisement broadcast throughout the country:

"October 14, 1912.

"The City of Sumter hereby announces that applications will be received from now till December the first for the office of City Manager of Sumter.

"This is a rapidly growing manufacturing city of 10,000 population, and the applicant should be competent to oversee public works, such as paving, lighting, water supply, etc.

"An engineer of standing and ability would be preferred.

"State salary desired and previous experience in municipal work.

"The City Manager will hold office as long as he gives satisfaction to the commission. He will have complete administrative control of the city, subject to the approval of the board of three elected commissioners.

"There will be no politics in the job; the work will be purely that of an expert.

"Local citizenship is not necessary, although a knowledge of local conditions and traditions will of course be taken into consideration.

"A splendid opportunity for the right man to make a record in a new and coming profession, as this is the first time that a permanent charter position of this sort has been created in the United States.

"At the request of the City Commissioners these applications will be filed with the Chamber of Commerce of Sumter, A. V. Snell, Secretary."

This attracted nation-wide attention. Every engineering journal of any prominence published it as news. Replies to the number of 150 came in, nearly all from trained civil engineers, the greater proportion of whom had had municipal experience.

Thus did Sumter emulate the practice of German cities, which never select their Burgomasters for political reasons, but solely for ability—a practice which has resulted in the growth of a distinct profession of municipal administration. In January, 1913, the first city manager was selected—Mr. M. M. Worthington, a former civil engineer, a resident of Virginia, in the employ of the Southern Railway. Mr. Worthington immediately showed the advantages of his training by putting into effect a cost system by which he saved more than half his first year's salary on one or two items of expenditure. By keeping proper account of the cart service in the public works department, he will save the city nearly $5,000 a year.

SPREAD OF THE MOVEMENT.

Sumter had not been operating long under the system when the town of Hickory, N. C. (population 3,716), became interested in a new city charter. One of her leading citizens discovered the Lockport law and proceeded to adapt it to his town. A charter was drawn up which followed the Lockport provisions *verbatim*, except that the city manager was charged with certain specific engineering duties, and that the council, instead of being chosen at large, was to be selected by wards.

The people accepted the charter in April, 1913, and, as in the case of Sumter, the city manager was chosen from the outside.

The Hickory charter was picked up by the commission in Morganton, N. C. (population 2,713). Making a few very slight changes in the Hickory charter, the citizens of this town took it up to the Capitol and had it enacted as their basic local law.

At this point the city manager plan ceases to be an exclusive Southern institution. In September, 1912, the cities of Ohio were emancipated from the state legislature by constitutional amendment. They were henceforth no longer required to go down to Columbus whenever they wanted to issue a bond for street improvement or to hire a new clerk. They could now do what Anglo-Saxon towns could do a thousand years ago: run their own local affairs as their local consciences and good sense dictated, instead of having to appeal to the wisdom of the up-state farmers.

DAYTON, O.

Immediately after the adoption of the home-rule movement, the Ohio cities began to talk of the charter revision, and if any one of them was more eager for self-government than another, it was Dayton (population 116,577). This city has a large number of civic and improvement societies which are constantly on the lookout for the "best things going" for their city. Sumter had recently adopted the new plan and the Chamber of Commerce was sending out pamphlets broadcast. Some of these fell into good hands in Dayton, and it was but a very short time before the Chamber of Commerce and the Bureau of Municipal Research and a variety of organizations had decided to insist upon the city manager idea as the starting point for a new charter. After an interruption on account of the flood, the local campaign was brought to its conclusion. By this time the city manager sentiment was so overwhelming that the ticket of charter freeholders nominated by the Citizens' Committee and committed to the new plan was elected on May 20, 1913, by a more than two to one majority. The commission fulfilled its obligations and produced what is perhaps the most advanced city charter ever drawn for a large American city. The original Lockport law was followed closely, with the single incidental variation that the city manager may be recalled by popular election in the same manner as an elective officer.

At about the same time as the Dayton movement, there sprung up a very strong interest in the plan in Youngstown and Elyria. In both these cities, before the charter revision commissioners had proceeded far with their deliberations, they became convinced of the virtues of the city manager plan, and both of them drafted charters along this line, again sticking close to the Lockport law. The Youngstown charter, however, provided that the members of the council should be nine in number, and that they should be nominated from wards but elected at large, thus emphasizing the fact that the Short Ballot does not require the abolition of local representation. Another and more serious deviation from the model charter was the provision that the city manager, at the time of his appointment, must be a resident of Youngstown for a period of five years. The reason for this was not a scientific one, but had its genesis in a certain local prejudice against giving such an important public office to a non-resident.

The only deviation in the Elyria charter was the provision which made the solicitor, city clerk, auditor and treasurer direct employees of the commission instead of the city manager, as the Lockport law provided. In the case of the solicitor and the clerk, it was pointed out that these officers had a very intimate and direct relationship to the council or commission in the shaping of its policies and the keeping of its records. The auditor and treasurer, so it was thought, should act as administrative checks upon the city manager.

Both the Youngstown and Elyria charters were defeated by the people. This was due on the one hand to the very vigorous opposition of the politicians, and on the other to the insufficient publicity given to the charter provisions.

OTHER OHIO CITIES

Success, however, again met the city manager plan in Springfield (population 46,921), which adopted its new charter on August 26, 1913. The Springfield charter follows closely the one drawn up in Dayton, except that, like the Elyria charter, it takes certain of the general officers out of the control of the city manager and puts them under the commission.

The next Ohio city to be influenced was Sandusky, where at the present writing a charter commission is in session, which is committed to the city manager plan.

It is also possible in Ohio still to amend the municipal code so as to permit the cities, without the somewhat troublesome procedure of electing a charter convention and framing a charter, to adopt ready-made forms of city government. Accordingly, there was passed in the session of 1913 a law which permits any city to come under one of three forms of government—the federal, the commission and the city manager plans. It was a distinct gain for this radically new type of city government to get recognition like this in a large state like Ohio.

THE MOVEMENT IN THE WEST.

Going back to March, 1913, we find that the city manager idea took root in a small city in California—Whittier (population 4,550). The charter framers in this town, which enjoys home rule privileges like the Ohio cities, got hold of the Lockport law and proceeded to draft a charter with that as a basis. As in some other communities, a considerable opposition was developed on the part of the politicians and the ill-informed, and owing to these facts and to certain incidental features of the charter, it went down to defeat.

La Grande, Ore. (population 4,843), adopted the plan on October 1.

In Arizona three towns have become actively interested in the city manager plan, Douglas, Phoenix and Bisbee.

In Douglas (population 6,437) a city manager charter of what may now be referred to as the conventional type was drawn up, but for reasons not unlike those operative in Whittier, was defeated. This result, however, did not deter the charter forces in Phoenix (population 11,134), for they drew up a charter on very much the same lines which was adopted by a three to one maority on October 11, 1913. The Phoenix charter departed from its precedent in fixing a definite salary for the city manager, and stipulating that he must be a resident of Phoenix at the time of his appointment. Most of the advocates of the plan regard both these provisions as serious departures from the type. As to the salary stipulation, the charter commissioners felt that the figure they set was high enough so as not to interfere with the responsibility of the governing body. The residence requirement, however, was put in on account of certain provisions of the state constitution.

Another very active field of operation is Minnesota. At the last session of the legislature one of the representatives dropped into the legislative hopper a copy of the original Lockport bill with practically no changes. This bill passed the lower house, but in the rush of business was not reported out of the Senate. Later on, several cities in the state (which is in the home rule class) were introduced to the city manager idea; Little Falls (population 6,078) votes on Oct. 28, 1913, Brainerd (population 8,526) has a city manager charter ready and a vote will soon be taken upon it.

Another southern city which voted on tl October was Waycross, Ga. (population election here was adverse.

POTENTIAL PROGRESS.

Such is the obvious progress of the mo real growth is not measured by these limi act, providing for commission governmen class cities in Pennsylvania, was drawn that it will be possible after the terms of mission expire, to reduce the salaries o sioners. The president of the Allied Civ is largely responsible for the adoption of no secret of the fact that the bill was so second commission in any of these cities cut their own salaries down to a nominal vote the amount thus saved to the salary ager. Already there is a great deal of ta such a step in several of the Pennsylvani

The adoption of the new plan by Dayto more attention than the Galveston or Des M

As this article is written a most signifi just taken place. Tacoma, Wash., has been under a charter of the Des Moines ty fulfilled expectations. To quote the M opinion, the commission form of governm in Tacoma has not been a success. The log-rolling and trading. Instead of one have five, each one objecting to the contro itself." The Mayor definitely comes out change to the city manager plan, and t vancement League in the same city supp stand.

Dallas is revising her charter, and the citizens there who are urgently advising Lockport system.

There is a great likelihood that in the National Socialist party, the members of localities have usually been opposed to c ernment, will endorse the city manager p democratic and best suited to carry out th their large social program involves. Tl however, on a more representative form is provided in the Lockport plan. By tl model charter, which has been prepared Thompson, head of the National Informa the party, the members of the council w by the Hare plan of proportional repres insures a voice for minorities and preserv of the Short Ballot.

The Theory of the New Controlled Executive Plan*

By Richard S. Childs, Secretary, The National Short Ballot Organization.

The recent adoption by Sumter, S. C., of a new type of commission plan of government with the appointive city manager, is important. It is the first time in the United States that a municipal chief executive has been made appointive and put under continuous control instead of independent and under intermittent control.

Pending the appearance in America of this principle, the short ballot movement was headed for a stone wall. For in demanding the reduction of the mischievous multiplicity of elective offices, we are met by the question "what offices would you make appointive and who would appoint them?" The natural and easy answer is to follow the tendency of the times and advocate casting all appointive power on the nearest chief executive. In New York state, for example, the New York Short Ballot Organization has presented constitutional amendments to the legislature, the effect of which is to give the governor control by appointment over the rest of the state ticket, namely, the secretary of state, state treasurer, attorney general, comptroller and state engineer and surveyor. It is easy to point to the parallel of the United States government for justification, or to the state of New Jersey.

The matter of safeguards on the appointing power is brought up. The politician takes it for granted that the state senate will have power to confirm or reject the appointments of the governor. The New York amendment, however, recognized the fact that the senate habitually utilizes the power of confirmation to accomplish a theft of the whole power of appointment. Forthwith, the responsibility of the governor for the appointments becomes something of a myth, and public control is baffled by the inability of the people to know whether it was the governor who made a given appointment, or some senator. For while the number of rejections by a senate may apparently not be large, the real number of rejections is very large indeed. The governor may not even informally ask the senators, or the boss who rules them, if this or that nomination will be acceptable, knowing well the limitations which the politicians will set upon him.

The history of the president's appointive power and its constriction by "senatorial courtesy" shows evils similar to those in New York state.

Likewise, in cities where the council must confirm the appointments of the mayor, an interchange of authority occurs and the council soon controls the patronage without the corresponding responsibility.

With such cases in mind, the New York Short Ballot Organization drafted its amendment so as to give the governor power to appoint these minor state officers, without confirmation, and with power to dismiss at pleasure. The amendment, consistent with this principle, went beyond the offices which are now elective and made the governor's power of unconfirmed appointment complete throughout the whole administration, so far as the constitution was concerned.

The mayor of New York City has similar power over all the department heads. He may appoint and remove without oversight by anybody, and this is considered one of the most modern and progressive features of the charter.

The National Municipal League's model charter conferred this absolute power on the mayor.

This is the present orthodox principle among reformers. The purpose is to clear the lines of responsibility from all entanglements; to make it impossible for an official charged with neglect to say "It wasn't my fault;" to get single-headed government instead of many-headed.

The opposition promptly complains that this is over-concentration of power. The politicians, fearful of the appearance of any machine except their own, argue that the chief executive would use his enlarged patronage to build up a new machine. Of course, we answer that a new machine once in a while by way of variety, might be a good thing and that we would have the boss of the new machine right where we could hit him full and square.

Nevertheless, it is my belief that there is a measure of soundness in the opposition to uncontrolled appointive power and that we must eventually give to the opponents of it a better answer than to say that it is at least better and safer than the confirmation plan.

In no other democratic country do the people subject themselves so to the mercies of individual caprice as we already do. And, as I have shown, reformers are ready to carry it still further. In many of our cities it may fairly be said that the mayor holds half the city power within his personal grasp. Certainly if we take into account his ability to misuse patronage and veto like chessmen, the mayor comes pretty near being a majority in

*Reprinted from the "National Municipal Review," January, 1913.

many of our city governments. In this matter we are unique among the nations, and it is curious that a country which appears most afraid of a strong government, and in which the Jeffersonian idea appears dominant, should be the one in which single individuals are entrusted with greater uncontrolled power than anywhere else in Christendom.

An instance of the dangers involved is New York City, where the mayor recently had it within his power to upset the subway situation whenever he pleased, and frequently it seemed to the people of the town that he was likely to do so. He expressed opposition to what he called "cornfield routes" for subways and wanted the new tubes built where there was already the greatest number of passengers. If that one man had happened to be impervious to argument, future generations in New York City might have been condemned to live upon an insignificant fraction of the land which lay within a few miles of city hall, with congestion piled on congestion, instead of congestion being relieved by the opening up of new spaces.

Similarly, the mayor of New York was charged with responsibility for an epidemic of crime, by reason of his causing sharp punishment of policemen who ventured to use their clubs. Matters reached a point where a gang of toughs could successfully forbid policemen to pass beyond the corner of a certain carbarn.

After the terrible Asch factory fire in New York, two important bills, aiming at fire prevention, came before the mayor for acceptance. One represented the best thought of the public-spirited citizens of the town and the most careful draftsmanship. The mayor, without giving anybody a chance to explain, rejected it because he thought his pet enemy, Hearst, had prepared it, and proceeded to sign the inferior measure.

Whether my statements are just to the mayor or not, it is obvious that things fully as serious as this are easily conceivable, and a plan of government which permits the whims or failings of a single man to swing such vast interests, even temporarily, is not thoroughly sound.

The chief ground for complaint against the uncontrolled-executive plan is, however, not its perilous strength, but the fact that the presence of these obvious perils compels us to withhold from our administrators the powers they need. They need not only complete undivided appointive power, but power to use their own discretion, power to make new rules, as they go along, to fit new situations, power to be agents instead of dummies of the law's minutiæ.

Our municipal, state and national legislatures now must undertake to control by continuous and detailed legislation a multitude of highly technic ought to be left to empowered adminis The legislatures cannot safely delegate administrators because they cannot hold tors answerable for results and subject to

The New York City government undert such holocausts as the Asch fire. There is vention bureau, placed according to cu theories, under the mayor's single control. the mayor is independent and uncontroll possible to confer the vast necessary p fire prevention bureau without running th vast powers may be used improperly opinionated executive, in which case the appeal and all hope of reform must be ha personality of the next mayor.

Another great and vital feature of loc New York City is the building code. aldermen make it and the mayor appro isters it. The present method has develo dals and the code is chronically out of da business and costly to the people. Th would be to have an appointive administ code board, served by an expert bureau to enact the code and keep it up to date If we attempt this at present we have alternatives: (1) To let the mayor have sponsibility for the building code board dismiss the members and appoint new on This overstrains our willingness to depend of one man. (2) To let the mayor appc confirmation by the council. This forks sponsibility and the principle has proven practice. (3) To let the mayor appoint th board, but give the members long terms that no one may or can alter a majority his term. This puts power beyond prom trol, prevents the retrieving of mistakes i and delays and baffles attempts at impro as attempts at corruption. Thus Gover been almost impotent in certain importan he was elected to carry through in New certain of his so-called subordinates have ures and silently defy his efforts to instal The people cannot be expected to analyze duly hold him blameless. He has no redr have the people, and there is nothing to the years to roll round before reform c Power ought not thus to be delegated be responsible representatives of the people.

The recall puts a touch of flexibility into the plan of electing independent chief executives. So far as the recall goes, I favor it. But it is at best, clumsy, unwieldy and expensive. The horse needs a hand on the rein. It is not always wise to give him his head and then unhitch him and buy another horse if he turns off the road to nibble the grass.

Upon a state legislature or a city legislature, i. e., a *group* of men who act in group, we willingly confer greater powers than we dare give *one* man, and all these large powers can, without diminution, be boldly and flexibly administered through a *controlled* chief executive.

Such is the new office which has just been created in Sumter, S. C. The new charter of this little city (10,000 population) modifies the commission plan by making the commissioners act as a board, never singly, and perform all executive work through an appointive city manager, who holds office subject to their pleasure. The city manager may be hired from out of town and is simply the expert servant of the commission.

Suppose New York adopted this plan by enlarging its present board of estimate and making it a supreme board of directors with no other elective officers to detract from its authority. That board of directors could hire a chief executive to carry out all its orders in proper co-ordination. There could be under this continuously controlled executive a building code board and a fire prevention board, for instance, to which could be safely sublet all the powers necessary to the proper regulation of buildings and the prevention of conflagrations. Then the public would have the right to disregard all details and simply hold the directors responsible for results.

After the Asch fire nobody suffered politically except George McAneny, the borough president, and he was not responsible at all. But if a building burned and people died in it the public could with perfect justice demand of our proposed board of directors—"What did you let this happen for? You had plenty of power to prevent it!" And the directors, apologizing, would turn privately to their city manager and repeat, "What is the reason? Did you appoint real experts or amateurs on that fire prevention board? Didn't you have inspectors enough? Or money enough? What do you need to prevent another fire?" And the manager, fearing lest he lose his job for having thus gotten his superiors into trouble, will tear things loose in the fire board to locate and punish the cause of the inefficiency and see that proper new provisions are made to prevent forever the repetition of any such disaster.

We cannot secure such a condition now because we dare not give to an uncontrolled executive such vast administrative discretion.

The controlled-executive plan filters everything through a group. It reduces the personal equation. Without loss of administrative unity, it abolishes one-man power. A single man may have his ups and downs, his freaks and fancies, his militant points and his passive ones, his natural bents and moods, his pet departments and projects. A board, or commission, or council, or parliament, has none of these things—to a group such excesses are relatively impossible. Even if all the members were cranks, their combined judgment would be reliable—they would neutralize each other.

This plan corresponds to the general manager under the board of directors in a business corporation. It gives the stability of the combined judgment of many men on matters of policy, but leaves execution to a single-headed controlled executive establishment.

The controlled-executive plan goes far beyond the recall of the mayor. Its executive can be bounced out of office in less time than it takes to print the blanks for a recall petition.

There are many other weaknesses of the independent-executive plan of government, all of which are corrected by the controlled-executive idea. I will simply name them.

1. The independence of the executive destroys continuity of the administrative policy. One mayor is a crank on finance and taxes, and devotes his attention to improving those matters, to the neglect of other departments which do not interest him. His successor leaves the financial reforms uncompleted and follows his own hobby of parks and schools.

2. Election of administrators is unsound in principle, for the choice of an administrator is no more a natural popular function than the choice of an engineer or a landscape architect. Administration of modern cities is an expert's job and the best experts are not necessarily good vote-getters.

3. The independent executive constitutes a separate city government and the attempt to compel him to work in harmony with the other "city governments" creates a costly and cumbersome mass of red tape. The council, for instance, in appropriating funds for the mayor to spend, will try to regulate the details of the expenditure, thus perhaps compelling what later in the course of the expenditure may be found to be extravagance or unwise economies or misdirected work.

4. The independence of the executive destroys unity

in the government. A city ought to have one government, not several. Pulling and hauling, deadlocks, friction and delays, trading of influence and the need of a boss to hold the ramshackle together and make it progress—all result from two-headed government.

Putting a chief executive under continuous control of a responsible group of men abolishes these evils. A moment's reflection will show that it is the universal plan in corporations and in all associations employing paid servants. It is likewise a standard plan in governments outside of the United States.

In foreign countries the parliament el the prime minister, who in turn control tion. The *magistrat* of a German ci power of appointment over the whole a hired by the council and subject to co by it.

I believe the best way to go about into practice is by giving encouragem spread adoption of the Sumter plan. T cessful in cities, will in time, spread to c to states.

Council plan and the only plan for the government of large cities which has always succeeded. It differs from the typical American plan of government in that the council is really important, there being no other elective officers. The ballot on election day is the size of a postal card containing the names of two or three candidates for one office, namely, member of council from the ward.

The ward plan involves the two perils of log-rolling and gerrymander smaller perils, however, than machine rule. The proportional representation idea, on the other hand, is untried as yet and our large cities would shrink from so academic a proposal.

The people in either of these circumstances would not need the guidance of the politicians in order to mark their ballots. The candidate fighting for election in a constituency of reasonable size would not need the help of the politicians in conducting his canvass. When elected he would have the people to thank and no one else. The people thus would hold the same undisputed control over their public servants as they do in the small commission cities.

Will the Commission Plan Succeed in Large Cities?

Yes.

JOHN MACVICAR, COMMISSIONER OF DES MOINES.

One of the objections most frequently urged against the Commission plan is based on the size of the cities for which it is proposed. On the one hand, it is said that it is not adaptable to small cities, and on the other, that it is not suitable for large cities. I can see no real merit in either of these objections. Whether cities are large or small, they all alike suffer from the division of authority, the Ward system, and from the mixing of municipal business with partisan machine politics. All private business, after it attains proportions beyond the personal supervision of one man, is conducted by organizations constructed on practically the same principle—that of placing power and responsibility with heads of departments; and it seems reasonable that a municipal system which proves correct in a city of 100,000 people should work equally well in a city of 25,000 or 1,000,000.

Mayor Gaynor says that he sees no novelty in Commission government; that the governing Board of New York City is composed of eight men, the Mayor, President of the Council, and the Comptroller, elected at large, and a President of each of the five Boroughs. True, New York has a Board of fifty Aldermen, but their powers are nominal, being simply the power to grant licenses and in a limited way to pass ordinances. At no time in the history of New York has she had as good service rendered by her municipal government as under this form, and if this governing Board were granted all powers and had the advantage of being non-partisan, with the democratic features of referendum and recall added, it would scarcely endanger the government of that City, but rather, I believe, insure more efficient results.

I have read with a good deal of care the reasoning of Mr. Richard S. Childs, in which the new plan is highly recommended for Cities of moderate size, but is declared to be not adapted to large Cities because, in general, "making the multitude hear," in a large City, is so vast a task that no one but an expert politician, or one who has expert politicians at his service, can hopefully undertake it. The writer believes that in such Cities as Pittsburg, Buffalo, and Baltimore the size of the electorate as compared with those now governed by Commissions, is sufficient to change completely the nature of the battle ground, and make it necessary to divide these great masses of population into large districts, which candidates may cope with more hopefully. The writer, it appears to me, approaches the problem from the wrong end, and in a real misapprehension of what happens in a Commissioned-governed City. Even in the smaller Cities, these things are not "managed" by candidates or committees or organizations of any kind, but by the citizens as a whole, acting as one body, very much as the people of the United States, City and country alike, act quite directly in electing our President and Vice-President. There are in New York, without much doubt, a thousand men of different callings as well known to their fellow New Yorkers as most of the Presidential candidates become. They are business and professional men, financiers, politicians, and, in various ways, men of mark. If New York was soon to elect a Commission of five men to conduct five great comprehensive subdivisions of its municipal business, men would be brought into prominence by the newspapers and by all the agencies of publicity in which great Cities abound. The importance of the issue would impress itself upon the people. New men, now unable or unwilling to compete for civic honors, would be attracted into the municipal arena. Most of these novices would fail to catch the public eye, but others, men of inherent force, like Mr. Jerome, would succeed. All would, at the primary, have to take their places on the official ballot in alphabetical order. No political organization could prevent any of its members who desire to be candidates from entering the race and dividing its forces. No one could surely fortell which would be the ten highest names on the long list securing the nominations. The method of voting would exclude all merely local favorites and the representatives of mere cliques or clannish elements of the population. At the final election five of these ten men presented in the same fair fashion of the alphabetical order would be elected. That they would represent as intelligent a choice as is exercised in a Presidential election and that, with the government of New York divided among them, they would as certainly respond to public sentiment as do the Commissioners of our smaller Cities, I cannot see much reason to doubt. The business of New York City is an enormous business, almost appalling in its demands upon those who administer it. In a sense, it is even now conducted by something approximating a Commission; but I firmly believe that the people and the press of New York, acting together under the real Commission system, could make efficient democracy a shining reality in our greatest City. They could, I believe, accomplish this while the personal machine which Mr. Childs has conjured up as a necessity for a candidate was being organized; and after it was organized it could not be used. Certainly, that objection falls of its own weight.

Preferential Voting.

By Robert Tyson, Ex-Secretary of the American Proportional Representation League.

When adopting the Commission plan of municipal government, the city of Grand Junction, Colo., added an interesting improvement over any previous city charter: she adopted preferential voting, and thereby secured the following advantages:

1. Abolition of primary elections.
2. A clear majority at one balloting.
3. Freedom of nomination: that is, several candidates representing a given policy can be nominated for one office without dividing the vote and thereby defeating the policy.

There are several plans or systems of preferential voting, but only two are in actual practical operation:

1. The Grand Junction plan, devised by Hon. James W. Bucklin, and now forming part of the charter of that city.
2. The Hare or Ware plan now used for legislative elections in West Australia, and which has been frequently used in "meeting-room" elections.

In each of these systems the ballot is so arranged that the voter may mark a first choice, a second choice, a third choice, etc. In each of them, if any candidate obtains a clear majority of first-choice votes, that decides the election, and the other choices are not used. But if no candidate gets a majority of first choices, then the other choices are used to get a majority for the most popular candidate.

As to marking the ballots, the Grand Junction plan provides three columns, headed respectively "first choice," "second choice," and "third choice." The voter puts crosses in these columns opposite the names of the candidates he votes for; and if there is a fourth choice, etc., this is put in the last column. But in Australia, there is only one column opposite the candidates, and the voter uses the actual figures 1, 2, 3, etc. Whether crosses or figures should be used is a mere matter of detail, and perhaps not a necessary part of either plan.

Of course, the voter does not mark more than *one* choice for the *same* candidate.

It is in the counting or canvassing of votes that the chief difference between the two plans appears.

The Grand Junction Method.

(See the Charter of Grand Junction, Colo., Sec. 22.)

The Hare Plan.

1. At each precinct the ballots are sorted, according to the first-choice votes, into as many heaps as there are candidates, no heed being paid to other choices. While this is being done, a tally of the first-choice votes is being made. Scrutineers for candidates may check the correctness of this work as it proceeds. At the conclusion of the sorting the tallies for each candidate are added up. The number of first-choice votes for each candidate is thus ascertained, and may be at once given to the newspaper reporters. Then the precinct officer ties the sorted ballots up as separated, labels them, puts them, with the tally sheets, back into the ballot box, and immediately delivers the box to the city clerk.

2. No ballot shall be spoiled if the intention of the voter be clearly evident from his marking; and if part of his choices are vitiated by defective marking the remainder of his choices shall be given effect if possible.

3. On the arrival of the first ballot boxes at the city hall, the election board commences the count by putting together in a compartment for each candidate the bundles of ballots cast for him, the tallies from the corresponding polling subdivisions being successively added together as the work proceeds. The bundles of ballots are not untied at this stage. When the ballot boxes have been received from all polling subdivisions, if the tally reports thus collated show a clear majority for any candidate, the counting is finished, subject, perhaps, to a careful recount next day if such be the custom or the law.

4. If by the operation of the foregoing rules no candidate has yet a majority, the tally clerks proceed to name the candidate who has the smallest number of first-choice votes. The chief election officer then declares that candidate "out of the count," and the tally clerks write the word "out" opposite the name. The officer then unties the bundles of ballots of the excluded candi date, and transfers the ballots, one by one, to such other candidates as are marked second choice thereon, subject to being stopped by the operation of rule 6. As he does

this he calls out the name to which each ballot is transferred, and the clerks keep tally in the column next beyond that containing the first-choice totals. With only three candidates, there will now be either a clear majority or a tie.

5. If at any stage of the counting any candidate gets a clear majority of all the votes, such candidate is duly elected, and the counting thereupon proceeds no further, unless it is desirable that the counting be continued so as to show the final standing of each candidate.

6. If there are more than three candidates, and none has yet a majority, the tally clerks add the transferred votes to the original totals, and announce what candidate is then at the bottom of the poll. This lowest candidate is declared "out," marked with the word "out" on the tally sheets, and his ballots are transferred and tallied in the manner already described. If in the course of the transfers the name of a candidate already "out of the count" should appear, that name is passed over, and the name of the next choice is taken instead.

7. This process is repeated, if necessary, until only two candidates remain, and the one having a majority is the elected one.

8. A tie between two or more candidates is to be decided in favor of the one having the greatest number of original first-choice votes. If all are equal in that respect, then the greatest number of original second-choice votes decides; and so on with further choices, if necessary. If this will not decide the tie, then all the tied candidates are to be declared "out" unless the election of one of them is necessary to fill a seat, in which case it is a tie at the top of the poll, and rule 9 applies.

9. In the event of a tie at the top of the poll, and which cannot be decided by the operation of rule 8, the tie shall be decided by casting lots.

Which is the Better System?

To help in a decision between these competing systems, I will briefly point out the advantages and drawbacks of each.

Taking the Grand Junction plan first, it has been objected that when there is no majority by first choices, the method of using second choices practically gives each voter *two* votes, and that the result of the counting of this second vote may be to defeat the voter's first choice. Similarly when the third-choice votes are added to the first and second choices, the counting of a voter's third choice may help to defeat his first. Consequently, voters may largely refrain from marking any but first choices; and if they do that then the basis of the preferential vote is gone.

An advantage claimed for the Grand Junction plan is that the ballots need not be looked at by the central election board, but only the tally-sheets.

To the Hare plan it is objected that both ballots and tally sheets must go to the central office, and that some transferring of ballots may have to be done there.

The advantages claimed for the Hare plan are that the counting at the precincts is shorter and simpler, because only the first choices are tallied; also that no voter can possibly hurt the chance of his first-choice candidate by marking second and third choices, and consequently there is no inducement to refrain from marking subsequent choices. The reason for this is that when a second-choice has to be used in the count, it is *substituted* for the first-choice on the same ballot, not *added* to the first choice. This holds good in regard to third and subsequent choices.

A Civil Service Law for Commission Cities.

ELLIOT H. GOODWIN, SECRETARY OF THE NATIONAL CIVIL SERVICE REFORM LEAGUE.

Sec. 1.

The Council[1] shall appoint three persons as civil service commissioners to serve one for two years, one for four years and one for six years. Each alternate year thereafter, the Council[1] shall appoint one person as the successor of the member whose term shall expire, to serve for six years.[2] Any vacancy shall be filled by the Council[1] for the unexpired term. Not more than two of the members shall be adherents of the same political party and no member shall hold any other salaried public office. The Council[1] may remove a commissioner during his term of office only by a unanimous vote and upon stating in writing the reasons for removal and allowing him an opportunity to be heard in his own defence.

Sec. 2.

The Commission shall appoint a Chief Examiner at an annual salary of \$———[3] who shall also act as Secretary. This position shall be in the competitive class. The Commission may appoint such other subordinates as may, by appropriation, be provided for.

Sec. 3.

The civil service of the city is hereby divided into the unclassified and the classified service.

The unclassified service shall comprise:

(a) All officers elected by the people.

(b) All members of executive boards.[4]

(c) One deputy and one secretary to each principal executive officer.

(d) Superintendents, principals and teachers in the school system of the city.[5]

(e) All judges and one secretary to each.

The classified service shall include all other positions now existing or hereafter created.

[1] Or "Mayor" in those cities in which the appointing power is lodged in the Mayor.

[2] If the term of the Mayor is one year, the terms of the Commissioners should be three years, one expiring each year.

[3] This amount should be stated but will vary according to the size of the city. In all cases it should be made large enough to secure the services of a competent and high-grade man.

[4] i. e., the School Board.

[5] Only where the school system is under the jurisdiction of a school board distinct from the city government.

Sec. 4.

The Commission shall prescribe, amend and enforce rules for the classified service which shall have the force and effect of law, shall keep minutes of its proceedings and records of its examinations and shall make investigations concerning the enforcement and effect of this chapter and of the rules. It shall make an annual report to the Council.[6]

The rules shall provide:

(1) For the classification of all positions in the classified service.

(2) For open, competitive examinations to test the relative fitness of applicants for such positions.

(3) For public advertisement of all examinations at least ten days in advance in at least one newspaper of general circulation and by posting a notice in the City Hall.

(4) For the creation of eligible lists upon which shall be entered the names of successful candidates in the order of their standing in examination. Such lists shall remain in force not longer than two years.

(5) For the rejection of candidates or eligibles who fail to comply with the reasonable requirements of the Commission in regard to age, residence, sex, physical condition or who have been guilty of crime or of infamous or disgraceful conduct or who have attempted any deception or fraud in connection with an examination.

(6) For the appointment of the person[7] standing highest on the appropriate list to fill a vacancy.

(7) For a period of probation not to exceed six months before appointment or promotion is made complete, during which period a probationer may be discharged or reduced with the consent of the Commission.

(8) For temporary employment without examination with the consent of the Commission, in cases of

[6] Or "Mayor."

[7] Or "one of the three persons." The State Constitution in New York has been held to require the certification of more than one name for each vacancy and in New York, Massachusetts, the Federal service and frequently elsewhere, the rule for certifying three names is in force. The rule for certifying the highest name only is best suited to small cities where candidates are few. It is, however, the rule in Chicago.

emergency and pending appointment from an eligible list. But no such temporary employment shall continue longer than sixty days nor shall successive temporary employments be allowed.

(9) For transfer from one position to a similar position in the same class and grade and for reinstatement within one year of persons who without fault or delinquency on their part are separated from the service or reduced.

(10) For promotion based on competitive examination and records of efficiency, character, conduct and seniority. Lists shall be created and promotions made therefrom in the same manner as prescribed for original appointment. An advancement in rank or an increase in salary beyond the limit fixed for the grade by the rules shall constitute promotion. Whenever practicable vacancies shall be filled by promotion.

(11) For suspensions for not longer than thirty days and for leaves of absence.

(12) For discharge or reduction in rank or compensation after appointment or promotion is complete only after the person to be discharged or reduced has been presented with the reasons for such discharge or reduction, specifically stated, and has been allowed a reasonable time to reply thereto in writing. The reasons and the reply must be filed as a record with the Commission.

(13) For the appointment of unskilled laborers in the order of priority of application after such tests of fitness as the Commission may prescribe.

(14) For the adoption and amendment of rules only after public notice and hearing. The Commission shall adopt such other rules, not inconsistent with the foregoing provisions of this section, as may be necessary and proper for the enforcement of this chapter.

Sec. 5.

In case of a vacancy in a position requiring peculiar and exceptional qualifications of a scientific, professional or expert character, upon satisfactory evidence that competition is impracticable and that the position can best be filled by the selection of some designated person of recognized attainments, the Commission may, after public hearing and by the affirmative vote of all three Commissioners, suspend competition, but no such suspension shall be general in its application to such position and all such cases of suspension shall be reported, together with the reason therefor, in the annual reports of the Commission.

Sec. 6.

All examinations shall be impartial and shall deal with the duties and requirements of the position to be filled. When oral tests are used a complete record of questions and answers shall be made. Examinations shall be in charge of the Chief Examiner except when members of the Commission act as examiners. The Commission may call on other persons to draw up conduct or mark examinations and when such persons are connected with the city service it shall be deemed a part of their official duty to act as examiners without extra compensation.

Sec. 7.

All persons in the city service holding positions in the classified service as established by this chapter at the time it takes effect shall retain their positions until discharged, reduced, promoted or transferred in accordance therewith. The Commission shall maintain a civil list of all persons in the city service, showing in connection with each name the position held, the date and character of every appointment and of every subsequent change in status. Each appointing officer shall promptly transmit to the Commission all information required for the establishment and maintenance of said civil list.

Sec. 8.

No treasurer or other public disbursing officer shall pay any salary or compensation for service to any person holding a position in the classified service unless the payroll or account for such salary or compensation shall bear the certificate of the Commission that the persons named therein have been appointed or employed and are performing service in accordance with the provisions of this chapter and of the rules established thereunder. Any taxpayer of the city may maintain an action in any civil court of record to recover for the city treasury any sums paid contrary to the provisions of this section from the person or persons authorizing such payment or to enjoin the Commission from attaching its certificate to a payroll or account for services rendered in violation of the provisions of this chapter or of the rules established thereunder.

Sec. 9.

In any investigation conducted by the Commission it shall have the power to subpoena and require the attendance of witnesses and the production thereby of books and papers pertinent to the investigation and to administer oaths to such witnesses.

Sec. 10.

No person in the classified service, or seeking admission thereto, shall be appointed, reduced or removed or in any way favored or discriminated against because of his political opinions or affiliations.

Sec. 11.

No officer or employee of the city shall, directly or indirectly, solicit or receive, or be in any manner concerned in soliciting or receiving, any assessment, subscription or contribution for any political party or political purpose whatever. No person shall, orally or by letter, solicit, or be in any manner concerned in soliciting, any assessment, subscription or contribution for any political party or purpose whatever from any person holding a position in the classified service.

Sec. 12.

No person holding a position in the classified service shall take any part in political management or affairs or in political campaigns further than to cast his vote or to express privately his opinions.

Sec. 13.

Any person wilfully violating any of the provisions of this chapter, or of the rules established thereunder shall be guilty of a misdemeanor.[6]

[6] In case the general penal laws of the State do not provide a penalty for general misdemeanors for which no special penalty is provided, a specific penalty should be provided in this section.

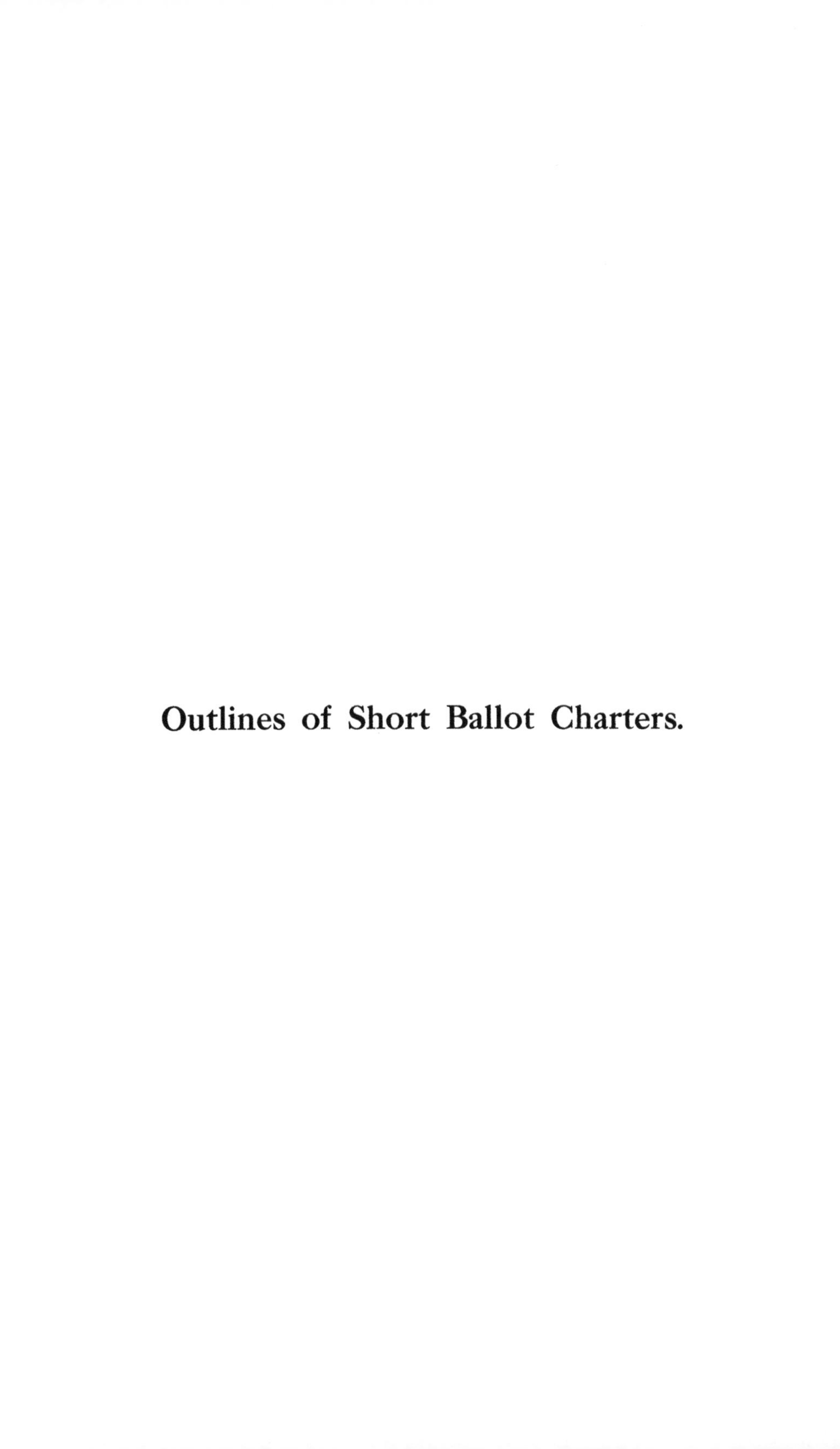

Outlines of Short Ballot Charters.

Outlines of Short Ballot Charters.

THE ELEMENTS OF THE COMMISSION STRUCTURE.

The Commission Plan of Government for cities is a plan of organization or structure and is not necessarily related to the question of Home Rule as against Centralization, or any other phase of the city problem which is chiefly concerned with the general powers of municipal corporations.

In the matter of organization the measure of power conferred upon municipalities varies in different sections of the country; the states fall naturally into groups, according to the general relationship between the state and its public corporations. In the Northwestern and Pacific states, the general tendency is to allow a larger measure of home rule. As a consequence of this fact, we find that the following states, which permit Commission Government, allow the municipalities, under certain conditions, to construct their own charters:

Michigan,
Minnesota,
Oregon,
Washington (cities of over 20,000 population),
California (cities of over 3,500 population).

Oklahoma also permits cities of over 2,000 population to draft a home rule charter through a Board of Freeholders.

The tendency in the Middle West and South has been to cover the field of municipal powers in the form of general statutes. The Illinois Constitution, for example, prohibits the enactment of special legislation with reference to cities and a statute provides a specific form of government which is applicable to all, with the exception of Chicago. Since the inception of the Commission Government movement, most of these states have enacted a general statute permitting the cities to choose between the older form and the Commission form. No state as yet prescribes the Commission form for any city, although at the present writing (January 21, 1911), there is some discussion in favor of such a move in the state of Kansas. The following states have general permissive Commission Government statutes which specify a particular form:

Iowa (cities of over 7,000 population),
Illinois (cities of less than 200,000 population),
Kansas (cities of over 2,000 population),
New Mexico (cities of over 3,000 population),
North Dakota (cities of over 2,000 population),
South Dakota (cities of the first, second or third class),
Wisconsin,
Kentucky (second class cities),
Mississippi,
Texas (cities under 10,000 population),
Louisiana,
South Carolina.

In the remaining states in which Commission Government is now permissible, the adoption of the form necessitates a special act of the legislature, which is presented to the people of the city for ratification. These states are:

Idaho,
Texas (cities of over 10,000 population),
Massachusetts,
Tennessee,
West Virginia.

There has apparently been much imitation of the features in the Commission Government law of the neighboring states. It has seemed best therefore, in this portion of the book, to group the documentary material according to localities rather than in the order of adoption.

CONSTANT FACTORS IN COMMISSION GOVERNMENT.

The fact that any city is listed in the succeeding pages presumes that it has in its political structure, two elements:

First, there must be a unification of the powers of the city, and the corresponding responsibility for the exercise of those powers, in the hands of a small body of men, in order to secure the "conspicuousness" in the full significance of that term, which is the essence of the Short Ballot. This unification of powers and responsibilities carries with it as a necessary corollary, the elimination of the sharp line between legislative and executive authority. The Commission Plan frankly breaks with the long standing tradition that there must be a complete separation of the powers of Government.

Second, there must be an abolition of the wards of the city as election units. This does not mean necessarily that Commissioners may not be nominated from wards, but it does mean that they must be elected by the voters of the city at large. So much, at least, must be conceded to the universal practice thus far.

THE TYPICAL STRUCTURE OF COMMISSION GOVERNMENT.

In reducing these principles to a working basis, the framers of Commission Government laws have followed certain typical features of the Galveston and Iowa Acts. They have nearly always bridged over the gap between the legislative and the executive functions by means of a personal union. That is, the Commission acts collectively in a legislative capacity, and individually in an administrative capacity. Whether this personal union will continue to be observed; whether such a union is good political practice—these are questions outside the scope of this introduction. In the common application of this principle the activities of the city Government are divided into four departments, each presided over by a member of the Board. Ordinarily, there is a Commissioner of Finance, a Commissioner of Public Safety, and either one or two Commissioners to look after the physical interests of the city. One of these is usually in charge of the Public Utilities in which the city is interested.

In the usual Commission form, the Mayor has no separate powers beyond those which belong to the first among peers. A deviation from this principle, however, has been made in a number of cities, characteristically in Texas and Oklahoma. In many of these even the veto power is preserved. The variation, if carried too far, however, is serious enough to warrant their elimination from the list of Short Ballot cities. The idea of unification also precludes the election of any other officers. Most cities have been consistent in this respect, but a few have retained the popular election of one or two general officials like the Auditor or Treasurer. It is difficult to say just how much of this inconsistency should be permitted and still allow the city to be retained in the Short Ballot list. In the following pages we have drawn the line at two, but have made an exception in one or two cases.

THE VARIABLE ELEMENTS OF THE PLAN.

Upon this simple foundation of the municipal structure, varied forms have been built, and it is these variations that the outlines undertake to bring out.

The Commission Organization:

The *title* of the Board of Commissioners varies in different parts of the country, and in some degree reflects the local feeling toward the central governing body and some of the traditions of government. New England has adopted the name "Municipal Council" in place of the older name "Common Council." Some of the western communities, on the other hand, have conservatively kept the term "Council," while others have shown their slight regard for the dictionary, by adopting the title "Board of Commissioners." The *number* of Commissioners varies, in general, with the population. The standard number is five, including the Mayor, but most of the small places have three. One or two cities have more than five. The method of *removal* of Commissioners is sometimes the Recall, but often the method prescribed in the original Charter of the city is retained in addition. The *salary* granted to the Commissioners is a fair index, when taken in connection with the population of the city, to the importance which is attached to the position. The *distribution of functions* among the individual members of the Board is usually made by the Board itself, but in some instances by the Mayor. In one or two cities the designation is made at election time.

General Powers of Commission:

The powers of the Commission, as stated above, normally include all the corporate powers. The outline of each charter as given in these pages, brings out in words as nearly as possible, the same as those of the organic act, the method by which the general powers are devolved upon the new Board. The exercise of these broad powers carries with it wide authority to create and discontinue agencies within the local government, in the shape of departments, bureaus, etc.

The Mayor:

The same variations as are indicated in the case of the Commission as a whole, have been indicated in the case of the Mayor, and the same observations hold good in the main with reference to that office.

Other Elective Officers:

The outline will show in each case how much of a deviation from the standard number of elective officers has been made in the case of each charter. The Board of Education and the whole school organization has been completely ignored in the Digest, inasmuch as the school organization throughout the country generally is a part of the state administration having, in a great many cases, a separate corporate existence.

Protection for Municipal Franchises

with Model Sections for a Commission Government Charter

Delos F. Wilcox, Ph.D., Author of "Municipal Franchises" and Chief of the Bureau of Franchises of the Public Service Commission for the First District, New York.

In the drafting of a city charter, it is not necessary that a hard and fast franchise policy should be worked out in detail and embodied in the city's fundamental law. The extent of the city's powers with reference to public utilities should be defined; the procedure of franchise granting should be exactly set forth; the general principles to which all franchises must conform should be clearly stated; and the governmental machinery for exercising control of public utility construction, maintenance, service and rates should be outlined.

The city should keep continuous control of the maintenance, equipment, location in the streets, extension, service and rates of public utilities because the available space in the streets is so limited and the demands upon it are so great as to make it imperative for the public authority to keep a continuous control of the distribution and redistribution of this space for various public uses, and the utilities are so vitally related to the growth and welfare of the city as to render it imperative for the city to be at all times in a position to compel the maintenance of the plant at the highest practicable standard of efficiency, with adequate equipment, safe and sufficient service, reasonable expansion and rates as near cost as is consistent with the gradual amortization of the capital and a fair annual return on the investment.

Experience shows that this continuous control cannot be effectively exercised in large cities directly by the city council, the board of commissioners, the department of public works, the city attorney or any other general body or officer having multifarious other duties to perform. In all cities of considerable size, say 50,000 or more population, a separate department, bureau or board should be established to provide for the necessary inspections, investigations and reports preliminary to the issuing of final orders to the companies by the council, the mayor or other supervisory authority. In smaller cities this jurisdiction, perhaps, can more readily be assumed by the regular city officials. In all cases the activities of the local authorities should be supplemented as to matters of state or interurban jurisdiction by the work of a state public service commission or department. As a means to the effective exercise of reserved powers of control, the city should grant only indeterminate franchises, so that the operating company of a public utility can be thrown out of the streets and a new one put in its place whenever the one in possession manifests a persistent unwillingness to conform to public regulations. Provision should be made, however, requiring the city to purchase or to find a purchaser for the physical property of the operator whose franchise is terminated.

The following "model" sections for a commission charter have been drafted and are submitted, not with the expectation that they will be embodied, without change or supplementation, in any particular charter law, but that they may form a basis for the working out of rational charter provisions relative to franchises and public utilities, consistent with the constitution and laws of the state and the local conditions of the city or cities affected by them:

ARTICLE ..

FRANCHISES AND PUBLIC UTILITIES.

Section 1. City's right to own and operate.

The city shall have power to acquire, construct, maintain and operate any or all public utilities requiring the permanent occupation of the streets on, above or below the surface thereof with fixtures. The city may acquire, lay, maintain and own all fixtures located in the streets and public places necessary for the operation of public utilities, and may in like manner acquire, construct, maintain and own public utility plants, whether for manufacture or distribution, or both, outside of the streets either within or without the corporate limits of the city. For the purpose of acquiring utilities or plants now or hereafter owned by private individuals or corporations, or of acquiring any real estate or easements required for the construction, maintenance, enlargement or operation of a public utility, the city shall have the power of eminent domain both within and without its corporate limits, but such power may be exercised outside the corporate limits only in accordance with general laws intended to give equal protection to all cities and towns within the state.

Sec. 2. Accounts of public utilities owned by the city.

The city, when owning any public utility, shall keep the books of accounts for such public utility distinct from other city accounts and in such a manner as to show the true and complete financial result of such city ownership, or ownership and operation, as the case may be. Such accounts shall be so kept as to show the actual cost to such City of the public utility owned; all cost of maintenance, extension and improvement; all operating expenses of every description, in case of such City operation; the amounts set aside for sinking fund purposes; if water or other service shall be furnished for the use of such public utility without charge, the accounts shall show, as nearly as possible, the value of such service, and also the value of such similar service rendered by the public utility to any other City Department without charge; such accounts shall also show reasonable allowance for interest, depreciation and insurance, and also estimates of the amount of taxes that would be chargeable against such property if owned by a private corporation. The Board of Commissioners shall cause to be printed annually for public distribution, a report showing the financial results, in form as aforesaid, of such City ownership or ownership and operation.

Sec. 3. City may grant franchises or lease public utility plants.

Subject to the limitations contained in this charter and in the constitution and general laws of the state, the city may grant franchises to private individuals or corporations authorizing them to place fixtures in the streets and public places for the operation of any public utility, but no such franchise shall be given for the construction and operation of a plant to compete with an already existing plant owned by the city, and no perpetual franchise shall ever be granted. The city may also lease street fixtures or a complete utility plant owned by it to a private individual or corporation for operation, but no such lease shall be for a longer period than ten years, and the making of any such lease shall be subject to the same restrictions as to procedure and approval as are in this article prescribed in the case of franchises.

Sec. 4. Unused franchises.

All franchises or special privileges in the streets and public places heretofore granted by any public authority, which are not now in actual use or enjoyment, or which the grantees thereof have not in good faith commenced to exercise at the time of the adoption of this charter, are hereby declared forfeited and of no validity, except that if the time fixed in any franchise for the commencement of the exercise thereof has not expired, such franchise shall not be deemed forfeited by this section. Every franchise hereafter granted shall prescribe the period, which shall not be more than one year from the date of the final approval thereof, within which construction shall be in good faith commenced, and any failure on the part of the grantee to comply with such provision or any subsequent failure of the grantee to continue in good faith to exercise the franchise shall render the franchise subject to repeal by ordinance without compensation therefor, and in case of such repeal any property of the grantee situated within the limits of the streets or public places of the city shall thereupon revert to and become the absolute property of the city as a penalty for such default.

Sec. 5. Strict construction of grants.

All franchises or privileges for the occupation of the streets shall be strictly construed in favor of the city and no such franchise or privilege shall be held to have been granted unless granted in clear and unmistakable terms.

Sec. 6. Repeal of duplicating franchises.

Every person or corporation owning or operating a public utility, wholly or partly within the limits of the city, having fixtures in the streets or public places thereof at the time this charter goes into effect, shall within sixty days thereafter file with the city clerk a sworn statement duly authenticated describing the franchise or franchises under which such utility is operated and in case such individual or corporation claims the right to operate such utility under two or more franchises covering the same area, such individual or corporation shall designate the particular grant under which such utility is thereafter to be operated, and if such franchise is valid all other duplicating franchises claimed by such individual or corporation shall thereupon be repealed by ordinance. If any such individual or corporation fails to elect the particular franchise under which operation is to be continued the Board of Commissioners shall forthwith designate the same and proceed to repeal all other duplicating grants claimed by such individual or corporation and shall take such steps as may be necessary to procure a final adjudication of the franchise rights of such individual or corporation, unless such designation and repeal are accepted in writing by the parties in interest within 60 days after the date thereof. No franchise hereafter granted shall be transferable by the grantee except with the city's approval expressed by ordinance, and in case any franchise heretofore granted shall at any future time be acquired by any individual or corporation already having a franchise for a similar purpose, then such individual or corporation shall forthwith and within thirty days thereafter file written notice with the city clerk stating which of said franchises is to be used in operation, and thereafter the Board of Commissioners shall at once repeal by ordinance such other franchise or franchises not so designated, and if such individual or corporation fails to make such designation then such franchise to be used in operation shall be designated by the Board of Commissioners and such other franchise or franchises shall be immediately repealed.

Sec. 7. Franchise procedure—Publication—Referendum.

Franchises shall be granted only by ordinance, which shall be published in its final form at least four weeks before its final passage. Publication shall be once a week for four weeks in full in not less than two daily newspapers of general circulation in the city, or, in lieu thereof, publication in like manner of a brief resumé of such ordinance with reference to the place at the city hall where copies of such ordinance printed in full may be secured upon application in person or by mail. In case of any proposed street railway franchise, in addition to the publication hereinabove provided for, a full printed copy of such ordinance shall be posted in some conspicuous place on each side of the streets to be occupied by the railroad in every block along the route. Such notices shall be posted at least four weeks before the final passage of any such ordinance and shall give notice of the place and a time not less than two weeks subsequent to such posting, at which place and time a public hearing shall be held on such proposed franchise before the Board of Commissioners or the Bureau of Franchises and Public Utilities, hereinafter provided for. If after such notice and public hearing the terms of such proposed ordinance are changed in any respect, there shall be a new publication as hereinbefore provided for, but the ordinance need not again be posted unless the route has been changed, and then only along the new or changed route. In case any ordinance granting a franchise receives upon final passage the affirmative votes of all the members of the Board of Commissioners, it shall go into effect at the end of sixty days thereafter if accepted in writing by the grantee, unless within such sixty days a referendum petition, signed by qualified voters of the city in number equal to ten per cent. of the total number of votes cast at the last preceding municipal election for all candidates for the office of mayor, be filed with the city clerk asking that such franchise ordinance be submitted to a vote of the electors for approval or rejection, and in case such petition is so filed no such ordinance shall be of any force or effect whatever until it has been approved by the electors by majority vote of those voting thereon at a general or special election. In such case, the ordinance shall be submitted at a general election unless the Board of Commissioners shall determine to submit it at a special election. Any franchise ordinance voted for by a majority but not by all of the commissioners shall be submitted to the electors for ratification at a general or a special election, as the Board of Commissioners may determine, and the Board of its own motion may submit any franchise ordinance to a referendum vote, but no such ordinance shall in any case be submitted at a general or special election held less than thirty days subsequent to the determination to submit such ordinance.

Sec. 8. Damages to abutting property.

The consent of abutting property owners shall not be required for the laying or erection of any public utility fixtures in the streets, but any such property owners not having voluntarily consented to the construction of any such utility fixtures in front of his premises shall be entitled to recover from the owner of such fixtures the actual amount of damages suffered by him on account thereof less any benefits received therefrom, the amounts of such damages and benefits to be ascertained by suit in the proper court commenced within three years from the date of the laying or erection of such fixtures.

Sec. 9. Franchise ordinances initiated by petition.

Franchise ordinances may be initiated by petition of not less than twenty per cent. of the qualified electors, to be determined as in the case of referendum petitions, but no such ordinance so initiated shall be submitted to referendum vote until it has been laid before the Board of Commissioners and a public hearing has been held thereon. If, after such hearing, the Board shall not within sixty days from the filing of such petition pass the ordinance by unanimous vote in its original form, the Board shall forthwith prepare and publish a report thereon and may propose an alternative or amended ordinance and shall cause the proposed ordinance in its original form and any such alternative or amended ordinance to be published as hereinbefore required and submitted to popular vote at a general or special election, for approval or rejection, but neither of such propositions shall be deemed adopted unless it receives an affirmative majority of all the votes cast at such election. In case both measures receive a majority of all votes cast, only that measure shall be effective which receives the higher number of affirmative votes.

Sec. 10. Grants for spur tracks.

Revocable permits for laying spur tracks across or along streets and public places for not to exceed 500 feet in any one stretch, to connect a railroad with any warehouse, factory or other establishment needing switching facilities shall not be considered to be franchises, as that term is used in this Article, but such permits may be granted and revoked by the Board of Commissioners from time to time in accordance with such terms and conditions as may be prescribed by general ordinance. Such general ordinance shall, however, be subject to the same procedure, including publication and the right of initiative and referendum, as any franchise ordinance.

Sec. 11. Renewal and extension franchises.

The renewal of any franchise heretofore or hereafter granted, or the modification of the conditions of any such franchise, or the extension of the application of any such franchise to additional streets or areas not covered by the original grant or brought under such franchise by the Board of Commissioners in the exercise of its reserved power to order extensions of plant or service, shall be by ordinance subject to all the conditions as to procedure, including among other things publication and the initiative and referendum, which are applicable to original franchise ordinances as prescribed in this Article.

Sec. 12. Reserved right of regulation.

The grant of every franchise or privilege shall be subject to the right of the city, whether in terms reserved or not, to make all regulations which shall be necessary to secure in the most ample manner the safety, welfare and accommodation of the public, including among other things the right to pass and enforce ordinances to require proper and adequate extensions of service, and to protect the public from danger or inconvenience in the operation of any work or business authorized by the grant of the franchise, and the right to make and enforce all such regulations as shall be reasonably necessary to secure adequate, sufficient and proper service, extensions, and accommodations for the people and to insure their comfort and convenience without discrimination either as to class or as to kind of service rendered or to be rendered at the option of the people, or in the price charged or to be charged for such service.

Sec. 13. Franchises to be indeterminate—City's right to purchase.

Every franchise ordinance shall provide for the maintenance of the plant and fixtures to be constructed thereunder at the highest practicable standard of efficiency at all times and shall provide for the amortization of at least that portion of the capital invested in plant and fixtures within the limits of public streets and places within a period fixed by the franchise, which shall not in any case be more than thirty years from the commencement of operation of the utility, or, in case of the renewal of a franchise heretofore granted, shall not be more than twenty years from the date of such renewal. Every franchise, whether original or renewal, hereafter granted shall be subject to the right of the city, at the expiration of a specified period which shall be not more than ten years from the commencement of operation thereunder and at specified intervals of not more than five years thereafter, to terminate the grant and take over the property necessarily or conveniently used in the operation of such utility to render service within the city limits or within its immediate suburbs, either for municipal operation or for muncipal ownership and lease to some other individual or corporation for operation, or for purchase and operation by some other individual or corporation designated by the city and to be known as the city's licensee. In case of such termination of the franchise and such purchase of the plant and property used in connection therewith, the purchase price shall be ascertained as may be prescribed in the franchise itself, but in no case shall any bonus be paid on account of the termination of the franchise in excess of a sum equal to 15 per cent. on the valuation of the physical property, and in arriving at such valuation deduction shall be made to the full amount of the amortization of capital provided for up to the date of such purchase. All renewals and replacements of plant and fixtures, to the full extent of the original cost of the portions of plant and fixtures so renewed or replaced, shall be paid for as a part of maintenance and shall not be charged to capital account. The cost of all additions, betterments and extensions actually and properly charged to capital account shall be subject to the amortization provisions of the franchise as original cost of construction as of the date when such additions, betterments and extensions are constructed.

Sec. 14. Accounts and reports of utilities operated under franchises.

Every person or corporation operating a public utility within the limits of the city by virtue of a franchise or right, whether heretofore or hereafter granted, shall keep books of account according to forms prescribed by the Board of Commissioners, showing in detail the assets, financial obligations, and monetary operations of such utility. In case any such utility extends in its operation beyond the boundaries of the city and to other communities not properly considered suburban to the city, the books of account referred to shall be kept separately for the portion of the utility operated within the city limits or for the portion which the city would have the right or be obligated to buy in case of the termination of the franchise, and for the utility as a whole, as the Board of Commissioners may from time to time prescribe: Provided, that if a public service commission or any other lawful authority shall be given the power by law to prescribe the forms of accounts for public utilities throughout the state or throughout any district of which the city is a part, the forms so prescribed shall be controlling as far as they go, but the Board of Commissioners may prescribe more detailed forms for the utilities within its jurisdiction. Every person or corporation operating a public utility in whole or in part within the city limits shall file with the city clerk an annual report of the status and financial transactions of such utility. The forms of these reports, the dates within which they must be filed and the penalties for failure to file them as required shall be prescribed from time to time by the Board of Commissioners. The forms of such reports shall be consistent with the forms of accounting in force during the year covered by the reports, but the Board of Commissioners may at any time, with reasonable notice, call upon the owner or operator of any franchise utility for such supplementary or special information in regard to such utility as the Board may desire, and such information shall forthwith be furnished if it is possible for the owner or operator of the utility to do so. The Board of Commissioners may at any time directly or by its agents examine all the books and papers of the owner or operator of such utility so far as they relate directly or indirectly to the property or business of the utility within the city limits or within the jurisdiction of the city to purchase the plant. The reports of the owner or operator of every such utility shall be public documents, open to inspection at all reasonable times in the office of the city clerk. Such reports and information secured by the examination of the books of the utility may, in the discretion of the Board of Commissioners, be published and distributed to those desiring copies thereof. The Board of Commissioners shall have the right annually or oftener to audit the accounts of any utility operated by a private person or corporation within the jurisdiction of the Board, and shall provide for a complete audit of the accounts of any such utility relating to construction work hereafter done for the purpose of authoritatively fixing from time to time the amount of the legitimate investment therein. The Board may of its own motion institute an investigation of the necessary and legitimate investment in any utility now constructed or in operation for the purpose of determining the capital value of such utility at the date when this charter goes into effect. No allowance shall be made in the valuation of any public utility plant for appreciation or depreciation of land values subsequent to the adoption of this charter and subsequent to the purchase of the land used for such utility, and no allowance shall be made for appreciation in the cost of construction on account of paving or other changes in the condition or uses of the streets until such additional cost has actually been incurred in connection with renewals or replacements of plant.

Sec. 15. Taxation and compensation.

The city shall have no power to levy any tax upon property located within the street limits and actually and necessarily devoted to public utility purposes. Upon movable property and property outside of the street limits the city may levy only such taxes as are levied on other property of a like or similar nature within the city limits and not devoted to the use of any public utility: Provided, that the city may require the owner or operator of any street railway, railroad or spur track lying within the street limits to lay, maintain and renew the pavements between the rails and the tracks and for a distance of not more than two feet on either side outside of the tracks, and to remove snow and ice therefrom and to sprinkle the entire roadway to a width of not more than fifty feet, or the city may require the owner or operator of any such tracks to pay into the city treasury the reasonable cost of such paving and maintenance if done by the city directly. No compensation for any utility franchise shall be paid to the city until the earnings of the utility are adequate to pay all legitimate operating expenses and taxes, to maintain the plant at the highest practicable standard of efficiency, to provide a return of not less than five per cent. upon the capital actually and necessarily invested in the utility and to set aside an annual sum sufficient, with its accumulations, to amortize the entire capital investment within the street limits within the period required in the franchise. A franchise ordinance may prescribe that, after such charges have been fully met, the net profits of the utility shall be divided between the owner of such franchise, the employees actually engaged in the operation of the utility and the city in such proportions as shall be fixed in such ordinance. No moneys received by the city as its share of the profits of any utility operated under a franchise shall ever be used for the general purposes of the city, but all such moneys shall be placed in a separate fund to be used only for the acquisition, construction or extension of public utility plants owned or to be owned by the city.

Sec. 16. Rates—Free Service.

Every franchise hereafter granted shall prescribe a maximum initial rate or rates for the service or commodity to be supplied, which rate or rates may be regulated and adjusted from time to time at intervals prescribed in the franchise and in the manner therein prescribed, but the rates prescribed in the original grant as accepted by the grantee shall never be so reduced by the city as to render the utility unable to meet the charges enumerated in section 15 of this Article as necessarily preceding the payment of compensation to the city: Provided, that city policemen, city firemen and United States letter carriers, while in uniform and actually engaged in the performance of their official duties, shall be permitted to ride on the street cars without the payment of fare, but in no other way shall any franchise holder be required to render any free or reduced-rate service to the city or any department or officer thereof except as compensation for the franchise subject to the restrictions contained in section 15 of this Article.

Sec. 17. Records to be kept.

Forthwith upon the adoption of this Charter, the Board of Commissioners, either directly or through such department, bureau, commission or office as may be established or designated for the purpose, shall take measures to create and thereafter maintain the following records:

First. A Street Record, which shall contain such maps, documents, diagrams and indices as may be required to show by ready reference for every street in the city the location and history of all utility fixtures therein for the full width of the street between the adjacent property lines, whether on, above or below the surface, whether located at specific points or running along or merely crossing such street.

Second. A Franchise Record, indexed and of proper form in which shall be transcribed accurate and correct copies of all franchises or grants by the city to any person or corporation to construct or operate any public utility. The index of said record shall give the name of the grantee and thereafter the name of any assignee thereof. Such record shall be a complete history of all franchises granted by the city and shall include a comprehensive and convenient reference to actions, contests or proceedings at law, if any, affecting the same.

Third. A Public Utility Record, for every person or corporation owning or operating any public utility under any franchise granted by the city, into which shall be transcribed accurate and correct copies of each and every franchise granted by the city to such person or corporation or which may be controlled or acquired by him or it, together with copies of all annual reports and inspection reports, as herein provided, and such other matters of information and public interest as the Board of Commissioners or the Bureau of Franchises and Public Utilities may from time to time acquire. All annual and inspection reports shall be published once in one daily newspaper of general circulation published in the city, or shall be printed and distributed in pamphlet form, or both, as the Board of Commissioners may deem best, and in case annual reports are not filed and inspections are not made as provided, the mayor shall in writing report to the Board the reason therefor, which report shall be transcribed in the record of the person or corporation owning or controlling such franchise or grant and shall be published once in one daily newspaper of general circulation published in the city, or shall be printed and distributed in pamphlet form, or both, as the Board may deem best.

The provisions of this section shall apply to all persons or corporations operating or having the right to operate under any franchise now in force or hereafter granted by the city.

Sec. 18. Control of street spaces—Joint use of fixtures—Relocation of fixtures.

The city shall have and forever retain the right to control the distribution of space in, over, under or across all public streets and places to be occupied by the fixtures of the various utilities from time to time occupying such streets and public places, and the Board of Commissioners may at any time require the owner of utility fixtures in the streets and public places of the city to share with the city or with any other person or corporation holding a franchise from the city the use of such fixtures for a proper rental and to the extent that such joint use shall be safe and shall not unreasonably interfere with the service being rendered or to be rendered by the owner of such fixtures. In case the admission of an additional utility to a particular street, or the enlargement or necessary relocation of the fixtures of an existing utility, or the carrying out of any public improvement in such street, shall at any time, in the judgment of the Board of Commissioners, require the readjustment of public utility fixtures in the street, the Board may require such readjustment and may prescribe the method by which it shall be carried out and by which the expense thereof shall be borne. It shall be an obligation assumed by the grantee of any public utility franchise to remove, readjust and relocate such grantee's fixtures in the streets wholly or partly at his own expense, as may be prescribed by the Board of Commissioners, when said Board deems such removal, readjustment or relocation necessary in the public interest for the most economical use of the street spaces available for public purposes, including therein all franchise utilities.

Sec. 19. Bureau of Franchises and Public Utilities.

There shall be established by ordinance a Bureau of Franchises and Public Utilities at the head of which shall be an officer to be appointed by the Board. Such officer shall be an expert in franchise matters and shall be provided with such legal, accounting, engineering, clerical and general assistance as may be required to enable him to perform his duties. It shall be the duty of such officer to keep a diligent oversight of the operation of all public utilities operated under franchises and to report to the Board all failures of any person or corporation to comply with the terms of the franchise or franchises under which such person or corporation is operating. Such officer shall hear and attend to all complaints lodged by citizens in regard to the operation of any public utility not operated by the city itself, and from time to time, as occasion may arise, he shall recommend to the Board of Commissioners the adoption of such measures as may seem to him wise or necessary to secure adequate and safe service and the full protection of the public interests in connection with the operation of any utility. No ordinance granting a franchise, or regulating, or in any manner relating to a public utility not operated by the city itself, whether initiated by petition or not, shall be passed without having first been referred to such officer for investigation and for his written recommendations thereon. Other duties relating to franchises or public utilities may at any time be conferred upon him by the Board of Commissioners.

Sec. 20. Other terms and conditions may be imposed.

Every franchise hereafter granted by the city shall be held subject to all the terms and conditions in this Article contained whether or not such terms or conditions shall be specifically mentioned in such franchise. Nothing in this Article contained shall operate to limit in any way, except as specifically stated, the discretion of the Board of Commissioners or of the electors of the city in imposing terms and conditions in connection with any franchise grant, but such grant may contain additional conditions not included herein, and may contain restrictions or provisions of any nature which may be deemed by said Board of Commissioners and said electors to be in the public interest, provided only that such restrictions and provisions shall not be inconsistent with the provisions of this charter or of the Constitution and general laws of the state.

The Practice of the Recall

By H. S. Gilbertson, Assistant Secretary of The Short Ballot Organization.

Most of the questions inspired by the rapid acceptance of the Recall are answered, in one fashion or another, in the history of that institution down to the present time, if a number of isolated instances of its actual use can be said to constitute a history.

The first occasion for the use of the Recall came in 1904. A certain Mr. Davenport, one of the Los Angeles councilmen, made himself unpopular in his ward, and especially to the labor element there, by a vote on a public printing contract. He was alleged also to have had connection with the liquor interests and to have taken money for voting for a permit to an offensive slaughter house in the residence district. The typographical union started a petition. An election was held and Davenport was recalled. He undertook to retain his seat in the council and to collect his salary, but without success. He then applied to the Supreme Court of California for a writ of mandamus to compel the Council to allow his petition. On purely technical grounds, based upon the failure of the City Clerk to observe a minor provision of the charter, this was granted. A second election, however, was held. Davenport carried but one of the sixteen precincts of his ward. His opponent received 63 per cent. of the votes cast. Again he appealed to the courts for relief, but the same court which had granted his former petition refused to take jurisdiction on what it considered an extra judicial matter.

In 1906 a councilman named Reynolds in the city of San Diego, Cal., was made the subject of a Recall petition on the ground that he had voted for a certain ordinance regulating the sale of liquors, and that he had repeatedly voted to disregard petitions to refer ordinances which were filed in conformity with the provisions of the charter to a vote of the people. The City Council in this instance, without consulting the City Attorney, ignored the recall petition and covered their negligence with a plea that the provisions of the charter which bore on the recall were unconstitutional. Legal proceedings continued for many months until three days before the end of the officer's term. No vote was ever taken on the matter.

After this the Recall was not used directly for five years, but the threat of its use in at least one instance caused city officials in Los Angeles to reverse their policies. On this occasion the Council in the face of an overwhelming popular protest, voted to give away a valuable franchise in the Los Angeles river bed. Preparations for recall proceedings were made, but before petitions were in the field the councilmen realized the hopelessness of their position and nullified the franchise.

The first use of the Recall in the case of a mayor is that of Mr. A. C. Harper, of Los Angeles. Mr. Harper, elected in 1906, had not been long in office when it began to appear that his appointments were not directed primarily by considerations of public interest, but with a view to satisfying office seekers. Within a year after his election the city prosecutor complained of laxness in the enforcement of laws. The responsibility for this condition clearly lay with the mayor and an appointee of his on the police commission. The charge was made, and supported by specific evidence, that the mayor and police commissioner were protecting vice. This, however, the mayor vigorously denied with a challenge to an investigation of the matter before the grand jury. The grand jury happened to be in session at the time and the matter was immediately taken up. After months of investigation a majority report was filed, which found that the laws relating to vice were sufficiently definite, and were quite enforceable, but had been neglected by the administration. The jury, however, refused to file information on the ground that, since the investigation had begun, the laws had been enforced. A minority report, however, definitely charged the mayor and the police officials with complicity with the vicious elements in the city. (Harper had also shown his incapacity by the appointment of a certain Ed. Kern to the Board of Public Works, who was notoriously unfit for this position.) In the face of this evidence, the Municipal League in Los Angeles, in the spring of 1909, assumed the responsibility for a Recall campaign. The outcome was the unseating of Harper and the election of George Alexander as mayor.

The Los Angeles charter provisions attracted early attention in a number of the Pacific Coast cities. The idea appealed particularly to a group of public spirited citizens in the city of Seattle as a possible means of reaching a certain Councilman whose public conduct was unbecoming in a representative, and whose personal demeanor was decidedly offensive. In 1906 a Recall amendment was inserted in the Seattle charter.

No serious occasion arose for putting this instrument into practical use until the latter part of 1910. It was directed this time against the mayor, who happened to be the same Hiram C. Gill who had attracted adverse attention four years before while a member of the City Council. Gill's term of office would expire in about a year, so that his administration had been given a thorough test. He had irritated the general public through his opposition to public improvements. He had seemed to play into the interests of the local, privately owned electric lighting company. He had opposed the establishment of a municipal garbage crematory. But the most serious opposition to his administration arose on account of his conduct of police affairs. Gambling and other forms of vice were known to flourish under police protection. At length the City Council on November 21, 1910, through a committee of five of its members, made an investigation and brought specific charges of maladministration. The thing, however, which gave a vivid, personal touch to the police question was the appointment of a Chief of Police by the name of Wappenstein.

In his defence of the charges, both before and during the recall discussion, Gill antagonized his opposition by the vulgar and offensive language which he used in public and by his effort to shift the responsibility for the shortcomings of his administration upon the City Council. The work of conducting the Recall election devolved upon the Public Welfare League, which outlined and organized a campaign very much on the same lines which were perfected in the case of Mayor Harper in Los Angeles. The Recall election, which took place on Feb. 8, 1911, resulted in the choice of a successor in Mr. George B. Dilling.

In none of these cases has the city been under the commission form of government at the time the Recall was invoked. But in 1907 Dallas adopted it into its charter. Three years later her School Board outraged public sentiment by the dismissal of two teachers, presumably without due cause. Thirty-five per cent. of the voters petitioned for a Recall election and the board was removed.

In the spring of 1911, a movement was started in Huron, S. D., a city operating under the commission form, to recall the mayor and Council. The mayor assigned as the primary cause of this action the increased rate of taxation. This year (which was the first under the commission plan) for the first time the commissioners provided for a sinking fund to meet outstanding bonded indebtedness. This meant an increase in taxes of about $25,000. A sufficient number of petitioners was secured to cause the recall to be submitted to popular vote at the regular spring election. The effort, however, failed.

Simultaneously with the Huron movement a campaign was started in Tacoma for the recall of the mayor and City Council. The outward condition which induced this step was the lack of harmony in the Council. Out of this trouble was said to have resulted a degree of inefficiency which reflected serious discredit on the commission plan of government that had been put in operation only about eleven months before.

The chief offender seems to have been the mayor, Mr. A. V. Fawcett, a citizen of some wealth with a long record of office seeking which was heavily clouded with scandal. The Recall as directed against the mayor had its origin with the Labor Council, which claimed that he had favored both non-union and non-resident labor in the construction of public buildings. Labor laid the blame for the existing industrial depression at the door of the city government. When the recall movement got under way other causes for dissatisfaction were revealed. It came to public notice that the mayor had failed and even refused to enforce the vice laws. He had also neglected to observe the charter provisions relating to the civil service and to the establishment of a uniform system of municipal accounting. He had opposed the establishment of branch libraries. In the first nine months the general budget had increased $100,000 over the corresponding period the previous year. On these grounds a recall petition was secured, and after a vigorous campaign the mayor was recalled. A month later two of the commissioners were similarly removed.*

Ten years ago it was generally assumed in this country that the direct participation of the citizen in government was fulfilled if he cast his ballot for his various delegated representatives at fixed intervals. The fact that popular control had no direct channel of expression between times, even in the face of intolerable political evils, was

* The use of the Recall in Everett, Wash., and in San Bernardino, Cal., and in two Oregon cities has been reported. The writer was unable, however, to get at the facts.

never great cause for regret. This, in fact, is the view of conservative publicists of the present time, who, taking their stand on legal precedent, go even further and aver that interference from the people between regular elections by direct vote is something unthinkable in representative government. Such interference they hold to be of the essence of pure democracy, something quite apart from the republican form which the framers of the constitution sought to guarantee.

With the reception of the Recall into good legal standing this limited interpretation of citizenship was rudely shaken. Originating in theory in the so-called "Imperial Mandate" of the Populist party of Kansas the innovation was so revolutionary that the men who introduced it into the Los Angeles charter found it necessary to keep its real nature secret and ride it in on the backs of other measures. But one day it got recognition from the California Court of Appeals in terms as follows:

"Responsible government is the very foundation of the Republican system, and there appears no reason why a representative should not be made to retire at any time, at the request of the people as well as at the end of a fixed period. This is not deemed incompatible with a republican form of government in France and several of the South American states. It is similar in principle and application to the customs or rules which makes the ministry the real government of England answerable at all times for its failure to meet the approval of the electorate of that country on some measure or question of policy."

Thus did the court clear away the popular misunderstanding that the Recall is nothing more than a new way of getting rid of bad officials on accepted statutory grounds. The Recall sets loose a new set of influences. We can remove an officer who may be personally and politically pure, for no other reason than the vague one that his conduct is unbecoming in a representative. Thus in April, 1911, an election was held in Huron, S. D., to recall the mayor and Council because they had provided for an increase in the tax levy to liquidate the bonded indebtedness. There were no accusations of malfeasance or misfeasance. This political nature of the Recall is shown no less clearly in the form in which it is cast, than in the ends which it seeks to accomplish. When the people ballot at a Recall election it is not a choice between removal and no removal, but a choice between men, one of whom is the incumbent in office.* The ballots ordinarily contain a statement of the causes upon which the removal is sought but this serves merely as a general guide to the voter and is not a formal accusation of guilt in any sense.

Neither is the principle of the Recall in any way related to the action which takes place when a delegate from one government to another is relieved of his mission. Ambassadors to foreign countries are affected in this way. Ambassabors, however, are not true representatives with wide discretion, but merely agents of the home government awaiting orders at the end of the telegraph wire. Whatever discretion is exercised has its inspiration in the Department of Foreign Affairs. Under some of the state constitutions framed in 1776 delegates to Congress were subject to recall, and delegates from Pennsylvania were actually removed in this manner. But here, again, the men in question were regarded in the light of mere agents of sovereign states.

A much closer parallel is the workings of the English parliamentary system. The Septennial Act sets a definite limit to the length of a parliamentary session. But in practice no recent parliament has ever lived out its allotted time. Before the lapse of seven years it has always become known by certain signals, which every one understands, that resort must be had to a new expression of the popular will. It then becomes the simple duty of the Crown to order a new election. The initiative comes from above. Under the Recall "we, the people," have taken the constitution literally and have decided to take the initiative into our own hands. The English custom is to recall the whole party. In the United States we usually direct our fire against one man. This, however, is not always so. Dallas recalled a school board, Huron, S. D., and Tacoma sought to recall their entire Council. In all three cases the issues were matters of administrative policy.

So much for definition. In practice the virtue of the Recall lies in the insecurity of tenure which it creates. Public office becomes in fact, as formerly in theory, a trust, which the electors may cause to be transferred at any time. In legislative and political usage there is obviously a delicate adjustment to be observed when we balance the factors that make for security and those that make for insecurity of tenure; for public office in the United States is none too attractive, even as it is, to men of appropriate talents and training. Should we not be loath to increase its instability by purchasing responsibility at the risk of cheapening the office in the eyes of prospective candidates?

* Not always, however. The Modesto, Calif., charter requires an election on the simple question of removal.

The suggested danger seems to be mostly hypothetical. Legislation and political usage, thus far, have supplied adequate immunities and compensations for any evil that might result from the loosening up process.

Coincident with the gradual acceptance of the Recall principle has grown up the tendency to lengthen the terms of elective officers. Whereas the first commission government legislation specified the two year term, the more recent general laws, as a rule, specify a four year term.

One important immunity is the percentage of petitioners (in relation to the total vote cast for mayor at the last preceding election) required to initiate Recall proceedings. The favorite number is twenty-five; in some places it is as low as fifteen; in San Francisco, which is not a commission governed city, it is ten; in Dallas, where the Recall has been successfully invoked, it is thirty-five. In the few years that the Recall has been incorporated in the city charters, the twenty-five per cent. petition seems to have been, in itself, a sufficient bulwark against actions based upon trivial causes. Frequent instances are on record of recall petitions being instituted for trivial reasons, and subsequently dropped for lack of a sufficient number of signatures.

Another legal immunity, incorporated in many of the laws, is the period of grace after the beginning of his term during which an officer may not be recalled. This period varies from three months in Colorado Springs to one year in New Jersey. The law in the latter state also provides that no second recall may be filed against an officer.

More significant, however, than these immunities of a formal character are those which inhere in the political practice of the electors themselves. Those prophets who have predicted that the people with this new political axe in easy reach would be swinging it at frequent intervals have been disappointed. Mob rule, so often the subject of earnest warnings, has failed to raise its head as yet. The Recall, to date, has been invoked successfully only where a clear case has been established, showing that an officer has violated, willfully and flagrantly, what will generally be understood as better public sentiment in the community. In the case of the mayors in Los Angeles, Seattle and Tacoma the issues took on a distinctly moral aspect on account of the questions of police administration involved. In San Diego the councilman openly defied the charter. In Los Angeles Councilman Davenport was convicted as a too friendly friend of "special interests." In Dallas the demand was for fair play to certain individuals. On the other hand, in Huron, where the question was one purely of financial policy, the recall was unsuccessful. Thus the available evidence, in the infancy of this new institution, ought to be sufficient to allay the fears of those who profess a horror of popular control.

In respect to the publicity which accompanies Recall proceedings, the officials indicted by popular opinion have had a hearing, whose thoroughness is unique in American city politics. Through the simplicity of the situation, attention is directed to one, or a very small group of persons, and a single set of issues. Ideal "Short Ballot" conditions prevail, and there is no confusing the voter as to what is going on; no outside assistance is needed. The verdict of the election for good or evil, is the people's verdict. Recall campaigns, too, have been the source of intense popular interest. Newspaper space was used up in great abundance in the mayoralty campaigns, and every available public auditorium was employed. The most accurate index of public interest, however, was the large vote which, in some cases, has exceeded that cast in a presidential year. Popular interest in the processes of a Recall is not always impartial and judicial, to be sure. Personalities naturally come prominently to the fore through the very simplicity of the situation.

Such, in the limited range of cases, has been the atmosphere of the new popular tribunal, a court whose fairness on the whole is certainly not open to serious criticism. In this tribunal the defendants have almost invariably ignored the political nature of the contest and rested their cases on legal technicalities. They have not met the issues on their merits. Fawcett, in Tacoma, failed to appear in public in his own defence. Gill in Seattle and Harper in Los Angeles fought removal in the courts at every conceivable loophole in the law. It is something of a tribute to the capacity of the people for fair dealing which has been rendered by the courts in recent opinions. One of these has already been quoted. One or two more will bear citation. Judge Albertson in one of the Seattle cases said:

"We must not hunt for obscure reasons to thwart the will of the people. This court cannot pass upon all the intricate questions involved on the spur of the moment. Where there is any doubt in the court's mind as to the charter provisions, it ought to be decided in the free expression of popular will. It is suggested by the plaintiff that the expense of such recall provisions should be avoided in view of the questions involved and uncertainty as to legal procedure, but the court cannot consider the matter of expense that is authorized by law. The people have adopted the charter amendment recognizing the expense and it is not for the court to say no."

Judge Hanford, in affirming this decision in the United States Circuit Court of Appeals, was equally liberal in his construction of the law involved:

"It is a matter of right or wrong between these parties. With the plaintiff only the payment of his tax is involved. The defendant stands here for the orderly conduct of an election authorized under the laws of the state. It is a matter that affects the whole community. The court should be very slow in tying the hands of the officers of the city in a case of this kind."

On the whole, the Recall seems to have rendered a decent account of itself to say the least. Its wide application in cities operating under the Commission plan has certainly not resulted in disaster. Whether, through its indirect moral influence, it has kept the peoples' representatives in the straight and narrow way is something which cannot be determined without the aid of psychological investigations, a process beyond the resources of the present writer.

The Lockport Proposal.*

By F. D. Silvernail, Consulting Engineer, Lockport, N. Y.

Municipal conditions in the city of Lockport are much the same as in many others which have suffered from the typical ills of American democracy. The city has a population somewhat under 20,000, and has been ruled for years by a triumvirate of bosses. Popular control has been a negligible quantity, and the rule of the self-appointed trio has been anything but one responsive to the will of the people of the city. As a natural consequence of the aloofness of the government, needed improvements have been delayed for years at a stretch, and when actually undertaken, have been executed in a most inefficient and expensive manner. It was these conditions which led the Lockport Board of Trade to become sponsor for the plan of municipal organization which has come to be known as the "Lockport Proposal," which was embodied in a bill introduced into the 1911 session of the New York legislature and supported by the Commission Government Association of New York State.

The "Lockport plan" is built upon the same basic principle as the Des Moines commission government law, but it aims to correct what seem to many to be illogical features of that plan. The commission government movement is based primarily upon the theory of the union of legislative and administrative powers in the hands of a small body of men who are the sole responsible agents of the people. It is a theory, borne out in practice, that this small group of men, because of their conspicuous position, tend to feel a responsibility to their constituents in a degree which virtually restores government to the people. The Des Moines plan, however, does not carry this theory of responsibility to its logical conclusion. The commission of five men are not collectively responsible for the acts of the municipality. Neither are the individual commissioners. At first blush these statements may startle some readers, but note carefully the following hypothetical situation. Let us suppose that the majority of the commission have passed an ordinance providing for the repavement of the main thoroughfare. Let us suppose that the commissioner of streets and public property was not a member of the majority which passed the resolution, and happens also to be a man of independent ideas. What action can the responsible commission take to force one of its own number to execute its orders? Now suppose another situation: The commissioner of streets is desirous of placing electroliers in the public squares. Public sentiment is clamoring for such action, but on looking over his annual budget, the commissioner finds that it is insufficient to cover this added expense. He applies to the commission for a larger appropriation and they refuse. In that case, who is responsible for the inaction of the city government? Cases of such conflict have actually been brought forward in some of the commission governed cities.

Under the Lockport plan responsibility would be vested in five men, acting always collectively. They would meet with no such difficulty in enforcing their orders as in the case cited, for the party responsible for the actual execution of orders would not be one of their own number but an appointive creature of theirs—the city manager. In short, the Lockport plan is an exact parallel of the organization of a private business corporation, with the city council corresponding to the board of directors and the city manager to the general manager. This city manager is the unique feature of the "Lockport plan." But while it is a unique proposal in the organization of city governments, it is by no means novel in other forms of organization. Not only have private corporations reached what appears to be their ultimate form in this particular type of organization, but it is the plan which operates in large school systems throughout the United States, in which the superintendent of schools corresponds to the city manager. It is also a very close approximation to the German type of city government, in which the Burgomeister is the central administrative agent and the council is the ultimate responsible body, which lays down the policy of the municipality. Of course, the German cities look back upon a totally different set of traditions from the American. Still, the naked question of municipal administration is not one which is concerned with the political genius of a people. Certainly, under the "Lockport proposal," the voice of the people has just as effective a medium as under the Des Moines plan. And, once we concede this fact, there remains the simple question of best organization.

* Reprinted, by permission, from the Annals of the American Academy, Philadelphia, 1911.

The "Lockport proposal" looks forward to a time when municipal government will be conducted by real experts. To suppose that popular election in the great majority of cases will secure expert service seems almost fatuous. Even the most educated of our citizens must fail if called upon to choose, let us say, between the technical qualifications of two candidates for a position which requires an engineer's training. On the other hand, an appointive expert could be found to take general charge of the city administration who could select trained assistants under the most favorable conditions. The city manager himself would, supposedly, be a rather high salaried officer and might be taken from any part of the country. There would seem to be in this country ample material from which to choose such an officer. In the event that such a proposal should receive wide adoption, it is easily conceivable that there would arise in the United States a class of municipal experts. The profession would be a most alluring one to men of talent and vision, and it seems hardly too much to suppose that we would come to have a combination of democracy and municipal efficiency which has never before been effected.

The Lockport plan, again, has certain possibilities which seem to place it on a higher level as a democratic instrument than the ordinary commission plan. The latter system has been strongly advocated by "business" interests. Labor, for this reason, has frequently looked askance at the movement, and perhaps not always without some just cause. In order to achieve true democracy, every important element in the city should be represented in the council, but if every councilman is to be both a representative of certain class interests and desires, and also a municipal expert, what is labor to gain? Many men who would prove most excellent representatives of labor would fail when confronted with problems of municipal administration. What is a barber, for example, apt to know about the administration of finance? And yet that same barber may be the truest representative and best spokesman of labor in the community. The "Lockport plan" would not embarrass him by requiring him to take charge of a department, but would simply require him to exercise his representative functions on the council.

The salaries which are usually paid under the commission plan are not sufficiently large in all cases to attract real experts. If the best brains of the community were required simply to pass judgment on policies and leave the execution of those policies to a salaried chief executive, many men of large calibre would be willing to devote to the city's business the small amount of time and energy which such a commissionership would require.

On the whole, then, it seems as though the "Lockport plan" has made a certain contribution to the solution of the twofold problem of municipal government in this country, viz.: that of securing administrative efficiency, which at the same time preserves all the essentials of democracy.

Aside from the features above noted, the Lockport plan embodies the usual minor features of the commission plan, including non-partisan nominations, elections at large, initiative, referendum, recall, etc. One minor feature, however, should be noted, viz.: nominations by deposit. Under this plan, the candidate, in lieu of a petition, may put up a deposit of fifty dollars, in order to have his name appear on the ballot. In case he receives fifteen per cent. or more of the total vote cast, or turns out to be, in other words, a serious candidate, his deposit is returned. This method is borrowed from the Canadian election law, and is believed to be a wise alternative to the system of nomination by petition.

Outlines of Short Ballot Charters

(Replacing pages of original publication.)

THE so-called Commission government movement involves plans of reorganization rather than the extension of the powers of the cities. No consistent reference to the general powers of municipal corporations, therefore, appears in the following pages.

FORMS OF COMMISSION GOVERNMENT LEGISLATION

An important distinction should be noted in the forms of legislation, especially as they bear upon the relationship between the city and the state government. We find in practice three general types. Thus in eight states the system of home rule in one form or another prevails to a greater or less extent. These states are:

Arizona.
California (cities of over 3,500 population).
Colorado.
Michigan.
Minnesota.
Oklahoma (cities of over 2,000 population).
Oregon.
Washington (cities of over 20,000 population).

But a more usual type of legislation, however, is the general permissive law by which any city of a specified class may adopt the new form of government by petition of a given percentage of the voters and popular vote. One state (Utah) makes the Commission plan of government mandatory for cities of the first and second classes. The following states have one or more general laws permitting the adoption of Commission government:

Alabama.	Montana.
California (cities of less than 10,000 population).	Nebraska.
	New Jersey.
	New Mexico.
Idaho.	North Dakota.
Illinois.	South Carolina.
Iowa.	South Dakota.
Kansas.	Texas.
Kentucky (second-class cities).	Utah.
	Wisconsin.
Louisiana.	Washington.
Mississippi.	Wyoming.

In the remaining states in which Commission government has been adopted by any city, the adoption necessitates a special act of the legislature which has in nearly every case thus far been presented to the people of the city for ratification. The following states belong in this classification:

Florida.	North Carolina.
Georgia.	Tennessee.
Maine.	Texas (cities of over 10,000 population).
Maryland.	
Massachusetts.	West Virginia.

In the growth of the Commission government idea, localities have tended apparently to imitate their neighbors' legislation. It has seemed best, therefore, to group the documentary material in this portion of the book, according to localities rather than in the order of adoption.

BASIC FEATURES OF COMMISSION GOVERNMENT.

The listing of any city in the succeeding pages presumes that it has in its political structure two elements:

First: There must be unification of the powers of the city and a corresponding responsibility for the exercise of those powers in a small body of men. The members of this body ordinarily constitute the only elective officers of the city. Slight variations of this rule, however, are allowed in our classification. (*See "Definition of Short Ballot Charter," p.* 10201.)

Second: The wards of the city as election units are eliminated. Such at least is the universal practice of Commission government charters to date, although in some of the southern states commissioners are nominated from wards and elected by the people of the city at large.

THE TYPICAL FORM OF COMMISSION GOVERNMENT

In reducing the above principles to a working basis, the framers of Commission government laws have followed certain typical features of the Galveston charter and the Iowa statutes. Thus, they have ignored the idea of the separation of powers and have made the legislative and executive departments identical in personnel. That is, the Commission acts collectively in the directive or legislative capacity and individually in an executive capacity. Commonly, the activities of the city government are divided into as many departments as there are commissioners, and each department is presided over by a member of the Commission. The mayor is often the head of a department known as the department of Public Affairs. The other departments are variously designated so as to include police functions and the general oversight of the fiscal and physical affairs of the city. The functions of these several departments are determined by ordinance when the theory of Commission government is carried out consistently. Some charters, however, undertake to define in some detail what the work of these departments shall be. It lies within the power of the Commission at any time to change the designation of commissoners to different departments.

In the usual Commission form, the Mayor has no separate powers beyond those which belong to the first among peers. A deviation from this principle, however, has been made in a number of cities, characteristically in Texas and Oklahoma. In many of these even the veto power is preserved. The variation, if carried too far, however, is serious enough to warrant their elimination from the list of Short Ballot cities. The idea of unification also, as stated before, precludes the election of any other officers. Most cities have been consistent in this respect, but a few have retained the popular election of one or two general officials like the Auditor or Treasurer. It is difficult to say just how much of this inconsistency should be permitted and still allow the city to be retained in the Short Ballot list. In the following pages we have drawn the line at two, but have made an exception in one or two cases.

THE VARIABLE ELEMENTS OF THE PLAN.

Upon this simple foundation of the municipal structure, varied forms have been built, and it is these variations that the outlines hereafter undertake to bring out.

The Commission Organization:

The *title* of the Board of Commissioners varies in different parts of the country, and in some degree reflects the local feeling toward the central governing body and some of the traditions of government. Massachusetts has adopted the name "Municipal Council" in place of the older name "Common Council." Some of the wes ern communities, on the other hand, have conservative kept the term "Council," while others have shown the slight regard for the dictionary, by adopting the tit "Board of Commissioners."

The *number* of Commissioners varies, in general, wi the population. The standard number is five, includi the Mayor, but most of the smaller cities have thr One or two cities have more than five.

The method of *removal* of Commissioners is sometim the Recall, but often the method prescribed in the ori inal Charter of the city is retained in addition.

The *salary* granted to the Commissioners is a fair i dex, when taken in connection with the population of t city, to the importance which is attached to the positio

The *distribution of functions* among the individu members of the Board is usually made by the Boa itself, but in some instances by the Mayor. In sor cities the designation is made by popular election.

General Powers of Commission:

The powers of the Commission, as stated above, nc mally include all the corporate powers of the city, e pressed in a variety of ways. The outline of each chart as given in these pages, brings out in words as nearly possible, the same as those of the organic act, the meth by which the general powers are devolved upon t Board. The exercise of these broad powers carries wi it wide authority to create, consolidate and discontin agencies within the local government, in the shape departments, bureaus, etc.

The Mayor:

The same variations are indicated as in the case of t Commission as a whole, and the same observations hc good in the main with reference to this office.

Other Elective Officers:

The outlines show in each case how much deviati from the standard number of elective officers has be made in the case of each charter. The Board of Edu tion and the whole school organization have been alm practically ignored, inasmuch as the school organizati throughout the country generally is a part of the st administration having, in a great many cases, a separ corporate existence. In one or two instances, howe (see Cartersville, Ga., and Sacramento, Cal.), the edu tional functions are vested in the City Commission.

Appointments:

Wherever possible the outline enumerates the appointed officers and indicates the manner of their appointment. The former is a good indication of the scope and of the distribution of the administrative powers of the city. A considerable variation in the manner of appointment is to be noted.

INCIDENTAL FEATURES OF THE COMMISSION PLAN.

Incidental to the Commission government movement are certain efforts to secure better municipal conditions otherwise than through this simple change in structure. These are associated in most minds so closely with the Commission plan that they seem properly to have a place in this volume.

Civil Service Provisions:

Many of the larger cities have taken advantage of reorganization to insert provisions in their charters looking toward a more systematic and equitable manner of appointing subordinate officers and employees in the Civil Service. Civil Service provisions, too, are sometimes held to be a necessary "check" on the great power of the Commissions. A brief notice of any such provision is noted in each case.

Elections:

The development in the matter of election reform has been mainly in the direction of eliminating partisan control. Most of the Commission Government charters contain provisions for non-partisan primaries, on the ballots of which names of candidates are to be placed by a petition of a specified number of qualified electors. The outline indicates the number or *percentage of petitioners* required in each case. *The basis for the computation in nearly every case is the total vote cast at the last preceding municipal election.** The Preferential system (see Charters of Grand Junction, Colo., and Spokane, Wash.) of voting is another incident of the Commission movement.

The Initiative:

The Initiative operates normally in the following manner: The ordinance proposed is submitted to the Board of Commissioners by a petition of a certain number of the voters or a percentage of the total vote cast at the last preceding municipal election. The Board of Commissioners then have the option of (1) taking the initiative into their own hands and passing the proposed ordinance, or (2) submitting the same to the voters at either a general or special election. The outlines indicate the *number or percentage * of petitioners* required to effect popular legislation in this way.

The Referendum:

Wherever the Referendum is in operation, any ordinances passed by the City Council, except one for the immediate preservation of the public health or safety, is suspended from operation for a given period of days or weeks. During its period of suspension every ordinance is subject to a protest, in the form of a petition against its final passage. If the petition is sufficient in all respects the Board of Commissioners must either (1) rescind its former action, or (2) submit the ordinance to people for their approval or disapproval.

Measures bearing the stamp of popular approval or disapproval through the operation of the Initiative or Referendum, may be reversed only through the operation of the same process.

The Recall:

The recall of elective public officers requires a petition of a certain *specified percentage* * or number of the voters as in the case of the Initiative and Referendum. When the sufficiency of the petition has been established, the Board of Commissioners must call an election for filling a prospective vacancy in the position of the officer sought to be removed. The officer in question may be a candidate for re-election. If at the recall election he does not receive the highest number of votes, he is thereby automatically removed from office. The regular election provisions usually apply to removal elections. Many of the charters provide for an interval of immunity after the installation of the officer, during which the recall petition may not be filed. A number of interesting variations from this form are to be noted, *e. g.*, Sacramento and Modesto, Cal.

Franchises:

There is a strong tendency in the cities re-organizing under the Commission Plan to prohibit the grant of exclusive franchises or franchises covering a longer period than fifty years. In many of the cities franchises

*Throughout the Outlines, unless a statement to the contrary is made, this basis of computation applies wherever reference is made to a number or percentage of the ballots cast for the highest office at the last preceding municipal election.

must be submitted to popular vote. Other restrictions are noted.

Special Features:

Various cities have inserted in their charters a variety of special features, either in the direction of greater publicity to the acts of the Commissioners or of business efficiency. These features are noted in a number of cases.

TABLE OF AMENDMENTS AND CORRECTIONS.

Since the original publication of the volume some errors and omissions have been pointed out. In a number of the laws important amendments have been made. To meet these conditions we have reprinted the pages containing the outlines of the South Dakota and Wisconsin laws. Other items are noted herewith:

Massachusetts

The State Civil Service Law applies to all cities.

Haverhill (p. 31001).

Under *Referendum* insert:

Twenty-five per centum petition.

North Dakota (p. 35, 401)

Initiative, Referendum and Recall were added by Chapter 67, Laws of 1911. A twenty-five per centum petition is necessary in each case. Abandonment of the act after six years is also provided for by popular election based upon a forty per centum petition.

Kansas (First class cities) (p. 34, 501)

In cities of between 30,000 and 60,000 population the mayor is required to devote at least six hours a day to the duties of his office; in cities of over 60,000 population the mayor and commissioners are required to devote their entire time to the duties of their offices. In cities of the first class of less than 30,000 population the mayor and council are restricted in the amount of taxes to be levied for various purposes.

(Second class cities) (p. 34563)

The words "*Commissioner-Departments*" should be followed by: (1) Fire, Police and Health, (2) Streets and Public Utilities, (3) Education, Finance and Revenue.

Illinois

The Commission government law (p. 34201) was amended in 1911 so as to continue the application of an act of April 2, 1903, to certain cities of between 7,000 and 100,000 inhabitants, relating to the appointment and discharge of employees of the police and fire departments.

The percentage of petitioners to initiate recall proceedings was reduced from seventy-five to fifty-five.

Mississippi (p. 36301)

This should not have been entitled a home-rule law. The form of the statute is very general.

HAVERHILL

(SPECIAL ACT APPROVED JUNE 3, 1908, ENABLING THE CITY TO ADOPT CERTAIN FEATURES OF THE COMMISSION PLAN, TO BE SUPPLEMENTED BY ORDINANCE. ACCEPTED BY THE CITY. ORDINANCE PASSED FEB., 1909.)

Commission-Organization:

Title: Municipal Council.

Number: Five, including Mayor.

Term: Two years, partial renewal.

Removal: Recall.

Salary: Eighteen hundred dollars.

Commissioner-Departments: 1, Finances; 2, Public Safety and Charities; 3, Streets and Highways; 4, Public Property. Designation by Municipal Council.

General Commission Powers:

Those formerly exercised by the City Council, Board of Mayor and Aldermen, Board of Aldermen and Common Council.

Special Requirements:

Monthly statements of Receipts and Disbursements.

Mayor:

Term: Two years.

Salary: Twenty-five hundred dollars.

Removal: Recall.

Powers in Relation to Commission: No veto power. Treasurer is authorized to sign notes; majority of Council countersign. Not a head of a Department but exercises general supervision.

Special Requirements: Assumes duties of heads of Departments during their disability.

Appointments:

The powers of nomination, appointment, confirmation and election which were formerly vested in the Mayor and Aldermen, City Council, Board of Aldermen and Common Council, are to be exercised by the Municipal Council, and the Mayor retains simply his right to vote on these matters like the other members of the Municipal Council.

Election Provisions:

Non-partisan primaries. Petitions require twenty-five signatures. Not over two candidates for each office at second election.

Initiative:

Twenty-five per centum petition (special election). Ten per centum petition (general election).

Referendum:

No provision.

Recall:

Twenty-five per centum petition.

GLOUCESTER

(AN ACT OF THE LEGISLATURE AMENDATORY TO THE CHARTER, CHAP. 611, LAWS OF 1908, APPROVED JUNE 11, 1908. ACCEPTED BY THE VOTERS OF THE CITY.)

Commission-Organization:

Title: Municipal Council.

Number: Five, including Mayor.

Term: One year.

Removal: Charter provisions.

Salary: One thousand dollars.

Commissioner-Departments: No designation.

General Commission Powers:

Those formerly exercised by the Mayor and Aldermen, Board of Aldermen, City Council and Common Council.

Special Requirements:

Monthly financial statements.

Mayor:

Term: One year.

Salary: Twelve hundred dollars.

Removal: Charter provisions.

Powers in Relation to Commission: Votes at meetings of Council. No veto power.

Appointments:

Manner: By Municipal Council.

Civil Service Provisions: None.

Election Provisions:

Contained in original Charter.

Initiative:

Twenty-five per centum petition (special election).

Referendum:

Twenty-five per centum petition (special election). The Council may submit questions of its own initiative.

Recall:

No provisions.

Franchises:

All franchise grants to be submitted to popular vote.

Special Features:

A member of the Municipal Council is chosen President thereof, to act in the absence of the Mayor.

TAUNTON

(SPECIAL CHARTER. AN ACT OF THE GENERAL COURT, APPROVED MAY 26, 1909. ADOPTED NOV. 2, 1909. IN EFFECT JAN. 1, 1910.)

Commission-Organization:

Title: Municipal Council.

Number: Nine and Mayor.

Term: Two years. Partial renewal.

Salary: Five hundred dollars.

Removal: Original Charter provisions.

Commissioner-Departments: The administrative functions of the city are performed by appointive officials.

General Commission Powers:

All powers and duties formerly exercised by the Mayor and Aldermen, Board of Aldermen, City Council, Common Council, under any general or special act.

Mayor:

Term: Two years.

Salary: Twelve hundred dollars.

Removal: Original Charter provisions.

Powers in Relation to Commission: President of the Council.

Appointments:

Manner: The Mayor appoints, subject to the approval of the Municipal Council, a Chief of Police and a City Solicitor. Appointment of all other non-elective officers by the Municipal Council.

Civil Service Provisions: None.

Election Provisions:

Names placed on primary ballot by petition of twenty-five voters. Partisan elections. General State Law applies where not in conflict.

Initiative:

No provision.

Referendum:

No provision.

Recall:

No provision.

LYNN

(Special Charter. An Act of the Legislature, Chapter 602, Laws of 1910, approved June 10, 1910.)

Commission-Organization:

Title: Municipal Council.

Number: Five, including Mayor.

Term: Two years. Partial renewal.

Removal: Recall.

Salary: Three thousand dollars.

Commissioner-Departments: 1, Public Safety; 2, Finance; 3, Streets and Highways; 4, Water and Water Works; 5, Public Property. Designations at election. The scope of each department is determined in the Charter (*q. v.*).

General Commission Powers:

The powers and duties under the general and special acts formerly exercised by the Mayor, Board of Mayor and Aldermen, Board of Aldermen, City Council, Common Council, Board of Public Works and Public Water Board.

Special Requirements:

Monthly financial statements. All resolutions, etc., appropriating money in excess of $500 or involving contracts above that amount, must be proposed in writing and notice given at least one week in advance in a daily newspaper, except an order for immediate preservation of public peace, health and safety.

Mayor:

Term: Two years.

Salary: Thirty-five hundred dollars.

Removal: Recall.

Powers in Relation to Commission: Presides over Council.

Appointments:

Enumeration: City Clerk, City Treasurer, Collector of Taxes, City Auditor, Purchasing Agent, Board of Overseers of the Poor, City Engineer, City Physician, Board of Health, City Solicitor, Board of Park Commissioners, Board of Sinking Fund Commissioners, Board of Library Trustees, Board of Assessors, and seven assistant Assessors. The terms of appointive officers continue indefinitely.

Manner: Appointments to office are subject to a publication of a list of vacancies in positions to be filled in a daily newspaper, in response to which the candidate for such offices may file application. The terms of officers, unless fixed by the act, continue indefinitely. The Commissioner in charge of departments is required to keep a record, subject to inspection, of all persons appointed or employed by the City, and of all persons suspended or removed, and the grounds for their removal.

Civil Service Provisions: None.

Election Provisions:

Non-partisan primaries. Petitions of twenty-five signatures.

Initiative:

Twenty-five per centum petition (special election).
Ten per centum petition (general election).

Referendum:

Twenty-five per centum petition (special election).

Ten per centum petition (general election).

Recall:

Twenty-five per centum petition.

Special Features:

The act calls for general meetings of the registered voters, which must be held three weeks after the filing of a petition, notice of which must be given on the front page of at least one daily newspaper not less than three times within two weeks after the filing of the petition. The presiding officer is chosen at the meeting, and any officer so requested in the petition is required to attend and to lay before the meeting any facts, documents or other information relative to the subject matter of the petition. (*See Charter.*)

LOWELL

An Act of the Legislature (Chap. 645, Laws of 1911) amending the City Charter, ratified by popular vote Nov. 7, 1911.

Commission Organizations:

Title: Municipal Council.

Number: Five, including Mayor.

Term: Two years. Partial renewal of the Council each year.

Removal: Recall.

Salary: Twenty-five hundred dollars.

Commissioner-Departments: 1. Public Safety (mayor) including sub-departments of police, health, poor and legal claims.

2. Finance, including sub-departments of treasury, auditing, purchasing, assessing, sinking funds, tax collection, registration of voters and city clerk.
3. Streets and Highways, including sub-departments of highways, street lighting, street watering, sewers and drains and engineering.
4. Waterworks, including all offices connected with water supply and fire protection.
5. Public Property and Licences, including sub-departments of buildings, parks, public grounds, cemeteries, electricity, weights and measures and license commission. Designation to departments is made by the Municipal Council.

"The Municipal Council shall determine the policies to be pursued and the work to be undertaken in each department, but each Commissioner shall have full power to carry out the policies or to have the work performed in his department, as directed by the Municipal Council."

General Commission Powers:

The powers previously exercised by the mayor, aldermen, common councilmen, members of the Board of Charities, Board of Trustees of Public Cemeteries and Water Board and Board of Police.

Special Requirements:

Monthly financial statements. No order, resolution, contract, etc., involving a liability of more than $500 may be passed without previous publication, except emergency measures passed by a four-fifths vote.

The Commissioner of Finance is required to have a complete examination of the city's books made annually.

Mayor:

Term: Two years.

Salary: Three thousand dollars.

Removal: Recall.

Powers: No veto power; presides at meetings of the Municipal Council.

Appointments:

Enumeration: City Clerk, Treasurer, Collector of Taxes, City Auditor, Purchasing Agent, Superintendent of Streets, Superintendent of Waterworks, City Engineer, City Physician, Board of Health (3), Board of Park Commissioners† (5), City Solicitor, Chief of the Fire Department, Superintendent of Police, Sealer of Weights and Measures, Board of Sinking Fund Commissioners (3), Board of Assessors (3), License Commissioners (chosen for a period of six years).

Manner: Enumerated officials by vote of the Municipal Council; subordinates by the Commissioner in charge for an indefinite term.

Civil Service Provisions:

Civil Service Provisions: The Civil Service Law of the state applies.

Election Provisions:

Non-partisan nominations; names placed on ballot at preliminary election on petition of twenty-five voters. The two persons receiving the highest number of votes at the preliminary election are the candidates at the annual (or special) election.

Initiative:

Twenty per centum petition (special election).
Ten per centum petition (general election).

Referendum:

Fifteen per centum petition.

Recall:

Twenty per centum petition.

---

*See Lynn, Mass., Charter (p. 31007) for provisions regarding publication of vacancy lists and keeping of public record of employees. These provisions have been introduced into the Lowell Charter.

†Their powers and duties as previously defined are not to be disturbed.

SALEM

(SPECIAL CHARTER, AN ACT OF THE LEGISLATURE APPROVED MAY 4, 1912. ADOPTED BY POPULAR VOTE NOV. 5, 1912.)

Commission Organization:

Title: City Council.

Number: Four, including mayor.

Term: Three years. Partial renewal.

Removal: Recall.

Salary: Two thousand dollars.

Commissioner-Departments:

1. Public Safety (mayor); including functions of police and fire, electrical affairs, inspection of wires, weights and measures, legal affairs, claims, licenses (except liquor licences), registration of voters, office of city clerk and other business not otherwise provided for in charter or ordinance.
2. Finance; including budget matters, auditing, assessment, collection of revenues, sinking funds, purchase of supplies, city printing and all financial matters not impairing authority of the board of assessors.
3. Public Works, including supervision of streets, sidewalks, street lighting, street watering, collection of ashes, public water supply, sewers, bridges and engineering.
4. Public Property, including supervision and enforcement of building laws, construction and maintenance of buildings (except school buildings), cemeteries, parks and shade trees.
5. Public Health, including supervision of public health, city hospitals, care of the poor, soldiers' relief, military and state aid, inspection of milk and vinegar, meats, provisions and food, inspection of animals, collection of garbage and the work of the city physician.

Mayor:

Term: Three years.

Removal: Recall.

Salary: Twenty-five hundred dollars.

Powers in relation to commission: Presides at meetings of the council. No veto power.

Appointments:

Enumeration: (1) City Clerk, three members of the board of assessors, Purchasing Agent. (2) City Solicitor, City Marshal, Chief Engineer of the Fire Department, City Messenger, City Electrician, three members of the Board of Registers of Voters, five members of the Board of Commissioners of Trust Funds. (3) City Treasurer, City Collector and City Auditor. (4) City Engineer, Commissioner of Streets and Water Works. (5) Inspector of Buildings, five members of the Board of Park Commissioners and a Superintendent of Parks and Shade Trees. (6) City Physician and three members of the Board of Health.

Manner: Group (1) by Council. Group (2) by the Mayor. Group (3) by the Director of Finance (except the Boards of License Commissioners and of Trust Funds, who are chosen as provided by law). Group (4) by the Director of Public Works. Group (5) by the Director of Public Property. Group (6) by the Director of Public Health. Two weeks preceding any appointment to any office established by the charter or by ordinance, the appointing officer is required to publish and post notice that such office is to be filled. Not less than two or more than four days prior to the actual appointment the appointing officer must publish and post the names of all applicants for the same.

Civil Service Provisions: The general state law applies.

SALEM—Continued

Election Provisions:

Non-partisan primaries and general city elections. Names are placed upon the primary ballot by petition of fifty voters. The ballots at the regular election contain the names of a number equal to twice the number to be elected to any office, receiving the highest number of votes at the preliminary election. But any person receiving a majority of all votes cast at a preliminary (primary) election is declared elected, without further submission of his name to the voters; provided that at such preliminary election at least eighty per centum of the registered vote of the city is cast.

Initiative:

Twenty-five per centum petition (general or special election).

Referendum:

Fifteen per centum petition (special or gen election).

Recall:

Twenty-five per centum petition. No recall du the first six months of office.

Special Features:

General meetings of the voters must be called u petition of three hundred of such voters. I requested at the meeting, or demanded in the p tion, any city official must attend the meeting, a if called upon, present any facts, document other information relative to the subject matte the petition.

LAWRENCE

(Special Charter, being Part 2 of Chap. 621, Laws of 1911 (approved June 30, 1911), ratified by popular vote Nov. 7, 1911).

Commission Organizations:

Title: City Council.

Number: Five, including Mayor.

Term: Two years; partial renewal annually.

Removal: Recall.

Salary: Twenty-five hundred dollars.

Commissioner-Departments: 1. Finance and Public Affairs (mayor), including sub-departments and boards connected with treasury, auditing, purchasing, assessing, sinking fund, tax collection, claims, registration of voters, city clerk and legal affairs.

2. Engineering, including sub-departments, etc., connected with highways, street watering, sewers and drains, water and waterwork, bridges and engineering.
3. Public Safety, including sub-departments etc., of police, fire, lighting, wiring, weights and measures and conduits.
4. Public Property, including sub-departments of buildings, parks and public grounds.
5. Public Health, including sub-departments, etc., of health, city physician, poor and public hospitals.

Designation to departments is made by vote of the City Council.

General Commission Powers:

The powers formerly exercised by the City Council, Board of Aldermen, Common Council, Board of Engineers of the Fire Department and Water Board.

"The City Council shall determine the policies to be pursued and the work to be undertaken in each department, but each Commissioner shall have full power to carry out the policies or to have the work performed in his department, as directed by the City Council."

Special Requirements:

Monthly financial statements.

Mayor:

Term: Two years.

Salary: Thirty-five hundred dollars.

Removal: Recall.

Powers: No veto power. Presides at meetings of the City Council.

*Appointments:**

Enumeration: City Clerk, City Treasurer, Collector of Taxes, City Auditor, City Solicitor, Purchasing Agent, Assessors, Sinking Fund Commissioners, Trustees of Public Library, Directors of the Cemetery, Overseers of the Poor.

Manner: Enumerated officials by majority of the City Council; subordinates appointed by the Commissioner in charge.

Civil Service Provisions: The Civil Service Law of the state applies.

Initiative:

Twenty-five per centum petition (special election). Ten per centum petition (general election).

Referendum:

Twenty-five per centum petition (general or special election).

Recall:

Twenty-five per centum petition.

Franchises:

No general franchise granted until approved by popular vote at an annual city election.

Special Features:

(*See this title in outline of Lynn, Mass., Charter,* p. 31007).

*See Lynn, Mass., Charter (p. 31007) for provisions regarding publication of vacancy lists and keeping of public record of employees. These provisions have been introduced into the Lawrence Charter.

MASSACHUSETTS STATUTE

AN ACT OF THE LEGISLATURE, (CHAPTER 267, LAWS OF 1915), APPROVED BY THE GOVERNOR, MAY 20, 1915, APPLICABLE TO ALL CITIES EXCEPT BOSTON, UPON ADOPTION BY POPULAR VOTE.)

PLAN "A"—GOVERNMENT BY MAYOR AND COUNCIL ELECTED AT LARGE

Governing Body:

Title: City Council.
Number: Nine, elected at large.
Terms of Office: Two years, partial renewal annually.
Salary: Fixed by the Council, but not to exceed five hundred ($500) dollars per annum.

Mayor:

The Mayor is elected by the people for a term of two years and is the chief executive officer of the city. His salary is determined by the City Council but may not exceed $5,000 per year. May exercise veto power subject to two-thirds vote of the City Council.

ppointments:

All heads of departments and members of municipal boards, as their terms of office expire, but excluding the School Committee, officials appointed by the Governor, and Assessors where they are elected by the people, are to be appointed by the Mayor without confirmation. The Mayor may remove any head of a department by filing with the City Clerk a statement of the reasons for such removal.

Election Provisions:

Non-partisan ballots.

PLAN "B"—GOVERNMENT BY MAYOR AND COUNCIL ELECTED BY DISTRICTS AND AT LARGE

Governing Body:

Title: City Council.
Number: In cities having more than seven wards, fifteen, one to be elected from each ward and the remainder at large.
In cities having seven wards or less, eleven, one from each ward and the remainder at large.
Term: Two years; partial renewal annually.
Salary: Fixed by the City Council but not to exceed five hundred ($500) per year.

Mayor:

See *Mayor* under "Plan A."

Appointments:

Made by the Mayor as in "Plan A," but with the exception of the solicitor, subject to confirmation by the City Council. Officers removed by the Mayor have a right to a hearing before the City Council.

PLAN "C"—COMMISSSION FORM.

Governing Body:

Title: City Council.
Number: Five, including Mayor.
Terms of Office: Two years; partial renewal annually.
Salary: Fixed by the Council, but not to exceed five thousand ($5,000) dollars for the Mayor nor four thousand ($4,000) for the other members of the Commission.
Commissioner Departments: (1) administration (Mayor), (2) finance, (3) health, (4) public works, (5) public property.

PLAN "D"—GOVERNMENT BY MAYOR, CITY COUNCIL AND CITY MANAGER.

Governing Body:

Title: City Council.
Number: Five, including Mayor.

Terms of Office: Two years; partial renewal annually.

Salary: The City Council may establish a salary for its members, not exceeding five hundred ($500) dollars.

Mayor:

Is that member of the Council who, at the election at which three members of the City Council are elected, receives the highest number of votes. He is the presiding officer of the City Council, but has no veto power. He receives such salary, not to exceed two thousand ($2,000) dollars, as the City Council may determine.

City Manager:

Title: City Manager.

Qualifications: Appointed for merit only, and need not be a resident of the city when appointed.

Tenure: At the pleasure of the City Council.

Powers and Duties: The usual powers and duties exercised by city managers (see Dayton, p. 34003).

Salary: Fixed by ordinance.

PROVISIONS APPLICABLE TO ALL

Appointments:

The City Clerk, under each of the plan by the Council.

Election Provisions:

No primary or caucus for municipal o be held. Candidates for Mayor, City (members of the School Committee a to be nominated as set forth in Sec. 1 II, Chap. 835, Laws of 1913.

Initiative:

Twenty per centum petition (special ele

Eight per centum petition (general ele

Referendum:

Twelve per centum petition (regular election).

Recall:

No provisions.

GARDINER

(SPECIAL CHARTER. AN ACT OF THE LEGISLATURE, APPROVED AUG. 11, 1911, RATIFIED BY POPULAR VOTE SEPT., 1911.)

Commission-Organization:

Title: City Council.

Number: Three, including Mayor. Partial renewal annually.

Term: Three years.

Removal: Recall.

Salary: One thousand dollars.

Commissioner-Departments: 1, Accounts and Finances (Mayor) including sub-departments of valuation, assessment, collecting, purchasing, accounting, auditing, treasury, sinking fund, claims, schools, public library, city clerk, printing; 2, Public Safety and Charities, including sub-departments of fire, police, poor, city almshouse, soldiers' relief and state aid, licenses, elections, legal affairs, parks, public buildings, liquor agency, health, inspection of buildings, inspection of animals, weights and measures, etc.; 3, Streets and Highways, including sub-departments of streets, sidewalks, culverts, bridges, street lighting, electrical affairs, street watering and cleaning, sewers, engineering, harbor, etc. Designation to departments on regular election ballot.

General Commission Powers:

All executive, legislative and judicial powers and duties formerly exercised by Mayor, Aldermen, Common Council, Assessors, Overseers of the Poor and Street Commissioner.

Mayor:

Term: Three years.

Removal: Recall.

Salary: Twelve hundred dollars.

Powers: Presides over meetings of the Council. No veto power.

Appointments:

Enumeration: City Clerk, Treasurer, Auditor, Purchasing Agent, Collector of Taxes, Superintendent of Streets and Highways, Chief of Police and Chief of Fire Department, City Solicitor, City Physician, Civil Engineer, Member of School Committee, Trustee of Gardiner Water District, Director of Public Library.

Manner: By majority vote of the Council for a term of three years, but subject to removal in the same manner at any time.

Election Provisions:

Nominations made at a preliminary election, on the ballots of which the names of candidates are placed by petition of not less than twenty-five voters, in the form of individual certificates. The two persons receiving the highest number of votes at the preliminary election are the candidates at the second election. The ballots must contain no party designation.

Initiative:

Twenty-five per centum petition, but not less than 250 signatures (special election).
Ten per centum petition (regular election).

Referendum:

Twenty-five per centum petition, but not less than 250 signatures (special election).
Ten per centum petition (general election).

Recall:

Twenty-five per centum petition, but not less than 250 signatures.

BUFFALO

(SPECIAL CHARTER, AN ACT OF THE LEGISLATURE (CHAP. 217, LAWS OF 1915); ADOPTED BY POPULAR VOTE NOV. 3, 1914.)

Commission-Organization:

Title: The Council.
Number: Five, including Mayor.
Term: Four years.
Removal: By the Governor.
Salary: Seven thousand ($7,000) dollars.
Commissioner Departments: (1) Public Safety (Mayor), (2) Finance and Accounts, (3) Public Affairs, (4) Public Works, (5) Parks and Public Buildings.

Mayor:

Term: Four years.
Removal: By the Governor.
Salary: Eight thousand ($8,000) dollars.
Powers and Duties: It is the duty of the Mayor to acquaint himself with the conduct of each of the other city departments and to report thereon to the council with such recommendations as he may deem advisable.

Appointments:

Enumeration: (1) Corporation Counsel, Superintendent of Education, Assessor (or Assessors) Street Commissioner, Building Commissioner, Health Commissioner, Chief of Fire Department, Chief of Police, Superintendent of Markets, Superintendent of the Poor, Board of Education, City Engineer, City Treasurer and City Auditor. (2) The Civil Service Commission.
Manner: Enumerated officers in group (1) by the Council, subject to removal by them at any time; deputies and subordinates by the Council, on the nomination of the councilman in charge of the department.
Civil Service Provisions: The Civil Service Commission is appointed by the Council for a term of four years and its members are removable upon charges and after a hearing.

Election Provisions:

Non-partisan primaries and elections. Names placed on primary ballot on petition of three hundred (300) electors. Candidates equal to twice the number of vacancies to be filled, for Commissioner and Mayor respectively are the candidates at the regular election.

Initiative:

No provisions.

Referendum:

Five per centum petition (special election, unless a general election is to be held within ninety days). Not more than one special election shall be held within a period of six months.

Recall:

No provisions.

NEW YORK STATUTE

AN ACT OF THE LEGISLATURE, APPROVED APRIL 18, 1914, APPLICABLE TO ANY CITY OF THE SECOND OR THIRD CLASS, WHEN ADOPTED AT A GENERAL OR SPECIAL ELECTION CALLED UPON PETITION OF TEN PER CENTUM OF THE VOTERS.*

PROVISIONS APPLICABLE TO EACH PLAN

Governing Body:

Title: Council.

Terms of Office: Four years. Partial renewal biennially.

Mayor:

In addition to other powers granted under the specific plans, the mayor has custody of the seal of the city and is required to authenticate the acts of the council and all instruments authorized to be authenticated; exercises other powers conferred by law upon the mayor of the city, if not inconsistent with this act.

Appointments:

Civil Service: The State law applies. Civil Service Commission appointed by the mayor or council.

City Clerk: Appointed by the council.

dicial Officers:

If elected before adoption of this act they continue to be elected, but if formerly appointive, will be appointed by the city council under Plans A, B and C, or by the Mayor under Plans D, E and F.

Boards of Education:

Not affected by this act; controlled in all respects by the charter or other law operative before adoption of this act.

Election Provisions:

The general laws of the state apply. These require the holding of partisan primaries, with provision for independent nominations. The ballot is of the so-called "Massachusetts" type, with the party emblem opposite the name of each candidate.

Initiative:

No provisions.

Referendum:

No provisions.

Recall:

No provisions.

PLAN A. (LIMITED COUNCIL)

Governing Body:

Number: Five (or three, in cities having less than 25,000 inhabitants, if voters so determine) including mayor. Election at large.

Salary:

Population		
less than	8,000	four hundred dollars.
" 8,000 to	10,000	five hundred dollars.
" 10,000 to	15,000	twelve hundred dollars.
" 15,000 to	20,000	seventeen hundred dollars.
" 20,000 to	30,000	two thousand dollars.
" 30,000 to	40,000	twenty-five hundred dollars.
" 40,000 to	75,000	thirty-five hundred dollars.
" 75,000 to	100,000	four thousand dollars.
" over	100,000	forty-five hundred dollars.

The salary of the mayor in each case is one-fourth greater than the amount indicated in the foregoing schedule.

Administration:

The council is required to divide the administration of the city's affairs into departments and make rules and regulations concerning the same. Each member of council is designated the head of one or more departments, over which he has special oversight and direction, subject to the ordinances of the council and the provisions of this act.

Mayor:

Must attend, and preside at, meetings of the council, but has no veto power. Is required to acquaint himself with the affairs of every department and report thereon, from time to time, to the council.

* Based upon vote cast for mayor at last previous election; not over 2,000 signatures required in any city.

Appointments :

Qualifications, powers and duties and compensation of all necessary officers and employees are determined by the council. The council employs and may remove any and every officer and employee.

PLAN B. (LIMITED COUNCIL WITH COLLECTIVE SUPERVISION)

Governing Body:

Number: Same as Plan A.

Salary:

Population less than 10,000: three hundred dollars.
" 10,000 to 25,000: five hundred dollars.
" 25,000 to 50,000: seven hundred and fifty dollars.
" 50,000 to 100,000: one thousand dollars.
" over 100,000: twelve hundred dollars.

Administration :

The council is required to divide the administration of the city's affairs into departments and make rules and regulations concerning the same. The individual members of the council do *not* serve as heads of departments, these positions being filled by appointment by the city council.

Appointments:

Same as Plan A.

Mayor:

Same as Plan A.

PLAN C. (LIMITED COUNCIL WITH APPOINTIVE CITY MANAGER)

Governing Body:

Number: Five, including mayor, in third class cities; seven, including mayor in second class cities; all elected at large.

Salaries:

Population less than 10,000: three hundred dollars.
" 10,000 to 25,000: five hundred dollars.
" 25,000 to 50,000: seven hundred dollars.
" 50,000 to 100,000: one thousand dollars.
" over 100,000: twelve hundred dollars.

Administration—City Manager:

Administrative and executive powers vested in a city manager, appointed by the council, to hold office during their pleasure. The duties of the city manager are to (1) be the administrative head of the city government; (2) see that within the city the laws of the state and the ordinances, resolutions and by-laws of the council are faithfully executed; (3) attend all meetings of the council, and recommend for adoption such measures as he shall deem expedient; (4) make reports to the council from t upon the affairs of the city, keep the c advised of the city's financial condition, a financial needs; (5) prepare and submit t a tentative budget for the next fiscal yea

Appointments:

The council determines upon the numb powers, duties and compensation of offic ployees, but appointments to all offices ments are made by the City Manager.

Mayor:

Is required to preside at all meetings of is official head of the city for the service cess, and under the military law, and monial purposes; has no veto power.

PLAN D. (SEPARATE EXECUT LEGISLATIVE DEPARTMEN

Governing Body:

Number: Five, not including mayor (cities of less than 25,000 population, i so decide); elected at large.

Salaries: One-half the amounts sched Plan A.

Administration :

Under the control of the mayor (see infra).

Mayor :

Exercises the executive and administrat May veto an ordinance or resolution which veto may be overridden by a t vote. His salary is three times that o man.

Appointments :

Mayor appoints all officers of the city law or ordinance to be appointed.

PLAN E. (LEGISLATIVE DEP CONSISTING OF NINE COUNCI

Same as Plan D. except that the counci nine persons elected at large.

PLAN F. (LEGISLATIVE DEP CONSISTING OF COUNCILMEN E BY DISTRICTS)

Same as Plan D. except that the counci as many members as there are wards and one councilman shall be elected ward.

PENNSYLVANIA STATUTE

(Third Class Cities)

(AN ACT OF THE LEGISLATURE, APPROVED JUNE 18, 1913, APPLICABLE TO ALL CITIES OF THE THIRD CLASS*, WITHOUT REFERENDUM, AND TO BOROUGHS OF OVER 10,000 INHABITANTS WHICH SHALL BECOME CITIES OF THE THIRD CLASS.)

Commission—Organization:

Title: Council.

Number: Five, including mayor.

Term: Two years.

Removal: Statutory provisions.

†*Salary:* Fixed by ordinance; not to be less than two hundred and fifty nor more than three thousand dollars a year; not to be increased or diminished during any term of office.

For the first term under this act: Population less than 15,000, $300.00; population between 15,000 and 30,000, $750.00; population between 30,000 and 50,000, $2,000.00; population between 50,000 and 70,000, $2,500.00; population over 70,000, $3,000.00.

Commissioner-Departments: 1, Public Affairs (Mayor); 2, Accounts and Finance; 3, Public Safety; 4, Streets and Public Safety; 5, Parks and Public Property. Designation by the Council.

Mayor:

Term: Four years.

†*Salary:* Not less than five hundred nor more than thirty-five hundred dollars per year.

For the first term under this act: Population less than 15,000, $500.00; population between 15,000 to 30,000, $1,200.00; population from 30,000 to 50,000, $2,500.00; population from 30,000 to 70,000, $3,000.00; population over 70,000, $3,500.00.

Removal: Statutory provisions.

Powers: Supervision of all city departments; is required to keep the Council informed as to general and financial needs and condition of the city.

Other Elective Officers:

Controller: Elected for a term of four years.

Appointments:

Enumeration: City Treasurer, City Clerk, City Solicitor, City Assessor.

Manner: By majority vote of the council.

Civil Service Provisions: None.

Election Provisions:

Non-partisan primaries and elections; names of candidates are placed upon the ballot by petition of twenty-five voters. Candidates receiving the highest number of votes at the primary, equal to twice the number of offices to be filled, are the candidates at the regular election.

Initiative:

Twenty per centum petition (special or general election).

Referendum:

Twenty per centum petition (special or general election).

Recall:

No provisions.

*Including all those having a population of over 10,000 except Philadelphia, Pittsburgh and Scranton.

†This provision, as some of the originators of the law have frequently pointed out, permits the adoption of the city manager plan by local action. By fixing the salaries of the commissioners at a low figure, it is feasible to devote the amount thus saved to the salary of the executive.

CUMBERLAND

(An Act repealing certain sections of, and additional to, the Code of Public Laws of Maryland. Approved Apr. 11, 1910.)

Commission-Organization:

Title: City Council.

Number: Five, including Mayor.

Term: Two years.

Removal: Expulsion by three-fifth vote of Council for dereliction of duty.

Salary: Twelve hundred dollars.

Commisioner-Departments: 1, Police and Fire; 2, Streets and Public Property; 3, Water and Electric Light; 4, Finance and Revenue. Designation by Council.

General Commission Powers:

To regulate the organization, management and operation of all departments of the city and whatever agencies may be created for the administration of its affairs.

Special Requirements:

The Health Officer, Attorney, Engineer, Auditor and Chief of Fire and Police Departments, are required to attend all regular meetings of the Mayor and City Council at which their presence is requested by any member thereof. They have the privilege of participating in the discussion of any matters relating to their special departments, but have no votes. Quarterly financial statements.

Mayor:

Term: Two years.

Salary: Fifteen hundred dollars.

Removal: Expulsion by three-fifth vote of Council for dereliction of duty.

Powers in relation to Commission: The Mayor has the right to vote upon all questions, but has no power to countermand any orders given by a Commissioner of any department or "in any manner whatsoever to interfere with the authority of any Commissioner in his own department."

Special Requirements: Must devote at least six hours a day to the duties of his office.

Appointments:

Enumeration: City Clerk, Treasurer, Collector, Attorney, Auditor, Chief of Fire Department, Chief of Police Department, Health Officer, Superintendent of Water and Electric Light Works, Engineer and Assistant Engineer of Water Works.

Manner: By Mayor and Council. Any appointive officer may be removed by the Mayor and Council for incompetency after notice and a hearing.

Civil Service Provisions: None.

Election Provisions:

Nomination to Primary Elections on petition of one hundred voters. The number of candidates at the second election is twice the number of offices to be filled.

Initiative:

No provisions.

Referendum:

No provisions.

Recall:

No provisions.

NEW JERSEY STATUTE

(An Act of the General Assembly permitting any city to adopt its provisions by special election, called upon petition of twenty per centum of the voters.* Approved April 25, 1911.)

Commission-Organization:

Title: Board of Commissioners.

Number: Cities under 10,000 population, three. Cities over 10,000 population, five; including Mayor.

The number of Commissioners may be decreased to three or increased to five in any city, by ordinance.

Term: Four years.

Removal: Recall.

Salaries: In cities of the first, second and third classes:

Population over 200,000; not over, $5,000.
Population between 90,000 and 200,000, $3,000.
Population between 40,000 and 90,000, $2,000.
Population between 20,000 and 40,000, $1,500.
Population between 10,000 and 20,000, $1,200.
Population between 5,000 and 10,000, $750.
Population between 2,500 and 5,000, $500.
Population between 1,000 and 2,500, $350.
Population between 500 and 1,000, $200.
Population less than 500, $50.

In cities of the fourth class:

Population over 90,000, not over, $5,000.
Population between 40,000 to 90,000, $3,000.
Population between 20,000 to 40,000, $2,500.
Population between 10,000 to 20,000, $2,000.
Population between 5,000 to 10,000, $1,500.
Population between 2,500 to 5,000, $1,250.
Population between 1,000 to 2,500, $1,000.
Population between 500 to 1,000, $500.
Population less than 500, $250.

Commissioner-Departments: 1. Public Affairs (Mayor). 2. Revenue and Finance. 3. Public Safety. 4. Streets and Public Improvements. 5. Parks and Public Property. In cities having only three Commissioners, Departments No. 1 and No. 3 and Departments No. 4 and 5 are consolidated.

General Commission Powers:

All administrative, judicial and legislative powers formerly possessed and exercised by the Mayor and City Council, and all other executive and legislative bodies in the city.

Special Requirements:

Monthly financial statements.

Mayor:

The Mayor is not elected as such, but is designated to the position by the Commission from among its own number.

Term: Four years.

Removal: Recall.

Powers in relation to Commission: Presides at all meetings; no veto power.

Salary: In cities of the first, second and third classes:

Population over 200,000, not over $5,500.
Population between 90,000 and 200,000, $3,500.
Population between 40,000 and 90,000, $2,500.
Population between 20,000 and 40,000, $1,800.
Population between 10,000 and 20,000, $1,500.

* The votes cast in favor of the adoption of the act must equal at least thirty per centum of the votes cast for members of the General Assembly at the last preceeding general election.

Population between 5,000 and 10,000, $1,000.
Population between 2,500 and 5,000, $750.
Population between 1,000 and 2,500, $500.
Population between 500 and 1,000, $250.
Population less than 500, $75.

In cities of the fourth class:

Population over 90,000, not over, $5,500.
Population between 40,000 and 90,000, $4,000.
Population between 20,000 and 40,000, $3,000.
Population between 10,000 and 20,000, $2,500.
Population between 5,000 and 10,000, $2,000.
Population between 2,500 and 5,000, $1,500.
Population between 1,000 and 2,500, $1,250.
Population between 500 and 1,000, $750.
Population less than 500, $500.

Appointments:

The Board of Commissioners has power to create such boards and appoint such officers as it may deem necessary for the conduct of the affairs of the city. Any officer may be removed at any time for cause after a public hearing.

Civil Service Provisions: The Civil Service Law, approved April 10, 1908, is operative in such cities as have accepted its provisions in the case of all employees holding office at the time of the adoption of this act.

Election Provisions:

Non-partisan primaries; nomination by petition of twenty-five voters. Candidates equal in number to twice the number of offices to be filled, receiving the highest number of votes at the primary election, are the candidates at the municipal election.

Initiative:

Fifteen per centum petition (special or general election).

Ten percentum petition (general election).

Referendum:

Fifteen per centum petition (special or general election).

Recall:

Twenty-five per centum petition. No recall petition may be filed in the first twelve months of office or more than once against any officer.

Abandonment of Act:

Operation under this act may be discontinued after six years, by special election, called upon petition of twenty-five per centum of the voters.

VIRGINIA STATUTE

An act of the legislature, approved March 13, 1914, applicable to every city having less than 100,000 inhabitants, when adopted at a special election called upon petition of 25 per cent of the electors qualified to vote at the last preceding municipal election.

I. GENERAL COUNCILMANIC PLAN.

Governing Body:

Title: Council.

Term of Office: Four years.

Number: Population less than 10,000—three* or five, elected at large.

Population 10,000 to 20,000—three, five or seven, elected at large or by wards.*

Population 20,000 to 30,000—three, five, seven or nine, to be elected at large or by wards.

Population over 30,000—three,* five, seven, nine or eleven, to be elected at large or by wards.

Any city operating under this plan, or any town, may appoint any person who is a qualified resident of such city or town, to be known as "city manager," and to perform such duties as the council may require of him and for such compensation as they may allow. Such officer is subject to removal by the council at any time.

II. MODIFIED COMMISSION PLAN.

Governing Body:

Title: Council.

Terms of Office: Four years.

Number: Three*, or five, elected at large.

Appointments:

Manner: By the Council, subject to removal by that body at any time except as especially provided by law.

Under this plan, the council selects one of its own number to preside over its meetings, with the title of mayor, and assigns each one of its members to particular administrative duties.

*The choice of a particular plan of government is indicated on the ballot, with propositions fixing the number and compensation of councilmen for the particular city and, in some cases, determining whether election shall be by wards or at large.

III. CITY MANAGER PLAN.

Governing Body:

Number: Population less than 10,000—three or five, elected at large.

Population over 10,000—five* to eleven.

Terms of Office: Four years.

City Manager:

Administrative and executive powers. The administrative and executive powers of the city, including the power of appointment of officers and employees, are vested in an official to be known as the City Manager, who shall be appointed by the council at its first meeting, or as soon thereafter as practicable, and hold office during the pleasure of the council; he shall receive such compensation as shall be fixed by the council by ordinance.

General Duties of the City Manager.

1. The City Manager shall see that within the city the laws, ordinances, resolutions and by-laws of the council are faithfully executed.
2. Attend all meetings of the council, and recommend for adoption such measures as he shall deem expedient.
3. Make reports to the council from time to time upon the affairs of the city; keep the council fully advised of the city's financial condition, and its future financial needs.
4. Prepare and submit to the council a tentative budget for the next fiscal year.
5. He shall perform such other duties as may be prescribed by the council not in conflict with the foregoing, and shall be bonded as the council may deem necessary.

(See also "Appointments").

Appointments:

Manner: By the city manager, subject to removal by him (except those in the financial, legal and judicial departments and the clerical and other attendants of the council).

Under this plan the council selects one of its own number to preside over its meetings, who becomes, thereupon, *ex-officio* mayor.

PROVISIONS APPLICABLE TO EACH PLAN.

Elections:

The general state law providing for partisan elections only, applies.

Initiative, Referendum, and Recall:

No provisions.

HUNTINGTON

(SPECIAL CHARTER. AN ACT OF THE LEGISLATURE, CHAP. 3, LAWS OF 1909.)

Commission-Organization:

Title: Board of Commissioners.

Number: Four, including Mayor.

Term: Three years.

Removal: By Citizens' Board, only for causes mentioned in State Constitution (*Art. IV, Sec. 6*).

Salary: Fifteen hundred dollars.

Commissioner-Departments: 1, Fire, Police and Law; 2, Finance, Taxation and Public Utilities; 3, Streets, Sewers, Wharves, Public Buildings and Grounds; 4, Health and Charity. Designation by Mayor.

General Commission Powers:
The corporate powers of the City.

Special Requirements:
Meetings held at least once a week.

Mayor:
The Commissioner receiving the highest number of votes at the general election of members, is Mayor of the City. If two or more Commissioners receive an equal number of votes at such election, they decide which shall be Mayor by casting lots.

Term: Three years.

Salary: Eighteen hundred dollars.

Removal: By Citizens' Board.

Powers: The Mayor is presiding officer of the Board of Commissioners, and in the capacity of Commissioner has the right to vote on any question arising before the Board, but in his capacity of presiding officer, has no vote by which to decide the question on which there is a tie vote.

Other Elective Officers:
Citizens' Board.

Appointments:

Enumeration: The enumerated appointive officers of the City are the City Clerk, Treasurer, Auditor, Police Judge, City Attorney, Chief of Police, Chief of Fire Department, City Engineer, Health Officer, and other officers created by the Board of Commissioners.

Manner of Appointment: By Board of Commissioners, for a term of three years.

Civil Service Provisons: The Board of Commissioners act in the capacity of Civil Service Board.

Election Provisions:
Candidates for members of the Board of Commissioners and the Citizens' Board are nominated by Convention, Primary or Petition, but no political party may nominate more than three persons for the office of member of the Board of Commissioners, and no two of these may be from the same Ward, and not more than eight persons from each Ward of the City for the office of members of the Citizens' Board. The Charter provides further "that there shall not be printed on any ticket, on any ballot to be voted at the Municipal Election, for the election of officers of the City, more than three names for the office of members of the Board of Commissioners, nor more than eight names for members of the Citizens' Board. Every person nominated to the office of Commissioner is required to file with the City Clerk a statement of the political party to which he claims allegiance."

Initiative:
See note on Citizens' Board.

Referendum:
See note on Citizens' Board.

Recall:
See note on Citizens' Board.

Franchises:
Franchises may not become effective until after a regular or special meeting of the Citizens' Board, at which meeting they may be vetoed. (*See text of Charter for further franchise provisions, Art. XII, Secs. 61 to 63.*)

Special Features:

The Citizens' Board: The Citizens' Board of the City of Huntington is comprised of sixteen persons from each Ward of the City, voted for and elected by Wards. It has the power of veto on all franchises or ordinances passed by the Board of Commissioners by a majority vote of its members. It is also authorized to hear, consider and act on charges against any member of the Board of Commissioners, and after having heard proof of such charges, to remove the Commissioner and declare his office vacant by a two-thirds vote. (*See text of Charter.*)

PARKERSBURG

(SPECIAL CHARTER. AN ACT OF THE LEGISLATURE, PASSED FEBRUARY 29, 1911, RATIFIED BY POPULAR VOTE MARCH 21, 1911.)

Commission-Organization:

Title: Council.

Number: Five including Mayor.

Term: Three years.

Removal: Recall.

Salary: Two thousand dollars.

Commissioner-Departments: 1. Public Affairs (Mayor); 2. Accounts and Finance; 3. Public Safety; 4. Streets, Parks and Public Property; 5. Water Works and Sewers.

General Commission Powers: All the executive, legislative and judicial powers conferred upon cities, etc., by the general laws of the state and this act.

Special Requirements: Monthly financial statements.

Mayor:

Term: Three years.

Salary: Three thousand dollars.

Removal: Recall.

Powers in Relation to Commission: Presides at meetings of Council. No veto power.

Appointments:

Enumeration: City Clerk, Solicitor, City Civil Engineer, Chief of Police, Chief of Fire Department, City Collector, Street Commissioner, Police Judge.

Manner: By majority vote of Council. All officers removable at pleasure of Council.

Civil Service Provisions: Council must appoint a board of three members, whose jurisdiction extends to applications for all positions in the departments of police, fire and water works.

Election Provisions:

Nomination by petition of twenty-five voters. The two candidates receiving the highest number of votes for Mayor, and the eight for Councilmen, at the primary, are the candidates at the general election.

Initiative:

Twenty percentum petition (special election); ten percentum petition (regular election).

Referendum:

Twenty percentum petition (special or general election).

Recall:

Twenty percentum petition.

Franchises:

Every franchise must be in the form of an ordinance. No franchise to be granted for a longer period than thirty years.

BLUEFIELD

(SPECIAL CHARTER, LAWS OF WEST VIRGINIA, 1909, PAGE 1.)

Commission-Organization:

Title: Board of Affairs.

Number: Four, including Mayor.

Term: Four years.

Removal: By Council for causes mentioned in Art. IV, Sec. 6 of the Constitution.

Salary: Fifteen hundred dollars (maximum).

Commissioner-Departments: 1, Finance; 2, Public Safety; 3, Police; 4, Streets. Designation by Mayor.

*Mayor:**

Term: Four years.

Salary: Fifteen hundred dollars (maximum).

Removal: By Council for causes mentioned in Art. IV, Sec. 6 of the Constitution.

Powers in Relation to Commission: Presides over meetings.

Appointments:

Enumeration: Treasurer, Auditor, Police Judge, City Solicitor, Chief of Police, Chief of Fire Department, City Engineer, Superintendent of Highways, Health Commissioner.

Manner: Board of Affairs.

Civil Service Provisions: None.

* After 1911 the person receiving the highest number of votes for members of Board of Affairs, is Mayor for second half of term. There are several complications in connection with this provision.

Election Provisions:

Nomination by petition, convention or primary. No party may nominate more than twice the number of officials to be elected. Candidates must file statements of party affiliation.

Initiative:

No provision.

Referendum:

No provision.

Recall:

No provision.

Franchises:

Must be approved by the Council.

Must be approved by the Council (see "*Special Features*").

The Council:

The Council is composed of four persons elected *from each Ward,* not more than two of whom may be of the same political party, for a term of two years.

The Council has power to veto any ordinance or franchise granted by the Board of Affairs. It may demand any papers, records, information, etc., of the Board or any City official. It may also make recommendations to the Board on any subject pertaining to City government. If charges are filed with the Council against any member of the Board, the Council shall hold a hearing, and by a two-thirds vote may remove such member (*see "Citizens' Board" in outline of Huntington, W. Va. Charter, and text of same*).

WHEELING

(SPECIAL CHARTER, AN ACT OF THE LEGISLATURE, ADOPTED BY POPULAR VOTE MAY 27, 1915.)

Governing Body:

Title: City Council.

Number: Nine, one nominated from each ward and nine at large.

Term: Two years.

Removal: Recall.

Salary: Five ($5.00) dollars for each regular meeting.

The Mayor:

Elected by the City Council from among their own number. He is official head of the city for the purpose of serving civil process and for all ceremonial purposes.

The City Manager:

Title: City Manager.

Qualifications:

Powers and Duties: Exercises the usual powers of a city manager (see Dayton, p. 34003). His authority over the officers and departments of the city is described as follows:

"The City Manager shall have authority to provide for the appointment of such officers, the appointments of whom are not vested in the Council, as shall be necessary or proper to carry into effect any authority, power, capacity or jurisdiction which is or shall be vested in the City of Wheeling, or in the Council thereof, or in such City Manager; to grant, in writing, to the officers so appointed the powers necessary or proper for the purposes above mentioned; to define their duties in writing; to allow them reasonable compensation (said compensation to be approved by Council), and to require and take of all or any of them such bonds, obligations or other writings as he shall deem necessary or proper to insure the proper performance of their several duties." (Part of Sec. 14.)

Appointments:

Enumeration: City Manager, City Clerk, City Solicitor, Judge of Police Court, Chief of Police and Commissioners of loans and bond issues.

Manner: Enumerated officers by the City Council; all others by the City Manager.

Civil Service Provisions: The City Council is empowered to appoint a Civil Service Commission for the purpose of examining applicants for positions in the fire, water and health departments. This Commission is to consist of three citizens, not more than one of whom shall be of the same political party.

Election Provisions:

Names submitted in municipal primary by petition. Non-partisan ballots. The candidates in each ward and at large receiving the highest and the next highest number of votes are the candidates at the general election.

Initiative:

Fifteen per centum petition (special election).
Ten per centum petition (general election).

Referendum:

Limited to changes in the boundaries of the city and franchises.

Fifteen per centum petition (general or special election).

Recall:

Twenty per centum petition.

HIGH POINT

(Special Charter, ratified Feb. 27, 1909. Public Laws 1909, Chapter 395.)

Commission-Organization:

Title: City Council.

Number: Nine*, including Mayor. Two councilmen from each of the four wards, but elected at large.

Term: Two years—no partial renewal provision.

Salary: Two dollars per meeting. Not over two meetings each month.

Commissioner-Departments: 1, Finance and Revenue; 2, Police and Fire; 3, Streets and Cemeteries; 4, Water Works and Sewerage; 5, Public Buildings and Property; 6, Lights and Lighting; 7, Purchasing; 8, Auditing. Designation by Mayor.

General Commission Powers:

The City Council has control over all departments of the city and has power to "make and enforce such rules and regulations as they may see fit and proper for and concerning the organization, management and operation of all departments of the city and whatever agencies can be created for the administration of its affairs."

Special Requirements:

Monthly statements of Receipts and Disbursements.

Mayor:

Term: Two years.

Salary: Not to exceed Five hundred dollars.

Removal: By majority vote of all commissioners, after proper hearing.

Powers in relation to Commission: Veto power. May vote on questions of sustaining veto.

Special Requirements: Charged especially with enforcement of franchise provisions.

Appointments:

Enumeration: The principal appointive officers of the city are the Auditor, Attorney, Recorder, Assessor and Collector of Taxes, Treasurer, Chief of Police, Engineer, Superintendent of Water Works and Sewerage, and Sexton.

Manner of Appointment: Each member of the Council has the right to propose and name employees in the departments under his supervision, but a majority of the Council have power to reject any such proposal and to discharge any employee except the City Attorney, Recorder and Auditor. The term of appointed officers is one year.

Election Provisions:

The Council makes all necessary regulations in keeping with the state law. Partisan elections. Expense of primary elections paid by the city.

Initiative:

No provision.

Referendum:

No general provision.

Recall:

No provision.

Franchises:

No grant of franchise, unless submitted to a vote of the people, for a longer period than thirty years. No grant for a longer period than fifty years. The Referendum of all franchises is compulsory on petition of five hundred voters.

---

* The number of officers to be voted for at one time is unusually large. The Charter, however, conforms in general to the Definition given on page 10201.

WILMINGTON

(Special Charter, an Act of the General Assembly, Ratified by that Body March 3, 1911; Ratified by the Voters of the City by Popular Election.)

Commission-Organization:

Title: Council.

Number: Five elected from wards by the voters of the city, but no two councilmen shall be from the same ward.

Term: Two years.

Removal: Recall.

Salary: Determined by the Council; not less than eight hundred dollars or more than nineteen hundred dollars.

Commissioner-Departments: 1. Public Affairs. 2. Accounts and Finance. 3. Public Safety. 4. Streets, Wharves and Public Improvements. 5. Water and Sewerage.

General Commission Powers:

Those formerly exercised by the Mayor, Board of Aldermen, Board of Audit and Finance, Water and Sewerage Commission, the Street Commission, Police and Fire Commission, and all other executive and administrative officers of the City.

Special Requirements:

Monthly itemized financial statements must be filed by the individual commissioners.

*Mayor:**

Term: Two years.

Salary: Determined by the Council; not less than eight hundred dollars or more than nineteen hundred dollars.

Removal: Recall.

Powers: Presides at all meetings of the Council. May vote on motion or reserve his vote to be cast in case of a tie.

* The candidate for Councilman who receives the highest number of votes is **ex-officio** Mayor, and Commissioner of Public Affairs.

Appointments:

Enumeration: Clerk and Treasurer, Collector, City Attorney, Chief of Police, Chief of Fire Department, City Engineer, Superintendent of Streets, three Library Trustees.

Manner: By majority vote of the Council. Removal in same manner except as specifically provided.

Civil Service Provisions: The Council must appoint three Commissioners to serve without compensation.

Election Provisions:

Non-partisan primaries; nomination by petition of twenty-five voters. The names of the two candidates from each ward who receive the highest number of votes at the primary are placed on the ballots at the general election.

Initiative:

Thirty-five percentum petition (special election). Ten percentum petition (general election).

Referendum:

Thirty-five percentum petition.

Recall:

Thirty-five percentum petition (special election). Ten percentum petition (general election).

GREENSBORO

SPECIAL CHARTER, AN ACT OF THE GENERAL ASSEMBLY, RATIFIED JAN. 17, 1911, ADOPTED BY POPULAR VOTE FEB., 1911.)

---

ommission-Organization:

Title: Board of Commissioners.

Number: Three, including Mayor.

Term: Two years.

Removal: Recall.

Salary: Twenty-four hundred dollars.

Commissioner-Departments: (1) Public Works, including construction and repair of streets, etc., erection of public buildings, enforcement of laws relating to streets, public squares, etc., public service, utilities. (2) Public Safety, including police and fire departments, fire alarm systems, public lighting. (3) Public Accounts and Finances (Mayor), including purchases for the city, collections of taxes and water rents, issuance of licenses or permits, accounting and public records, collection of franchise fees and accounts of public service corporation.

Commissioners are elected to specific departments.

ieneral Commission Powers:

All the legislative powers, functions and duties conferred upon the city or its officers.

pecial Requirements:

The Commissioners are required to devote their entire time to the service of the city.

layor:

Term: Two years.

Salary: Twenty-six hundred dollars.

Removal: Recall.

ther Elective Officers:

Judge of the Municipal Court.

ppointments:

Enumeration: City Clerk, City Attorney.

Manner: Enumerated officers elected by the Board of Commissioners. The selection of other officers and employees may be made by the Board itself or delegated to the individual Commissioner. Departmental officers may be suspended or removed by the Commissioner in charge, but such action may be reviewed by the Board. The City Treasurer is one of the Commissioners other than the Mayor.

Civil Service Provisions:

None.

Election Provisions:

Nominations are made at a primary election, on the ballots for which names are placed by sworn request of the candidate and the payment by him of five dollars. The two candidates for each office receiving the highest number of votes are the candidates at the municipal election.

Initiative:

Twenty-five per centum petition (special election).

Referendum:

Twenty-five per centum petition (special election).

Recall:

Twenty-five per centum petition. The municipal judge is not subject to recall.

Franchises:

No franchise granted except after ratification by a two-thirds vote of the people at a general or special election. No franchise for a longer period than fifty years. Every franchise must contain provision for its forfeiture and for the maintenance of the property of the grantee in good condition. The city expressly reserves the right to exercise full police power over public utilities.

Special Features:

The Board of Commissioners is *ex-officio* Board of Education.

HICKORY

(Replacing original page of same number)

(SPECIAL CHARTER, AN ACT OF THE LEGISLATURE, RATIFIED BY POPULAR VOTE MAR. 17, 1913.)

Governing Body:

Title: City Council.

Number: Five, including four aldermen and the Mayor.

Term: Two years.

Removal: Recall.

Salary: One dollar per meeting, but not over sixty dollars in any year (the City Council meets weekly), except the member who may be designed City Treasurer.

Mayor:

ARTICLE V.

Sec. 1. The power and duties of the mayor shall be such as are conferred upon him by this charter, together with such others as are conferred by the city council in pursuance of the provisions of this act, and no others.

Sec. 2. He shall preside at all meetings of the city council and shall have the right to vote upon all questions. He shall be recognized as the official head of the city by the courts for the purpose of serving civil processes, and by the public for all ceremonial purposes. He shall have power to administer oaths.

Sec. 3. Such functions not enumerated in this charter as are conferred upon the mayor by the general laws of the state shall be exercised by the city manager, unless the city council designate some other person to exercise same.

Sec. 4. During the disability of the mayor, the functions of his office shall devolve upon some member of the city council designated by that body at its first meeting in May of each and every year.

The City Manager:

ARTICLE VI.

Sec. 1. There shall be chosen by the city council an officer to be known as the city manager, who shall be the administrative head of the city government.

Sec. 2. Before entering upon the duties of his office, the city manager shall take and subscribe an oath that he will faithfully perform the duties of his office and shall execute a bond, with an incorporated bonding company or companies as surety or sureties, in favor of the city for the faithful performance of his duties. The amount of the bond shall not be less than seven thousand five hundred dollars, and may be increased or a new bond required by the city council whenever it may deem it advisable.

Sec. 3. The term of the city manager shall be at the pleasure of the city council.

Sec. 4. The city manager shall not be personally interested in any contracts to which the city is a party, for the supplying the city materials of any kind.

Sec. 5. It shall be his duty to attend all meetings of and to recommend to the city council, from time to time, such measures as he shall deem necessary or expedient for it to adopt, and to furnish it with any necessary information respecting any of the departments under his control. He shall accurately keep the minutes of the city council.

Sec. 6. He shall transmit to the hands of the several departments written notice of all acts of the city council relating to the duties of their departments, and he shall make designation to officers to perform duties ordered to be performed by the city council.

Sec. 7. He shall sign all contracts, licenses and other public documents on behalf of the city, as the city council may authorize and require.

Sec. 8. He shall have access at all times to the books, vouchers and papers of any officer or employee of the city, excepting the city treasurer's books, and shall have power to examine, under oath, any person connected therewith.

Sec. 9. He shall have power to revoke licenses pending the action of the city council.

Sec. 10. He shall have authority and charge over all public works, the erection of buildings for the city, the making and construction of all improvements, paving, curbing, sidewalks, streets, bridges, viaducts, and the repair thereof; he shall approve all estimates of the cost of public works, and recommend to the city council the acceptance or rejection of the work done or improvements made; he shall have control, management and direction of all public grounds, bridges, viaducts and public buildings; he shall have control of the location of street car tracks, telephone and telegraph poles and wires; he shall have charge of the water sheds from which the city takes its supply of water, pumping stations, pipe lines, filtering apparatus, and all other things connected with or incident to the proper supply of water for the city; and shall secure all rights of way and easements connected with the water works or sewerage systems or the extension of the streets, etc.

All the powers enumerated, however, shall be exercised subject to the supervision and control of the city council.

Sec. 11. He shall have power to suspend, fine and dismiss any member of the police, fire, water works and sewerage and street departments in the interest of discipline. But any officer, appointed or elected by the City Council to a position in said department, who has been suspended, fined or dismissed, may appeal to the City Council at any of its regular meetings, and it shall review his case, affirm, or modify or reverse the order of the manager and make any restitution within the law which it may deem advisable. The City Manager shall promptly report all suspensions, fines and dismissals as hereinafter provided in the article in reference to the police powers of the City of Hickory.

Sec. 12. The officers and other employees of the police department, fire department, street department, and the water works and sewerage department shall be elected for a term of one year, from a list submitted to the City Council by the City Manager, and if the City Council is unable or refuses to elect from the list so furnished, it shall call on the City Manager from time to time for other lists, which it shall be his duty to furnish.

Appointments:

Enumeration: City Manager, City Attorney, City Treasurer, City Physician, the Board of School Visitors, Superintendent of Schools, the Judge of the Municipal Court.

City Manager for a term of one year.

Subordinate positions in the Health Department are filled in like manner from lists supplied by the City Physician, and in the school department from lists supplied by the Superintendent of Schools. (The Board of School Visitors has only inquisitorial functions.)

Civil Service Provisions: None.

Election Provisions:

Names placed upon primary ballot on petition of twenty-five voters. The names of candidates equal

aldermen are elected

Initiative:

Twenty-five per centum election).

Referendum:

Twenty-five per centum election).

Recall:

Twenty-five per centum

ELIZABETH CITY

(General Charter, an Act of the Legislature (Chap. 341, Laws of 1915) approved March 8, 1915).

Governing Body:

Title: Board of Aldermen.
Number: Eight (two from each ward).
Term: Two years.
Removal: Statutory provisions apply.
Salary: Three ($3) dollars for each regular and two ($2) dollars for each special meeting.

Mayor:

Presides at meetings of the Board of Aldermen and is the official head of the city for the service of civil process. He also has the veto power upon ordinances, contracts and franchises. His salary is not to exceed one hundred ($100) dollars per annum.

The City Manager:

Title: City Manager.
Powers and Duties: Exercises the usual powers of a city manager. He is purchasing agent of the city and is generally responsible for the conduct of all departments under his control.
Salary: Fixed by the Board of Aldermen; not to exceed twenty-four hundred ($2,400) dollars per year.

Appointments:

Enumeration: (1) City Manager, Health Officer, City Attorney, (2) City Auditor, City Tax Collector, Street Commissioner, Chief of Fire Department, Harbor Master, Chief of Police, Building Inspector.
Manner: Group (1) by the Board of Aldermen. Group (2) by the Board of Aldermen upon the recommendation of the City Manager.

Election Provisions:

The State laws apply.

Initiative:

No provisions.

Referendum:

No provisions.

Recall:

No provisions.

SOUTH CAROLINA STATUTE

(AN ACT APPROVED FEB. 22, 1910, NO. 277, ACTS AND RESOLUTIONS OF THE GENERAL ASSEMBLY. APPLICABLE TO CITIES OF BETWEEN 20,000 AND 50,000 POPULATION WHICH MAY ADOPT ITS PROVISIONS BY POPULAR VOTE AT A SPECIAL ELECTION CALLED UPON PETITION OF TWENTY PER CENTUM OF THE VOTERS.)

Commission-Organization:

Title: Council.

Number: Five, including Mayor.

Term: Four years. Partial renewal.

Removal: Recall.

Salary: Two thousand dollars.

Commissioner-Departments: One Councilman is Police Commissioner. Other departments to be created by Council. Designation by Mayor.

General Commission Powers:

All the legislative, executive and judicial powers of the City.

Special Requirements:

Councilmen required to devote entire time to the service of the City.

Mayor:

Term: Four years.

Salary: Twenty-five hundred dollars.

Removal: Recall.

Powers in Relation to Commission: Presides at meetings. No veto power.

Appointments:

Manner: By Council, except positions under Civil Service Rules.

Civil Service Provisions: Commission of three established. Terms, six years. Partial renewal.

Election Provisions:

Party nominations and elections regulated by the Charter.

Initiative:

Twenty per centum petition (special election).

Referendum:

Twenty per centum petition (special election).

Recall:

Twenty per centum petition, which is addressed to the Governor.

Abandonment of Act:

Operation under this act may be discontinued after six months, by popular election.

The City of **Columbia** *has adopted this act.*

SOUTH CAROLINA STATUTE

(An Act of the Legislature, February 23, 1912, Passed Without the Assent of the Governor. Applicable to Cities Having a Population Between 7,000 and 20,000 and Those Between 50,000 and 100,000 When Adopted Therein at a Special Election Called Upon Petition of Twenty-five Per Centum of the Electors.*)

Commission-Organization:

Title: City Council.

Number: Population 7,000 to 10,000; four, including mayor.

In all others, five, including mayor.

Term: Four years. Partial renewal biennially.

Removal: Recall.

Salary: Population 7,000 to 10,000; fixed by the city council. Population 10,000 to 20,000; twelve hundred dollars. Population over 50,000; four thousand dollars.

Commissioner - Departments: Determined by the Council. Designation by the Mayor, but reassignments may be made, when necessary, by vote of the council.

General Commission Powers:

All legislative, executive and judicial powers and duties, including the power to establish subordinate offices and to assign to the same their appropriate duties.

Mayor:

Term: Four years.

Salary: Population 7,000 to 10,000; fixed by the council.** Population 10,000 to 20,000; eighteen hundred dollars. Population over 50,000; five thousand dollars.

Removal: Recall.

Appointments:

Enumeration: City Attorney.

Manner: By the council.

Civil Service Provisions: The City Council is required to appoint a commission of three members to serve for overlapping terms of six years. The classified service includes departments of fire, police and public health.

Election Provisions:

No party primaries unless requested by the chief officer of the city organization of the party. Otherwise elections are conducted as provided for by general state laws.

Initiative:

Twenty per centum petition (special election).

Referendum:

Twenty per centum petition (special election).

Recall:

Twenty per centum petition.

Abandonment of Act:

Any city may abandon operation under this act after six years by the same procedure as employed for its adoption.

SPECIAL PROVISIONS FOR THE CITY OF SUMTER.

This act contains a special section providing for an election in the city of Sumter on the second Tuesday of June, 1912, at which the voters were given an option between the usual commission form and the city manager form. Under the first of these there would have been a mayor and two councilmen who would have received salaries, respectively, of $1,200 and $1,000 per year. Under the second form (which was adopted), the mayor and two councilmen receive salaries, respectively, of $300 and $200 per year, and they are required to appoint and fix the salary of a "city manager."

The portion of the section relating to the city manager reads as follows:

> "If a majority of the ballots cast at the election provided for herein shall be in favor of having a manager (city manager), then, in that event, the mayor and councilmen when elected shall not distribute the powers of said council among the members of the same; but shall employ a male person of sound discretion and of good moral character, not of their number, of such salary and upon such terms as they may decide, who shall be subject to such rules and regulations as may be provided by said councilmen."

*Special provision is made for cities between 4,000 and 10,000 inhabitants and for the cities of Sumter and Florence, both having a population of between 7,000 and 10,000. The provisions of the act are not applicable to Georgetown and Orangeburg Counties.

**The salary of the Mayor of Florence is fixed at $2,200.

CARTERSVILLE

(Special Charter, an act of the Legislature, approved August 18, 1911, ratified by popular vote, October 4, 1911.)

Commission-Organization:

Title: Board of Commissioners.

Number: Three, including Mayor.

Term: Two years.

Removal: Recall.

Salary: Five hundred dollars.

Commissioner - Departments: 1, Public Affairs (mayor), including all matters relating to taxation, finance, public utilities and revenue, auditing, Public Utilities and Finance; 2, Streets, Parks and Sewers; 3, Public Safety, Property and Schools. The functions and subdivisions of departments and designation of commissioners to each department are determined by the Board of Commissioners.

General Commission Powers:

All executive, administrative and legislative powers formerly vested in the mayor and board of aldermen, water, light and bond commission, board of school commissioners.

Special Requirements:

Quarterly itemized financial statements.

Mayor:

Term: Two years.

Salary: Fifteen hundred dollars.

Removal: Recall.

Powers: All powers and duties formerly vested and imposed upon the mayor not inconsistent with this act. No veto power.

Appointments:

Enumeration: None.

Manner: By the Board of Commissioners.

Civil Service Provisions: All employees must be chosen with reference to merit and fitness.

Election Provisions:

Nominations at non-partisan primaries; names placed on the ballot on petition of ten voters. Candidates to twice the number to be elected to each office receiving the highest number of votes are the candidates at the general election.

Initiative:

Twenty-five per centum petition (special election). Ten per centum petition (general election).

Referendum:

Ten per centum petition (general or special election).

Recall:

Twenty-five per centum petition.

Franchises:

No franchise to be granted except by ordinance subject to referendum, the expense of any special election for submitting a franchise to be borne by the grantee.

ST. PETERSBURG

(SPECIAL CHARTER, ADOPTED BY POPULAR VOTE, RATIFIED BY THE LEGISLATURE, 1913.)

Commission-Organization:

Title: Board of Commissioners.

Number: Three, including mayor.

Term: Six years. Partial renewal biennially.

Removal: Recall.

Salary: Twenty-four hundred dollars.

Commissioner-Departments:

1. Public Affairs, Revenue and Finance, including matters involving relation of the city to the government of the county, the state, the United States, and other municipalities; supervision of all boards and of the offices of City Atorney, City Judge, City Clerk; supervision of all financial affairs, including offices of City Treasurer, Auditor, Tax Assessor and Tax Collector.

2. Public Safety, including supervision over police, sanitary and health departments.

3. Public Works and Public Utilities, including supervision of construction, maintenance and operation of streets, avenues and alleys, wharves, docks, slips, quays and other water front property and all public utilities.

Commissioners are elected to specific departments, and are required to devote their entire time to the service of the city.

General Commission Powers:

Enumerated in detail in the charter, but including all the corporate powers.

Mayor:

Term: Six years.

Salary: Twenty-five hundred dollars.

Removal: Recall.

Powers: Presides over Board, but has no veto power.

Appointments:

Enumeration: City Clerk, City Attorney, Municipal Judge, Treasurer, City Physician, Auditor, City Engineer, Chief of Police and Fire Chief.

Manner: Enumerated officers by majority vote of the Board of Commissioners. Each commissioner has power to appoint and remove administrative heads and employees of subdivisions of his dedepartment.

Civil Service Provisions: None.

Election Provisions:

Names are placed upon ballot by petition of twenty-five voters. Preferential Voting.

Initiative:

Fifteen per centum petition (General or special election).

Referendum:

Twenty per centum petition. No recall petition may be filed during the first three months of office.

City Manager:

At any time at least two years after the beginning of operation under this act the Board of Commissioners at a special or general election may submit the question (or, it may be submitted under the Initiative) whether or not there shall be a City Manager, with a board of five commissioners. In the event that the question is decided affirmatively, five commissioners are to be elected, who shall exercise the legislative power. This board shall select the City Manager, who shall receive a salary of $5,000 for the first year, after which his salary may be fixed annually by the Board of Commissioners. The city manager shall have full control and charge of all business and departments of the city and the power to employ and discharge any employee or servant of the city not provided for otherwise in the charter. Each member of the Board of Commissioners shall receive a salary of $300 a year.

ST. AUGUSTINE

(An Act of the Legislature of 1915, adopted by popular vote June 7, 1915.)

Governing Body:

Title: City Commission.
Number: Three, elected at large.
Term: Three years; partial renewal annually.
Removal: Recall.
Salary: None.

Mayor:

Elected by the city commission from among their own number. Exercises powers and duties identical with those of the mayor of Dayton, O. (see p. 34003).

City Manager:

The powers and duties of the city manager are the usual ones conferred upon this officer. In addition to his other duties he is required to act as purchasing agent for the city.

His salary is to be fixed by the City Commission at not less than three thousand ($3,000) dollars.

Enumeration: (1) City Manager, City Attorney, Municipal Judge, (2) City Auditor and Clerk, Chief of Police, Chief of Fire Department, City Treasurer and Collector.

Election Provisions:

Non-partisan elections: names placed upon ballot upon petition of electors equal to two per cent. of those registered. Candidates receiving in the primary the highest number of votes equal to twice the number of vacancies to be filled are the candidates at the regular election.

The general election laws of the state apply in so far as they are not in conflict with the charter.

Sec. 12. "No candidate for the office of City Commissioner shall make any personal canvass among the voters to secure his nomination or election or the nomination or election of any other candidate in the same election whether such candidate be for municipal, county, state or other office. He may cause notice of his candidacy to be published in the newspapers and may procure the circulation of a petition for his nomination; but he shall not personally circulate such petition, nor by writing solicit anyone to support him or vote for him. He shall not expend or promise any money, office, employment or any other thing of value to secure a nomination or election, but he may answer such inquiries as may be put to him and may declare his position publicly upon matters of public interest, either by addressing public meetings or by making like statements for newspaper publication or general circulation. A violation of these provisions, or any of them, shall disqualify him from holding the office if elected and the person receiving the next highest number of votes, who has observed the foregoing conditions, shall be entitled to the office."

Initiative:

*Five per centum petition (for submission to the City Commission. An additional *five per centum is required for submission to the electors, if the City Commission fails to approve the proposed ordinance.

Referendum:

*Fifteen per centum petition (general election). Twenty-five per centum (special election).

Recall:

*Twenty per centum petition.

The question submitted at the election is the simple one of recall. If a single vacancy is created, it is filled by the remaining members of the Commission. If more than one vacancy is created a special election is required.

Special Feature:

The charter contains a unique statement of the official relations between the City Commission and the City Manager, which is reproduced here in full:

Sec. 10. "All powers of the city except such as are vested in the jurisdiction of the Municipal Court and except as otherwise provided by this charter, or by the Constitution of the State, are hereby vested in the City Commission; and, except as otherwise provided by this charter, or by the constitution of the state, the City Commission may, by ordinance or resolution prescribe the manner in which any power of the city shall be exercised. Neither the Commission nor any of its members shall dictate the appointment of any person to office or employment by the City Manager or in any manner prevent the City Manager from exercising his own judgment in selecting the personnel of his administration. The Commission and its members shall deal with the administrative service solely through the City Manager and neither the Commission nor any member thereof shall give orders to, nor make requests of, any of the subordinates of the City Manager, either publicly or privately. Any such dictation, orders, requests, or other interference upon the part of a member of the City Commission with the administration of the city shall constitute a misdemeanor and upon conviction thereof before a court of competent jurisdiction, any member of the City Commission so convicted shall be fined not exceeding two hundred dollars or be imprisoned not exceeding six months, or both, at the discretion of the court, and shall be removed from office."

* Registered voters.

KENTUCKY STATUTE

(An Act of the Legislature, approved Mar. 21, 1910, Chapter 50, Laws of 1910, applicable to second class cities upon adoption at popular election, called upon petition of twenty-five per centum of the voters.)

Commission-Organization:

Title: Board of Commissioners.

Number: Five, including Mayor.

Term: Four years.

Removal: By vote of four members after hearing.

Salary: Three thousand dollars.

Commissioner-Departments: 1, Public Affairs; 2, Public Finance; 3, Public Safety; 4, Public Works; 5, Public Property.

General Commission Powers:

All the legislative, executive and judicial powers of the City.

Special Requirements:

Monthly financial statements.

Mayor:

Term: Four years.

Salary: Thirty-six hundred dollars.

Removal: By unanimous vote of Commissioners.

Powers in Relation to Commission: Presides at meetings of Board. No veto power.

Appointments:

Manner: By majority of the Board.

Civil Service Provisions: None.

Election Provisions:

Nomination by petition of one hundred voters. No party designation.

Initiative:

Twenty-five per centum petition (regular election).

Referendum:

Twenty-five per centum petition (regular election).

Recall:

No provisions.

Operation under this act may be discontinued after four years by popular election and petition of thirty-three and a third per centum of the voters.

The City of **Newport** *has adopted this act.*

MEMPHIS

(SPECIAL CHARTER. CHAPTER 298, TENNESSEE LAWS OF 1909, APPROVED APR. 27, 1909.)

This Act provides for the amendment of Chapter 11 of the Acts of 1879 and stipulates that the name of the Board of Fire and Police Commissioners be changed to the "Board of Commissioners of the City of Memphis."

Commission-Organization:

Title: Board of Commissioners.

Number: Five, including Mayor.

Term: Four years.

Removal: Original Charter provisions.

Salary: Three thousand dollars.

Commissioner-Departments: 1, Public Affairs and Health; 2, Fire and Police; 3, Streets, Bridges and Sewers; 4, Accounts, Finances and Revenues; 5, Public Utilities, Grounds and Buildings. Designation by the Board.

General Commission Powers:

All the powers and duties formerly vested in the Board of Fire and Police Commissioners, the Board of Public Works and the Legislative Council.

Mayor:

Term: Four years.

Salary: Six thousand dollars.

Powers in Relation to Commission: No veto power. Has general supervision over office of City Attorney, Judge and City Court Clerks, City Clerk, Superintendent of the Public Health Department and the City Paymaster.

Removal: Original Charter provisions.

Appointments:

Enumeration: City Attorney, City Judge, City Engineer, City Clerk, Chief of Police, Chief of Fire Department, City Paymaster, City Chemist, Superintendent of Health Department, Clerk of City Court, City Plumbing Inspector, City Meat Inspector, City Boiler Inspector, Collector of License and Privilege Taxes, Wharfmaster, Marketmaster, City Veterinary Surgeon, Gas and Electric Light Inspector, City Harnessmaker, Inspector of Weights and Measures, Superintendent of City Hospital, Electric Inspector, Building Inspector.

Manner: Principal officers elected by the Board. Their terms and salaries are fixed in the Charter. Minor officers nominated by the individual Commissioners and elected by the Board.

Civil Service Provision: Board of three appointed by the Commission. Terms, three years. Removable on vote of four Commissioners for cause.

Initiative:

No provision.

Referendum:

No provision.

Recall:

No provision.

CHATTANOOGA

(SPECIAL CHARTER, AN ACT OF THE LEGISLATURE, APPROVED FEBRUARY 9, 1911, HOUSE BILL NO. 43, SUPPLEMENTED BY SENATE BILL 418 AND HOUSE BILL 451, SESSION OF 1911.)

---

ommission-Organization:

Title: Board of Commissioners.

Number: Five, including Mayor.

Term: Four years.

Removal: Recall.

Salary: Twenty-two hundred and fifty dollars.

Commissioner-Departments: 1. Public Affairs and Finance. 2. Fire and Police. 3. Streets and Sewers. 4. Education and Health. 5. Public Utilities, Grounds and Buildings.

eneral Commission Powers:

All executive, administrative, legislative and judicial powers formerly possessed by the Mayor, General Council, Board of Aldermen, Councilmen, Board of Public Works, Board of Public Safety, Board of Public Health, Board of School Commissioners, Board of Park Commissioners and other executive and administrative officers of the city.

Special Requirements:

Monthly itemized financial statements.

Mayor:

Term: Four years.

Salary: Three thousand dollars.

Removal: Recall.

Powers: Has veto power, and has vote on question of sustaining his own veto. Has all other powers vested in Mayor at the time of the adoption of this act, which are not inconsistent therewith.

Other Elective Officers:

City Judge and City Attorney, who are subject to removal by the Recall.

Appointments:

Enumeration: City Auditor, City Treasurer, Clerk of the City Court, City Engineer, City Physician, whose terms of office and duties are the same as those provided by the previous law under which the city operated.

Manner: By majority vote of the Commissioners. Removal at any time in the same manner. But officials in office at the time of the adoption of this act may be removed only for cause.

Civil Service Provision: The Board of Commissioners must, by ordinance, establish a Civil Service Commission of three members.

Election Provisions:

Non-partisan primaries. Nomination by petition of twenty-five voters. The number of candidates chosen is twice the number of offices to be filled at the second election.

Initiative:

Twenty-five percentum petition (special election).

Referendum:

Twenty-five percentum petition.

Recall:

Thirty percentum petition.

Special Features:

The public schools are under the control of one of the Commissioners, who supersedes the Board of School Commissioners. But the Board of Commissioners may create a Board of Education.

KNOXVILLE

(SPECIAL CHARTER, AN ACT OF THE LEGISLATURE, APPROVED JULY 1, 1911. ADOPTED BY THE PEOPLE AUGUST 26, 1911.)

Commission-Organization:

Title: Board of Commissioners.

Number: Five, including Mayor.

Term: Four years.

Salary: Three thousand dollars.

Removal: Recall.

Commissioner-Departments: 1, Public Affairs (Mayor); 2, Accounts and Finance; 3, Public Safety; 4, Streets and Public Improvements; 5, Parks and Public Property. Designation by the Council.

General Commission Powers:

All executive, legislative and judicial powers formerly exercised by the Mayor, Board of Aldermen, Board of Public Works, Board of Health, Board of Park Commissioners, Board of Water Works Commissioners, the Comptroller, City Engineer, etc.

Special Requirements:

Monthly financial statements.

Mayor:

Term: Four years.

Salary: Thirty-five hundred dollars.

Removal: Recall.

Powers: Presides at meetings of the Board. No veto power.

Appointments:

Enumeration: Recorder and Treasurer, City Attorney, Library Trustees, Chief of Police, Chief of Fire Department, Market Master.

Manner: By majority vote of the Board of Commissioners, subject to removal for cause.

Civil Service Provisions: The Board of Commissioners are required to appoint a Board (three) of Civil Service Commissioners.

Election Provisions:

The election provisions of the old law apply, together with the additional sections of the new charter, relating to "corrupt practice."

Initiative:

Forty per centum petition (special election).
Twenty-five per centum petition (general election).

Referendum:

Twenty-five per centum petition (special or general election).

Recall:

Forty per centum petition.

Franchises:

Every franchise grant is subject to the general referendum provisions of the charter.

Special Features:

The Board of Commissioners elect a Sinking Fund Commission.
The Board of Commissioners are limited as to the tax rate.

OHIO STATUTE

(AN ACT OF THE LEGISLATURE 1913, APPLICABLE TO ANY CITY AFTER ADOPTION BY THE VOTERS THEREOF AT A SPECIAL ELECTION CALLED UPON PETITION OF TEN PER CENTUM OF THE ELECTORS.**)

COMMISSION PLAN*

Commission-Organization:

Title: Commission.

Number: Population under 10,000; three. Population 10,000 and over; five.

Term: Four years. Partial renewal biennially.

Commissioner-Departments: The commission may, at its discretion, assign the direction or supervision of particular departments or branches to the individual commissioners; but such action does not release the commission as a whole from responsibility for the condition of any department or branch of government so assigned.

General Commission Powers:

The powers conferred upon municipalities by the constitution of Ohio, and any additional powers which have been conferred upon municipalities by the general assembly, unless the exercise of such powers shall have been expressly conferred upon some other authority or reserved to the people.

Appointments:

Enumeration: Clerk, Treasurer, Auditor and Solicitor; but provision may be made by ordinance for the performance of the duties of Clerk and Treasurer by the same person.

Manner: By majority vote of the Commission.

CITY MANAGER PLAN

Governing Body:

Title: Council.

Number: Less than 10,000 population; five. From 10,000 to 25,000 population; seven. More than 25,000 population; nine.

Term: Four years. Partial renewal biennially.

Powers of Governing Body:

As under Commission plan.

The City Manager:

Appointment and Tenure: By the Council, to hold office during their pleasure.

Qualifications: Must take official oath and give official bond. No residence requirement.

Salary: Fixed by the Council.

Powers and Duties: (a) to see that the laws and ordinances are faithfully executed; (b) to attend all meetings of the council at which his attendance may be required by that body; (c) to recommend for adoption to the council such measures as he may deem necessary or expedient; (d) to appoint all officers and employees in the classified service of the municipality, subject to the provisions of this act and the civil service law; (e) to prepare and submit to the council such reports as may be required by that body, or as he may deem advisable to submit; (f) to keep the council fully advised of the financial condition of the municipality and its future needs; (g) to prepare and present to the council a tentative budget for the next fiscal year; (h) to perform such other duties as the Council may determine by ordinance or resolution.

Appointments:

As under the Commission Plan.

THE FEDERAL PLAN

Governing Body:

Title: Council.

Number: Population less than 10,000; five. Population 10,000 to 25,000; seven. Population 25,000 to 50,000; nine. For each additional 25,000 inhabitants over 50,000; one, but in no case may the total number of councilmen be greater than fifteen.

** May not be submitted while an election for submitting the question of framing a local charter under the home-rule provision of the constitution is pending.

* The petition for the adoption of this act must specify one and only one form to be voted upon.

Term: Four years.

General Powers of Governing Body: All legislative power.

Mayor:

Term: Elected by the people for four years.

Powers: Has veto power, which may be overruled by a two-thirds vote of the Council. The executive power is vested in this officer together with the heads of departments. He is required (a) to see that the laws are enforced; (b) to recommend to the council for adoption such measures as he may deem necessary or expedient; (c) to keep the Council fully advised of the financial condition and future needs of the municipality; (d) to prepare and submit to the council such reports as may be required by that body; (e) to appoint, whenever he deems it necessary, competent, disinterested persons not exceeding three in number, to examine without notice the affairs of any department officer or employee; (f) to perform such other duties as the Council may determine.

Appointments:

Enumeration: Director of Public Service, Director of Public Safety, Solicitor and Treasurer. (The Council may provide for combining the offices and duties of directors of Public Service and Public Safety.)

Manner: Enumerated officers, except the auditor, by the mayor; removable by him without assignment of reasons. The heads of departments have power to appoint, remove and determine the functions, number and salaries of subordinates. This power is subject, however, to the rules and regulations of the Civil Service Commission.

Special Features:

The Board of Control, consisting of the mayor, the auditor and the heads of departments appointed by the mayor, is required to hold stated meetings at least twice a week and to keep a record of its proceedings. No ordinance or resolution involving any expenditure of money for public improvements shall be passed until it shall have been approved by this Board, except upon a two-thirds vote of the Council.

PROVISIONS APPLICABLE TO EACH PLA

The Auditor:

Elected by the Council (or Commission).

Civil Service Provisions:

A commission of three members, which admini the state civil service law, is to be appointe the council, whose members are removabl that body after notice and a public hearing.

Salaries of Councilmen:

Fixed by ordinance, but may not be changed du the terms of office of the incumbent.

Election Provisions:

Ballots are to be without party marks or desi tions. The names of candidates are printe rotation, the name of each candidate being pl at the head of the list in one of as many seri there are candidates to be voted for.

Candidates at the regular municipal election e to the number of places to be filled, who rece the highest number of votes, are to be decl elected.

The Initiative:

All laws pertaining to the Initiative and Ref dum in municipalities are applicable to operating under this act.

Referendum:

See "Initiative."

**Recall:*

Fifteen per centum petition.

In case the officer is not recalled, the city i quired to reimburse him for his legitimat penses at the recall election, but not excee fifty per centum of the sum which is perm by law to spend as a candidate for his office regular election.

Abandonment of Act:

Any city operating under this act may aband after five years and may adopt any other of government provided for herein, by sp election, called upon petition of ten per ce of the electors.

* Submitted as an optional proposition with that of the ad of the act.

DAYTON

(Home Rule Charter, drafted by a board of fifteen elected freeholders. Adopted by the people Aug. 12, 1913.)

Governing Body:

Title: Commission.
Number: Five.
Term: Four years. Partial renewal biennially.
Removal: Recall.
Salary: Twelve hundred dollars (Mayor, $1,800).

Mayor:

Sec. 36. The mayor shall be that member of the commission who, at the regular municipal election at which the three commissioners were elected, received the highest number of votes, except that at the first regular municipal election held under this charter the mayor shall be the commissioner receiving the highest number of votes. In case two candidates receive the same number of votes, one of them shall be chosen mayor by the remaining members of the commission. In event of a vacancy in the office of mayor, the remaining members of the commission shall choose his successor for the unexpired term from their own number. The mayor shall be the presiding officer, except that in his absence a president protempore may be chosen. The mayor shall exercise such powers conferred and perform all duties imposed upon him by this charter, the ordinances of the city and the laws of the state. He shall be recognized as the official head of the city by the courts for the purpose of serving civil processes, by the Governor for the purposes of the military law, and for all ceremonial purposes.

Sec. 37. In the event the commissioner who is acting as mayor shall be recalled, the remaining members of the commission shall select one of their number to serve as mayor for the unexpired term. In the event of the recall of all of the commissioners, the person receiving the highest number of votes at the election held to determine their successors shall serve as the Mayor.

City Manager:

Sec. 47. The commission shall appoint a city manager who shall be the administrative head of the municipal government and shall be responsible for the efficient administration of all departments. He shall be appointed without regard to his political beliefs and may or may not be a resident of the city of Dayton when appointed. He shall hold office at the will of the commission and shall be subject to recall as herein provided.

Sec. 48. Powers and Duties of the City Manager. The powers and duties of the city manager shall be

(a) To see that the laws and ordinances are enforced.

(b) To appoint and, except as herein provided, remove all directors of departments and all subordinate officers and employees in the departments in both the classified and unclassified service; all appointments to be upon merit and fitness alone, and in the classified service all appointments and removals to be subject to the civil service provisions of this charter;

(c) To exercise control over all departments and divisions created herein or that may be hereafter created by the commission;

(d) To attend all meetings of the commission, with the right to take part in the discussion but having no vote;

(e) To recommend to the commission for adoption such measures as he may deem necessary or expedient;

(f) To keep the commission fully advised as to the financial condition and needs of the city; and

(g) To perform such other duties as may be prescribed by this charter or be required of him by ordinance or resolution of the commission.

Sec. 49. Salary. The city manager shall receive such salary as may be fixed by ordinance of the commission.

Sec. 50. Investigations by the City Manager. The city manager may without notice cause the affairs of any department or the conduct of any officer or employee to be examined. Any person or persons appointed by the city manager to examine the affairs of any department or the conduct of any officer or employee shall have the same power to compel the attendance of witnesses and the production of books and papers and other evidence, and to cause witnesses to be punished for contempt, as is conferred upon the commission by this charter.

Appointments:

Enumeration: (1) City Manager, Civil Service Board, Clerk of the Commission. (2) City Attorney, Director of Public Service, Director of Public Welfare, Director of Public Safety, Director of Finance. (3) The following subordinate officers: Health Officer, Chief of Police, Fire Chief, City Accountant, City Treasurer, City Purchasing Agent.

Manner: Group (1) by the Commission. Groups (2) and (3) by the City Manager.

Civil Service Provisions: The following officers are in the unclassified service: Those elected by the people, the City Manager, the heads of departments and divisions of departments, members of appointive boards, the Clerk of the Commission, and the deputies and secretaries of the City Manager, and one assistant or deputy and one secretary for each department.

All other positions are in the classified service in the competitive, non-competitive or labor divisions, and are under the regulations of the Civil Service Board.

Election Provisions:

Non-partisan nominations and elections. Names are placed on the ballot at the primary election by petition of two per centum of the registered voters.

Candidates to twice the number of offices to be filled, receiving the highest number of votes at the primary are the candidates at the second election.

Initiative:

Ten per centum petition* to bring the ordinance to the attention of the council; additional fifteen* per centum petition after thirty days to have it submitted to the people (special election).

Referendum:

Twenty-five per centum petition* (special election).

Recall:

Twenty-five per centum petit
No recall petition may be fi
months of office. The que
arated from that of the ch
the name of the officer sou
not appear as a candidate
The recall may be applied to

*Registered vote.

SPRINGFIELD

(HOME RULE CHARTER, DRAFTED BY A BOARD OF FIFTEEN ELECTED FREEHOLDERS. ADOPTED BY THE POPULAR VOTE AUG. 26, 1913.)

Governing Body:

Title: City Commission.
Number: Five.
Term: Four years. Partial renewal biennially.
Removal: Recall.
Salary: Five hundred dollars.

Mayor:

Sec. 6. President. The city commission shall at the time of organizing elect one of its members as president and another as vice-president for terms of two years. In case the members of the city commission, within five days after the time herein fixed for their organization meeting, are unable to agree upon a president or a vice-president of such commission, then a president, or a vice-president, or both, as the occasion may require, shall be selected from all the members of such commission by lot conducted by the city solicitor; who shall certify the result of such lot upon the journal of the commission.

The president shall preside at all meetings of the commission and perform such other duties consistent with his office as may be imposed by it; and he shall have a voice and vote in its proceedings, but no veto. He may use the title of mayor in any case in which the execution of legal instruments of writing or other necessity arising from the general law of the state so requires; but this shall not be construed as conferring upon him the administrative or judicial functions of a mayor under the general laws of the state.

The president of the city commission shall be recognized as the official head of the city by the courts for the purpose of serving civil process, by the governor for the purpose of military law, and for all ceremonial purposes. He may take command of the police and govern the city by proclamation during times of public danger or emergency, and he shall himself be the judge of what constitutes such public danger or emergency. The powers and duties of the president shall be such as are conferred upon him by this charter, together with such others as are conferred by the city commission in pursuance of the provisions of this charter, and no others.

If the president be temporarily absent from the city, or become temporarily disabled from any cause, his duties shall be performed during such absence or disability by the vice-president. In the absence of both president and vice-president the other members of the city commission shall select one of their number to perform the duties of president.

City Manager:

Sec. 15. Appointment. The city commission shall appoint a city manager, who shall be the administrative head of the municipal government under the direction and supervision of the city commission, and who shall hold office at the pleasure of the city commission. He shall be appointed without regard to his political beliefs and need not be a resident of the city at the time of his appointment. During the absence or disability of the city manager, the city commission may designate some properly qualified person to execute the functions of the office.

Sec. 16. Powers and Duties. The powers and duties of the city manager shall be:

(a) To see that the laws and ordinances are enforced.

(b) Except as herein provided, to appoint and remove all heads of departments, and all subordinate officers and employees of the city; all appointments to be upon merit and fitness alone, and in the classified service all appointments and removals to be subject to the civil service provisions of this charter.

(c) To exercise control over all departments and divisions created herein or that hereafter may be created by the commission.

(d) To see that all terms and conditions imposed in favor of the city or its inhabitants in any public utility franchises are faithfully kept and performed; and upon knowledge of any violation thereof to call the same to the attention of the city solicitor, who is hereby required to take such steps as are necessary to enforce the same.

(e) To attend all meetings of the commission, with the right to take part in the discussions, but having no vote.

(f) To recommend to the commission for adoption such measures as he may deem necessary or expedient.

(g) To act as budget commissioner and to keep the city commission fully advised as to the financial condition and needs of the city; and

(h) To perform such other duties as may be prescribed by this charter or be required of him by ordiance or resolution of the commission.

Sec. 17. Head of Departments. Excepting the departments of city solicitor, auditor, treasurer, sinking fund and civil service, and until otherwise provided by the city commission, any existing department now under the control of a special board, such as library, hospital and park, the city manager shall be the acting head of each and every department of the city until otherwise directed by the commission; but with the consent and approval of the commission, he may appoint a deputy or chief clerk to represent him in any department of which he is the acting head. No member of the city commission shall directly interfere with the conduct of any department, except at the express direction of the commission.

Sec. 18. Platting Commissioner. The city manager shall also be the platting commissioner of the city, and he shall exercise the authority and discharge the duties of that office under the provisions of the general law of the state applicable thereto, except as the same may be modified by the city commission.

Appointments:

Enumeration: City Manager, City Solicitor, City Auditor, City Treasurer, Purchasing Agent, Sinking Fund Commissioner, Civil Service Commission.

Manner: Enumerated officers by the City Commission; all others by the City Manager, subject to Civil Service provisions.

Civil Service Provisions: The general laws of the state apply.

Election Provisions:

Non-partisan primaries and general elections. Designations on the primary ballot are made by petition of not less than two (2) per centum of the registered voters in the city. Each signer of such petition must pledge himself to vote for the person named as a candidate in such petition, and the candidate must accept the designation before his name may appear on the ballot.

Candidates equal to twice the number of vacancies to be filled, receiving the highest number of votes at the primary, are the candidates at the general election.

Initiative:

Five per centum petition for submission to the City Commission. An additional five per centum petition is required for submission of the ordinance to the voters at a general election, in the event of its rejection by the City Commission or its passage in a different form from the original. But before any ordiance is so submitted to the voters it must have been approved as to its
City Solicitor.

If the number of petitioners in
amount in the aggregate to twen
of the registered voters, the ordi
mitted at an election held for th

Referendum:

Fifteen per centum petition* (ge
Twenty-five per centum petition*

Recall:

Fifteen per centum petition.

The question of recall is separa
from that of the election of a
officer or officers sought to be re

Candidates to succeed such office
nated by petition of five per ce
tered voters without resort to a

No petition for the recall of any
within six months after the beg
of office.

*Registered voters.

MIDDLETOWN

(Home Rule Charter, drafted by a board of freeholders; adopted by popular election Aug. 8, 1913.)

Commission—Organization.

Title: City Commission.

Number: Five.

Term: Four years. Partial renewal bienially.

Removal: Recall.

Salary: Five hundred dollars.

Commissioner-Departments: No designation of commissioners is made by charter, nor is any provision made for the making of such designation, or for distribution of functions among their members by the City Commission. The chairman of the City Commission is designated the executive head of the city "for the time being."

Appointments:

Enumeration: Clerk, Treasurer, Auditor, Attorney, City Engineer, Civil Service Commission. (The non-salaried Boards of Health and Library Trustees and the Park Commissioners are continued.)

Manner: Enumerated officers by the City Commission.

Civil Service Provisions: The Civil Service Commission of three members is required to enforce the Civil Service law of the state.

Election Provisions:

*Names placed upon the ballot by petition of five per centum of the electors of the city. Ballots are to be without party designations of any kind. Elections are to be held in the same manner as for members of the Board of Education.

Initiative:

Twenty per centum petition.

†*Referendum:*

Ten per centum petition.

Recall:

Twenty per centum petition. Nominations of candidates to succeed the officer sought to be removed are made by petition of ten per centum "of the total ballots cast at the last general municipal election."

The question of removal is separated on the ballot from that of the election of a successor and the name of the officer whose removal is sought does not appear on the ballot as a candidate to succeed himself.

*Apparently based upon the registered vote.
†The registered vote, but not so in the case of the Initiative or Recall.

SANDUSKY

(HOME RULE CHARTER, DRAFTED BY A BOARD OF ELECTED FREEHOLDERS; ADOPTED BY POPULAR VOTE MAY 25, 1914.)

Governing Body:

Title: City Commission.
Number: Five.
Term: Four years. Partial renewal biennially.
Removal: Recall.
Salary: Four hundred ($400) dollars per year.

Mayor:

The president of the City Commission, elected by that body from its own membership, presides at meetings of the Commission, but has no veto power; uses the title of "mayor" in the execution of legal documents, when the state law requires; is to be recognized by the courts as head of the city for the service of civil process, by the governor for the purposes of the military law and for all ceremonial purposes; may take command of the police in times of great public danger.

His salary is fixed at one thousand dollars per year.

City Manager:

The qualifications, methods of appointment, powers and duties of this office are identical with those set forth in the Springfield, O., charter (q. v.).

Appointment:

Enumeration: City Manager, City Solicitor, City Treasurer, Clerk of the City Commission. The City Commission is authorized to appoint advisory boards to assist the City Manager.

Manner: The City Manager appoints all heads of departments except the Solicitor (law department) and the city treasurer, who are appointed by the commission.

Civil Service Provisions: The City Commission is required to establish civil service rules for the appointment, promotion, reduction and removal of members of the Police and Fire departments, and may establish such rules for other officers and employees of the city.

Election Provisions:

Ballots are non-partisan. Nominations made by petitions numbering five per centum of the total vote cast at the last preceding municipal election. There is but one election. Candidates equal to the number of vacancies receiving the highest number of votes are declared elected.

Initiative:

The general state law applying to cities.

Referendum:

The general state law applying to cities.

Recall:

Ten per centum petition.

A single vacancy is filled by the remaining members of the Commission. If two or more members are removed, successors are elected in the manner provided for general elections.

ASHTABULA

(HOME RULE CHARTER, DRAFTED BY AN ELECTED CHARTER COMMISSION; ADOPTED BY POPULAR VOTE NOVEMBER 3, 1914.)

Governing Body:

Title: Council.

Number: Seven. Partial renewal biennially.

Term: Two years.

Removal: Recall.

Salary: One hundred ($100) dollars per year.

Mayor:

The provisions relating to the President (mayor) are identical with those in the Sandusky, O., charter (q. v.) except as to salary. His salary is fixed at one hundred and fifty ($150) dollars per year.

City Manager:

The qualifications, methods of appointment, powers and duties of the city manager are identical with those set forth in the Springfield, O., charter (q. v.).

Appointments:

Enumeration: City Manager, City Solicitor, City Treasurer.

Manner: Enumerated officers by the Council; others by the City Manager.

Civil Service Provisions: The Council is required to appoint a Commission of three members, which is governed by the general civil service law of the state.

Elect on Provisions:

Proportional representation (Hare Plan). The full text of the election provisions follows:

NOMINATION OF CANDIDATES

Sec. 42. Candidates for the elective offices of the City shall be nominated by petition only. Each petition shall contain the name of the candidate, giving his place of residence with street and number, if any, shall specify the office for which he is nominated, and if only one candidate is to be elected to the office named in the petition, it shall be signed by the qualified electors of the City not less in number than five (5) per cent. of the total number of registered voters therein. If more than one candidate is to be elected to the office named, it shall be signed by not less than two (2) per cent. of the total number of registered voters in the City.

Such petitions shall contain a provision that each signer thereto thereby pledges himself to support and vote for the candidate whose nomination is therein requested, and each elector signing a petition shall add to his signature his place of residence giving street and number, if any, voting precinct, and date of signing. All signatures shall be made with ink or indelible pencil, and no elector shall sign the nominating petition of more than one candidate for the same office.

Signers of such petitions shall insert in them the names of five electors as a committee who may fill vacancies caused by death or withdrawal. The signatures of all the petitioners need not be appended to one paper, but to each separate paper there shall be attached an affidavit of the circulator thereof, stating the number of signers thereto, that each person signed in his presence on the date mentioned, that each signature is that of the person it purports to be, and that all other statements therein are true to the best of his knowledge and belief.

Each circulator of a nominating petition or paper of a candidate for the Council shall file a copy of the same with the Clerk of Council and before so filing shall attach his affidavit that it is a true copy of such nomination paper, and it shall be the duty of the Clerk of Council to combine and preserve all copies of the nominating papers or petitions of candidates elected to the Council during their respective terms of office.

Such petitions shall not be signed by any elector more than sixty days prior to the day of the election and such petitions shall be filed with the Board of Deputy State Supervisors of Elections of Ashtabula County, Ohio, not less than thirty-five days prior to the day of said election.

Sec. 46-1. Ballots for the election of members of the Council shall be marked according to the following rules and the same shall be printed at the top of each ballot under the head of "Directions to Voters:" Put the figure 1 opposite the name of your first choice for the Council. If you want to express also second, third, and other preferences, do so by putting the figure 2 opposite the name of your second choice, the figure 3 opposite the name of your third choice, and so on. You may express thus as many preferences as you please. This ballot will not be counted for your second choice unless it is found that it cannot help your first; it will not be counted for your third choice unless it is found that it cannot help either your first or your second; etc. The more choices you express, the surer you are to make your ballot count for one of the candidates you favor.

A ballot is spoiled if the figure 1 is put opposite more than one name. If you spoil this ballot, tear it across once, return it to the election officer in charge of the ballots, and get another from him.

Sec. 46-2. Ballots cast for the election of members of the Council shall be counted and the results determined by the election authorities according to the following rules:

(a) No ballot shall be declared invalid except one on which the first choice of the voter cannot be clearly ascertained. A ballot marked with a cross opposite one name, but with no other mark, shall be treated exactly as if it had been marked with a figure 1 opposite the same name, but with no other mark.

(b) The ballots shall first be sorted and counted at the several voting precincts according to the first choice of the voters. The valid ballots so cast for each candidate shall be sorted into two groups, that of valid ballots on which the voter's second choice is clearly indicated and that of valid ballots on which his second choice is not clearly indicated. Each such group shall be tied up by itself and properly marked on the outside and the two for each candidate shall then be tied up in one bundle which shall also be properly marked on the outside. All the bundles thus made up at a precinct, together with the invalid ballots and a record of all the ballots cast at the precinct, showing the number of invalid ballots, the number of valid ballots, the total number of first-choice ballots for each candidate, and the number of ballots in each of the two groups of first-choice ballots received by each candidate, shall be forwarded to the Board of Deputy State Supervisors of Elections, as directed by that Board and the counting of the ballots shall proceed under its direction.

(c) First-choice votes for each candidate shall be added and tabulated as the first count.

(d) The whole number of valid ballots shall then be divided by a number greater by one than the number of seats to be filled. The next whole number larger than the quotient thus obtained shall be the quota or constituency.

(e) All candidates the number of whose votes on the first count is equal to or greater than the quota shall then be declared elected.

(f) All votes obtained by any candidate in excess of the quota shall be termed the surplus of that candidate.

(g) The surpluses shall be transferred, successively in order of size from the largest to the smallest. Each ballot of the surplus that is capable of transfer shall be transferred to and added to the votes of continuing candidates, according to the highest available preference on it.

(h) "Ballots capable of transfer" means ballots from which the preference of the voter for some continuing candidate can be clearly ascertained. "Continuing candidates" means candidates who have not been declared elected or defeated.

(i) The particular ballots to be taken for transfer as the surplus of such candidate shall be obtained by taking as nearly an equal number of ballots as possible from the first-choice ballots, capable of transfer, that have been cast for the candidate in each of the different precincts of the city. All such surplus ballots shall be taken as they may happen to come in the different packages without selection.

(j) After the transfer of all surpluses the votes standing to the credit of each candidate shall be counted and tabulated as the second count.

(k) After the tabulation of the second count (or after that of the first count if no candidate received a surplus on the first) the candidate lowest on the poll as it then stands shall be declared defeated and all his ballots capable of transfer shall be transferred to the continuing candidates, each ballot being transferred to the credit of that continuing candidate preferred by the voter. After the transfer of these ballots a fresh count and tabulation shall be made. In this manner candidates shall be successively declared defeated, and their ballots capable of transfer transferred to continuing candidates, and a fresh count and tabulation made. After any tabulation the candidate to be declared defeated shall be the one then lowest on the poll.

(l) Whenever in the transfer of a surplus or of the ballots of a defeated candidate the votes of any candidate shall equal the quota, he shall immediately be declared elected and no further transfer to him shall be made.

(m) When candidates to the number of seats to be filled have been declared elected, all other candidates shall be declared defeated and the count shall be at an end; and when the number of continuing candidates shall be reduced to the number of seats to be filled, those candidates shall be declared elected and the count shall be at an end; and in this case the ballots of the last candidate defeated need not be transferred.

(n) If at any count two or more candidates at the bottom of the poll have the same number of votes, that candidate shall first be declared defeated who was lowest at the next preceding count at which their votes were different. Should it happen that the votes of these candidates are equal to each other on all counts, lots shall be drawn to decide which candidate shall next to declared defeated.

(o) In the transfer of the ballots of any candidate who has received ballots by transfer, those ballots shall first be transferred upon which the defeated candidate was first choice.

(p) On each tabulation a count shall be kept of those ballots which have not been used in the election of some candidate and which are not capable of transfer, under the designation "Non-transferable ballots."

(q) Every ballot that is transferred from one candi[dat]e to another shall be stamped or marked so that its en[tire] course from candidate to candidate throughout the count [can] be conveniently traced. In case a recount of the ballot[s is] made, every ballot shall be made to take in the recount [the] same course that it took in the first count unless ther[e is] discovered a mistake that requires its taking a diffe[rent] course, in which case such mistake shall be corrected [and] any changes made in the course taken by ballots that ma[y be] required as a result of such correction. The particular bal[lots] the course of which is to be changed in the recount as a re[sult] of such corrections shall be taken as they happen to co[me] without selection.

(r) So far as may be consistent with good order and [with] convenience in the counting and transferring of the bal[lots,] the public, representatives of the press, and especially candidates themselves shall be afforded every facility being present and witnessing these operations.

Initiative:

Ten per centum petitions (for submission to Council and to electors at a general election).

Referendum:

See "Initiative" provisions.

Recall:

Twenty-five per centum petitions. If not over [two] members of the Council are removed at [one] election, vacancies are filled by the remair[ning] members for the remainder of the unexp[ired] term. If three or more members are so remo[ved] the Council is required to call a special elec[tion] for the choice of their successors, but candid[ates] are not designated on the ballots to succeed [par]ticular members removed.

APPLICATION

Sec. 48. Any member of the Council, provided for in [this] Charter, may be removed from office by petition.

PROCEDURE

Sec. 49. A petition for the recall of a member of [the] Council shall be signed by at least twenty-five per cent [of] the total number of registered voters in the municipality, [but] no such petition shall be valid unless it contains the [sig]natures of at least seventy-five per cent. of the electors [who] signed the nomination petition of the member whose reca[ll is] requested. The signatures to the petition need not al[l be] appended to one paper, but the signatures of those [who] signed the nominating petition of the member whose re[call] is sought shall be upon one paper separate from those [con]taining the other signatures.

NOTICE

Sec. 53. At the expiration of said period of thirty [days] the Clerk of the Council shall certify upon such peti[tion] whether the signatures thereto amount to at least twe[nty-] five (25) per cent. of the registered voters of the City [and] include the signatures of seventy-five per cent. of the e[lec]tors who signed the nominating petition of the member wh[ose] removal is asked for. If the petition does contain the ne[ces]sary signatures he shall at once serve notice of the fact u[pon] the Council, and upon the receipt of such notice the mem[ber] named in the petition shall be deemed removed from o[ffice] and the vacancy shall be filled as provided in section [of] the Charter as herein amended.

ILLINOIS STATUTE

(An Act of the Legislature approved Mar. 9, 1910, an amendment to the General City Act of Apr. 10, 1872. Any city operating under the general act, having a population not exceeding 200,000, may adopt its provisions by popular election based upon a petition of ten per cent. of the votes cast for mayor at the last preceding municipal election.)*

Commission-Organization:

Title: Council.

Number: Five, including Mayor.

Term: Four years.

Removal: Recall.

Salary: Under 2,000 population, $40 per annum.
2,000 to 5,000 population, $100 per annum.
5,000 to 10,000 population, $400 per annum.
10,00 to 15,000 population, $900 per annum.
15,000 to 20,000 population, $1,700 per annum.
20,000 to 30,000 population, $2,000 per annum.
30,000 to 40,000 population, $3,000 per annum.
40,000 to 60,000 population, $3,500 per annum.
60,000 to 80,000 population, $4,000 per annum.
80,000 to 100,000 population, $4,500 per annum.
100,000 to 200,000 population, $5,500 per annum.

Commissioner-Departments: 1, Public Affairs (Mayor); 2, Accounts and Finances; 3, Public Health and Safety; 4, Streets and Public Improvements; 5, Public Property. Designation made by Council.

General Commission Powers:

"The Council shall have and possess, and the Council and its members shall exercise all executive and legislative powers and duties now had, possessed and exercised by the mayor, city council, president and board of trustees of villages, board of library trustees, city clerk, city attorney, city engineer, city treasurer, city comptroller, and all other executive, legislative and administrative officers in cities or villages now or hereinafter organized and incorporated under the general corporation law of the State of Illinois for the incorporation of cities and villages, except that in each city or village organized under and adopting the provisions of this Act the board of local improvements, provided for in and by Act entitled "An Act concerning local improvements," approved June 14, 1897, in force July 1, 1897, and all Acts amendatory thereto, shall be and remain a separate and distinct body, with all the rights, powers and duties and authority in said Act contained, and except also, that nothing herein contained shall apply or extend or pertain to or in any way effect the park and driveway officers now or hereafter elected under the particular laws pertaining thereto, and except also that nothing in this Act shall in any way extend or pertain to or effect any public school law in operation in any municipality which may adopt this Act, anything in this present Act contained to the contrary notwithstanding."

Special Requirements:

Monthly statements of Receipts and Disbursements.

Mayor:

Term: Four years.

Salary: Under 2,000 population, $50 per annum.
2,000 to 5,000 population, $250 per annum.
5,000 to 10,000 population, $600 per annum.
10,000 to 15,000 population, $1,200 per annum.
15,000 to 20,000 population, $2,000 per annum.
20,000 to 30,000 population, $2,500 per annum.
30,000 to 40,000 population, $3,500 per annum.
40,000 to 60,000 population, $4,000 per annum.
60,000 to 80,000 population, $4,500 per annum.
80,000 to 100,000 population, $5,000 per annum.
100,000 to 200,000 population, $6,000 per annum.

Removal: Recall.

Powers in relation to Commission: No veto power.

(Over.)

* Unincorporated communities of at least three hundred inhabitants may adopt the Commission features when incorporating under the General City Act.

Appointments:

Enumeration: City Clerk, Corporation Counsel, City Attorney, Assistant City Attorney, Treasurer, Comptroller, City Physician, Chief of Police, Chief of Fire Department, Market Master, three Library Trustees.

Manner: Majority vote of the Council.

Civil Service Provisions: The law of Mar. 20, 1895, is operative.

Election Provisions:

Non-partisan primaries; names placed on ballots by petition of twenty-five electors. At the second election the number of candidates is twice the number to be voted for.

Initiative:

Twenty-five per centum petition (special election)
Ten per centum petition (general election).

Referendum:

Ten per centum petition (general or special election.)

Recall:

Seventy-five per centum petition.

Franchises:

Subject to a compulsory referendum at a general or special election.

Abandonment of Commission Plan:

Any city or village which has operated under this Act may abandon organization thereunder by popular vote after four years.

The following cities have adopted this act: **Carbondale, Decatur, Dixon, Elgin, Kewanee, Moline, Ottawa, Rochelle, Rock Island, Springfield, Jacksonville, Spring Valley, Waukegan, Hillsboro.**

IOWA STATUTES

(AN ACT, APPROVED MAR. 29, 1907, ENABLING CITIES OF THE FIRST CLASS, INCLUDING THOSE OF 25,000 POPULATION AND OVER, TO ADOPT A SPECIFIED FORM OF COMMISSION GOVERNMENT. ANY CITY OF THIS CLASS MAY ADOPT THE ACT BY POPULAR ELECTION ON PETITION OF TWENTY-FIVE PER CENTUM OF THE VOTERS. BY AN ACT APPROVED MAR. 30, 1909, THE PROVISIONS OF THIS EARLIER LAW WERE EXTENDED TO CITIES HAVING SEVEN THOUSAND POPULATION AND OVER.)

Commission-Organization:

Title: Council.

Number: In cities having between 7,000 and 25,000 population, three, including Mayor.

In cities having over 25,000 population, five, including Mayor.

Term: Two years.

Removal: Recall.

Salary:

Population 7,000 to 10,000,	$450.
Population 10,000 to 15,000,	900.
Population 15,000 to 25,000,	1,200.
Population 25,000 to 40,000,	1,800.
Population 40,000 to 60,000	2,500.
Population over 60,000,	3,000.

Commissioner-Departments: In cities over 25,000 population: 7, Public Affairs; 2, Accounts and Finance; 3, Public Safety; 4, Streets and Public Improvements; 5, Parks and Public Property. Designation by the Council.

General Commission Powers:

"All the executive, legislative, and administrative powers formerly exercised by the Mayor, City Council, Board of Public Works, Park Commissioners, Board of Police and Fire Commissioners, Board of Water Works, Trustees, Board of Trustees, Solicitor, Assessor, Treasurer, Auditor, City Engineer, and other executive and administrative officials in a city of the first class and those operating under special charter."

Special Requirements:

Monthly statements of Receipts and Disbursements.

Mayor:

Term: Two years.

Salary:

Population 7,000 to 10,000,	$600.
Population 10,000 to 15,00	1,200.
Population 15,000 to 25,000,	1,500.
Population 25,000 to 40,000,	2,500.
Population 40,000 to 60,000,	3,000.
Population over 60,000,	3,500.

Removal: Recall.

Powers in relation to Commission: Presides over Council. No veto power.

Other Elective Officers:

None.

Appointments:

Enumeration: City Clerk, Solicitor, Assessor, Treasurer, Auditor, Civil Engineer, City Physician, Marshal, Chief of Fire Department, Market Master, Street Commissioner, three Library Trustees, and Police Judge in cities which have no Superior Court. In cities of less than 25,000 population, the Mayor and Council may dispense with some of these officers at their discretion.

Manner: By majority vote of the Council. Any officer or assistant may be removed by Council except as specially provided.

(*Over.*)

Civil Service Provisions: Council may establish a Board of three. Appointed by the Council for a term of six years. Partial renewal. The Civil Service provisions of the act apply to all apointive officials and employees of the city except the general officials acting under the immediate supervision of the Commissioner in charge, election officials, and the Mayor's secretary and Assistant Solicitor.

Election Provisions:

Non-partisan primaries; names placed on ballot by petition of twenty-five signatures.

Initiative:

Twenty-five per centum petition (special election).

Ten per centum petition (general election).

Referendum:

Twenty-five per centum petition (special election).

Ten per centum petition (general election).

Recall:

Twenty-five per centum petition (general or special election).

Abandonment of Act:

Operation under the Act may be discontinued after six years by a majority vote of the electors at a special election, based upon a twenty-five per centum petition.

The following cities have voted to adopt this act: **Burlington, Cedar Rapids, Davenport, Des Moines, Fort Dodge, Keokuk, Marshalltown, Sioux City.**

IOWA STATUTE

(AN ACT OF THE LEGISLATURE APPROVED MAY, 1915, APPLICABLE TO CITIES AND INCORPORATED TOWNS ORGANIZED UNDER CHAPTER 14-C OF THE SUPPLEMENT TO THE CODE, 1913, WHEN APPROVED AT A SPECIAL ELECTION, CALLED UPON PETITION OF TWENTY-FIVE PER CENTUM OF THE ELECTORS.)

Governing Body:

Title: Council.

Number: Population 25,000 and over, five. Population less than 25,000, three.

Terms: Two years; partial renewal annually.

Removal: Recall.

Salaries: None.

Mayor:

Elected by the Council from its own number; acts as presiding officer; is official head of the city for the service of civil process and may take charge of the police in times of public danger.

City Manager:

Title: City Manager.

Qualifications: The Council in making the appointment of a manager, may consider the qualification or fitness only of the person appointed; he shall be appointed without regard to his political affiliations, and need not be a resident of the city or town, at the time of his appointment. During the absence or disability of the City Manager the Council may designate some properly qualified person to perform and execute the duties of his office.

Powers and Duties: Exercises all of the usual powers of similar officers, e. g., City Manager of Dayton, O. (see p. 34003). In addition, he is specially charged with the management of numerous public works, e. g., streets, sewers, markets, sewage disposal plants, municipal lighting works, transportation and recreation facilities. He is given active charge over the police and fire departments and over the issuance of licenses.

Salary: Fixed by the Council.

Appointments:

Those of Police Judge or Magistrate, Solicitor or Corporation Counsel, Assessor and Board of Review of Assessments and members of the Library Board are made by the Council; all others by the City Manager.

Election Provisions:

Non-partisan nominations; names placed upon primary ballot by petition of at least ten electors, in the manner prescribed by Section 1087-a-13 of the supplement to the Code, 1913. It is a misdemeanor for the City Manager to take part in political activity of any sort; except the casting of a vote.

Initiative:

See general statute, page 34301.

Referendum:

See general statute, page 34301.

Recall:

See general statute, page 34301.

MISSOURI STATUTE

(AN ACT OF THE LEGISLATURE OF 1913, APPLICABLE TO ALL CITIES OF THE THIRD CLASS * WHICH MAY ADOPT ITS PROVISIONS AT A SPECIAL ELECTION CALLED UPON PETITION OF 25 PER CENTUM OF THE VOTERS.)

Commission Organization:

Title: The Council.

Number: Population 3,000 to 12,000, three; population 12,000 to 20,000, four; population 20,000 to 30,000, five.

Term: Two years.

Removal: Recall.

Salary: Population 3,000 to 15,000, fixed by ordinance; population 15,000 to 22,000, $1,100; population 22,000 to 30,000, $1,500.

Commissioner-Departments: 1, Public Affairs (Mayor); 2, Accounts and Finance; 3, Public Safety; 4, Streets and Public Improvements; 5, Parks and Public Property. Designation by the Council. In cities of less than 20,000 population, two departments may be assigned to a councilman.

General Commission Powers:

All executive, legislative and judical powers formerly exercised by all officials and boards of the city.

Mayor:

Term: Two years.

Removal: Recall.

Salary: Population 3,000 to 15,000, fixed by ordinance; population 15,000 to 22,000, $1,500; population 22,000 to 30,000, $2,000.

Powers: Presides at meetings of the Council.

Appointments:

Enumeration: City Clerk, Attorney, Assessor, Treasurer, Auditor, Civil Engineer, City Physician, Marshal, Chief of Fire Department, Police Judge, Market Master, Street Commissioner, three library trustees; but in cities of less than twenty thousand inhabitants only such officers need be appointed as the mayor and councilmen may deem necessary.

Manner: By majority vote of the Council.

Civil Service Provisions: In cities of between twenty thousand and thirty thousand inhabitants, the council is required to appoint two civil service commissioners. The civil service sections relate to all except enumerated officials, commissioners, unskilled laborers, election officials, the mayors' secretary and assistant attorney.

Election Provisions:

Non-partisan elections: names placed upon primary ballot on petition of twenty-five voters. Names of candidates equal in number to twice the number of places to be filled, receiving the highest number of votes at the primary are placed on the ballot at the regular election.

Initiative:

Twenty-five per centum petition (special election).
Ten per centum petition (general election).

Referendum:

Twenty-five per centum petition (special election).

Recall:

Twenty-five per centum petition.

* Those having a population of between 3,000 and 30,000; not including those having a population of between 30,000 and 75,000, see p. 34403.

MISSOURI STATUTE

(AN ACT OF THE LEGISLATURE APPLICABLE TO ALL CITIES HAVING MORE THAN 30,000 AND LESS THAN 75,000 INHABITANTS, WHICH MAY ELECT TO BECOME CITIES OF THE SECOND CLASS AT A SPECIAL ELECTION TO BE HELD OCT. 7, 1913.)

Commission-Organization:

Title: Council.

Number: Five, including mayor.

Removal: Recall.

Salary: Eighteen hundred dollars.

Commissioner-Departments: 1, Public Safety and Public Affairs (Mayor), including oversight of police and fire departments and contracts; 2, Health and Sanitation, including supervision of the Board of Health and its officers and employees, and the enforcement of laws for public health; 3, Revenue, including enforcement of all laws relating to assessment and collection of taxes, inspection and audit of all accounts, the purchase and distribution of all supplies, supervision of all printing for the city; 4, Public Property and Public Utilities, including the maintenance of all public utility plants owned by the city and the enforcement of regulations concerning, and collection of revenues derived from the same, the control of parks and playgrounds, supervision of public buildings, enforcement of franchise agreements, supervision of cemeteries; 5, Streets and Public Improvements, including supervision of streets, alleys, sidewalks, etc., not otherwise provided for, supervision of the erection of public works.

General Commission Powers:

The corporate powers of the city.

Mayor:

Term: Four years.

Salary: Twenty-four hundred dollars.

Removal: Recall.

Powers: Presides at meetings of the council, but has no veto power.

Appointments:

Enumeration: City Attorney, City Clerk, Chief of Police, City Engineer, City Physician.

Manner: The City Clerk by the Council, the Chief of Police and City Attorney by the Mayor; the City Engineer by the Commissioner of Streets and Public Improvements; the City Physician by the Commissioner of Public Health and Sanitation. These officers hold office at the pleasure of appointing power.

Civil Service Provisions: Provision is made for a Civil Service Board of four members to be appointed by the Mayor, subject to confirmation by the Council. This board is required to classify "all employments in the various city departments of administration for open competition, and free examination for fitness and for an eligible list from which vacancies can be filled."

Election Provisions:

Names of candidates are placed on primary ballot by payment of a fee of ten dollars, and designations are for the specific commissionerships (or mayoralty). Every candidate may file with his statement of intention to become a candidate a platform or declaration of principles not to exceed three hundred words, to be printed by the city, and the city clerk is required to mail a copy of the same to each registered voter, on or before five days preceding the primary election. Names of candidates are placed upon the ballot in the order of filing a statement of principles.

The names of the two candidates receiving the highest number of votes for each office at the primary are placed upon the ballot at the regular election.

Initiative:

Fifteen per centum petition (general or special election).

MISSOURI STATUTE—Continued

Referendum:

Ten per centum petition (special or general election). Five per centum petition (general election).

Recall:

Twenty per centum petition. No officer may be removed during the first three months of his term.

The question submitted at the recall election is the simple one of removal, a second election being held, if necessary, to fill the vacancy.

KANSAS STATUTE FOR FIRST CLASS CITIES

(An Act of the Legislaturre, Approved Mar. 2, 1907 (Chapter 114) permitting cities of the first class to adopt the form of government specified herewith, at a special election provided for the purpose. Amended by Chap. 74, Laws of 1909.)

Commission-Organization:

Title: Board of Commissioners.

Number: Five, including Mayor.

Term: Two years.

Removal: Recall.

Salary: Population 15,000 to 20,000, not over $1,000 per annum.
Population 20,000 to 30,000, not over $1,600 per annum.
Population 30,000 to 40,000, not over $1,500 per annum.
Population 40,000 to 60,000, not over $1,800 per annum.
Population over 60,000, not over $3,000 per annum.

Commissioner-Departments: 1, Police and Fire; 2, Finance and Revenue; 3, Streets and Public Improvements; 4, Parks and Public Property; 5, Streets, Waterworks and Lighting.

General Commission Powers:

Succeeds to the powers formerly exercised by the Mayor and Council.

Special Requirements:

Quarterly reports of receipts and disbursements.

Mayor:

Term: Two years.

Salary: Population 15,000 to 20,000, not over $1,800 per annum.
Population 20,000 to 30,000, not over $2,000 per annum.
Population 30,000 to 40,000, not over $2,000 per annum.
Population 40,000 to 60,000, not over $2,500 per annum.

Removal: Recall.

Powers in Relation to Commission: No veto power.

Special Requirements: Ex-officio Commissioner of Fire and Police Departments.

Appointments:

Enumerated: The City Attorney, City Clerk, City Treasurer, City Auditor, City Engineer, Superintendent of Streets, Superintendent of Water Works, Secretary of Water Works, Chief of Police, City Physician, Judge of the Police Court, Superintendent of Public Parks, City Assessor, Fire Marshal

Manner of Appointment: By majority vote of Board. The Board of Commissioners has power to remove the principal officers for neglect of duty or malfeasance in office. Subordinates removed by majority vote with or without cause.

Civil Service Provisions: Commissioners must appoint a board of three.

Election Provisions:

Nomination is by petition, in all cities, under the Commission form. (*Chapter* 74, *Laws of* 1909.)

Initiative:

Twenty-five per centum petition (special election).
Ten per centum petition (general election).

Recall:

Twenty-five per centum petition.

Franchises:

No franchise for a longer period than twenty years.
No exclusive franchises.

Abandonment of Act:

Any city having operated under this act for more than four years may abandon such organization, by popular election, on petition of twenty-five per centum of the electors.

The following cities have adopted this act: **Hutchinson, Kansas City, Leavenworth, Topeka, Wichita.**

KANSAS STATUTE FOR SECOND CLASS CITIES

(An Act of 1909 (Senate Bill No. 52) permitting cities of the Second Class (those having from 2,000 to 15,000 population) to adopt, by special election the form of commission government specified herein.)

Commission-Organization:

Title: Board of Commissioners.

Number: Three, including Mayor.

Term: Three years (partial renewal annually).

Removal: Recall.

Salary: Population 2,000 to 5,000, $250 per annum.
Population 5,000 to 7,000, $500 per annum.
Population 7,000 to 10,000, $900 per annum.
Population 10,000 to 15,000, $1,000 per annum.

Commissioner-Departments: Education, Finance and Revenue. Has usual powers of School Boards. His appointments must be confirmed by a majority of the Board of Commissioners.

General Commission Powers:

Successors of Mayor and Council, and Board of Education.

Special Requirements:

Monthly financial statements.

Mayor:

Term: Three years.

Salary: Population 2,000 to 5,000, $300 per annum.
Population 5,000 to 7,000, $700 per annum.
Population 7,000 to 10,000, $1,000 per annum.
Population 10,000 to $15,000, $1,200 per annum.

Removal: Recall.

Powers in relation to Commission: President of Commission, ex-officio Commissioner of Police, Fire and Health.

Appointed Officers:

Enumeration: City Attorney, City Clerk, City Treasurer, Police Judge, City Engineer, City Marshal, Fire Chief.

Manner: By majority vote of Board, for a term of two years. Board may remove for cause.

Election Provisions:

Names placed on primary ballots on petition of twenty-five signatures. Number of candidates voted for at second election is twice the number of offices to be filled.

Initiative:

Twenty-five per centum petition (special election).

Ten per centum petition (general election).

Referendum:

No general provision (*See "Franchises"*).

Recall:

Twenty-five per centum petition.

Franchises:

Limited to twenty years. No exclusive franchises. Adequate compensation to City. All franchises subject to Referendum.

Abandonment of Commission Plan:

Any City having operated under the law for more than six years, may abandon such organization by popular election, on petition of ten per centum of the qualified voters.

The following cities have voted to adopt this act: **Anthony, Abilene, Coffeyville, Cherryvale, Council Grove, Dodge City, Emporia, Eureka, Girard, Independence, Iola, Marion, Neodesha, Parsons, Pittsburg, Wellington.**

NEBRASKA STATUTE

(AN ACT OF THE LEGISLATURE, APPROVED 1911. APPLICABLE TO CITIES HAVING A POPULATION OF 5,000 OR MORE, ON ADOPTION AT SPECIAL ELECTION, CALLED UPON PETITION OF TWENTY-FIVE PER CENTUM OF THE VOTERS.)

Commission-Organization:

Title: Council.

Number: In cities of over 100,000 population, seven.
In cities of 25,000 to 100,000 population, five.
In cities of 5,000 to 25,000 population, three.

Term: The same as under previous law governing the city.

Removal: Recall.

Salary: Population over 100,000, $4,500 per annum.
Population between 40,000 and 100,000, $2,000 per annum.
Population between 25,000 and 40,000, $1,000 per annum.
Population between 7,000 and 25,000, $1,000 per annum.
Population between 5,000 and 7,000, $300 per annum.

Commissioner-Departments: Population over 100,000: 1, Public Affairs (Mayor); 2, Accounts and Finances; 3, Police, Sanitation and Public Safety; 4, Fire Protection and Water Supply; 5, Street Cleaning and Maintenance; 6, Public Improvements; 7, Parks and Public Property.

Population 25,000 to 100,000: 1, Public Affairs (Mayor); 2, Accounts and Finances; 3, Public Safety; 4, Streets and Public Improvements; 5, Parks and Public Property.

Population 5,000 to 25,000: 1, Public Affairs and Public Safety; 2, Accounts and Finances; 3, Streets, Public Improvements and Public Property.

General Commission Powers:

All executive, legislative and judicial powers formerly exercised by the Mayor, Council, Water Commissioners or Water Board, Light Commissioners, Board of Police and Fire Commissioners, Park Commissioners, Excise Board, Fire Warden.

Mayor:

The Mayor is selected by the Council from among their own number.

Term: (*See term of Commissioners.*)

Removal: Recall.

Salary: Population over 100,000, $5,000 per annum.
Population between 40,000 and 100,000, $2,500 per annum.
Population between 25,000 and 40,000, $1,500 per annum.
Population between 7,000 and 25,000, $1,300 per annum.
Population between 5,000 and 7,000, $500 per annum.

Appointments:

Enumeration: The Council may appoint as many officers, provided for by existing law, as may be necessary for the economical administration of the government of the city, and may create new offices and employments.

Manner: By the Council, subject to their removal at their pleasure.

*Civil Service Provisions:**

None.

* "In cities of the metropolitan class" no member of the departments of police, sanitation, public safety, fire department, or water supply, may be employed or discharged for political reasons. No officer may be discharged except after a public hearing. In cases of peremptory suspension the Council must hear charges at its second meeting following. No specific provision for Civil Service Board.

NEBRASKA

Election Provisions:

The names of candidates are placed upon the primary election ballot by petition of 25 voters in cities of over 5,000 and less than 25,000 inhabitants, of 100 voters in cities of over 25,000 inhabitants. Candidates are required to pay the City Treasurer a filing fee to aid in the expense of holding the primary.

The names of the candidates are "rotated" by the printer so that they appear in a different position on the ballots for each election district.

Candidates to the number of twice the number of offices to be filled, receiving the highest number of votes cast at the primaries, are the candidates at the second election.

Initiative:

Twenty-five per centum petition (special election).
Fifteen per centum petition (general election).

MICHIGAN HOME RULE STATUTE

By an Act of the Legislature (*Act* 279, *P. A.* 1909), the State of Michigan authorized the adoption of "Commission" government in cities by a Home Rule Law which specified certain obligatory, permissive and prohibitory provisions for future City Charters. By *Section* 3 (*m*), provision is made, by implication, for the election of a Council at large. By *Section* 4 (*p*), provision is made for altering, amending or repealing any special act effecting any existing Municipal Department except the public schools. By *Section e*, however, the City is prohibited to adopt a Charter amendment except by a majority vote of the electors voting at a general or special election. By *Section* 18, specific provision was made for the City to revise its Charter by the submission of the question to the electors either on the initiative of two-thirds of the legislative body of the City, or by an initiatory twenty per centum petition of the electors as provided in *Section* 25 of this Act.

HARBOR BEACH

(HOME RULE CHARTER. ADOPTED APR. 4, 1910.)

Commission-Organization:

Title: Council.

Number: Five, including Mayor.

Term: One year.

Removal: Vote of majority of Council upon charges.

Salary: None.

Commissioner-Departments: 1, Water Works; 2, Streets, Sidewalks and Sewers; 3, Accounts and Finances; 4, Public Safety and Public Property.

General Commission Powers:

Legislative and Executive.

Mayor:

Term: One year.

Salary: None.

Removal: Vote of majority of Council.

Powers in Relation to Commission: President of Council. Has vote on all matters (*see "Appointments"*).

Appointments:

Enumeration: City Clerk, City Treasurer, City Attorney, City Marshal, Street Commissioner, City Surveyor, City Assessor, Chief Engineer of the Fire Department and two members of the Board of Review of Assessments.

Manner: By Mayor, with consent of Council.

Civil Service Provisions: None.

Election Provisions:

Non-partisan primaries, names placed on ballot by petition.

Initiative:

No provision.

Referendum:

No provision.

Recall:

No provision.

PORT HURON

(HOME RULE CHARTER, ADOPTED DEC., 1910, IN EFFECT JAN., 1, 1911.)

Commission-Organization:

Title: Mayor and City Commissioners.

Number: Five, including Mayor.

Term:

Removal: By Commission on charges.

Salary: Twelve hundred dollars.

Commissioner-Departments: 1, Public Affairs; 2, Accounts and Finances; 3, Public Safety; 4, Streets and Public Improvements; 5, Parks and Public Property.

Designation to Departments by the Commission.

General Commission Powers:

All the corporate powers of the city.

Special Features: Uniform Municipal Accounting System prescribed.

Mayor:

Term:

Removal: By Commission, for specified causes (wilful neglect of duty, etc.).

Salary: Two thousand dollars.

Powers in relation to Commission: Presides at meetings.

Appointed Officers:

Enumeration: Clerk, Treasurer, Assessor, City Attorney, Superintendent of Public Works, Parks and Cemeteries, Chief of Police, Physician, Chief of Fire Department, Chief Engineer of Water Works, and eleven Supervisors, (one for each Election Precinct).

Manner: By Commission

Election Provisions:

Non-partisan elections. Names go on ballot by petition of one hundred and not more than one hundred and twenty-five names. The two names for each office receiving the highest number of votes at the primary election go on ballots at the second election.

Initiative:

Twenty-five per centum petition (special or general election).

Referendum:

Twenty-five per centum petition (special or general election).

Recall:

No provisions.

Special Features:

The Board of Commissioners select a Supervisor for each Election Precinct. These Supervisors, together with the Assessor, City Attorney and the four City Commissioners, constitute the representation of the City of Port Huron on the Board of Supervisors of the County.

BATTLE CREEK

(Home-Rule Charter, Drafted by a Board of Charter Commissioners, Adopted by Popular Vote April 7, 1913.)

Commission-Organization:

Title: Commission.

Number: Five, including Mayor.

Term: Two years. Partial renewal biennially.

Removal: By four-fifths vote of the Commission for cause after notice and hearing.

Salary: Three hundred dollars.

Commissioner-Departments: 1. Public Affairs, including all legal matters, all work of the City Attorney and City Clerk.

2. Accounts and Finance, including the work of the City Treasurer, the collection of fines, fees, licenses, water rates and other charges for public utilities.

3. Public Buildings and Grounds, including supervision and care of all public buildings, parks, waterworks, plants and public grounds and utilities owned or leased by the city.

4. Public Safety, including police department, fire department, health department, the conduct and operation of city hospitals and grounds and the inspection of plumbing, electric wiring, elevators, fire escapes and buildings.

5. Public Works, including all construction work, care of streets and alleys, side and cross walks, waterworks, water pipes, sewers, bridges, conduits, culverts, street lighting, paving, grading, opening of streets, street cleaning, plumbing inspection.

Designation by the Mayor.

General Commission Powers:

All the corporate powers of the city; all executive, legislative and judicial powers formerly exercised by the Mayor, aldermen, Common Council, Board of Public Works, Police Commissioner, Board of Health and all other officers.

Mayor:

Term: Two years.

Removal: By four-fifths vote of the commission for cause after notice and hearing.

Salary: Five hundred dollars.

Powers: Is executive head of the city; presides over the meetings of the Commission, but has no veto power.

Other Elective Officers:

*Justices of the Peace, Constables.

Appointments:

Enumeration: Clerk, Treasurer, City Atorney, Assessor, Board of Review (4 members), Health Officer, City Engineer, Chief of Police, Captain and Policemen, Firemen.

Manner: By the Commission.

Civil Service Provisions: None.

Election Provisions:

Non-partisan nominations and general election. Designations for nominating election are made by petition of not less than five nor more than ten signatures from each of the fifteen election precincts.

The two candidates for mayor and the eight candidates (or four, when two commissioners are to be elected) receiving the highest number of votes at the primary, are the candidates at the regular election.

Initiative:

No provisions.

Referendum:

No provisions.

Recall:

No provisions.

* Technically, city officers in Michigan, but county officers in most states.

WISCONSIN STATUTE

(AN ACT OF THE LEGISLATURE, APPROVED JUNE 15, 1909 (CHAPTER 48, LAWS OF 1909), APPLICABLE TO CITIES OF THE SECOND, THIRD AND FOURTH CLASSES AFTER ADOPTION BY THE PEOPLE THEREOF AT A SPECIAL ELECTION. THE QUESTION OF ADOPTION IS SUBMITTED ON PETITION OF TWENTY-FIVE PER CENTUM.)

Commission-Organization:

Title: City Council.

Number: Three, including Mayor.

Term: Four years. Partial renewal.

Removal: Charter provisions.

*Salary:** Over 40,000 population, $4,500.
30,000 to 40,000 population, $4,000.
20,000 to 30,000 population, $3,500.
15,000 to 20,000 population, $3,000.
10,000 to 15,000 population, $2,500.
7,500 to 10,000 population, $2,000.
5,000 to 7,500 population, $1,500.
3,500 to 5,000 population, $1,200.
2,500 to 3,500 population, $1,000.
Under 2,500 population, $700.

Commissioner-Departments: No fixed designation. Council may determine same.

General Commission Powers:

The powers formerly exercised by the Council and the several administrative and executive departments.

Mayor:

Term: Six years.

Removal: Charter provisions.

Powers in Relation to Commission: President of Council. No veto power.

*Salary:** Over 40,000 population, $5,000.
30,000 to 40,000 population, $4,500.
20,000 to 30,000 population, $4,000.
15,000 to 20,000 population, $3,500.
10,000 to 15,000 population, $3,000.
5,000 to 7,500 population, $2,000.
3,500 to 5,000 population, $1,500.
Under 2,500 population, $1,000.

Appointments:

Enumeration: City Clerk, Corporation Counsel, Comptroller, Superintendent of Streets.

Manner: By majority of Council.

Civil Service Provisions: None.

Election Provisions:

Names placed on primary ballots by petition of twenty-five signatures. Non-partisan elections.

Initiative:

No provision.

Referendum:

Twenty per centum petition (general or special election). Not applicable to franchises.

Recall:

No provision.

Abandonment of Act:

Operation under this statute may be abandoned by popular vote after six years.

* Minimum.

The following cities have adopted this act: **Appleton, Eau Claire.**

BIRMINGHAM

(Applicable to Cities Having a Population of 100,000 and Over, Without Reference to a Popular Vote. Approved March 31, 1911.)

Commission-Organization:

The first Board of Commissioners under this act is to consist of the Mayor of the city at the time this act is approved, who is to hold office for two years, and two other commissioners appointed by the Governor for terms of three and four years, respectively. At the expiration of these terms the Commissioners are to be elected by the voters. The title of the "Mayor" is dropped and the head of the Commission is known as "President."

Title: Board of Commissioners.

Number: Three, including Mayor.

Term: Three years, partial renewal annually.

Removal: Recall.

Salary: Seven thousand dollars.

Commissioner-Departments: 1. Public Justice. 2. Streets, Parks and Public Property and City and Public Improvements. 3. Accounts, Finances and Public Affairs. The Commissioner appointed for the four years' term and his successors are vested with ample judicial power in relation to the ordinances of the city.

General Commission Powers:

All strictly municipal legislative, executive and judicial powers formerly exercised by the Mayor and Board of Aldermen, Board of Police Commissioners, and any and all other boards, commissioners and officers.

Appointments:

Manner: All officers and employees are chosen, and are subject to removal, by the Board of Commissioners at their pleasure.

Elections:

Non-partisan nominations on petition* of five hundred persons qualified to vote at the coming election. Second election within one week if necessary to secure majority. No positive prohibition of partisan nominations by convention or caucus, etc.

Initiative:

No provisions.

Referendum:

No provisions.

Recall:

Petitions signed by three thousand persons qualified to vote for successor to officer sought to be removed.

Franchises:

Franchise grants may not take effect for nearly thirty days after passage by the Board, during which time they may be submitted to a referendary vote, in petition of one thousand signatures.

Special Features:

The Governor is authorized at any time to have all the books and accounts of the city examined by the State Examiner of Public Accounts, the cost of the examination to be paid by the city.

---

* Filed with the Probate Judge of the County.

ALABAMA STATUTE

(AN ACT OF THE LEGISLATURE, APPROVED APRIL 8, 1911, AUTHORIZING THE ADOPTION OF THE COMMISSION FORM OF GOVERNMENT BY ANY CITY NOT WITHIN THE SPHERE OF ANY OTHER LAW AUTHORIZING THIS FORM; SUBMITTED TO A POPULAR VOTE ON PETITION OF A NUMBER OF ELECTORS EQUAL TO ONE PER CENTUM OF THE POPULATION, ON BASIS OF THE LAST PRECEDING FEDERAL CENSUS.)

Commission-Organization:

Title: Board of Commissioners.

Number: Three.*

Term: Three years. Partial renewal annually.

Removal: Recall.

Salary: The amount is fixed by ordinance subject to the following schedules:

Population 7,500 to 15,000: $1,500 per annum; population 15,000 to 50,000: at the rate of $100 for each 1,000 of the population; over 50,000 population: $1,000 for each 10,000 population; but in no case to exceed $7,500.

Commissioner-Departments: The Board determines the distribution of functions and each member is the head of a department. One of the number is Mayor, with no veto power but such other powers as are conferred upon him by the Board.

General Commission Powers:

All powers formerly possessed by the Mayor or governing body or bodies by whatsoever name called except school boards.

Mayor:

See "*Commissioner-Departments.*"

Appointments:

The Board of Commissioners is given full power to prescribe and change at any time, the powers, duties and titles of all officers of the city.

Election Provisions:

Nomination by petition of three percentum of the voters. Party nominations are not forbidden. The system of voting is prescribed as follows:

* The mayor at the time of the adoption of the act, becomes a Commissioner until October 1st, of the year in which his term office would have expired. The other two commissioners are elected in all cases.

Sec. 11.

At elections for commissioners under this act the ballots shall be substantially in the following form:

For commissioner of the city of..................
(insert name of city) for term ending September 30th, 19....

FIRST CHOICE.

Put cross mark opposite candidate of your first choice.

..........A. B.
..........C. D.
..........E. F.
..........G. H.
..........I. J.
..........K. L.
..........M. N.

SECOND CHOICE.

Put cross mark opposite candidate of your second choice. Second choice must not be same name voted for on first choice.

..........A. B.
..........C. D.
..........E. F.
..........G. H.
..........I. J.
..........K. L.
..........M. N.

At such election the names of all candidates for commissioner who have qualified as such as above provided shall be printed on the ballots in alphabetical order under the heading "First Choice" and again under the heading "Second Choice." If more than one office is to be filled the ticket shall be extended so as to likewise present the names of the candidates for the other offices. Each qualified elector may vote for a first and second choice for each office to be filled, but no vote of any qualified elector for first choice for any office or offices shall be rejected or not counted because of the absence of or any invalidity in his vote for second choice, nor shall any vote of any qualified elector for second choice for any office or offices be rejected or not counted because of the absence of or any invalidity in his vote for first choice. At all such elections the candidate or candidates receiving the highest number of first choice votes for the office or offices to be filled shall be declared elected thereto; provided, such highest number of votes be not less than a majority of the whole number of ballots cast. Should any office remain unfilled by reason of the failure of any candidate to receive a majority of the first choice votes cast, then the first choice and second choice votes of each candidate shall be added together and the candidate or candidates who shall have received the highest number of first and second choice votes together shall be declared elected; provided, such number be not less than a majority of the whole number of votes cast. Should any office still remain unfilled by reason of the failure of any candidate to receive votes equal to a majority of the ballots cast, such vacancy or vacancies shall be filled by another election to be held not less than ten nor more than fifteen days thereafter. At such second election the ballots shall have printed theron only the names of those two candidates who receive the highest number of first choice and second choice votes, when added together at the first election; and the number of candidates whose names shall be printed on said second election ballot shall not exceed two for each office to be filled. In case of a tie vote between two candidates each of whom receives a majority of first choice votes, the one shall be deemed to have the highest number who shall have received the highest number of second choice votes. In case of a tie vote between two unelected candidates who receive an equal number of first choice and second choice votes, when added together, the one shall be deemed to have the highest number who shall have received the highest number of first choice votes. No defect in the form of ballot or technicality or inaccuracy in such election, or in the call, notice or conduct thereof, shall invalidate such election if the same was in substance fairly conducted and the will of the people fairly expressed thereat. Except as is otherwise provided in this act, all elections for commissioners hereunder shall be conducted as provided by the general laws of this State applicable thereto, and at the expense of the city in which such election is held.

Initiative:

No provision.

Referendum:

No general provisions; but see "*Franchises.*"

Recall:

Twenty-five percentum petition.

Franchises:

Franchise grants must be submitted to popular vote on petition of a number of voters determined by the ratio of one to every three hundred inhabitants of the city upon payment by the grantee of a deposit to cover the estimated cost of a special election.

Special Features:

The Governor is authorized, at any time, to have the books of the city examined by a State Examiner of Public Accounts, who is to be paid by the city.

Abandonment of Act:

Operation under this act may be abandoned after six years, by special election called upon petition of twenty percentum of the voters.

MONTGOMERY*

(CLASS "C" CITIES)

(AN ACT OF THE LEGISLATURE, APPROVED APRIL, 1911, APPLICABLE TO CITIES HAVING A POPULATION OF MORE THAN TWENTY-FIVE THOUSAND AND LESS THAN FIFTY THOUSAND.)

Commission-Organization:

Title: Board of Commissioners.

Number: Five, including mayor.

†*Term:* Four years.

Removal: Recall.

Salary: Three thousand dollars.

Commissioner-Departments: 1, Public Affairs; 2, Accounts and Finances; 3, Justice; 4, Streets and Parks; 5, Public Property and Public Improvements. Designation by Board.

General Powers of Commission:

All the municipal powers, legislative, executive and judicial, previously possessed and exercised by the mayor and board of aldermen, board of police commissioners and any other and all boards except the county board of health. The board of education is a separate body.

President: (*Mayor*)

Term: Four years.

Salary: Forty-five hundred dollars.

Removal: Recall.

Appointments:

Manner: By majority vote of the Board of Commissioners.

Civil Service Provisions: Employees must be chosen with reference to fitness and without reference to party affiliations. No provision for Civil Service Board.

Election Provisions:

Non-partisan elections. Nomination by petition of one hundred qualified voters. Secondary election is held if necessary for any office.

Initiative:

No provisions.

Referendum:

Twenty-five per centum petition.

Recall:

Petitions of one thousand voters.

Franchises:

No exclusive franchises. Board of Commissioners has access to all books and papers of any grantee of a franchise at any time. City preserves the right to purchase the property of the grantee for just compensation. No franchise may be leased, assigned or otherwise alienated without the express consent of the city.

Abandonment of Act:

Operation under this act may be abandoned after four years by popular election based upon petition of one thousand voters.

---

*This law, though a general statute in form, is applicable only to the City of Montgomery.

†The mayor of the city at the time of the passage of this act is ex-officio mayor for four years under this act. The other members of the first commission are appointed by the Governor.

ALABAMA STATUTE *

(CLASS "D" CITIES)

(AN ACT OF THE LEGISLATURE, APPROVED APRIL 21, 1911, APPLICABLE TO CITIES HAVING A POPULATION OF MORE THAN ONE THOUSAND AND LESS THAN TWENTY-FIVE THOUSAND (CLASS "D" CITIES). ADOPTED BY POPULAR VOTE CALLED UPON PETITION OF VOTERS EQUAL TO THREE IN EVERY ONE HUNDRED OF POPULATION.)

Commission-Organization:

Title: Board of Commissioners.

Number: Three, including Mayor.

Term: Three years. Partial renewal annually.

Removal: Recall.

Salary: In cities of over 7,000 population, $1,200. In cities of less than 7,000 population, $900.

Commissioner-Departments: 1, Public Safety and Public Health; 2, Streets, Parks, City and Public Property and City and Public Improvements; 3, Accounts, Finance and Public Affairs. Designation by the Board.

General Powers of Commission:

All powers, executive, legislative and judicial, formerly possessed and exercised by the mayor and board of aldermen, board of police commissioners and all other boards and commissions excepts boards of education.

President:

Selected by the Board of Commissioners from among their own number.

Term: Three years.

Removal: Recall.

Special Powers: All powers formerly possessed by the mayor of the city, except the power of veto.

Appointments:

Manner: By the Board of Commissioners.

Civil Service Provisions: Employees must be selected solely with regard to fitness and without regard to political affiliations. No provision for competitive examinations.

Election Provisions:

Non-partisan elections: Names placed upon ballot on petition of voters equal in number to one to every hundred of population. A secondary election is held, if necessary, to secure majority.

Initiative:

No provision.

Referendum:

No provision.

Recall:

Twenty-five per centum petition.

---

*The law provides for the appointment of the first commission by the Governor.

PONTIAC

(Home Rule Charter, Drafted in Accordance with the General Home Rule Law [Act 279, P. A. 1909]. Adopted January, 1911.)

Commission-Organization:

Title: Commission.

Number: Three, including Mayor.

Term: Three years. Partial renewal.

Removal: Recall.

Salary: Two thousand dollars.

Commissioner-Departments: 1. Public Safety. 2. Finance. 3. Water Supply. 4. Public Utilities. 5. Streets and Public Improvements. 6. Sewers and Drainage. The Mayor is Commissioner of Departments No. 1 and No. 2. Designation by Commission of one of their own number to headship of Departments No. 3 and No. 4 (Commissioner of Public Improvements) and one to Departments No. 5 and No. 6 (Commissioner of Public Utilities).

Special Requirements:

Monthly financial statements.

Mayor:

Term: Three years.

Salary: Two thousand dollars.

Removal: Recall.

Appointments:

The City Attorney, Chief of Fire Department, Chief of Health Department, appointed by the Mayor at the request, and subject to the confirmation of the Commission, removable at their pleasure. The two Commissioners appoint the City Engineer. Other appointments by the Commissioner in charge.

Civil Service Provisions:

None.

Election Provisions:

Non-partisan primaries; names placed on ballot on petition of twenty-five voters. The two (or four) candidates receiving the highest number of votes are the candidates at the second election.

Referendum:

Twenty percentum petition (general or special election).

Initiative:

Twenty percentum petition (special election); five percentum petition (general election).

Recall:

Twenty percentum petition.

Franchises:

No franchise for a longer period than thirty years. No franchise to be leased or assigned except as provided in the terms of the grant. The city may require the grantees of franchises to allow the use of its tracks, poles, wires, etc., by any other corporation, upon the payment of a reasonable rental. No franchise not revocable by the Commission at any time may be granted except after reference to a popular vote, the expenses of submission to be paid by the grantee. No franchise granted without fair compensation to the city, which compensation shall not be in lieu of any lawful taxation. The enumeration of particular matters in the charter which must be included in every franchise may never be construed so as to impair the right of the Commission to insert such other conditions, restrictions, etc., in franchises, as it shall deem proper in order to protect the interests of the city.

WYANDOTTE

(HOME RULE CHARTER, DRAFTED IN ACCORDANCE WITH PROVISIONS OF THE GENERAL HOME RULE LAW [ACT 279, P. A. 1909]. ADOPTED FEBRUARY, 1911.)

Commission-Organization:

Title: City Commission.

Number: Five, including Mayor.

Term: Two years.

Removal: Recall.

Salary: Two hundred and fifty dollars.

Commissioner-Departments: 1. Public Affairs. 2. Finance and Revenue. 3. Public Safety. 4. Streets, Sewers and Public Property. 5. Municipal Service. Designation by Commission.

General Commission Powers:

The corporate powers.

Special Requirements:

Monthly financial statements. Must observe uniform system of accounting provided by state law.

Mayor:

Term: Two years.

Salary: Two hundred and fifty dollars.

Removal: Recall.

Powers in Relation to Commission: General supervision of city departments. No veto.

Other Elective Officers:

City Clerk, City Treasurer, holding office for one year.

Appointments:

Enumeration:
City Assessor.

Manner:
By a majority vote of Commission.

Election Provisions:

Non-partisan primaries. Names placed on ballots by petition of twenty-five voters. The two (or four) candidates receiving the highest number of votes at the primary are the candidates at the second election.

Initiative:

Twenty-five percentum petition (special election); ten per centum petition (general election).

Referendum:

Twenty-five percentum petition (special or general election).

Recall:

Twenty percentum petition.

Special Features:

City Assessor and other supervisors of election constitute the representation of the city on the County Board of Supervisors.

FREMONT

(HOME RULE CHARTER, DRAFTED BY A CHARTER CONVENTION; ADOPTED BY POPULAR VOTE NOVEMBER 7, 1911; APPROVED BY THE GOVERNOR OCTOBER 4, 1911.)

Commission-Organization:

Title: City Commission.

Number: Three, including Mayor.

Term: Two years. Partial renewal annually.

Removal: By statutory procedure.

Salary: Three dollars for each regular meeting, but not over $150 in one year.

Commissioner-Departments: 1, Public affairs, including matters relating to police, fire and health; all legal matters; 2, Finance and Revenue, including matters relating to license, collection of water and electric light rates, preparation of the annual budget, the distribution of funds authorized by the City Commission, the maintenance of the proper balance in each fund, the payment of bonds and interest owing by the city; 3, Public Property, including matters relating to streets, alleys, sidewalks, parks, bridges, public buildings and the maintenance and repair of same and all franchises.

Other matters may be assigned to these departments by the City Commission.

General Commission Powers:

All the corporate powers of the city.

The Mayor:

Term: Two years.

Salary: Same as commissioners.

Removal: By statutory procedure.

Powers: Has general administrative supervision, but no veto power.

Appointments:

Enumeration: Treasurer, Clerk, two members of the Board of Registration, Chief of the Fire Department.

Manner: By the mayor with the confirmation of the Commission. Any officer so appointed may be removed or discharged by him at any time, or by any two members of the Commission on presentation of reasons for such removal in writing. Assistants and laborers may be appointed by heads of departments.

Election Provisions:

Non-partisan primaries; names placed upon ballot on petition of fifteen and not more than forty voters. The number of candidates equal to twice the number of places to be filled, elected at the primary, are the candidates at the general election.

Initiative:

No provisions.

Referendum:

No provisions.

Recall:

No provisions.

Franchises:

No franchise for a larger period than thirty years. No exclusive franchise. The City Commission reserves the right to fix a reasonable schedule of rates for public service, which shall not prohibit the grantee from earning at least 10 per cent. on the amount of actual cash investment in the city over and above reasonable operating expenses. Every franchise must provide for adequate compensation for its grant. Every franchise must be approved by popular vote at a general or special election. The City Commission has the right to purchase the franchise and property of any company operating a public utility plant, and may provide for the use of the grantee's property by other persons upon payment of a reasonable compensation therefor.

JACKSON

(HOME RULE CHARTER, DRAFTED BY AN ELECTIVE CHARTER COMMISSION; ADOPTED BY POPULAR VOTE, Nov. 3, 1914.)

Governing Body:

Title: City Commission.

Number: Five, including mayor. Partial renewal biennially.

Term: Four years.

Removal: In the manner provided by general law.

Salary: Five Hundred ($500) dollars per annum.

Mayor:

Elected by the people for a term of two years. Is authorized to exercise the powers conferred upon sheriffs to suppress disorder. Receives a salary of seven hundred and fifty ($750) dollars annually.

City Manager:

Sec. 30. The City Manager shall have charge of the administration of municipal affairs under the direction and supervision of the City Commission.

Sec. 31. He shall designate one of his subordinates as Assistant Manager, who, unless it is otherwise provided by the City Commission, shall perform all the duties of the City Manager in case of his absence from the City or temporary disability.

Sec. 32. He shall manage and supervise all public improvements, works and undertakings of the City except as otherwise provided in this charter. He shall have charge of the construction, repair and maintenance of streets, sidewalks, bridges, pavements, sewers, and of all public buildings or other property belonging to the City. He shall manage and control all the city utilities and shall be charged with the preservation of property, tools and appliances of the City. He shall have charge of the cleaning, sprinkling and lighting of streets and public places.

Sec. 33. It shall be the further duty of the City Manager, except as otherwise provided in this charter:

(a) To take active control of the fire, police and engineering departments of the City and to engage such assistants therein as shall be provided for in this charter or by the City Commission.

(b) To see that all terms and conditions imposed in favor of the City or its inhabitants in any public franchise are faithfully kept and performed and that ordinances and laws relating to the City are enforced.

(c) To attend all meetings of the City Commission, with the right to take part in the discussions, but having no vote.

(d) To recommend to the City Commission for adoption such measures as he may deem necessary or expedient.

(e) To prepare the annual budget and to keep the City Commission fully advised as to the financial condition and needs of the City.

(f) To exercise and perform all administrative functions that are not imposed by this charter or by act of the City Commission upon some other official.

(g) To perform all other duties prescribed by this charter or required of him by the City Commission.

Sec. 55. The City Manager shall be a man of good business and executive ability, and, if practicable, a civil or mechanical engineer. He may or may not be a resident or elector of the City at the time of his appointment, but other things being equal, preference shall be given to a citizen of Jackson. In the case of special technical skill, such as City Engineer, Health Officer or Librarian, the City Commission may, if need be, appoint non-residents of the City.

Appointments:

Enumeration: (1) City Manager, City Clerk, City Treasurer, City Attorney, City Physician, Health Officer, Sanitary Inspector, one supervisor from each ward, and one or more building inspectors. (2) Chief of Police, Chief of Fire Department.

Manner: Group (1) by the City Commission. Group (2) by the City Manager with the approval of the City Commission.

Civil Service Provisions: None.

Election Provisions:

Non-partisan ballots used at primaries and elections. Names of candidates placed upon the ballot on petition of not less than one hundred or more than one hundred and fifty qualified electors.

Candidates equal to twice the number of vacancies to be filled receiving the highest number of votes at the primary are the candidates on the second year.

Initiative:

Ten per centum petition.

Referendum:

Fifteen per centum petition.

Recall:

Removal of elective officers is effected in the manner provided by general state law.

CADILLAC

(HOME RULE CHARTER, DRAFTED BY A BOARD OF ELECTED CHARTER COMMISSIONERS. ADOPTED BY POPULAR VOTE DEC. 9, 1913).

Governing Body:

Title: Commission.

Number: Five, including Mayor. The four commissioners are nominated from "voting precincts" but elected at large.

Term: Four years.

Removal: Recall.

Salary: None.

The Mayor:

Elected for two years; not to receive any compensation. His powers and duties are not defined in the charter.

City Manager:

CHAPTER XI.

Section 1. The general manager shall be the administrative head of the municipal government under the direction and supervision of the Commission. He shall not hold any other public office or employment, except that of notary public, and shall not be interested in the profits or emoluments of any contract, job, work, or service for the city.

Sec. 2. Before entering upon the duties of his office he shall take the official oath and shall execute a bond in favor of the city for the faithful performance of his duties in such sum as shall be fixed by the Commission.

Sec. 3. The general manager shall have power to appoint and remove officers and members of all boards and commissions not included within regular department officers; all officers appointed by the general manager shall serve until removed by him or until their successors have been appointed and have qualified.

Sec. 4. It shall be the duty of the general manager, except as otherwise specifically provided in this charter:

(a) To take active control of the fire, police, and engineering departments of the city, and to engage such assistants therein as shall be herein provided.

(b) To see that, within the city, the laws of the state and the ordinances, resolutions and by-laws of the Commission are enforced and faithfully executed.

(c) To supervise, under the direction of the Commission, the administration of the affairs of the city.

(d) To attend all meetings of the Commission, and to recommend to that body from time to time such measures as he shall deem necessary or expedient for it to adopt.

(e) To draw up resolutions and ordinances for adoption by the Commission and furnish them with any necessary information respecting any of the departments under his control.

(f) To keep the Commission advised of the financial condition and future needs of the city.

(g) To prepare and submit to the Commission such reports as may be required by that body, and to draw up an annual report which shall consolidate the special reports of the several departments.

(h) To revoke licenses, pending the action of the Commission.

(i) To sign warrants of arrest, and to cause arrests for infraction within the city of the laws of the state, and the ordinances and other regulations of the city.

(j) To administer oaths and take affidavits.

(k) To appoint persons to fill all places for which no other mode of appointment is provided.

(l) To sign such contracts, deeds and other public documents on behalf of the city, as the Commission may authorize and require.

(m) To exercise and perform all other executive and administrative functions and duties, unless other designation shall be made by this charter or by act of the Commission.

(n) To manage and control all charitable, correctional and reformatory institutions and agencies belonging to the city; to enforce all laws, ordinances and regulations relative to the preservation and promotion of the public health, the prevention and restriction of disease, the prevention, abatement and suppression of nuisances, and the sanitary inspection and supervision of the production, transportation, storage and sale of food and foodstuffs, and the supervision of weights and measures; to cause a complete and accurate system of vital statistics to be kept; and in time of epidemic, to enforce such quarantine and isolation regulations as may be appropriate to the emergency.

Sec. 5. The general manager shall have exclusive control of the stationing and transfer of all patrolmen and other officers and employes constituting the police force, under such rules and regulations as the Commission may prescribe. He shall have the exclusive management and control of such other officers and employes as shall be employed in the administration of the affairs of the department. The police force shall be composed of such officers, patrolmen and other employes as may be provided by ordinance of the Commission. In case of riot or other emergency, the mayor may appoint additional patrolmen and officers for temporary service, who need not be in the classified list of such division.

Sec. 6. No person shall act as special policeman, special detective, or other special officer for any purpose whatsoever, except upon written authority from the general manager. Such authority shall be exercised only for a specified time, not to exceed three months.

Sec. 7. The general manager shall have exclusive control of the stationing and transfer of all firemen and other officers and employes constituting the fire department, under such rules and regulations as the Commission shall prescribe, and shall have the exclusive management and control of such other officers and employes as may be employed in the administration of the affairs of the department. The fire department shall be composed of such other officers, firemen and employes as may be provided by ordinance of the Commission. In case of riot, conflagration, or like emergency, the mayor may appoint additional firemen and officers for temporary service, who need not be in the classified service.

Sec. 8. The general manager shall have the exclusive right to suspend any of the officers or employes in the respective departments who may be under his management and control, for incompetence, gross neglect of duty, gross immorality, drunkenness, failure to obey orders given by the proper authority, or for any other just and reasonable cause. If any officer or employe be suspended, as herein provided, the general manager shall forthwith in writing certify the fact to the Commission, together with the cause for the suspension, and the Commission shall render judgment thereon, which judgment, if the charge be sustained, may be suspension, reduction in rank, or dismissal; and such judgment in the matter shall be final, except as otherwise hereinafter provided. The general manager, in any such investigation, shall have the same power to administer oaths, and secure the attendance of witnesses and the production of books and papers, as is conferred on the Commission.

Sec. 9. The general manager shall manage and supervise all public improvements, works and undertakings of the city except as otherwise provided in this charter. He shall have charge of the construction, improvement, repair, and maintenance of streets, sidewalks, alleys, lanes, squares, bridges, viaducts, aqueducts, public highways, sewers, drains, ditches, culverts, streams, and water courses and of all public buildings. He shall manage and control market houses, crematories, sewage disposal plants and farms and shall enforce all the obligations of privately owned or operated public utilities enforceable by the city. He shall have the charge of the making and preservation of all surveys, maps, plans, drawings and estimates for such public work; the cleaning, sprinkling and lighting of streets and public places; the collection and disposal of waste; the preservation of tools and appliances belonging to the city and pertaining to the functions of the departments. He shall manage all municipal water, lighting, heating, power and transportation enterprises. He shall manage and control the use, construction, improvement, repair, and maintenance of all recreational facilities of the city, including parks, playgrounds, public gymnasiums, public bath houses, and social centers. He shall have charge of the engineer of the city, who shall be the deputy general manager of public service.

Sec. 10. The general manager may, without notice, cause the affairs of any department, or the conduct of any officer or employe to be examined. Any person or persons appointed by the general manager to examine the affairs of any department or the conduct of any officer or employe shall have the same power to compel the attendance of witnesses, and the production of books and papers and other evidence, and to punish for contempt, as is conferred upon the Commission or a committee thereof by this charter.

Sec. 11. The general manager shall be entitled to a seat in the Commission, and shall have the right to introduce ordinances and resolutions and to take part in the discussion of all matters coming before the Commission; but he shal[l] no vote therein.

Sec. 12. During a vacancy in the office or the disabi[lity of] the general manager the Commission shall designate properly qualified person to execute the functions of the

Appointments:

Enumeration: General (City) Manager, City [...] City Treasurer, City Assessor and members [...] boards except the Board of Education.

Manner: Enumerated Officers by the Commi[ssion], all others by the General Manager.

Civil Service Provision: None.

Election Provisions:

Elected Provisions: Nominations by petition [...] per centum of the voters in the constituenc[y]

Preferential voting, with first, second and [...] choices.

Initiative:

Fifteen per centum petition.

Referendum:

Twenty-five per centum petition.

Recall:

Thirty-five per centum petition.

The question of removal is separated on the [...] from that of the selection of a successor [...] officer sought to be removed.

MANISTEE

(HOME RULE CHARTER, DRAFTED BY AN ELECTIVE BOARD OF CHARTER COMMISSIONERS. ADOPTED BY POPULAR VOTE DEC. 17, 1913).

Governing Body:

Title: Council.
Number: Five, including mayor.
Term: Five years, one member elected each year.
Removal: Recall.
Salary: None.

Mayor:

(Portion of Article IV.)

Sec. 13. The powers and duties of the mayor shall be such as are conferred upon him by this Charter, together with such others as are conferred by the Council pursuant to the provisions of this Charter and no others.

Sec. 14. He shall be President of the City Council and shall exercise all the powers conferred and perform all the duties imposed upon the presiding officer of the Council by the Charter. He shall appoint all standing and special committees of the City Council. He shall be recognized as the official head of the City by the courts for the purpose of serving civil process, by the Governor for the purposes of the military law, and for all ceremonial purposes.

Sec. 15. The Mayor shall have the power to take command of the peace and to govern the city by proclamation during the times of great public danger, and this right shall not be abridged or abrogated.

Sec. 16. During the disability of the Mayor, the functions of his office shall devolve upon some member of the City Council designated by that body.

Sec. 17. He shall exercise all other powers and perform all other duties conferred and imposed by the general law upon Mayors of cities, except other designation shall be made by this Charter or by act of the Council.

City Manager:

(Portion of Article VI.)

Sec. 10. There shall be chosen by the City Council an officer to be known as the City Manager, who shall be the administrative head of the City Government.

Sec. 11. Before entering upon the duties of his office the City Manager shall take the official oath required by law and shall execute a bond in favor of the City for the faithful performance of his duties in such sums as shall be determined upon by the City Council.

Sec. 12. The City Manager shall not be personally interested in any contracts to which the City is a party for supplying the City with materials or labor of any kind.

Sec. 13. It shall be his duty to attend all meetiings of, and to recommend to, the City Council, from time to time such measures as he shall deem necessary or expedient for it to adopt. He shall prepare matters for consideration at meetings of the City Council, and furnish them with any necessary information respecting any of the departments.

He shall, at such times as the Council shall require, present reports from the several departments and shall draw up an annual report which shall consolidate the special reports of the several departments; he shall present to the City Council annually an itemized estimate of the financial needs of the several departments for the ensuing year.

Sec. 14. He shall transmit to the heads of the several departments written notice of all acts of the City Council relating to the duties of their departments, and he shall make designations of officers to perform duties ordered to be performed by the City Council.

Sec. 15. He shall sign such contracts, licenses and other public documents, on behalf of the City, as the City Council may authorize and require.

Sec. 16. He shall have access at all times to the books, vouchers and papers of any officer or employee of the City and shall have power to examine, under oath, any person connected therewith. It shall be his duty, either in person or by the aid of a competent assistant, to know the manner in which the accounts of the City are kept.

Sec. 17. He shall have power to revoke licenses pending the action of the City Council.

Sec. 18. During the disability of the City Manager the City Council shall designate some properly qualified person to execute the functions of the office.

Appointments:

Enumeration: City Clerk, City Treasurer, City Manager, City Attorney and three Assessors.

Manner: Enumerated and non-enumerated officers by majority vote of the Council, to hold office during their pleasure.*

Election Provisions:

Non-partisan preferential ballot (first and second choices). Names placed on ballot on petition of twenty-five electors.

Initiative:

Fifteen per centum petition.

Referendum:

Twenty-five per centum petition.

Recall:

Ten per centum petition for submission at general election; twenty-five per centum if at special election.

No recall petition may be filed against any officer during the first six months of office.

* Although it is customary to give the power of appointment to the City Manager, it is assumed that, under this charter, the actual disposition of the appointing power will be subject to an understanding as to policy between the Council and the City Manager.

WISCONSIN STATUTE

(REVISED TO 1912)

(An Act of the Legislature, approved June 15, 1909 (Chapter 48, Laws of 1909), as amended by Chapter 67A, Laws of 1911, applicable to cities of the second, third and fourth classes after adoption by the people thereof at a special election. The question of adoption is submitted on petition of twenty-five per centum.)

Commission-Organization:

Title: City Council.

Number: Three, including Mayor.

Term: Four years. Partial renewal annually.

Removal: Recall and statutory provisions.

**Salary (minimum):* Over 40,000 population, $4,500.
30,000 to 40,000 population, $3,500.
20,000 to 30,000 population, $3,000
15,000 to 20,000 population, $2,500.
10,000 to 15,000 population, $2,000.
7,500 to 10,000 population, $1,200.
5,000 to 7,500 population, $1,000.
3,500 to 5,000 population, $750.
2,500 to 3,500 population, $500.
Under 2,500 population, $400.

Commissioner-Departments: The Council may create any general department and designate one of its members as head thereof.

General Commission Powers:

The powers formerly exercised by the Council and the several administrative and executive departments.

Mayor:

Term: Six years.

Removal: Recall and statutory provisions.

Powers in Relation to Commission: President of Council. No veto power.

**Salary:* Over 40,000 population, $5,000.
30,000 to 40,000 population, $4,000.
20,000 to 30,000 population, $3,500.
15,000 to 20,000 population, $3,000.
10,000 to 15,000 population, $2,500.
7,500 to 10,000 population, $1,500.
5,000 to 7,500 population, $1,200.
3,500 to 5,000 population, $1,000.
2,500 to 3,500 population, $600.
Under 2,500 population, $500.

Appointments:

Enumeration: City Clerk, Corporation Counsel, Comptroller, Superintendent of Streets.
Manner: By majority of Council.
Civil Service Provisions: None.

Election Provisions:

Names placed on primary ballots by petition of twenty-five signatures. Non-partisan elections.

Initiative:

Twenty-five per centum petition (special election).
Fifteen per centum petition (general election).

Referendum:

Twenty per centum petition (general or special election). Not applicable to franchises.

Recall:

Petition equal to one-third of all votes cast in the city for governor at last general election.

Abandonment of Act:

Operation under this statute may be abandoned by popular vote after six years.

---

*No salary may be increased except by vote of the people at a general election or by increase of population.

MINNESOTA HOME RULE STATUTE

(An Act of the Legislature, Chap. 170, S. F. 465, approved Apr. 10, 1909.)

Sections 748 *to* 755, *inclusive, of the Revised Laws of* 1905, were amended so as to incorporate in the law provisions which would permit the establishment of the Commission form of government and non-partisan primaries and elections for all municipal officers. The Commission form under this act goes into effect as an amendment to the City Charter. The Board of Freeholders is authorized to provide in a Home Rule Charter that all elective officers, including the Mayor and members of the Council, shall be elected at large or otherwise. It is authorized also to provide that all candidates at general municipal elections shall be nominated by a primary election and that there shall or shall not be any party designation or mark indicating that the candidate is a member of a party.

Under Section 3 of the act provision is made for assigning to each member of the Council certain designated administrative duties.

Section 4 authorizes the Board of Freeholders to provide for the recall of elective officers on the basis of a petition, the size of which is left to their own determination.

MANKATO

(Home Rule Charter, drafted by a charter commission; adopted by popular vote, 1910.)

Commission-Organization:

Title: Council.

Number: Five, including Mayor.

Term: Two years.

Removal: Recall.

Salary: Six hundred dollars.

Commissioner-Departments: 1, Public Health, Sanitation, Police and General Welfare; 2, Accounts and Finances; 3, Parks, Public Grounds, Buildings and Fire Protection; 4, Waterworks and Sewers; 5, Streets and Alleys. Designation to departments by majority vote of the Council.

General Commission Powers:

"It shall exercise the corporate power of the city. and subject to the limitations of the Charter shall be vested with all powers of legislation in municipal affairs adequate to a complete system of local government, consisted with the constitution of the state."

The Mayor:

Term: Two years.

Salary: Nine hundred dollars.

Removal: Recall.

Special Functions: Is charged with general oversight of the City's accounts and of the affairs of public utility corporations. No veto power.

Other Elective Officers:

Judge and special Judge of the Municipal Court.

Appointments:

Enumeration: City Clerk, Assessor, Treasurer, City Attorney, City Engineer, Chief of Police, Chief of Fire Department and Health Commissioner.

Manner: By majority vote of the Council; removal in the same manner.

Election Provisions:

Names placed on primary ballot on petition of twenty-five electors. Non-partisan primaries. Candidates equal to twice the number to be voted for receiving the highest number of votes are the candidates at the general election.

Initiative:

Twenty per centum petition (special election).
Ten per centum petition (general election).

Referendum:

Twenty per centum petition (general or special election).

Recall:

Twenty per centum petitions. No recall petition may be filed during the first three months of office. No official recalled or resigning while recall proceeding are pending may be elected or appointed to any city office within one year.

Franchises:

Every ordinance granting a franchise is required to state the maximum price of service charged; the city retains the right to fix a reasonable charge for such service. The maximum length of time for which a franchise may be granted is twenty-five years. Every franchise must contain a provision for forfeiture in case of non-compliance with its terms.

ST. PAUL

(HOME RULE CHARTER; DRAFTED BY CHARTER COMMISSION; ADOPTED BY POPULAR VOTE MAY 7, 1912.)

Commission-Organization:

Title: Council.

Number: Seven, including mayor.

Term: Two years.

Removal: Recall.

Salary: Forty-five hundred dollars.

* *Commissioner-Departments:* 1, Finance; 2, Public Works; 3, Public Safety; 4, Education; 5, Parks and Playgrounds; 6, Public Utilities. Designation by the Mayor.

General Commission Powers:

The legislative authority is vested in the Council. The administrative functions of the individual commissioners are set forth in detail in the charter and not delegated in the usual way by the Council.

Mayor:

Term: Two years.

Removal: Recall.

Salary: Five thousand dollars.

Powers: Presides over the Council; may exercise power of veto over ordinances, which may be overruled by majority of all members of the Council; assigns commissioners to the several departments; may remove any appointive officers or employee of the city, except one appointed by the Comptroller.

Other Elective Officers:

The Comptroller, who is ex officio Civil Service Commissioner.

† Two judges of the municipal court and such justices of the peace as are provided by general law.

Appointments:

Enumeration: The following general officers. Corporation Counsel, City Clerk, Chief of Police, Chief of Fire Department, Superintendent of Schools, Commissioner of Health, whose salaries are fixed in the charter. Numerous other minor officers in the several departments are enumerated.

Manner: Various.

Civil Service Provisions: The Comptroller is ex-officio Civil Service Commissioner. Every officer and employee not specifically exempted is in the classified service.

Election Provisions:

Non-partisan primaries; names placed on ballot on petition of fifty voters. Candidates at the primary receiving the highest number of votes to twice the number of places to be filled are the candidates at the regular election.

Initiative:

Ten per centum petition (general election).
Twenty per centum petition (special election)

Referendum:

Eight per centum petition (special or general election).

Recall:

Twenty-five per centum petitions. No recall during the first or last six months of office.

Special Features:

This charter varies from and is less elastic than the usual "commission" type in a number of important respects. The powers of the Council and the individual commissioners are stated in much greater detail. Administrative procedure, which is dealt with by ordinance or by executive order, as, for example, the budget, is regulated by charter. The independent comptroller has civil service powers. The council has no general power to create, abolish and consolidate departments.

---

* The duties of each elected officer are set forth in the charter in elaborate detail.

† The municipal courts in many states are treated as parts of a general state system, and justices of the peace as county officers. For purposes of comparison between various states and cities, this volume admits charters in which these officers are elective, provided that the strictly administrative departments of the government are organized on a short ballot basis.

DULUTH

(Home Rule Charter, drafted by a Charter Commission, adopted by popular vote Dec. 3, 1912.)

Commission Organization:

Title: City Council.

Number: Five, including mayor.

Term: Four years.

Removal: Recall.

Salary: Four thousand dollars; ($4,500 when city has 100,000 inhabitants; $5,000 when city has 150,000 inhabitants).

Commissioner-Departments: 1, Public Affairs; 2, Finance; 3, Public Works; 4, Public Safety; 5, Public Utlities. Designation by the Council. Members are required to devote their entire time to the service of the city.

General Commission Powers:

Legislative and executive authority of the city.

Mayor:

Term: Four years.

Salary: Same as commissioners.

Removal: Recall.

Powers: Presides over the Council; no veto power.

Appointments:

Enumeration: City Clerk, Auditor, Assessor, Purchasing Agent (at the discretion of the council), Attorney.

Manner: Enumerated officers by the council, with power of removal at any time. Individual commissioners have power to appoint administrative heads, deputies, clerks, assistants, laborers and servants in their departments subject to Civil Service provisions. But by four-fifths vote the council may remove any appointee of any commissioner.

Civil Service Provisions: A board of three members to be appointed by the Council is required to provide for the classification of all employees except day laborers, "enumerated" officers, election boards, special policemen, special detectives and other temporary employees; for competitive examination; for an eligible list; for a period of probation before employment is made permanent, and for promotion on the basis of merit, experience and record.

Election Provisions:

Names of candidates placed upon ballots by petition of fifty voters; the candidate, in accepting nomination, is required to take oath that he is not the nominee or representative of, nor has received support from any political party or committee representing any political party or organization.

Preferential voting, with first, second and additional choices, but commissioners are voted for in a group and not separately as under the Grand Junction charter.

Expenditures by or in behalf of candidates are limited to those incurred for printing and distributing literature and holding public meetings.

Initiative:

Twenty per cent. petition (special election).
Ten per cent. petition (general election).

Referendum:

Twenty per centum petition (special election).
Ten per centum petition (general election).

Recall:

Twenty-five per centum petition. No recall in the first three months of office.

MONTANA STATUTE

(AN ACT OF THE LEGISLATURE, SUBSTITUTE HOUSE BILL No. 263, SESSION OF 1911, APPLICABLE TO CITIES OF THE FIRST, SECOND AND THIRD CLASSES UPON ADOPTION AT SPECIAL ELECTION CALLED UPON PETITION OF 25 PER CENTUM* OF THE VOTERS.)

Commission-Organization:

Title: Council.

Number: In cities of the third and second classes, and cities of the first class of less than 25,000 population, three including Mayor; in cities of over 25,000 population, five including Mayor.

Term: Two years. Partial renewal.

Removal: Recall.

Salary: In cities of the third class:

Less than 3,000 population	$500
More than 3,000 population	900
In cities of the second class	1,500
In cities of the first class:	
Less than 30,000 population	2,500
Between 30,000 and 50,000 population	3,000
More than 50,000 population	3,500

Commissioner-Departments: 1, Accounts, Finance and Public Property (Mayor); 2, Public Safety and Charity; 3, Streets, Public Improvements and Parks. Or, if five commissioners: 1, Public Affairs (Mayor); 2, Accounts and Finance; 3, Public Safety and Charity; 4, Streets and Public Improvements; 5, Parks and Public Property. Designation to departments by the Council.

General Commission Powers:

All executive, legislative powers and duties formerly possessed and exercised by the Mayor, City Council, Board of Public Works, Park Commissioners, Board of Police and Fire Commissioners, Board of Water Works, Trustees, Board of Library Trustees, Attorney, Assessor, Treasurer, Auditor, City Engineer, and all other executive and administrative offices organized under the general municipal corporation laws.

Special Requirements:

Monthly financial statements.

Mayor:

Term: Two years.

Salary: In cities of the third class:

Less than 3,000 population	$600
More than 3,000 population	1,000
In cities of the second class	1,650
In cities of the first class:	
Less than 30,000 population	3,000
Between 30,000 to 50,000 population	4,000
More than 50,000 population	4,500

Removal: Recall.

Powers in relation to Commission: No veto power. General supervision.

Appointments:

Enumeration: City Clerk, City Treasurer, City Attorney, City Auditor, City Engineer, City Physician, Chief of the Fire Department, Commissioner of Weights and Measures, Street Commissioner, Library Trustees, Cemetery Trustees.

Manner: By a majority vote of the Council. Removal in the same manner. Civil Service provisions apply to all appointive officers except the above, and laborers, election officials, and Mayor's Secretary and Assistant Attorney.

Civil Service Provisions: The Council is required to appoint a Commission of three members to hold office for six years, with partial renewal of the Commission every two years.

Election Provisions:

Nomination by petition of twenty-five voters. The two candidates for Mayor and the four (or eight) candidates for Councilmen receiving the highest number of votes at the primary are the candidates at the municipal election.

Initiative:

Twenty-five per centum* petition (special election). Ten per centum* petition (general election).

Referendum:

Twenty-five per centum* petition (general or special election).

Recall:

Twenty-five per centum* petition.

Franchises:

All ordinances for the grant, renewal or extension of franchises must be submitted to a popular vote.

Abandonment of Act

Operation under this act may be abandoned after six years by popular election called upon petition of twenty-five per centum* of the voters.

* Based upon registration, not upon vote cast at first preceding municipal elections.

NORTH DAKOTA STATUTE

(AN ACT APPROVED MAR. 20, 1907, PERMITTING CITIES OF NOT LESS THAN 2,000 INHABITANTS TO ADOPT BY POPULAR VOTE, THE FORM OF COMMISSION GOVERNMENT SPECIFIED HEREIN. THE QUESTION OF ADOPTION MAY BE SUBMITTED ON PETITION OF TEN PER CENTUM OF THE ELECTORATE.)

Commission-Organization:

Title: Board of Commissioners.

Number: Five, including President.

Term: Four years.

Removal: No provision.

Salary: Not specified.

Commissioner-Departments: 1, Police and Fire Commissioner; 2, Commissioner of Streets and Public Improvements; 3, Water Works and Sewerage Commissioner; 4, Commissioner of Finance and Revenue. Designation by Council.

The specific manner in which the powers conferred upon the Board of Commissioners shall be performed is "not specifically pointed out," but the Board "may provide by ordinance the details necessary for the full exercise of such power."

General Commission Powers:

The Board of Commissioners are the legal successors of the Mayor and Board of Aldermen.

President:

Term: Four years.

Salary: Not specified.

Removal: No provision.

Powers in Relation to Commission: Presides over Commission.

Appointments:

Enumeration: Treasurer, Auditor, Attorney, one or more Assessors, Physician, Street Commissioner, Chief of the Fire Department, Board of Public Works, one or more Policemen.

Manner: By majority vote of the Council.

Civil Service Provisions: None.

Election Provisions:

The system of voting is cumulative: "Each voter shall be allowed as many votes for the candidates of City Commissioners as there are Commissioners to be elected, such votes being distributed among the candidates as the voter shall see fit; no voter shall be allowed to cast more votes than candidates to be elected."

Initiative:

No provision.

Referendum:

No provision.

Recall:

No provision.

The following cities have adopted this act: **Bismar**

SOUTH DAKOTA STATUTE

(REVISED TO 1912)

(Chapter 86, Laws of 1907, as amended by Chapters 57 and 158, Laws of 1909, creating a new class of cities known as Cities under Commission, enabling any city of the first, second or third class to adopt the Commission Form of Government. Amended by Chapter 97, Laws of 1911.)

Commission-Organization:

Title: Board of Commissioners.

Number: Five, including mayor.

Number: Five or three,* including mayor.

Removal: Recall.

Salary: Population 2,000 or less, $25.00 per annum. Fifty dollars additional for each one thousand or major fraction thereof.

In cities of 10,000 population or more, $600, but may be fixed at $1,500 by popular vote.

In cities governed by three commissioners, having a population between 3,500 and 10,000, not exceeding $1,000; in cities of less than 3,500 population, $400.

Commissioner-Departments: 1, Police and Fire; 2, Streets and Public Property; 3, Water Works and Sewerage; 4, Finance and Revenue; or 1, Public Property, Police and Fire; 2, Water Works and Sewerage.

General Commission Powers:

All the corporate powers.

Mayor:

Term: Five years.

Salary: Population 2,000 or less, $25.00 per annum. Fifty dollars additional for each additional one thousand or major fraction thereof.

In cities of 10,000 population or over, $1,200, but may be fixed at $2,000 if so authorized by popular vote.

In cities governed by three commissioners, having a population between 3,500 and 10,000, not exceeding $1,200; in cities of less than 3,500, $600.

Removal: Recall.

Powers in Relation to Commission: President of Board. No veto power. Has supervision of public buildings and lighting.

Appointments:

Enumeration: City Treasurer, City Assessor, City Auditor, Police Justice, City Justice of the Peace, City Attorney, City Engineer.

Manner: By a majority vote, for a term of one year.

Election Provisions:

Any voter may become a candidate at the annual election by a petition of not less than twenty-five nor more than one hundred and fifty voters. If no candidate for any office receives a majority of all votes cast therefor a secondary election is held. No party designations on ballots. Separate ballot for School Directors.

Initiative:

Five per centum petition (special election).

Referendum:

Five per centum petition (special election).

The proposition voted on may refer to the whole, or a portion of an ordinance.

Recall:

Fifteen per centum petition.

Election of successor requires a majority of votes cast; a secondary election is held if necessary.

Franchises:

Must be submitted to popular vote.

Special Features:

The annual appropriation ordinance must contain the annual tax levy, which must not exceed twenty mills on each dollar of assessed valuation, exclusive of sums devoted to interest and sinking funds. Tax levy for schools is limited to twenty-five mills.

* At the option of the city.

GALVESTON

(An Act approved Mar. 30, 1903, Chap. 37, Laws of 1903, amending the Charter of April 18, 1901.)

Commission-Organization:

Title: Board of Commissioners.

Number: Five, including Mayor.

Term: Two years.

Removal: Statutory provisions.

Salary: Twelve hundred dollars.

Commissioner-Departments: 1, Police and Fire; 2, Streets and Public Property; 3, Water and Sewerage; 4, Finance and Revenue. The designations by the Board of Commissioners.

General Commission Powers:

All the corporate powers.

Mayor:

(Complete title, "Mayor-President.")

Term: Two years.

Salary: Two thousand dollars.

Removal: Statutory provisions.

Powers in Relation to Commission: Full voting privileges. No veto power.

Special Requirements: Must devote at least six hours a day to the duties of his office.

Appointments:

Enumeration: Secretary, Attorney, Recorder, Judge of the Corporation Court, Assessor and Collector of Taxes, Chief of Police and Chief of Fire Department, Engineer, who is Superintendent of Streets; Auditor, Secretary of Water Works and Sewerage Departments, Harbor Master, Sexton, Superintendent of Water Works and Sewerage, Engineer of Water Works, Assistant Engineer of Water Works. These officers hold office for a period of two years.

Manner: By majority vote of Council. Removal with or without cause. The several Commissioners are required to prepare for the Board of Commissioners a list of recommendations of persons for appointment to the various minor positions.

Civil Service Provisions: None.

Election Provisions:

The general laws of the State apply.

Initiative:

No provisions.

Referendum:

No provisions.

Recall:

No provisions.

Franchises:

No franchise for longer period than fifty years. All franchises subject to taxation.

HOUSTON**

(SPECIAL CHARTER. AN ACT OF THE LEGISLATURE, CHAP. 15, SPECIAL LAWS OF 1905. AMENDED BY POPULAR VOTE OCTOBER 15, 1913.)

Commission—Organization:

Title: City Council.

Number: Five, including Mayor.

Term: Two years.

Removal: Recall.

Salary: Twenty-four hundred dollars.

Commissioner-Departments:

No. 1, Tax and Land. No. 2, Fire.

No. 3, Streets and Bridges. No. 4, Water.

Commisisoners are elected to designated departments and are required to devote so much of their time to the service of the city as may be necessary to the discharge of their duties.

Mayor:

Term: Two years.

Salary: Seventy-five hundred dollars.

Removal: Recall.

Powers: Veto power; but as a member of Council may vote on question of overruling veto.

Special Requirements: Must devote entire time to service of the city.

Other Elective Officers:

The Comptroller, who receives a salary of $3,600 per year.

Appointments:

Enumeration: By ordinance.

Manner: The Mayor has power to appoint, subject to confirmation by the City Council, such heads of departments in the administrative service as may be created by ordinance, and has power to appoint and remove all officers and employees in the service of the city, for cause.

Civil Service Provisions: A commission of three is created. Members are to be appointed by the Mayor, subject to confirmation by the Council; one is to be a member of the City Council.

Election Provisions:

Preferential ballot with first, second and third choices is used in the primaries and is prepared by the executive committee of the political party. But the preferential system does not go into effect until the charter amendment is supplemented by ordinance.

Initiative

* Fifteen per centum petition (special election).

Referendum:

* Ten per centum petition (special election).

Recall:

Applies to elective and appointive offices.

* Twenty-five per centum petitions. No member sought to be recalled may pass upon the sufficiency of the petitions for the same.

No petition for removal may be filed within the first year after the beginning of the officer's term.

A special election is held to fill any vacancy caused by recall.

**This page supersedes page of same number and title of original publication and is brought up to date to amendment of Oct. 15, 1913. For text of original charter, see page 51, 101 et seq.

*Based on total vote cast for mayor and commissioners at the last preceding Democratic primary.

GREENVILLE

(SPECIAL CHARTER. AN ACT OF THE LEGISLATURE, 1909.)

Commission-Organization:

Title: City Council.

Number: Three, including Mayor.

Term: Two years.

Salary: Twelve hundred dollars.

Commissioner-Departments: No designation in Charter. Council assigns duties.

General Commission Powers:

All the powers conferred upon the City.

Special Requirements:

Must devote entire time to duties of office.

Mayor:

Term: Two years.

Salary: Twelve hundred dollars.

Removal: Impeachment by majority of Council.

Powers in Relation to Commission: Veto power.

Special Requirements:

Must devote entire time to duties of office.

Other Elective Officers:

Assessor and Collector, City Attorney, City Marshal, City Clerk.

Appointments:

Manner: Heads of Departments created by ordinance. The City Council appoints and may remove officers and employees for cause.

Civil Service Provisions: None.

Election Provisions:

City Council prescribes regulations. Political parties recognized. Nomination petitions provided for. Candidates for office of Alderman are voted for by number.

Initiative:

No provision.

Referendum:

No provision.

Recall:

No provision.

Franchises:

Referendum on petition of one hundred voters. Council, of its own motion, may submit franchise questions.

Special Features:

The office of City Treasurer is let by contract to the "highest and best bidder." (*See outline of Dallas.*) Public utilities owned by the City may not be disposed of except by a vote of sixty per centum of the taxpayers.

DALLAS

(Special Charter. An Act of the Legislature, Approved Apr. 13, 1907, Amended 1909.)

Commission-Organization:

Title: Board of Commissioners.

Number: Five, including Mayor.

Term: Two years.

Removal: Recall.

Salary: Three thousand dollars.

Commissioner-Departments: 1, Police and Fire; 2, Streets and Public Property; 3, Water Works and Sewerage; 4, Finance and Revenue. Designation by Board.

General Commission Powers:

All powers conferred on the City, except as otherwise provided (see *"Special Features"*).

Special Requirements:

Monthly statements of receipts and disbursements. Commissioners must give entire time to service of City. Meetings at least three times a week.

Mayor:

Term: Two years.

Salary: Four thousand dollars.

Removal: Recall.

Powers in Relation to Commission: Ex-officio President of Board and exercises all powers of members thereof.

Veto power, but the Mayor may vote upon the question of sustaining the veto.

Appointments:

Nomination by Mayor, subject to confirmation of Board (see *"Special Features"*).

Civil Service Provisions: None.

Election Provisions:

Partisan and independent nominations.

Candidates for Mayor and members of the Board of Commissioners are voted for separately and are designated on the official ballot as candidate for "Commissioner No. 1" or "Commissioner No. 2," etc., in accordance with the written requests which each candidate files with the City Secretary.

In the event of a candidate's not receiving a majority of all votes cast for any office at the first election, the Mayor calls a second election. On the ballots of the second election, the two persons receiving the first and second highest number of votes cast for each office are placed upon the official ballot.

Independent candidates for the office of Mayor and member of the Board of Commissioners may have their names placed upon the ballot at the annual election, by filing a petition signed by one hundred voters.

Initiative:

Fifteen per centum petition (special election).
Five per centum petition (general election).

Referendum:

Fifteen per centum petition (general or special election).

Recall:

Thirty-five per centum petition.

Franchises:

No exclusive franchises. All franchises must have three readings. Petition of five hundred voters required for submitting any franchise at an annual election. No franchise for longer period than twenty years.

(Over.)

Special Features:

The presidents of the banks situated in the City of Dallas are constituted a nominating Board which may, by a majority vote, name a candidate for the office of Auditor of the City.

There is a Park Board of five, of which the Mayor is a member, four of whom are appointed by the Mayor, subject to the confirmation of the Board of Commissioners, who serve for a period of two years. This Board has exclusive jurisdiction over the control, management and maintenance of the public buildings in the City of Dallas, with power to acquire in the name of the City, land for park purposes, except as herein otherwise provided.

The office of City Treasurer is let by contract in the manner herein specified:

"The office of City Treasurer shall be let by contract to the highest and best bidder in the discretion of the Board of Commissioners. The Board of Commissioners shall, not less than thirty days prior to the expiration of the term of office of the present City Treasurer, and every two years thereafter, advertise for bids for the said office, stating what said bids shall specify and the terms on which such bids shall be received. The Treasurer appointed by contract shall nevertheless be an officer of the city and subject to the same duties as a Treasurer otherwise elected. Said Treasurer shall give such bond as the Board of Commissioners may require, conditioned for the faithful discharge of his duties. He shall receive and securely keep all moneys belonging to the city, and make all payments for the same upon an order signed by the Mayor and countersigned by the Auditor, except that payments from the school funds shall be upon an order signed by the president of the Board of Education, countersigned by the Auditor and attested by the secretary of said board; provided, that no order shall be paid unless it shows upon its face that the Board of Commissioners or Board of Education, as the case may be, has ordered its issuance, and for what purpose. He shall render a full and correct statement of his receipts and payments to the Board of Commissioners at their first regular meeting in every month, and at such other time as the Board of Commissioners may require. He shall perform such other acts and duties as the Board of Commissioners may require, and shall receive for his services five (5) dollars per annum."

Art. IV. Sec. 8.

FORT WORTH

(SPECIAL CHARTER. AN ACT OF THE LEGISLATURE, 1907, CHAPTER 7, SPECIAL LAWS OF 1907, APPROVED FEB. 26, 1907.)

Commission-Organization:

Title: Board of Commissioners.

Number: Four, excluding Mayor.

Term: Two years.

Removal: Recall.

Salary: Three thousand dollars.

Commissioner-Departments: 1, Police and Fire; 2, Streets and Public Property; 3, Water Works, Sewerage and Light; 4, Finance and Revenue. Designations by Mayor.

General Commission Powers:

Those formerly exercised by the Mayor and Board of Aldermen.

Special Requirements:

Monthly financial statements.

Mayor:

Term: Two years.

Salary: Thirty-six hundred dollars.

Removal: Recall.

Powers in Relation to Commission: Presides at meetings.

Other Elective Officers:

Assessor, Collector of Taxes and City Attorney.

Appointments:

Enumeration: Treasurer, Recorder, Secretary, Marshal, Fire Chief, Secretary of Water Works, Sewerage and Lights, Auditor, Physician, Engineer and Electrician.

Civil Service Provisions: None.

Election Provisions:

Texas general laws.

Initiative:

No provisions.

Referendum:

Twenty per centum petition (general or special election).

Recall:

Twenty per centum petition.

Franchises:

All franchises subject to taxation.

BEAUMONT

(Amendment to the Charter [Chap 12, Laws of 1899]. Texas Special Laws of 1907, Page 817, Approved Apr. 18, 1907.)

Commission-Organization:

Title: Board of Commissioners.

Number: Seven, including Mayor. Two Commissioners from each Ward elected at large.

Term: Two years.

Removal: Statutory provisions.

Salary: Fixed by Council prior to election.

Commissioner-Departments: Administrative duties performed by appointive officers, who are directly responsible to the Council.

General Commission Powers:

Powers formerly exercised by the City Council. All other officers are responsible to the Board of Commissioners.

Mayor:

Term: Two years.

Salary: Fixed by Council prior to election.

Removal: Statutory provisions.

Powers in Relation to Commission: Veto power.

Appointments:

Enumeration: City Marshal, City Attorney, City Secretary, Assessor and Tax Collector, City Treasurer, City Recorder, City Health Officer, City Engineer, City Scavenger, Street Commissioner, Chief of Fire Department.

Manner: By the Council on the nomination of the Mayor.

Civil Service Provisions: None.

Initiative:

No provisions.

Referendum:

No provisions.

Recall:

No provisions.

DENISON

(Special Charter. An Act of the Legislature, Laws of 1907, Chapter 33.)

Commission-Organization:

Title: City Council.

Number: Three, including Mayor.

Term: Two years.

Removal: Recall.

Salary: Fifteen hundred dollars.

General Commission Powers:

"Full power except as herein otherwise provided to exercise all the powers conferred upon the City."

Special Requirements:

Meets daily in administrative session at the call of the Mayor.

Mayor:

Term: Two years.

Salary: Eighteen hundred dollars.

Removal: Recall.

Powers in Relation to Commission: Veto power (*see "Appointments"*).

Appointments:

Manner: By Mayor, who may remove at any time.
Civil Service Provisions: None.

Election Provisions:

Candidates for Alderman are designated as "No. 1" or "No. 2" on official ballots and voted for separately. Council determines manner of holding elections.

Initiative:

No provisions.

Referendum:

See *"Franchises."*

Recall:

Twenty per centum petition.

Franchises:

No franchise granted except by a vote of the people; expense of special election to be borne by applicants. No franchise for over thirty years.

AUSTIN

(Special Charter. An Act of the Legislature, approved Mar. 24, 1909.)

Commission-Organization:

Title: City Council.

Number: Five, including Mayor.

Term: Two years.

Removal: Recall.

Salary: Two thousand dollars.

Commissioner-Departments: 1, Public Affairs; 2, Receipts, Disbursements and Accounts; 3, Parks and Public Property; 4, Streets and Public Improvements; 5, Police and Public Safety.

General Commission Powers:

All corporate powers. All executive, legislative and judicial powers formerly possessed and exercised by the Mayor, City Council, Water, Light and Power Commissioner, etc., except Fire Department.

Councilmen obliged to vote on all questions (certain exceptions specified).

Mayor:

Term: Two years.

Salary: Twenty-five hundred dollars.

Removal: Recall.

Power (General): (*See "Appointments."*) Has all powers not otherwise assigned.

Appointments:

Manner of Appointment: Nomination by Mayor, subject to confirmation of Council, for chief officers. Individual commissioners may nominate subordinates. Appointments hold for two years.

Election Provisions:

Nomination by a non-partisan primary; names placed on ballots on petition of twenty-five voters. Wards retained for voting purposes.

Initiative:

Twenty-five per centum petition (special election).

Referendum:

Twenty-five per centum petition (general or special election).

Recall:

Twenty-five per centum petition.

Special Features:

The office of City Treasurer is let by contract to the and best bidder." (*See outline of Dallas Charter.*)

CORPUS CHRISTI

(SPECIAL CHARTER. AN ACT OF THE LEGISLATURE, APPROVED MAR. 15, 1909.)

Commission-Organization:

Title: City Council.

Number: Five, including Mayor.

Term, Two years.

Removal: Recall.

Salary: Five hundred dollars.

Commissioner-Departments: 1, Public Affairs; 2, Receipts, Disbursements and Accounts; 3, Parks and Public Property; 4, Streets and Public Improvements; 5, Police and Public Safety. Designation by Council.

General Commission Powers:

"All the powers of the City."

Mayor:

Term: Two years.

Salary: Eighteen hundred dollars.

Removal: Removable by impeachment. Recall.

Powers in Relation to Commission: Veto power.

Appointments:

By City Council subject to removal at any time; but officer so removed is entitled to a written statement of causes.

Civil Service Provisions: None.

Election Provisions:

Partisan and Independent nominations.

Initiative:

No general provisions.

Referendum:

No general provisions.

Recall:

Thirty-three and one-third per cent. petition.

Franchises:

If grant is for more than thirty years, must be submitted to a popular vote. Council must submit any franchise, on petition of applicants, the expense of election to be paid by them. All franchises subject to referendum on twenty-five per centum petition.

Special Features:

Office of Treasurer let by contract to the "highest "highest and best bidder." (*See outline of Dallas Charter.*)

TEXAS STATUTE

(AN ACT OF LEGISLATURE, CHAP. 106, LAWS OF 1909, APPROVED MAR. 25, 1909, BY WHICH CITIES OF LESS THAN 10,000 POPULATION, WHETHER INCORPORATED OR UNINCORPORATED, MAY ADOPT THE COMMISSION FORM OF GOVERNMENT BY POPULAR VOTE.)

A petition of ten per centum of the voters may be addressed to the County Judge in the case of the uninporated villages, towns and cities, requesting that the community be allowed to adopt the act.

The Commission consists of three members, one of whom is Mayor.

Sessions of the Commission are held once a month for one day, and the Commissioners receive a compensation of five dollars per diem.

The Commission has authority to appoint a Clerk, who performs the duties of Clerk, Assessor, Collector of Taxes and Treasurer. It has "all the duties, authority and powers conferred by the general laws of the State in force at the time of the taking effect of the Act applying to City Councils of villages, towns and cities of less than ten thousand" population.

[The Secretary of State keeps no official record of the cities operating under this act. The statute is drawn up in loose form and is ambiguous in several particulars.]

MARSHALL

(Special Charter. An Act of the Legislature.)

Commission-Organization:

Title: City Council.

Number: Nine and Mayor. Three chosen from each Ward, but elected at large.

Term: Two years. Partial renewal.

Removal: By City Council after trial.

Salary: Five dollars per session, not over $150 in one year.

Commissioner-Departments: No designation in Charter.

Mayor:

Term: Two years.

Salary: Not over eighteen hundred dollars.

Removal: By City Council after trial.

Powers in Relation to Commission: Veto power.

Special Requirements: Must devote entire time to duties of his office.

Other Elective Officers:

City Secretary, Chief of Police.

Appointments:

Enumeration: Treasurer, Assessor and Collector of Taxes, City Secretary, City Attorney, Chief of Police, City Engineer.

Manner: By the Council for a term of two years.

Civil Service Provisions: None.

Election Provisions:

The general State law applies.

Initiative:

No provisions.

Referendum:

The Council may make regulations.

Recall:

No provisions.

PORT ARTHUR

(SPECIAL CHARTER, AN ACT OF THE LEGISLATURE, APPROVED MARCH, 1911.)

Commission-Organization:

Title: Commission.

Number: Three, including Mayor.

Term: Two years.

Removal: By the District Court of the County.

Salary: Not over fifteen hundred dollars; the amount to be determined by the Commission.

Commissioner-Departments: 1, Public Affairs; 2, Public Records and Finance; 3, Public Property and Improvements; 4, Public Order and Safety. The Mayor is assigned to the Department of Public Affairs in addition to his assignment to one of the other departments. Designation by the Commission.

General Commission Powers:

All the legislative, executive and administrative powers and duties.

Mayor:

Term: Two years.

Removal: By the District Court of the County.

Powers in relation to Commission: Presides at meetings of the Commission. No veto power.

Salary: Not over fifteen hundred dollars.

Appointments:

Enumeration: City Attorney, City Health Officer, City Depository, Recorder, Chief of Police, Harbor Master, City Clerk, City Engineer.

Manner: By the Commissioner in charge subject to confirmation by the Commission.

Civil Service Provisions: The Commission is authorized to adopt Civil Service regulations to govern the appointment of persons to any appointive position in any department of the city.

Election Provisions:

All candidates are nominated by direct primary election by precincts and not more than three candidates for commissioner may be nominated in each of the three commissioner-precincts. But a candidate may be nominated in a precinct other than that of his residence. Simple announcement of candidacy filed with City Clerk is sufficient to place names on the primary ballot. Election is at large. Candidates are voted for by number. Preferential voting (for first and second choice) is provided for.

Initiative:

No provisions.

Referendum:

No General provisions.

Recall:

No provisions.*

Franchises:

Rights of city to water front, etc., may be alienated only by a two-thirds vote of the tax paying electors. No franchise for a longer period than twenty-one years.

Special Features:

The office of City Depository is let by contract to the highest bidder.

The annual budget is submitted to a vote of the tax payers of the city, without petition. Any items therein may be approved or rejected.

*An officer's salary may be disapproved at the annual budget election.

AMARILLO

(HOME RULE CHARTER, DRAFTED BY A CHARTER COMMISSION. ADOPTED BY POPULAR ELECTION NOVEMBER 18, 1913.)

Governing Body:

Title: City Commission.
Number: Three, including mayor.
Term: Two years.
Removal: Recall.
Salary: Ten dollars for each regular meeting; but regular meetings may not be held oftener than once a week.

Mayor:

Sec. 11. **Duties of the Mayor.** The mayor of the city shall be the presiding officer of the Commission, except that in his absence a Mayor protempore may be chosen; he shall be entitled to vote as a member of the Commission; sign all bonds; be the official head of the city, and exercise all powers and perform all duties imposed upon him by this Charter and by the ordinances of the city.

City Manager:

Sec. 20. **City Manager.** The Commission shall appoint a City Manager, who shall be the administrative head of the municipal government, and shall be responsible for the efficient administration of all departments; he may or may not be a resident of the City of Amarillo when appointed, and shall hold his office at the will of the Commission.

Sec. 21. **Powers and Duties of the City Manager.** The City Manager shall see that the laws and ordinances of the city are enforced;

Appoint all appointive officers or employes of the city, with the advice and consent of the Commission (such appointments to be upon merit and fitness alone), and remove all officers and employes appointed by him;

Exercise control and supervision over all departments and offices that may be created by the Commission, and all officers and employes appointed by him;

Attend all meetings of the Commission with a right to take part in the discussion, but having no vote;

Recommend, in writing, to the Commission such measures as he may deem necessary or expedient;

Keep the Commission fully advised as to the financial condition and needs of the city, and

Perform such other duties as may be prescribed by this Charter, or be required of him by ordinance or resolution of the Commission.

Appointments:

See "City Manager."

Election Provisions:

The office of mayor and each commissionership is separately designated on the ballot.

A majority vote is necessary to choice, and a second election is held, if necessary.

The general election laws of Texas apply in so far as they are not inconsistent with the charter.

Initiative:

The proposed ordinance must be accompanied by a statement of not less than five persons that they are to be considered a filing committee.

Twenty-five per centum petitions.

After the certification of the sufficiency of the petitions, the City Commission is required to hold a public hearing upon the proposed ordinance and to mail to each member of the filing committee, notice of such hearing.

Referendum:

Conducted under the same conditions as the Initiative.

Recall:

Twenty-five per centum petitions, but one-fifth of those petitioning must certify that they voted for the officer sought to be recalled.

The question of recall is separated on the ballot from that of the election of a successor.

No recall petition may be filed against any officer within six months after his election or within six months after an election for his recall.

TAYLOR

(HOME RULE CHARTER, DRAFTED BY A BOARD OF ELECTED FREEHOLDERS; ADOPTED BY POPULAR VOTE, APRIL 6, 1914.)

Governing Body:

Title: Board of Commissioners.

Number: Five.

Term: Two years. Partial renewal annually.

Removal: Statutory methods.

Salary: Two dollars for each meeting, but not for more than two meetings in any month; no commissioner to receive compensation for meetings at which he is not present.

Mayor:

The Board of Commissioners elects one of its own number chairman.

City Manager:

ARTICLE VII

Sec. 2. The board of commissioners shall choose, for a term of two years, a city manager.

He shall be chosen solely on the basis of administrative qualifications from among all the candidates who apply in answer to public advertisements.

ARTICLE IX.

Sec. 1. The City Manager shall be the chief executive officer of the city, and shall receive such compensation as may be provided by the Board of Commissioners. He shall be subject to removal by the Board of Commissioners on three months notice. He may demand written charges and a public hearing on the same before the Board of Commissioners at any time between the issuance of the order of removal and the date on which it takes effect.

The manager shall be responsible to the board of commissioners for the proper administration of all the affairs of the city.

Sec. 2. The manager shall make recommendations to the board of commissioners on all matters concerning the administration of the city, and in no case (save when the board of commissioners is considering the removal of the manager himself) shall the board of commissioners act without first having asked the opinion in writing of the manager on that point.

ARTICLE XI.

Sec. 1. The City Manager shall prepare and submit to the Board of Commissioners an annual budget on the basis of estimates of the expenses of the various departments of the city. These departmental estimates, showing the expenses of the departments for the preceding year and indicating wherein increases or diminutions are recommended for the ensuing year, shall be printed in one of the city newspapers for two weeks before submission by the manager to the commission, and printed copies of the estimates shall be available to any citizen upon request to the manager. The manager shall make up the budget and submit it to the board of commissioners. Due notice shall be made of the time when the budget is to be discussed by the commissioners and printed copies of the budget as recommended by the manager shall be available to any citizen at least one week before date set for the discussion in the commission. This discussion shall be in open meeting, and at least three hours shall be given to hearing protests and objections, if any, oral or written, to any item or items in the budget, or to omissions therefrom.

Sec. 3. Monthly Reports. The city manager shall make to the board of commissioners a monthly report in writing showing in detail the receipts and disbursements for the preceding month. These reports of the city manager, after first having been passed upon by the board of commissioners, shall be published each month in some newspaper published in the city.

ARTICLE XVII.

Sec. 7. Vacancies in City Manager, How Filled. Until a city manager shall have been chosen, or in event of a vacancy occurring in the office of manager, the Board of Commissioners shall select one of its members to perform the duties of manager.

Appointments:

Enumeration: City Manager, City Attorney, Recorder of the Corporation Court, Auditor, Board of Equalization.

Manner: Enumerated officers by the Board of Commissioners; all others by the City Manager, subject to the approval of the Board of Commissioners.

Civil Service Provisions: None.

Election Provisions:

Preferential plan with first, second and third choices, by means of ballots containing no partisan or other designation. The general laws of the state apply, in so far as they are not inconsistent with the charter provisions.

Initiative:

Petition of at least three hundred and fifty voters.

Referendum:

Petition of at least three hundred and fifty voters.

Recall:

No provisions.

TYLER

(HOME RULE CHARTER, DRAFTED BY A BOARD OF ELECTED CHARTER COMMISSIONERS; ADOPTED BY POPULAR VOTE APRIL 6, 1915.)

Governing Body:

Title: Commission.
Number: Five, elected at large.
Term: Two years; partial renewal annually.
Removal: Recall.
Salary: None.

City Manager:

Title: City Manager.
Powers and Duties: Is "responsible to the commission for the proper administration of all affairs of the city." His enumerated powers are substantially those of the city manager at Dayton, O. (see p. 34003). See also *"Appointments."*
Tenure: Appointed by the Commission for a term of two years; is removable upon three months' notice and may demand written charges and an opportunity to be heard in his own defense.
Salary: To be not less than eighteen hundred ($1,800) dollars nor more than thirty-six hundred ($3,600) dollars.

Appointments:

The heads of all departments are in charge of a director, to be appointed by the City Manager and removable by him (except the department of education), such appointments to be subject to the approval of the commission. Each director must be chosen with reference to his particular qualifications in the field of work assigned to him and must possess such minimum requirements in training and experience as the Commission shall determine.

Election Provisions:

Non-partisan preferential ballot with first, second and third choices.

Initiative:

*Thirty per centum petition (regular or special election); but no proposition may be adopted unless fifty per centum of the vote of the city is cast.

Referendum:

*Thirty per centum petition.

Recall:

*Thirty per centum petition. No recall election may be held until the member shall have been in office at least one year, nor until a year after any previous election for the recall of the same officer.

* Registered electors.

SHERMAN

HOME RULE CHARTER, DRAFTED BY A BOARD OF ELECTED CHARTER COMMISSIONERS; ADOPTED BY POPULAR VOTE MARCH 6, 1915.

Governing Body:

Title: Council-Commission. *Partial renewal.
†*Number:* Sixteen, including mayor.
Term: Two years.
Removal: Recall.
Salary:

The Council meets once in every two months. From their own number the councilmen select two (who may be recalled by them at any time) to act with the mayor as the City Commission. The City Commission meets once a week, and, subject to the conditions noted, exercises the usual powers of the governing bodies, including the power to select, control and remove the City Manager.

Mayor:

The mayor is elected, as such, by the people. His duty is to act as president of the Council and chairman of the Commission. He is to receive a salary of twenty-five (25) dollars per month in addition to his salary as commissioner.

He is required to make an audit of the city's finances at least once a year.

City Manager:

The city manager is appointed by the City Commission and exercises the usual powers of city managers. There is no restriction in the charter as to residence at the time of appointment.

Appointments:

Enumeration: (1) City Manager, City Clerk. (2) Directors of the departments of Law, city attorney, public service, public welfare, public safety and finance, chief of fire department, chief of police.

Election Provisions:

Nomination by petition of ten percentum of the qualified voters.

Ballots are to be without party designations and names on ballots are to be rotated so that each name is printed an equal number of times.

Initiative:

Ten per centum petition for submission to the Council-Commission.

Additional fifteen per centum for submission to the electorate.

Referendum:

Ten per centum petition for submission to the Council-Commission.

Additional fifteen per centum for submission to the electorate.

Recall:

Twenty-five per centum petition. Before recall election is held, nomination of successors must be made by the filing of a petition of ten per centum of the qualified voters, as in regular elections. No recall petition shall be filed against an officer until he has held office for six months.

Special Feature:

The city commission, upon its own motion, or upon the application of the City Manager, may create a city plan board, a public health board, or such other unpaid advisory boards as it may deem deem necessary.

---

* Section seven of the charter provides that "to the end that a part of the city council may be elected each year," seven members of the council are "requested" to resign thirty days before the first annual election under the charter. The designation of the members to resign is to be determined by lot.

† While this provision is not precisely in accord with our definition of a commission-manager charter (see p. —) it is felt that under local conditions in a community no larger than Sherman the citizens have far less difficulty in obtaining accurate information concerning candidates than in larger communities. In other respects the charter conforms to the general definition.

TULSA

(Charter framed by a Board of Freeholders. Adopted July 3, 1908. Approved Jan. 5, 1909.)

Commission-Organization:

Title: Board of Commissioners.

Number: Five, including Mayor.

Term: Two years.

Removal: Recall.

Salary: Twelve hundred dollars.

Commissioner-Departments, Designation: 1, Police and Fire Commissioner; 2, Streets and Public Property; 3, Water Works and Sewerage; 4, Finance and Revenue. Commissionerships are voted for by number; but such number bears no relation to the designation of the individual Commissioners after election.

General Commission Powers:

All the corporate powers.

Special Requirements:

Monthly financial statements.

No final action concerning any special Department may be taken in the absence of the Commissioner, unless the matter has been made the special order of the day at the previous meeting of the Board, or such action is taken at a regular meeting of the Board.

Mayor:

Term: Two years.

Salary: Fifteen hundred dollars.

Removal: Recall.

Powers in relation to Commission: Has veto power, but may vote on question of sustaining his own veto. May vote on confirmation of appointments. President of the Board. Special oversight over contracts and franchises.

Other Elective Officers:

City Auditor.

Appointments:

Manner: City Attorney nominated by the Mayor, subject to confirmation of the Board of Commissioners, the Mayor having no vote on the confirmation. Judge of the Municipal Court, and the four members of the Park Board are nominated by the Mayor, subject to confirmation, the Mayor being entitled to vote on the question.

Civil Service Provisions: None.

Election Provisions:

Commissioners are chosen by number. Recognition of political parties and candidates. A second election is held if no candidate for a given office has received a majority of votes at the first.

Initiative:

Constitutional provisions.

Referendum:

Constitutional provisions.

Recall:

Thirty-five per centum petition.

Franchises:

No grant, renewal or extension without approval of majority of voters at a general or special election. Initiative on franchise questions on a twenty-five per centum petition. No exclusive franchises.

ARDMORE

(Special Charter, drafted by Board of Freeholders, adopted Nov. 17, 1908, approved Jan. 7, 1909.)

Commission-Organization:

Title: Board of Commissioners.

Number: Four, excluding Mayor; one from each Ward, but elected at large.

Term: Four years.

Salary: Six hundred dollars.

Removal: Recall.

Commissioner-Departments: Distribution of functions and designations to Departments made by the Board.

General Commission Powers:

Legislation.

Mayor:

Term: Four years.

Salary: Fifteen hundred dollars.

Removal: Recall.

Powers in Relation to Commission: Vested with executive authority, veto power, general supervision, presides at Board meetings. (*See Appointments.*)

Appointments:

Enumeration: City Treasurer, City Clerk, Chief of Fire Department, City Engineer, Judge of Municipal Court, City Attorney.

Manner: By Mayor, with advice and consent of the Board of Commissioners; subordinates, by Commissioner in charge of Department, with consent of Board. No Civil Service provisions.

Election Provisions:

General State Law.

Initiative:

Twenty-five per centum petition (general election). Constitutional provisions.

Referendum:

Twenty-five per centum petition (general election). Constitutional provisions.

Recall:

Thirty per centum petition.

Franchises:

None granted, renewed or extended except by authority or approval of majority of qualified electors expressed at a general or special election.

Parties requesting submission of questions at a special election are required to deposit amount to cover expenses of same.

Special Features:

Public corporations are under the control of a Board of Commissioners appointed by the Mayor, with the advice and consent of the City Commissioners. Public parks are under the control of a Park Board of three, appointed in the same manner. This Board has power to acquire in the name of the City, land and other property for park purposes.

ENID

(CHARTER FRAMED BY A BOARD OF FREEHOLDERS ELECTED APR. 27, 1909. ADOPTED SEP. 22, 1909. IN EFFECT DEC. 20, 1909.)

Commission-Organization:

Title: Board of Commissioners.

Number: Four, including Mayor.

Term: Two years.

Removal: Recall.

Salary: Fifteen hundred dollars.

Commissioner-Departments: 1, Police and Fire; 2, Streets, Alleys and Public Property; 3, Water Works and Sewage. Designation by Board.

General Commission Powers:

All powers conferred upon the City.

Mayor:

Term: Two years.

Salary: Fifteen hundred dollars.

Removal: Recall.

Powers in Relation to Commission: President of Board. No vote except on confirmation of appointments and in cases of tie vote.

Appointments:

Manner:

Judge of Police Court, Chief of Police, City Policemen, City Attorney, Chief of Fire Department and Firemen, appointed by Police Commissioner.

The City Engineer, City Street Commissioner, Inspector of Public Works, City Board of Health, City Board of Park Commissioners, City Inspector of Weights and Measures, Inspector of Milk and Dairies, appointed by the Commissioner of Streets, Alleys and Public Property.

The City Clerk, City Superintendent of Water Works, Engineer and Assistant Engineer of Water Works and Police Matron, appointed by the Commissioner of Water Works and Sewage.

The City Engineer, City Assessor, City Enumerator, City Library Board, Humane Agent and other appointees, appointed by the Commissioner of Finance and Revenue.

All appointments of Commissioners are subject to the confirmation of a majority vote of the Board of Commissioners as a whole. Commissioners making appointments of City officers have no vote on the confirmation of same.

Election Provisions:

Candidates are elected by number. Partisan and Independent nominations.

Initiative:

Constitutional provisions (*See Appendix*).

Referendum:

Constitutional provisions (*See Appendix*).

Recall:

Thirty per centum petition.

Franchises:

All franchise grants must be submitted to taxpayers' election.

McALESTER

(CHARTER DRAFTED BY A BOARD OF FREEHOLDERS, ELECTED JAN. 4, 1910.)

Commission-Organization:

Title: Mayor and Commissioners.

Number: Two, and Mayor.

Term: Three years: Partial renewal.

Removal: Recall.

Salary: Twenty-five hundred dollars.

Commissioner-Departments: 1, Public Works; 2, Finance; 3, Public Health and Safety (Mayor).

General Commission Powers:

"All executive authority is vested in the Mayor and Commissioners." "All legislative authority is vested in the City Council."

Special Requirements:

Monthly statements of Receipts and Disbursements. Must devote entire time to service of the City.

Mayor:

Term: Three years.

Salary: Twenty-five hundred dollars.

Removal: Recall.

Powers in Relation to Commission: No veto power.

Special Requirements: Must devote entire time to service of the City.

Other Elective Officers:

Municipal Judge, Board of Inspection.

Appointments:

Enumeration: City Clerk, City Attorney, Assessor, Chief of Police, City Physician, Fire Chief and City Engineer.

Manner: City Clerk, and City Attorney by majority vote of Council. Other officers by the Commissioner in charge.

Civil Service Provisions: None.

Election Provisions:

Follow general laws of the State, recognizing partisan and independent candidates.

Initiative:

Constitutional provisions.

Referendum:

Constitutional provisions.

Recall:

Twenty-five per centum petition. No recall during first four months after installation.

Franchises:

Public utility franchises must be submitted to a popular vote. Upon petition of twenty-five per centum of the electors, a special election must be called for the grant or renewal of a franchise.

Special Features:

The Charter calls for the election of a Board of three Freeholders, who constitute the Board of Inspection, and who cause the accounts of the City to be inspected once, at least, per annum, by an expert accountant and are required to make recommendations regarding the accounts to the City Council.

BARTLESVILLE

(Drafted by a Board of Freeholders, elected Apr. 5, 1910. Adopted by the people Aug. 2, 1910.)

Commission-Organization:

Title: Board of Commissioners.

Number: Three, including Mayor.

Term: Three years. Partial renewal.

Removal: Recall.

Salary: Two thousand dollars, subject to increase by popular vote.

Commissioner-Departments: 1, Public Affairs (Mayor); 2, Finance and Supplies; 3, Highways and Public Improvements.

General Commission Powers:

All corporate powers except as otherwise provided.

Special Requirements:

Quarterly statements of finances and proceedings. Commissioners must devote entire time to duties of office.

Mayor:

Term: Three years.

Salary: Two thousand dollars.

Removal: Recall.

Powers in Relation to Commission: Presides at meetings of Board. Votes on all questions. No veto power.

Appointments:

Enumeration: City Attorney, City Treasurer, City Assessor, Board of Parks and Cemeteries, Board of Library Trustees.

Manner: By the Commissioner in charge, subject to confirmation by the Board.

Civil Service Provisions: None.

Election Provisions:

State regulation, with provision for partisan primaries and independent nominations.

Initiative:

Constitutional provision.

Referendum:

Constitutional provision.

Recall:

Twenty-five per centum petition. No Recall in first four months after installation.

Franchises:

No franchise granted except with approval of people at general or special election. No franchise for over twenty-five years; city to have option of acquiring the property of public utility corporations upon payment of fair valuation at termination of the grant.

SAPULPA

(CHARTER DRAFTED BY A BOARD OF FREEHOLDERS, ELECTED APR. 5, 1910.)

Commission-Organization:

Title: Board of Commissioners.

Number: Four, including Mayor.

Term: Two years.

Removal: Recall.

Salary: Eighteen hundred dollars.

Commissioner-Departments: 1, Finance; 2, Public Works; 3, Public Safety. The Commissioner of Finance is ex-officio Treasurer. The Commissioner of Public Works is ex-officio Superintendent of Streets and Water Works.

General Commission Powers:

Such powers as are not reserved in the Constitution by the Initiative and Referendum to the people.

Mayor:

Term: Two years.

Salary: Two thousand dollars.

Removal: Recall.

Powers in relation to Commission: Presides at meetings. Has casting vote. Veto power.

Appointments:

Enumeration: City Clerk, City Auditor, City Attorney, City Engineer, City Assessor, Chief of Police, Chief of Fire Department, Judge of Police Court, City Physician.

Manner: Enumerated officers by Mayor, subject to the confirmation of the Board.

Civil Service Provisions: None.

Election Provisions:

Nomination by petition. Non-partisan elections. Second election if majority is received by no candidate at first.

Initiative:

Twenty-five per centum petition. (Elections as per Article XVIII of the Constitution.)

Referendum:

Twenty-five per centum petition. (Elections as per Article XVIII of the Constitution.)

Recall:

Twenty-five per centum petition.

Franchises:

City reserves right to fix charges for public utility service. No exclusive franchises. No franchises for more than twenty-five years. Franchises submitted on petition of twenty-five per centum of the electors.

DUNCAN

(HOME-MADE CHARTER DRAFTED BY A BOARD OF FREEHOLDERS. ADOPTED AUG. 16, 1910.)

Commission-Organization:

Title: Board of Commissioners.

Number: Three, including Mayor.

Term: Three years. Partial renewal.

Removal: Recall.

Salary: Four hundred and eighty dollars.

Commissioner-Departments: 1, Department of General Administration (Mayor); 2, Public Comfort, Health and Safety; 3, Public Works and Property.

General Commission Powers:

All legislative, executive and judicial powers.

Special Requirements:

Meetings must be held once a month. Monthly financial statements.

Mayor:

Term: Three years.

Salary: Six hundred dollars.

Removal: Recall.

Powers in Relation to Commission: President of the Board. No veto power.

Appointments:

Enumeration: City Clerk, Assessor, Treasurer, City Weigher, City Attorney, Municipal Judge, Chief of Police, City Physician, City Chemist, Sewer Inspector, Fire Chief, Gas Inspector, Building Inspector, Sidewalk Inspector, City Engineer, Auditor and Street Repairer.

Manner: By the Commissioner in charge.
Civil Service Provisions: None.

Election Provisions:

Officers "nominated by primary election (or proposed by petition) and elected at large by primary election as provided by the General Election Laws of the State of Oklahoma." It is unlawful for any candidate for office to promise employment or any article of value for the purpose of obtaining votes.

Initiative:

Constitutional provisions (*See Appendix*).

Referendum:

Constitutional provisions (*See Appendix*).

Recall:

Twenty-five per centum petition.

Franchises:

No exclusive franchises. City reserves right to regulate the charges for public service. Applicants for franchises must bear expense of election for submitting the question of the grant.

OKLAHOMA CITY

(HOME RULE CHARTER, DRAFTED BY A BOARD OF FREEHOLDERS, ELECTED NOVEMBER 8, 1910.)

Commission-Organization:

Title: Board of Commissioners.

Number: Five, including Mayor.

Term: Four years. Partial renewal every two years.

Removal: Recall.

Salary: Thirty-six hundred dollars.*

Commissioner-Departments: 1. Public Affairs (Mayor). 2. Accounting and Finance. 3. Public Safety. 4. Public Works. 5. Public Property. The Police Department is in charge of the Mayor.

General Commission Powers:

The legislative powers of the city.

Special Requirements:

Monthly financial statements.

Mayor:

Term: Four years.

Removal: Recall.

Powers in Relation to Commission: Presides at meetings of the Board. No veto power.

Salary: Four thousand dollars:*

Appointments:

Enumeration: Municipal Counsellor, Assistant Municipal Counsellor, Municipal Judge, Treasurer, Chief of Police, Chief of Fire Department, Assessor, Auditor, Clerk, Civil Engineer, City Physician, Street Commissioner, Superintendent of Water Works, five Library Trustees, Board of Park Commissioners.

Manner: Enumerated officials by majority vote of the Board of Commissioners. Other officials are appointed by the Commissioner in charge, subject to the confirmation of the Board, for a term of two years.

Civil Service Provisions: A board of three members established by the Charter; partial renewal of the board annually.

Initiative:

Cf. Appendix, p. 91,101.

Referendum:

Cf. Appendix, p. 91,101.

Recall:

Thirty-five percentum petition; containing at least 2500 signatures. No recall petition may be filed in the first six months of office.

Franchises:

No exclusive franchises. The city reserves the right to fix the rates at which service may be rendered by public service corporations.

The Board of Commissioners has power to impose an annual tax on gross receipts, a per capita tax on passengers transported, a license tax on cars used in transporting passengers, and all other taxes authorized by the Constitution and laws of the state and the charter.

Applicants for franchise grants must bear the expense of submitting questions to popular election.

* Provision is made for increase in salary when the population of the city reaches 100,000.

LAWTON

(Home Rule Charter, Adopted by popular vote Sept., 1911—Approved by the Governor.)

Commission-Organization:

Title: Board of Commissioners.

Number: Three, including Mayor.

Term: Two years.

Removal: Recall.

Salary: Two thousand dollars.

Commissioner-Departments: 1, Public Safety; 2, Finance; 3, Public Property; the Commissioners are elected to departments specified on the regular election ballot.

Each Commissioner has "actual management and control as superintendent and director in the affairs of his department."

"Any person, firm or corporation, feeling aggrieved at the decision or action of any one of the Commissioners in the transaction of the business of his department, shall have the right to appeal from said decision to the Board of Commissioners, by serving a written notice of such appeal upon the Commissioner within five days from the time of such decision or action."

General Commission Powers:

All the powers of the city.

Special Requirements:

Monthly departmental reports to the Commission are required.

Quarterly financial statements are required of the Board.

Mayor:

No officer is designated Mayor, but the Board elects one of its number chairman. This member presides at meetings of the Board, signs bonds and other instruments, administers oaths, and on him are served all legal processes against the city. He also performs the functions of City Clerk.

Appointments:

Enumeration: Municipal Judge, City Attorney (but the city may employ the services of a firm of attorneys).

Manner: Enumerated officers by a majority vote of the Commission; all others by the Commissioner in charge.

Civil Service Provisions:

It is the duty of the Board of Commissioners to provide, by ordinance, for the creation of a Board of Civil Service Commissioners "when the population of the city of Lawton shall have reached twenty thousand."

Election Provisions:

Names are placed upon the primary ballot on petition of twenty-five electors. The two persons receiving the highest number of votes at the primary are candidates at the second election. But names may also be placed upon the general election ballot by petition of twenty per centum of the voters of the city. Names of candidates are rotated by the printer of the ballots in such a way as to bring each name at the top of the list of candidates on an equal number of ballots.

Initiative:

Constitutional Provisions.

Referendum:

Constitutional Provisions.

Recall:

An original petition of ten signatures is filed in the office of one of the Commissioners not affected. This Commissioner is required to deliver a copy of the petition thus filed to the Commissioner affected and to cause it to be published in a local newspaper. During such publication any qualified voter may appear before the Commission who publishes the petition and sign the same. An election must be called upon the establishing of the genuineness of signatures equal to fifteen per centum of the highest number of votes cast for any Commissioner at the last municipal election.

The question submitted to the voters is the simple one of removal, but a primary election is held simultaneously and, if a majority of the votes are for removal, the selection of a successor is made at a subsequent election in the same manner as at a regular election. No recall petition may be filed within four months after the election of any officer.

COLLINSVILLE

(Home Rule Charter, drafted by an elective charter convention; filed November 24, 1914.)

Governing Body:

Title: Board of Commissioners.
Number: Three.
Terms: Three years.
Removal: Recall.
Salary: Five ($5) dollars per meeting.

Mayor:

The Board of Commissioners elects one of its number chairman, who is required to sign all ordinances, papers and documents of the Board.

Manager:

The "Business Manager" is "vested with the executive and judicial power and authority of the city, subject to supervision and control by the Board of Commissioners." He is required to make nominations for appointment to all offices, which shall be confirmed by the Board and to make a monthly financial statement.

ntments:

Enumeration: The Board may establish such offices and employments as may be necessary.
Manner: See "City Manager."
Civil Service Provisions: None.

Election Provisions:

Non-partisan primaries and general elections. Names of candidates are required to be rotated on the ballot. In cases where no candidate receives a majority of all votes cast, a second election is held.

Initiative:

The provisions of the constitution and general laws of the state are applicable.

Referendum:

See "Initiative."

Recall:

Twenty-five per centum petition.
No recall petition may be filed against an officer until four months after the beginning of his term. The recall election decides merely the question of removal, vacancies being filled by the remaining Commissioners or by popular election.

ARKANSAS STATUTE

(Cities of the First Class)

ACT OF THE LEGISLATURE, 1913, APPLICABLE TO CITIES HAVING A POPULATION OF BETWEEN 18,000 AND 40,000.)

mission Organization:

itle: Board of Commissioners.

umber: Five, including mayor.

erm: Four years. Partial renewal biennially.

emoval: Recall.

alary: Two thousand dollars.

Commissioner-Departments: Department of Public Affairs (Mayor), including functions of police judge, police department, city jail and relations with other municipalities; Commissioner No. 1 (Accounts and Finance), including functions of city clerk, tax collection, licensing, renting, printing and custody of city's funds (unless board of commissioners shall otherwise provide); Commissioner No. 2 (Health and Public Safety), including functions of fire and health department, city hospitals, building, lighting and heating departments, gas, electrical, plumbing and building inspection, collection and disposal of garbage, sanitation and sewerage; Commissioner No. 3 (Streets and Public Improvements), including opening, grading, paving, lighting, cleaning, repairing and sprinkling streets; sewer viaduct and bridge construction, sidewalks and crossings and functions of city engineering department; Commissioner No. 4 (Parks and Public Property), including charge of water works, parks, libraries and other property not delegated to other departments. Commissioners are elected to designated departments.

ieral Commission Powers:

All executive, legislative and judicial powers formerly exercised by the mayor, city council, board of public affairs and all other officers in cities of the first class.

Mayor:

Term: Four years.

Removal: Recall.

Salary: Twenty-four hundred dollars.

Powers: Is chief executive officer of the city, presides at all meetings of the council, but has no veto power; supervises all departments.

Appointments:

Enumeration: City Clerk, City Attorney, City Engineer, Chief of Police, City Physician, Chief of Fire Department.

Manner: By the Board of Commissioners.

Civil Service Provisions: The Board of Commissioners is required to appoint a Civil Service Board of three members, for terms of six years, expiring in rotation. The classified service includes all appointive offices and employees except those enumerated above and laborers.

Election Provisions:

Non-partisan primaries; names of candidates placed on ballot by petition of fifty voters and deposit of $10. The names of the two candidates receiving the highest number of votes at the primary are placed on the ballot at the regular election.

Candidates are prohibited from expending, to secure election, a sum greater than ten per centum of one year's salary of the office for which they are respectively candidates. No candidate may, directly or indirectly, use or cause to be used, more than one vehicle at any election for the purpose of transporting voters to the polling places and such vehicle may be used only to transport old or infirm persons.

ARKANSAS STATUTE—Continued

Initiative:

Twenty-five per centum (special election).
Fifteen per centum (general election).

Referendum:

Twenty-five per centum (special or general election).

Recall:

Thirty-five per centum petition. The election is held on the simple question of removal.

Franchises:

Any franchise may be submitted to popular v petition of twenty-five per centum.

Abandonment of Act:

Any city operating under this act may aband same by special election called upon the ini of twenty-five per centum of the electors four years of operation.

LOUISIANA STATUTE

(An Act approved Apr. 7, 1910, applicable to all cities having a population of at least seventy-five hundred, except New Orleans, Monroe, Baton Rouge and Lake Charles, upon adoption by popular vote. The question of adoption may be submitted on a petition of thirty-three per centum of the voters of the city.)

Commission-Organization:

Title: Council.

Number: In Cities over 25,000 population, five, including Mayor.

In Cities less than 25,000 population, three, including Mayor.

Term: Four years.

Removal: Recall.

Salary: Population 7,500 to 10,000, not more than $1,000.
Population 10,000 to 15,000, not more than $1,500.
Population 15,000 to 20,000, not more than $2,000.
Population 25,000 to 40,000, not more than $2,000.
Population 40,000 to 60,000, not more than $2,400.
Over 60,000 population, not more than $2,500.

Commissioner-Departments:

In Cities of over 25,000 population: 1, Public Affairs and Public Education (Mayor); 2, Accounts and Finance; 3, Public Safety; 4, Public Utilities; 5, Streets and Parks.

In Cities of less than 25,000 population: 1, Accounts, Finances and Public Utilities; 2, Public Safety, Streets and Parks.

General Commission Powers:

All the executive, legislative, judiciary and administrative powers.

Mayor:

Term: Four years.

Salary: Population 7,500 to 10,000, not more than $1,500.
Population 10,000 to 15,000, not more than $2,000.
Population 15,000 to 20,000, not more than $2,500.
Population 25,000 to 40,000, not more than $3,000.
Population 40,000 to 60,000, not more than $3,500.
Over 60,000 population, not more than $4,000.

Removal: Recall.

Appointments:

Enumeration: City Attorney, Secretary-Treasurer and Tax Collector, Auditor, Civil Engineer, City Physician.

Manner: The principal administrative officers are chosen by a majority vote of the Council, and removable in like manner at any time.

Civil Service Provisions: None.

Election Provisions:

Thirty-three per centum petition (special election).

Referendum:

Thirty-three per centum petition (special election).

Recall:

Thirty-three per centum petition.

Franchises:

Public Utility franchises must be submitted to popular vote at a special election.

The following cities have adopted this act: **Shreveport.**

NEW ORLEANS

(AN ACT OF THE LEGISLATURE, APPROVED JULY 11TH, 1912. ADOPTED BY POPULAR VOTE AUG. 28, 1912.)

Commission Organization:

Title: Commission Council.

Number: Five, including mayor.

Term: Four years.

Removal: In the manner provided in the state constitution.

Salary: Six thousand dollars.

Commissioner-Departments: 1, Public Affairs, including subdivisions of Law, Civil Service and Publicity; 2, Public Finances, including subdivisions of Assessment of Private Property, Receipts and Expenditures of Public Money and Accounts of Public Money; 3, Public Safety, including subdivisions of Fire Prevention and Relief, Police, Health and Charity and Relief; 4, Public Utilities, including subdivisions of Public Service Corporations and Franchises; 5, Public Property, including subdivisions of Streets and Alleys, Park and Playgrounds, Public Buildings and Public Baths. Designation by the council: The Board of Commissioners of the Police Department consists of the Mayor, the Commissioner of Public Safety and one other commissioner selected by the Commission Council. The Board of Commissioners of the Fire Department consists of the Mayor, the Commissioner of Public Safety and one other commissioner selected by the Commission Council. The Board of Health consists of the mayor, the Commissioner of Public Safety and three other members at large to be selected by the Commission Council.

General Commission Powers:

All executive, legislative and other powers and duties formerly exercised by all municipal officers in the city of New Orleans.

Mayor:

Term: Four years.

Salary: Ten thousand dollars.

Removal: In the manner provided in the constitution.

Powers: Has general supervision of city departments; signs all contracts, bonds and other instruments requiring the assent of the city; is ex-officio a member of each board, commission or body authorized by charter or ordinance.

Appointments:

Enumeration: The following, whose compensation is fixed in the charter, are appointed by the Commission Council: City Attorney, City Notary, Judges and Clerks of the Recorder's Court, Clerk of the Commission Council, Auditor of Public Accounts, Chief Engineer of the Fire Department Superintendent of Police, Superintendent of Public Health, City Engineer and City Chemist. The City Engineer may appoint one, and the City Attorney two assistants, whose compensation is fixed in the charter.

Manner: All officers not enumerated above must be chosen in accordance with the rules governing the Classified Civil Service under Act 89 of 1900. Any officer chosen by the Commission Council may be removed at any time by a vote of four members. The Civil Service Board consists of the Mayor and two commissioners to be selected by the Commission Council.

Civil Service Provisions: Cf. foregoing section.

Elective Provisions:

The general election laws of the state apply.

Initiative:

* Thirty per centum petition (special election).

Referendum:

* Thirty per centum petition (special election).

Recall:

No provision.

*Registered vote. Each signer must make affidavit that he has read and understands the ordinance.

MISSISSIPPI HOME RULE LAW

By an enabling act, approved Mar. 31, 1908, (*Chapter* 108, *Laws of* 1908), all Cities of the State have the option of coming under a Commission government law, which provides that there shall be an Aldermanic body composed of three or five members to be elected at large, one of the number to be voted for as Mayor.

The powers and duties of Mayor and Aldermanic bodies and of all elective municipal officers are devolved upon the *Mayor and Commissioners* and subordinate officers under the Commission form. Additional power is given to the Commission to appoint all necessary subordinate officers not specified in the City Charter to be elective, and to prescribe the duties of subordinate officers both elective and appointive, and to fix the salaries and to remove all such officers for cause.

Franchises are subject to Compulsory Referendum. Commission must hold at least weekly meetings for the purpose of conferring, also formal meetings must be held once a month, in which the record of the preceding month's work must be made. All elected municipal officials must attend these meetings.

If a petition charging misconduct against any official, signed by ten voters, is presented to the Mayor, the latter must at once order an investigation of such officer.

In order to adopt this form of government, a petition must be circulated and signed by at least ten per centum of the voters. This petition must show the number of Commissioners, time that each Commissioner must devote to public duties, salaries per month, amount of bond to be given and a statement of such other officers as the municipality may desire to elect.

If the election carries, the Governor issues a Charter. The Municipality may amend this Charter by local election so far as the number of Commissioners, time required of each, salary and bond are concerned.

[*The following cities have adopted charters* in pursuance of this act:* **Clarksdale, Hattiesburg.**]

* Text not available for first edition of this publication.

MISSISSIPPI STATUTE

(An Act of the Legislature applicable to all cities upon adoption at a special election called upon petition of ten per centum of the qualified electors. Chapter 120, Laws of 1912. Approved March 15, 1912.)

Commission-Organization:

Title: Council.

Number: Three, including Mayor.

Term: Four years.

Removal: Statutory procedure.

Salary: Fixed by ordinance, approved by popular vote.

Commissioner-Departments: Defined and designated by ordinance, each member of the council being the head of one department.

General Powers of Commission:

All legislative, executive and judicial powers previously exercised by the mayor and board of aldermen and all other officers, commissioners, trustees, boards, etc.

Note also the following provisions (Sec. 24):

"Sec. 24. When any city operating under the provisions of this act shall desire to extend, diminish or limit the powers and duties to be exercised by the Council of such city or the members thereof, the same may be done as follows: The Council may adopt an ordinance so extending, diminishing, or limiting the powers or duties to be exercised by such Council or the members thereof, as desired, and shall, after the passage and adoption thereof by the Council, submit the same for the approval of the qualified electors of such city at a general or special election to be held not less than thirty, nor more than sixty days after the adoption of such ordinance by the Council. If at such election, a two-thirds majority of the qualified electors of such city voting thereon shall be in favor of such ordinance, then a certified copy of such ordinance, together with all proceedings thereon, including a copy of the returns of such election, shall be submitted to the Governor, who shall submit the same to the Attorney-General for his opinion. If the Attorney-General be of the opinion that the said ordinance is consistent with the Constitution and the laws of the United States, and of the Constitution of this State, and not inconsistent with the provisions of this Act, the Governor shall thereupon approve such ordinance, and the same shall be thereupon recorded, at the expense of such municipality, in the office of the Secretary of State, and in the ordinance book of such city, and when so recorded, shall have the force and effect of law."

Special Requirements:

Quarterly financial statements.

Mayor:

Term: Four years.

Removal: Statutory procedure.

Salary: See provisions re other commissioners.

Special Powers: President of the Council; has general supervision of all departments.

Appointments:

Manner: By majority vote of the Council.

The following provisions (Sec. 19a) for the removal of appointees of the Council should be noted:

"Sec. 19a. Any officer or employee of any city operating under this Act, elected, appointed or employed by the Council, may, in addition to being discharged or removed at any time by the Council, be discharged or removed by the qualified electors of such city in the following manner: One or more petitions, signed and sworn to as required of other petitions, under this Act, demanding of the Council the removal or discharge of any such officer or employee, shall be filed with the City Clerk, all of which petitions, if more than one, shall be of like tenor and effect, and shall contain a statement of the grounds for which removal or discharge is sought. One of the signers of each petition shall also make oath before an officer competent to administer oaths, that the causes for removal or discharge contained in such petitions, are, as he believes, true in substance and in fact. If the petition or petitions after being verified, examined and certified by the Clerk, as provided for in this Act, shall be found

(Over)

to be insufficient, the Council shall, at its next regular meeting, either remove or discharge such officer or employee, or order and fix the date for holding a special election not less than thirty nor more than sixty days from the date of such order; which election shall be conducted, returned and the results thereof declared in all respects as other municipal elections. The ballots used at said special elections shall be in the following form:

"For the Removal of (name of officer or employee sought to be removed).

"Against the Removal of (name of officer or employee sought to be removed)."

If at such election a majority of those voting shall vote for the removal of such officer or employee, he shall *ipso facto* be removed or discharged.

No petition shall be circulated for the removal or discharge of any such officer or employee until after such petition, signed by at least twenty-five qualified electers of such city, shall have been published in some newspaper published in such city for a period of ten days.

If the City Clerk is sought to be removed under this section, the petition provided for herein shall be filed with the Mayor, or one of the Councilmen, who shall deal therewith in all respects the same as the Clerk is required to do with similar petitions.

Election Provisions:

Nomination for the Council are made at party primaries in the manner prescribed by state law. A plurality vote is sufficient for choice at the official election.

Initiative:

Any ordinance providing for the undertakin construction of any public work or improv and providing for the necessary funds th may be adopted by petition of twenty-fiv centum of the qualified electors and a ma vote at a general or special election. But petitions must, before being submitted, b proved as to legality by the Attorney-Gener

Referendum:

Twenty-five per centum petition.

Recall:

Not applicable to electiove officers. See *"Ap ments"* (*supra*).

Franchises:

No exclusive franchises; no franchise for a period than twenty-five years. Every fra must be approved by popular vote.

Abandonment of Act:

Operation under this act may be discontinue six years.

COLORADO SPRINGS

(Charter framed by a Charter Convention Mar. 20, 1909; adopted May 11, 1909.)

Commission-Organization:

Title: Council.

Number: Five, including Mayor.

Term: Four years. Partial renewal.

Removal: Recall.

Salary: Two thousand dollars.

Commissioner-Departments: 1, Water and Water Works (Mayor); 2, Finance; 3, Public Safety; 4, Public Works and Property; 5, Public Health and Sanitation. Designation by Council.

General Commission Powers:

All the powers of the city except as otherwise provided, subject to the distribution and delegation of the same provided in Charter or by ordinance.

Special Requirements:

Monthly statements of receipts and disbursements. Must establish a system of uniform accounts.

Mayor:

Term: Four years.

Salary: Thirty-six hundred dollars.

Removal: Recall. Also by vote of four members of the Council.

Powers in Relation to Commission: Veto on items in appropriation measures.

Special Requirements: Specially charged with the supervision of franchises and public utilities.

Appointments:

Manner: Heads of Departments, deputies and principal assistants created by Charter or by ordinance, other employees except day laborers, appointed by the Mayor upon the recommendation of the Commissioner in charge. Mayor appoints all officers and employees whose election or appointment is not otherwise provided for.

Civil Service Provisions: Charter provides a Board of three. Terms, six years. Partial renewal.

Election Provisions:

Names go on primary ballots by petition of twenty-five signatures. Non-partisan elections. Second election, if necessary to secure majority for any candidate. The use of carriages on election day is prohibited.

Initiative:

Fifteen per centum petition (special election).

Five per centum petition (general election).

Referendum:

Fifteen per centum petition (general or special election).

Council of its own motion may submit questions to popular vote.

Recall:

Thirty per centum petition. No recall within first six months after installation.

Franchises:

No franchise grant except by vote of the people. No exclusive franchises. No franchise for over twenty-five years. Council may grant revocable permits to use the streets.

GRAND JUNCTION

(FRAMED BY A CHARTER CONVENTION AUG. 6, 1909. ADOPTED SEPT. 14, 1909.)

Commission-Organization:

Title: City Council.

Number: Five, including Mayor.

Term: Four years.

Removal: Recall.

Salary: Twelve hundred dollars.

Commissioner-Departments: 1, Public Affairs; 2, Finance and Supplies; 3, Highways; 4, Health and Civic Beauty; 5, Water and Sewers.

The Commissioner of Public Affairs is Judge of the Corporation Court and head of the Police and Fire Departments of the City, and Superintendent of public utilities not owned and managed directly by the City.

The Commissioner of Finance and Supplies is ex-officio City Treasurer and Purchasing Agent of the City. He is also City Collector.

The Commissioner of Health and Civic Beauty has general supervision of parks and shade trees, and has power to supervise the architectural beauty of the City and to make recommendations as to color, style, and character of buildings, painting, sidewalks, etc.

General Commission Powers:

All the legislative, executive and administrative powers.

Special Requirements:

The City Council has no power to make contracts of any kind, or leases of City property, the operation of which extend beyond the time of the new Commissioner's election at any general municipal election.

Mayor:

Term: Four years.

Salary: Fifteen hundred dollars.

Removal: Recall.

Powers in Relation to Commission: President of Council. Votes on all questions. No veto power.

Appointments:

By nomination of the heads of the departments, subject to confirmation of the City Council and subject to removal by the Council at any time.

Civil Service Provisions: A Civil Service Commission is established and consists of three members whose powers and duties are determined by ordinance, but appointments may not be made until Jan. 1, 1913.

Election Provisions:

Nominations to elective offices upon petition of twenty-five voters. The ballots for the election of officers provide for a system of preferential voting. (*See full text of election provisions in text of G. J. Charter, and also article by Robert Tyson.*)

Initiative:

Ten per centum petition based upon vote for Governor at last general election, (for submission at special election), five per centum petition (general election).

Referendum:

Ten per centum petition (as above), general or special election.

Recall:

Twenty per centum petition. No recall petition in first three months after installation.

Franchises:

Franchises relating to streets, alleys and public places are granted only upon the vote of the qualified tax paying electors.

DENVER

(Amendments to the City and County Charter, submitted under the Initiative and adopted by popular vote Feb. 14, 1913.)

Commission Organization:

Title: Council.

Number: Five, including Mayor.

Term: Four years. Partial renewal every two years.

Removal: Recall.

Salary: Five thousand dollars.

Commissioner-Departments: 1, Property, exercising functions of County Clerk and Recorder of Deeds, City Clerk, Recorder, Public Utilities Commission, Park Commission, Playgrounds Commission, Building Inspector, Inspector of Electric Wiring and Plumbing, Boiler and Elevator Inspector and Electrician; 2, Finance, exercising functions of County Treasurer and County Assessors, City Treasurer, City Assessor, Commission of Supplies and Excise Commissioner; 3, Safety, exercising functions of Sheriff, Department of Fire, Police and Excise (except those relating to Excise): 4, Improvements, exercising functions of County Surveyor, Board of Public Works, Engineer, Commissioner of Highways, Superintendent of Street Sprinkling and Art Commission; 5, Social Welfare, exercising functions of County Superintendent of Schools and County Coroner, Commissioner of Charity and Correction, Library Commission, Health Commissioner and Market Master. Commissioners are elected to particular departments but may be transferred from one department to another by affirmative vote of four members.

General Commission Powers:

All legislative powers possessed by the city and county, except as otherwise provided in the amendment adopted Feb. 14, 1913.

The Mayor:

Selected by the Council from their own number and removable at their pleasure; acts as presiding officer but has no veto power.

Other Elective Officers:

Election Commissioner.

Auditor.

Appointments:

Enumeration: Two Justices of the Peace and two constables appointed by the Council.

Manner: The Commissioner of each department is authorized to appoint all officers, commissions, boards and employees assigned to his department.

Civil Service Provisions: The original charter (1904) provided for a commission of three, appointed by the mayor.

Election Provisions:

Preferential voting with first, second and third choices when the number of candidates for any office is more than two. Names placed upon ballot by petition of not less than one hundred voters. Each candidate in his letter of acceptance is required to make affidavit that he is not a candidate, directly or indirectly, of any political party, or of any person, firm, or corporation owning, interested in, or intending to apply for any franchise, license or contract with the city.

Initiative:

Five per centum petition (general election).

Fifteen per centum petition (special election).

Referendum:

Five per centum petition (general election).

Fifteen per centum petition (special election).

Recall:

Twenty-five per centum petition.

MONTROSE

(Home Rule Charter, drafted by an elected charter convention. Adopted by popular vote January 14, 1914.)

Governing Body:

Title: City Council.
Number: Five.
Term: Two years.
Removal: Recall.
Salary: Ten (10) dollars per month.

Mayor:

The City Council elects from its own number one member who acts as presiding officer, with the title of mayor, but with no veto power.

City Manager:

Sec. 36. The City Manager shall have the following powers and duties:

First: To appoint and remove all officers and employees in his departments necessary to carry out the duties imposed upon him by Section 65, Article VII, of this charter, or any other duties imposed upon him by this charter, or the City Council, except as herein otherwise provided, and to fix their compensation. He shall not appoint any relative of his to any office of trust.

Second: To attend all meetings of the City Council with right to take part in any discussion and to recommend to the City Council such measures as he may deem necessary or expedient; but he shall have no vote.

Third: To keep the City Council fully advised as to the financial condition and needs of the City.

Fourth: To perform such other duties as may be prescribed by this charter or be required of him by ordinance or resolution of the City Council.

Sec. 37. The City Manager shall receive a salary not to exceed Eighteen Hundred Dollars ($1,800.00) per annum.

Sec. 46. The City Manager shall be the purchasing and sales agent for all personal property for the city and shall procure all supplies, issuing a requisition therefor. Such requisition shall be in writing, and shall state the quality, quantity and kind of material required, whether urgency demands that the order be made by wire, whether the supplies should come by express or otherwise, and the probable cost thereof, in detail, if known. Except in case of emergency he shall advertise for competition proposals for any supplies in a newspaper, or by circular letters, or other means, sent to several competitive dealers where estimated cost exceeds One Hundred Dollars ($100.00), and competitive bids shall be kept on file in the office of the City Manager.

Sec. 65. The City Manager shall, in accordance with the Revised Statutes of Colorado of 1908 and all amendatory acts thereto and subject to the supervision and control of the City Council in all matters, and the ordinances of the city, manage and have charge of the construction, improvements, repairs, and maintainance of streets, sidewalks, alleys, lanes, bridges, viaducts and other public highways; of water works, sewers, drains, ditches, culverts, canals, streams and water courses, gutters and curbing; of all public buildings, of boulevards, squares and other public places and grounds belonging to the city or dedicated to public use, except parks and play grounds; the cleaning, sprinkling and lighting of streets and public places, the collection and disposal of waste, and the care and preservation of all tools, appliances and personal property belonging to the city. He shall have supervision of issuing building permits, the inspecting of plumbing, wiring and weights and measures. He shall also have charge of the enforcement of all the obligations of privately owned or operated public utilities enforceable by the city.

Appointments:

Enumeration: City Manager, City Attorney, Police Magistrate, Board of Library Commissioners and Board of Cemetery and commissioners.
Manner: Enumerated officers by the City Council; all others by the City Manager.
Civil Service Provisions: None.

Election Provisions:

The general laws of the state apply.

Initiative:

Five per centum petition (general election.
Fifteen per centum petition (special election).

Referendum:

Five per centum petition (general election).
Fifteen per centum petition (special election).

Recall:

Twenty-five per centum petition. The procedure followed is that set forth in Article XXI of the Constitution of Colorado.

UTAH STATUTE

(AN ACT OF THE LEGISLATURE, 1911. MANDATORY FOR ALL CITIES OF THE FIRST AND SECOND CLASSES.)

Commission-Organization:

Title: Board of Commissioners.

Number: In cities of the first class: five, including Mayor. In cities of the second class: three, including Mayor.

Term: Four years. Partial renewal every two years.

Removal: In the manner prescribed by previous statutes.

Salary: In cities of the first class having more than 20,000 population, $3,600; less than 20,000 population, not less* than $500 nor more than $1,500 per annum.

Commissioner-Departments: 1, Public Affairs and Finance (Mayor); 2, Water Supply and Water Works; 3, Public Safety; 4, Streets and Public Improvements; 5, Parks and Public Property. Designation by the Board of Commissioners.

General Commission Powers:

All powers formerly exercised by the Mayor, City Council and Board of Public Works.

Special Requirements:

Monthly financial statements.

Mayor:

Term: Four years.

Removal: In the manner prescribed by previous statutes.

Powers in relation to Commission: Presides at meetings of Board. No veto power.

Salary: In cities of the second class having more than 20,000 population, $4,200; having less than 20,000 population, not less* than $600 nor more than $2,000 per annum.

Other Elective Officers:

Auditor, for a term of two years.

Appointments:

Enumeration: City Recorder, City Treasurer, City Attorney.

Manner: By majority vote of the Board.

Election Provisions:

Partisan nominations may be made by convention, but all candidates must file a petition of nomination signed by one hundred voters. Candidates to twice the number of offices to be filled, receiving the highest number of votes cast at the primary election, are the candidates at the general election.

Initiative:

No provisions.

Referendum:

No provisions.

Recall:

No provisions.

* Fixed by the City Council at least 15 days prior to the election of Commissioners.

NEW MEXICO STATUTE

(Laws of 1909, Page 236, approved Mar. 18, 1909.)

This act permits cities of over 3,000 population, according to the latest school census, to incorporate under it, and any city by a petition of five hundred voters, addressed to the Mayor and Council or to the County Board of Commissioners, if the community is not organized, may have the question of its adoption submitted at a special election.

The act provides for the election of three commissioners as follows:

1. Commissioner of Public Works and Public Safety.
2. Commissioner of Accounts and Finance.
3. Commissioner of Public Property and Public Improvement.

The Mayor is ex-officio president of Public Works and Public Property. The three Commissioners are elected at large for two years and receive no salary. Together they constitute the City Council. The City Clerk is also elected. Provision is made for the selection by the Mayor and Councilmen of the "Superintendent of Public Affairs" whose duties are outlined as follows:

Sec. 10.

After the organization of any city council under this act it shall employ a competent person, who shall be designated as the "superintendent of city affairs," who, before entering upon the discharge of his duties, shall file his oath of office and enter into a bond to the city of not less than $5,000, and more, if required by the city council by resolution, for the faithful performance of his duties as in the duty of said "superintendent of city affairs,' to take charge of all public matters of the city, under the direction of the mayor and the city council; to direct street improvement, care for and repair all streets and all public improvements, and to direct the use, extension, repair and maintenance of all public utilities; to see that the city is kept in proper sanitary condition and safe for life and property. And it shall be his duty to submit to the mayor and the city council at the regular meeting of the city council, held in the month of March of each year, a detailed estimate, as near as is practicable, of the expense of maintaining streets, alleys, public grounds, of keeping a proper sanitary condition, and the estimate and expense of any improvement which may be necessary and contemplated by said superintendent, the mayor and city council, and he shall make such recommendations to said mayor and city council as may seem to the best interests of the city, and he shall, at all times, when necessary, consult the mayor and city council upon all matters pertaining to the city's welfare and the comfort and convenience thereof. The mayor and city council may change, alter and reduce estimates, the cost of improvement and repairs of streets, alleys and other matters pertaining to the city's affairs; or said mayor and city council may increase said estimates and enlarge any and all improvements or repairs to be made. It is contemplated in this act that the superintendent shall, with the advice and consent of the city council, direct all public matters of the city in which the inhabitants of the city are interested, either directly or indirectly and which pertains to the city's affairs, the comfort and convenience of its people. Said general superintendent shall give his entire time and attention to the city's affairs, and for which he is employed, and he shall not, at any time engage in any work or occupation and his compensation shall be as may be determined by the mayor and the city council and fixed by resolution, and shall not be increased or diminished for two years after being so determined and fixed, or during the period of his employment without his consent.

The second part of the act provides an alternative form, by which the Mayor and not less than two nor more than four commissioners may be entrusted with the government of the city. The salary of the Mayor in this case is fixed at eighteen hundred dollars and that of the Commissioners at fourteen hundred dollars and none of them may be otherwise employed.

The City of **Roswell** *is organized under the first form provided in this Act.*

NEW MEXICO STATUTE

(Repealing Statute Approved March 18, 1909. This Page Replaces Former One of Same Number.)
(AN ACT OF THE LEGISLATURE, APPLICABLE TO ANY CITY OF NOT LESS THAN 3,000 INHABITANTS, WHEN ADOPTED BY POPULAR VOTE AT A SPECIAL ELECTION CALLED UPON PETITION OF TWENTY-FIVE PER CENTUM OF THE ELECTORS THEREIN.)

Commission-Organization:

Title: Commission.

Number: Three, including mayor.

Term: Two years.

Removal: Statutory procedure.

Salary: Not over nine hundred dollars.

Commissioner - Departments: Determined by ordinance. Designation by the Commission.

General Commission Powers:

The corporate powers of the city.

Mayor:

Term: Two years.

Removal: Statutory procedure.

Salary: Not over one thousand dollars.

Powers: Presides over Commission; no veto power.

Appointments:

Enumeration: City Attorney, Treasurer, Civil Engineer, City Physician, Marshal, Chief of Fire Department.

Manner: By majority vote of the Council.

Civil Service Provisions: None.

Election Provisions:

The general laws of the state apply.

Initiative:

No provisions.

Referendum:

No provisions.

Recall:

No provisions.

WYOMING STATUTE

(An Act of the Legislature approved Feb. 21, 1911. Applicable to cities formerly operating under special charters, having a population exceeding 10,000, cities of the first class, and cities and towns having a population of not less than 7,000, when adopted by popular election called upon petition of 15 per centum of the registered voters.)

Commission-Organization:

Title: Council.

Number: Three, including Mayor.

Term: Four years, except in cities of the first class, in which the term is two years.

Removal: Recall.

Salary: $2,000, unless fixed at a less amount by ordinance.

Commissioner-Departments: 1, Public Affairs (Mayor); 2, Accounts, Finance, Parks and Public Property; 3, Streets and Public Improvements. Designation to departments by the Council. The two commissioners are police judges, but any city may, by ordinance, provide other methods of filling these positions.

General Commission Powers:

All legislative, executive, judicial and other powers and duties formerly possessed and exercised by the Mayor, City Council and other executive and administrative officers of the city.

Special Requirements:

Monthly itemized financial statements. (The State Examiner is required to make an annual examination of the accounts of the city.)

Mayor:

Term: Four years, except in cities of the first class, in which the term is two years.

Removal: Recall.

Salary: $2,400, unless fixed at a less amount by ordinance.

Appointments:

Enumeration: City Clerk, Attorney, Treasurer, Civil Engineer, Health Officer, Chief of Police, Chief of Fire Department. The salaries of these officers are fixed by the statute.

Manner: By majority vote of the Council; removals at any time in the same manner.

Civil Service Provisions:

None.

Election Provisions:

Nomination for primary election on petition of twenty-five electors. The two candidates for Mayor and the four candidates for commissioner receiving the highest number of votes at the primary are the candidates at the second election. But no primary election is held unless the number of candidates exceeds two and four respectively. Non-partisan ballots.

Initiative:

Twenty-five per centum petition.

Referendum:

Thirty-five per centum petition (special election). Ten per centum petition (general election).

Recall:

Twenty-five per centum petition.

SAN DIEGO

(An Amendment to the Charter. Senate Concurrent Resolution of Jan. 12, 1909.)

Commission-Organization:

Title: Common Council.

Number: Four and Mayor.

Term: Four years.

Removal: Recall.

Salary: Two thousand dollars.

Commissioner-Departments: 1, Finance, Ways and Means; 2, Police, Health and Morals; 3, Public Streets and Buildings; 4, Fire and Sewers; 5, Water. Designation by Council.

General Commission Powers:

All powers formerly exercised by the Common Council, the Board of Public Works and Boards of Fire and Police Commissioners.

Mayor:

Term: Four years.

Salary: Two thousand dollars.

Removal: Recall.

Powers in Relation to Commission: Not a member of Council, but has general supervision of the administration of the city's affairs; has veto power.

Other Elective Officers:

City Treasurer.

Appointments:

Enumeration: City Attorney, City Clerk, City Engineer, Chief of Fire Department.

Manner: Enumerated officers by majority vote of Common Council. Members of the Boards of Health, Cemetery and Park Commissioners, and Auditor, by Mayor, subject to confirmation of the Common Council.

Election Provisions:

Non-partisan primaries; names placed on ballot by petition. The two candidates or groups of candidates receiving the highest number of votes at the primary are candidates at the regular election.

Initiative:

Fifteen per centum petition (special election).
Five per centum petition (general election).

Referendum:

Seven per centum petition (special or general election).

Recall:

Twenty-five per centum petition.

Franchises:

No exclusive franchises. Every franchise grant subject to right of Common Council to repeal or change.

BERKELEY

(CHARTER DRAFTED BY A BOARD OF FREEHOLDERS, RATIFIED AT A POPULAR ELECTION JAN. 30, 1909.)

Commission-Organization:

Title: Council.

Number: Five, including Mayor.

Term: Four years.

Removal: Recall.

Salary: Eighteen hundred dollars.

Commissioner-Departments: 1, Finance and Revenue; 2, Public Health and Safety; 3, Public Works; 4, Public Supplies. Designation by the Council.

General Commission Powers:

All corporate powers of the city.

Mayor:

Term: Two years.

Salary: Twenty-four hundred dollars.

Removal: Recall.

Powers in relation to Commission: Votes on all questions in Council. No veto power.

Special Requirements: Especially charged with oversight of contracts and public utilities.

Other Elective Officers:

Auditor.

Appointments:

Enumeration: The chief officials of the city are the City Clerk, City Assessor, Treasurer, Collector, Attorney, Engineer, Chief of Police, Fire Chief, Street Superintendent, Health Officer and five Library Trustees.

Manner: The chief officials are appointed and removable by a majority vote of the Council. The Council may consolidate the functions and duties of two or more officers, and may determine the manner of appointment of subordinates.

Civil Service Provisions: Council authorized to establish a Civil Service Commission, to act without compensation. Partial renewal.

Election Provisions:

Names of candidates placed on primary election ballot on petition of twenty-five voters. Second elections, if necessary to secure majority for any office.

Initiative:

Fifteen per centum petition (special election).

Five per centum petition (general election).

Referendum:

Ten per centum petition (general or special election). The Council may, of its own initiative, submit questions to popular vote.

Recall:

Twenty per centum petition. No recall petition in first three months after installation.

Franchises:

All franchises subject to a Compulsory Referendum. No franchise to be assigned without the consent of the Council.

MODESTO

(SPECIAL CHARTER, DRAWN BY A BOARD OF FREEHOLDERS, ELECTED APR. 11, 1910. ADOPTED SEP. 14, 1910. SUBJECT TO THE FORMAL APPROVAL OF THE LEGISLATURE AT ITS SESSION OF 1911.)

Commission-Organization:

Title: Council.

Number: Five, including Mayor.

Term: Four years. Partial renewal.

Removal: Recall.

Salary: None, unless authorized by popular vote.

Commissioner-Departments: 1, Finance and Revenue; 2, Public Health and Safety; 3, Public Works; 4, Public Supplies. Designation by the City Council.

General Commission Powers:

All corporate powers.

Special Requirements:

Monthly financial statements.

Mayor:

Term: Four years.

Salary: None, unless authorized by popular vote.

Removal: Recall.

Powers: Especially charged with oversight of public utility corporations. President of the Council.

No veto power.

Appointed Officers:

Enumeration: City Clerk, Auditor, Assessor, Treasurer, Collector, Attorney, Engineer, Chief of Police, Fire Chief, Street Superintendent, Building Inspector, Sewer Inspector, Health Officer and five Library Trustees.

Manner: Majority vote of the Council. Manner of appointing deputies to be determined by ordinance.

Civil Service Provisions: The City Council is authorized to establish a Civil Service Commission.

Election Provisions:

Non-partisan primaries; names placed on ballots by petition of twenty-five voters. Not more than two candidates for each office at second election.

Initiative:

Twenty-five per centum petition (special election).
Fifteen per centum petition (general election).
Not more than one special election in a period of twelve months.

Referendum:

Twenty-five per centum petition (special election).

Recall:

Fifteen per centum petition. The question submitted at the Recall election is the simple one, whether the officer shall or shall not be removed. A successor, if any, is chosen at a subsequent election.

Franchises:

Compulsory Referendum of all franchises. No exclusive franchises.

Special Features:

The City Council is authorized to establish a Uniform System of Accounts.

OAKLAND

(A Charter drafted by a Board of Freeholders, elected July 6, 1910. Adopted Dec. 8, 1910. Subject to the formal approval of the Legislature at its session of 1911.)

Commission-Organization:

Title: City Council.

Number: Five, including Mayor.

Term: Four years. Partial renewal.

Removal: Recall.

Salary: Thirty-six hundred dollars.

Commissioner-Departments: 1, Public Affairs; 2, Revenue and Finance; 3, Public Health and Safety; 4, Public Works; 5, Streets. Council makes designations by a majority vote. The Department of Public Affairs, which is under supervision of the Mayor, deals with matters in which the State is brought into relation with the government of the United States, of the State, and the County and other municipalities. The Commissioner of Finance is ex-officio member of the Board of Education.

General Commission Powers:

All the general powers of the City.

Special Requirements:

The installation of a uniform system of accounts is mandatory.

Mayor:

Term: Four years.

Salary: Forty-two hundred dollars.

Removal: Recall.

Powers: President of Council. No veto power. Especially charged with the supervision of public utility corporations.

Other Elective Officers:

Auditor, who is ex-officio Assessor.

Salary: Thirty-six hundred dollars.

Appointments:

Enumeration: There are certain officers designated as "Chief Officials" as follows: City Attorney, City Treasurer, City Engineer, Chief of Police, Chief of Fire Department, City Superintendent, Health Officers, Superintendent of Electrical Department; but the Council may, by vote of four members, consolidate the functions of two or more Chief Officials by a vote of three members, and the Board may remove any of the Chief Officials of the City. The salaries of these officials and of the principal subordinates are fixed by the Charter.

Manner: The appointment of the "Chief Officials" is made, with certain designated exceptions, by the Commissioner in charge, subject to the confirmation of the Council. The City Attorney and the City Clerk are appointed by the Council. Provision is made for a Board of Library Directors—five in number, appointed by the Mayor, subject to confirmation of the Council. The Board of Play-Ground Directors, appointed in the same manner, has exclusive control over play-grounds and the exclusive right to elect and superintend construction of buildings thereon for playground purposes. Directors are authorized to employ and appoint superintendents and assistants. The Board of Park Directors, appointed in like manner, has exclusive control and management of parks and public grounds, with power to erect municipal buildings thereon and to employ assistants.

Civil Service Provisions: A Board of three is appointed by the Mayor, subject to confirmation by the Council. Partial renewal.

Election Provisions:

Double elections. Non-partisan primary. Nomination by petition of not less than fifty nor more than two hundred and fifty individual certificates. Commissioners are elected by number.

Initiative:

Five per centum petition (general election).

Fifteen per centum petition (special election).

(Over.)

Two or more ordinances proposed for the purpose of securing the same result may be submitted at the same time and the voter may choose between any ordinance or none, or may express his preference for any one. If the majority of votes on the first action is affirmative, then the ordinance receiving the highest number of votes becomes law and the others fail of passage.

Referendum:

Ten per centum petition, but not less than 2,000 signatures. (General or special election.) The Council of its own initiative, may submit any question at a general election.

Recall:

Fifteen per centum petition. The petition contai the answer of the officer sought to be removed the reasons given for removal. A subsequent r call of the same officer requires a twenty p centum petition. No recall during the first si months of office.

Franchises:

Compulsory Referendum of all franchises.

VALLEJO

(HOME RULE CHARTER, DRAFTED BY A BOARD OF FREEHOLDERS, BY AUTHORITY OF ARTICLE XI OF THE CONSTITUTION. ADOPTED FEBRUARY, 1911.)

Commission-Organization:

Title: Council.

Number: Three, including Mayor.

Term: Four years. Partial renewal.

Removal: Recall.

Salary: Eighteen hundred dollars.

Commissioner-Departments: 1. Finance and Supplies (Mayor). 2. Public Health and Safety. 3. Public Works. Designation by Council.

General Commission Powers:

The corporate powers.

Special Requirements:

Must establish a uniform system of accounts.

Mayor:

Term: Four years.

Salary: Twenty-four hundred dollars.

Removal: Recall.

Powers in Relation to Commission: Specially charged with the supervision of public utilities.

Other Elective Officers:

Auditor, who is ex-officio Assessor.

Appointments:

Enumeration: City Clerk, Treasurer, who is ex-officio Tax Collector, Attorney, Engineer, Chief of Police, Fire Chief, Street Superintendent, Health officer, three Library Trustees.

Manner:

Chief officials by the Council. The Council may provide for the appointment and removal of subordinates.

Civil Service Provisions:

The Council has power to establish a Commission.

Election Provisions:

Non-partisan primaries; nomination by petition of twenty-five voters. A second election is held if necessary to secure a majority. Councilmen voted for by number.

Initiative:

Fifteen percentum petition (special election); five percentum petition (general election).

Referendum:

Ten percentum petition (general or special election).

Recall:

Fifteen percentum petition. No recall in the first six months of office.

Franchises:

(Follows closely the provisions of the Berkeley, Cal., Charter, q. v.)

SANTA CRUZ

(HOME RULE CHARTER, DRAFTED IN PURSUANCE OF ARTICLE XI. OF THE CONSTITUTION, BY A BOARD OF FREEHOLDERS, ELECTED NOVEMBER 3, 1910, ADOPTED BY POPULAR ELECTION FEBRUARY 1, 1911; RATIFIED BY THE LEGISLATURE, 1911.)

Commission-Organization:

Title: Council.

Number: Five, including Mayor.

Term: Four years. Partial renewal every two years.

Removal: Recall.

Salary: Nine hundred dollars.

Commissioner-Departments: 1. Public Affairs (Mayor). 2. Revenue and Finance. 3. Public Health and Safety. 4. Public Works: 5. Streets and Parks. Designation by the Council.

General Commission Powers:

The Corporate powers of the city.

Mayor:

Term: Two years.

Removal: Recall.

Powers in Relation to Commission: President of the Council. No veto power.

Salary: Twelve hundred dollars.

Other Elective Officers:

An Auditing Committee of three members.

Appointments:

Enumeration: The "chief officials" are the City Attorney; Police Judge; Treasurer, who is *ex-officio* Tax Collector; City Clerk, who is *ex-officio* Assessor; Chief of Police; Chief of Fire Department; Assistant Chief of the Fire Department; Health Officer; Street Superintendent; Superintendent of the Electrical Department; Plumbing and Building Inspector; Superintendent of Water Works; five Library Trustees.

Manner: The City Attorney and five Library Trustees are appointed by the Mayor; the Police Judge, the Superintendent of the Electrical Department and the Plumbing and Building Inspector, by the Commissioner of Public Safety; the Treasurer by the Commissioner of Revenue and Finance; the City Clerk by the Council; the City Engineer and the Street Superintendent by the Commissioner of Streets and Parks; the Superintendent of Water Works by the Commissioner of Public Works.

All these appointments are subject to the confirmation of the Council. The term of the Police Judge is four years. Appointments to other positions are made by the Commissioner in charge.

Civil Service Provisions: None.

Election Provisions:

Non-partisan primaries; nomination by petition of twenty-five voters. In case no candidate is elected to any office at the first election, a second election is held at which the two persons receiving the highest number of votes at the first election are the candidates.

Initiative:

Twenty percentum petition (special election). Ten percentum petition (general election).

Referendum:

Twenty percentum petition (special election). Ten percentum petition (general election).

Recall:

Fifteen percentum petition. No recall petition in the first three months of office.

Franchises:

No exclusive franchises. No franchise to run for a longer period than thirty-five years. The city reserves the right to fix the charges at which service shall be rendered to the city by public utility companies.

Special Features:

The Auditing Committee (elected) is required to employ an accountant to examine the books of all administrative officers and the proceedings of the City Council in relation to the purchase of supplies, letting of contracts, payment of salaries and wages and to report in writing the purchase of any supplies at a cost exceeding the market rate.

MONTEREY

(HOME RULE CHARTER, DRAFTED IN PURSUANCE OF ARTICLE XI. OF THE CONSTITUTION, BY A BOARD OF FREEHOLDERS, ELECTED JULY 25, 1910; RATIFIED BY THE LEGISLATURE, 1911.)

---

mmission-Organization:

Title: Council.

Number: Five, including Mayor.

Term: Four years. Partial renewal every two years.

Removal: Recall.

Salary: Two hundred dollars.

Commissioner-Departments: 1. Finance and Revenue. 2. Public Health and Safety. 3. Public Works. 4. Public Supplies. Designation by the Council.

neral Commission Powers:

All powers vested in the city.

ayor:

Term: Two years.

Salary: Two hundred and fifty dollars.

Powers in Relation to Commission: President of Council; especially charged with supervision of public utility companies.

ppointments:

Enumeration: The "chief officials" are the City Clerk, Auditor, Assessor, Treasurer, Police Judge, Collector, Attorney, Engineer, Chief of Police, Fire Chief, Street Superintendent, Building Inspector, Sewer Inspector, Health Officer, five Library Trustees.

Manner: "Chief Officials" by majority vote of the Council. Subordinate officers and employees in a manner to be determined by Council.

Civil Service Provisions: None.

Election Provisions:

Nomination by petition of twenty-five voters. No primary elections. The candidates receiving the highest number of votes, equal in number to the offices to be filled, are declared elected.

Initiative:

Twenty percentum petition (special election). Ten percentum petition (general election).

Referendum:

Twenty-five percentum petition (general or special election).

Recall:

Twenty-five percentum petition.

SAN LUIS OBISPO

(Home Rule Charter Drafted by a Board of Freeholders, in Pursuance of Article XI. of the Constitution. Adopted by Popular Vote September 12, 1910; Ratified by the Legislature 1911.)

Commission-Organization:

Title: Council.

Number: Five, including Mayor.

Term: Four years. Partial renewal every two years.

Removal: Recall.

Salary: Five hundred dollars.

Commissioner-Departments: 1. Finance and Revenue. 2. Public Health and Safety. 3. Public Works. 4. Public Supplies. Designation by the Council. The Commissioner of Finance and Revenue is *ex-officio* member of the Board of Education.

General Commission Powers:

"The Corporate powers of the city."

Special Requirements:

The Council must prescribe a uniform system of accounts.

Mayor:

Term: Two years.

Salary: Six hundred dollars.

Removal: Recall.

Powers: President of the Council. No veto power.

Special Requirements: Must annually employ a certified public accountant, who has "unlimited privileges of investigation" into all the affairs of all officers, etc., of the city. Is especially charged with supervision of public utility companies subject to municipal control.

Other Elective Officers:

City Clerk.

Appointments:

Enumeration: The "chief officials" are the City Treasurer, Attorney, Collector, Engineer, Chief of Police, Street Superintendent, five Library Trustees, and Fire Chief.

Manner: The "chief officials" are appointed, subject to removal at any time, by a majority vote of the Council. But the Chief of Police and Fire Chief are to be nominated by the Commissioner of Public Safety, and the Street Superintendent by the Commissioner of Public Works. The Council has power to determine the mode of appointment, etc., of minor offices and employments.

Election Provisions:

Nomination by petition of twenty-five voters; (no primaries are held).*

Initiative:

Twenty-five percentum petition (special election). Ten percentum petition (general election).

Referendum:

Twenty-five percentum petition (special election). Ten percentum petition (general election).

Recall:

Twenty-five percentum petition. No recall petition may be filed during the first three months of office.

Franchises:

No franchise to run for a longer period than thirty-five years. The city reserves the right to fix the rates at which service may be rendered under the franchise and to take over the property of the grantee at the expiration of the franchise period on payment of a fair valuation therefor.

* An alternative proposition providing for a second election in case a majority of the votes cast should not be received by any candidate, was rejected by the voters.

CALIFORNIA STATUTE

[The following is the text of the portion of the Statutes of California relating to the government of cities of the fifth class (those having a population of 3,000 to 10,000). The matter in Roman is old law (Chapter VI of Chapter XLIX of the Statutes, approved Mar. 13, 1883). The matter in italics is additional to the Statutes (Chapter 418, of the Laws of 1911, approved April 10, 1911). Similar additions were made to the Statutes for cities of the sixth class. (Sections 852a and 852b.)]

Sec. 751. Officers.

The government of said city shall be vested in a Board of Trustees, to consist of five members; a Board of Education, to consist of five members; and whenever a free public library and reading room is established therein, five Trustees thereof; a Recorder, a Treasurer, a City Attorney, a Clerk, a Marshal, an Assessor, and such subordinate officers as are hereinafter provided for.

Sec. 752. Election and terms of office.

The members of the Board of Trustees and of the Board of Education, and the Assessor, Marshal, Treasurer and Recorder shall be elected by the qualified voters of said city, at a general municipal election to be held therein on the second Monday in April in each odd-numbered year. The Marshal, Assessor, Treasurer, and Recorder shall hold office for a period of two years from and after the Monday next succeeding the day of such election, and until their successors are elected and qualified. Members of the Board of Trustees and of the Board of Education shall hold office for a period of four years from and after the Monday next succeeding the day of such election, and until their successors are elected and qualified; provided, that the first Board of Trustees and Board of Education elected under the provisions of this Act shall at their first meeting so classify themselves by lot, as that three of their members shall go out of office at the expiration of two years and two at the expiration of four years. The City Attorney shall be appointed by the Board of Trustees, and shall hold office during the pleasure of the Board of Trustees. The Board of Trustees may, in their discretion, appoint a Poundmaster, to hold office during the pleasure of the Board; also a Superintendent of Streets and a City Engineer, both of whom shall hold office during the pleasure of the Board, and both of which offices may be held by the same person.

Sec. 752a.

The board of trustees may at any time submit to the electors at any municipal or at any special election to be held for that purpose, an ordinance to divide the administration of the municipality into five departments and provide for the assignment of its several members to be heads of such respective departments and to be appointed as the commissioners of such respective departments; provided, that if a department of public health be created the commissioner in charge may be given the powers and duties of the municipal board of health, and such health board be thereby abolished. Such ordinance shall define the duties, powers and responsibilities of each commissioner and may require such commissioner to devote a specified number of hours of each business day to the performance of such duties, in which event such commissioner may receive a compensation, the amount of same to be fixed by said ordinance. The board may by majority vote, subject to the provisions of this section, assign its several members to be and appoint them as the respective commissioners of such several departments, and may by like vote from time to time change such assignment and appointment. It may assign employees to one or more departments, may require an officer or employee to perform duties in two or more departments, and may make such other rules and regulations as may be necessary or proper to the efficient and economical conduct of the business of the municipality. The substance of the ordinance so proposed shall be printed on the ballots used at such election substantially as follows. Shall the administration of the municipality be divided into five departments as follows: (insert the five departments of government proposed and briefly designate the powers and duties conferred upon each and the compensation each commissioner or head of department shall receive), "Yes" and "No" so printed in connection therewith that the voters may express their choice. The returns of the election shall be canvassed and declared as at other municipal elections and if it appears that a majority of the votes cast at such election were in favor of the ordinance, such ordinance shall take effect and be in force on the tenth day thereafter.

The board of trustees may submit to the electors at any municipal election or at a special election to be held for that purpose, the question as to whether the elective officers, or any of them, other than trustees, shall be appointed by said board, instead of being elected as provided in the preceding section. The question so submitted shall be printed on the ballots used at such election substantially as follows: "Shall the board of trustees hereafter appoint the.................... (naming the offices) of the city (or town) of...............," with the words "Yes" and "No" so printed in connection therewith that the voters may express their choice. The returns of the election shall be canvassed and declared as at other municipal elections and if it appears that a majority of the votes cast on any such proposition were in favor of the appointment of such officers or any of them, then at the expiration of the terms of office of any such officials then in office, and on the occurrence of a vacancy in any such offices, such elective officers or any of them for the appointment of whom such majority vote was so cast, shall thereafter be appointed by the board of trustees and hold office during the pleasure of such board.

Sec. 753.

[The Clerk, Treasurer, etc., are to execute bonds and take the constitutional oath of office.]

Sec. 754. Vacancies.

Sec. 755. Compensation.

The members of the Board of Trustees shall receive no compensation whatever, except while acting as a Board of Equalization. The Clerk, Treasurer, Assessor, Marshal, City Attorney, and Recorder shall severally receive, at stated times, a compensation to be fixed by ordinance by the Board of Trustees, which compensation shall not be increased or diminished after their election, or during their several terms of office. Nothing herein contained shall be construed to prevent the Board of Trustees from fixing such several amounts of compensation, in the first instance, during the term of office of any such officer, or after his election. The compensation of all other officers shall be fixed from time to time by the Board of Trustees.

SACRAMENTO

(Home Rule Charter, drafted by a Board of Freeholders, adopted by popular vote Nov. 7, 1911, subject to ratification by the Legislature.)

Commission Organizations:

Title: City Commission.

Number: Five, including President.

Term: Five years, one member being elected each year.

Removal: Recall.

Salary: Thirty-six hundred dollars.

Commissioner-Departments: (1) Public Works, (2) Streets, (3) Public Health and Safety, (4) Education, (5) Finance. The specific functions of each Commissioner are laid down in the charter.

Designation to departments by vote of City Commission; no reassignment during the Commissioner's term except by four-fifths vote.

General Commission Powers:

All the powers vested in the City by enumeration in the charter or held under the Constitution and general laws of the state.

The President:

Elected by the Commission from their own number; has no special functions other than those of a presiding officer and ceremonial head of the city.

Appointments:

Enumeration: Officers of the First Class: City Attorney, City Assessor, City Treasurer, City Collector, City Auditor, City Clerk, City Engineer, Judge of the Police Court, Purchasing Agent.

Officers of the Second Class: City Librarian, Superintendent of Streets, Health Officer, Chief of Police, Chief of Fire Department, Municipal Employment Agent, City Machinist, City Building Inspector, City Electrician, City Engineer of the Waterworks.

Manner: Officers of the first class are appointed by the Commission and are given power to appoint deputies; officers of the second class are appointed by the Commissioner in charge and have no specific power to appoint deputies.

Civil Service Provisions: The City Commission is required by the Charter to establish a Civil Service Board of three members. Such members are subject to removal on vote of four members of the City Commission, after an opportunity for a public hearing.

Election Provisions:

Nomination to general municipal election on petition of not less than one hundred nor more than three hundred electors (individual certificates). A second election is held if necessary to secure a majority vote for any office, the two persons receiving the highest number of votes at the general election being the candidates.

Initiative:

Fifteen per centum petition (special election). Five per centum petition (general election).

The City Commission in publishing notice of the submission of the ordinance may include a statement not over 500 words in length, setting forth its reasons for not adopting the measure in question. In which case the proponents of the measure have the right to include in the public notice their reasons for requesting its adoption, but must bear the expense of such publication.

Referendum:

Fifteen per centum petition (special election). Five per centum petition (general election).

*Recall:**

Ten per centum petition (special or regular annual election), based upon vote registered at last municipal election.

No recall in the first six months of office.

The question submitted at the recall election is simply whether or not the officer shall be recalled. In case of an affirmative vote the vacancy is filled by the City Commission until a successor is chosen at the next annual election. In case a majority of the Commission is recalled, the City Clerk is required to fill the vacancies until filled by special election, which must be called by him within three days after the official canvass of the vote cast at the recall election. A second recall for any officer necessitates a twenty per centum petition (*registered* vote).

*(See pages 51901-2 for full text.)

Franchises:

No franchise, except for steam or interurban railroads, for longer period than twenty-five years; no franchise for a term extending beyond the corporate life of the grantee. Franchises for steam and interurban railroads not to extend for a longer period than thirty-five years.

The term of the franchise must specify the time at which the city may become possessor of the plant and property of the grantee.

No franchise may be alienated without the express consent of the city, given by ordinance; but a franchise may be included in a mortgage or deed of trust executed for the purpose of obtaining money for corporate purposes.

Every franchise for a steam or interurban railroad must, in express terms, admit the right of competing roads to make joint use of its tracks, etc., upon payment of a fair proportion of the cost of construction and maintenance.

Special Features:

The Board of City Commissioners is *ex officio* Board of Education.†

The Board is required to publish weekly an Official Gazette containing reports of the meetings of the Commission and a detailed financial statement, but no political matter.

†(See pp. 51901-2 for full text of Educational Article.)

STOCKTON

(HOME RULE CHARTER, DRAFTED BY A BOARD OF FREEHOLDERS. ADOPTED BY POPULAR VOTE OCTOBER 17, 1911.)

Commission-Organization:

Title: Council.

Number: Five, including Mayor.

Term: Four years. Partial renewal biennially.

Removal: Recall.

Salary: Twenty-four hundred dollars.

Commissioner-Departments: 1, Finance, Revenue and Public Supplies; 2, Public Health and Safety; 3, Public Works; 4, Audit. Designation by Council.

"As between any commissioner and the council the legislative determination or distribution of [such] duties, powers or subject matters by the council shall be final, but as between the people and any member of the council the inability or failure of such member to act wisely or effectively in the matters of such determination or distribution of such duties, powers or subject matters shall be a reason for his recall as provided elsewhere in this charter."

General Commission Powers:

All the corporate powers of the city.

Mayor:

Term: Four years.

Salary: Three thousand dollars.

Removal: Recall.

Special Powers: Has general administrative oversight, especially over the contracts and franchises. He is required to employ a certified public accountant annually to examine the books of the auditor.

Appointments:

Enumeration: City Clerk, Assessor, Tax-Collector, Attorney, Engineer, Chief of Police, Fire Chief, Street Superintendent, Health Officer and five library trustees.

Manner: By majority vote of the Council.

Civil Service Provisions: The Council is authorized to establish a civil service commission to administer rules and regulations made by the Council.

Election Provisions:

Non-partisan primaries; names placed on ballot on petition of not less than twenty-five nor more than thirty-five voters; a second election is held if necessary to secure a majority vote for any office.

Initiative:

Twenty per centum petition (special election).

Ten per centum petition (general election).

Referendum:

Twenty per centum petition. No recall petition may be filed in the first three months of office.

Budget Provisions:

The Commissioner of Finance, Revenue and Public Supplies is required to submit an annual estimate of receipts and expenditures for the ensuing year. The passage of the budget by the council is as follows:

"The council shall meet annually not later than thirty days prior to fixing the tax levy and make a budget of the estimated amounts required to pay the expenses of conducting the business of the city government for the next ensuing year. The budget shall be prepared in such detail as to the aggregate sum and the items thereof allowed to each department, office, board or commission as the council may deem advisable. No part of the items so allowed each department, office, board or commission shall be transferred to any other department, office, board or commmission, unless by unanimous consent and the consent of the department, office, board or commission affected."

Franchises:

The maximum length of any franchise is fixed at twenty-five years. Every franchise is made subject to the right of the city to prescribe and regulate rates, rentals, etc., charged for public service thereunder. Every franchise is subject to purchase by the city of the property and plant of the grantee at expiration. No franchise may be leased, assigned or alienated without the express consent of the city. The city, through its auditor, has the right to examine the books of any franchise holder at any time. Every franchise holder must report annually to the city auditor such facts as the council may require.

BAKERSFIELD

(HOME RULE CHARTER, DRAFTED BY A BOARD OF ELECTED FREEHOLDERS; ADOPTED BY POPULAR VOTE, 1915.)

Governing Body:

Title: Council.
Number: Seven (one elected from each ward).
Term: Two years.
Removal: Recall.
Salary: Fifty dollars per month.

Mayor:

The council elects one of its members president to exercise the usual powers of presiding officer but no veto power.

City Manager:

Sec. 35. The city manager shall have general supervision and direction of the administrative operation of the city government.

Sec. 36. The duties of the manager are:

1. To see that all the laws and ordinances are faithfully enforced by the heads of the departments;

2. To attend all meetings of the council at which his attendance may be required by that body;

3. To recommend for adoption to the council such measures as he may deem necessary or expedient;

4. To keep the council fully advised of the financial condition of the municipality and its future needs;

5. To prepare and submit to the auditor a tentative budget for the next fiscal year;

6. To appoint and remove, except as herein otherwise provided, all officers and subordinate officers and employees of the departments, in both the classified and unclassified service; all appointments to be upon merit and fitness alone;

7. To exercise control over all other departments and divisions that may be hereafter created by the council, and assigned to his management, not in conflict with the provisions of this charter;

8. To investigate all complaints, in regard to the service maintained by any and all public utilities in the city, and to take such proceedings as may be necessary to correct the abuse, if any.

Sec. 37. The city manager shall receive such salary as may be fixed by the council, and before entering upon the duties of his office, he shall take the official oath required by this article.

Appointments:

Enumeration: (1) City Manager, Treasurer, Assessor, Clerk, to serve during the pleasure of the council; auditor, police judge, public welfare commissioners for a term of two years.
(2) Chief of Police, Chief of Fire Department, City Engineer, Superintendent of Streets, Health Officer, Building and Plumbing Inspector.
Manner: Group (1) by the Council; Group (2) by the City Manager.
Civil Service Provisions: Appointments by the City Manager are to be made on the basis of merit and fitness.

Election Provisions:

Non-partisan primaries and elections: names placed on ballot by petition of twenty-five electors. The two candidates receiving the highest number of votes at the nominating election are the candidates at the general election, but any candidate receiving a majority of all votes cast at the first election is thereupon declared elected.

Initiative:

Twenty-five per centum petition.

Referendum.

Twenty-five per centum petition.

Recall:

Twenty-five per centum petition. Applies to all elected and appointive officials. The question submitted at the recall election is the simple question of removal; the successor is to be chosen at a subsequent election.

SAN JOSE

(Home Rule Charter, drafted by a board of freeholders elected by the people; adopted by popular vote April 19, 1915.)

Governing Body:

Title: Council.
Number: Seven.
Terms: Six years.
Removal: Recall.
Salary: Five (5) dollars per meeting, but not over twenty-five (25) dollars per month.

Mayor:

The Council elects a presiding officer from among its own members.

The City Manager:

Title: City Manager.
Powers and Duties: He is the official head of the city and exercises the powers and duties of mayors under the laws of California applicable to the city. He also exercises the usual powers of a City Manager in other cities (see Dayton, p. 34003). See *"Appointments."*

Appointments:

Enumeration: (1) City Manager, City Clerk, Civil Service Commission and City Planning Commission. (2) City Treasurer, City Engineer, City Attorney, Chief of Police Department, Chief of Fire Department, Board of Health, Health Officer, Superintendent of Parks, Board of Library Trustees.
Manner: Group (1) by the Council. Group (2) by the City Manager.
The Council may remove any officer appointed by it by an affirmative vote of four members after a public hearing, but the City Manager may be removed without such hearing. The City Manager in making removals is required to file a statement of the reasons for removal with the Civil Service Commission. The person whose removal is sought must have an opportunity to be heard in his own defense.
Civil Service Provisions: A Commission of three members is appointed by the Council for terms of six years. The classified service consists of all officers except (1) those elected by the people, (2) the City Manager, City Clerk, City Treasurer and City Attorney, (3) heads of departments and members of boards and (4) private secretaries and the first deputy of each officer.

Election Provisions:

Non-partisan nominations and elections. Names placed on the primary ballots on petition of 250 electors. Candidates equal to twice the number of vacancies to be filled, receiving the highest number of votes at the primary, are the candidates at the general election, but those receiving a majority of all votes cast at the primary are thereupon declared elected.

Initiative:

Twenty-five per centum petition (special election).
Fifteen per centum petition (general election).

Referendum:

Twenty-five per centum petition (special election).
Fifteen per centum petition (general election).

Recall:

Twenty-five per centum petition. No recall petition may be filed within six months of the beginning of the officer's term.

BAKER

(HOME RULE CHARTER, AUTHORIZED BY CHAPTER 226, LAWS OF 1907, IN EFFECT NOVEMBER, 1910.)

Commission-Organization:

Title: Board of Commissioners.
Number: Three including Mayor.
Term: Two years.
Removal: Recall.
Salary: Two thousand dollars.
Commissioner-Departments: 1. (Mayor) Public Affairs, Finance, Police and Pound, Municipal Court, Public Buildings, Parks and Library. General Supervision: 2. Highways, Streets, Sewers, Lighting; 3. Water, Fire, Sanitation. Designation to Departments at election.

General Commission Powers:

The legislative and administrative powers.

Special Requirements:

Quarterly financial statements. The Board may not make any lease of public property, the operation of which will extend over two years, nor dispose of any right or title of the city, the consideration of which shall exceed $2,000, without referring the same to a vote of the people. Commissioners must devote entire time to service of the city.

ayor:

Term: Two years.
Salary: Twenty-five hundred dollars.
Removal: Recall.
Powers in relation to Commission: President of the Board. May veto items in appropriation bills.

ppointments:

The Mayor appoints the heads of departments and all other employees, but only upon recommendation of the Commissioner in charge. The Mayor must also submit appointments to his own department to the Board. Appointees are removable at any time without cause.

Election Provisions:

Non-partisan nominations on petition of twenty-five signatures. Commissioners are voted for by groups designated by number on ballot.

Initiative:

The State Laws apply.*

Referendum:

The State Laws apply.*

Recall:

The State Laws apply.

Franchises:

No franchise granted except upon vote of the qualified tax-paying electors of the city, the question to be submitted on payment of deposit by grantee of the estimated expense of the election. Unused franchises declared forfeited. All power to regulate fares and other charges for public service is reserved to the people to be exercised by them either by ordinance of the Board or by direct legislation. No exclusive franchises. No franchise to be leased, assigned or otherwise alienated without the express consent of a majority of the Board. The Board has power to compel the joint use of tracks, poles, etc., with competing corporations on payment of reasonable compensation therefor by the latter. No franchise for a longer period than twenty-five years. No franchise without compensation to the city, including an annual payment of the gross proceeds arising from the use of the franchise. Every grant of a franchise must provide that the city may take over the property of the grantee on payment of fair compensation.

The Board has power to impose other restrictions, etc., than those enumerated in the Charter.

* Chap. 226, Laws of 1907.

PORTLAND

(HOME RULE CHARTER, DRAFTED BY A BOARD OF FREEHOLDERS; ADOPTED BY THE PEOPLE MAY 3, 1913.)

Commission-Organization:

Title: Council.

Number: Five, including mayor.

Term: Four years. Partial renewal biennially.

Removal: Recall.

Salary: Five thousand dollars.

Commissioner-Departments: 1, Public Affairs; 2, Finance; 3, Public Safety; 4, Public Utilities; 5, Public Improvements.

Designation by the Mayor, Commissioners and all other paid officers are required to devote their entire time to the service of the city.

General Commission Powers:

The Council exercises all powers and authority conferred upon the city by charter or general law, except such as is conferred expressly upon some other officer.

Mayor:

Term: Four years.

Salary: Six thousand dollars.

Powers: Has general supervision of the affairs of the city and is required to keep the Council informed thereon.

Presides at meetings of the Council, but has no veto power.

Required to institute litigation on behalf of the city (or may do so on his own motion) to annul or cancel franchises; may investigate the offices and accounts of any officer or employee of the city; is required to prepare the annual budget.

Other Elective Officers:

The Auditor, elected for a term of four years.

Appointments:

Enumeration: Treasurer, City Engineer, City Attorney, Municipal Judge, Purchasing Agent.

Manner: Enumerated officers by majority vote of the Council, to serve during their pleasure; but the officer sought to be removed is entitled to a written statement of the reasons for removal and to file a counter statement.

Civil Service Provisions: Provision is made for a Commission of three, appointed for terms of six years expiring in rotation, and for classification of employees, examinations, etc.

Election Provisions:

Nomination by petition of one hundred voters. Preferential voting with first, second and third choices. Ballots are to contain no partisan designation, but the views of any candidate on strictly municipal questions may be indicated in not more than twelve words.

Initiative:

The general laws and constitution of the state apply.

Referendum:

See "Initiative."

Recall:

See "Initiative."

Special Features:

The charter requires the Council to enact an administrative code providing for the powers and duties of the various departments, uniform standards; for the purchase of materials and supplies, for the appointment of a purchasing agent; for the publication, at least once in every six months, of charts or diagrams showing receipts and expenditures of the different departments; for the keeping of time records of employees for itemized cost accounting; for the housing and storing of supplies.

LA GRANDE

(HOME RULE CHARTER; DRAFTED BY A BOARD OF FIFTEEN ELECTED FREEHOLDERS; ADOPTED BY POPULAR VOTE, OCTOBER 1, 1913.)

Governing Body:

Title: Commission.

Number: Three.

Term: One year.

Removal: Recall.

Salary: Five dollars per meeting.

General Powers of Commission:

CHAPTER V.

Sec. 10. It shall be the duty of the Commission to enact ordinances, and they may repeal ordinances, as shall be required by the public good, take care that the business character and ability of the General Manager is sufficient to enforce the municipal law, perform his duties and services for the best interests and welfare of the municipal government, and in a careful, prudent and business-like manner, and the Commissioners shall be responsible to the city for the strict and efficient performance of his duties. They shall at each regular meeting investigate all matters of importance to the city coming to their attention, either by observation or by report; listen to petitions and grievances and suggestions which may properly be presented to them; obtain from the General Manager weekly reports and act upon them; take and approve all official undertakings which this Charter or the ordinances of the city may require; require any officer to give security for the faithful performance of his duties; and the Recorder shall endorse the approval of the Commission upon such undertaking, together with a reference to the book and page of the minutes where the approval is found, and attach his signature thereto; and the said Commission shall by ordinance limit and fix the salaries and compensation of all officers provided for by this Charter; provided, the salary of the General Manager shall not exceed thirty-six hundred dollars ($3600.00) per annum; and the Commission shall perform such other duties, and in the manner as may be prescribed hereafter by this charter.

Mayor:

CHAPTER V.

Sec. 3. The commissioners shall elect one of their number Chairman, at their first meeting in January, who shall be designated and known as the President of the City of La Grande. In case of vacancy as Chairman, such vacancy may be filled at any time by them. He shall preside at all meetings of the Commission, provided, that in his absence or inability to act then the Commission shall choose a Chairman pro tem. from among their number. The Chairman as such President of the City of La Grande shall approve and sign all rules, resolutions and ordinances adopted by the Commission in the manner hereinafter described. The term of such Chairman shall end with the year in which he is elected.

City Manager:

CHAPTER VIII.

Sec. 4. The General Manager shall have absolute control and supervision over all offices and employees of the City except the Commissioners and Municipal Judge, and shall have power to appoint all officers prescribed by this Charter, except the Commissioners and Municipal Judge, to employ such additional help as may be necessary to carry on and perform the business affairs and departmental work of the City. He shall have power to discharge, with or without cause, any person appointed or employed by him; he shall see that the business affairs of the municipal corporation are transacted in a modern, scientific and business-like manner and the services performed and the records kept shall be as nearly as may be like those of an efficient and successful private corporation; he shall be accountable to the Commission for his actions, conduct and management of the business and may be discharged at the will of the Commission, with or without cause; he shall perform such duties as may be required by the Charter or ordinances of the City or specially required of him by the Commission.

Appointments:

Enumeration: (1) General Manager, Municipal Judge, (2) City Recorder, Treasurer, City Attorney, Chief of Police, Chief of Fire Department, City Engineer, Superintendent of the Water System, City Health Officer, Street Superintendent.

Manner: Group (1) by the Commission, Group (2) By the General Manager, subject to removal by him, with or without cause.

Civil Service Provisions: None.

Election Provisions:

Preferential Voting with first, second and third choices.

Initiative:

The general statutes of Oregon are made applicable.

Referendum:

See "*Initiative.*"

Recall:

Twenty-five per centum petition.

TACOMA

(A Charter framed by a Board of Freeholders, elected June 8, 1909, in accordance with Article 11, Section 10, of the Constitution and an Act of the Legislature approved Mar. 4, 1895. Adopted Oct. 16, 1909.)

Commission-Organization:

Title: Mayor and Council.

Number: Five, including Mayor.

Term: Four years.

Removal: By vote of four members of the Council. Recall.

Salary: Thirty-six hundred dollars.

Commissioner-Departments: 1, Public Affairs, Health and Sanitation; 2, Public Safety; 3, Public Works, Streets, Improvements and Property; 4, Light and Water; 5, Finance. Designations by the Council. The Commissioner of Finance is ex-officio Treasurer.

General Commission Powers:

Special Requirements: Weekly sessions for legislative purposes. Daily sessions for administrative purposes. Monthly financial statements.

Mayor:

Term: Four years.

Salary: Four thousand dollars.

Removal: By vote of four members of the Council. Recall.

Powers in Relation to Commission: President of Council.

Other Elective Officers:

Comptroller: Term, four years. Exercises a general control over the fiscal affairs of the City.

Appointments:

Enumerated: Class B: City Clerk, City Attorney, City Engineer, Chief of Police, Fire Chiefs and other superintendents of departments which may be created by the Council.

Class C: Clerks and assistants and includes all persons employed in a clerical capacity, or as assistants to office.

Class D: All other employees.

Manner: The City Clerk and City Attorney by the Council. Other officers by the Commissioners in charge, subject to confirmation of the Council. The Mayor commissions all appointive officers.

Civil Service Provisions: A Board of three is established, to serve without compensation. Partial renewal.

Election Provisions:

Nomination to primary by petition of twenty-five individual certificates. Non-partisan ballots. Not more than two candidates at second election for each office to be filled. Campaign expenses of any candidate limited to five hundred dollars.

Initiative:

Twenty per centum petition (special election).
Five per centum petition (general election).

Referendum:

Fifteen per centum petition (general or special election).

Recall:

Twenty-five per centum petition (general or special election). No recall petition in first six months after installation.

Franchises:

Suspended for referendum on petition of twelve per centum of the voters. No exclusive franchises. No franchise to be leased or assigned without the consent of the Council.

SPOKANE

(HOME RULE CHARTER, DRAFTED BY A BOARD OF FREEHOLDERS. ADOPTED DEC., 1910.)

Commission-Organization:

Title: Council.

Number: Five, one of whom is elected Mayor by the Council.

Term: Four years. Partial renewal.

Removal: Recall.

Salary: Five thousand dollars.

Commissioner-Departments: 1, Public Affairs; 2, Finance; 3, Public Safety; 4, Public Works; 5, Public Utilities. Designation by Council.

General Commission Powers:

All the corporate powers.

Mayor:

Term: Four years.

Salary: Five thousand dollars.

Removal: Recall.

Powers in Relation to Commission: No veto power.

Presides over Council.

Appointments:

Enumeration: Clerk, Corporation Counsel, Treasurer, Auditor, City Engineer, Labor Agent, Purchasing Agent.

Manner: Enumerated officers by Council. Each Commissioner has power to appoint and remove the heads of subdivisions within his Department.

Civil Service Provisions: A Commission of three established. Appointed by the Council to serve for six years without compensation. Partial renewal.

Election Provisions:

Twenty-five individual nomination certificates required. There are no primaries, but a system of preferential voting similar to the Grand Junction, Colo. plan, (*q. v.*) is provided for. Election expenses of any candidate not to exceed two hundred and fifty dollars.

Initiative:

Fifteen per centum petition (special election).

Five per centum petition (municipal election).

Referendum:

Ten per centum petition (special or general election, at the discretion of the Council). The Council may, of its own motion, submit ordinances, etc.

Recall:

Twenty per centum petition (special election).

Fifteen per centum petition (municipal election).

Two or more elective officers may be removed by the same election.

Franchises:

No exclusive franchises. No franchise for over twenty-five years. Every street railway franchise to connect with any existing street railway franchise must expire on the same date as the existing franchise. Every renewal, continuance, or extension of existing franchises or grant of new franchises to succeed expiring franchise upon the same streets, in whole or in part, are to be limited so as to expire on the same date as the longest unexpired term of any franchise then held by the grantee.

Special Features:

A Park Board of ten members is established. They are to be appointed by the Council for a term of ten years. Partial renewal each year.

WASHINGTON STATUTE

(AN ACT OF THE LEGISLATURE PERMITTING CITIES OF FRO M 2,500 TO 20,000 INHABITANTS TO ADOPT ITS PROVISIONS BY POPULAR ELECTION CALLED UPON PETITION OF TWENTY-FIVE PER CENTUM OF THE VOTERS. APPROVED MARCH 17, 1911.)

Commission-Organization:

Title: City Commission.

Number: Three, inc. Mayor.

Term: Three years.

Removal: Recall.

Salary: Population 2,500 to 5,000, $250.
Population 5,000 to 8,000, $1,000.
Population 8,000 to 14,000, $1,800.
Population 14,000 to 20,000, $2,000.

Commissioner-Departments: 1. Public Safety (Mayor). 2. Finance and Accounting. 3. Streets and Public Improvements. Designation by the Council.

General Commission Powers:

All the corporate powers of the city.

Special Requirements:

Monthly financial statements.

Mayor:

Term: Three years.

Removal: Recall.

Powers in relation to Commission: No veto power;
Population 5,000 to 8,000, $1,200.
presides at all meetings of the Council.

Salary: Population 2,500 to 5,000, $500.
Population 8,000 to 14,000, $2,000.
Population 14,000 to 20,000, $2,500.

Appointments:

Enumeration: City Clerk.

Manner: By majority vote of the Commission; removable in like manner.

Civil Service Provisions: None.

Election Provisions:

Non-partisan primaries; nomination by petition of one hundred voters. The two (or four) candidates for each position, who receive the highest number of votes at the primary are the candidates at the second election.

Initiative:

Twenty-five per centum petition (special or general election).

Referendum:

Twenty-five per centum petition (special or general election).

Recall:

Twenty-five percentum petition. No recall in first six months of office.

Franchises:

All franchises must be approved by popular vote at a general or special election.

Abandonment of Act:

Operation under this act may be abandoned after six years by popular election, called upon petition of twenty-five per centum of the electors.

EVERETT

(HOME RULE CHARTER. DRAFTED BY A BOARD OF FREEHOLDERS. RATIFIED BY POPULAR VOTE APRIL 16, 1912.)

Commission-Organization:

Title: Council.

Number: Three, until the city shall have population of 50,000; thereafter, five.

Term: Four years.

Removal: Recall.

Salary: Two thousand dollars until the city has a population of 40,000; thereafter, $2,500, increasing at the rate of $500 for each additional 15,000 population, but not to exceed $5,000.

Commissioner-Departments: 1. Finance, including office of clerk and treasurer; 2, Safety, including police, fire and health departments; 3, Public Works, including departments of engineering, streets and sewers, city electrician, plumbing inspector, employment office, harbor master and port warden. Designation by popular election.

General Powers of Commission:

All powers not otherwise provided for. (The Library Board is given independent powers.)

Special Requirements:

Members of the Council are required to devote their time to the duties of their offices.

President (Mayor):

Term: Four years.

Removal: Recall.

Salary: Same as other commissioners.

Special Powers: Presides at meetings of council; no veto power.

Appointments:

Enumeration: City Clerk, Treasurer, City Attorney, City Engineer, Board of Sanitation and Health Officer, Park Board (5), Library Board (5). Enumerated officers, except Library Board (appointed by the Mayor), are appointed by the Council and are removable at any time.

Each commissioner has power to appoint and remove administrative heads of all subdivisions in his department, subject to the Civil Service regulations.

Civil Service Provisions: A civil service commission of three members is established.

Election Provisions:

Nomination by petition of twenty-five voters. Candidates receiving a majority of all votes cast at first election are elected thereby; a second election is held where necessary to receive a majority.

Initiative:

Fifteen per centum petition (special election). Five per centum petition (general election).

Referendum:

Ten per centum petition (general or special election).

Recall:

Twenty per centum petition. Petition must contain "specific statement of the grounds for removal." No recall petition to be filed during the first six months of office.

Franchises:

No exclusive franchises. No franchise for a longer period than twenty-five years. No franchise shall be granted without provision for proper compensation to the city therefor. The council retains the power to regulate rates and charges for public service, require the elevation or depression of tracks of railroads, to require reasonable extensions. Every grantee shall be required to present an annual report in such form as the Council shall require. Franchises may not be capitalized. Every franchise is subject to common use by other grantees upon payment of adequate compensation.

Taxation:

Tax levies are limited as to the amounts to be raised for parks and cemeteries, libraries and as to the total levy.

LEWISTON

(An Act amendatory to the special acts relating to the city. House Bill No. 121, Laws of 1907.)

Commission-Organization:

Title: Mayor and Council.

Number: Seven, including Mayor.

Term: Two years, partial renewal.

Removal: Recall.

Salary: Three dollars per session.

Commissioner-Departments: 1, Police; 2, Fire; 3, Streets; 4, Public Property; 5, Water Works and Sewerage; 6, Finance and Revenue.

General Commission Powers:

The corporate powers of the City.

Special Requirements:

Monthly financial statements.

Mayor:

Term; Two years.

Salary: Three hundred dollars.

Removal: Recall.

Powers in relation to Commission: Veto power; presides over Council. No vote except in case of tie and on question of removals.

Appointed Officers:

Enumeration: A Comptroller, who is ex-officio City Clerk; Collector of Water Rates and Registrar, a Police Judge, a Chief of Police, a Chief of the Fire Department, City Attorney, City Engineer, City Treasurer, City Assessor, City Health Officer, Superintendent of Water Works, Street Superintendent. One person may be appointed to one or more such office, except Comptroller. The Comptroller and the City Clerk have fixed terms and are removable only for cause.

Manner: By Mayor and Council, and removable at the will of Mayor and Council without cause. No fixed terms, except Comptroller and City Clerk.

Civil Service Provisions: Council has power to create a Civil Service Board.

Election Provisions:

Names placed on primary election ballot on petition of one hundred voters.

Initiative:

Fifteen per centum petition (special election).

Five per centum petition (general election).

Referendum:

Petition requires three hundred signatures. Submission at special election.

Recall:

The election for the recall of the officers is based upon a twenty-five per cent. petition. The cost of the extra help required by the City Clerk in preparing petitions for the recall, must be paid by the petitioners, who are required to deposit the sum necessary with the City Clerk. The recall may not be applied before the officer sought to be removed has been in office three months.

Special Features:

Officers who are heads of Departments have privilege of the floor at meetings of the Council when matters concerning their Department are under discussion.

IDAHO STATUTE

(APPLICABLE TO ALL CITIES OF THREE THOUSAND POPULATION AND OVER UPON ADOPTION BY POPULAR ELECTION HELD UPON PETITION OF TWENTY-FIVE PERCENTUM OF THE VOTERS. HOUSE BILL NO. 233, APPROVED MARCH 13, 1911.)

Commission-Organization:

Title: Council.

Number: Five, including Mayor.

Term: Four years. Partial renewal every two years.

Removal: Recall.

Salary:

From 3,000 to 7,000 population, $ 150.
From 7,000 to 10,000 population, 450.
From 10,000 to 15,000 population, 900.
From 15,000 to 25,000 population, 1,200.
From 25,000 to 40,000 population, 2,000.

Commissioner-Departments: 1. Public Affairs (Mayor). 2. Accounts and Finances. 3. Public Safety. 4. Streets and Public Improvements. 5. Parks and Public Property. Designation by the Council.

General Commission Powers:

All executive, legislative and judicial powers formerly exercised by the Mayor, City Council, Board of Public Works, Board of Library Trustees, etc.

Mayor:

Term: Two years.

Removal: Recall.

Powers in Relation to Commission: Presides over Council. No veto power. Charged with the general supervision of public utility companies.

Salary:

From 3,000 to 7,000 population, $ 300.
From 7,000 to 10,000 population, 600.
From 10,000 to 15,000 population, 1,200.
From 15,000 to 25,000 population, 1,800.
From 25,000 to 40,000 population, 3,000.

Appointments:

Enumeration: City Clerk, City Attorney, City Treasurer, City Engineer, City Physician, Chief of Police, Chief of Fire Department, Street Commissioner, Library Trustees, Police Judge.

Manner: By majority vote of the Council.

Civil Service Provisions: None.

Election Provisions:

Non-partisan nominations by petition of twenty-five signatures. The ballot regulations are, in part, as follows:

"The [ballot] form shall be set up with the names of candidates in the order in which they appear upon the form of official ballot prepared by the City Clerk: in printing each set of official ballots for the various election precincts or wards, the position of the names shall be changed in each office division as many times as there are candidates in the office division or group in which there are the most names; as nearly as possible, an equal number of ballots shall be printed after each change. In making the changes of position, the printer shall take the line of type at the top of each division and place it at the bottom of that division, shoving up the column so that the name that was second before shall be first after the change. After the ballots are printed, before being cut, they shall be kept in separate piles for each change of position and shall then be piled, taking one from each pile and placing it upon the pile to be cut, the intention being that every other ballot in the pile of printed sheets shall have the names in different positions. After the piles are made in this manner, they shall be cut and placed in blocks of one hundred (100) ballots in each block, every other ballot in such blocks to have the names in different positions, as nearly as practicable."

The City Clerk may cause questions submitted at a regular election to be printed on separate sheets.

Second elections are held, if necessary, to secure majorities for the offices to be filled.

Initiative:

Twenty-five percentum petition (special election). Ten percentum petition (general election).

"Such petitions shall be substantially as follows: We, the undersigned, being qualified electors of the city of ...., State of Idaho, hereby declare that we have read, or heard read at length, section by section, the proposed ordinance or measure hereto attached, and fully understand its contents, meaning and purpose, and believe it should become a law of the city for the following reasons: (here state the reasons is not more than two hundred (200) words). That we hereby request that such ordinance or measure be submitted to a vote of the people if not passed by the Council."

(NAME OF SIGNER.)
(STREET NUMBER.)

"Any number of copies of the petition and ordinance thereto attached may be circulated at the same time and all shall be considered as one petition, but each petition must be verified by at least one (1) qualified elector, which verification shall state that affiant knows that all of the persons whose names are signed to the petition are qualified electors of the city, and that each signer, prior to placing his name upon the petition, read, or heard read at length, section by section, the proposed ordinance or measure thereto attached. Such verification may be made before any notary public."

Referendum:

No provision.

Recall:

Thirty-five percentum petition (special election). Twenty percentum petition (general election) No recall in the first three months of office.

Franchises:

No franchise for a longer period than thirty years The city reserves the right to regulate the rates a which public service shall be rendered. Every franchise must provide that the city may take ove the plant of the grantee at the end of the fran chise period on payment of a fair valuation there for. No franchise may be alienated or assigne without the express consent of the City Counci Ordinances granting franchises must contain pro visions prohibiting the corporation holding th same from issuing capital stock on account of th franchise value.

Abandonment of Act:

This act may be abandoned after six years' opera tion thereunder, by special election called upo petition of twenty-five percentum of the voters.

PHOENIX

(*Revised; destroy earlier leaf of same number*)

(HOME RULE CHARTER, DRAFTED BY A BOARD OF FREEHOLDERS; ADOPTED BY POPULAR VOTE OCT. 11, 1913.)

Governing Body:

Title: Commission.

Number: Five, including mayor.

Term: Two years. Partial renewal annually.

Removal: Recall.

Salary: Five dollars per meeting, but not to exceed three hundred dollars per year.

Mayor:

CHAPTER V.

Sec. 1. The Mayor. The mayor shall be the chief executive of the city, and ex-officio chairman of the commission, and shall see that the ordinances thereof are enforced.

Sec. 2. The mayor shall annually and from time to time give the commission information relative to the affairs of the city, and recommend for its consideration such matters as he may deem expedient.

Sec. 3. The mayor shall be recognized as the official head of the city by the courts for the purpose of service of civil process upon the city and instituting any action or proceeding at law or equity for and in behalf of the city, and appearing in any manner before the courts on behalf of the city; he shall be recognized by the governor and other State officials as the chief and official head of the city.

Sec. 4. The mayor shall take command of the police and govern the city by proclamation during times of great danger.

City Manager:

CHAPTER III.

Sec. 4. The City Manager shall be appointed by the Commission and shall hold his office until removed by a vote of three-fifths of the Commission voting affirmatively therefor.

CHAPTER VI.

Sec. 1. The Manager. Subject to the control of the Commission, the Manager shall have the general supervision and direction of the administrative operation of the city government; he shall supervise and direct the official conduct of all appointive city officers except the Auditor, City Attorney, City Clerk, City Treasurer and City Magistrate; he shall supervise the performance of all contracts made by any person for work done for the City, and in that behalf represent the City except as it may be otherwise provided in this Charter; he shall make all purchases of materials or supplies for the City, subject to the provisions of this Charter, and see that the same are received as contracted for; he shall employ and discharge from time to time, as occasion requires, all employees of the City appointed by him by and with the consent and approval of the Commission; he shall appoint all officers of the City the appointment or election of whom is not otherwise provided for in this Charter, and may remove them when the interests of the City require; he shall make a written report to the Commission at its first meeting in each month of the state of the condition and business affairs of the City; and he shall, whenever required by the Commission, make a written or verbal report, as may be indicated by the Commission, in detail of any particular matter relating to the affairs of the City within his supervision; he shall require monthly reports, or may require them oftener, from each of the officers of the City appointed by him of the business and condition of such office, and shall submit the same to the Commission upon its request therefor. All reports required by the Charter or by ordinance shall be in writing, except that the Commission, in the case of reports other than the monthly reports herein required, may direct them to be verbal; and likewise the Manager may direct reports other than the monthly reports herein provided for to be made verbally. All written reports shall be safely kept by the proper officers as a part of the records of the City, and be open to the inspection of the electors of the City during office hours.

Sec. 2. It shall be his duty, as well as that of the mayor, to see that all of the ordinances of the city are enforced.

CHAPTER X.

Sec. 3. The salaries of the City Manager, City Auditor and all other City officers, except the City Magistrate, whose compensation is or may be fixed by the Commission, may be changed, increased or modified by ordinance of the Commission as it may deem proper and necessary.

Appointments:

Enumeration: (1) City Manager, City Magistrate, City Auditor, (2) City Clerk, City Treasurer, City Assessor, City Collector, City Attorney, City Engineer, Chief of Police, Fire Chief, Superintendent of Streets.

Manner: Group (1) by the Commission, Group (2) by the City Manager.

Civil Service Provisions: None.

Election Provisions:

Names placed on the ballot at the primary on petition of three per centum of the total vote cast for mayor at the last preceding general municipal election.

Ballots at primaries and regular elections are without party designations.

Candidates receiving, at the primary, a majority of all votes cast for any office are thereupon elected.

A second election is held if necessary to secure a majority vote to fill one or more vacancies.

Initiative:

Fifteen per centum petition (special election).

Referendum:

Ten per centum petition (special election).

Recall:

Twenty-five per centum petition.

No recall petition may be filed during the first six months of any officer's term.

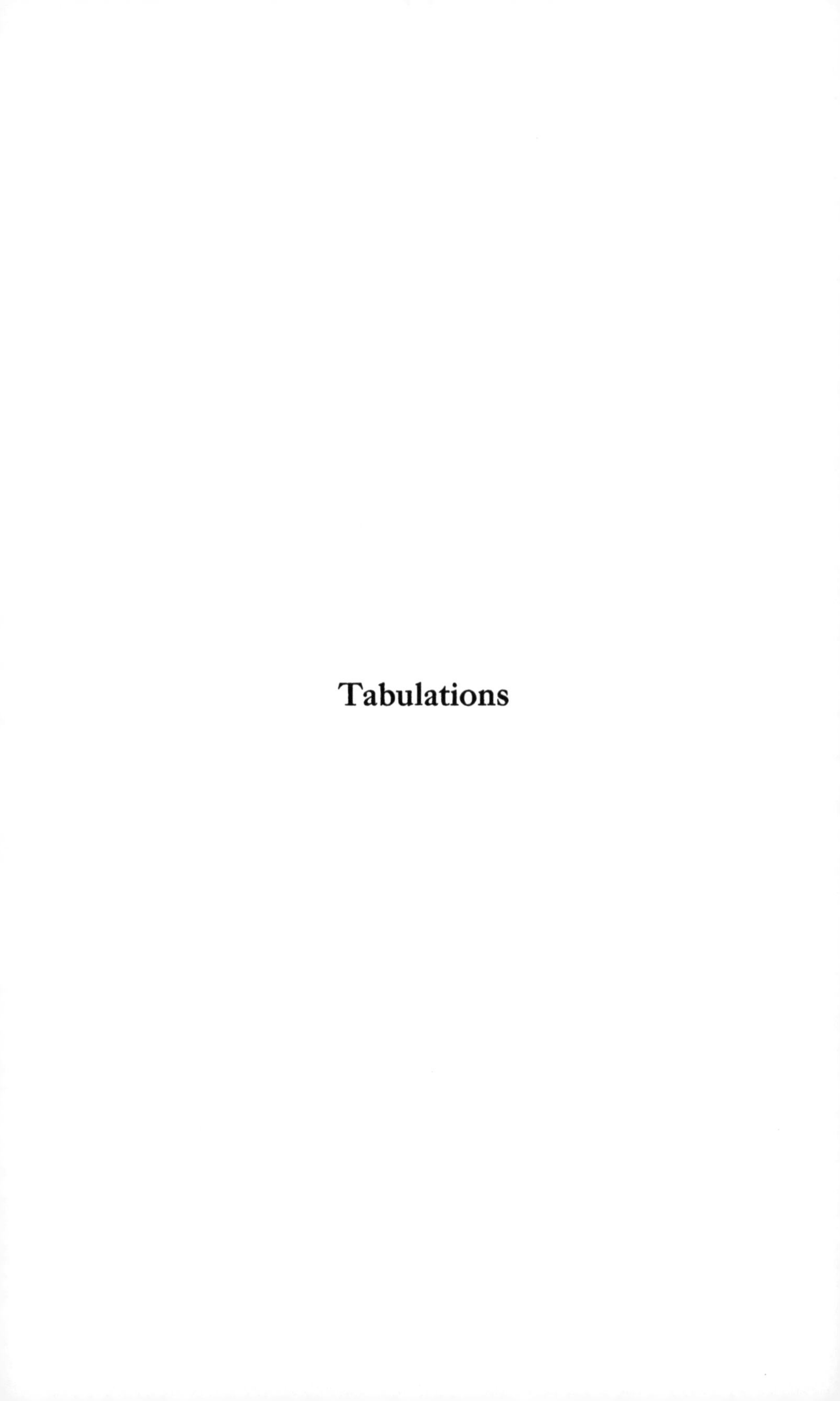

Tabulations

CITIES OF OVER 100,000 POPULATION

CITY	Population	Form	Date of Act*	Date in Operation	Commissioners			Mayor		Outline Reference
					No.†	Salary	Term	Salary	Term	
Oakland, Cal.....	150,174	H. R.	Dec. 8, 1910	July 1, 1911	5	$3600	4	$4200	4	38007
Memphis, Tenn...	131,105	Sp. Act	Apr. 27, 1909		5	3000	4	6000	4	33801
Spokane, Wash....	104,402	H. R.	Dec. 1910	1911	5	5000	4	5000	4	38303

*If Statute or special act of legislature, date of Governor's approval; if Home Rule Charter, date of popular election. †Including Mayor.

GENERAL STRUCTURE

41002

CITIES OF 25,000 TO 100,000 POPULATION

CITY STATE	Population	Form	Date of Act*	Date in Operation	Commissioners			Mayor		Outline Reference
					No.†	Salary	Term	Salary	Term	
Dallas, Tex.	92,104	Sp. Act	Apr. 13, 1907	1907	5	$3000	2	$4000	2	36007
Lynn, Mass.	89,336	Sp. Act	June 10, 1910	1910	5	3000	2	3500	2	31007
Des Moines, Iowa	86,368	Stat.	Mar. 29, 1907	1907	5	3000	2	3500	2	34301
Tacoma, Wash.	83,743	H. R.		May 3, 1910	5	3600	2	4000	2	38301
Kansas City, Kan.	82,331	Stat.	Mar. 2, 1907	Apr. 8, 1910	5	3000	2	4000	2	34501
Houston, Tex.	78,800	Sp. Act	1905	July, 1905	5	2400	2	4000	2	36003
Ft. Worth, Tex.	73,312	Sp. Act	Feb. 26, 1907	1907	5	3000	2	3600	2	36009
Wichita, Kan.	52,450	Stat.	Mar. 2, 1907	Apr. 1, 1909	5	1800	2	2500	2	34501
Springfield, Ill.	51,678	Stat.	Mar. 10, 1910	1911	5	3500	4	4000	4	34201
Sioux City, Iowa	47,828	Stat.	Mar. 29, 1907	Apr. 4, 1910	5	2500	2	3000	2	34301
Haverhill, Mass.	44,115	Sp. Act	June 3, 1908	1908	5	1800	2	2500	2	31001
Topeka, Kan.	43,684	Stat.	Mar. 2, 1907	Apr. 6, 1910	5	1800	2	2500	2	34501
Davenport, Iowa	43,028	Stat.	Mar. 29, 1907		5	2500	2	3000	2	34301
Berkeley, Cal.	40,434	H. R.		July 1, 1909	5	1800	4	2400	2	38003
San Diego, Cal.	39,578	H. R.	Jan. 12, 1909	1909	5	2000	4	2000	4	38001
Galveston, Tex.	36,981	Sp. Act	Mar. 30, 1903	1903	5	1200	2	2000	2	36001
Taunton, Mass.	34,259	Sp. Act	Mar. 26, 1909	Jan. 1, 1910	10	500	2	1200	2	31005
Cedar Rapids, Iowa	32,811	Stat.	Mar. 29, 1907	Jan. 1, 1908	5	1800	2	2500	2	34301
Huntington, W. Va.	31,161	Sp. Act	1909	June 1909	4	1500	3	1800	3	33201
Decatur, Ill.	31,140	Stat.	Mar. 9, 1910	1910	5	3000	4	3500	4	34201
Newport, Ky.	30,309	Stat.	Mar. 21, 1910	Jan. 1912	5	3000	4	3600	4	33701
Austin, Tex.	29,860	Sp. Act	Mar. 24, 1909	Apr. 19, 1909	5	2000	2	2500	2	36015
Colorado, Spgs., Colo.	29,078	H. R.	May 11, 1909	July 27, 1909	5	2000	4	3600	4	37001
Shreveport, La.	28,015	Stat.	Apr. 7, 1910	Nov. 15, 1910	5	2000‡	4	3000‡	3	36301
Columbia, S. C.	26,319	Stat.	Feb. 22, 1910	1910	5	2000	3	2500	4	33401

*If Statute or special act, date of Governor's approval; if Home Rule Charter, date of popular election. ‡Maximum. †Including Mayor.

41011

CITY, STATE	Population	Form	Date of Act*	Date in Operation	Commissioners			Mayor		Outline Reference
					No.†	Salary	Term	Salary	Term	
Elgin, Ill..........	25,976	Stat.	Mar. 9, 1910	1911	5	2000	4	2500	4	34210
Muskogee, Okla...	25,278	H, R.	Sept. 26, 1910		5	2500		3000		36115

CITIES OF 5000 TO 25000 POPULATION

CITY STATE	Population	Form	Date of Act‡	Date in Operation	Commissioners No.†	Commissioners Salary	Commissioners Term	Mayor Salary	Mayor Term	Outline Reference
Gloucester, Mass	24,398	Sp. Act	June 11, 1908	1909	5	$1000	1	$1200	1	31003
Burlington, Iowa	24,324	Stat.	Mar. 30, 1909	Apr. 4, 1910	3	1200	2	1500	2	34301
Beaumont, Tex.	20,640	Sp. Act	Apr. 18, 1907		7	Fixed by Council	2	Fixed by Council	2	36011
Leavenworth, Kan	19,363	Stat.	Mar. 2, 1907	1908	5	1000*	2	1800*	2	34501
Port Huron, Mich	18,863	H. R.	Dec. 1910	Jan. 1911	5	1200		2000		35003
Eau Claire, Wis	18,310	Stat.	June 15, 1909	Apr. 19, 1910	3	3000	3	3500	3	35101
Hutchinson, Kan	16,364	Stat.	Mar. 7, 1907	1909	5	1000*	2	1800*	2	34501
Denison, Tex	15,632	Sp. Act.	1907	Apr. 1907	3	1500	2	1800	2	36013
Ft. Dodge, Iowa	15,543	Stat.	Mar. 30, 1909	Apr. 1911	3	1200	2	1500	2	34301
Pittsburg, Kan	14,755	Stat.	1909		3	1000	3	1200	3	34503
Sioux Falls, S. D	14,094	Stat.	Oct. 1, 1909	1909	5	625	5	625	5	35501
Keokuk, Iowa	14,008	Stat.	Mar. 30, 1909	Apr. 11, 1910	3	900	2	1200	2	34301
Enid, Okla.	13,799	H. R.	Sept. 22, 1909		4	1500	2	1500	2	36105
Marshalltown, Iowa	13,374	Stat.	Mar. 30, 1909	Apr. 1, 1911	3	900	2	1200	2	34301
McAlester, Okla.	12,954	H. R.	Jan. 4, 1910	Oct. 4, 1910	3	2500	3	2500	3	36107
Coffeyville, Kan	12,687	Stat.	1909	1910	3	1000	3	1200	3	34503
Parsons, Kan	12,463	Stat.	1909	Apr. 18, 1910	3	1000	3	1200	3	34503
Sherman, Tex	12,412									
Hattiesburg, Miss	11,733	H. R.		1910						
Marshall, Tex	11,452	Sp. Act	1910	Apr. 15, 1910	10	150*	2	1800*	2	36023
Bluefield, W. Va	11,188	Sp. Act	1909	1909	4	1500	4	1500	4	33203
Independence, Kan	10,480	Stat.	1909	Apr. 28, 1909	3	1000	3	1200	3	34503
Amarillo, Tex	9,957			1911						
Ottowa, Ill	9,535	Stat.	Mar. 9, 1910	1911	5	400	4	600	4	34201
Emporia, Kan	9,058	Stat.	1909	1910	3	900	3	1000	3	34503

*Maximum. ‡If Statute or special act, date of Governor's approval; if Home Rule Charter, date of popular election. †Including Mayor.

41021

CITY, STATE	Population	Form	Date of Act	Date in Operation	Commissioners			Mayor		Outline Reference
					No.	Salary	Term	Salary	Term	
Iola, Kan.	9,032	Stat.	1909	Apr. 1910	3	$900	3	$1000	3	34503
Greenville, Tex.	8,850	Sp. Act	1907	Mar. 10, 1907	3	1200	2	1200	2	36005
Ardmore, Okla.	8,618	H. R.	Nov. 17, 1908	1909	5	600	4	1500	4	36103
Corpus Christi, Tex.	8,222	Sp. Act	Mar. 15, 1909	Apr. 1909	5	500	2	1800	2	36015
Newton, Kan.	7,862	Stat.	1909	Apr. 18, 1910	3	900	3	1000	3	34503
Grand Junction, Colo.	7,754	H. R.	Sept. 14, 1909	Nov. 2, 1909	5	1200	4	1500	4	37003
Dixon, Ill.	7,216	Stat.	Mar. 9, 1910	1911	5	400	4	600	4	34201
Wellington, Kan.	7,034	Stat.	1909	1910	3	900	3	1000	3	34503
Minot, N. D.	6,188	Stat.	Mar. 20, 1907	Apr. 1909	4	$5.00 per session	4	150	4	35401
Bartlesville, Okla.	6,181	H. R.	Aug. 2, 1910	1910	3	2000	3	2000	3	36109
Bismark, N. D.	5,443	Stat.	Mar. 20, 1907	1909	5	Not specified	4	Not specified	4	35401
Carbondale, Ill.	5,411	Stat.	Mar. 9, 1910	1911	5	400	4	600	4	34201

POPULAR CONTROL

CITIES OF OVER 100,000 POPULATION

CITY,	Initiative		ecall			ITY, STATE	Initiative		erendum		
	Spec. Elec.	Reg. Elec.	Spec. Elcc.	Reg. Elec.			Spec. Elec.	Reg. Elec.	Spec. Elec.	Reg. Elec.	
Oakland, Cal.	15	5	10	10							
Memphis, Tenn...... ...	—	—	—	—							
Spokane, Wash.	15	5	10	10							

Percentages (OF TOTAL VOTE CAST AT LAST MUNICIPAL ELECTION) REQUIRED ON PETITION FOR SPECIAL AND REGULAR ELECTION.

41202

CITY, STATE	Initiative		Referendum		Recall
	Spec. Elec.	Reg. Elec.	Spec. Elec.	Reg. Elec.	

CITY, STATE	Initiative		Referendum		Recall
	Spec. Elec.	Reg. Elec.	Spec. Elec.	Reg. Elec.	

CITIES OF 25,000 TO 100,000 POPULATION

ITY,	Initiative		Referendum		Recall
	Spec. Elec.	Reg. Elec.	Spec. Elec.	Reg. Elec.	
Dallas, Tex.	15	5	15	15	35
Lynn, Mass.	25	10	25	10	25
Des Moines, Iowa.	25	10	25	10	25
Tacoma, Wash.	20	5	15	15	25
Kansas City, Kan.	25	10			25
Houston, Tex.	—	—	—	—	—
Ft. Worth, Tex.	—	—	20	20	20
Wichita, Kas.	25	10			25
Springfield, Ill.	25	10	10	10	75
Sioux City, Iowa.	25	10	25	10	25
Haverhill, Mass.	25	10	—	—	25
Topeka, Kan.	25	10			25
Davenport, Iowa.	25	10	25	10	25
Berkeley, Cal.	15	5	10	10	20
San Diego, Cal.	15	5	7	7	25
Galveston, Tex.	—	—	—	—	—
Taunton, Mass.	—	—	—	—	—
Cedar Rapids, Iowa.	25	10	25	10	25
Huntington, W. Va.	—	—	—	—	—
Decatur, Ill.	25	10	10	10	75
Newport, Ky.	—	25	—	25	—
Austin, Tex.	25	25	25	25	25
Colorado Springs, Colo.	15	5	15	15	30

CITY	Initiative				Recall
	Spec. Elec.	Reg. Elec.	Spec. Elec.	Reg. Elec.	
Shreveport, La.	33		33		33
Columbia, S. C.	20		20		20
Muskogee, Okla.	x	x	x	x	—
Elgin, Ill.	25	10	10	10	

Percentages (OF TOTAL VOTE CAST AT LAST MUNICIPAL ELECTION REQUIRED ON PETITION FOR) SUBMISSION OF QUESTIONS AT SPECIAL AND REGULAR ELECTION. X **Constitution Provisions.**

CITY, STATE	Initiative		Referendum		Recall	CITY, STATE	Initiative		Referendum		Recall
	Spec. Elec.	Reg. Elec.	Spec. Elec.	Reg. Elec.			Spec. Elec.	Reg. Elec.	Spec. Elec.	Reg. Elec.	

41212

CITIES OF 5,000 TO 25,000 POPULATION

CITY, STATE	Initiative Spec. Elec.	Initiative Reg. Elec.	Referendum Spec. Elec.	Referendum Reg. Elec.	Recall
Gloucester, Mass.	25	25	25	25	—
Burlington, Iowa	25	10	25	10	25
Beaumont, Tex.	—	—	—	—	—
Leavenworth, Kan.	25	10			25
Port Huron, Mich.	25	25	25	25	—
Eau Claire, Wis.	—	—	20	20	—
Hutchinson, Kan.	25	10			25
Denison, Tex.	—	—	—	—	20
Ft. Dodge, Iowa	25	10	25	10	25
Pittsburg, Kan.	25	10			25
Sioux Falls, S. D.	5	—	5	—	15
Keokuk, Iowa	25	10	25	10	25
Enid, Okla.	x	x	x	x	30
Marshalltown, Iowa	25	10	25	10	25
McAlester, Okla.	x	x	x	x	25
Coffeyville, Kan.	25	10			25
Sherman, Tex.	—	—	—	—	—
Hattiesburg, Miss.	—	—	—	—	—
Marshall, Tex.	—	—	—	—	—
Bluefield, W. Va.	—	—	—	—	—
Independence, Kan.	25	10			25
Amarillo, Tex.	—	—	—	—	—
Ottowa, Ill.	25	10	10	10	75
Emporia, Kan.	25	10			25
Iola, Kan.	25	10			25
Greenville. Tex.	—	—	—	—	—
Ardmore, Okla.	—	25	—	25	30
Corpus Christi, Tex.	—	—	—	—	33⅓
Newton, Kan.	25	10			25
Grand Junction, Colo.	10	5	10	10	20
Dixon, Ill.	25	10	10	10	75
Wellington, Kan.	25	10	—	—	25
Minot, N. D.	—	—	—	—	—
Bartlesville, Okla.	x	x	x	x	25
Bismark, N. D.	—	—	—	—	—
Carbondale, Ill.	25	10	10	10	75

41221

Percentages (OF TOTAL VOTE CAST AT LAST MUNICIPAL ELECTION) REQUIRED ON PETITION FOR SUBMISSION OF QUESTIONS AT SPECIAL OR REGULAR ELECTIONS. **X Constitution Provisions.**

41222

CITY, STATE	Initiativ		ndum		Recall	CITY, STATE	Ini tiv		rend		Recall
	Spec. Elec.	Reg. Elec.	Spec. Elec.	Reg. Elec.			Spec. Elec.	Reg. Elec.	Spec. Elec.	Reg. Elec.	

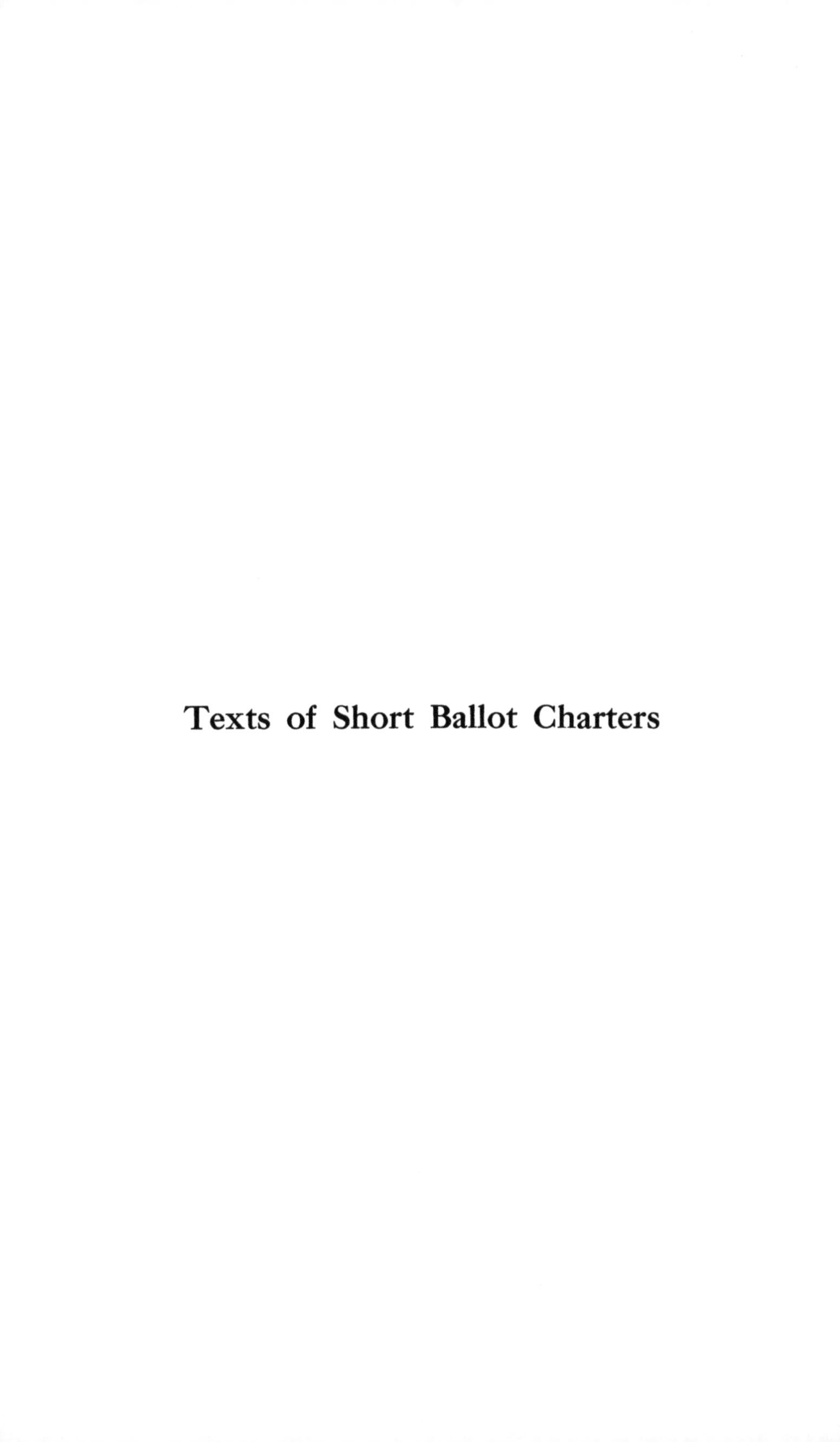

Texts of Short Ballot Charters

CHARTER OF GALVESTON, TEXAS

AN ACT TO AMEND "AN ACT TO INCORPORATE THE CITY OF GALVESTON AND TO GRANT IT A NEW CHARTER AND TO REPEAL ALL PRE-EXISTING CHARTERS," APPROVED APRIL 18, 1901, AND TO REPEAL ALL LAWS IN CONFLICT THEREWITH.

(CHAPTER 37, LAWS OF 1903)

Be it enacted by the Legislature of the State of Texas:

Section 1. Enacting clause. Corporate powers, duties, obligations, Corporate seal.

That all the inhabitants of the City of Galveston shall continue to be a body politic and corporate, with perpetual succession, by the name and style of the "City of Galveston," and as such they and their successors by that name shall have, exercise and enjoy all the rights, immunities, powers, privileges and franchises now possessed and enjoyed by said city, and herein granted and conferred; and shall be subject to all the duties and obligations now pertaining to or incumbent on said city as a corporation, not inconsistent with this Act, and may ordain and establish such acts, laws, regulations and ordinances, not inconsistent with the Constitution and laws of this State, as shall be needful for the government, interest, welfare and good order of said body politic; and under the same name shall be known in law, and be capable of contracting and being contracted with, suing and being sued, implead and being impleaded, answering and being answered unto, in all courts and places and in all matters whatever; may take, hold and purchase, lease, grant and convey such real and personal or mixed property or estate as the purposes of the corporation may require, within or without the limits thereof, and may make, have and use a corporate seal, and change and renew the same at pleasure.

Sec. 2. Corporate limits.

Sec. 3. City wards.

Sec. 4. City property.

[Vested in Corporation.]

Sec. 5. Mayor and Commissioners — first election of. Places of election and manner of holding. Cost of election; how paid. Canvassing returns. Mayor to be President; members of Board; tenure of office. Regular city elections; time appointed for. Places of election and manner of holding. Canvassing returns. Mayor and Commissioners. Qualifications and term of office. Municipal government. Time for qualifying.

As soon as practicable, and within sixty days after this Act shall take effect, it shall be the duty of the Commissioners' Court of Galveston County to order an election to be held in the City of Galveston, at which election the qualified voters of the City of Galveston shall select a Mayor and four Commissioners, who shall constitute the Board of Commissioners of the City of Galveston, and said Commissioners' Court shall fix the time and places in said city for holding said election, and the manner of holding the same shall be governed by the laws of the State of Texas governing general elections. The cost of such election shall be paid by the County of Galveston, but shall be refunded to said county by the City of Galveston. On the Tuesday following said election, or as soon thereafter as practicable, the said Court shall canvass the returns and declare the election of the candidates receiving the highest number of votes.

The Mayor shall be President of said Board of Commissioners, and the members of said Board shall hold office until their successors are elected and qualified.

On the second Tuesday in May, 1905, and in each second year thereafter, the Board of Commissioners of said city for the time being shall cause to be held in said city an election for their successors in office. In ordering such election the Board of Commissioners of the City of Galveston shall determine the places in the City of Galveston for holding such election, and the manner of holding same shall be governed by the laws of the State of Texas regulating general elections. On the Tuesday following such election the Board shall canvass the returns and declare the election of the candidates receiving the highest number of votes. The Mayor and each of the said four Commissioners shall not be less than twenty-five years of age, citizens of the United States, and for five years immediately preceding their election residents of the City of Galveston, and shall hold office for two years from and after the date of their qualification and until their successors shall have been duly elected and qualified. Said Board of Commissioners shall constitute the municipal government of the City of Galveston.

Each of said Commissioners, within ten days after the official announcement of his election or appointment, as the case may be, shall qualify as required by this Charter and the Constitution and laws of the State, and failing so to do, his office shall become vacant.

Sec. 6. Commissioners successors of Mayor and Aldermen. Board of Commissioners—power of. Mayor-President. Directors in corporations.

The President and other members of the Board of Commissioners elected under this Act, and their successors in office, shall be held and deemed, in law and in fact, the successors of the Mayor and Aldermen of said City of Galveston, and upon the qualification of said President and the other members of said Board of Commissioners, all the powers, rights and duties of the Mayor and Board of Aldermen of the said city shall cease; and from and after the passage hereof the said Board of Commissioners shall have and exercise all the rights, powers and duties of the Mayor and Board of Aldermen of cities as may be conferred by the Constitution and laws of this State, and shall have and exercise all the rights, powers and duties conferred upon them or either of them by the terms of this Act.

The President of the said Board shall be Mayor, and shall have and exercise all the rights, powers and duties of Mayor conferred by the Constitution and laws of this State, and all those conferred by the terms of this Act. The Mayor shall be the President of the Board, and shall be named and styled "Mayor-President of the Board of Commissioners for the City of Galveston," and wherever the words Mayor or President occur in this Act they and each of them shall be held and construed as identical terms, descriptive of the President of the Board of Commissioners for the City of Galveston; and wherever the said city has heretofore, under the decree or judgment of any court, or under any law, ordinance or resolution, been entitled to representation through the Mayor of said city and one or more of the Aldermen thereof on the Board of Directors of any incorporated company in which the said city may own stock or be interested, it shall hereafter be represented on any such Board of Directors by the President of said Board of Commissioners and by two other members of said Board, to be selected by said Board.

Sec. 7. Board of Commissioners—style of. (Amended, Acts 1905.) Salaries. President—duties, salary, etc.

Said Mayor and Commissioners shall, collectively, constitute and be known as the "Board of Commissioners of the City of Galveston." They shall take an oath to faithfully perform the duties of their said office, and each shall receive as compensation for his said services, beginning June 1, 1905, the sum of twelve hundred dollars ($1,200) per annum, payable in equal monthly installments, except that the President of said Board shall receive a salary of two thousand dollars ($2,000) per annum, payable in equal monthly installments, and the said President shall devote at least six hours a day to the duties of his office and to the affairs of said city.

Sec. 8. Bond and oath of Mayor and Commissioners. Bonds; how payable and conditioned. Officers appointed by majority vote.

That the Mayor and each Commissioner, before entering upon the duties of his office, shall give bond payable to the Governor of the State, for the use and benefit of said city, in the sum of five thousand dollars, conditioned for the faithful discharge of his duty, with two or more good and sufficient sureties, to be approved by the County Judge of Galveston County, and shall in addition to taking the oath prescribed by the Constitution of the State also take an oath that he is not under direct or indirect obligation to appoint or elect any person to any office, position or employment under said government.

The said Board of Commissioners shall, by a majority vote of all the members thereof, have the power to appoint all officers and subordinates in all departments of the said city.

Sec. 9. Removal of Commissioners.

Any member of said Board of Commissioners may be removed for the same reason and in the same manner as county officers.

Sec. 10. Resignation or removal of Mayor or Commissioners. Vacancy; election to fill. Mayor pro tem.

Resignation by the Mayor or any Commissioner elected under this Act shall be made in writing to the Board of Commissioners for their action thereupon. In case of the removal of the Mayor or of any Commissioners from the territorial limits of said city, such removal shall ipso facto be deemed to create a vacancy in his office. In case of any vacancy from any cause in the office of Mayor, or any Commissioner, the Board of Commissioners shall fill such vacancy by appointment until the next succeeding regular election; provided, such election is not more than ninety days off, and the person so appointed shall possess all the qualifications required by this Charter for this office; but should such election be more than ninety days off, this said office shall be filled by an election called for that purpose according to law. In case of vacancy in the office of Mayor, from any cause, the Board of Commissioners may appoint one of their number to act as Mayor pro tem until such vacancy is filled as provided for in this section, and such Mayor pro tem shall have and exercise all the powers and duties of Mayor while he so acts, and his acts shall have the same force and validity.

Sec. 11. Oaths administered by Commissioners and Secretary.

Each Commissioner and the Secretary of the Board of Commissioners shall be, and they are hereby, authorized to administer oaths in the municipal affairs and government of the city.

Sec. 12. Rules and regulations; Commissioners to make and enforce. Commissioners' departments—designation of heads; powers; duties. Police and Fire Commissioner. Commissioner of Streets and Public Property. Waterworks and Sewerage Commissioner. Commissioner of Finance and Revenue.

Said Board of Commissioners so constituted shall have control and supervision over all the departments of said city, and to that end shall have power to make and enforce such rules and regulations as they may see fit and proper for and concerning the organization, management and operation of all of the departments of said city and whatever agencies may be created for the administration of its affairs.

They shall, by a majority vote of all said Commissioners, designate from among their members one Commissioner who shall be known as "Police and Fire Commissioner," and who shall have under his special charge the enforcement of all police regulations of said city and general supervision over the fire department thereof; and one Commissioner, to be known as the "Commissioner of Streets and Public Property," who shall have under his special charge the supervision of the streets, alleys, public grounds and property of said city, and be charged with the duty of lighting the streets, and keeping the streets, alleys, public grounds and property in a clean and sanitary condition, and with the enforcement of all rules and regulations necessary to these ends, and who shall also have under his special charge the supervision of all public improvements, except as herein otherwise provided, and shall see that all contracts therefor are faithfully complied with, and that the conditions of the grant of any franchise or privilege are faithfully complied with and performed; and one Commissioner, to be known as the "Waterworks and Sewerage Commissioner," who shall have under his special charge the construction, maintenance and operation of the waterworks and sewer system and departments of said city, and shall see to the enforcement of all regulations with respect to said departments and with respect to all the revenues pertaining thereto; and one Commissioner who shall be known as the "Commissioner of Finance and Revenue," who shall have under his special charge the enforcement of all laws for the assessment and collection of taxes of every kind, and the collection of all revenues belonging to said city from whatever source the same may be derived, and who shall also examine into and keep informed as to the finances of such city.

Sec. 12a. President has right to vote. Board may compel witness' attendance; also production of books and papers. Contempt—punishment for. Process—issuance of; how served.

The President of said Board shall have the right to vote as a member thereof on all questions which may arise. Said Board of Commissioners shall have the power to summon and compel the attendance of witnesses, and the production of books and papers before them whenever it may be necessary for the more effective discharge of their duties, and shall have power to punish for contempt of said Board with the same fines and penalties as the County Judge may punish for contempt of the County Court. All process necessary to enforce the powers conferred by this section shall be signed by the President of the Board and attested by the Secretary thereof, and shall be served by any member of the police force of said city.

Sec. 13. President—powers and duties. Claims—audited; approval of. Financial statements.

That the President of said Board of Commissioners shall be the executive officer of said city, and shall see that all the laws thereof are enforced. The Commissioner named as the head of each department shall audit all accounts or claims against it, unless he be absent or fail or refuse so to do, in which event, the President shall appoint another Commissioner to act in his stead during his absence or to audit claims and accounts as the said Commissioner shall fail or refuse to act upon; but before payment all accounts shall be acted upon and approved by at least two members of said Board of Commissioners. Said Board shall require a statement to be published in January, April, July and October of each year, in the official newspaper of said city, showing a full, clear and complete statement of all taxes and other revenues collected and expended during the preceding quarter, indicating the respective sources from which the moneys are derived, and also indicating the disposition made thereof.

Sec. 14. Riots—President's duties as to. Special police summoned. Failing to appear; penalty for.

That whenever the President of the Board of Commissioners shall deem it necessary in order to enforce the laws of the city, or to avert danger, or protect life or property, in case of a riot or any outbreak, or calamity or public disturbance, or when he has reason to fear any serious violation of law or order, or any outbreak, or any other danger to said city or the inhabitants thereof, he shall summon into service, as a special police force, all, or as many of the citizens as in his judgment and discretion may be necessary and proper; and such summons may be by proclamation or order, addressed to the citizens generally, or those of any ward of the city or subdivision thereof, or such summons may be by personal notification; such special police, while in service, shall be subject to the orders of the President of the Board of Commissioners, shall perform such duties as he may require, and shall have the same power while on duty as the regular police force of said city; and any person so summoned, and failing to obey, or appearing and failing to perform any duty that may be required by this Act, shall be fined in any sum not exceeding one hundred dollars.

Sec. 15. (Amended Acts 1905.) Acting President—appointment of; compensation of. President receives no salary, when.

In case the President of said Board is unable to perform the duties of his office by reason of temporary or continued absence or sickness, the said Board shall appoint by ballot, by a majority vote of all the members thereof, one of their number to act in his stead, whose official designation shall be "Acting President of the Board of Commissioners," and the Commissioner so appointed shall be invested with all the powers, and shall perform all the duties of the President of said Board during such absence or sickness, and shall receive the salary of the said President during such vacancy; **Provided,** that it shall continue for ten days or longer, and during such absence in excess of ten days the President shall receive no salary; **Provided, further,** that the Commissioner receiving compensation as Acting President shall not receive his salary as Commissioner for the same time he receives compensation as Acting President.

Sec. 16. Regular meetings of the Board. Quorum. Commissioners' department—no action as to business of, unless. Special meetings; how called; business of. Legislative sessions open.

Said Board of Commissioners shall meet at least once every week in regular meeting at such time as shall be fixed by said Board, at the City Hall or other designated place in said city, to consider and take under advisement and act upon such business as may come before them. A majority of said Board shall constitute a quorum for the transaction of all business, but no action of said Commissioner shall be effective unless upon a vote of a majority of such quorum, and no final action shall be taken in any matter concerning the special department of any absent Commissioner unless such business has been made a special order of the day, or such action is taken at a regular meeting of the Board.

Special meetings may be called by the President of said Board, or by any two members thereof, at any time, to consider only such matters as shall be mentioned in the call for said meeting, and written notice thereof shall be given to each member of said Board.

All legislative sessions of said Board, whether regular or called, shall be open to the public.

Sec. 17. Lawmaking power of Board. Publication of ordinances. Proof of publication. Revised ordinances not published. Ordinances take effect, when. Ordinances evidence in Court.

The Board of Commissioners of said city shall be vested with the power and charged with the duty of making all laws or ordinances not inconsistent with the Constitution and laws of this State, touching every object, matter and subject within the local government instituted by this Act. Every ordinance imposing any penalty, fine, imprisonment or forfeiture for a violation of its provisions shall, after the passage thereof, be published in every issue of the official newspaper for ten (10) days successively (excluding Sundays), and proof of such publication by the printer or publisher of such newspaper made before any officer authorized to administer oaths and filed with the Secretary of the Board of Commissioners, or any other competent proof of such publication, shall in all courts be conclusive evidence of the legal publication and promulgation of such ordinances; **Provided,** that amendments and corrections made in digesting and revision for publication in book form need not be so published.

Ordinances passed by the Board of Commissioners and requiring publication shall take effect and be in force from and after the tenth publication thereof unless it be otherwise expressly provided in such ordinance. Ordinances passed by the Board of Commissioners and not requiring publication shall take effect and be in force from and after their passage, unless it shall therein otherwise expressly be provided. All ordinances of the city, when printed and published and bearing on the title page thereof the words "Ordained and published by the Board of Commissioners of the City of Galveston," or words of like import, shall be prima facie evidence of their authenticity and shall be admitted and received in all courts and places without further proof.

Sec. 18. Ordinances; style of.

The style of all ordinances shall be, "Be it ordained by the Board of Commissioners of the city of Galveston," but such caption may be omitted when said ordinances are published in book form or are revised and digested under the order of the Board.

Sec. 19. Charter officers; appointment of. Terms of office. All officers qualified voters.

The Board of Commissioners at their first meeting after their qualification, or so soon thereafter as possible shall select the following officers, to-wit: a secretary, a treasurer, an attorney, a recorder or judge of the Corporation Court, an assessor and collector of taxes, a chief of police, a chief of the fire department, an engineer who shall also be superintendent of streets, an auditor, a secretary of waterworks and sewerage departments, a harbor master, a sexton, a superintendent of waterworks and sewerage, an engineer of the waterworks, an assistant engineer of the waterworks; and, if deemed necessary by the Board, an inspector of waterworks and sewerage plumbing, an assistant chief of police, an assistant chief of the fire department and an assistant city engineer. All said officers so elected shall hold their offices for two years, and until the election and qualification of their successors, unless removed by the said Board of Commissioners under the authority vested in it by this Act. No one shall be eligible to appointment or election to the foregoing offices or any of them unless he be at the time of his appointment a qualified voter in the City of Galveston.

[Remainder of section relates to the duties, compensation, etc., of the City Secretary, Treasurer, Assessor and Collector, Attorney, Auditor, Health Physician, Eng eer, Harbor Master, Superintendent of Waterworks a Sewerage, Engineer of Waterworks, Inspector of Wat works and Sewerage and Sexton.]

Sec. 20. Police and Fire Departments.

Said Board of Commissioners shall have full power authority to establish and maintain a police departm to be composed of a Chief of Police, an Assistant Chief Police, two sergeants and such number of patrolmen policemen as such Board may deem necessary, said offic and members of said police department to be appointed, their compensation and duties to be fixed, defined and re lated as hereinafter provided; and shall also have power authority to establish and maintain a fire department, procure fire engines and other apparatus for the extingui ment of fires, and provide engine houses for keeping preserving the same, and said fire department shall be c posed of a Chief of the Fire Department, an Assistant Cl of the Fire Department, and such number of firemen as Board may deem necessary, the officers and members of fire department to be appointed and their compensation duties to be fixed, defined and regulated as hereinafter vided.

At the first meeting of said Board of Commissioners a their qualification, or as soon thereafter as possible, it s be the duty of the Commissioner who may be selected Police and Fire Commissioner to prepare and present to Board of Commissioners in writing his recommendations persons for appointment, both in said police and fire dep ments, based on the integrity of character and physical intellectual capacities of the applicants for such positio and the said Board of Commissioners shall, upon recei such recommendations, select therefrom proper persons fill such positions in the departments respectively as may by them deemed wise and necessary; and upon the fai or refusal of said Police and Fire Commissioner to pre said recommendations at the second regular meeting of Board, it shall thereafter proceed to elect proper per to fill such positions; **Provided,** however, that so far a may be practicable and consistent with good order, discip and improvement of the public service, it shall be the of said Police and Fire Commissioner to prefer in rec mendations to said Board for appointment to the police fire departments, respectively, those men who have pr themselves capable, good and efficient in the perform of their duties, and the said Board shall give due weigh such recommendations; **Provided,** however, that the C of Police and Chief of the Fire Department shall have power to temporarily suspend any subordinate officer member of their departments, respectively, for reasons s factory to said Chief of Police or Fire Department, as case may be, and to appoint some person to discharge duties of such suspended officer or member until the gro of such suspension can be inquired into by the Police Fire Commissioner; and it shall be the duty of the chie whose department such suspension shall occur to report same in writing within three (3) days, with the rea therefor, to the said Police and Fire Commissioner, and to furnish such suspended officer or member with a thereof within like time. Said Police and Fire Commissioner is hereby invested with exclusive jurisdiction to hear and determine any and all charges against any member of the police and fire departments for infractions of discipline, disobedience of orders, incompetency, corruption, malfeasance or nonfeasance in office, for violation of any of the rules or regulations prescribed for the government of said police and fire departments, or for any conduct unbecoming an officer or member of the said departments, respectively; and every officer and member of the police and fire departments shall obey all lawful rules and regulations prescribed by said Board of Commissioners for the government of said police and fire departments on pain of dismissal, or such lighter punishment, either by suspension, reduction or forfeiture of pay, or otherwise, as the said Police and Fire Commissioner may adjudge; **Provided,** however, that all charges or complaints against the Chief of Police or the Chief of the Fire Department shall be heard and determined by said Board of Commissioners as provided in this Act in case of trial before said Board of Commissioners. In case of any charges or complaints made under the provisions of this section against any member of said fire or police departments within the jurisdiction of the Police and Fire Commissioner, he shall have the power to administer oaths to summon and compel the attendance of witnesses before him, and to examine such witnesses upon any matter where it may be necessary to the discharge of his duties.

The Chief of Police shall attend upon the court which may be designated by law for the trial of offenses arising under this Act, under any ordinance, rule or regulation enacted by the Board of Commissioners pursuant to this Act, and shall promptly and faithfully execute all writs and process issuing from said court. He shall be the chief police officer of said city and shall have like power with the sheriff of the county to execute the writ of search warrant. He shall be active in quelling riots, disorders and disturbances of the peace within the limits of the said city, and shall take into custody all persons so offending against the public peace, and shall have the authority to take suitable and sufficient bail for the appearance before said court of any person charged with an offense within the jurisdiction of said court; and it shall be his duty to arrest all persons who shall obstruct or interfere with him in the execution of the duties of his office, or who shall be guilty of disorderly conduct, or any disturbance whatever. To prevent a breach of the peace, or to preserve quiet and good order, he shall have authority to close any theatre, barroom, ballroom, drinking house or any other place or building of public resort, and in the prevention and suppression of crime and the arrest of offenders within said city, he shall have, possess and execute like power, authority and jurisdiction as the sheriff of a county under the laws of this State. He shall receive a salary of not exceeding fifteen hundred ($1500) dollars per annum. He shall give such bond for the faithful performance of his duties, and perform such other duties, and possess such other powers, rights and authority, in addition to those herein provided, as the Board of Commissioners may require and confer upon him, not inconsistent with the Constitution and laws of this State and the provisions of this Act. In case of absence, sickness or inability to act, of the Chief of Police, said Police and Fire Commissioner shall have the power, and it shall be his duty, to designate some other member of said police department as Acting Chief of Police during the period of such absence, sickness or inability to act of said Chief of Police.

The Chief of the Fire Department shall be charged with the duty of superintending and directing the extinguishing of fires and preservation and safe-keeping of all fire engines, hose and other apparatus used in connection therewith; he shall have the power, and it is hereby made his duty, to keep away from the vicinity of any fire all idle, disorderly and suspicious persons, and to compel all officers of the city and all other persons to aid in the extinguishment of fires and the preservation of property exposed to danger thereat, and in preventing goods from being stolen, and generally to carry out and enforce such regulations for the prevention and extinguishment of fires as may be by said Board of Commissioners deemed expedient.

The Assistant Chief of the Fire Department shall receive as compensation for his services the sum of not exceeding twelve hundred ($1200) dollars per annum. The Assistant Chief of Police shall receive as compensation for his services the sum of not exceeding twelve hundred ($1200) dollars per annum; **Provided,** however, that neither the Assistant Chief of the Fire Department nor the Assistant Chief of Police shall be appointed unless deemed necessary by the Board of Commissioners.

Sec. 20a.

[Relates to captains, firemen and engineers, salaries, etc.]

Sec. 21. Officers—further and other duties may be prescribed. Compensation of, fixed by Board. All officers to give bonds. New bonds. Vacancies.

Said Board of Commissioners shall have power from time to time to require further and other duties of all officers whose duties are herein prescribed, and to define and prescribe the powers and duties of all officers elected to any office under this Act whose duties are not herein specially mentioned, and to fix their compensation when not herein fixed. They shall also require bonds to be given to said city by all officers for the faithful performance of their duties, and shall require a new bond from any officer whenever in the judgment of said Board the existing bond is insufficient, and whenever such new bond is required he shall perform no official act until said bond shall be given and approved. The Board of Commissioners shall provide for the filling of vacancies in all offices not herein provided for, and in all cases of vacancy the same shall be filled only for the unexpired term.

Sec. 22. Old Board and officers continued. Acts validated.

The present Board of Commissioners, officers and employees of said city of Galveston shall continue in office and in the exercise of their functions until the Mayor and Commissioners provided for herein are elected as herein provided and have qualified and shall otherwise provide. And all acts done or to be done, and proceedings taken or had or to be taken, or had by or under authority of said present Board of Commissioners in pursuance of or in compliance with said Act of the Legislature, approved April 18, 1901, or this Act, are hereby validated and confirmed to all intents and purposes as though no question had ever been made concerning the authority of said present Board of Commissioners.

Sec. 23. Ordinances continued in force.

All ordinances, regulations or resolutions now in force in the city of Galveston, and not in conflict with this act, shall remain in force under this Act until altered, modified or repealed by the Board of Commissioners herein provided for.

Sec. 24.

[No salary to exceed $900. Fees prohibited, except fees paid to city. City Electrician; salary.]

Sec. 25. Terms of office. Vacancies, how filled.

The duration of all offices created by this Act, or by any ordinance pursuant to this Act passed by the Board of Commissioners of said city, shall never exceed two years; **Provided,** nevertheless, that the incumbent of any such office shall continue to perform the duties thereof until his successor is duly qualified. In case of vacancy in the Board of Commissioners of said city, such vacancy shall be filled in the manner provided in Section 10 of this Act for the unexpired term, and in case of vacancy in any other office in said city the Board of Commissioners thereof shall fill such vacancy for the unexpired term.

Sec. 26.

[Officers to attend meetings of Board.]

Sec. 27. Official bonds—how payable.

All official bonds required under this Act, except the bonds of the members of the Board of Commissioners, shall be made payable to the City of Galveston, and shall be in such form and with such sureties as the Board of Commissioners may prescribe.

Sec. 28. City not to give bond in judicial proceedings.

It shall not be necessary in any action, suit or proceeding of any kind in which the city of Galveston is a party, for any bond, undertaking or security to be executed by or in behalf of said city, but all such actions, suits, appeals or proceedings shall be conducted in the same manner as if such bond, undertaking or security had been given, and said city shall be liable to the same extent as if they had been duly given and executed.

Sec. 29. Board to create or discontinue offices. Remove officers. Fix compensation of. All officers qualified voters.

The Board of Commissioners shall have authority from time to time to create and fill and discontinue offices and employments other than herein prescribed according to the date of their appointment be qualified voters of the city and in their discretion, by a majority vote of all the members of the Board; to remove, for or without cause, the incumbent of any such office or employment, and may, by order or otherwise, prescribe, limit or change the compensation of such officers or employees. All officers of the city shall at the date of their appointment be qualified voters of the City of Galveston.

Sec. 30. Officers sick or absent, substitute for.

In case of sickness or absence or inability from any cause on the part of any official to perform his duties, the Board of Commissioners may provide for the performance of such duties by a temporary substitute of such officer, or otherwise, as they may deem best, and the acts performed by such substitute or otherwise, as said Board may direct, shall be deemed as valid for all intents and purposes as though performed by the said official himself.

Sec. 31. Breaches of duty of city officials; liability. District Attorney to prosecute. Right of Board to deal with.

All of the officials of said city charged with disbursing, safe-keeping or performing any other acts touching the taxes or other revenues of said city now due or that may hereafter become due, shall be liable for any and all breaches of duty touching the same, as are the State and county officials in regard to like services and acts, and may be proceeded against criminally and civilly in the same way. It shall be the duty of the District Attorney of the district in which said city of Galveston is situated to enforce all such remedies, civilly and criminally, just as in the case of State officers; **Provided,** that nothing in this section shall impair the jurisdiction of the Board of Commissioners in respect to such offenses, as provided in this Act, but all such remedies shall be deemed and held to be cumulative.

Sec. 32. Officers—removal of for incompetency, etc. Notice to accused. Board to try charges. Accused entitled to counsel. Vote on charges. Judgment entered.

The Board of Commissioners shall have the power to remove any officer for incompetency, inefficiency, corruption, mal-conduct, malfeasance, or non-feasance in office, or such other causes as may be prescribed by ordinance after due notice in writing, and opportunity to be heard in his defense, under the rules and regulations hereinafter set forth. That whenever charges are preferred in writing under oath, and filed with the President of said Board by any person against any such officer for any or all of the offenses named or provided for as above, it shall be his duty to have the accused duly served with a copy of such charges and shall set a day to inquire into the truth of such charges and shall notify the accused and the other members of the said Board, and the witnesses for and against the accused to be present, and the said Board of Commissioners shall constitute a Court to try and determine said case and they are hereby invested with exclusive jurisdiction to hear and determine said charges, and may continue the investigation from day to day, upon proper showing, to enable the accused or prosecutor to get material evidences before said Board. The accused shall have the right to be heard in person or by counsel, and said Board shall likewise be represented by counsel, if they desire it. Upon the conclusion of the investigation and argument of the case, a vote shall be taken on each charge and specification, and if a majority of all members of said Board vote to sustain either of the charges against the accused, said Board shall enter or cause to be entered its judgment in which shall be recorded the vote of each member of the Board upon the several charges and specifications, and an order shall be entered removing the accused from his office and declaring the same vacant. But if the vote is otherwise, the accused shall be declared "not guilty," and judgment entered accordingly.

Sec. 33.

[Relates to the management of the John Sealy Hospital.]

Sec. 34.

[Defines the powers of local government; enactment of measures for public health, opening of streets, establishment of hospitals, regulation of vagrancy, erection of buildings, exclusion of paupers from the city, regulation of slaughter houses, regulation of street railroads, disposition of sewerage, issuance of licenses, regulation of public amusements, etc.]

Sec. 35. Condemnation for streets, drains, and sewers, and other public purposes. (Amended, Acts 1905.) Removal of buildings unauthorized on shores and waters. Nuisances—abatement of. Notice to owners. Cost of, charge on property.

To pass ordinances for the condemnation of property for the purpose of opening the streets of the city, and for the construction and maintenance of drains, sewers, and combination drains and sewers, and other public purposes, conforming the mode and manner of such condemnation to the rules prescribed for cities and towns by the general laws of the State, and to prohibit or remove, at the expense of the owner thereof, all buildings or structures on the shores or in the waters within the limits of the city where the same are not permitted or authorized by law; to define nuisances, and by adequate penalties to prevent or abate, or upon reasonable notice, which in case of a non-resident may be made through the mails or by publication in a newspaper, to require or cause the abatement and removal of all nuisances within the city, and for a distance of five miles outside of the same, at the cost and expense of the person or persons responsible therefor, or who may own, occupy or control the premises on which said nuisances exist, and the cost and expense of removing or abating said nuisances from such premises shall be assessed against the same and against the owner thereof, and shall be a lien on said premises and enforceable in any court of competent jurisdiction; and said Board of Commissioners shall have full power to pass and adopt all such ordinances as may be necessary or proper to make effective and enforce the provisions and requirements herein expressed.

Sec. 36. Dead carcass and other unwholesome matters—removal of.

Sec. 37. Harbor and channel—dredging, cleansing, protection of. Wharves—to erect and regulate erection of. Public property—to fill and improve; use of, regulated. Channel and harbor—protection of.

The said Board of Commissioners shall have the power to do any and all acts necessary to preserve the harbor and dredge out, widen or deepen the channel of the harbor of the City of Galveston, to prevent any use of the same or any act in relation thereto inconsistent with the public health, or calculated to render the waters of the same, or any part thereof, impure or offensive, or tending in any degree to fill up or obstruct the said channel; and to prevent and punish the casting, throwing or depositing therein of any stone, shell or other substance, logs or floating matter, and to prevent and remove all obstructions therein and to punish the authors thereof. It shall also have the power to erect and to regulate the erection of wharves fronting the channel, or their extension in such manner as may be by it deemed for the public interest, to fill or cause to be filled or otherwise improved any property belonging to said City of Galveston, or under its control, and to do any and all acts necessary and proper to promote the use and availability of such property for the purposes of commerce and in aid of the preservation and protection of the said harbor of Galveston and the channel therein.

Sec. 38. Deep water—to procure; appropriations.

The Board of Commissioners shall have power to promote and secure the obtaining and maintenance of deep water in the harbor of Galveston and from said harbor into the Gulf of Mexico, and to that end may appoint and employ such agent or agents as they may deem necessary or expedient and appropriate and expend any sum of money not exceeding three thousand ($3,000) dollars per annum.

Sec. 39. Hawkers, peddlers, pawnbrokers, etc.—licensed; prohibited; regulated. Dealers in bankrupt stocks—same. Licensing generally.

To license, tax, regulate, suppress and prevent hawkers, peddlers, pawnbrokers and dealers in all kinds of junk and second-hand goods, wares and merchandise, itinerant or transient venders of clothing or wearing apparel, articles of bedding or merchandise of any description whatever, dealers in bankrupt or fire stocks or damaged stocks of any kind, or any other business or occupation which in the opinion of said Board shall be the proper subject of police regulation.

Sec. 40. Bathing and swimming, regulated. (Amended Acts, 1905.) Buildings, etc., on beach.

The Board of Commissioners shall have power to regulate and determine the time and place of bathing and swimming in the waters adjoining or within said city and to prevent any obscene or indecent exposition, exposure or conduct; to regulate by general ordinance the character and construction, and prohibit the use for any improper or unlawful purposes of bath houses, pavilions, restaurants, fishing piers and other structures in the waters adjacent to the beach of the city; to regulate the construction of approaches to such structures so as to not unreasonably obstruct or interfere with the drive on said beach; and to exercise a general police control along said beach and in the waters adjacent thereto.

Sec. 41. Railroad tracks—removal for non-user. Railroad tracks—change location of. Lien for cost of removal.

The Board of Commissioners shall have power to require, on due notice, all railway companies owning tracks within the city limits which may have been or may hereafter be abandoned by them, by non-user, to move such tracks and to restore at their own expense the streets or way upon which such abandoned track is located to proper grade. The Board of Commissioners shall have power at any time to change the location and to remove or cause to be removed the railway track or tracks on any street or avenue from one portion of the street to another, and to effect and enforce such change of location or removal in such mode as may be prescribed by ordinance or otherwise and at the expense of the owner or operator thereof, and to secure the payment thereof shall have a lien on all the property of said railway companies.

Sec. 42. Official journal.

The Board of Commissioners shall, as soon as may be after the commencement of each fiscal year, contract as they may by ordinance or resolution determine, with a public newspaper of such city as the official paper thereof, and to continue as such until another is selected, and shall cause to be published therein all ordinances, notices and other matter required by this Act, or by the ordinances of said city, to be published.

Sec. 43. Public library—establishment of. Donation of books, etc., for.

The Board of Commissioners shall have authority, by ordinance duly enacted, to provide for the establishment and maintenance of a free public library in the City of Galveston, and to this end may make appropriations in amounts within their discretion; and may receive donations of books, papers, magazines, periodicals, or other property or money for the benefit of and maintenance of such public library.

Sec. 44. Auditing accounts; collection of revenues and assets; payment of liabilities and expenses. Fiscal year. Budget—making of. Reserve fund—unexpended portion of, how disposed of. Appropriations in excess of budget—prohibited; punished; void. Estimates for budget by heads of departments. Certified to. Details and objects of. Budget allowances not to be changed, except. Salaries, etc., changed by unanimous vote, except. Board may make loan. Deficiency—pro-rata abatement of allowances. Excess of revenue to general fund. Each commissioner shall file itemized report of money expended.

The Board of Commissioners shall have full authority over the financial affairs of the city, and shall provide for the collection of all revenues and other assets, the auditing and settlement of all accounts, and in the exercise of a sound discretion make appropriation for the payment of all liabilities and expenses. The fiscal year of the city shall begin March 1st of each year. In the month of February of each year, or as soon thereafter as practicable, the Board shall make a careful estimate of the probable revenues for the next fiscal year, and apportion the same to the several departments of the City Government, including a reserve fund of twenty-five thousand ($25,000.00) dollars, to be used only in the case of extraordinary emergencies which could not have been foreseen before their occurrence. Any unexpended portion of said reserve fund created for any year shall constitute a part of such reserve fund for the ensuing year. Any member of the said Board of Commissioners who shall knowingly vote for, or in any manner aid or promote, the passage or adoption of any ordinance, legislation or other act of said Board increasing the appropriation for the expenses of said city beyond the estimate aforesaid, unless the actual revenues shall have exceeded such estimate, and in such event beyond such actual revenue, shall thereby vacate his office and shall be guilty of malfeasance in office and shall be removed from his office in the manner provided for in this Act, and any appropriation over and above the said estimated revenues shall be void. Such estimate or budget shall be prepared in such detail and as to the aggregate sum and the items thereof, as the said Board shall deem advisable, and in order to enable the said Board to properly prepare such estimate, the heads of all departments shall, at least thirty (30) days before the said estimate is hereby required to be made, send to the said Board, in writing, estimates of the amounts needed for the conduct respectively of each department of said city for the next ensuing fiscal year. Such estimates shall be certified to by the parties making them, and shall specify in detail the objects thereof, and items required for the respective departments, including a statement of each of the salaries of the officers, employees, deputies and subordinates in each department. It shall be the duty of the said Board of Commissioners, when assembled for the consideration of said budget, to consider and investigate the estimate prepared by said officers, to hold daily sessions, if necessary, for the consideration and adoption of said budget. After said budget shall have been duly passed and adopted, said Board of Commissioners shall not have the power to increase the amounts fixed therein, whether by insertion of new items or otherwise, beyond the estimated revenues, unless the actual revenues shall exceed such estimate, and in such event beyond such actual revenue, and the said several sums as therein fixed shall be and become appropriated after the beginning of the next ensuing fiscal year for the several purposes therein named, to be used by the said Board of Commissioners and the several departments of said government for the purposes therein named; **Provided,** that the salaries as so fixed by the Board and the other provisions of the budget may at any time be changed by the unanimous vote of the full Board, except that the said reserve fund shall not be changed nor shall any funds appropriated for the use of one department be diverted to the use of another, and no loan shall be authorized or made to pay any deficiency arising from a failure to realize sufficient income from taxation to meet the amounts provided for in said budget, but the said Board of Commissioners may borrow money for its use in anticipation of the receipt of taxes levied for any one year, and pledge, as security, the uncollected taxes for any such year; **Provided,** however, that the money so borrowed for this purpose shall not exceed in any one year the sum of one hundred thousand ($100,000.00) dollars. In case of any deficiency there shall be a pro rata abatement of all appropriations contained in said budget, and in case of any surplus arising in any fiscal year by reason of an excess of income received from the estimated revenues over the expenditures for such year, the said surplus shall be credited to the general fund of said city, and shall form part of the general fund for the next ensuing fiscal year. And each of said City Commissioners shall at the end of each fiscal year file with the Secretary an itemized report of all money expended by the department of which he is the head, showing for what and to whom such money was paid.

Sec. 45. Franchises—grant of. Forfeiture of—provided for. Advertisement of. Regulation and control of. Ordinance for. Terms and conditions; rates, fares and charges. Former grants preserved. Taxation of franchises.

No franchise or right in relation to any highway, avenue, street, lane or alley, either on, above or below the surface of the same, and no franchise or right in relation to any island or land covered by water that may belong to or be claimed by the City of Galveston, shall be granted by the Board of Commissioners to any person or corporation for a longer period than fifty (50) years. Every grant of any such franchise or right shall make provision by way of forfeiture of the grant or otherwise for the purpose of compelling compliance with the terms of the grant, and to secure efficiency of public service at reasonable rates, and the maintenance of the property in good condition throughout the full term of the grant. Before any grant of any such franchise or right shall be made the proposed specific grant, embodied in the form of a brief advertisement prepared as may be directed by ordinance of the Board of Commissioners, shall be published at the expense of the applicant for at least three (3) days in the official journal of said city. When the grant of any franchise or right is made, the city shall not part with, but shall expressly reserve, the right and duty at all times to exercise in the interest of the public full superintendence, regulation and control in respect to all matters connected with the police powers of said city. Before any such grant of any such franchise or right shall be made, the proposed specific grant shall be embodied in the form of an ordinance, with all such terms and conditions as may be right and proper, including a provision as to the rates, fares and charges, if the grant provides for the charging of rates, fares and charges. All legal ordinances, resolutions or acts heretofore passed or had by the said city, making any grant or concession, or vesting any property, right, interest or franchise, shall remain unaffected by the repeal of the charter of said city and amendments thereto hereinafter provided for. Any and all rights, privileges and franchises heretofore or hereafter granted to or held by any person, firm or corporation in the streets, alleys, highways or public grounds or places in said city shall be subject to taxation by said city separately from and in addition to the other assets of such person, firm or corporation, and the Board may require the rendition and assessment thereof accordingly; **Provided**, that no assessment separately for franchises, rights or privileges shall be made prior to January 1, 1905.

Sec. 46.

[Relates to regulation of speed of vessels, etc.]

Sec. 47. City not liable for damages caused by grade raising or for defects in streets, etc.

That the said City of Galveston shall not be liable in damages for any injury or injuries to persons or to property caused by filling, raising, grading or elevating any property within the City of Galveston, or in the prosecution of any public improvement in said city, or on account of any defect of any street, sidewalk or other public place.

Sec. 48.

[Relates to construction of breakwaters, etc.]

Sec. 49.

[Relates to exemption of city funds.]

Sec. 50. No evidence of debt to be issued, except. Expenses limited to current revenue. Current revenue alone liable for debts contracted. Public property, moneys, etc., exempt from seizure, execution of attachment for debt.

That said Commissioners shall not issue any bonds, notes, script or other evidence of indebtedness, except as provided in this Act, and shall in no event contract for work, material or services in excess of the amount of the estimated revenues for the current year and the funds on hand applicable to such purposes; and all parties contracting with said Commissioners for work, material or services shall look alone to the revenues for that year, and to such funds as may be applicable for such purposes at the date of any such contract, and the revenues of no subsequent year shall be appropriated or used to meet any such deficit; and no property, real or personal, owned or held by said City of Galveston for public use, for governmental purposes, or in trust for the public, shall ever be subject to execution or attachment, or seizure under any legal process, for any debt heretofore or hereafter created by said City of Galveston; and all taxes due, or money in the hands of the officers charged with the collection of taxes, or any other revenues belonging to said city, shall be exempt from seizure under attachment, execution, garnishment or any other legal process.

Sec. 51. Vehicles—regulating, licensing. Porters and other occupations licensed and regulated. Amended. Charges for carriage fixed. Protection provided. Licenses, called to be used on street.

The Board shall have power to license, tax and regulate the owners of all vehicles in the city of Galveston regulate hackmen, draymen, omnibus drivers and drivers of baggage wagons, porters, automobiles, bicycles, electric motors of any kind and all others pursuing like occupation, with or without vehicles, and prescribe their compensation, and provide for their protection, and make it a misdemeanor for any person to attempt to defraud them of any legal charge for services rendered; and to tax, regulate, license and restrain runners for steamboats, railroads, stages and public houses, and enforce the collection of all such taxes by proper ordinances; and all revenue collected under the provisions of this section, or any ordinance passed in pursuance thereof, shall be used only for the improvement of the streets and alleys of said city. This section shall not be construed to apply to street cars.

Sec. 52. Delinquent taxes unappropriated—disposition of.

That the said Board of Commissioners of said city is authorized to apropriate all delinquent taxes against which no demands are outstanding, and after the purposes for which said taxes were levied have been fulfilled and satisfied, to any proper municipal purposes, and the said Board is empowered, at the end of each fiscal year thereafter, to declare such residue of all said delinquent taxes a surplus fund; and to direct that the same, when collected, be carried in bulk as a surplus account, subject to appropriation by said Board for proper municipal purposes, under the provisions of this Act.

Sec. 53.

[Property exempt from taxation.]

Sec. 54.

Ad valorem taxes—levy of. Real property defined. Personal property defined. Taxes, when due. Rate of interest on. Discount allowed. Penalty assessed.

Sec. 55. Assessment and collection of taxes regulated. Tax lists and inventories. Assessments—how and when made. Penalties. State law to govern. Penalty for not assessing.

Said Board of Commissioners shall have power to provide by ordinance for the assessing and prompt collection of all taxes, and to regulate the manner, mode and form of making out, and swearing to, tax lists or inventories, and the appraisement of property therein, and to prescribe how and when property shall thus be rendered, and shall also prescribe the number and form of assessment rolls and fix and define the duties and powers of the Assessor and Collector, and adopt such measures and regulations, and prescribe and enforce such penalties, as they may deem advisable, to secure the due and proper assessment of all property within the limits of said city, and the collection of the taxes thereupon, conforming the said manner and mode of rendering property for assessment, and the assessment thereof, as near as may be, to that provided by law for the rendition and assessing of property for State and County purposes, and until the passage of such ordinances, the said Board of Commissioners and the Assessor and Collector of Taxes shall be governed in their procedure and acts in relation to the assessment and collection of said notes as provided by the laws of this State relating to the assessment and collection of State and County taxes. If any person shall fail or refuse to render his property for taxation under oath in form and manner as required by the Board of Commissioners, or otherwise by law, when called upon and requested so to do by the Assessor and Collector of Taxes, he shall be punished by fine of not less than five ($5) dollars nor more than twenty-five ($25) dollars for each day during which he shall so fail or refuse.

Sec. 56 to 65.

[These sections relate to the procedure to be observed in the levying and collection of taxes.]

Sec. 66. Street railroads. Tax assessment against. Compel repair and safe carriage, ample accommodations, etc. Rate of travel. Penalties for violations. To fill, grade and pave between tracks. Railroad failing after notice, city may have work done. Cost collected—lien for.

The Board of Commissioners shall have power to assess and collect the ordinary municipal taxes upon city or horse railroads, and to compel the said city railroad com panies to keep their roads in repair, and to restrain the rat of travel so as not to exceed seven miles per hour, and t compel said city railroads to supply ample accommodatio for the safe and convenient travel of the people on any stree where their tracks may run. The Board of Commissioner may enforce these regulations by proper ordinance, wit suitable penalties for all violation of said ordinances. When ever the said Board of Commissioners shall determine to fil grade, pave or otherwise improve any street or avenue, an over and upon which, or any portion thereof, there may b tracks and roadbed of any railroad company, the said rai road company shall, upon notice, fill, grade, pave or other wise improve the portion of said street or avenue so occu pied by it, between the rails of said tracks and for one foo on each side of said rails, with such material and in suc manner as has or may be provided by said Commissioner for the improvement of the other portions of such street o avenue. Upon failure so to do, after thirty days' notice, th said Board may so improve such street or avenue betwee said rails and for one foot on each side thereof for accoun of said railroad company, and for all sums so expended, an legal interest thereon, the City of Galveston shall have first lien on the roadbed, franchises and other property o said railroad company and, if not paid upon demand, sui may be brought by said city to recover said indebtednes and for the forclosure of said lien.

Sec. 67. Funding bonds—issuance of. Interest rate. Ol bonds—how retired. Bonds to be refunded.

(a) The city of Galveston shall have the power to i sue bonds to the amount of not exceeding $3,100,000 such denomination as the Board of Commissioners may d termine, payable at such time, not to exceed fifty years, they may determine and as may be agreed to by the holde of such bonds, bearing interest, payable semi-annually, at rate to be agreed on by the holders of such bonds and t Board of Commissioners; said interest rate, however, not exceed five per cent per annum, but the City of Galvest shall have the right to select by lot, as interest coupons said bond mature, sufficient of the bonds to retire at n exceeding par, not less than two per cent per annum of t total bond outstanding of each issue into the sinking fu thereof. These bonds are to be issued for the purposes refunding such of the outstanding bond issues of the City Galveston as are hereinafter specified; that is to say, a su cient number of said bonds so authorized to be issued sh be in lieu and instead of the outstanding forty-year limit debt bonds of 1881; a sufficient number of said bonds authorized to be issued shall be in lieu and instead of t waterworks, street improvement and city hall bonds ou standing; a sufficient number thereof shall be in lieu a instead of the forty-year limited debt bonds of 1891 ou standing; a sufficient number thereof shall be in lieu a instead of the general indebtedness funding bonds of 18 outstanding; a sufficient number thereof shall be in li and instead of the general indebtedness funding bonds a proved September 8, 1897, outstanding; a sufficient numb thereof shall be in lieu and instead of bonds outstandi issued for the establishment and maintenance of a sewera system in pursuance of an ordinance of the City of Galveston passed December 16, 1897, and the amendment thereof passed August 21, 1899.

Tax levy for 1881 bonds.

(b) The Board of Commissioners of the city of Galveston shall have power to levy, assess and collect an annual ad valorem tax not exceeding twenty cents on the one hundred dollars valuation of all property subject to taxation within said city in order to provide for the payment of interest at such rate as may hereafter be determined by the Board of Commissioners of said City of Galveston, not to exceed five per cent per annum, and to create a sinking fund of not less than two per cent per annum on such amount of the total bonds remaining unpaid of the issue of what is known as the forty-year limited debt bonds of 1881, and refunding bonds, respectively, issued in lieu of same.

Tax levy for waterworks, street improvement and city hall bonds.

(c) The Board of Commissioners of the city of Galveston shall have the power to levy, assess and collect an annual ad valorem tax not exceeding sixteen and four-tenths cents on the one hundred dollars valuation of all property subject to taxation within said city, in order to provide for the payment of interest at such rate as may hereafter be determined by the Board of Commissioners, not to exceed five per cent per annum, and to create a sinking fund of not less than two per cent per annum on such amount of the total bonds remaining unpaid of the issue of what is known as the waterworks, street improvement and city hall bonds, and refunding bonds, respectively, issued in lieu of same.

Tax levy for 1891 bonds.

(d) The Board of Commissioners of the city of Galveston shall have the power to levy, assess and collect an annual ad valorem tax not exceeding thirty-three cents on the hundred dollars valuation of all property subject to taxation within said city, in order to provide for the payment of interest at such rate as may hereafter be determined by the Board of Commissioners, not to exceed five per cent per annum, and to create a sinking fund of not less than two per cent per annum on said amount of the total bonds remaining unpaid of the issue of what is known as the forty-year limited debt bonds of 1891, and refunding bonds, respectively, issued in lieu of same.

Tax levy for 1895 bonds.

(e) The Board of Commissioners of the city of Galveston shall have power to levy, assess and collect an annual ad valorem tax of not exceeding five and five-tenths cents on the one hundred dollars valuation of all property subject to taxation within said city, in order to provide for the payment of interest at such rate as may hereafter be determined by the Board of Commissioners, not to exceed five per cent per annum, and to create a sinking fund of not less than two per cent per annum on such amount of the total bonds remaining unpaid of the issue of what is known as the general indebtedness refunding bonds of 1895, and refunding bonds, respectively, issued in lieu of same.

Tax levy for 1897 bonds.

(f) The Board of Commissioners of the city of Galveston shall have power to levy, assess and collect an annual ad valorem tax of not exceeding five cents on the one hundred dollars valuation of all property subject to taxation within the said city, in order to provide for the payment of interest at such rate as may hereafter be determined by the Board of Commissioners, not to exceed five per cent per annum, and to create a sinking fund of not less than two per cent per annum on such amount of the total bonds remaining unpaid of the issue of what is known as the general indebtedness refunding bonds of 1897, and refunding bond, respectively, issued in lieu of the same.

Tax levy for sewer bonds. Board of Commissioners may determine upon less rate of interest—how. Rate when bondholders fail to consent.

(g) The Board of Commissioners of the city of Galveston shall have power to levy, assess and collect an annual ad valorem tax of not exceeding ten cents on the one hundred dollars valuation of all property subject to taxation within said city, in order to provide for the payment of interest at such rate as may hereafter be determined by the Board of Commissioners, not to exceed five per cent per annum, and to create a sinking fund of not less than two per cent per annum on such amount of the total bonds remaining unpaid of the issue of what is known as the sewer bonds and refunding bonds, respectively, issued in lieu of same; **Provided,** however, that the said Board of Commissioners shall not determine upon a less rate of interest than five per cent per annum upon any outstanding legal bonds of the City of Galveston, except and unless with the consent of the holders of such bonds, respectively, and if the holder or holders of any such bonds do not so consent to a less rate of interest than five per cent per annum, then and in that case the bond or bonds of any such holder or holders not so consenting shall bear interest at the rate of five per cent per annum.

Tax levy limited to above rates for account of refunding bonds. For bonds not funded tax rates remain as heretofore.

(h) This Act shall not be so construed as to authorize the Board of Commissioners of the City of Galveston to levy, or to assess, or to collect any tax in excess of the rates mentioned in this section, for the purpose of paying the interest on, or creating a sinking fund for, any series of either the outstanding bonds or the refunding bonds mentioned in this section; **Provided,** however, that if any of such outstanding bonds be not refunded then and in that case said Board of Commissioners shall have power to levy, assess and collect such rate of taxation to pay the interest on, and to create a sinking fund for, such bonds not refunded as does not exceed the rate of taxation prescribed in any legal ordinance, resolution or act heretofore passed by the City Council of the City of Galveston, or Act of Legislature heretofore passed relating thereto, providing for the issuance and payment of either principal or interest of any such outstanding legal, unpaid and unrefunded bonds of the City of Galveston.

Interest and sinking funds. Special funds. Bonds signed by President, etc. To be forwarded to Comptroller for registration.

(i) Each of said funds so created shall be a special fund for the purposes aforesaid, and shall not be drawn upon or diverted for any other purpose, and the City Treasurer of said City of Galveston shall honor no draft upon said fund, except to pay the interest upon, or to redeem the bonds for which each or either of said funds was created under the provisions of this section. All bonds issued as refunding bonds shall be signed by the President of the Board of Commisioners and countersigned by the Secretary of said Board, and shall be payable at such place as may be fixed by ordinance of said Board of Commissioners. It shall be the duty of the President of said Board of Commissioners when such bonds are issued to forward the same to the Comptroller of the State of Texas, whose duty it shall be to register them in a book kept for that purpose, and to endorse on each bond registered his certificate of registration.

Funding Act to be published.

(j) Immediately upon the qualification of the Commissioners of the City of Galveston, to be appointed and elected as provided in this Act, or as soon thereafter as practicable, it shall be their duty to make publication of the terms and this funding act; but the passage of this Act shall be and is hereby deemed sufficient notice to the holders of the present bonds of the City of Galveston now standing.

Commissioners to fix terms, interest, etc., for refunding, etc.

(k) The manner of exchange of refunding bonds, their date of issuance, rate of interest, maturity and all other details of the issuance of the new bonds is hereby left to the Board of Commissioners under such rules and regulations as a majority of them shall prescribe, not inconsistent with the provisions of this Act.

Release by bondholder of uncollected taxes. Released taxes to be applied to floating debt and general fund.

(l) The acceptance and consummation by any creditor of the exchange of bonds provided by this Act shall of itself operate to assign and transfer to said municipal corporation all his rights to, and claims against, the uncollected taxes or other assets whatever of said municipal corporation, including whatever funds there may be, either in bonds, money or other securities, held in either interest or sinking funds of the issue so exchanged or refunded, with the right in said municipal corporation to enforce the same either in its own name or in the name of the creditor, and the funds that may be realized therefrom are to be paid to the Treasurer of said municipal corporation, and they are hereby devoted and appropriated to the payment of the present floating debt of the City of Galveston; and after that is paid to go in the general fund for any proper municipal purposes, so far as is not inconsistent with the terms of this Act.

Sinking fund—investment of. Some series purchased to be cancelled. Bond or evidence of debt to be cancelled. Unmatured coupons to be surrendered with bonds redeemed.

(m) Said Board of Commissioners shall have the power, and it is made their duty, from time to time as they may determine whenever as much as five thousand ($5000) dollars shall have accumulated in the sinking fund of any series of bonds, to invest the same in bonds of any such series, in bonds of said City of Galveston, in bonds of the State of Texas, or in bonds of the United States, as may be deemed most advantageous by said Board; **Provided,** however, that when bonds of any particular series have heretofore been or may hereafter be purchased for the sinking fund of the same series, said bonds shall be cancelled and retired. It shall be the duty of said Board of Commissioners upon the surrender of any evidence of indebtedness for which a new bond is to be issued under the provisions of this Act, and before the said bond is delivered, to cancel the evidence of indebtedness so surrendered with a punch or by writing across the face thereof that it is cancelled, so that it can not be again used. All matured interest coupons shall be surrendered with the bonds, and no bond shall be received or refunded from which unmatured interest coupons are detached, unless such coupons are produced and surrendered with the bond.

Bond register to be kept. Payment of bonds or coupons to be noted in register.

(n) Said Board of Commissioners shall also keep, or cause to be kept, for and on behalf of the City of Galveston, a complete bond registry and set of books, showing all bonds issued, the date and amount thereof, the rate of interest, maturity, etc., of all bonds or other indebtedness surrendered under the provisions of this Act, and all the other transactions of such Board having reference to the refunding of the indebtedness of said city. When bonds or their coupons are paid, their payment or cancellation shall be noted in said registry, and the said book so required shall be kept safely among the records of the said City of Galveston.

No taxing power except that provided by charter.

(o) Said Board of Commissioners shall have power to impose, levy and collect ad valorem taxes, poll taxes, occupation taxes, license taxes and such other taxes as are specially authorized by this charter, but shall not exercise any other taking power.

Officers punished for breach of trust in like manner as State officers.

(p) That for any violation of the trusts imposed upon the officers or agents of the City of Galveston employed under this Act, the same consequences shall follow, civilly and criminally, that result from any breach of trust or willful violation of duty imposed by law upon any of the officers of the State of Texas charged with the discharge of like duties, and for a breach of trust or willful violation of duty in respect thereof, upon conviction, they shall be punished in like manner as is or may be provided by the penal laws of the State of Texas.

Sec. 68. Grade raising—appointment of board of engineers. Grade established. Compensation of Board.

The Board of Commissioners of said city of Galveston shall have the power and they are hereby authorized to appoint a board of engineers, to consist of three competent and skilled engineers, who shall devise and report to said Board of Commissioners plans and specifications, with estimates of the cost, for elevating, filling and grading the avenues, streets, sidewalks, alleys and lots of the City of

Galveston so as to protect said city from overflow from the waters of the gulf, and to secure sufficient elevation for drainage and sewerage. When the report of said board of engineers has been adopted by the Board of Commissioners, all filling, raising and grading in said city shall be done with reference to the grades thus established. The Board of Commissioners are authorized to spend out of the general revenue of the city a sum not to exceed ten thousand ($10,000) dollars to pay for the expenses of said board of engineers.

Sec. 69.

Bonds, issued for grade raising. Maximum amount. Interest rate. First filling begin, where. Grade raising territory defined. Second in point of time. Amount allowed for raising grade of streets. Raising buildings to grade. May be done by city; how paid for. Raising of buildings at cost of owner and to be paid for by him. Grade Raising Board—appointment of. Powers and duties of Board. All proposed plans and work to be reported to and approved by City Commissioners. Salary, bond and oath. Terms of offices.

Sec. 70. State tax donations—how applied. (Amended, Acts 1905.) Tax levy for grade raising bonds.

All moneys that have been or may be donated or appropriated by the State of Texas to the city of Galveston shall be applied to and used for the purpose of paying the interest upon and providing a sinking fund of not less than two per cent per annum for the redemption of the two million dollars ($2,000,000) of bonds, the issuance of which is provided for in the preceding section (No. 69), and said Board of Commissioners shall have the power and are hereby authorized to levy and cause to be assessed and collected for the year 1902 and annually thereafter, for the purpose of providing such interest and sinking fund, an ad valorem tax of not to exceed sixty cents on the one hundred dollars cash value of all real, personal and mixed property within the corporate limits of the said City of Galveston, or that may be taxable therein on the first day of January of each and every year, except so much thereof as may be exempted by the Constitution and laws of this State or of the United States.

Sec. 71. Wharf Company dividends to supplement tax for grade raising.

In addition to the ad volarem tax provided for in section 70 of this Act, said Board of Commissioners may, except so far as the same are otherwise disposed of by this Act, also hypothecate and pledge the annual dividends and income that may be received by the city from its stock in the Galveston Wharf Company, or so much thereof as will, when added to the money received each year from the ad valorem tax provided for in said section 70, be sufficient to pay the interest and sinking fund upon the bonds authorized to be issued under said section 69 that are then outstanding.

Sec. 71a. Bonds for duplicate main. Rate of interest. Proceeds, how used. Tax levy for. Redemption of bonds.

The Board of Commissioners of the city of Galveston is hereby authorized and empowered to issue the bonds of the city of Galveston in the denomination of $100.00, or multiples thereof to the amount of $100,000.00, said bonds to be payable not more than fifty years after their date, and bearing interest payable semi-annually at a rate not to exceed five per cent per annum. Said bonds shall not be sold or otherwise disposed of at less than par, and their proceeds shall be used and expended exclusively for the construction of a duplicate water main across Galveston Bay. And it is hereby made the duty of the Commissioners of the City of Galveston whenever said bonds are issued, to levy and cause to be assessed and collected annually for the purpose of providing for the payment of the interest on said bonds, and a sinking fund of two per cent, an ad valorem tax not to exceed 3 cents on the $100.00 cash value of all real, personal and mixed property within the corporate limits of said City or that may be taxable therein, on the first day of January of each and every year, except so much thereof as may be exempted by the Constitution and laws of this State or of the United States; from taxation. The City of Galveston shall have the right at any time to select by lot and redeem any of the aforesaid bonds with the sinking funds that may accrue from taxation, or with any of the funds said City may have for that purpose. It being expressly understood that the said Board of Commissioners may set aside and appropriate annually, in addition to the sinking fund aforesaid, all surplus revenues arising from the City waterworks, which may be used for the redemption of these bonds.

Sec. 71b. Bonds for erection of public free schools. Rate of interest. Proceeds, how used. City Treasurer to disburse. Tax levy for.

In addition to the power to issue any and all other bonds as elsewhere or otherwise provided in or by the Charter of said City of Galveston, the said City of Galveston shall have the power and it is hereby authorized to issue from time to time, or at any one time, bonds of said City to the amount of Fifty Thousand Dollars ($50,000.00) of the denomination of one hundred dollars ($100.00), or any multiple thereof, payable forty years after their date and bearing interest payable semi-annually, at a rate of not exceeding five per cent per annum, which said bonds shall be sold for cash at not less than par, and the proceeds thereof shall be used, and expended for the construction, erection, equipment, improvement, maintenance and repair of public free school houses in said City under the direction, and upon the requisition of the Board of Trustees of the public free schools of said City, and no part thereof shall ever be used or expended for or diverted to any other purpose whatsoever; and said proceeds shall be paid over, as and when received, to the Treasurer of said City, and said Treasurer shall pay out and disburse the same only upon the requisition, order or warrants of said Board of Trustees, signed by the President of said Board and countersigned by its Secretary, without other authority for such disbursement, and without any warrant drawn by the Auditor of said City of Galveston and signed by the President of the Board of Commissioners of said City, and countersigned by the Commissioner of Finance and Revenue, under the seal of the Board of Commissioners of the City of Galveston. The Board of Commissioners of the City of Galveston shall have the power and are hereby authorized to levy and cause to be assessed and collected annually for the purpose of paying the interest upon said bonds and providing a sinking fund for the redemption thereof, of not less than two per cent per annum, an ad valorem tax sufficient to pay said interest and provide said sinking fund upon all real, personal and mixed property situated or owned in said City of Galveston, or that may be taxable therein on the first day of January of each and every year, except so much of said property as may be exempted from taxation by the Constitution and laws of this State or of the United States. Said fund for the payment of said interest and the accumulation of said sinking fund shall not be diverted to or used, expended or drawn upon for any other purpose whatsoever, and the City Treasurer of the said City shall honor no draft or requisition of any kind whatsoever upon said fund, except to pay the interest upon or redeem said bonds.

Sec. 71c. Bonds for grading, raising, etc. Rate of interest. Tax levy for.

The Board of Commissioners of the city of Galveston shall have power and are hereby authorized to issue from time to time bonds of the city of Galveston in the denomination of $100.00 or multiples thereof, to the amount of $300,000.00, payable not more than fifty years after their date, with the right of the City to select by lot and redeem with the sinking fund any of them twenty (20) years after their issuance, and bearing interest, payable semi-annually, at a rate of not to exceed 4½ per cent per annum. Said bonds shall not be sold or otherwise disposed of at less than par and their proceeds shall be used and expended exclusively for the grading, raising, filling, drainage, paving or otherwise improving the avenues, streets and sidewalks in such parts or portions of the City of Galveston as may be designated and selected by said Board of Commissioners. And said Board of Commissioners shall have the power and are hereby authorized to levy and cause to be assessed and collected annually upon the issuance of said bonds, an ad valorem tax not to exceed ten cents on the $100.00 cash value of all real, personal and mixed property within the corporate limits of the City of Galveston, or that may be taxable therein, except so much thereof as may be exempted by the Constitution and laws of this State, or of the United States, to pay the interest and sinking fund of not less than 2 per cent upon said bonds.

[Sec. 71d omitted from charter.]

Sec. 71e. Aid in constructing causeway. Bonds for construction of causeway. Redemption of bonds. Rate of interest. Tax levy for. Bonds to be voted on before issued.

The Board of Commissioners of the city of Galveston be and the same are hereby authorized to aid and assist the County of Galveston in the construction of a causeway across Galveston Bay from the main land to Galveston Island opposite the limits of the said City of Galveston, by appropriating out of any funds that may be available for that purpose, a sum not to exceed $20,000.00 in any one year for a period of ten years. And in the event no funds of said City may be available for the purpose aforesaid, then the said Board of Commissioners, for the purpose of aiding and assisting said County of Galveston in the construction of said causeway, shall have the power and are hereby authorized to issue from time to time bonds of the City of Galveston in the demonination of $100.00, or multiples thereof, to an amount not exceeding $200,000.00, payable not more than fifty years after their date, with the right of the city to select by lot and redeem with the sinking fund or otherwise any of said bonds twenty years after their issuance, bearing interest, payable semi-annually at a rate not to exceed 4½ per cent. per annum. Said bonds shall not be sold or otherwise disposed of at less than par and their proceeds shall be used and expended exclusively to aid and assist the County of Galveston in the construction of said causeway. And said Board of Commissioners shall have the power and are hereby authorized to levy and cause to be assessed and collected annually upon the issuance of said bonds, an ad valorem tax not to exceed ten cents on the $100.00 cash value of all real, personal and mixed property within the corporate limits of the City of Galveston, or that may be taxable therein, except so much thereof as may be exempted by the Constitution and laws of this State, or of the United States, to pay the interest and provide a sinking fund of not less than 2 per cent upon said bonds.

The bonds provided for in this Act shall not be issued by the Board of Commissioners of the City of Galveston unless their issuance shall be authorized by the votes of a majority of the qualified voters of the City of Galveston, who are property taxpayers residing in said City, voting at an election upon the question of the issuance of said bonds, as required by Chapter CXLIX of the acts of the Twenty-sixth Legislature of the State of Texas, approved May 26th, 1899.

Sec. 72. Grade raising tax, etc., a special trust fund.

Each tax authorized under this Act to be levied, assessed and collected for the purpose of paying the interest and sinking fund upon any bonds issued under this Act shall be, and the same is hereby declared to be, a trust fund for the purpose of paying the interest upon and providing a sinking fund for the redemption of the respective bonds for which it was levied; and when collected, the money thereupon shall never be diverted from the purpose for which it was levied, nor used for any other purpose. Any dividend or income that may be pledged to secure the interest and sinking fund upon any of the bonds authorized to be issued under this Act shall also be, and is hereby declared to be a trust fund, and shall never be used for any other purpose than that for which the same may be hypothecated or pledged.

Sec. 73. President to make financial reports to Comptroller. Certified to by Auditor. Printed as public document. Submitted to Legislature. Shall contain what Comptroller to examine city finances; may appoint examiner. Examiner may administer oaths and summon witnesses.

The President of the said Board of Commissioners shall cause to be prepared and make stated financial reports at least as often as once every six (6) months to the Comptroller of the State of Texas in accordance with forms and methods and at times to be prescribed by said Comptroller. All such reports shall be certified as to their correctness by the auditor of said city. Such reports shall be printed as a part of the public documents of the State, and be submitted by the Comptroller of the State to the Legislature at each regular session next succeeding the making of such reports. Such reports shall contain an accurate statement in summarized form and also in detail of the financial receipts of the city from all sources, and of the expenditures of the city for all purposes, together with a statement in detail of the debt of said city at the date of said report and of the purposes for which said debt has been incurred as well as such other information as may be required by said Comptroller of the State. Said Comptroller of the State shall have power, and it is also made his duty, by himself or by some competent person or persons appointed by him, to examine into the affairs of the financial department of said city; on every such examination inquiry shall be made as to the financial condition and resources of the city, and whether the requirements of the Constitution and laws have been complied with, and into the methods and accuracy of the accounts of the said city, and as to such other matters as the said Comptroller may prescribe. The Comptroller of the State and every such examiner appointed by him shall have power to administer an oath to any person whose testimony may be required on any such examination, and to compel the appearance and attendance of any such person for the purpose of any such examination and the production of books and papers. A report of each examination shall be made and shall be a matter of public record in the office of said Comptroller.

Sec. 74.

Proposals for work to be advertised for. Bids to be opened. Bids to be recorded. When acted on. Contractor to give bond. Board to approve bond. Contracts awarded, see majority vote. Signed by whom. Contract to be recorded. Estimates by heads of departments. Approval of. No Commissioner to be interested in contracts. Punishment for. Work may be done by day labor. Eight hours constitute day's work, except.

Sec. 75. Suits by or against city—citizens not disqualified as witnesses or jurors in. Officers of city exempt from jury services.

That no person shall be an incompetent judge, justice, witness or juror by reason of his being an inhabitant or freeholder in the city of Galveston, in any action or proceeding in which said city may be a party interested, and all officers and employees of said city shall be exempt from jury service while holding office or in the employ of said city.

Sec. 76. Surplus receipts for account of bond funds, applied to general purposes.

At the end of each fiscal year, if an amount should have accrued from taxation, or revenue received from dividends on stocks or surplus receipts, or earnings from any source, which are now or will be hereafter pledged to be applied to the interest and sinking funds for the protection of all classes of outstanding bonds, or bonds to be hereafter issued, should exceed two per cent for sinking fund, then and in that event the surplus, if any, over and above said two per cent sinking fund, can be used for the purpose of making general improvements, or otherwise, as the Commissioners may determine.

Sec. 77. Printed ordinances admitted in evidence. Existing ordinances remain in force.

The printed or published ordinances and other acts of the government of said city purporting to have been printed or published under the authority of the Board of Commissioners or other municipal government of said city shall be received as evidence of the ordinances and acts therein contained. Certified copies of ordinances shall also be received in evidence. All ordinances, resolutions, rules and regulations now in force in the City of Galveston and not in conflict with the provisions of this Act shall remain in force under this Act until altered, amended or repealed by said Board after this Act takes effect.

Sec. 78 and 78a.

[Relate to the establishment and powers of Corporation Court, and to the city's agreement with the Wharf Company.]

Sec. 79. Act of 1876, etc., repealed. Repeal does not affect ordinances, etc., of city council. Rate of tax on refunding bonds fixed. Obligations, etc., of city not impaired.

(93.) That an act entitled "An Act to incorporate the city of Galveston and grant it a new charter," passed on the 2d day of August, 1876, and all other acts relative to the incorporation of the City of Galveston, as well as all amendments to the Charter of said city, be and the same are hereby repealed, excepting, however, all legal ordinances, resolutions or acts heretofore passed by the City Council of Galveston and any provisions of said Charter of 1876, and amendments and acts relating thereto providing for the issuance and payment of either principal or interest of outstanding legal unpaid bonds of the City of Galveston; **Provided,** that the rate of taxation hereafter fixed in any ordinance providing for the issuance of refunding bonds shall not exceed the rate levied in the ordinance under which the bonds to be refunded were issued; **Provided,** further, that nothing in this Act shall be taken or construed to impair the obligations of outstanding legal contracts of the City of Galveston.

Sec. 80. All courts, etc., to take cognizance of this act.

(94.) This act shall be taken and held to be a public law and all courts and tribunals shall take judicial cognizance and knowledge of the contents and provisions hereof and it shall not be necessary to plead or prove such contents or provisions.

Sec. 81. Repealing clause.

(Section 3 of bill.) That all laws and parts of laws in conflict with this Act be and the same are hereby repealed.

Sec. 82. Emergency clause.

(Section 4 of bill.) That the fact that there is no Corporation Court in said city of Galveston, and the administration of the law therein is in consequence greatly hindered, and that the other changes hereby made in the Charter of said city are urgently needed for the better administration of its affairs, creates an emergency and an imperative public necessity requiring that the constitutional rule that bills shall be read on three several days be suspended, and that this Act shall take effect and be in force from and after its passage, and it is therefore so enacted.

[Approved March 30, 1903.]

ANNOTATIONS—GALVESTON, TEXAS CHARTER.

A. A. BROWN, ET AL., VS. CITY OF GALVESTON, 97 TEXAS, PAGE 1.

Constitutional Law—City Charter—Government Conferred on Board of Commissioners.—The following questions are submitted to this court by the Court of Civil Appeals.

"1. Did the city of Galveston have authority under the act of the Legislature, approved April 18, 1901, granting it a new charter and repealing all preexisting charters to enact and enforce the ordinances by virtue of which the right to collect the license tax was claimed?

"2. Were the charter and ordinances authorizing the collection of the tax in conflict with the Constitution of this State on taxation?

"3. Did the court below err in sustaining the motion to dissolve the injunction and in dismissing the petition?"

The charter of the City of Galveston (act of April 18, 1901) in conferring upon a president and a board of commissioners, a majority appointed by the Governor, the power of governing this city usually committed to a mayor and city council, was not void as violating art. 6, sec. 3, of the Constitution, giving all qualified electors the right to vote for mayor and all other executive offices; nor was it beyond the power of the Legislature to enact as being in derogation of an inherent right of local self government by municipalities arising, by implication, from history and tradition in the State. (Op. 8-10.)

Same—Legislature—Implied Limitation.

2. The principles on which restriction of the powers of the Legislature may be implied discussed, and various sections of the Constitution compared and not to show a limitation of the power to permit municipal government to appointive officers. (Pp. 10-12.)

Powers of Government—Distribution—Limitation.

3. All political power is inherent in the people of the State (Const. art. 1, sec. 2) and it is to them that the right of self government is secured (Cont. art. 1, sec. 1). These powers are distributed among the department of the State Government (Cont. art. 2); and all the powers of the people which may properly be exercised in the formation of laws against which there is no inhibition expressed or implied in the Constitution, are conferred upon the Legislature. (Cont. art. 3, sec. 1.) (Pp. 12-15.)

THE COURT DREW ITS CONCLUSIONS FROM THE FOLLOWING CASES:

Ex parte Lewis, which was decided by the Court of Criminal Appeals in this State, reported in the Southwestern Reporter, volume 73, page 811.

Lytle v. Halff, 75 Texas, 132; Harris County v. Stewart, 91 Texas, 143; Cooley, Const. Lim., 200, 201; Cleburne v. Railway Co., 66 Texas, 461; Suth. Stat. Const., sec. 262; Bear v. Marx, 63 Texas, 301; Nevada v. Swift, 11 Nev., 134; People v. Hurlburt, 24 Mich., 44; Allor v. Wayne Co. Auditors, 43 Mich., 76; Davock v. Moore, 63 N. W. Rep., 424; Geake v. Fox, 63 N. E. Rep., 19; State v. Denny, 118 Ind., 449.

State v. Moores, 55 Neb., 840, which have been overruled by the Supreme Court of that State in the case of Redell v. Moores, 55 Law Rep. Ann., 740, decided by the Supreme Court of Nebraska, directly overruled by State v. Moores, before cited.

From the many authorities which support the position of the Nebraska court we cite: Newport v. Horton, 22 R. I., 196; Americus v. Perry, 114 Ga., 871; Harris v. Wright, 121 N. C., 172; Philadelphia v. Fox, 64 Pa. St., 169; State v. Hunter, 38 Kan., 578; Luehrman v. Taxing District, 2 Lea., 425; People v. Wood, 15 N. Y., 532; Nevada v. Swift, 11 Nev., 128.

In our own State the doctrine is well settled that a municipal corporation can exist only by and through an act of the Legislature of the State, and that it has no power not granted by the charter and can have no officer not provided for by law. Blessing v. Galveston, 42 Texas, 641; Pye v. Peterson, 45 Texas, 312; Vosburg v. McCrary, 77 Texas, 568.

CHARTER OF HOUSTON, TEX.

AN ACT TO GRANT A NEW CHARTER TO THE CITY OF HOUSTON, HARRIS COUNTY, TEXAS; REPEALING ALL LAWS OR PARTS OF LAWS IN CONFLICT HEREWITH AND DECLARING AN EMERGENCY.

(CHAPTER 17, SPECIAL LAWS OF 1905.)

ARTICLE I.

ection 1. Corporate Name.

ec. 2. Boundaries.

ec. 3. Platting of Property.

ARTICLE II.

ection 1. Corporate Powers.

The City of Houston, made a body politic and corporate y this act, shall have perpetual succession, may use a ommon seal, may sue and be sued, may contract and be ontracted with, implead and be impleaded in all courts and laces and in all matters whatever, may take, hold, and purhase lands as may be needed for the corporate purposes of aid city, and may sell any real estate or personal property wned by it, perform and render all public services, and, hen deemed expedient, may condemn property for public se, and may hold, manage and control the same; such conemnation proceedings to be governed and controlled by the aw now in force in reference to the condemnation of the ight of way of railroad companies and the assessment of amages therefor, and shall be subject to all the duties and bligations now pertaining to or incumbent upon said city s a corporation not in conflict with the provisions of this ct, and shall enjoy all the rights, immunities, powers, privieges and franchises now possessed and enjoyed by said city nd herein granted and conferred.

ec. 2. Powers of Ordinance.

ec. 3. Real Estate, etc., Owned by City.

ec. 4. Street Powers.

ec. 5. To Regulate Street and Electric Railway Companies.

ec. 6. To Regulate Rates of Public Utilities.

The City Council shall have the power by ordinance to fix nd regulate the price of water, gas and electric lights, and o regulate and fix the fares, tolls and charges of local telehones and exchanges; of public carriers and hacks, whether ransporting passengers, freight or baggage, and generally o fix and regulate the rates, tolls or charges of all public tilities of every kind.

To fix and regulate the fares and charges of electric or treet railway companies, and shall require by ordinance, nder proper penalties, that any street railroad using any of he streets of the city shall for one fare give a transfer from ny of its lines to any other line in the city, whether such ther line be owned by it or any other company, and in addiion to the penalties to be prescribed by ordinance for the ailure to give transfers, shall have the right by mandamus or ther proper remedy in any court of competent jurisdiction to enforce any ordinance requiring the giving of transfers by any street railroad company; and in addition thereto the City of Houston may recover of the street railway company the sum of twenty-five dollars as penalty and liquidated damages for each and every failure to give a transfer.

It shall be unlawful to continue, amend or extend any street railroad franchise, without binding any such railroad to give universal transfers, under provisions to be fixed by general ordinance.

Sec. 7.

[May own waterworks.]

Sec. 8. Fires.

[City has power to enact ordinances for protection against fire.]

Sec. 9. Wharves and Docks.

Sec. 10. Markets.

Sec. 11. Charities and Corrections.

Sec. 12. Fines for Violation of Ordinances.

Sec. 13. Corporation Court.

The magistrate of said court shall be known as the "Judge of the Corporation Court," who shall be a qualified voter, and shall be appointed by the Mayor and confirmed by the City Council, and shall hold his office for two years, unless sooner removed by the Mayor and City Council, and shall receive such salary as may be fixed by ordinance.

It shall be the duty of the Mayor, as soon as practicable after the passage of this act, to nominate some suitable person to the City Council, to be by it confirmed, for the position of Judge of the Corporation Court, who shall discharge the duties of said office under the terms and provisions of the State law creating said court, and also subject to the provisions of this act.

There shall be a clerk or clerks of said court, with such deputies as may be created or provided by ordinance by the City Council, who shall be appointed by the Mayor, and shall be subject to removal at any time by the Mayor or City Council, and shall receive such salary as may be fixed by the City Council.

[Paragraphs on power and duties of clerks omitted.]

Sec. 14. Schools.—The City of Houston an Independent School District.

The City of Houston shall constitute an independent school district, subject to the general school laws of the State, except where in conflict with this act, and the city shall have authority to levy and collect taxes and appropriate funds for the support and maintenance of the public schools within its limits.

School Trustees—How Appointed, Terms of Office, etc.

The trustees to constitute the school board of said city shall hereafter be appointed by the Mayor, and confirmed by the Council, but the trustees now in office shall continue to serve till the expiration of their respective terms; and all vacancies caused by death, resignation, or other cause, shall be filled by appointment in the same manner for the unexpired term. The regular term of members of the school board shall be two years, and the regular appointment of members shall be made at the first meeting of the Council in May of each year, or as soon thereafter as practicable, and the necessary number of trustees shall be appointed to take the places of those whose terms have expired.

Right of Mayor to Veto any Pecuniary Liability.

No order, resolution, or vote of the school board by which any pecuniary liability shall be incurred, or any funds expended or appropriated, shall become effective until ten days after the same is adopted, and a certified copy thereof furnished to the Mayor, and the Mayor may at any time during said period veto the same by filing his objections thereto in writing with the secretary of the school board, who shall enter the objections at large upon the minutes of the board; said order, resolution or vote shall become void, unless at the next meeting of the board it shall again be adopted over the veto by the affirmative votes of at least five members, whose names shall be entered upon the minutes of the board.

City Treasurer Custodian of Funds.

[Paragraphs relating to disbursements of school funds omitted.]

(Members of school board not to receive any compensation.)

Sec. 15.

[Paragraphs on certain regulations concerning public health omitted.]

Sec. 16. Peace and Good Order.

[Relates to police regulations.]

Sec. 17. Franchises.

The right of control, easement, user and the ownership of and title to the streets, highways, public thoroughfares and property of the City of Houston, its avenues, parks, bridges, and all other public places and property are hereby declared to be inalienable, except by ordinance duly passed by a majority of all the members of the City Council and approved by the Mayor, and no grant of any franchise, or lease, or right to use the same, either on, along, through, across, under or over the same by any private corporation, association or individual, shall be granted by the City Council, unless submitted to the vote of the legally qualified voters of said city, for a longer period than thirty years; provided, however, that whenever application is made for any grant of franchise, lease, right or privilege in or to the streets and public thoroughfares of the City of Houston by any person or corporation, if they so request, the Council shall submit the same at an election called for said purpose, the expense of which shall be borne by the applicant for said franchise, and at said election, if the majority of the votes cast by the legally qualified voters shall be in favor of making said grant as applied for, said grant may be made for such a term of years as is specified in the ordinance submitting the same at said election; provided, however, that no grant shall be made or authorized for a longer period than fifty years.

The City Council may also, upon its own motion, submit all applications or ordinances requesting the granting of franchises or special privileges in or to the streets, public thoroughfares and highways of the City of Houston, to an election, at which the people shall vote upon the propositions therein submitted; the expense of which election shall be paid by the applicant, or applicants, therefor. No such franchise shall ever be granted until it has been read in full at three regular meetings of the Council, nor shall any such franchise, grant, right or easement ever be made to any private individual, corporation or association, unless it provides for adequate compensation or consideration therefor, to be paid to the City of Houston, and in addition to any other form of compensation, grantee shall pay annually such a fixed charge as may be prescribed in the franchise. Such grant under and any contract in pursuance thereof shall provide that upon the termination of the grant, the grant, as well as the property, if any, of the grantee, in the streets, avenues and other public places, shall thereupon, without other or further compensation to the grantee, or upon the payment of a fair valuation therefor (the mode of ascertaining which shall be determined in the grant), be and become the property of the City of Houston, and the grantee shall never be entitled to any payment or valuation because of any value derived from the franchise or the fact that it is or may be a going concern, duly installed and operated.

Every such grant shall make adequate provision by way of forfeiture of the grant, or otherwise, to secure efficiency of public service at reasonable rates, and to maintain the property in good order throughout the life of the grant.

The City Council may also inspect and examine, or cause to be inspected and examined at all reasonable hours, any books of account of such grantee, which books of accounts shall be kept and such reports made in accordance with the forms and methods prescribed by the City Council, which, as far as practicable, shall be uniform for all such grantees.

Sec. 18. Referendum.

Whenever application is made to the City Council of the City of Houston for any such grant or franchise, lease or right to use the streets, public highways, thoroughfares or public property of the City of Houston, as is provided for in the preceding section of this act, or whenever an ordinance is introduced in the City Council proposing to make the grant of any franchise, lease or right to use the public highways, streets, thoroughfares and public property of the City of Houston, publication of said ordinance of such proposed grant or right to use the streets, public thoroughfares and highways of said city shall be made by publishing the ordinance as finally proposed to be passed, which shall not thereafter be changed, unless again republished, setting forth in detail all the rights, powers and privileges granted or proposed to be granted, in some daily newspaper published in the City of Houston, once a week for three consecutive weeks, which ublication shall be made at the expense of the applicant or he person or persons desiring said grant, and no such grant hall be made, or ordinance passed, until after publication in he manner aforesaid, nor shall any such ordinance confirm- ag or making any such grant, lease or right to use the treets, public highways and thoroughfares of the City of Iouston take effect or become a law or contract, or vest any ight in the applicants therefor, until after the expiration of hirty days after said ordinance has been duly passed by the ity Council and been approved by the Mayor.

Pending the passage of any such ordinance or during the ime intervening between its final passage and approval by he Mayor, and the expiration of the thirty days before which time it shall not take effect, it is hereby made the duty f the City Council to order an election, if requested so to do y written petition signed by at least five hundred legally ualified voters of said city, at which election the legally ualified voters of said city shall vote for or against the pro- osed grant as set forth in detail by the ordinance conferring le rights and privileges upon the applicants therefor, which aid ordinance shall be published at length and in full in the all for said election made by the Mayor, and if at said elec- ion the majority of the votes cast shall be for said ordinance nd the making of said proposed grant, the same shall there- pon become effective; but if a majority of the votes cast at aid election so held shall be against the passage of said rdinance and the making of said grant, said ordinance hall not pass, nor shall it confer any rights, powers or rivileges of any kind whatever upon the applicants therefor, nd it shall be the duty of the City Council, after canvassing he vote of said election to pass an ordinance repealing the rdinance which has been by it passed, if the same has been assed.

No grant of franchise, or lease or right of user, in, upon, long, through, under or over the public streets, highways r public thoroughfares of the City of Houston shall be made r given, nor shall any rights of any kind whatever be con- erred upon any person, private corporation, individual or ssociation of any kind whatever, except the same be made y ordinance duly passed by the City Council, nor shall any xtension or enlargement of any rights or powers previously ranted to any corporation, person or association of persons, a, upon, along, through, under or over the streets of the City of Houston be made, except in the manner and subject o all of the conditions herein provided for in this act for the naking of original grants and franchises; provided, however, hat the provisions of this section shall not apply to the ranting of sidetrack or switch privileges to railway com- anies for the purpose of reaching, and affording railway onnection and switch privileges to the owners or users of ny industrial plants; it being the intention to permit the City Council to grant such rights or privileges to railway ompanies whenever in their judgment the same is expedient, ecessary or advisable.

ec. 19. Contracts for Services.

No contract shall ever be made which binds the city o pay for personal services to be rendered for any stated eriod of time; but all contracts involving a personal service hall be restricted to the doing of some particular act or thing, and upon its completion no further liability shall exist on the part of the city.

Nor shall the City of Houston or any one acting for it make any contract for supplies for the current use of any depart- ment of the municipality for a longer period than ninety days, and so far as practicable, all supplies purchased for the use of any or all of the departments of said city shall be made or let upon competing prices therefor.

No contract shall be entered into until after an appro- priation has been made therefor, nor in excess of the amount appropriated, and all contracts, whenever practicable, shall be made upon specifications, and no contract shall be binding upon the city unless it has been signed by the Mayor and countersigned by the Controller, and the expense thereof charged to the proper appropriation, and whenever the con- tract charged to any appropriation equals the amount of said appropriation, no further contracts shall be countersigned by the Controller.

All contracts, of whatever character, pertaining to public improvement, or the maintenance of public property of said city, involving an outlay of as much as one thousand dollars ($1,000.00) shall be based upon specifications to be prepared and submitted to and approved by the Mayor and City Coun- cil, and after approval by the Mayor and City Council, adver- tisement for the proposed work, or matters embraced in said proposed contract, shall be made, inviting competitive bids for the work proposed to be done; which said advertisement shall be put in a daily newspaper not less than ten times. All bids submitted shall be sealed, shall be opened by the Mayor in the presence of a majority of the aldermen, and shall remain on file in the Mayor's office and be opened to public inspection for at least forty-eight hours before any award of said work is made to any competitive bidder. The Council shall determine the most advantageous bid for the city, and shall enter into contract with the party submitting the lowest secure bid, but shall always, in every advertise- ment of public work or contract involving as much as one thousand dollars ($1,000.00), reserve the right to reject any and all bids. Pending the advertisement of the work or con- tract proposed, specifications therefor shall be on file in the office of the Mayor, subject to the inspection of all parties desiring to bid.

ARTICLE III.

Sections 1-14. Taxation.

Taxing power limited to specified purposes: General ex- penses, interest, sinking fund; certain property exempt; pro- cedure in assessment and taxation, etc.

Section 15. Board of Appraisement.

There shall be a Board of Appraisement in said city, which shall be composed of two Aldermen and the As- sessor and Collector of Taxes, or such officer or employee designated by the City Council to perform the duties of an Assessor and Collector of Taxes.

The two aldermanic members of said board shall be ap- pointed by the Mayor not later than the first day of May of each year, and said board shall as soon as possible after the completion of all or any one of the Assessment rolls by the

Assessor and Collector, or other person designated therefor by the City Council, meet and carefully examine said roll or rolls, and properly and equitably adjust and equalize the taxable values thereon, thus continuing until they have adjusted and equalized the valuation on all property on said rolls, under such regulations as may be prescribed by the City Council by ordinance, and after the completion of said work, said board shall make due report of its action to the City Council.

Said board, constituted as herein provided, shall continue for a period of one year, and shall be a standing committee to which all matters relative to taxes shall be referred. The members of said board shall not receive any further compensation or extra compensation by reason of their services as members of said Board of Appraisement, nor as members of said standing committee on taxes.

In case of dissatisfaction with the decision of said Board of Appraisement by any taxpayer, an appeal from the decision of said Board of Appraisement may be had to the City Council of the City of Houston, but such appeal must be by written petition, specifically stating the things complained of, and by the dissatisfied taxpayer be filed with the City Secretary before the expiration of thirty days after said board has finally examined and passed upon the delinquent rolls of said city and made its final report to the Mayor and City Council, as herein provided. The decision of the City Council in all cases of appeal from the decision of the Board of Appraisement shall be final and binding, and no appeal shall be allowed from the decision of the City Council.

[Paragraph relating to procedure omitted.]

ARTICLE IV.

Section 1. Authority to Issue Bonds.

The City Council shall have the power and authority by ordinance duly passed, if it so elects, to borrow money on the credit of the city for permanent improvements, to an amount not to exceed one hundred thousand dollars ($100,000.00) in any one year, and may issue bonds of the city therefor. It may also have the power, and is hereby expressly authorized to issue bonds for the purpose of refunding bonds of the city of previous issues; provided, the bonds may be refunded at a lower rate of interest than the bonds proposed to be retired draw.

No bonds shall be issued for any purpose except for the purpose of making permanent improvements, which shall not exceed one hundred thousand dollars ($100,000.00) in any one year, and for the purpose of refunding bonds of the city of previous issues, unless an election be duly ordered by the Mayor and City Council, and if at said election a majority of the vote polled shall be in favor of creating such debt, it shall be lawful for the City Council to make the issuance of bonds as proposed in the ordinance submitting the same at the election so held, but if a majority of the vote polled shall be against the creating of such debt, it shall be unlawful for the City Council to issue the bonds.

In all elections to determine the expenditure of money for the assumption of debt, only those shall be qualified to vote who pay taxes on property in said city, and are legally qualified voters in said City of Houston; provided, that no poll tax for the payment of debts thus incurred shall be levied upon the persons debarred from voting in relation thereto.

No bonds shall be issued drawing more than five per cent. interest per annum, and they shall be invalid if sold for less than par and accrued interest, and all bonds shall express upon their face the purpose for which they are issued.

[Paragraphs relating to sinking fund and penalties for diversion of funds omitted.]

Sec. 2. Bayou.

[Power granted to acquire certain lands.]

Sec. 3. Fees.

Within its corporate limits, the City of Houston shall be the local agent of the State government for the enforcement of the State laws, in all cases wherein the Corporation Court of the City of Houston has jurisdiction, and all fines or penalties imposed by said court, including all costs incident thereto, and assessed against the parties so fined, are by this act declared to be due and owing to, and shall be payable to the City of Houston, and in all cases where fees are allowed, the officers making the arrest, or the attorney prosecuting said causes in said Corporation Court, said fees shall be payable to, and shall hereby become due and owing to the City of Houston.

[Paragraph relating to perquisites omitted.]

Sec. 4. Sidewalks.

Sec. 5. Vestibule Cars.

ARTICLE V.

Section 1. Elective Officers.

The administration of the business affairs of the City of Houston shall be conducted by a Mayor and four Aldermen, who, together, shall be known and designated as the City Council, each and all of whom shall be elected by the qualified voters of the city at large, and who shall hold their respective offices for two years from and after the next city election, or until their successors are elected and qualified, unless sooner removed, as is provided by this act; provided, however, that all of the present officers of the City of Houston, who were elected at a city election held in said city, on the fourth day of April, A. D. 1904, pursuant to the provisions of an act passed by the Twenty-eighth Legislature of the State of Texas, entitled: "An Act to provide a charter for the City of Houston, Harris County, Texas, repealing all laws or parts of laws in conflict herewith, and declaring an emergency"; except the Mayor, Aldermen and City Attorney, shall hold their respective offices, unless sooner removed by the Mayor for cause, and receive the compensation now fixed therefor, until the expiration of two years from and after the date of their election on the fourth day of April, 1904, and qualification thereunder.

Compensation of all officers, except the Mayor and Aldermen, shall be fixed by the City Council, which may increase or diminish the same at will, or abolish entirely any office at any time, except as to the officers above mentioned, and until their two years' term of office expires.

In case a primary election is held pursuant to the call or ınder the direction of any political party, or of any assoiation of individuals for the nomination of candidates for the ffices of Mayor and Aldermen, the candidates or persons oted for in said primary election shall be voted for at large y all of the legally qualified voters in said city, it being the urpose of this act to nominate and elect at large in said city he Mayor and Aldermen, without restricting the nomination f candidates for either position to any smaller designated erritory within the limits of said city, and any primary elecion held for the purpose of nominating candidates who shall tand for election at a city election in said city at which said rimary the candidates for Mayor and Aldermen are not oted for, as herein provided, shall be absolutely illegal, and o person so nominated at said primary election shall be ligible to election at a general election, nor shall he hold any ffice if elected thereto after nomination in a primary wherein the voters at large in said city did not participate in said rimary election.

ec. 2. Appointive Officers.

The Mayor shall have power to appoint, subject to conrmation by the City Council, such heads of departments ı the administrative service of the city as may be created by rdinance, and shall have power to appoint and remove all fficers or employes in the service of the city for cause, whenver in his judgment the public interests demand or will be etter subserved thereby; and no officer whose office is reated by ordinance shall hold the same for any fixed term, ut shall always be subject to removal by the Mayor or may e removed by the City Council. In case of such removal, if ne officer or employe so removed requests it, the Mayor or ity Council, as the case may be, shall file in the public rchives of the city a written statement of the reason for hich the removal was made.

ARTICLE VI.

ection 1. The Mayor.

The chief executive and administrative officer of the city nall be a Mayor, who shall be a citizen of the United tates, a qualified voter, residing for five consecutive years nmediately before his election within the city limits, nd a bona fide owner of real estate for at least two years efore his election, and shall hold his office for two years, nd until his successor is elected and qualified, unless sooner moved as provided by this act.

ec. 2. Mayor Pro Tem.

At the first regular meeting of the City Council after the duction of the newly elected Mayor and Aldermen in fice, the Mayor shall nominate, subject to confirmation y the City Council, one of the Aldermen who shall be known nd designated as "Mayor Pro Tem," and shall continue to old the title and the office until the expiration of the term office for which he was elected as Alderman, but shall reive no extra pay by reason of being or acting Mayor Pro em.

ec. 3. Disability of the Mayor.

If for any reason the Mayor is absent from the city, ck or unable to perform the duties of his office, the Mayor Pro Tem shall act as Mayor, and during such absence or disability shall possess all of the powers and perform all of the duties of the Mayor, except that he shall not, independent of the City Council, appoint or remove any officer or head of any department from office, which officer or head of department was appointed by the Mayor, unless the Mayor shall be absent, or disabled for a period of at least sixty days.

Sec. 4. Vacancy.

In case of the death, resignation or permanent disability of the Mayor, or whenever a vacancy in the office of Mayor shall occur for any reason, the Mayor Pro Tem shall act as Mayor, and shall possess all of the rights and powers of the Mayor, and perform all of his duties, under the official title, however, of "Mayor Pro Tem" until an election is ordered by the City Council to fill the vacancy in the office of the Mayor. Said election, should a vacancy occur in the office of Mayor, shall be called by the City Council and held within thirty days thereafter, and notice by publication given for at least twenty days, as may be required by law.

Sec. 5. Removal of the Mayor.

In case of misconduct, inability or willful neglect in the performance of the duties of his office, the Mayor may be removed from office by the City Council by majority vote of all the Aldermen elected, but shall be given an opportunity to be heard in his defense, and shall have the right to have process issued to compel the attendance of witnesses, who shall be required to give testimony, if he so elects. The hearing, in case of impeachment of the Mayor, shall be public and a full and complete statement of the reasons for such removal, if he be removed, together with the findings of facts as made by the Council, shall be filed by the City Council in the public archives of the city, and shall be and become a matter of public record.

Pending the charge of impeachment against the Mayor, the City Council may suspend him from office for a period of not exceeding thirty days, and if upon final hearing the conclusions and findings of the City Council are that the Mayor be impeached and removed from office, such findings shall be final.

Sec. 6. Veto Power of the Mayor.

Every ordinance, resolution or motion of the City Council, shall, before it takes effect, be presented to the Mayor for his approval and signature. If he approves it, he shall sign it; if he disapproves it, he shall specify his objection thereto in writing by the next regular meeting of the City Council, and return the same to the City Council, with such disapproval. If he does not return it with such disapproval, nor sign it, it shall upon the expiration of the time for its return to the City Council with his disapproval, be in effect and force, the same as if he had approved it.

The City Council may, in case of the veto of any ordinance or resolution by the Mayor, pass the same over the veto of the Mayor by a majority vote, but in all such cases the Mayor shall not be deprived of his right to vote as a member of the City Council by reason of the veto. In case the Mayor's veto is sustained, the matter shall not again come before the Council within six months, but in ordinances or resolutions making appropriations, the Mayor may veto any or every item therein, but such veto shall only extend to the items so vetoed, and those which he approves shall become effective, unless passed over his veto in the manner above specified.

Sec. 7. General Powers of the Mayor.

The Mayor shall have and exercise such powers, prerogatives and authority, acting independently of or in concert with the City Council, as are conferred by the provisions of this act, or as may be conferred upon him by the City Council, not inconsistent with the general purposes and provisions of this charter, and shall have the power to administer oaths, and shall sign all contracts and shall have the right and authority at any time to remove any officer or employe of the city subject to the provisions of this act; provided, however, he shall not have the right to remove one of the Aldermen of the city or the Controller, except by acting in concert with the other Aldermen as the City Council.

In case of the disability or absence of the Judge of the Corporation Court, the Mayor, or in the absence or disability of the Mayor, the Mayor Pro Tem, shall act as Judge of the Corporation Court.

Sec. 8. Annual Budget.

It shall be the duty of the Mayor from time to time to make such recommendations to the Council as he may deem to be for the welfare of the city, and on the second Monday of March of each year to submit to the Council the annual budget of the current expenses of the city for that fiscal year, each item in which may be increased, reduced or omitted by the Council, subject to the veto power of the Mayor.

The fiscal year of the City of Houston is hereby designated, beginning with the first day of March of each year and closing with the last day of Febraury next ensuing thereafter.

Sec. 9. Salary of the Mayor.

The salary of the Mayor of the City of Houston shall be four thousand dollars per annum, which said salary shall be payable in equal monthly installments. The Mayor shall devote his entire time to looking after the business and administration affairs of said city, or performing such duties as may devolve upon or be encumbent upon him to perform, and if for any reason, except in case of sickness or on business for the city, the Mayor shall absent himself from the city or fail or refuse to perform and discharge the duties of his office, for a period of time exceeding fifteen days, he shall not be allowed any compensation for such time, exceeding fifteen days, as he may fail to perform the duties of his office, but his salary shall for each and every day during such time and in excess of the fifteen days, be ratably reduced and deducted from his next monthly payment.

ARTICLE VII.

Section 1. City Council.

There shall be a City Council of the City of Houston, which shall consist and be composed of a Mayor and four Aldermen, with full power and authority, except as herein otherwise provided, to exercise all powers conferred upon the city subject to the veto power of the Mayor as hereinbefore provided.

Sec. 2. Qualification of Aldermen.

No person shall be elected an Alderman unless he be a citizen of the United States, and shall have been for five years immediately preceding such election a citizen of the City of Houston, and for two years prior to his election a bona fide owner of real estate in said city.

All Aldermen shall be elected by a vote of the people at large, and if nominated by any political party or organizatio as a candidate at any primary election, said nomination shal be made by voting for the candidate at large in said city.

No person shall be eligible to office who shall have bee nominated in any primary election in a ward or precinct o the city, or in any manner which will prevent the voters a large in said city from exercising the privilege of voting fo or against said candidate.

Sec. 3. Judge of Elections.

The City Council shall be the judge of the election an qualification of its own members, subject to review by th courts, in case of contest.

Sec. 4. Restrictions Upon Members of the Council.

[Specifies the usual restrictions imposed upon councilmen as to holding other public offices, being intereste in contracts, etc.]

Sec. 5. Rules of the Council.

Sec. 6. Meetings of the Council.

Sec. 7. Vacancies.

In case of the death, resignation, removal from the city or disqualification arising from any cause, of any Alderman, his office shall thereupon become vacant and an election shall be ordered by the City Council to elect his successor.

Sec. 8.

The City Council shall, consistent with the provisions o this act, have power to establish any office that may in i opinion be necessary or expedient for the conduct of th city's business or government, and may fix its salary an define its duties; provided, however, that all offices e tablished by the Council shall be subject to discontinuanc or be abolished by the Council at any time, and any e cumbent of any office, except the Controller, may be remove at any time by the Mayor, with or without the concurrenc of the Council; and in no case shall any officer or employ of the city be entitled to receive any compensation or emol ment of any office which may be abolished, or from whic he may be removed, except for services rendered to the dat when the office was abolished or the encumbent removed.

[Paragraph requiring officers to give bonds omitted.

Sec. 9.

[Mayor or City Council to investigate departments.

Sec. 10.

[Paragraph on appropriations to departments omitted.]

Sec. 11. Business Sessions.

For the purpose of conducting and transacting the ordinary business and administrative affairs of the city, the City Council shall be continuously in executive session, or open and ready to be convened therefor at any time, and at such hours as the Mayor may designate, and it is hereby declared to be the duty of every member of the City Council to attend at all times the executive sessions which may be called by the Mayor, or in case of his failure to call the same, by a majority of the members of the City Council, whenever they deem it expedient to do so.

Sec. 12. Salary.

The Aldermen shall each receive a salary of twenty-four hundred dollars ($2,400.00) per annum, payable in equal monthly installments, and shall devote their entire time to the service of the city, and shall perform all of the duties required by this act, and such other administrative duties as may be allotted or designated by the Mayor, from time to time.

The Council may remove at any time any Alderman by majority vote, for inattention to the affairs of the city, misconduct, or any grounds sufficient in judgment of the Council for removal.

ARTICLE VIII.

CITY CONTROLLER.

Section 1. Manner of Election.

The City Council shall at its first meeting in May, 1906, or as soon thereafter as it may be disposed to do so, and bi-ennially thereafter, elect a Controller, who shall hold his office for two years or until his successor is elected and qualified in the manner prescribed above, and who shall not be removed except by impeachment proceedings of the City Council, at which proceedings he shall be given ample opportunity to be heard, and may be represented by counsel, with the right to summon witnesses and compel the production of books and papers upon process duly issued by the City Council.

It shall require a majority vote of all the members of the City Council, which shall be a matter of record, to impeach the Controller.

Sec. 2. Duties of the Controller.

Sec. 3. Controller to keep books of account. All warrents to be signed by Controller and Mayor. No moneys to be disbursed without this warrant.

Sec. 4. Annual report of Controller. To be able to report at any time on state of city finances.

Sec. 5. Right to Examine the Books of the Grantees of Public Franchises.

The City of Houston shall have the right to regulate the rates, fares, tolls and charges to be collected from the public by any holders, owners, operators, persons or incorporations enjoying any grants or franchises from the City of Houston, pertaining to public utilities, including furnishing of lights, water, telephones and street car service, etc., pertaining to a public or quasi-public duty, and the right and authority is hereby given to the Mayor to require the City Controller or such other officer or employee as may be designated, to examine, carefully inspect all of the books, accounts, papers and documents, as well as the property of such persons or corporations using and enjoying any of said grants or franchises from the City of Houston as above stated, and to make such reports of said examination as required by the Mayor or City Council, when deemed necessary, for the following purposes:

1. When such franchise or grant was made upon the consideration and agreement that the City of Houston should receive a per cent. or portion of the revenue derived from the use of said grant or franchise.

2. When the persons or corporations above referred to have listed their property for taxation at a valuation deemed by the City Council or the Mayor to be below its actual value, or fails to list the same for taxation.

3. When the City Council desires to fix the rates, fares, tolls and charges which said persons or corporations above described shall charge the public for water, lights, transportation or other services rendered or furnished under the franchises granted to it or them by the City of Houston, and the information is desired or deemed necessary by the Mayor or City Council as a basis upon which to fix a proper rate.

4. When the Mayor or City Council have directed the individuals or corporations above specified to extend their lines and service, or to improve their service in any manner necessary for the public comfort and convenience, or to make improvements and betterments of their property, and such persons or corporations demur thereto on the ground that the income from their property used under said franchise is not sufficient to justify the same.

Such examinations and reports provided for in this section are for the purpose of ascertaining the value of the property and the income derived from it, and the reasonable expense for its operation.

ARTICLE IX.

GENERAL PROVISIONS.

Section 1. Actions by Citizens.

Any citizen who is a property taxpayer of the City of Houston may maintain an action in the proper court to restrain the execution of any illegal, unauthorized or fraudulent contract or agreement on behalf of said city, and to restrain any disbursing officer of said city from paying any illegal, unauthorized or fraudulent bills, claims or demands against said city, or any salaries or compensation to any person in its administrative service whose appointment has not been made in pursuance of the provisions of law and the regulations in force thereunder. And in case any such illegal, unauthorized or fraudulent bills, claims or demands, or any such salary or compensation, shall have been paid, such citizen may maintain an action in the name of said city against the officer making such payment and the party receiving the same, or either, or both, to recover the amount so paid, and such amount, after deducting all expenses of the action shall be paid into the city treasury; provided, however, that the court may require such citizens to give security to indemnify the city against costs of court, unless the court shall decide that there was reasonable cause for bringing the action. The right of any property taxpayer of the city to bring an action to restrain the payment of compensation to any person appointed to or holding any office, place or employment in violation of any of the provisions of this act, shall not be limited or denied by reason of the fact that said office, place or employment shall have been classified as, or determined to be, not subject to competitive examination; provided, however, that any judgment or injunction granted or made in any such action shall be prospective only, and shall not affect payments already made or due to such persons by the proper disbursing officers.

In case of any unsatisfied judgment, or any suit or process of law against said city, any five or more citizens who are freeholders of said city shall, upon petition, accompanied by affidavit that they believe that injustice will be done to said city in said suit or judgment, be permitted to intervene and inquire into the validity of said judgment, or defend said suit or action as fully and completely as the officers of said city would by law have the right to do.

Sec. 2.

[Elections are regulated by the City Council. Two paragraphs omitted.]

The City Council may, consistent with the other provisions of this act, and conforming to all the provisions of the State law regulating primary elections in cities and towns, in so far as the same may be applicable, prescribe the manner and method of holding primary elections by all political parties or political organizations of any kind whatsoever, and to determine the rules that shall obtain with respect to the representation the respective parties or candidates may be entitled to at the polls; may prescribe an official ballot, official returns, etc., and the expense of all primary elections held for the purpose of nominating candidates of any political party or organization for city officers shall be borne and paid for by the City of Houston.

Sec. 3. Petitions.

The petitions provided for in this act need not be on paper, and may be printed or written, but the signatures thereto must be the autograph signatures of the persons whose names purport to be signed. To each signature the house address of the signer must be added, and the signature must be made, acknowledged or proved before an officer authorized by law to take acknowledgments and proof of deeds. The certificate of such officer under his official seal that a signature was so made and ackuowledged or proved shall be sufficient proof of the genuineness of the signature for the purposes of this act. The signing of another's name, or of a false or fictitious name, to a petition, or the signing of a certificate falsely stating either that a signature was made in presence of the officer or acknowledged or proved before him, shall be punishable as a forgery.

Sections 4 to 14, inclusive.

[Relate to the public nature of the act, the validity of existing ordinances, the position of existing officers, evidence of ordinances, the city's exemption from giving bond, exemption of public property from execution, sale, the competence of persons as judge, liability of city for damages.]

Sec. 15. Ownership and Regulation of Public Utilities.

The right is hereby granted to the City of Houston to acquire its public utilities, such as gas, water and electric light works, and underground, surface and elevated street railways, subways, or underground conduit systems for electric light, power, telephone, telegraph and other wires used for the purpose of transmitting any electric service. That such utilities may be purchased by a payment in cash of twenty-five per cent. of such price, the balance in annual installments, including interest, to be paid out of the revenues of such utility, and that such works so purchased shall stand pledged as security for the payment of the amount due thereon, but that no judgment shall be rendered against the city upon any deferred note, requiring the city to pay any specified sum of money, but said judgment shall be merely one of foreclosure, divesting and depriving the city of the possession of the property so purchased but not paid for, in which event the city shall forfeit and lose only the cash payment of twenty-five per cent. of the agreed price, without liability or judgment in any sum for the unpaid purchase price; provided, that no purchase or expenditure shall be made under this section, unless the same shall first have been submitted to the vote of the qualified tax-paying voters at an election to be held exclusively for that purpose.

And the right is hereby expressly granted to the City of Houston to regulate all public utilities in said city and to require efficiency of public service, and to require all persons or corporations to discharge the duties and undertakings for the performance of which the respective franchises were made.

Sec. 16. Improvement Districts.

The City Council may, and upon petition shall, divide the city or any portion of the corporate territory thereof, into "Improvement Districts," clearly defining the limits and boundaries of each district; and shall have the right and is hereby authorized to borrow money on the credit of any improvement district so created in the city, and issue bonds therefor for the purpose of constructing and laying permanent sidewalk improvements in such district, but every proposition to borrow money on the credit of any improvement district for permanent sidewalk improvements therein shall be submitted to the qualified tax-paying voters living within and owning property in such district, and shall distinctly specify the purpose for which the loan is desired, and the permanent sidewalk improvements proposed to be constructed. If said proposition be sustained by a majority of the votes cast in such election in such district, such loan shall be lawful......etc.

Sec. 17.

[Relates to calling election for change in government.]

Sec. 18.

[Relates to repeal of laws in conflict.]

IOWA COMMISSION GOVERNMENT LAWS.

AN ACT TO PROVIDE FOR THE GOVERNMENT OF CERTAIN CITIES, AND THE ADOPTION THEREOF BY SPECIAL ELECTION "ADDITIONAL TO TITLE V OF THE CODE."

(CHAPTER 48, LAWS OF 1907.)

Be it enacted by the General Assembly of the State of Iowa:

Section 1. Cities Affected.

That any city of the first class, or with special charter, now or hereafter having a population of twenty-five thousand or over, as shown by the last preceding state census, may become organized as a city under the provisions of this act by proceeding as hereinafter provided.

Sec. 2. Petition—Question Submitted—Results Certified—Election of Officers.

Upon petition of electors equal in number to twenty-five percentum of the votes cast for all candidates for mayor at the last preceeding city election of any such city, the mayor shall by a proclamation, submit the question of organizing as a city under this act at a special election to be held at a time specified therein, and within two months after said petition is filed. If said plan is not adopted at the special election called, the question of adopting said plan shall not be resubmitted to the voters of said city for adoption within two years thereafter, and then the question to adopt shall be resubmitted upon the presentation of a petition signed by electors equal in number to twenty-five per centum of the votes cast for all candidates for mayor at the last preceding general city election.

At such election the proposition to be submitted shall be, "Shall the proposition to organize the city of (name of a city), under chapter (naming the chapter containing this act) of the acts of the Thirty-second General Assembly be adopted?" and the election thereupon shall be conducted, the vote canvassed, and the result declared in the same manner as provided by law in respect to other city elections. If the majority of the votes cast shall be in favor thereof, the city shall thereupon proceed to the election of a mayor and four (4) councilmen, as hereinafter provided. Immediately after such proposition is adopted, the mayor shall transmit to the Governor, to the Secretary of State, and to the county auditor, each a certificate stating that such proposition was adopted.

At the next regular city election after the adoption of such proposition, there shall be elected a mayor and four (4) councilmen. In the event, however, that the next regular city election does not occur within one year after such special election, the mayor shall, within ten days after such special election, by proclamation, call a special election for the election of mayor and four councilmen, sixty days' notice thereof being given in such call; such election in either case to be conducted as hereinafter provided.

Sec. 3. Statutes Applicable—Existing Ordinances, Resolutions, etc.

All laws governing cities of the first class and not inconsistent with the provisions of this act, and sections 955, 956, 959, 964, 989, 1,000, 1,023 and 1,053 of the Code now applicable to special charter cities and not inconsistent with the provisions of this act shall apply to and govern cities organized under this act. All by-laws, ordinances and resolutions lawfully passed and in force in any such city under its former organization shall remain in force until altered or repealed by the council elected under the provisions of this act. The territorial limits of such city shall remain the same as under its former organization, and all rights and property of every description which were vested in any such city under its former organization, shall vest in the same under the organization herein contemplated, and no right or liability either in favor of or against it, existing at the time, and no suit or prosecution of any kind shall be affected by such change, unless otherwise provided for in this act.

Sec. 4. Elective Officers—Vacancies—Terms of Office.

In every such city there shall be elected at the regular biennial municipal election, a mayor and four councilmen.

If any vacancy occurs in any such office the remaining members of said council shall appoint a person to fill such vacancy during the balance of the unexpired term.

Said officers shall be nominated and elected at large. Said officers shall qualify and their terms of office shall begin on the first Monday after their election. The terms of office of the mayor and councilmen or aldermen in such city in office at the beginning of the terms of office of the mayor and councilmen first elected under the provisions of this act shall then cease and determine, and the terms of office of all other appointive officers in force in such city, except as hereinafter provided, shall cease and determine as soon as the council shall by resolution declare.

Sec. 5. Candidates—How Nominated—Primary Election Ballot—Canvass of Vote—Result Published—Municipal Election.

Candidates to be voted for at all general municipal elections at which a mayor and four councilmen are to be elected under the provisions of this act shall be nominated by a primary election, and no other names shall be placed upon the general ballot except those selected in the manner hereinafter prescribed. The primary election for such nomination shall be held on the second Monday preceding the general municipal election. The judges of election appointed for the general municipal election shall be the judges of the primary election, and it shall be held at the same place, so far as possible, and the polls shall be opened and closed at the same hours, with the same clerks as are required for said general municipal election.

Any person desiring to become a candidate for mayor or councilman shall, at least ten days prior to said primary election, file with the said clerk a statement of such candidacy, in substantially the following form:

State of Iowa.......................County.—ss.

I, (......................) being first duly sworn, say that I reside at ....street, city of.................. county of................... State of Iowa; that I am a qualified voter therein; that I am a candidate for nomination to the office of (mayor or councilman) to be voted upon at the primary election to be held on the.............. Monday of ...., 19......and I hereby request that my name be printed upon the official primary ballot for nomination by such primary election for such office.

(Signed) ....

Subscribed and sworn to (or affirmed) before me by....... .... on this ....day of 19....

(Signed)......................

and shall at the same time file therewith the petition of at least twenty-five qualified voters requesting such candidacy. Each petition shall be verified by one or more persons as to the qualifications and residence, with street number, of each of the persons so signing the said petition, and the said petition shall be in substantially the following form:

PETITION ACCOMPANYING NOMINATING STATEMENT.

The undersigned, duly qualified electors of the city of ....and residing at the places set opposite our respective names hereto, do hereby request that the name of (name of candidate) be placed on the ballot as a candidate for nomination for (name of office) at the primary election to be held in such city on the.....................Monday of .... 19... We further state that we know him to be a qualified elector of said city and a man of good moral character and qualified in our judgment for the duties of such office.

Immediately upon the expiration of the time of filing the statements and petitions for candidacies, the said city clerk shall cause to be published for three successive days in all the daily newspapers published in the city, in proper form, the names of the persons as they are to appear upon the primary ballots and if there be no daily newspaper, then in two issues of any other newspapers that may be published in said city; and the said clerk shall thereupon cause the primary ballots to be printed, authenticated with a fac-simile of his signature. Upon the said ballot the names of the candidates for mayor, arranged alphabetically, shall first be placed, with a square at the left of each name, and immediately below the words "Vote for one." Following these names, likewise arranged in alphabetical order, shall appear the names of the candidates for councilman, with a square at the left of each name, and immediately below the names of such candidates shall appear the words, "Vote for four." The ballots shall be printed upon plain, substantial white paper, and shall be headed:

CANDIDATES FOR NOMINATION FOR MAYOR AND COUNCILMEN OF————CITY AT THE PRIMARY ELECTION.

but shall have no party designation or mark whatever. The ballots shall be in substantially the following form:

(Place a cross in the square preceding the names of the parties you favor as candidates for the respective positions.)

OFFICIAL PRIMARY BALLOT.

CANDIDATE FOR NOMINATION FOR MAYOR AND COUNCILMEN OF————CITY AT THE PRIMARY ELECTION.

☐ For Mayor.
(Name of Candidate)
(Vote for one.)

☐ For Councilman,
(Name of Candidate)
(Vote for four.)

Official ballot attest:

(Signature)

....

City Clerk.

Having caused said ballots to be printed, the said city clerk shall cause to be delivered at each polling place a number of said ballots equal to twice the number of votes cast in such polling precinct at the last general municipal election for mayor. The persons who are qualified to vote at the general municipal election shall be qualified to vote at such primary election, and challenges can be made by not more than two persons, to be appointed at the time of opening the polls by the judges of election; and the law applicable to challenges at a general municipal election shall be applicable to challenges made at such primary election. Judges of election shall, immediately upon the closing of the polls, count the ballots and ascertain the number of votes cast in such precinct for each of the candidates, and make return thereof to the city clerk, upon proper blanks to be furnished by the said clerk, within six hours of the closing of the polls. On the day following the said primary election the said city clerk shall canvass said returns so received from all the polling precincts, and shall make and publish in all the newspapers of said city at least once, the result thereof. Said canvass by the city clerk shall be publicly made. The two candidates receiving the highest number of votes for mayor shall be the candidates and the only candidates whose names shall be placed upon the ballot for mayor at the next succeeding general municipal election, and the eight candidates receiving the highest number of votes for councilman, or all such candidates, if less than eight, shall be the candidates and the only candidates whose names shall be placed upon the ballot for councilman at such municipal election.

All electors of cities under this act who by the laws governing cities of the first class and cities acting under special charter would be entitled to vote for the election of officers at any general municipal election in such cities, shall be qualified to vote at all elections under this act; and the ballot at such general municipal election shall be in the same general form as for such primary election, so far as applicable, and in all elections in such city the election precincts, voting places, method of conducting the election, canvassing the votes and announcing the results, shall be the same as by law provided for election of officers in such cities, so far as the same are applicable and not inconsistent with the provisions of this act.

Sec. 5-A. Services for Hire—Penalty.

Any person who shall agree to perform any services in the interest of any candidate for any office provided in this act, in consideration of any money or other valuable thing for such services performed in the interest of any candidate shall be punished by a fine not exceeding three hundred dollars ($300), or be imprisoned in the county jail not exceeding thirty (30) days.

Sec. 5-B. Bribery on Illegal Voting—Penalty.

Any person offering to give a bribe, either in money or other consideration, to any elector for the purpose of influencing his vote at any election provided in this act, or any elector entitled to vote at any such election receiving and accepting such bribe or other consideration; any person making false answer to any of the provisions of this act relative to his qualifications to vote at said election; any person wilfully voting or offering to vote at such election who has not been a resident of this State for six months next preceding said election, or who is not twenty-one years of age, or is not a citizen of the United States; or knowing himself not to be a qualified elector of such precinct where he offers to vote; any person knowingly procuring, aiding or abetting any violation hereof shall be deemed guilty of a misdemeanor and upon conviction shall be fined a sum not less than one hundred dollars ($100), nor more than five hundred dollars ($500), and be imprisoned in the county jail not less than ten (10) nor more than ninety (90) days.

Sec. 6. Council—Quorum—Mayor to Preside.

Every such city shall be governed by a council, consisting of the mayor and four councilmen, chosen as provided in this act, each of whom shall have the right to vote on all questions coming before the council. Three members of the council shall constitute a quorum, and the affirmative vote of three members shall be necessary to adopt any motion, resolution or ordinance, or pass any measure, unless a greater number is provided for in this act. Upon every vote the yeas and nays shall be called and recorded, and every motion, resolution or ordinance shall be reduced to writing and read before the vote is taken thereon. The mayor shall preside at all meetings of the council; he shall have no power to veto any measure, but every resolution or ordinance passed by the council must be signed by the mayor, or by two councilmen, and be recorded, before the same shall be in force.

Sec. 7. Council—Powers and Duties—Departments.

The council shall have and possess and the council and its members shall exercise all executive, legislative and judicial powers and duties now had, possessed and exercised by the mayor, city council, board of public work, park commissioners, board of police and fire commissioners, board of water works trustees, board of library trustees, solicitor, assessor, treasurer, auditor, city engineer, and other executive and administrative officers in cities of the first class and cities acting under special charter. The executive and administrative powers, authority and duties in such cities shall be distributed into and among five departments, as follows:

1. Department of PUBLIC AFFAIRS.
2. Department of ACCOUNTS AND FINANCE.
3. Department of PUBLIC SAFETY.
4. Department of STREETS AND PUBLIC IMPROVEMENTS.
5. Department of PARKS AND PUBLIC PROPERTY.

The council shall determine the powers and duties to be performed by, and assign them to the appropriate department; shall prescribe the powers and duties of officers and employees; may assign particular officers and employees to one or more of the departments; may require an officer or employee to perform duties in two or more departments; and may make such other rules and regulations as may be necessary or proper for the efficient and economical conduct of the business of the city.

Sec. 8. Departments—Superintendents—Officers and Assistants.

The mayor shall be superintendent of the department of Public Affairs, and the council shall at the first regular meeting after election of its members designate by majority vote one councilman to be superintendent of the department of Accounts and Finances; one to be superintendent of the department of Public Safety; one to be superintendent of the department of Streets and Public Improvements; and one to be superintendent of the department of Parks and Public Property; but such designation shall be changed whenever it appears that the public service would be benefitted thereby.

The council shall, at said first meeting, or as soon as practicable thereafter, elect by majority vote the following officers: A city clerk, solicitor, assessor, treasurer, auditor, civil engineer, city physician, marshal, chief of fire department, market master, street commissioner, three library trustees, and such other officers and assistants as shall be provided for by ordinance and necessary to the proper and efficient conduct of the affairs of the city; and shall appoint a police judge in those cities not having a superior court. Any officer or assistant elected or appointed by the council may be removed from office at any time by vote of a majority of the members of the council except as otherwise provided for in this act.

Sec. 9. Power to Create and Discontinue Offices.

The council shall have power from time to time to create, fill and discontinue offices and employments other than herein prescribed, according to their judgment of the needs of the city; and may by majority vote of all the members remove any such officer or employe, except as otherwise provided for in this act; and may by resolution or otherwise prescribe, limit or change the compensation of such officers or employes.

Sec. 10. Office in City Hall—Salaries.

The mayor and council shall have an office at the city hall, and their total compensation shall be as follows: In cities having by the last preceding State or National census from 25,000 to 40,000 people, the annual salary of the mayor shall be $2,500, and of each councilman $1,800. In cities having by such census from 40,000 to 60,000 people, the mayor's annual salary shall be $3,000, and that of each councilman $2,500; and in cities having by such census over 60,000 population, the mayor's annual salary shall be $3,500, and that of each councilman $3,000. Such salaries shall be payable in equal monthly installments.

Any increase in salary occasioned under the provisions of this scale by increase in population in any city shall commence with the month next after the official publication of the census showing such increase therein.

Every other officer or assistant shall receive such salary or compensation as the council shall by ordinance provide, payable in equal monthly installments.

The salary or compensation of all other employes of such city shall be fixed by the council and shall be payable monthly or at such shorter periods as the council shall determine.

Sec. 11. Meetings—President of Council—Vice-President.

Regular meetings of the council shall be held on the first Monday after the election of councilmen, and thereafter at least once each month. The council shall provide by ordinance for the time of holding regular meetings, and special meetings may be called from time to time by the mayor or two councilmen. All meetings of the council, whether regular or special at which any person not a city officer is admitted, shall be open to the public.

The mayor shall be president of the council and preside at its meetings, and shall supervise all departments and report to the council for its action all matters requiring attention in either. The superintendent of the department of Accounts and Finances shall be vice-president of the council, and in case of vacancy in the office of mayor, or the absence or inability of the mayor, shall perform the duties of the mayor.

Sec. 12. Ordinances and Resolutions—Franchises.

Every ordinance or resolution appropriating money or ordering any street improvement or sewer, or making or authorizing the making of any contract, or granting any franchise or right to occupy or use the streets, highways, bridges or public places in the city for any purpose, shall be complete in the form in which it is finally passed, and remain on file with the city clerk for public inspection at least one week before the final passage on adoption thereof. No franchise or right to occupy or use the streets, highways, bridges or public places in any city shall be granted, renewed or extended, except by ordinance, and every franchise or grant for interurban or street railways, gas or water works, electric light or power plants, heating plants, telegraph or telephone systems, or other public service utilities within said city, must be authorized or approved by a majority of the electors voting thereon at a general or special election, as provided in section 776 of the Code.

Sec. 13. Officers and Employees—What Prohibited.

No officer or employe elected or appointed in any such city shall be interested, directly or indirectly, in any contract or job for work or materials, or the profits thereof, or services to be furnished or performed for the city; and no such officer or employe shall be interested directly or indirectly in any contract or job for work or materials, or the profits thereof, or services to be furnished or performed for any person, firm or corporation operating interurban railway, street railway, gas works, water works, electric light or power plant, heating plant, telegraph line, telephone exchange, or other public utility within the territorial limits of said city. No such officer or employe shall accept or receive, directly or indirectly, from any person, firm or corporation operating within the territorial limits of said city, any interurban railway, street railway, gas works, water works, electric light or power plant, heating plant, telegraph line or telephone exchange, or other business using or operating under a public franchise, any frank, free ticket or free service, or accept or receive, directly or indirectly, from any such person, firm or corporation, any other service upon terms more favorable than is granted to the public generally. Any violation of the provisions of this section shall be a misdemeanor, and every such contract or agreement shall be void.

Such prohibition of free transportation shall not apply to policemen or firemen in uniform; nor shall any free service to city officials heretofore provided by any franchise or ordinance be affected by this section. Any officer or employe of such city who, by solicitation or otherwise, shall exert his influence directly or indirectly to influence other officers or employes of such city to adopt his political views or to favor any particular person or candidate for office, or who shall in any manner contribute money, labor, or other valuable things to any person for election purposes, shall be guilty of a misdemeanor, and upon conviction shall be punished by a fine not exceeding three hundred dollars ($300) or by imprisonment in the county jail not exceeding thirty (30) days.

Sec. 14. Civil Service Commissioners—Duties—Powers of Council.

Immediately after organizing the council shall by ordinance appoint three civil service commissioners, who shall hold office, one until the first Monday in April in the second year after his appointment, and one until the first Monday in April of the fourth year after his appointment, and one until the first Monday in April of the sixth year after his appointment. Each succeeding council shall, as soon as practicable after organizing, appoint one commissioner for six years, who shall take the place of the commissioner whose term of office expires. The chairman of the commission for each biennial period shall be the member whose term first expires. No person while on the said commission shall hold or be a candidate for any office of public trust. Two of said members shall constitute a quorum to transact business. The commissioners must be citizens of Iowa, and residents of the city for more than three years next preceding their appointment.

The council may remove any of said commissioners during their term of office for cause, four councilmen voting in favor of such removal, and shall fill any vacancy that may occur in said commission for the unexpired term. The city council shall provide suitable rooms in which the said civil service commission may hold its meetings. They shall have a clerk, who shall keep a record of all its meetings, such city to supply the said commission with all necessary equipment to properly attend to such business.

(a) Oath of Office.

Before entering upon the duties of their office, each of said commissioners shall take and subscribe an oath, which shall be filed and kept in the office of the city clerk, to support the Constitution of the Unted States and the State of Iowa, and to obey the laws, and to aim to secure and maintain an honest and efficient force, free from partisan distinction or control, and to perform the duties of his office to the best of his ability.

(b) Examinations—Results Certified.

Said commission shall, on the first Monday of April and October of each year, or oftener if it shall be deemed necessary, under such rules and regulations as may be prescribed by the council, hold examinations for the purpose of determining the qualifications of applicants for positions, which examinations shall be practical and shall fairly test the fitness of the persons examined to discharge the duties of the position to which they seek to be appointed. Said commission shall as soon as possible after such examination, certify to the council double the number of persons necessary to fill vacancies, who, according to its records, have the highest standing for the position they seek to fill as a result of such examination, and all vacancies which occur, that come under the civil service, prior to the date of the next regular examination, shall be filled from said list so certified; provided, however, that should the list for any cause be reduced to less than three for any division, then the council or the head of the proper department may temporarily fill a vacancy, but not to exceed thirty days.

(c) Removals and Discharges—Appeals.

All persons subject to such civil service examinations shall be subject to removal from office or employment by the council for misconduct or failure to perform their duties under such rules and regulations as it may adopt, and the chief of police, chief of the fire department, or any superintendent or foreman in charge of municipal work, may peremptorily suspend or discharge any subordinate then under his direction for neglect of duty or disobedience of his orders, but shall, within twenty-four hours thereafter, report such suspension or discharge, and the reason therefor, to the superintendent of his department, who shall thereupon affirm or revoke such discharge or suspension, according to the facts.

Such employee (or the officer discharged or suspending him) may, within five days of such ruling, appeal therefrom to the council, which shall fully hear and determine the matter.

(d) Witnesses—Annual Report—Rules and Regulations.

The council shall have the power to enforce the attendance of witnesses, the production of books and papers, and power to administer oaths in the same manner and with like effect, and under the same penalties, as in the case of magistrates exercising criminal or civil jurisdiction under the statutes of Iowa.

Said commissioners shall make annual report to the council, and it may require a special report from said commission at any time; and said council may prescribe such rules and regulations for the proper conduct of the business of the said commission as shall be found expedient and advisable, including restrictions on appointments, promotions, removals for cause, roster of employes, certification of records to the auditor, and restrictions on payment to persons improperly employed.

(e) Penalties.

The council of such city shall have power to pass ordinances imposing suitable penalties for the punishment of persons violating any of the provisions of this act relating to the civil service commission.

(f) Officers and Employees Affected.

The provisions of this section shall apply to all appointive officers and employes of such city, except those especially named in section 8 of this act, commissioners of any kind (laborers whose occupation requires no special skill or fitness), election officials, and mayor's secretary and assistant solicitor, where such officers are appointed; provided, however, that existing employes heretofore appointed or employed after competitive examination or for long service under the provisions of chapter 31, acts of the Twenty-ninth General Assembly, and subsequent amendments thereto, shall retain their positions without further examination unless removed for cause.

All officers and employees in any such city shall be elected or appointed with reference to their qualifications and fitness, and for the good of the public service, and without reference to their political faith or party affiliations.

It shall be unlawful for any candidate for office, or any officer in any such city, directly or indirectly, to give or promise any person or persons any office, position, employment, benefit, or anything of value, for the purpose of influencing or obtaining the political support, aid or vote of any person or persons.

Every elective officer in any such city shall, within thirty days after qualifying, file with the city clerk, and publish at least once in a daily newspaper of general circulation, his sworn statement of all his election and campaign expenses, and by whom such funds were contributed.

Any violation of the provisions of this section shall be a misdemeanor and be a ground for removal from office.

Sec. 15. Monthly Itemized Statement—Annual Examination.

The council shall each month print in pamphlet form a detailed itemized statement of all receipts and expenses of the city and a summary of its proceedings during the preceding month, and furnish printed copies thereof to the state library, the city library, the daily newspapers of the city, and to persons who shall apply therefor at the office of the city clerk. At the end of each year the council shall cause a full and complete examination of all the books and accounts of the city to be made by competent accountants, and shall publish the result of such examination in the manner above provided for publication of statements of monthly expenditures.

Sec. 16. Appropriations.

If, at the beginning of the term of office of the first council elected in such city under the provisions of this act, the appropriations for the expenditures of the city government for the current fiscal year have been made, said council shall have power, by ordinance, to revise, to repeal or change said appropriations and to make additional appropriations.

Sec. 17. Terms Defined.

In the construction of this act the following rules shall be observed, unless such construction would be inconsistent with the manifest intent, or repugnant to the context of the statute:

1. The words "councilman" or "alderman" shall be construed to mean "councilman" when applied to cities under this act.

2. When an office or officer is named in any law referred to in this act, it shall, when applied to cities under this act, be construed to mean the office or officer having the same functions or duties under the provisions of this act, or under ordinances passed under authority thereof.

3. The word "franchise" shall include every special privilege in the streets, highways and public places of the city, whether granted by the State or the city, which does not belong to the citizens generally by common right.

4. The word "electors" shall be construed to mean persons qualified to vote for elective officers at regular municipal elections.

Sec. 18. Removal of Elective Officers—Procedure—Election of Successors.

The holder of any elective office may be removed at any time by the electors qualified to vote for a successor of such incumbent. The procedure to effect the removal of an incumbent of an elective office shall be as follows: A petition signed by electors entitled to vote for a successor to the incumbent sought to be removed, equal in number to at least twenty-five per centum of the entire vote for all candidiates for the office of mayor at the last preceding general municipal election, demanding an election of a successor of the person sought to be removed shall be filed with the city clerk, which petition shall contain a general statement of the grounds for which the removal is sought. The signatures to the petition need not all be appended to one paper, but each signer shall add to his signature his place of residence, giving the street and number. One of the signers of each such paper shall make oath before an officer competent to administer oaths that the statements therein made are true as he believes, and that each signature to the paper appended is the genuine signature of the person whose name it purports to be. Within ten days from the date of filing such petition the city clerk shall examine and from the voters' register ascertain whether or not said petition is signed by the requisite number of qualified electors, and, if necessary, the council shall allow him extra help for that purpose; and he shall attach to said petition his certificate, showing the result of said examination. If by the clerk's certificate the petition is shown to be insufficient, it may be amended within ten days from the date of said certificate. The clerk shall, within ten days after such amendment, make like examination of the amended petition, and if his certificate shall show the same to be insufficient, it shall be returned to the person filing the same; without prejudice, however, to the filing of a new petition to the same effect. If the petition shall be deemed to be sufficient, the clerk shall submit the same to the council without delay. If the petition shall be found to be sufficient, the council shall order and fix a date for holding the said election, not less than thirty days or more than forty days from the date of the clerk's certificate to the council that a sufficient petition is filed.

The council shall make, or cause to be made, publication of notice and all arrangements for holding such election, and the same shall be conducted, returned and the result thereof declared, in all respects as are other city elections. The successor of any officer so removed shall hold office during the unexpired term of his predecessor. Any person sought to be removed may be a candidate to succeed himself, and unless he requests otherwise in writing, the clerk shall place his name on the official ballot without nomination. In any such removal election, the candidate receiving the highest number of votes shall be declared elected. At such election if some other person than the incumbent receives the highest number of votes the incumbent shall thereupon be deemed removed from the office upon qualification of his successor. In case the party who receives the highest number of votes should fail to qualify, within ten days after receiving notification of election, the office shall be deemed vacant. If the incumbent receives the highest number of votes he shall continue in office. The same method of removal shall be cumulative and additional to the methods heretofore provided by law.

Sec. 19. Petitions for Ordinances—Adoption or Submission—How Repealed or Amended.

Any proposed ordinance may be submitted to the council by petition signed by electors of the city equal in number to the percentage hereinafter required. The signatures, verification, authentication, inspection, certification, amendment and submission of such petition shall be the same as provided for petitions under section 18 hereof.

If the petition accompanying the proposed ordinance be signed by electors equal in number to twenty-five per centum of the votes cast for all candidates for mayor at the last preceding general election, and contains a request that the said ordinance be submitted to a vote of the people if not passed by the council, such council shall either

(a) Pass said ordinance without alteration within twenty days after attachment of the clerk's certificate to the accompanying petition or

(b) Forthwith after the clerk shall attach to the petition accompanying such ordinance his certificate of sufficiency, the council shall call a special election, unless a general municipal election is fixed within ninety days thereafter, and at such special or general municipal election, if one is so fixed, such ordinance shall be submitted without alteration to the vote of the electors of said city.

But if the petition is signed by not less than ten nor more than twenty-five per centum of the electors, as above defined, then the council shall, within twenty days, pass said ordinance without change, or submit the same at the next general city election occurring not more than thirty days after the clerk's certificate of sufficiency is attached to said petition.

The ballots used when voting upon said ordinance shall contain these words: "For the Ordinance" (stating the nature of the proposed ordinance), and "Against the Ordinance" (stating the nature of the proposed ordinance). If a majority of the qualified electors voting on the proposed ordinance shall vote in favor thereof, such ordinance shall thereupon become a valid and binding ordinance of the city; and any ordinance proposed by petition, or which shall be adopted by a vote of the people, cannot be repealed or amended except by a vote of the people.

Any number of proposed ordinances may be voted upon at the same election, in accordance with the provisions of this section; but there shall not be more than one special election in any period of six months for such purpose.

The council may submit a proposition for the repeal of any such ordinance or for amendments thereto, to be voted upon at any succeeding general city election; and should such proposition so submitted receive a majority of the votes cast thereon at such election, such ordinance shall thereby be repealed or amended accordingly. Whenever any ordinance or proposition is required by this act to be submitted to the voters of the city at any election, the city clerk shall cause such ordinance or proposition to be published once in each of the daily newspapers published in said city; such publication to be not more than twenty or less than five days before the submission of such proposition or ordinance to be voted on.

Sec. 20. Ordinances—When Effective—Petitions of Protest.

No ordinance passed by the council, except when otherwise required by the general laws of the State or by the provisions of this act, except an ordinance for the immediate preservation of the public peace, health or safety, which contains a statement of its urgency and is passed by a two-thirds vote of the council shall go into effect before ten days from the time of its final passage and if during said ten days a petition signed by electors of the city equal in number to at least twenty-five percentum of the entire vote cast for all candidates for mayor at the last preceding general muncipal election at which a mayor was elected, protesting against the passage of such ordinance, be presented to the council, the same shall thereupon be suspended from going into operation, and it shall be the duty of the council to reconsider such ordinance; and if the same is not entirely repealed, the council shall submit the ordinance, as is provided by sub-section b of section 19 of this act, to the vote of the electors of the city, either at the general election or at a special municipal election to be called for that purpose; and such ordinance shall not go into effect or become operative unless a majority of the qualified electors voting on the same shall vote in favor thereof. Said petition shall be in all respects in accordance with the provisions of said section 19, except as to the percentage of signers, and be examined and certified to by the clerk in all respects as is therein provided.

Sec. 21. Abandonment of Commission Plan of Government—Procedure.

Any city which shall have operated for more than six years under the provisions of this act may abandon such organization hereunder, and accept the provisions of the general law of the State then applicable to cities of its population, or if now organized under special charter, may resume said special charter by proceeding as follows:

Upon the petition of not less than twenty-five percentum of the electors of such city a special election shall be called, at which the following proposition only shall be submitted: "Shall the city of (name the city) abandon its organization under chapter — of the acts of the Thirty-second General Assembly and become a city under the general law governing cities of like population, or if now organized under special charter shall resume said special charter?"

If the majority of the votes cast at such special election be in favor of such proposition, the officers elected at the next succeeding biennial election shall be those then prescribed by the general law of the State for cities of like population, and upon the qualification of such officers such city shall become a city under such general law of the State; but such change shall not in any manner or degree affect the property, right or liabilities of any nature of such city, but shall merely extend to such change in its form of government.

The sufficiency of such petition shall be determined, the election ordered and conducted, and the results declared, generally as provided by section 18 of this act, in so far as the provisions thereof are applicable.

Sec. 22. Petitions.

Petitions provided for in this act shall be signed by none but legal voters of the city. Each petition shall contain, in addition to the names of the petitioners, the street and house number in which the petitioner resides, his age and length of residence in the city. It shall also be accompanied by the affidavit of one or more legal voters of the city stating that the signers thereof were, at the time of signing, legal voters of said city, and the number of signers at the time the affidavit was made.

Sec. 23. In Effect.

This act, being deemed of immediate importance, shall take effect and be in force from and after its publication in The Register and Leader and Des Moines Capital, newspapers published in Des Moines, Iowa.

[Approved March 29, A. D. 1907.]

AN ACT TO AMEND THE LAW AS IT APPEARS IN SECTION TEN HUNDRED FIFTY-SIX-A THIRTY-SIX (1056-A 36) OF THE SUPPLEMENT TO THE CODE, 1907, RELATING TO THE GOVERNMENT OF CERTAIN CITIES AND THE RECALLING OF ELECTIVE OFFICERS THEREIN.

(CHAPTER 65, LAWS OF 1909.)

Be it enacted by the General Assembly of the State of Iowa:

Section 1. Statement of Candidacy-petition-ballot-form.

That section ten hundred fifty-six-a thirty-six (1056a-36) of the supplement to the code, 1907, be amended by inserting after the word "elections" at the end of the thirty-fourth (34) line in said section the following:

"So far as applicable, except as otherwise herein provided, nominations hereunder shall be made without the intervention of a primary election by filing with the clerk at least ten (10) days prior to said election, a statement of candidacy accompanied by a petition signed by electors entitled to vote at said special election equal in number to at least ten per centum of the entire vote for all candidates for the office of mayor at the last preceding general municipal election, which said statement of candidacy and petition shall be substantially in the form set out in section ten hundred fifty-six-a twenty-one (1056-a 21) of the supplement to the code, 1907, so far as the same is applicable, substituting the word 'special' for the word 'primary' in such statement and petition, and stating therein that such person is a candidate for election instead of nomination.

The ballot for such special election shall be in substantially the following form:

OFFICIAL BALLOT.

Special election for the balance of the unexpired term of................as..........................

For..........................

(Vote for one only)

(Names of Candidates)

☐ ....

☐ ....

Name of present encumbent

Official ballot attest:

(Signature)

....

City Clerk.

Sec. 2. In Effect.

This act being deemed of immediate importance shall take effect and be in force from and after its passage and approval and publication in the Des Moines Register and Leader and Des Moines Capital, newspapers published in Des Moines, Iowa.

[Approved April 16, A. D. 1909.]

GOVERNMENT OF CERTAIN CITIES.

(CHAPTER 64, LAWS OF 1909.)

Be it enacted by the General Assembly of the State of Iowa:

Section 1. Repeal—cities affected.

That section ten hundred fifty-six-a seventeen (1056-a17) of chapter fourteen-c (14-c) of the supplement to the code, 1907, be and the same is hereby repealed and the following enacted in lieu thereof.

"Cities having by the last preceding state or national census a population of seven thousand or over, including any such city acting under special charter, may become organized as a city under the provisions of this act by proceeding as hereinafter provided."

Sec. 2. Repeal—petition—question submitted—result certified—election of officers.

That section ten hundred fifty-six-a eighteen (1056-a18) of chapter fourteen-c (14-c) of the supplement to the code, 1907, be and the same is hereby repealed and the following enacted in lieu thereof:

"Upon petition of electors equal in number to twenty-five per centum of the votes cast for all candidates for mayor at the last preceding city election of any such city, the mayor shall, by proclamation, submit the question of organizing as a city under this act at a special election to be held at a time specified therein, and within two months after said petition is filed; provided, however, that in case any city is located in two or more townships said petition shall be signed by twenty-five per centum of the qualified electors of said city residing in each of said townships. If said plan is not adopted at the special election called, the question of adopting said plan shall not be re-submitted to the voters of said city for adoption within two years thereafter, and then the question to adopt shall be re-submitted upon the presentation of a petition signed by electors as hereinbefore provided, equal in number to twenty-five per centum of the votes cast for all candidates for mayor at the last preceding general city election. At such election, the proposition to be submitted shall be, "Shall the proposition to organize the city of (name the city), under chapter fourteen-c (14-c) of the supplement to the code, 1907, as amended by the acts of the thirty-third general assembly, be adopted?", and the election thereupon shall be conducted, the vote canvassed, and the result declared in the same manner as provided by law in respect to other city elections. If the majority of the votes cast shall be in favor thereof, cities having a population of twenty-five thousand and over shall thereupon proceed to the election of a mayor and four councilmen, and cities having a population of seven thousand, and less than twenty-five thousand, shall proceed to the election of a mayor and two councilmen, as hereinafter provided. Immediately after such proposition is adopted, the mayor shall transmit to the governor, to the secretary of state, and to the county auditor, each a certificate stating that such proposition was adopted. At the next regular city election after the adoption of such proposition there shall be elected a mayor and councilmen. In the event, however, that the next regular city election does not occur within one year after such special election the mayor shall, within ten days after such special election by proclamation call a special election for the election of a mayor and councilmen, sixty days' notice thereof being given in such call; such election in either case to be conducted as hereinafter provided."

Sec. 3. Statutes relating to cities of second class applicable.

That section 1056-a19 of chapter 14-c of the supplement to the code, 1907, be and the same is hereby amended by inserting after the word "first" and before the word "class" in the first line thereof the words "and second."

Sec. 4. Elective officers.

That section 1056-a20 of chapter 14-c of the supplement to the code, 1907, be and the same is hereby amended by striking out the first sentence of said section and inserting in lieu thereof the following:

"In every city having a population of twenty-five thousand and over there shall be elected at the regular biennial municipal election a mayor and four councilmen, and in every city having a population of seven thousand and less than twenty-five thousand; there shall be elected at such election a mayor and two councilmen."

Sec. 5. Repeal—candidates—how nominated—primary election—ballot—canvass of vote—result published—municipal election.

That section ten hundred fifty-six-a twenty-one (1056a21) of the supplement to the code, 1907, be repealed and the following enacted in lieu thereof:

"Candidates to be voted for at all general municipal elections at which a mayor and councilmen are to be elected under the provisions of this act shall be nominated by a primary election, and no other names shall be placed upon the general ballot except those selected in the manner hereinafter prescribed. The primary election for such nomination shall be held on the second Monday preceding the general municipal election. The judges of election appointed for the general municipal election shall be the judges of the primary election, and it shall be held at the same place, so far as possible, and the polls shall be opened and closed at the same hours, with the same clerks as are required for said general municipal election. Any person desiring to become a candidate for mayor or councilman shall, at least ten days prior to said primary election, file with the said clerk a statement of such candidacy, in substantially the following form:

State of Iowa ....County, ss.

I (————) being first duly sworn, say that I reside at.......street, city of ...., county of..........., state of Iowa; that I am a qualified voter therein; that I am a candidate for nomination to the office of (mayor or councilman) to be voted upon at the primary election to be held on the.............Monday of............19..., and I hereby request that my name be printed upon the official primary ballot for nomination by such primary election for such office.

(Signed)..... ....

Subscribed and sworn to (or affirmed) before me by.... ....on this...........day of ....19....

(Signed) ....

and shall at the same time file therewith the petition of at least twenty-five qualified votors requesting such candidacy. Each petition shall be verified by one or more persons as to the qualifications and residence, with street number, of each of the persons so signing the said petition, and the said petition shall be in substantially the following form:

PETITION ACCOMPANYING NOMINATING STATEMENT.

The undersigned, duly qualified electors of the city of ....and residing at the places set opposite our respective names hereto, do hereby request that the name of (name of candidate) be placed on the ballot as a candidate for nomination for (name of office) at the primary election to be held in such city on the.............Monday of ....19... We further state that we know him to be a qualified elector of said city and a man of good moral character and qualified in our judgment for the duties of such office.

Names of Qualified Electors	Number	Street

Immediately upon the expiration of the time for filing the statements and petitions for candidacies, the said city clerk shall cause to be published for three successive days in all the daily newspapers published in the city, in proper form, the names of the persons as they are to appear upon the primary ballot, and if there be no daily newspaper, then in two issues of any other newspapers that may be published in said city; and the said clerk shall thereupon cause the primary ballots to be printed, authenticated with a fac-simile of his signature. Upon the said ballot the names of the candidates for mayor, arranged alphabetically, shall first be placed, with a square at the left of each name, and immediately below the words "Vote for One." Following these names, likewise arranged in alphabetical order, shall appear the names of the candidates for councilmen, with a square at the left of each name, and below the names of such candidates shall appear the words, "Vote for four," or "Vote for two," as the case may be. The ballot shall be printed upon plain, substantial white paper, and shall be headed:

CANDIDATES FOR NOMINATION FOR MAYOR AND COUNCILMEN OF————CITY AT THE PRIMARY ELECTION.

but shall have no party designation or mark whatever. The ballots shall be in substantially the following form:

(Place a cross in the square preceding the names of the parties you favor as candidates for the respective positions.)

OFFICIAL PRIMARY BALLOT.

CANDIDATES FOR NOMINATION FOR MAYOR AND COUNCILMEN OF————CITY AT THE PRIMARY ELECTION.

For Mayor

(Name of Candidate.)

(Vote for one.)

For Councilman

(Name of Candidate.)

(Vote for four) or (Vote for two) as the case may be.

Official Ballot attest:

(Signature) ....

City Clerk.

Having caused said ballots to be printed, the said city clerk shall cause to be delivered at each polling place a number of said ballots equal to twice the number of votes cast in such polling precinct at the last general municipal election for mayor. The persons who are qualified to vote at the general municipal election shall be qualified to vote at such primary election, and challenges can be made by not more than two persons, to be appointed at the time of opening the polls by the judges of election; and the law applicable to challenges at a general municipal election shall be applicable to challenges made at such primary election. Judges of election shall, immediately upon the closing of the polls, count the ballots and ascertain the number of votes cast in such precinct for each of the candidates, and make return thereof to the city clerk, upon proper blanks to be furnished by the said clerk, within six hours of the closing of the polls. On the day following the said primary election, the said city clerk shall canvass said returns so received from all the polling precincts, and shall make and publish in all the newspapers of said city, at least once, the result thereof. Said canvass by the city clerk shall be publicly made. The two candidates receiving the highest number of votes for mayor shall be the candidates, and the only candidates, whose names shall be placed upon the ballot for mayor at the next succeeding general municipal election, and in cities having a population of twenty-five thousand and over, the eight candidates receiving the highest number of votes for councilman, or all such candidates if less than eight, and in cities having a population of seven thousand and less than twenty-five thousand the four candidates receiving the highest number of votes for councilman, or all such candidates if less than four, shall be the candidates, and the only candidates whose names shall be placed upon the ballot for councilman at such municipal election. All electors of cities under this act who by the laws governing cities of the first and second class and cities acting under special charter would be entitled to vote for the election of officers at any general municipal election in such cities, shall be qualified to vote at all elections under this act; and the ballot at such general municipal election shall be in the same general form as for such primary election, so far as applicable, and in all elections in such city the election precinct, voting places, method of conducting election, canvassing the vote and announcing the results, shall be the same as by law provided for election of officers in such cities, so far as the same are applicable and not inconsistent with the provisions of this act."

Sec. 6. Council—quorum.

That section 1056-a 24 of chapter 14-c of the supplement to the code, 1907, be and the same is hereby amended by striking out all of said section beginning with the word "every" in the first line thereof down to and including the word "act" in the seventh line of said section and inserting in lieu thereof the following:

"Every city having a population of twenty-five thousand and over shall be governed by a council consisting of the mayor and four councilmen, and every city having a population of seven thousand and less than twenty-five thousand shall be governed by a council consisting of the mayor and two councilmen, chosen as provided in this act, each of whom shall have the right to vote on all questions coming before the council. In cities having four councilmen three members of the council shall constitute a quorum, and in cities having two councilmen, two members of the council shall constitute a quorum and in cities having four councilmen the affirmative vote of three members, and in cities having two councilmen the affirmative vote of two members shall be necessary to adopt any motion, resolution or ordinance, or pass any measure unless a greater number is provided for in this act."

Sec. 7. Council—powers and duties.

That section 1056-a 25 of chapter 14-c of the supplement to the code, 1907, be and the same is hereby amended by striking out all of said section beginning with the word "The" in the first line thereof and closing with the word "charter" in the eighth line thereof and inserting in lieu thereof the following:

"The council shall have and possess, and the council and its members shall exercise all executive, legislative and judicial powers and duties now had, possessed and exercised by the mayor, city council, solicitor, assessor, treasurer, auditor, city engineer and other executive and administrative officers in cities of the first and second class, and in cities under special charter, and shall also possess and exercise all executive, legislative and judicial powers and duties now had and exercised by the board of public works, park commissioners, the board of police and fire commissioners, board of water works trustees, and board of library trustees in all cities wherein a board of public works, park commissioners, board of police and fire commissioners, board of water works trustees, and board of library trustees now exist or may be hereafter created."

Sec. 8. Repeal—department superintendents—officers and assistants.

That section 1056-a 26 of chapter 14-c of the supplement to the code, 1907, be and the same is hereby repealed, and the following enacted in lieu thereof:

"The mayor shall be superintendent of the department of public affairs, and the council shall at the first regular meeting after election of its members designate by majority vote one councilman to be superintendent of the department of accounts and finances; one to be superintendent of the department of public safety; one to be superintendent of the department of street and public improvements; and one to be superintendent of the department of parks and public property; provided, however, that in cities having a population of less than twenty-five thousand there shall be designated to each councilman two of said departments. Such designation shall be changed whenever it appears that the public service would be benefitted thereby. The council shall, at said first meeting, or as soon as practicable thereafter, elect by majority vote the following officers: A city clerk, solicitor, assessor, treasurer, auditor, civil engineer, city physician, marshal, chief of fire department, market master, street commissioner, three library trustees, and such other officers and assistants as shall be provided for by ordinance and necessary to the proper and efficient conduct of the affairs of the city; provided, however, that in cities having a population of less than twenty-five thousand such only of the above named officers shall be appointed as may, in the judgment of the mayor and councilmen be necessary for the proper and efficient transaction of the affairs of the city. In those cities of the first class not having a superior court, the council shall appoint a police judge. In cities of the second class not having a superior court the mayor shall hold police court, as now provided by law. Any officer or assistant elected or appointed by the council may be removed from office at any time by vote of a majority of the members of the council, except as otherwise provided for in this act."

Sec. 9. Office in city hall—salaries.

That section ten hundred fifty-six-a twenty-eight (1056-a 28) of chapter fourteen-c (14-c) of the supplement to the code, 1907, be and the same is hereby amended by striking out all of said section beginning with the word "The" in the first line thereof, and ending with the figures and dollar mark "$3,000," in the third line from the top of page 214 as the same appears in the supplement to the code, 1907, and inserting in lieu thereof the following:

"The mayor and councilmen shall have an office at the city hall, and their total compensation shall be as follows: In cities having by the last preceding state or national census a population of 7,000 and less than 10,000 the mayor's annual salary shall be $600.00, and each councilman $450.00. In cities having by such census a population of 10,000 and less than 15,000 the mayor's annual salary shall be $1,200.00 and each councilman $900.00. In cities having by such census a population of 15,000 and less than 25,000 the mayor's annual salary shall be $1,500.00 and each councilman $1,200.00. In cities having by such census a population of 25,000 and less than 40,000 the mayor's annual salary shall be $2,500.00 and each councilman $1,800.00. In cities having by such census a population of 40,000 and less than 60,000, the mayor's annual salary shall be $3,000.00, and each councilman $2,500.00, and in cities having by such census a population of 60,000 or more the mayor's annual salary shall be $3,500.00 and that of councilman $3,000.00."

Sec. 10. Civil Service commissioners—terms.

That section 1056-a 32 of chapter 14-c of the supplement to the code, 1907, be and the same is hereby amended by striking out the first two sentences thereof and inserting in lieu thereof the following:

"In cities having a population of twenty-five thousand and over the council shall and in cities having a population of seven thousand and less than twenty-five thousand the council may immediately after organizing, by ordinance appoint three civil service commissioners who shall hold office, one until the first Monday in April of the second year after his appointment, one until the first Monday in April of the fourth year after his appointment, and one until the first Monday in April of the sixth year after his appointment; provided, however, that in all cases in which no civil commissioners are appointed by the council, the council shall have the same powers and shall exercise and perform all the duties devolving upon such commissioners, as provided for in this act. In cities wherein civil service commissioners have been appointed under the provisions of this act each succeeding council shall, as soon as practicable after organizing, appoint one commissioner for six years, who shall take the place of the commissioner whose term of office expires."

Sec. 11. Abandonment of commission plan of government.

That section 1056-a 39 of chapter 14-c of the supplement to the code, 1907, be and the same is hereby amended by striking out all of that portion of said section beginning with the word "Shall" in the ninth line thereof and closing with the word "charter" in the twelfth line and inserting in lieu thereof the following: "Shall the city of (name of city) abandon its organization under chapter 14-c of the supplement of the code, 1907, as amended by the acts of the thirty third general assembly, and become a city under the general law governing cities, or if now organized under special charter shall resume said special charter?"

Sec. 12. In effect.

This act being deemed of immediate importance shall take effect and be in full force from and after its publication in the Register & Leader and the Des Moines Capital, newspapers published at Des Moines, Iowa.

[Approved March 30, 1909.]

ANNOTATIONS—IOWA LAWS.

S. A. ECKERSON, APPELLANT, V. CITY OF DES MOINES, ET AL., APPELLEES; A. M. HUSTON, ET AL., INTERVENERS, APPELLANTS.

Action in equity for an injunctional decree. A. M. Huston and the board of park commissioners of the city of Des Moines intervened, and filed petitions respectively. The petition of plaintiffs and the several petitions of the interveners were held bad on demurrer, and from the ruling entered, plaintiffs and interveners appeal.—Affirmed.

Constitutional Law: Guaranty of Republican Form of Government:

Application of Constitutional Provision.

1. The provision of the United States Constitution guaranteeing to each State a republican form of government has application only to the form of State Government, and not to a system of local government provided by the States for their municipalities or other subdivisions; and chapter 48, Acts 32d General Assembly, providing for the government of certain municipalities is not in violation of such provision, in that it ignors the es-

sential features of a republican form of government by committing the executive, legislative and judicial departments to a single board of governing body.

Constitutional Law: Municipal Government: Distribution of Power:

2. Article 3, section 1 of the Constitution of Iowa providing that the government of the State shall be divided into three departments, legislative, executive and judicial, and the persons charged with the duty of exercising powers belonging to one department shall not exercise those pertaining to either of the others, has application only to the State government and not to that of municipalities; and the legislature has power to determine the manner in which municipal governments shall be administered, to designate the officers or agencies upon whom the duty shall rest and invest them with power to carry the government into operation; so that chapter 48, Acts 32d General Assembly, is not repugnant to said constitutional provision because investing a mayor and four councilmen, in certain cities, with legislative, executive and judicial powers.

Same: Local and Special Laws.

3. The purpose and intent of section 30, article 3 of the State Constitution is to prohibit individual corporate organization of cities, which is local as to place and special as to powers granted; and not the passage of laws applicable to a class of municipalities similarly conditioned, whether then existing or thereafter to come into existence. So that chapter 48, Acts 32d General Assembly, giving to cities of a certain population a special form of government is not repugnant to this provision of the constitution because local or special.

Same: Uniformity of Laws: Classification of Cities:

4. A legislative act providing a special form of government for cities of 25,000 population or over is not unconstitutional, because making an arbitrary classification which is unreasonable, and not based upon any distinction arising out of known fact conditions.

Same: Presumption as to Legality of Legislative Acts.

5. The question of whether conditions exist, calling for classification of cities and an exclusive grant of powers is to be determined, in the first instance, by the legislature; and in so doing it will be presumed that such conditions existed, whether specified in the act or not, and that the legislature acted advisedly and within its constitutional rights, unless the contrary appears from the law itself or extrinsic circumstances respecting its operation.

Same: General Laws: Uniformity of Operation.

6. The fact that it is possible, or even probable, that some one or more cities may not avail themselves of the provisions of an act granting special powers to the class of cities to which they belong, will not effect the uniform application of the law if all who do accept it are to be governed alike.

Same: Delegation of Legislative Power:

7. A law which is a complete enactment when it leaves the legislative department is not objectionable as a delegation of the legislative power, because containing a provision that it shall not become operative except upon a vote of the people to whom it is made applicable.

Same: Removal from Office:

8. A person in possession of a public office has no constitutional right thereto even for the full period of his term; and the legislature may provide for his removal from an office of its own creation, by a vote of the people of the municipality from which he was elected.

Same: "Initiative and "Referendum":

9. The legislature may provide that a popular vote may be resorted to in the enactment of municipal law; the provisions of the constitution vesting all legislative authority in the General Assembly having no application to the legislative power of city councils.

Same: Rights of Suffrage: Nomination: Ballots:

10. Chapter 48, Acts 32d General Assembly, which prescribes a form of government for certain cities, and provides that in preparing the primary ballot for the nomination of officers no names shall be placed thereon except those of persons who have filed a statement of candidacy, etc., does not intend thereby to abridge the right of voting for persons other than those named on the ballot, by inserting their names in writing, and hence is not repugnant to the constitutional provision guaranteeing the unrestricted right to vote for any person or to be a candidate for any office.

Municipal Organization: Election: Submission of Separate Question.

11. The validity of a special election, to organize a city government under the provisions of chapter 48

of Acts 32d General Assembly, is not affected by the fact that another and distinct proposition was also submitted at the same election.

Construction of Statutes: Park Boards:

12. Statutory repeals by implication are not favored; the statutes in apparent conflict will be construed so as to give effect to each if reasonably possible, especially when enacted by the same legislature. Under these rules chapters 42 and 48, so far as they relate to park boards, are both held to be existing law; one relating to park boards in cities generally, and the other to such boards in cities organized under chapter 48.

Constitutional Law:

1. Claiborne Co. v. Brooks, 111 U. S. 412 (4 Sup. Ct. 494, 28 L. Ed. 470): In re Pfahler (Cal. Sup.), (88 Pac. 270, 11 L. R. A. (N. S.) 1092. State v. King, 37 Iowa, 464; Hopkins v. Duluth, 81 Minn. 189 (83 N. W. 536); Brown v. Galveston, 97 Tex. 1 (75 S. W. 488); Kadderly v. Portland, 44 Or. 118 (74 Pac. 710, 75 Pac. 222); Williams v. Eggleston, 170 U. S. 304 (18 Sup. Ct. 617, 42 L. Ed. 1047). Kies v. Lowrey, 199 U. S. 233 (26 Sup. Ct. 27, 50 L. Ed. 167),

Constitutional Law:

2. Smith on Corporation, 153; Cooley on Constitutional Limitations, 133; 20 AM. & Eng. Ency., 1223. 116 Iowa 109.

Same: Local and Special Laws:

3. McAunich v. Railroad, 20 Iowa, 338; Haskel v. Burlington, 30 Iowa, 232; Owen v. Sioux City, 91 Iowa, 190; Tuttle v. Polk, 92 Iowa 433. Lastro v. State, 3 Tex. App. 363; Smith v. Grayson, 18 Tex. Civ. App. 153 (44 S. W. 921); Stone v. Wilson, 19 Ky. Law, 126 (39 S. W. 49); Ladd v. Holmes, 40 Or. 167 (66 Pac. 714, 91 AM. St. Rep. 457); State v. Mayor, etc., 52 N. J. Law, 32 (18 Atl. 694, 6 L. R. A. (N. S. 57); Allen v. Hirsch, 8 Or. 412. State v. Cooley, 56 Minn. 540 (58 N. W. 158); State v. Minor, 79 Minn. 201 (81 N. W. 912); In re Cleveland, 52 N. J. Law, 188 (19 Atl. 17, 7 L. R. A. 431); People v. Hoffman, 116 Ill. 587 (5 N. E. 596, 8 N. E. 788, 56 Am. Rep. 793); Lum v. Mayor, 72 Miss. 950 (18 South. 476); State v. Pond, 93 Mo. 606 (6 S. W. 468); Owen v. Baer, 154 Mo. 434 (55 S. W. 644). Tuttle v. Polk, supra; State v. Desmoines, supra; Page v. Middlerton, 114 Iowa, 378. People v. Kipley, 171 Ill. 44 (49 N. E. 229, 41 L. R. A. 775).

Same:

5. Santo v. State, 2 Iowa, 165; Richman v. Board, 77 Iowa, 513; Ogden v. Saunders, 12 Wheat. (U. S.) 213 (6 L. Ed. 606).

Same:

6. Dalby v. Wolf, 14 Iowa, 228; State v. King, 37 Iowa, 462; Lytle v. May, 49 Iowa, 224; State v. Forkner, 94 Iowa, 733; Adams v. Beloit, 105 Wis. 963 (81 N. W. 869, 47 L. R. A. 441); People v. Kipley, 171 Ill. 44 (49 N. E. 229, 41 L. R. A. 775).

Same:

7. Morford v. Unger, 8 Iowa, 82; Des Moines v. Hillis, 55 Iowa, 643; State v. Hoagland, 51 N. J. Law, 62 (16 Atl. 166); Clark v. Rogers, 81 Ky. 43; Opinion of Judges, 55 Mo. 295; Insurance Co. v. Swigert, 104 Ill. 653: Mayor v. Finney, 54 Ga. 317; Adams v. Beloit, 105 Wis. 363 (81 N. W. 869, 47 L. R. A. 441); Howard v. Railroad, 207 U. S. 463 (28 Sup. Ct. 141, 52 L. Ed.—).

Same: Removal:

8. Shaw v. Marshalltown, 131 Iowa, 128.

Same: Initiative and Referendum:

9. Taylor v. McFadden, 84 Iowa, 262; Hindman v. Boyd, 42 Wash. 17 (84 Pac. 609); Ex parte Anderson, 134 Cal. 69 (66 Pac. 194, 86 Am. St. Rep. 236).

Same: Right of Suffrage:

10. State v. Dillon, 32 Fla. 545 (14 South. 383, 23 L. R. A. 124); Cole v. Tucker, 164 Mass. 486 (41 N. E. 681, 29 L. R. A. 668); Bowers v. Smith, 111 Mo. 45 (20 S. W. 101, 16 L. R. A. 754, 33 Am. St. Rep. 491); Sanner v. Patton, 155 Ill. 553 (40 N. E. 290); People v. Shaw, 133 N. Y. 493 (31 N. E. 512, 16 L. R. A. 606); Detroit v. Rush, 82 Mich. 532 (46 N. W. 951, 10 L. R. A. 171); Eaton v. Brown, 96 Cal. 371 (31 Pac. 250, 17 L. R. A. 697, 31 Am. St. Rep. 225). Chamberlain v. Wood, 15 S. D. 216 (88 N. W. 109, 56 L. R. A. 187, 91 Am. St. Rep. 674). Com. v. Reeder, 171 Pa. 505 (33 Atl. 67, 33 L. R. A. 141).

Same: Municipal:

11.

Same: Constitution of Statutes:

12. Railroad v. Supervisors, 67 Iowa, 199; Lambe v. McCormick, 116 Iowa, 169. White v. Meadville, 177 Pa. 643 (35 Atl. 695, 34 L. R. A. 567); Hawes v. Fleighler, 87 Minn. 319 (92 N. W. 223);

Contra:

The case of Railroad v. Chicago, 166 U. S. 226 (17 Sup. Ct. 581, 41 L. Ed. 979), and other like cases cited by counsel, do not, in our view, have any bearing on the question as here made. In support of their position, counsel for plaintiffs rely upon Attorney General v. Detroit, 112 Mich. 1· (70 N. W. 450, 37 L. R. A. 211) and Whitcomb case, 120 Mass. 118 (21 Am. Rep. 502). In o opinion the cases thus cited do not reach the que tion as made on the record before us. As the boo in which they are to be found are generally acce sible, we shall not stop to discuss them.

STATE, EX REL. JONES, V. SARGENT, ET AL. (SUPREME COURT OF IOWA, JAN. 11, 1910.)

1. Municipal Corporation (Sects. 181 and 195*).

Offices—Appointment—Appointment from Dominant Political Party—Discretion in Appointing.

Cide Supp. 1907, Sec. 679d (Acts 29th Gen. Assem., p. 17, C. 31, Sec. 4), requiring the Mayor of cities having a population of more than 20,000 to appoint of fire and police commissioners, to be selected from the two leading political parties, so that, as far as practicable, two members of the board shall be members of the dominant party and one member a member of the party next in numerical strength, leaves some discretion in the mayor as to the practicability of appointing two members from the dominant party, and, where he offered the second appointment to four members of that party, who refused it, there was no abuse of discretion in appointing two members from the party next in numerical strength, in the absence of a showing of fraud or favoritism, though there were in the city more than 1,000 members of the dominant party.

The Court cited the following decisions in support of its opinions:

Sanborn v. Mason City, 114 Iowa, 189, 86 N. W. 286, is not in point; Edmonds v. Banbury, 28 Iowa, 267, 4 Am.; Atty. Gen. v. Board, 58 Mich. 213, 24 N. W. 887, 55 Am.; Shaw v. City of Marshalltown, 131 Iowa 128, 104 N. W. 1121, 10 L. R. A. (N. S. 825, s. c. in 9 Am.); Goodrich v. Mitchell, 68 Ka 765, 75 Pac. 1034, 64 L. R. A. 945, 104 Am.; Eck son v. City of Des Moines, 137 Iowa 453, 115 N. 177; Evansville v. State, 118 Ind. 426, 21 N. 267, 4 L. R. A. 93; Atty. Gen. v. Detroit, Supr Bowden v. Bedell, 68 N. J. Law 451, 53 Atl. 19 Rathbone v. Wirth, 150 New York 459, 45 N. E. 34 L. R. A. 408; Mayor v. State, 15 M. D. 379, Am. Dec. 572; Hovey v. State, 119 Ind. 386, N. E. 890; Atty. Gen. v. Board of Councilmen, Mich. 213, 24 N. W. 887, 55 Am.

J. Weaver, dissenting, cites the following:

State v. Van Beek, 87 Iowa 569, 54 N. W. 525, L. R. A. 622, 43 Am.; People v. Hurlbut, 24 Mi 44, 9 Am. Rep. 103; State v. Moores, 55 Neb. 4 76 N. W. 175, 41 L. R. A. 624; State v. Garbros 111 Iowa 500, 82 N. W. 959, 56 L. R. A. 570, Am.; Barker v. People, 3 Cow. (N. Y.) 686, 15 A Dec. 322; Atty. v. Board, 58 Mich. 213, 24 N. 887, 55 Am. Rep. 675; Brown v. Haywood, 4 Hei (Tenn.) 357; Louthan v. Com., 79 Va. 196, 52 A Rep. 626; Atty. Gen. v. Detroit, 58 Mich. 213, N. W. 887, 55 Am. Rep. 675; Pumpelly v. Owe 45 How. Prac. (N. Y.) 219; Bradshaw v. Rodge 20 Johns (N. Y.) 103; Commonwealth v. Plaist 148 Mass. 375, 19 N. E. 224, 2 L. R. A. 142, 12 St. Rep. 566.

CHARTER OF BERKELEY, CAL.

PREPARED AND PROPOSED BY A BOARD OF FREEHOLDERS ELECTED NOV. 21, 1908. RATIFIED BY THE QUALIFIED ELECTORS JAN. 30, 1909.

ARTICLE I.

NAME AND RIGHTS OF THE CITY.

Section 1. Name of the city.

The municipal corporation now existing and known as the Town of Berkeley shall remain and continue a body politic and corporate in name and in fact, by the name of the City of Berkeley, and by such name shall have perpetual succession.

Sec. 2. Rights and liabilities.

The City of Berkeley shall remain vested with and continue to have, hold and enjoy all property, rights of property and rights of action of every nature and description now pertaining to this municipality, and is hereby declared to be the successor of the same. It shall be subject to all the liabilities that now exist against this municipality.

ARTICLE II.

BOUNDARIES.

Section 3.

[Boundaries defined.]

ARTICLE III.

ELECTIONS.

Section 4. General and special municipal elections.

A municipal election shall be held in the City on the first Saturday in May in the year 1909, and on the first Saturday in April in 1911 and on the first Saturday in April in every second year thereafter, and shall be known as the general municipal election. A second election shall be held, when necessary, as provided in subdivision 22 of section 5, on the third Saturday after said general municipal election, and shall be known as the second general municipal election.

All other municipal elections that may be held by authority of this Charter or of general law shall be known as special municipal elections.

Sec. 5. Nomination and election of city officers.

(1) The mode of nomination and election of all elective officers of the City to be voted for at any municipal election shall be as follows and not otherwise:

Condition of candidacy.

(2) The name of a candidate shall be printed upon the ballot when a petition of nomination shall have been filed in his behalf in the manner and form and under the conditions hereinafter set forth.

Form of nomination petition.

(3) The petition of nomination shall consist of not less than twenty-five individual certificates, which shall read substantially as follows:

PETITION OF NOMINATION.

Individual certificate.

State of California,
County of Alameda,
City of Berkeley.
ss.

Prect. No. ....

I, the undersigned, certify that I do hereby join in a petition for the nomination of ....whose residence is at No. ....Street, Berkeley, for the office of........ ....to be voted for at the municipal election to be held in the City of Berkeley on the .... day of .... 19... and I further certify that I am a qualified elector and am not at this time a signer of any other petition nominating any other candidate for the above named office, or, in case there are several places to be filled in the above named office, that I have not signed more petitions than there are places to be filled in the above named office; that my residence is at No. .... Street, Berkeley, and that my occupation is ....

(Signed)..............................

State of California,
County of Alameda,
City of Berkeley.
ss.

.... being duly sworn, deposes and says that he is the person who signed the foregoing certificate and that the statements therein are true and correct.

(Signed)..............................

Subscribed and sworn to before me this ....day of .... 19....

....

(Notary Public or Verification Deputy.)

The petition of nomination of which this certificate forms a part shall, if found insufficient, be returned to............ at No. .... Street, Berkeley, Cal.

Forms to be supplied by the City Clerk.

(4) It shall be the duty of the City Clerk to furnish upon application a reasonable number of forms of individual certificates of the above character.

Requirements of certificate.

(5) Each certificate must be a separate paper. All certificates must be of a uniform size as determined by the City Clerk. Each certificate must contain the name of one signer thereto and no more. Each certificate shall contain the name of one candidate and no more. Each signer must be a qualified elector, must not at the time of signing a certificate have his name signed to any other certificate for any other candidate for the same office, nor, in case there are several places to be filled in the same office, signed to more

certificates for candidates for that office than there are places to be filled in such office. In case an elector has signed two or more conflicting certificates, all such certificates shall be rejected. Each signer must verify his certificate and make oath that the same is true before a notary public or a verification deputy, as provided for in this section. Each certificate shall further contain the name and address of the person to whom the petition is to be returned in case said petition is found insufficient.

Verification deputies.

(6) Verification deputies, under this section, must be qualified electors of the City and shall be appointed by the City Clerk upon application in writing signed by not less than five qualified electors of the City. The application shall set forth that the signers thereto desire to procure the necessary signatures of electors for the nomination of candidates for municipal office at an election therein specified, and that the applicants desire the person or persons whose names and addresses are given, appointed as verification deputies, who shall upon appointment be authorized and empowered to take the oath of verification of the signers of petitions of nomination. Such verification deputies need not use a seal, and shall not have power to take oaths for any other purposes whatsoever, and their appointments shall continue only until all petitions of nomination, under this section, shall have been filed by the City Clerk.

Date of presenting petition.

(7) A petition of nomination, consisting of not less than twenty-five individual certificates for any one candidate, may be presented to the City Clerk not earlier than forty-five days nor later than thirty days before the election. The Clerk shall endorse thereon the date upon which the petition was presented to him.

Examination of petitions by City Clerk.

(8) When a petition of nomination is presented for filing to the City Clerk, he shall forthwith examine the same, and ascertain whether it conforms to the provisions of this section. If found not to conform thereto, he shall then and there in writing designate on said petition the defect or omission or reason why such petition cannot be filed, and shall return the petition to the person named as the person to whom the same may be returned in accordance with this section. The petition may then be amended and again presented to the Clerk as in the first instance. The Clerk shall forthwith proceed to examine the petition as hereinbefore provided. If necessary, the Council shall provide extra help to enable the Clerk to perform satisfactorily and promptly the duties imposed by this section.

Withdrawal of Signature.

(9) Any signer to a petition of nomination and certificate may withdraw his name from the same by filing with the City Clerk a verified revocation of his signature before the filing of the petition by the Clerk, and not otherwise. He shall then be at liberty to sign a petition for another candidate for the same office.

Withdrawal of candidate.

(10) Any person whose name has been presented under this section as a candidate may, not later than twenty-five days before the day of election, cause his name to be with drawn from nomination by filing with the City Clerk a re quest therefor in writing, and no name so withdrawn shal be printed upon the ballot. If upon such withdrawal th number of candidates remaining does not exceed the numbe to be elected, then other nominations may be made by filin petitions therefor not later than twenty days prior to suc election.

Filing of petitions.

(11) If either the original or the amended petition of nom ination be found sufficiently signed as hereinbefore provided the Clerk shall file the same twenty-five days before the dat of the election. When a petition of nomination shall hav been filed by the Clerk it shall not be withdrawn nor adde to and no signature shall be revoked thereafter.

Preservation of petitions.

(12) The City Clerk shall preserve in his office for a perio of two years all petitions of nomination and all certificate belonging thereto filed under this section.

Election proclamation.

(13) Immediately after such petitions are filed, the Cler shall enter the names of the candidates in a list, with th offices to be filled, and shall not later than twenty days befor the election certify such list as being the list of candidate nominated as required by the Charter of Berkeley, and th Council shall cause said certified list of names and the office to be filled, designating whether for a full term or unexpire term, to be published in the proclamation calling the electio at least ten successive days before the election in not mor than two daily newspapers of general circulation publishe in the City of Berkeley. Said proclamation shall conform i all respects to the general State law governing the conduc of municipal elections, now or hereafter in force, except a above required.

Form of ballots.

(14) The City Clerk shall cause the ballots to be printe and bound and numbered as provided for by State law ex cept as otherwise required in this Charter. The ballots sha contain the list of names and the respective offices, as pu lished in the proclamation and shall be in substantially th following form:

General (or special) municipal election, City of Berkeley.

(Inserting date thereof.)

INSTRUCTIONS TO VOTERS: To vote, stamp or write cross (X) opposite the name of the candidate for whom yo desire to vote. All marks otherwise made are forbidde All distinguishing marks are forbidden and make the ballo void. If you wrongly mark, tear or deface this ballot, re turn it to the Inspector of Election, and obtain another.

Requirements of ballot.

(15) All ballots printed shall be precisely of the same siz quality, tint of paper, kind of type, and color of ink, so tha without the number it would be impossible to distinguish on ballot from another; and the names of all candidates printe upon the ballot shall be in type of the same size and styl A column may be provided on the right hand side for charte

amendments or other questions to be voted upon at the municipal elections, as provided for under this Charter. The names of the candidates for each office shall be arranged in alphabetical order, and nothing on the ballot shall be indicative of the source of the candidacy or of the support of any candidate.

Every nominee to be on ballot.

(16) The name of no candidate who has been duly and regularly nominated, and who has not withdrawn his name as herein provided, shall be omitted from the ballot.

Arrangement of offices on ballot.

(17) The offices to be filled shall be arranged in separate columns in the following order:

"For Mayor (if any) vote for one."
"For Auditor (if any) vote for one."
"For Councilman (if any) vote for (giving number)."
"For School Directors (if any) vote for (giving number)."

Space for voting cross.

(18) Half-inch square shall be provided at the right of the name of each candidate wherein to mark the cross.

Blank spaces for additional candidates.

(19) Half-inch spaces shall be left below the printed names of candidates for each office equal in number to the number to be voted for, wherein the voter may write the name of any person or persons for whom he may wish to vote.

Sample ballots.

(20) The Clerk shall cause to be printed sample ballots identical with the ballot to be used at the election and shall furnish copies of the same on application to registered voters at his office at least five days before the date fixed for such election, and shall mail one such ballot to each voter entitled to vote at such election, so that all of said sample ballots shall have been mailed at least three whole days before said election.

Vote necessary for election.

(21) In case there is but one person to be elected to an office, the candidate receiving a majority of the votes cast for all the candidates for that office shall be declared elected; in case there are two or more persons to be elected to an office, as that of Councilman or School Director, then those candidates equal in number to the number to be elected, who receive the highest number of votes for such office shall be declared elected; provided, however, that no person shall be declared elected to any office at such first election unless the number of votes received by him shall be greater than one-half the number of ballots cast at such election.

Second Election.

(22) If at any election held as above provided there be any office to which the required number of persons was not elected, then as to such office the said first election shall be considered to have been a primary election for the nomination of candidates, and a second election shall be held to fill said office. The candidates not elected at such first election, equal in number to twice the number to be elected to any given office, or less if so there be, who receive the highest number of votes for the respective offices at such first election, shall be the only candidates at such second election, provided, that if there be any person who, under the provisions of this subdivision, would have been entitled to become a candidate for any office except for the fact that some other candidate received an equal number of votes therefor, then all such persons receiving such equal number of votes shall likewise become candidates for such office.

The candidates equal in number to the persons to be elected who shall receive the highest number of votes at such second election shall be declared elected to such office.

Date of second election.

(23) The second election, if necessary to be held, shall be held three weeks after the first election.

Rules governing second election.

(24) All the provisions and conditions above set forth as to the conduct of an election, so far as they may be applicable, shall govern the second election, except that notice of election need be published twice only, and provided also that the same precincts and polling places shall, if possible, be used.

Failure of person elected to qualify.

(25) If a person elected fails to qualify, the office shall be filled as if there were a vacancy in such office, as hereinafter provided.

Informalities in election.

(26) No informalities in conducting municipal elections shall invalidate the same, if they have been conducted fairly and in substantial conformity to the requirements of this Charter.

Sec. 6. General election regulations.

(1) The provisions of the State law relating to the qualifications of electors, the manner of voting, the duties of election officers, the canvassing of returns, and all other particulars in respect to the management of elections, so far as they may be applicable, shall govern all municipal elections, provided that the Council shall meet as a canvassing board and duly canvass the election returns within four days after any municipal election.

Voting machines.

(2) In case voting machines shall be used at municipal elections, the Council shall have power, by ordinance, to modify the provisions of Section 5 so far as may be necessary to adapt them to the use of voting machines.

ARTICLE IV.

RECALL OF ELECTIVE OFFICERS.

Section 7. Applies to all elective officers.

(1) Every incumbent of an elective office, whether elected by popular vote or appointed to fill a vacancy, is subject to recall by the voters of the City. The procedure to effect such removal from office shall be as follows:

Petition for recall.

(2) A petition signed by qualified electors equal in number to twenty per centum of the entire vote cast for Mayor

at the last preceding general municipal election at which a Mayor was elected, demanding an election of a successor of the officer sought to be removed, shall be addressed to the Council and presented to the City Clerk. The petition may request such election to be held at a special municipal election or at the next general municipal election. The petition must contain a statement of the reasons for the demand.

Provisions of Section 5 apply.

(3) The provisions of Section 5 respecting the forms and conditions of the petition and the mode of verification and certification and filing shall be substantially followed, with such modifications as the nature of the case requires.

Election under recall petition.

(4) If the officer sought to be removed shall not resign within five days after the petition is filed by the City Clerk, and if the petition requests a special election, the Council shall cause a special election to be held within forty-five days to determine whether the people will recall said officer, or, if a general municipal election is to occur within sixty days, the Council may in its discretion postpone the holding of such election to such general municipal election.

Grounds of recall. Officer's justification.

(5) In the published call for the election there shall be printed in not more than two hundred words the reasons for demanding the recall of the officer as set forth in the Recall petition, and in not more than two hundred words the officer may justify his course in office.

Candidates. Election.

(6) The officer sought to be removed shall be deemed a candidate and, unless he resigns, his name shall be printed on the ballot. The nomination of other candidates and the election shall be in accordance with the provisions of Section 5.

Incumbent removed.

(7) The officer sought to be removed shall, if he do not resign, continue to perform the duties of his office until the election, and, if he fail of election, he shall be deemed removed from office.

No recall petition for the first three months.

(8) No recall petition shall be filed against any officer until he has actually held his office for at least three months.

Incapacity of recalled official.

(9) No person who has been recalled from an elective office, or who has resigned from such office while recall proceedings were pending against him, shall be appointed to any office within one year after such recall or resignation.

Further regulations.

(10) The Council may by ordinance make such further regulations as may be necessary to carry out the provisions of this section, and to adapt the provisions of Section 5 thereto.

ARTICLE V.

ELECTIVE OFFICERS.

Sec. 8. The Elective Officers.

The elective officers of the City shall be a Mayor, an Auditor, four Councilmen, and four School Directors.

The Council shall consist of the Mayor and four Councilmen, each of whom, including the Mayor, shall have the right to vote on all questions coming before the Council.

The Board of Education shall consist of four School Directors and the Councilman appointed to be Commissioner of Finance and Revenue, each of whom, including said Commissioner, shall have the right to vote on all questions coming before the Board.

Sec. 9. Elected at large.

The Mayor, Auditor, Councilmen and School Directors shall be elected at the general municipal election on a general ticket from the City at large.

Sec. 10. Eligibility of Mayor, Auditor, and Councilmen.

Sec. 11. Eligibility of School Directors.

Sec. 12. Vacancy in office of Mayor, Auditor or Councilman.

If a vacancy shall occur in the office of Mayor, Auditor or Councilman, the Council shall appoint a person to fill such vacancy. If at any municipal election held under subdivision 22 of Section 5 of this Charter a Mayor, Auditor or the required number of Councilmen be not elected by reason of a tie vote among any of the candidates therefor, then the Council after the qualification of the persons, if any, elected thereto at such election, shall appoint one of the persons, receiving such tie vote to fill such office as in the case of a vacancy therein. In each case the person so appointed shall hold office, subject to the provisions of the Recall until the next general municipal election.

Sec. 13. Vacancy in office of School Director.

If a vacancy shall occur in the office of School Director, the Board of Education shall appoint a person to fill such vacancy. If at any municipal election held under subdivision 22 of Section 5 of this Charter a School Director be not elected by reason of a tie vote among any of the candidates therefor, then the Board of Education after the qualification of the persons, if any, elected thereto at such election, shall appoint one of the persons receiving such tie vote, to fill such office as in case of a vacancy therein. In each case a person so appointed shall hold office, subject to the provisions of the Recall, until the next general municipal election.

Sec. 14. Mayor's and Auditor's term of office.

The Mayor and Auditor shall each hold office for a term of two years from and after the first day of July after his election, and until his successor is elected and qualified.

Sec. 15. Councilmen's term of office.

The Councilmen shall hold office for a term of four years from and after the first day of July after their election and until their successors are elected and qualified. Provided, that the Councilmen first elected under this Charter shall, at their first meeting, so classify themselves by lot that two of them shall hold office for two years and two of them for four years.

At each general municipal election after the first under this Charter, there shall be elected two Councilmen.

Sec. 16. School Director's term of office.

Sec. 17. Official bonds.

[Bond of Mayor and Auditor fixed at $10,000, of Councilmen at $5,000, of School Directors at $2.500.]

Sec. 18. Oath of office.

Sec. 19. Salaries.

(*See Outline.*)

Sec. 20. Administering oaths. Subpoenas.

ARTICLE VI.

THE MAYOR.

Section 21. The chief executive.

[Mayor has general oversight.]

Sec. 22. Mayor pro tempore.

[Chosen by Council.]

Sec. 23. Mayor's reports.

Sec. 24. Mayor to have City's books examined.

[Mayor to employ certified public accountant at least semi-annually.]

Sec. 25. Supervision of public utility companies.

[Mayor may institute proceedings for violations of law, etc.]

Sec. 26. Powers and duties prescribed by ordinance.

ARTICLE VII.

EXECUTIVE AND ADMINISTRATIVE DEPARTMENTS.

Sec. 27. The four municipal departments.

(These are: 1. Finance and Revenue; 2. Public Health and Safety; 3. Public Works; 4. Public Supplies.)

Sec. 28. Council to assign duties to the departments.

Sec. 29. The four Commissioners.

[Designation made by Council.]

Sec. 30. The chief officials.

The chief officials of the city shall be City Clerk, Assessor, Treasurer, Collector, Attorney, Engineer, Chief of Police, Fire Chief, Street Superintendent, Health Officer and five Library Trustees. They shall be appointed and may be removed by a majority vote of the Council. The Council, at any time when in its judgment the interests of the city so demand, may consolidate and place in charge of one such officer the functions and duties of two or more of such officers. The Council shall by ordinance prescribe the duties of all the chief officials.

The Council shall at the first regular meeting after the election of its members, or as soon thereafter as practicable, proceed to the appointment of the chief officials of the City and the determination of their duties as provided in this section.

Sec. 31. Subordinate officers and employees.

The Council shall have power by ordinance to create and discontinue offices, deputyships, assistantships and employments other than those prescribed in this Charter, to provide the modes of filling them, to prescribe the duties pertaining thereto, according to its judgment of the needs of the city, and to determine the mode of removing any such officer, deputy, assistant or employee, except as otherwise provided in this Charter.

Sec. 32. Compensation of officers and employees.

[Fixed by Council.]

Sec. 33. Reports of departments.

Sec. 34. Reports to be published.

Sec. 35. Councilman to hold no other office.

Sec. 36. Officers not to be interested in contracts or franchises.

Sec. 37. Political and religious tests.

[Charter prohibits.]

ARTICLE VIII.

THE COUNCIL.

Section 38. The Council, the governing body.

Sec. 39. President and Vice-President.

Sec. 40. Meetings of Council.

[Fixed by Council.]

Sec. 41. Meetings to be public.

Sec. 42. Quorum.

[Majority constitutes.]

Sec. 43. Rules of proceeding.

Sec. 44. Ordinances and resolutions.

(2) Ayes and noes.

(3) Majority vote of Council.

(4) Subject and title.

Enacting clause of ordinances.

(5) The enacting clause of all ordinances passed by the Council shall be in these words: "Be it ordained by the Council of the City of Berkeley as follows:"

Requirements of an ordinance.

(6) To constitute an ordinance a bill must before final action thereon be passed to print and published with the ayes and noes for two days, and, in case of any amendment being made thereto before the final adoption of the ordinance, must in like manner be republished as amended for not less than one day.

Ordinances required in certain cases.

(7) No action providing for any specific imporvements or the appropriation or expenditure of any public money, except sums less than five hundred dollars; for the appropriation, acquisition, sale or lease of public property; for the

levying of any tax or assessment; for the granting of any franchise; for establishing or changing fire limits, or for the imposing of any penalty, shall be taken except by ordinance; provided, that such exceptions be observed as may be called for in cases where the Council takes action in pursuance of a general law of the State.

(8) Reconsideration.

(9) Signing and attesting.

[Ordinances signed by Mayor and attested by City Clerk.]

Revision and amendment.

(10) No ordinance shall be revised, re-enacted or amended by reference to its title only; but the ordinance to be revised or re-enacted, or the section or sections thereof to be amended, or the new section or sections to be added thereto, shall be set forth and adopted in the method provided in this section for the adoption of ordinances.

(11) Repeal.

Ordinances granting franchises.

(12) No bill for the grant of any franchise shall be put upon its final passage within thirty days after its introduction, and no franchise shall be renewed before one year prior to its expiration.

(13) Record of City ordinances.

Sec. 45. Protection of absent commissioner.

No final action shall be taken in any matter concerning the special department of any absent Councilman unless such business has been made a special order of the day by action at a previous meeting of the Council, or such action is taken at a regular meeting of the Council.

Sec. 46. Publication of Charter and ordinances.

The Council, during the first year after its organization under this Charter and from time to time thereafter, shall cause all ordinances at such time in force to be classified under appropriate heads, and, together with or separately from the Charter of the City and such provisions of the Constitution and laws of the State as the Council may deem expedient, to be published in book form.

ARTICLE IX.

POWERS OF THE CITY AND OF THE COUNCIL.

Section 47. General powers of the City.

Without denial or disparagement of other powers held under the constitution and laws of the State, the City of Berkeley shall have the right and power:

Public buildings, works and institutions.

(1) To acquire by purchase, condemnation or otherwise, and to establish, maintain, equip, own and operate libraries, reading rooms, art galleries, museums, schools, kindergartens, parks, playgrounds, places of recreation, fountains, baths, public toilets, markets, market houses, abattoirs, dispensaries, infirmaries, hospitals, charitable institutions, jails, houses of correction and farm schools, work houses, detention homes, morgues, cemeteries, crematories, garbage collection and garbage disposal and reduction works, street cleaning and sprinkling plants, quarries, wharves, docks, waterways, canals, and all other public buildings, places, works and institutions.

Water, light, heat and power.

(2) To acquire by purchase, condemnation or otherwise, and to establish, maintain, equip, own and operate waterworks, gas works, electric light, heat and power works, within or without the City, and to supply the City and its inhabitants and also persons, firms and corporations outside the City, with water, gas and electricity.

Telephone, telegraph and transportation.

(3) To acquire by purchase, condemnation or otherwise, and to establish, maintain, equip, own and operate telephone and telegraph systems, cable, electric or other railways, ferries and transportation service of any kind.

Sale of products of public utilities.

(4) To sell gas, water, electric current and all products of any public utility operated by the City.

Land for public purposes.

(5) To acquire by purchase, condemnation or otherwise, within or without the City, such lands or other property as may be necessary for the establishment, maintenance and operation of any public utility or to provide for and effectuate any other public purpose; and to sell, convey, encumber and dispose of the same for the common benefit.

Lease of public utilities.

(6) To lease to corporations or individuals for the purpose of maintenance and operation any public utility owned by the City.

Bequests and donations.

(7) To receive bequests, gifts and donations of all kinds of property, in fee simple, or in trust for charitable and other purposes, and do all acts necessary to carry out the purposes of such bequests, gifts and donations, with power to manage, sell, lease or otherwise dispose of the same in accordance with the terms of the bequest, gift or trust, or absolutely in case such bequest, gift or trust be unconditional.

Borrowing money, bonds.

(8) To borrow money for any of the purposes for which the City is authorized to provide and for carrying out any of the powers which the City is authorized to enjoy and exercise and to issue bonds therefor; provided, that in the procedure for the creation and issuance of such bonded indebtedness the general laws of the State of California in force at the time such proceedings are taken shall be observed and followed.

Special tax.

(9) To raise money by a special tax, in addition to the annual tax levy provided in Section 57 of this Charter. To authorize such special tax, the provisions of Section 92 of Article XIII relating to the Initiative, or Section 94 of Article XIV relating to the Referendum, shall be followed and the levy of such tax must be approved by at least two thirds of the qualified electors who vote thereon. At such election the Council may be authorized, in cases where pub

lic necessity requires the expenditure of any sum so voted before the next succeeding tax levy, to borrow such sum and provide in the next succeeding tax levy for its repayment with interest at not exceeding five per cent. per annum. Or the Council may be authorized to levy a special tax each year for a period of years not exceeding three years in all, for any permanent municipal improvement, and the money so raised may be expended each year after the same is collected and available.

Joint ownership of water supply.

(10) To join with one or more cities incorporated under the Constitution and laws of the State in order to acquire and develop jointly a source or sources of water supply for municipal and domestic purposes and to construct the works necessary for their joint and several purposes and needs, and to unite with such cities in bond issues therefor.

Sue and defend.

(11) To sue and defend in all courts and places and in all matters and proceedings.

Sec. 48. Direct legislation by people.

The qualified voters of the City shall have power through the initiative and otherwise, as provided by this Charter and the general laws of the State, to enact appropriate legislation to carry out and enforce any of the above general powers of the City or any of the special powers of the Council.

Sec. 49. Powers of the Council enumerated.

[Subdivisions 1 to 62 relate to regulations dealing with the following subjects: Official seal; Violation of Charter and ordinances; Nuisances; Rewards; Police and Fire Departments; Police and fire alarm systems; Explosives; Inflammable materials; Engines and Boilers; Fire limits; Building regulations; Fire escapes; Precaution against fires; Provision for safety in theatres, halls, etc.; Provision for safety in streets; Improper use of streets; Weeds and rubbish on sidewalks; Billboards and signs; Dogs; Public pound; Cruelty to animals; Preservation of health; Dangerous and offensive occupations, disagreeable noises; Inspection of food products; Dairies; Lodging, tenement and apartment houses; Sewer connections; Garbage; Licensing businesses; Regulation of public vehicles; Weights and measures; Public shows, Gambling; Public order and decency; Taxation; Erroneously callected taxes; Fees; Mayor's urgency fund; Lease of lands owned by the City; Purchase of property under execution; Sale of useless personal property; Trusts; Street grades; Street work; Street opening; Light and water; Boulevards; Closed or abandoned streets; Waterfront and wharves; Regulation of public utility rates; Regulation of street railroads; Railroads to keep streets in repair, spur tracks; Regulation of poles and wires; Size and location of pipes; Elections; Establishment of a Civil Service Commission, a Civic Art Commission, a Park Commission, a Playground Commission, a Commission of Public Charities; Municipal ownership.]

ARTICLE X.

FINANCE AND TAXATION.

Sec. 50. The fiscal year.

The fiscal year of the City shall commence upon the first day of July of each year, or at such other time as may be fixed by ordinance.

Sec. 51. Tax System.

The Council shall by ordinance provide a system for the assessment, levy and collection of all City taxes not inconsistent with the provisions of this Charter.

The Council shall have power to avail itself by ordinance of any law of the State of California now or hereafter in force and comply with the requirements thereof whereby assessments may be made by the Assessor of the County in which the City of Berkeley is situated and taxes collected by the Tax Collector of said County for and on behalf of the City of Berkeley. Other provisions of this Charter concerning the assessment, levy and collection of taxes shall be subject to the provisions of any such ordinance while the same shall be in froce.

Sec. 52. Department estimates of annual requirements.

[Heads of departments send annual estimates to Commissioner.]

Sec. 53. Annual estimates of City's requirements and revenue.

On or before the first Monday in May in each year, or on such date in each year as shall be fixed by the Council, the Commissioner of Finance and Revenue shall submit to the Council an estimate of the probable expenditures of the City government for the next ensuing fiscal year, stating the amount required to meet the interest and sinking funds for the outstanding funded indebtedness of the City, and the wants of all the departments of the municipal government in detail, and showing specifically the amount necessary to be provided for each fund and department; also an estimate of the amount of income from fines, licenses and other sources of revenue exclusive of taxes upon property, and the probable amount required to be levied and raised by taxation.

Sec. 54. Annual budget.

Sec. 55. Board of Equalization.

Sec. 56. Annual tax levy.

Sec. 57. Limit of tax levy.

The tax levy authorized by the Council to meet the municipal expenses for each fiscal year shall not exceed, except as herein provided, the rate of one dollar on each one hundred dollars of the assessed value of all real and personal property within the City. The Council in making the levy shall apportion not less than thirty-five cents to the School Fund, unless the estimate of the Board of Education calls for a less amount. The remainder of such levy shall be placed in the general fund, which may be apportioned by the Council, except as otherwise provided in this Charter.

Sec. 58. Bond tax. Library tax.

The Council shall have power to levy and collect taxes in addition to the taxes herein authorized to be levied and collected, sufficient to pay the interest and maintain the sinking fund of the bonded indebtedness of the City and to provide for the establishment and support of free public libraries and reading rooms.

Sec. 59. Cash Basis Fund.

The Council shall create and maintain a permanent revolving fund, to be known as the Cash Basis Fund, for the purpose of putting the payment of the running expenses of the City on a cash basis. For this purpose the Council shall provide that, from the money collected from the annual tax levy and from money received from other sources, a sum equal to not less than two and one-half cents on each one hundred dollars of the assessed value of said property shall be placed in such fund until the accumulated amount in such fund shall be sufficient to meet all legal demands against the treasury for the first four months or other necessary period of the succeeding fiscal year.

The Council shall have power to transfer from the Cash Basis Fund to any other fund or funds such sum or sums as may be required for the purpose of placing such fund or funds, as nearly as possible, on a cash basis. It shall be the duty of the Council to provide that all money so transferred from the Cash Basis Fund be returned thereto before the end of the fiscal year.

Sec. 60. Tax liens.

Sec. 61. Duties of the Auditor.

Sec. 62. Money to meet warrants.

Sec. 63. Disposition of money collected.

Every officer collecting or receiving any moneys belonging to or for the use of the City shall settle for the same with the Auditor on or before the last day of each month, or at more frequent intervals as may be directed by the Council, and immediately pay all the same into the treasury, on the order of the Auditor, for the benefit of the funds to which such moneys severally belong. When the last day of the month falls upon Sunday or a legal holiday, the said payments shall be made on the next preceding business day. The Council may provide, in its discretion, for the deposit of the City moneys in banks in accordance with the State law.

Sec. 64. Uniform accounts and reports.

The Council shall prescribe uniform forms of accounts, which shall be observed by all officers and departments of the City which receive or disburse moneys. Whenever an act shall be passed by the State Legislature calling for uniform municipal reports, the City authorities shall be governed thereby.

ARTICLE XI.

Section 65. Public work and supplies—Form of contracts.

Sec. 66. Progressive payments on contracts.

Any contract may provide for progressive payments, if in the ordinance authorizing or ordering the work permission is given for such a contract. But no progressive payments can be provided for or made at any time which, with prior payments, if there have been such, shall exceed in amount at that time seventy-five per cent. of the value of the labor done and the materials used up to that time, and no contract shall provide for or authorize or permit the payment of more than seventy-five per cent. of the contract price before the completion of the work done under said contract and the acceptance thereof by the proper officer, department or board.

Sec. 67. Public work to be done by contract.

Sec. 68. Contracts for official advertising.

The Council shall let annually contracts for the official advertising for the ensuing fiscal year. For this purpose the Council shall advertise for five consecutive days, setting forth distinctly and specifically the work contemplated to be done, and asking for sealed proposals therefor. The proposals shall specify the type and spacing to be used at the rate or rates named in the bids. The Council shall let the contracts for such official advertising to the lowest responsible bidder publishing a daily newspaper in the City which is a newspaper of general circulation and has been in existence at the time of the awarding of the contract at least one year; provided, that the Council may reject any or all bids if found excessive, and advertise for new bids.

The newspaper to which the award of such advertising is made shall be known and designated as the "official newspaper."

Sec. 69. Contracts for lighting.

No contract for lighting streets, public buildings, places or offices shall be made for a longer period than one year nor shall any contract to pay for electric light or any illumination material at a higher rate than the minimum price charged to any other consumer be valid.

Sec. 70. Contracts for water.

No contract for supplying water for the use of the municipality in any of its departments shall be valid wherein the rates exceed those charged to other consumers.

Sec. 71. Hours of labor.

The maximum time of labor or service required of any laborer, workman or mechanic employed upon any municipal work, whether so employed directly by the City and its officers, or by a contractor or sub-contractor, shall be eight hours during any one calendar day.

Sec. 72. Collusion with bidder.

Any officer of the City, or of any department thereof who shall aid or assist a bidder in securing a contract to furnish labor, material or supplies at a higher price than that proposed by any other bidder, or who shall favor one bidder over another by giving or withholding information or who shall wilfully mislead any bidder in regard t the character of the material or supplies called for, or who shall knowingly accept materials or supplies of a quality inferior to those called for by the contract, or who shall knowingly certify to a greater amount of labor performed than has been actually performed, or to the receipt of a greater amount or different kind of material or supplies than has been actually received, shall be deemed guilty of malfeasance and shall be removed from office.

Sec. 73. Collusion by bidder.

If at any time it shall be found that the person to whom a contract has been awarded has, in presenting any bid or bids, colluded with any other party or parties for the purpose of preventing any other bid being made, then the contract so awarded shall be null and void, and the Council shall advertise for a new contract for said work, or provide for such public work to be done by the Department of Public Works.

ARTICLE XII.

FRANCHISES.

Section 74. Property rights of the City inalienable.

The rights of the City in and to its water front, wharf property, land under water, public landings, wharves, docks, streets, highways, parks and all other public places, except as otherwise provided in this Charter, are hereby declared inalienable.

Sec. 75. No use of streets without a franchise.

No person, firm or corporation shall ever exercise any franchise or privilege mentioned in this article except in so far as he or it may be entitled to do so by direct authority of the Constitution of California or of the Constitution or laws of the United States, in, upon, over, under and along any street, highway or other public place in the City unless he or it shall have obtained a grant therefor in accordance with the provisions of this article of this Charter.

Sec. 76. Franchises to use streets.

Every franchise or privilege to construct or operate street, suburban or interurban railroads along, upon, over or under any street, highway, or other public place or to lay pipes or conduits or to erect poles or wires or other structures in, upon, over, under or along any street, highway or other public place in the City for the transmission of gas or electricity, or for any purpose whatever, shall be granted upon the conditions in this article provided, and not otherwise.

Sec. 77. Applications for franchises.

(1) An applicant for a franchise or privilege shall file with the Council an application therefor, and thereupon the Council shall, if it propose to grant the same, advertise the fact of said application, together with a statement that it is proposed to grant the same, in the official newspaper of the City. The publication of such advertisement must run for ten successive days and must be completed not less than twenty and not more than thirty days before any further action can be taken on such application.

Conditions of grant.

(2) The advertisement must state the character of the franchise or privilege it is proposed to be granted, and if it be a street, suburban or interurban railroad, the route to be traversed; that sealed bids therefor will be opened at a stated time and place, and that the franchise will be awarded to the bidder offering to pay to the City during the life of the franchise the highest percentage of the gross annual receipts received from the use, operation or possession of the franchise, provided that such percentage be not less than two per cent. of said gross annual receipts during the first ten years, not less than three per cent. during the second ten years, not less than four per cent. during the third ten years, and not less than five per cent. for the rest of the life of the franchise.

Bidding for the franchise.

(3) At the time of opening the sealed bids, any responsible person, firm or corporation, present in person, or represented, may bid for such franchise or privilege not less than one-fourth of one per cent. of the gross annual receipts above the highest sealed bid therefor, and such bid so made may be raised not less than one-fourth of one per cent. of the gross annuual receipts by any other responsible bidder, and such bidding may continue until finally such franchise shall be struck off, sold and awarded by the Council to the person, firm or corporation offering the highest percentage of the gross annual receipts arising from the use, operation or possession of such franchise; provided that if, in the judgment of the Council, no adequate or responsible bid has been made, the Council may withdraw such franchise from sale or advertise for new bids.

Deposit as guarantee of good faith.

(4) Every application and bid for franchises under this article shall be accompanied by a cash deposit of two thousand dollars or a certified check therefor as a guarantee of the good faith of the applicant or bidder, and as a fund out of which to pay all expenses connected with such application and the granting of such franchise.

Upon the franchise being awarded, all deposits made by unsuccessful bidders shall be returned. The deposit of the successful bidder shall be retained until the filing and approval of the surety bond hereinafter provided for, whereupon the remainder of such deposit, after the payment therefrom of all expenses incurred by the City in connection with the advertising and awarding of such franchise, shall be returned.

Free competition in bidding.

(5) No clause or condition of any kind shall be inserted in any franchise or grant offered or sold under the terms of this article which shall directly or indirectly restrict free and open competition in bidding therefor, and no clause or provision shall be inserted in any franchise offered for sale which shall in any wise favor one person, firm or corporation as against another in bidding for the purchase thereof.

Bond.

(6) The successful bidder for any franchise or privilege awarded under this article shall file a bond running to the

City to be approved by the Council, in the penal sum by it to be prescribed and set forth in the advertisement for bids, conditioned that such bidder shall well and truly observe and faithfully perform each and every term and condition of such franchise and that in case of any breach of condition of such bond, the whole amount of the penal sum therein named shall be taken and deemed to be liquidated damages and shall be recoverable from the principal and surety upon such bond.

Such bond shall be filed with the Council within five days after such franchise is awarded, and within thirty days after the filing and approval of such bond such franchise shall by the Council be granted by ordinance to the person, firm, or corporation to whom it shall have been struck off, sold, or awarded, and in case such bond shall not be so filed, the award of such franchise shall be set aside and any money deposited in connection with the awarding of the franchise shall be forfeited and the franchise shall, in the discretion of the Council, be readvertised and again offered for sale in the same manner and under the same restrictions as hereinbefore provided.

Sec. 78. Life of franchises.

The maximum length of time for which a franchise or privilege to use the streets, highways, waters, or other public places of the City may be granted to any person, firm or corporation shall be thirty-five (35) years.

Sec. 79. Beginning and completion of work.

Work under any franchise granted in accordance with the terms of this article shall be commenced in good faith within not more than four months from the date of the final passage of the ordinance granting such franchise and if not so commenced within said time, said franchise shall be forfeited. Work under any franchise so granted shall be completed within the time fixed for such completion in the ordinance granting such franchise, which time shall be not more than three years from the date of the final passage of the ordinance granting said franchise, and if not so completed within said time, said franchise shall be forfeited; provided, that if good cause be shown, the Council may by resolution extend the time for completion thereof not exceeding three months.

Sec. 80. Service and accommodation.

The grant of every franchise or privilege shall be subject to the right of the City, whether reserved or not, to make all regulations which shall be necessary to secure in the most ample manner the safety, welfare and accommodations of the public, including among other things the right to pass and enforce ordinances to protect the public from danger or inconvenience in the operation of any work or business authorized by the grant of the franchise and the right to make and enforce all such regulations as shall be reasonably necessary to secure adequate, sufficient and proper service and accommodations for the people and insure their comfort and convenience.

Sec. 81. Rates and charges.

The grant of every franchise or privilege shall be subject to the right of the City, whether reserved or not, to prescribe and regulate the rates, fares, rentals or charges made for the service rendered under such franchise. The grant of every franchise for a street, suburban or interurban railroad shall provide that all United States mail carriers and all officials, policemen and firemen of the City shall at all times, while in the actual discharge of their duties, be allowed to ride on the cars of such railroad within the boundaries of the City, without paying therefor and with all the rights of other passengers.

Sec. 82. Right of City to assume ownership.

Every ordinance granting any franchise shall provide that at the expiration of the period for which the franchise was granted, or at any time before as stated in the ordinance, the City, at its election and upon the payment of a fair valuation therefor to be made in the manner provided in the ordinance making the grant, may purchase and take over to itself the property and plant of the grantee in its entirety, but in no case shall the value of the franchise of the grantee be considered or taken into account in fixing such valuation. Or it may be provided in the ordinance granting any franchise that the property and plant of the grantee shall, at the expiration of the period for which the franchise was granted, become the property of the City, without any compensation to the grantee.

Sec. 83. No conveyance necessary for City's ownership.

Every ordinance granting any franchise shall further provide that upon the payment by the City of a fair valuation in the manner provided in the ordinance, the plant and property of the grantee shall become the property of the City by virtue of the grant in payment thereunder, and without the execution of any instrument or conveyance. Or in case it is provided in the ordinance granting any franchise that the property and plant of the grantee shall, at the expiration of the period for which it was granted, become the property of the City without any compensation to the grantee, the property and plant of the grantee shall then become the property of the City by virtue of the grant and without the execution of any instrument or conveyance.

Sec. 84. Lease or assignment of franchise.

Any franchise granted by the City shall not be leased, assigned or otherwise alienated without the express consent of the City, and no dealings with a lessee or assignee on the part of the City to require the performance of any act or payment of any compensation by the lessee or assignee shall be deemed to operate as such consent; provided, that nothing herein shall be construed to prevent the grantees of such franchise from including it in a mortgage or trust deed executed for the purpose of obtaining money for corporate objects.

Sec. 85. Street sprinkling, cleaning and paving.

Every grant of any franchise or privilege in, over, under or along any of the streets, highways or public places in the City for railway purposes, shall be subject to the conditions that the person, firm or corporation, exercising or enjoying the same shall sprinkle, clean, keep in repair, and pave and repave so much of said street, highway or other public place as may be occupied by said railway as lies between the rails of each railway track, and between the lines of double track, and for a space of two feet outside of said tracks.

Sec. 86. Examination of company's books. Audit.

The City of Berkeley, by its Auditor, Deputy Auditor, or accountants authorized by the Auditor, or by the Council shall have the right at all reasonable times to examine all the books, vouchers and records of any person, firm or corporation exercising or enjoying any franchise or privilege granted by the City for the purpose of verifying any of the statements of gross receipts provided for, and for any other purpose whatsoever connected with the duties or privileges of the City or of such person, firm or corporation arising from this Charter or from the ordinance granting the franchise, and may audit the same at the end of each year.

Sec. 87. Annual Reports of Company.

Every person, firm or corporation operating any business under a franchise granted under this article shall file annually with the City Auditor on such date as shall be fixed by the Council a report for the preceding year.

Such report shall be in writing, verified by the affidavit of such person or persons, or officer of the corporation, as the Council shall direct, and shall contain a statement, in such form and detail as shall from time to time be prescribed by the Council of all the gross receipts arising from all the business done by said person, firm or corporation within the City of Berkeley for the year immediately preceding such report. Such report shall contain such further statements as may be required by the Council concerning the character and amount of business done and the amount of receipts and expenses connected therewith, and also the amount expended for new construction, repairs and betterments during such year.

Sec. 88. Payment of gross receipts.

The stipulated percentage of gross receipts shall be paid annually at the time of filing the annual report. Failure to pay such percentage shall work a forfeiture of the franchise. The provisions as to payment of gross receipts shall apply to every person, firm or corporation using or operating the works constructed under such franchise.

Sec. 89. Forfeiture for non-compliance.

Every ordinance granting any franchise or privilege shall provide for the termination and forfeiture thereof for any breach or failure to comply with any of the terms, limitations or conditions thereof, and in all such cases the Council shall have power to declare the termination and forfeiture of any such franchise or privilege, the same as though in each instance such power was expressly reserved.

Sec. 90. Reservation for belt lines.

No exclusive right or privilige shall ever be granted by the City or Council in, to or upon the bed of the Bay of San Francisco beyond the line of mean low tide; nor shall any structure be erected thereon so as to prevent the construction and operation of belt lines of railroads along the waterfront; and any franchise or permit for a railroad track in, over or upon the bed of the Bay of San Francisco shall be subject to the right of any other railroad or railroad company to use the same upon payment of a reasonable compensation therefor.

Sec. 91. Franchise not in use forfeited.

All franchises and privileges heretofore granted by the City which are not in actual use or enjoyment or which the grantees thereof have not in good faith commenced to exercise, shall be declared forfeited and invalid, unless such grantees or their assigns shall, within six months after this Charter takes effect, in good faith commence the exercise and enjoyment of such privilege or franchise.

ARTICLE XIII.

THE INITIATIVE.

Section 92. Direct legislation.

(1) Any proposed ordinance may be submitted to the Council by a petition signed by registered electors of the City equal in number to the percentage hereinafter required.

Provisions of Section 5 apply.

(2) The provisions of Section 5 of Article III respecting the forms and conditions of the petition and the mode of verification and certification and filing shall be substantially followed, with such modification as the nature of the case requires.

Fifteen per cent petition.

(3) If the petition accompanying the proposed ordinance be signed by electors equal in number to fifteen per centum of the entire vote cast for all candidates for Mayor at the last preceding general municipal election at which a Mayor was elected, and contain a request that said ordinance be submitted forthwith to the vote of the people at a special election, then the Council shall either:

(a) Pass said ordinance without alteration within twenty days after the attachment of the Clerk's certificate of sufficiency to the accompanying petition (subject to a referendary vote, under the provisions of Article XIV of this Charter); or,

(b) Within twenty-five days after the Clerk shall have attached to the petition accompanying such ordinance his certificate of sufficiency, the Council shall proceed to call a special election at which said ordinance without alteration shall be submitted to a vote of the people.

Five per cent petition.

(4) If the petition be signed by electors equal in number to at least five, but less than fifteen, per centum of the entire vote cast for all candidates for Mayor at the last preceding general municipal election at which a Mayor was elected, and said ordinance be not passed by the Council as provided in the preceding subdivision, then such ordinance, without alteration, shall be submitted by the Council to a vote of the people at the next general municipal election that shall occur at any time after twenty days from the date of the Clerk's certificate of sufficiency attached to the petition accompanying such ordinance.

Publication of Popular Ordinances.

(5) Whenever any ordinance or proposition is required by this Charter to be submitted to the voters of the City at any election either (a) the Council shall cause the ordinance or proposition to be printed and it shall be the duty of the Clerk to enclose a printed copy thereof in an envelope with a sample ballot and mail the same to each voter, at least three days prior to the election, or (b) the Council may order such ordinance or proposition to be printed in the official newspaper of the City and published in like manner as ordinances adopted by the Council are required to be published, and may order that such publication shall take the place of the printing and mailing of the ordinance or proposition and of the sample ballots as first above provided.

Election.

(6) The ballots used when voting upon such proposed ordinance shall contain the words, "For the Ordinance" (setting forth in full the title thereof and stating the general nature of the proposed ordinance) and "Against the Ordinance," (setting forth in full the title thereof and stating the general nature of the proposed ordinance). If a majority of the qualified electors voting on said proposed ordinance shall vote in favor thereof, such ordinance shall thereupon become a valid and binding ordinance of the City.

Several ordinances at one election.

(7) Any number of proposed ordinances may be voted upon at the same election, in accordance with the provisions of this article.

(8) Limit to special elections.

Repeal of popular ordinance.

(9) The Council may submit a proposition for the repeal of any such ordinance, or for amendments thereto, to be voted upon at any succeeding general municipal election; and should such proposition, so submitted, receive a majority of the votes cast thereon at such election, such ordinance shall be repealed or amended accordingly. An ordinance proposed by petition, or adopted by a vote of the people, cannot be repealed or amended except by a vote of the people.

Further regulations.

(10) The Council may, by ordinance, make such further regulations as may be necessary to carry out the provisions of this section, and to adapt the provisions of Section 5 of Article III thereto.

ARTICLE XIV.

THE REFERENDUM.

Section 93. Mode of protesting against ordinances.

No ordinance passed by the Council shall go into effect before thirty days from the time of its final passage except when otherwise required by the general laws of the State or by the provisions of this Charter respecting street improvements, and except the ordinance making the annual tax levy, and except an ordinance for the immediate preservation of the public peace, health or safety, which contains a statement of its urgency, and is passed by a four-fifths vote of the Council; provided, that no grant of any franchise shall be construed to be an urgency measure, but all franchises shall be subject to the referendum vote herein provided. If during said thirty days a petition signed by qualified electors of the City equal in number to at least ten per centum of the entire vote cast for all candidates for Mayor at the last preceding general municipal election at which a Mayor was elected, protesting against the passage of such ordinance, be presented to the Council, the same shall thereupon be suspended from going into operation and it shall be the duty of the Council to reconsider such ordinance, and if the same be not entirely repealed, the Council shall submit the ordinance, as is provided in Article XIII of this Charter, to the vote of the electors of the City, either at the next general municipal election or at a special election to be called for that purpose, and such ordinance shall not go into effect or become operative unless a majority of the qualified electors voting on the same shall vote in favor thereof. The provisions of Section 5 of Article III respecting the forms and conditions of the petition and the mode of verification and certification and filing shall be substantially followed, with such modifications as the nature of the case requires.

Sec. 94. Reference of measures to popular vote.

Any ordinance or measure that the Council or the qualified electors of the City shall have authority to enact, the Council may of its own motion submit to the electors for adoption or rejection at a general or special municipal election, in the same manner and with the same force and effect as is provided in this Charter for ordinances or measures submitted on petition. At any special election called under the provisions of this Charter, there shall be no bar to the submission of other questions to a vote of the electors in addition to the ordinances or measures herein provided for, if said other questions are such as may legally be submitted at such election. If the provisions of two or more measures approved or adopted at the same election conflict then the measure receiving the highest affirmative vote shall control.

Sec. 95. Further regulations.

The Council may, by ordinance, make such further regulations as may be necessary to carry out the provisions of this Article, and to adopt the provisions of Section 5 of Article III thereto.

ARTICLE XV.

THE PUBLIC SCHOOLS.

[The Public Schools are exempted from the general control of the Council. The latter are required to levy taxes to the amount certified by the Board of Education to be needed over and above the amounts received from the state and county funds.]

ARTICLE XVI.

MISCELLANEOUS.

[This article deals with matters incidental to the installation of the Charter, and defines the legal force of the instrument.]

CHARTER OF COLORADO SPRINGS, COLORADO.

FRAMED BY THE CHARTER CONVENTION MARCH 20, 1909. ADOPTED MAY 11, 1909.

We, the people of the City of Colorado Springs, under the authority of the Constitution of State of Colorado, do ordain and establish this Charter for the City of Colorado Springs.

ARTICLE I.

NAME, BOUNDARIES, ETC.

Section 1. Name, Boundaries, etc.

Sec. 2. Powers—Rights—Liabilities.

ARTICLE II.

ELECTIVE OFFICERS.

Section 3. Officers—Terms.

The elective officers of the City shall be a Mayor and four Councilmen, each of whom shall be elected at large by the qualified electors of the city. The term of all elective officers, except as otherwise provided herein, shall commence at 10 o'clock A. M., on the first secular day of May following their election, and, except as otherwise provided herein, shall be for four years and until their successors are elected and qualified; provided, however, that of the four Councilmen first elected under this Charter, the term of the two receiving the highest number of votes shall be for four years, and the term of the other two shall be for two years; and provided, further, that the terms of the elective officers first elected under this Charter shall commence at 10 o'clock A. M. on the third Tuesday following the first general municipal election held under this Charter and shall end at 10 o'clock A. M. of the first secular day of May following the election of their successors.

Sec. 4. Qualifications.

Sec. 5. Vacancy.

Sec. 6. Removal.

In case of misconduct, inability or willful neglect in the performance of the duties of his office, the Mayor or any Councilman may be removed from office by the Council by a vote of four members, but he shall be given an opportunity to be heard in his defense, and shall have the right to appear by counsel and to have process issue to compel the attendance of witnesses who shall be required to give testimony if he so elects. In such case the hearing shall be public and a full and complete statement of the reasons for such removal, if he be removed, together with the findings of fact as made by the Council, shall be filed by the Council with the Clerk, and shall be and become a matter of public record.

ARTICLE III.

THE COUNCIL.

Section 7. Legislative Powers.

[Vested.]

Sec. 8. President and Vice-President of Council.

The Mayor shall be President of the Council, and, when present, shall preside at all meetings. The Council shall elect one of its number to be Vice-President, who, during the absence or disability of the Mayor, or while any vacancy exists in the office of the Mayor, shall possess all of the powers and perform all of the duties of the Mayor, except that he shall not have any power of removal.

Secs. 9 to 15, inclusive.

[Deal with the legislative procedure, etc.]

Sec. 16. Ordinances Granting Franchises.

No proposed ordinance granting any franchise shall be put upon its final passage within sixty days after its introduction, nor until it has been published not less than once a week for six consecutive weeks in two daily newspapers of general circulation published in the City.

Sec. 17. Record of Ordinances.

Sec. 18. Proof of Ordinances.

Sec. 19. Publication of Charter and Ordinances.

The Council shall, as speedily as may be, and in any event within two years from the time of its organization under this charter, and from time to time thereafter, cause all ordinances at such times in force to be classified under appropriate heads, and to be published in book form, together with or separate from the Charter, and such provisions of the Constitution and laws of the State as the Council may deem expedient.

(Enumerates the usual ministerial functions of mayors of cities.)

Sec. 20. Power to Establish Offices.

The Council shall, consistent with the provisions of this Charter, establish any office, position or employment that may in its opinion be necessary or expedient, and fix the salary and duties thereof. It may at any time abolish the same, whereupon the salary attached thereto shall cease.

Sec. 21. Statements.

The Council shall cause to be printed each month in pamphlet form a detailed statement of all receipts and expenditures of the city and a summary of its proceedings during the preceding month and furnish printed copies thereof to the public library, the daily newspapers of the city and to persons who shall apply therefor at the office of the Clerk. Said statement shall also show the amount of water used during the preceding month and the amount of reserve water in storage at the end of that month.

Sec. 22. Vote of Council on Appointments.

All votes upon appointments shall be by roll call and recorded. The vote of three members shall be necessary for appointment.

ARTICLE IV.

THE MAYOR.

Section 23. Duties—Authority—Powers.

[Enumerates the usual ministerial functions of mayors of cities.]

Sec. 24. Veto Power.

In ordinances making appropriations, the Mayor may veto any or every item therein, but such veto shall only extend to the items so vetoed, and those which he approves shall become effective, and those which he disapproves shall not become effective, unless passed over his veto by the vote of four (4) members of the Council.

ARTICLE V.

EXECUTIVE AND ADMINISTRATIVE DEPARTMENTS.

Section 25. Distribution.

The executive and administrative powers, authority, and duties of the city, not otherwise herein provided for, shall be distributed among five departments, as follows:

Department of Water and Water Works,
Department of Finance,
Department of Public Safety,
Department of Public Works and Property,
Department of Public Health and Sanitation.

Sec. 26. Council Assign Duties.

Sec. 27. Commissioners of Departments—How Designated.

Sec. 28. Council May Change Designation.

Sec. 29. Commissioner May Employ or Discharge.

The Commissioner for each of the departments shall have the supervision and control of all the affairs and property belonging to such department, except as otherwise provided in this Charter, or by ordinance, subject to such regulations as may be prescribed by the Council. He may employ and discharge or delegate to any subordinate the power to employ and discharge day laborers and unskilled workmen.

ARTICLE VI.

DEPARTMENT OF WATER AND WATER WORKS.

Section 30. Department an Entity.

The Department of Water and Water Works shall embrace all property, rights and obligations of the City in respect of water and water works, and shall in so far as practicable be administered as an entity. To that end all contracts, records and muniments of title pertaining thereto shall be assembled and carefully preserved, and accounts shall be kept of its assets, liabilities, receipts and disbursements, separate and distinct from the accounts of any other department. Its revenue shall be so applied that as far as possible the department shall be self-sustaining.

Sec. 31. Commissioner Administer Department.

The Commissioner of Water and Water Works is charged with the administration of said department. He shall appoint all such officials, assistants and skilled employees as may be necessary, and may secure the services or advice of hydraulic engineers, special counsel and other experts for such compensation as may be approved by the Council. He shall take care that the water supply of the City is preserved from impairment or pollution and seasonably augmented so as to assure at all times a supply of potable water adequate for the growing needs of the City. To that end he shall cause comparative investigation to be made of all available reservoir sites and sources of such water supply and report thereon to the Council with his recommendations. He shall also prepare and submit to the Council measures for the storage and augmenting of the City's supply of water for ditch and irrigation purposes. He shall cause adequate measurements and tests to be made and record thereof preserved.

Sec. 32. Commissioner Fix Rates—Council Impose Fines.

He shall with the approval of the Council expressed by resolution, fix rates and establish regulations for the use of water by consumers and regulations for the orderly administration of the department. The Council shall by ordinance impose fines and penalties for the violation of any of said regulations.

Sec. 33. Duty of Commissioner as to Bonds.

He shall, as soon as may be after this Charter goes into effect, prepare with the advice of the Commissioner of Finance a measure for the retirement by purchase or redemption of the existing water bonds of the City through the issuance and sale hereby provided for of bonds of the City to mature not later than fifty years from their date, bearing interest at a rate not exceeding four per centum per annum and providing for payments into a sinking fund commencing not earlier than ten years from their date, said interest and sinking fund payments to be chargeable primarily upon the revenues of the department, and shall submit said measure to the Council for action thereon.

He shall from time to time in like manner prepare and submit to the Council for action thereon measures for such bond issues or other financing of the department's affairs as the needs of the City may require.

Sec. 34. Emergency Warrants.

ARTICLE VII.

DEPARTMENT OF FINANCE.

Secs. 35 to 48, inclusive.

[These Sections deal with the fiscal year (identical with calendar year); control of public moneys; adoption of existing law; assessor to certify to the Council amount of property assessed; estimates of expenses of the several departments to be annually furnished Mayor, who will thus present his budget; the Council to consider the budget, to estimate sum necessary to be raised by tax levy, and to make the proper levy appropriations; no liability without appropriation; special appropriations for 1909; collection of taxes (identical with state taxes); limitation of city indebtedness (city not to become indebted to an amount exceeding 3% of valuation of taxable property.]

ARTICLE VIII.

DEPARTMENT OF PUBLIC SAFETY.

Secs. 49 to 53, inclusive.

[These Sections deal with the maintenance of the police and fire departments, over which the Commisioner of Public Safety is to exercise control; a relief fund for these departments is provided; existing police court to continue as provided by Colorado statutes and to have exclusive original jurisdiction.]

ARTICLE IX.

DEPARTMENT OF PUBLIC WORKS AND PROPERTY.

Sec. 54. Commissioners Have Supervision.

ARTICLE X.

DEPARTMENT OF HEALTH AND SANITATION.

Secs. 55 to 60, inclusive.

[These Sections deal with assistants and employees; qualifications of the health officer and of the assistants; Commissioner of Health to have power of arrest; duty of physicians and householders regarding contagious disease.]

ARTICLE XI.

COMMISSIONS AND BOARDS.

Secs. 61 and 62.

[These Sections empower the existing Park Commissioners and directors of the public library to continue with their powers, etc., as under the Colorado statutes.]

ARTICLE XII.

FRANCHISES AND PUBLIC UTILITIES.

Section 63. Franchise Granted Upon Vote.

No franchise shall be granted by the City except upon the vote of the qualified tax-paying electors, and the question of its being granted shall be submitted to such vote upon deposit with the Treasurer of the expense (to be determined by the Treasurer) of such submission by the applicant for said franchise.

Sec. 64. Franchise Specify Streets.

All franchises or privileges hereafter granted shall plainly specify on what particular streets, alleys, avenues or other public property the same shall apply; and no franchise or privilege shall hereafter be granted by the City in general terms or to apply to the City generally.

Sec. 65. Power to Regulate Rates and Fares.

All power to regulate the rates, fares and charges for service by public utility corporations is hereby reserved to the people, to be exercised by them by ordinance of the Council or in the manner herein provided for initiating or referring an ordinance. Any right or regulation shall further include the right to require uniform, convenient and adequate service to the public and reasonable extensions of such service and of such public utility works.

Sec. 66. Ordinance in Plain Terms.

No franchise, right or privilege or license shall be considered as granted by any ordinance except when granted therein in plain and unambiguous terms and any and every ambiguity therein shall be construed in favor of the City and against the claimant under said ordinance.

Sec. 67. Issuance of Stock.

Every ordinance granting any franchise shall prohibit the issuing of any stock on account thereof by any corporation holding or doing business under said franchise, to an amount in excess of the sum which shall be fixed for said purpose by the Council whenever requested so to do by the holder of said franchise; the said sum as fixed by the Council shall consist of the following items, only, to wit:

(a) The sum necessarily expended by the grantee of said franchise in obtaining the same from the City; and

(b) The sum which is in the opinion of the Council reasonably sufficient to compensate said grantee for the time and services given by him in obtaining said franchise. Any violation of the terms of this section shall at the option of the City operate as a forfeiture of said franchise.

Sec. 68. License Tax.

The City shall have the right to license or tax street cars, telephones, gas meters, electric meters, water meters, or any other similar device for measuring service; also telephone, telegraph, electric light and power poles, subways and wires. The said license or tax shall be exclusive of and in addition to all other lawful taxes upon the property of the holder thereof.

Sec. 69. Special Privileges to Mail Carriers, Policemen and Firemen.

The grant of every franchise for a street, suburban or interurban railroad shall provide that all United States mail carriers and all policemen and firemen of the City in uniform shall at all times, while in the actual discharge of their duties, be allowed to ride on the cars of such railroad within the boundaries of the City without paying therefor and with all the rights of other passengers.

Sec. 70. Railroad Elevate or Lower Tracks.

The Council shall by ordinance require under proper penalties any railroad company, whether steam or electric, to elevate or lower any of its tracks running over, along or across any of the streets or alleys of the City, whenever in the opinion of the Council the public safety or convenience require.

Sec. 71. Franchise Provide for Safety, Etc.

The grant of every franchise or privilege shall be subject to the right of the City, whether in terms reserved or not, to make all regulations which shall be necessary to secure in the most ample manner the safety, welfare and accommodation of the public, including among other things the right to pass and enforce ordinances to require proper and adequate extensions of the service of such grant, and to protect the public from danger or inconvenience in the operation of any work or business authorized by the grant of the franchise and the right to make and enforce all such regulations as shall be reasonably necessary to secure adequate, sufficient and proper service, extensions and accommodations for the people and insure their comfort and convenience.

Sec. 72. Oversight of Franchise for Use of Water Reserved to City.

Every franchise, right or privilege which has been, or which may be hereafter granted, conveying any right, permission or privilege to the use of the water belonging to the City or to its water system, shall always be subject to the most comprehensive oversight, management and control in every particular by the City; and the rights of the City to such control for municipal purposes is retained by the City in order that nothing shall ever be done by any grantee or assignee of any such franchise, right or privilege which shall in any way interfere with the successful operation of the water works of the city, or which shall, or which shall tend to, divert, impair or render the same inadequate for the complete performance of the trust for the people under which such water works are held by the City.

Sec. 73. No Exclusive Franchise—Renewal.

No exclusive franchise shall ever be granted, and no franchise shall be renewed before one year prior to its expiration.

Sec. 74. No Franchise Leased, Except.

No franchise granted by the City shall ever be leased, assigned or otherwise alienated without the express consent of the City, and no dealing with the lessee or assignee on the part of the City to require the performance of any act or payment of any compensation by the lessee or assignee, shall be deemed to operate as such consent. No such franchise shall ever be assigned to any foreign corporation.

Sec. 75. No Extension or Enlargement of Franchise, Except.

No extension or enlargement of any franchise or grant of rights or powers previously granted to any corporation, person or association of persons, shall be made except in the manner and subject to all the conditions herein provided for in this Article for the making of original grants and franchises; **provided, however,** that the provisions of this Article shall not apply to the granting by ordinance of revocable licenses or privileges for side track or switch privileges to railway companies for the purpose of reaching and affording railway connection and switch privileges to the owners or users of any industrial plant, it being the intention to permit the City to grant such revocable licenses or privileges to railway companies whenever in its judgment the same is expedient, necessary or advisable, and whenever the application for such privileges is accompanied by the assent in writing of the owners of the major part in extent of the front feet of the lots or tracts of land of the block fronting on each side of any street, or parts of a street, over or on which it is desired to lay or construct such side tracks or switches.

Sec. 76. Provision for Common Use of Tracks, Poles, Etc.

Sec. 77. Mayor to Maintain General Supervision—Reports —Inspection.

Sec. 78. Books of Record and Reference.

The Mayor shall provide and cause to be kept in the office of the City Clerk, the following books of record and reference:

First.—A Franchise Record, indexed and of proper form, in which shall be transcribed accurate and correct copies of all franchises or grants by the City to any person, persons or corporation owning or operating any public utility. The index of said record shall give the name of the grantee and thereafter the name of any assignee thereof. Said record shall be a complete history of all franchises granted by the City and shall include a comprehensive and convenient reference to actions, contests or proceedings at law, if any, affecting the same.

Second.—A Public Utility Record, for every person, persons or corporation owning or operating any public utility under any franchise granted by the City, into which shall be transcribed accurate and correct copies of each and every franchise granted by the City to said person, persons or corporation or which may be controlled or acquired by them or it, together with copies of all annual reports and inspection reports, as herein provided, and such other matters of information and public interest as the Mayor may from time to time acquire. All annual and inspection reports shall be published once in two daily newspapers of general circulation published in the City, or printed and distributed in pamphlet form, as the Council may deem best, and in case annual reports are not filed and inspections are not made, as provided, the Mayor shall in writing report to the Council the reasons therefor, which report shall be transcribed in the Record of the person, persons or corporation owning or contolling said franchise or grant, and published once in two daily newspapers of general circulation published in the City, or printed and distributed in pamphlet form, as the Council may deem best.

The provisons of this section shall apply to all persons or corporations operating under any franchise now in force or hereafter granted by the city.

Sec. 79. Books of Account—Examination.

Sec. 80. Term [of Franchise] Not Longer Than Twenty-five Years—Compensation.

Sec. 81. City May Purchase—Procedure.

(a) Every grant of a franchise or right shall provide that the City may, upon the payment therefor of its fair valuation, to be made as provided in the grant, purchase and take over the property and plant of the grantee in whole or in part.

The procedure to effect such purchase shall be as follows:

When the Council shall, by resolution, direct that the Mayor shall ascertain whether any such property or part thereof, should be acquired by the City, or in the absence of such action of the Council, when a petition subscribed by ten per centum of the qualified taxpaying electors requesting that the Mayor shall ascertain whether any such property or part thereof should be acquired by the City, shall be filed with the Clerk, the Mayor shall forthwith carefully investigate said property and report to the Council—

(1) At what probable cost said property may be acquired.

(2) What, if any, probable additional outlays would be necessary to operate same.

(3) Whether, if acquired, it could be operated by the City at a profit or advantage in quality or cost of service, stating wherein such profit or advantage consists.

(4) Whether, if acquired, it could be paid for out of its net earnings, and if so, within what time, and

(5) Such other information touching the same as he shall have acquired.

Such report shall be made in writing, shall include a statement of facts in relation thereto with such particularity as will enable the Council to judge of the correctness of his findings, and immediately after submission to the Council, shall be filed with the Clerk, recorded in the Public Utility Record and published once in each of two daily newspapers of general circulation published in the City, or printed and distributed in pamphlet form, as the Council may deem best.

If a petition subscribed by twenty-five per centum of the qualified tax-paying electors of the City, requesting that the question whether or not the City shall acquire said property shall be submitted to a vote of the people, shall within sixty days after the filing of said report be filed with the Clerk, the Council shall provide by ordinance for the submission of the question to a vote of the qualified tax-paying electors.

(b) Every grant reserving to the City the right to acquire the plant as well as the property, if any, of the grantee situated in, on, above or under the public places of the City, or elsewhere, used in connection therewith, shall in terms specify the method of arriving at the valuation therein provided for and shall further provide that upon the payment by the City of such valuation the plant and property so valued, purchased and paid for shall become the property of the City by virtue of the grant and payment thereunder and without the execution of any instrument of conveyance; and every such grant shall make adequate provision by way of forfeiture of the grant, or otherwise, for the effectual securing of efficient service and for the continued maintenance of the property in good order and repair throughout the entire term of the grant.

(c) Whenever any plant or property shall become the property of the City of Colorado Springs, the City shall have the option at any time then or thereafter either to operate the same on its own account, or by ordinance to lease the same or any part thereof together with the franchise or right to use the streets or other public property in connection therewith for periods not exceeding twenty-five years under such rules and regulations as it may prescribe, or by ordinance to sell the same to the highest bidder at public sale.

Sec. 82. Matters in Charter Not to Impair Right of Council to Insert Other Matters in Franchise.

The enumeration and specification of particular matters in this Charter which must be included in every franchise or grant, shall never be construed as impairing the right of the Council to insert in such franchise or grant, such other and further matters, conditions, covenants, terms, restrictions, limitations, burdens, taxes, assessments, rates, fares, rentals, charges, control, forfeitures, or any other provision whatever, as the Council shall deem proper to protect the interests of the people.

Sec. 83. Revocable Permits.

ARTICLE XIII.

ELECTIONS.

Secs. 84 to 109, inclusive.

[These Sections follow closely the election provisions in the Berkeley, California, charter (*q. v.*]

[*See also outline of Colorado Springs charter.*]

Sec. 110. Use of Carriages on Day of Election.

No candidate for any elective office shall directly or indirectly use or cause to be used in aid of his candidacy on the day of any municipal election more than one carriage or other vehicle to aid voters to get to the polling places. Such carriage or other vehicle shall be used to transport only those voters who by reason of illness or other infirmity are unable to go to the polling places unless so transported. Any candidate desiring to use the same carriage or other vehicle above mentioned shall, not less than one day prior to the day of election, file in the office of the Clerk a statement of such desire on his part, which shall contain such a description of the carriage or vehicle he desires to use as will readily identify the same. No other carriage or vehicle than the one so described in the said statement shall be used by the said candidate, or by any committee or association promoting his candidacy for the purpose of conveying voters to the polling places on the day of election.

A violation of any of the provisions of this section by any candidate shall disqualify him from holding the office for which he is a candidate.

Every elective officer of the City shall, at the time he takes the oath of office, be required to take and subscribe an oath that he has not violated any of the provisions of this section.

Sec. 111. General Election Regulations.

ARTICLE XIV.

RECALL OF ELECTIVE OFFICERS.

Section 112. Applies to All Elective Officers.

Sec. 113. Petition for Recall.

[*See Outline.*]

Sec. 114. Petition May be Amended or New Petition Made.

Within ten days from the filing of said petition the Clerk shall ascertain by examination thereof and of the registration books and election returns whether the petition is signed by the requisite number of qualified electors, and shall attach thereto his certificate showing the result of such examination. He shall, if necessary, be allowed extra help by the Council.

If his certificate shows the petition to be insufficient, he shall within said ten days so notify in writing one or more of the persons designated on the petition as filing the same; and the petition may be amended at any time within ten days from the filing of the certificate. The Clerk shall within ten days after such amendment make like examination of the amended petition and attach thereto his certificate of the result. If still insufficient or if no amendment is made, he shall return the petition to one of the persons designated thereon as filing it, without prejudice, however, to the filing of a new petition for the same purpose.

Sec. 115. Election Under Recall Petition, Unless Officer Resigns.

Sec. 116. Candidates—Election.

Sec. 117. Incumbent Removed.

Sec. 118. No Recall Petition for First Six Months.

No recall petition shall be filed against any officer until he has actually held his office for at least six months.

Sec. 119. Incapacity of Recalled Officer.

ARTICLE XV.

THE INITIATIVE.

Secs. 120 to 128, inclusive.

[*See Berkeley, California, Charter, and Outline of Colorado Springs Charter.*]

ARTICLE XVI.

THE REFERENDUM.

Section 129. Mode of Protesting Against Ordinances.

[*See Berkeley, California, Charter.*]

Sec. 130. Reference by the Council.

The Council may, of its own motion, submit to electoral vote for adoption or rejection at a general or special municipal election any proposed ordinance or measure in the same manner and with the same force and effect as is provided in Article XV. If the provisions of two or more proposed ordinances or measures adopted or approved at the same election conflict, then the ordinance or measure receiving the highest affirmative vote shall control.

Sec. 131. Further Regulations.

The Council may, by ordinance, make such further regulations as it may deem necessary to carry out the provisions of this article.

ARTICLE XVII.

OFFICERS, EMPLOYEES AND SALARIES.

Section 132. Officers—Employees.

Secs. 132 to 141, inclusive.

[Differentiate between officers (Mayor, Councilmen, and Police Magistrate) and employees of the city; establishes office hours; fixes salaries (Mayor $3,600, Councilmen $2,000); salaries cease upon removal; appointment of clerk and attorney; positions of treasurer and auditor to continue as now until the Council provides otherwise; oaths of office; bonds; no city employee to receive any commission, etc., by reason of dealings with the city.]

Sec. 142. Religious or Political Opinions Not to Affect Appointment.

No appointment to position under the City government shall be made or be withheld by reason of any religious or political opinions or affiliations or political services, and no appointment to or selection for or removal from any office or employment, and no transfer, promotion, reduction, reward or punishment shall be in any manner affected by such opinions, affiliations or services.

Sec. 143. Provision for Official Books, Records, Etc.

Sec. 144. Payment of Debts.

Failure of any officer or employee promptly to pay any indebtedness contracted by him while in the service of the city shall be ground for his removal.

Sec. 145. Attend to Duties.

Sec. 146. City Attorney. Duties.

Sec. 147. Assistants.

ARTICLE XVIII.

CIVIL SERVICE.

Section 148. Commission.

There is hereby established a Civil Service Commission consisting of three members who shall serve without compensation.

The Council first elected after the adoption of this Charter shall, as soon as practicable thereafter, appoint one member of said Commission to serve for two years, another member to serve for four years, and a third member to serve six years. Biennially thereafter, one member shall be appointed by the Council to take the place of the member whose term shall next expire, so that one member shall be appointed every two years to serve for a period of six years. If a vacancy shall occur in the Commission, it shall be filled by appointment by the Council for the unexpired term.

Sec. 149. Commission Make Rules.

The Commission shall, with the approval of the Council, make such rules and regulations for the proper conduct of its business, as it shall find necessary or expedient. The Commission shall, among other things, provide for the classification of all employment in the Department of Public Safety and in the Department of Public Works and Property, for open, competitive and free examinations as to fitness; for an eligible list from which vacancies shall be filled; for a period of probation before employment is made permanent; and for promotion on the basis of merit, experience and record.

Sec. 150. Council Give Further Powers.

The Council whenever requested by the Commission may by ordinance confer upon the Commission such other or further rights, duties and privileges as may be necessary adequately to enforce and carry out the principles of Civil Service.

ARTICLE XIX.

GENERAL PROVISIONS.

Section 151. Present Form of Government Continue Until.

Except as otherwise in this article provided, the form of government existing in the city of Colorado Springs at the time of the adoption of this charter shall continue unaltered, and all officers and other persons in the service of the City at the time this charter takes effect, shall continue to serve as such and to receive the compensation therefor now provided by law or by ordinance, and to have and exercise the powers, authority and jurisdiction theretofore possessed by them respectively, until the elective officers first elected hereunder shall have qualified. Upon such qualification of said elective officers hereunder, the term of office of every officer or other person in the service of the City at the time this charter takes effect shall immediately cease and determine. Thereafter all of said officers (except the Mayor and aldermen) and all of said other persons in the service of the city at the time this charter takes effect shall continue to draw compensation at the same rate, and to exercise like powers, authority and jurisdiction as theretofore, until replaced, or until the Council shall otherwise provide.

Secs. 152 to 158, inclusive.

[Refer to the duty of the present officers (*i e.,* old regime) regarding the election of their successors; former ordinances not inconsistent with this charter to continue in force; penalty for violation; definition of misdemeanor; containing bonds, etc.; submission of charter amendments; and reservation of powers.]

CHARTER OF GRAND JUNCTION, COLORADO.

FRAMED BY THE CHARTER CONVENTION, AUG. 6, 1909, BY AUTHORITY OF ARTICLE XX OF THE CONSTITUTION. ADOPTED SEPT. 14, 1909.

(Election Provisions only.)

Secs. 2 to 5.

[Relate to time of holding elections, registration, etc.]

Sec. 6. Nomination and Election of Officers.

Sec. 7. Condition of Candidacy.

Sec. 8. Form of Nomination Petition.

The petition of nomination shall consist of not less than twenty-five (25) individual certificates, which shall read substantially as follows:

PETITION OF NOMINATION.
Individual Certificate.

STATE OF COLORADO,
County of Mesa,
City of Grand Junction.
ss.

I do hereby join in a petition for the nomination of ....whose residence is at No................Street, Grand Junction, for the office of..to be voted for at the municipal election to be held in the city of Grand Junction, on the.............day of......................19....; and I certify that I am a qualified elector, and am not at this time a signer of any other certificate nominating any other candidate for the above named office; that my residence is at No...........Street, Grand Junction, and that my occupation is............................

I also certify that I believe the above named person is especially qualified to fill the said office and is of a good moral character. I further certify that I join in this petition for the nomination of the above named person believing that he has not become a candidate as the nominee or representative of, or because of any promised support from any political party, or any committee or convention representing or acting for any political party.

(Signed)..........................

STATE OF COLORADO,
County of Mesa,
City of Grand Junction.
ss.

................................., being first duly sworn, deposes and says that he is the person who signed the foregoing certificate, and that the statements therein are true.

(Signed)..........................

Subscribed and sworn to before me this...............day of..........................., A. D. 19....

My commission expires.......................

....
Notary Public.

The petition of nomination, of which this certificate forms a part shall, if insufficient, be returned to.................. at No............................ Grand Junction.

Sec. 9. Forms Supplied by City Clerk.
Sec. 10. Requirements of Certificate.
Sec. 11. Date of Presenting Petition.
Sec. 12. Examination of Petition by City Clerk.
Sec. 13. Filing of Petitions.
Sec. 14. Withdrawal or Acceptance.
Sec. 15. Form of Acceptance.
Sec. 16. Preservation of Petitions, Etc.
Sec. 17. Election Notices.

The City Clerk shall, on the tenth day before every city election, certify a list of the candidates so nominated for office at such election, whose names are entitled to appear on the ballot, as being the list of candidates nominated as required by this charter, together with the offices to be filled at such election, designating whether such election is for a full or unexpired term; and he shall file in his office said certified list of names and the offices to be filled, and he shall cause to be published in a notice calling for such election, for three successive days before such election, in two daily newspapers of general circulation, and published in the city of Grand Junction, an election notice, which said notice shall contain a list of names of candidates, the offices to be filled, and the time and the places of holding such election.

Sec. 18. Preferential Ballot—Form.

The city clerk shall cause ballots for each general and special election to be printed, bound, numbered, endorsed, and authenticated, as provided by the constitution and laws of the State, except as otherwise required in this Charter. The ballots shall contain the full list and correct names of all the respective offices to be filled, and the names of the candidates nominated therefor. It shall be in substantially the following form with the cross (X) omitted when there are four or more candidates for any office. (When there are three and not more candidates for any office, then the ballot shall give first and second choice only; when there are less than three candidates for any office, all distinguishing columns as to choice, and all reference to choice, may be omitted.)

GENERAL (OR SPECIAL) MUNICIPAL ELECTION, CITY OF GRAND JUNCTION. (Inserting date thereof.)

Instructions.—To vote for any person, make a cross (X) in ink in the square in the appropriate column according to your choice, at the right of the name voted for. Vote your first choice in the first column; vote your second choice in the second column; vote any other choice in the third column; vote only one first and only one second choice. Do not vote more than one choice for one person, as only one choice will count for any candidate by this ballot. Omit voting for one name for each office, if more than one candidate therefor. All distinguishing marks make the ballot void. If you wrongly mark, tear, or deface this ballot, return it, and obtain another.

51501

Commissioners of Public Affairs.	First Choice	Second Choice	Third Choice.
John Doe			X
James Foe	X		
Louis Hoe			
Dick Joe		X	X
Richard Roe			
Commissioner of Highways.			
Mary Brown	X		
Harry Jones		X	
Fred Smith			
Commissioner of Water and Sewers			
Joe Black	X		
Robert White			

Sec. 19. Blank Spaces for Additional Candidates.

One space shall be left below the printed names of the candidates for each office to be voted for, wherein the voter may write the name of any person for whom he may wish to vote.

Sec. 20. Requirements of Ballots.

All ballots printed shall be identical, so that without the numerical number thereon it would be impossible to distinguish one ballot from another. Space shall be provided on the ballot for Charter Amendments or other questions to be voted on at the municipal elections, as provided by this charter. The names of candidates for each office shall be arranged in alphabetical order of the sur-names. Nothing on the ballot shall be indicative of the source of the candidacy, or of the support of any candidate. No ballot shall have printed thereon any party or political designation or mark, and there shall not be appended to the name of any candidate any such party or political designation or mark, or anything indicating his views or opinions.

Sec. 21. Sample Ballots.

Sec. 22. Canvass and Election.

As soon as the polls are closed, the election judges shall immediately open the ballot boxes, take therefrom and count the ballots, and enter the total number thereof on the tally sheet provided therefor. They shall also carefully enter the number of the first, second, and third choice votes for each candidate on said tally sheet and make return thereof to the city clerk as provided by law. No vote shall be counted for any candidate more than once on any ballot, all subsequent votes on that ballot for that candidate being void.

The person receiving more than one-half of the total number of ballots cast at such election as the first choice of the electors for any office shall be elected to that office; provided, that if no candidate shall receive such a majority of the first choice votes for such office, then and in that event, the name of the candidate printed on the ballot having the smallest number of first choice votes, and all names written on the ballot having a less number of votes than such last named candidate, shall be excluded from the count, and votes for such candidate or persons so excluded shall not thereafter be counted. A canvass shall then be made of the second choice votes received by the remaining candidates for said office; said second choice votes shall then be added to the first choice votes received by each remaining candidate for such office, and the candidate receiving the largest number of said first and second choice votes, if such votes constitute a majority of all ballots cast at such election, shall be elected thereto; and provided, further, that if no such candidate shall receive such a majority after adding the first and second choice votes, then and in that event, the name of the candidate then having the smallest number of first and second choice votes shall be excluded from the count, and no votes for such candidate so excluded shall thereafter be counted. A canvass shall then be made of the third choice votes received by the remaining candidates for such office; said third choice votes shall then be added to the first and second choice votes received by each remaining candidate for such office, and such remaining candidate receiving the highest number of first, second and third choice votes shall be elected thereto. When the name of but one person remains as a candidate for any office, such person shall be elected thereto regardless of the number of votes received.

A tie between two or more candidates is to be decided in favor of the one having the greatest number of first choice votes. If all are equal in that respect, then the greatest number of second choice votes determine the result. If this will not decide, then the tie shall be determined by lot, under the direction of the canvassing board.

Whenever the word "majority" is used in this section, it shall mean more than one-half of the total number of ballots cast at such election.

Sec. 23. Informalities in Election.

No informalities in conducting municipal elections shall invalidate the same, if they have been conducted fairly and in substantial conformity with the requirements of this charter.

Sec. 24. Use of Carriages on Day of Election.

No candidate for any elective office shall directly or indirectly use or cause to be used in aid of his candidacy on the day of any municipal election, more than one carriage or other vehicle to aid voters to get to the polling places. Such carriage or other vehicle shall be used to transport only those voters who by reason of illness or other infirmity are unable to go to the polling places unless so transported. Any candidate desiring to use the one carriage or other vehicle above mentioned shall, not less than one day prior to the day of election, file in the office of the clerk a statement of such desire on his part, which shall contain such a description of the carriage or vehicle he desires to use as will readily identify the same. No other carriage or vehicle than the one so described in the said statement shall be used by the said candidate, or by any committee or association promoting his candidacy for the purpose of conveying voters to the polling places on the day of election.

A violation of any of the provisions of this section by any candidate shall disqualify him from holding the office for which he is a candidate.

Every elective officer of the city shall, at the time he takes the oath of office, be required to take and subscribe an oath that he has not violated any of the provisions of this section.

Sec. 25. General Election Regulations.

Sec. 26. Voting Machines.

CHARTER OF HUNTINGTON, WEST VIRGINIA.

(CHAPTER 3, LAWS OF 1909.)

ARTICLE I.

THE CITY OF HUNTINGTON.

Section 1. The City of Huntington.

Secs. 2 and 3.

[Define the corporation limits and ward boundaries.]

ARTICLE II.

MUNICIPAL AUTHORITIES.

Secs. 4, 5 and 6.

[Define the municipal authorities (as four commissioners), and fix the powers of the commissioners.]

ARTICLE III.

CITIZENS' BOARD.

Section 7. Citizens' Board.

The city of Huntington shall have an additional board to that provided in section four of this act, to be known and styled the "Citizens' Board of the City of Huntington," and which shall be comprised of sixteen persons from each ward of the city, and who shall be voted for and elected by the voters of each ward respectively, and in the manner hereinafter prescribed.

Sec. 8.

The citizens' board shall, at its first meeting after a majority of the newly elected members thereof shall have qualified, elect one of its members president of the body, whose term of office shall run with the term of the members of the body electing him.

Sec. 9.

The city clerk shall be ex-officio clerk of the citizens' board, and shall perform such duties pertaining thereto as the board may require of him.

Sec. 10.

Whenever a majority of the newly elected members of the citizens' board shall have qualified, they shall enter upon the duties of their said offices, as a body, and supercede all the former members of said board.

Sec. 11.

If any person elected to the citizens' board fail to qualify as herein provided within sixty days after his said election, or shall, after having qualified, resign from the board, or move from the city, his office shall be vacated, and the citizens' board shall, by a majority vote of the members voting thereon, fill such vacancy for the unexpired term with some person from the same ward and of the same political party as the person whose vacancy of office is being filled.

Sec. 12.

The citizens' board, shall, likewise by a majority vote of the members voting thereon, fill any vacancy in the office of president of its body by electing another member of the board to the office of president for the unexpired term.

Sec. 13.

The right of veto on any franchise or ordinance passed by the board of commissioners is hereby conferred upon the citizens' board, in the manner prescribed in Article twelve of this act. Such veto shall be by a majority vote of all the members elected to said board (except as prescribed in Section Seventy-three of this act), and the vote thereon shall be taken by roll call of the members and entered of record in the minutes of the meeting.

Sec. 14.

The citizens' board shall have the right to hear, consider and act on charges against any member of the board of commissioners, and, after having heard proof of such charges, may remove such commissioner and declare his office vacant by a two-thirds vote of all the members elected on said board, and the vote thereon shall be by roll call of the members and entered of record in the minutes of the meeting. But before such commissioner shall be put to trial on such charges, he shall have at least ten days written notice of the nature of said charges, and the time and place of a hearing thereon before said citizens' board. If the citizens' board, after hearing of said charges, shall remove said commissioner from office, thereby declaring a vacancy in his said office of commissioner, it shall through its president or otherwise, cause its action thereabout to be at once certified to the board of commissioners.

Sec. 15.

No commissioner shall be removed from his office except for one of the causes mentioned in section six of Article IV of the Constitution of West Virginia.

Sec. 16.

The citizens' board shall make proper rules for its government not contrary or inconsistent with any of the provisions of this act or the authority vested in the board of commissioners; and it shall cause a record of its meetings and proceedings to be kept and recorded by its clerk in a well bound book, which shall remain in the custody and at the office of the city clerk and open to public inspection. The minutes of the meeting and proceedings of said board, after recordation and when signed by its president, shall be admitted as evidence in any court of record in this state.

ARTICLE IV.

DEPARTMENTS OF CITY GOVERNMENT.

Secs. 17, 18 and 19.

[Divide the government of the city into departments, and assign the commisioners to such departments; each commissioner to keep office hours.]

ARTICLE V.

THE MAYOR.

Secs. 20 to 23, inclusive.

[Relate to method of choosing Mayor (commissioner receiving majority of votes); in case of tie lots to be cast; vacancy to be filled by election of some commissioner; duties of the mayor.]

ARTICLE VI.

ADDITIONAL OFFICERS.

Sec. 24.

[Establishes a number of appointive offices.]

ARTICLE VII.

QUALIFICATION OF VOTERS.

Secs. 25 and 26.

[Fix the qualifications and registration of voters.]

ARTICLE VIII.

NOMINATIONS OF CANDIDATES.

Sec. 27.

Candidates to be voted for at any municipal election for members of the board of commissioners and members of the citizens' board may be nominated by convention, primary or petition in the manner and under the provisions now or hereafter prescribed by state laws relating thereto; *Provided, however,* that no political party shall nominate more than three persons for the office of members of the board of commissioners, no two of whom shall be from the same ward, and no more than eight persons in each ward of the city for the office of members of the citizens' board. If any certificate of nomination, or any petition for nomination, of candidates for either the board of commissioners or the citizens' board shall contain more names than prescribed in this section for such office, then the ballot commissioners shall take the first three names for board of commissioners and the first eight names for citizens' board as the nominees of such party for said respective offices. And, *provided, further,* that there shall not be printed on any ticket on any ballot to be voted at any municipal election for the election of officers of the city more than three names for the office of members of the board of commissioners nor more than eight names for the office of members of the citizens' board.

Sec. 28.

In case of the nomination of candidates to be voted for to fill vacancies on the board of commissioners, no political party shall nominate more than double the number to be elected and such nominations shall be certified, and the names of the nominees printed on the ballot, in the manner prescribed in section twenty-seven herein.

Sec. 29.

Every person so nominated for the office of commissioner shall, wthin five days after his nomination has been certified by the political party making the nomination, or a petition therefor shall have been filed, make, under oath, and file with the city clerk, a statement of the political party to which he claims allegiance; and, if nominated by two or more parties, he shall state to which of them he belongs. If such person fail to make the oath, and file the same, as herein prescribed, the ballot commissioners shall not place his name on the ballot to be voted at the approaching election.

ARTICLE IX.

ELECTIONS OF OFFICERS.

Sec. 30.

On the second Tuesday of May, 1909, and on the same day, in every third year thereafter, there shall be elected by the qualified voters of the whole city four commissioners, who shall hold their offices from the time of their qualification on and from the first Monday of the next succeeding June for the term of three years, and until their successors are elected and a majority thereof shall have qualified.

Sec. 31.

At the same election at which commissioners shall be elected, there shall also be elected, by the qualified voters of each ward of the city, sixteen members of the citizens' board, who shall at the time be residents of the ward from which they are elected, and who shall hold their offices from the time of their qualifications on and from the first Monday of the next succeeding June for the term of three years, and until their successors are elected and a majority thereof shall have qualified.

Sec. 32.

No person shall be eligible to the office of commissioner or member of the citizens' board except he be a citizen entitled to vote at the election at which commissioners are elected.

Sec. 33.

Not more than two persons whose names appear on any ticket of the ballot being voted at an election for members of the board of commissioners shall be elected to said office. The four candidates receiving the greatest number of votes shall be declared elected, provided that not more than two of the four candidates receiving the greatest number of votes shall be of the same political party, and if more than two candidates of the same political party receive the greatest number of votes, then the two of such party receiving the greatest number of votes shall be declared elected; and the votes for the other candidates of said party for said office shall be disregarded, and the two candidates of other political parties voted for at said election who receive the next greatest vote shall be declared elected; *provided, further,* that if the name of any such candidate be printed on more than one ticket of the ballot, he shall be considered the candidate of the party on which ticket he received the greatest number of votes at said election; and in order to ascertain that fact, the election officers, and the board of canvassers, shall make and keep a separate tally of the votes cast for such candidate on each ticket on which his name appears.

Sec. 34.

If two or more candidates receive an equal number of votes, for commissioner or member of the citizens' board, the canvassing board, before whom said election returns shall have been canvassed, shall decide between them according to the provisions and intent of this act as to eligibility of candidates and political parties and tickets to which they belong.

Sec. 35.

Not more than eight persons whose names appear on the ticket of any party being voted at an election for members of the citizens' board shall be elected to said office. The sixteen candidates receiving the greatest number of votes shall be declared elected, *provided,* that not more than eight of the sixteen candidates receiving the greatest number of votes shall be of the same political party.

Sec. 36.

All elections, of whatsoever kind, held under this act shall be conducted, returned and the result thereof ascertained and declared in the manner prescribed by the laws of the state relating to elections in so far as they are not in conflict or inconsistent with the provisions of this act.

Secs. 37 to 41, inclusive.

[Provide for contested elections, oaths and bonds of officers, terms and salaries.]

Sec. 42.

The salary of the commissioner shall be fifteen hundred dollars each per annum payable monthly as their services shall have been rendered; but the commissioner who shall be designated Mayor shall receive three hundred dollars in addition to his salary as commissioner, which shall be paid monthly as his services shall have been rendered.

Provided, however, that whenever the United States census of said city shall show its population to be as much as twenty thousand people, then each commissioner's salary shall be advanced to eighteen hundred dollars; and thereafter no advance in their salary shall be made except by an ordinance passed by the board of commissioners making such advance, which in no event shall exceed two thousand five hundred dollars, and which shall be subject to the veto of the citizens' board, as provided in section 13 of this act; and *provided, further,* that if the board of commissioners fail or refuse to make their appointments of all appointive officers for a period of thirty days, said commissioners thereafter and until such appointments shall have been made, shall forfeit their salary; and the mayor, city clerk and treasurer shall take official notice of such failure to fill said appointive offices, and shall not issue any order for nor otherwise pay to the commissioners their salary for the period of their failure to make said appointments.

Sec. 43.

The board of commissioners may, by ordinance, fix the salaries of all appointive officers, which shall be subject to the veto of the citizens' board, as provided in said section 13.

Secs. 44 and 45.

[Fix the pay of day laborers and leave the duties of appointive officers to the commissioners.]

ARTICLE X.

MEETINGS OF BOARD OF COMMISSIONERS.

Secs. 46 to 49, inclusive.

[Provide for regular (weekly) and special meetings of the Commissioners, for viva-voce and roll-call vote, and for detailed minutes.]

MEETINGS OF CITIZEN'S BOARD.

Sec. 50.

The citizens' board shall meet on the first Monday of each month, at an hour and at the place to be fixed by it by the rules governing its body.

Sec. 51.

Special meetings of the citizens' board may be called by its president, or any ten members thereof, or by the board of commissioners, or by the mayor, by notice published in two daily newspapers of the city of opposite politics, on three successive days, stating the time and object of the meeting. The holding of a special meeting of the citizens' board shall be *prima facia* evidence that the said notice required therefor was given as prescribed in this section.

ATTENDANCE OF WITNESSES, PUNISHING CONTEMPTS, ETC.

Sec. 52.

The board of commissioners and the citizens' board in the exercise of their respective powers and the performance of their respective duties, as prescribed by this act and by the laws of the state, shall have the power to enforce the attendance of witnesses, the production of books, and papers, and the power to administer oaths in the same manner and with like effect, and under the same penalties, as notaries public, justices of the peace and other officers of the state authorized to administer oaths under state laws; and said board of commissioners and said citizens' board shall have such power to punish for contempts as is conferred on county courts by section thirteen of chapter thirty-nine of the code. All process necessary to enforce the powers conferred by this act on the board of commissioners and citizens' board shall be signed by the mayor (or acting mayor) and the president of the citizens' board, respectively, and shall be executed by any member of the police force.

QUORUM.

Sec. 53.

A majority of the members of the board of commissioners and a majority of the members of the citizens' board shall be necessary for the transaction of business before said respective boards.

Sec. 54.

Whenever a vacancy, from any cause whatever, shall occur in the office of commissioner, and the time for a regular municipal election, as provided for in section 30 herein, is not within six months therefrom, then the board of commissioners shall call a special election at which the qualified voters of the city shall fill such vacancy by the election of some person thereto; but the person so elected must be eligible to hold said office and shall not be of the same political party or the same political faith as any two commissioners who at the time hold the office of commissioner. Such special election shall be governed by the laws of the state relating to elections and as prescribed in this act for regular elections.

Sec. 55.

If there shall occur at any one time two or more vacancies on the board of commissioners the citizens' board, by a majority vote of all the members elected thereto, shall fill such vacancies for the time being, but the person so appointed shall be of the same political party as the commissioner whose office was vacated and is being filled; and in no event shall such appointments be made so as to give any political party a majority on the board of commissioners.

Provided, before any such appointment shall become final the person so appointed shall make and file the oath required by section twenty-nine of this act; and after the filing of said oath the citizens' board may, if it so elects, by a majority vote of all members elected thereto, recall said appointments, or any one thereof, and such appointment from that time shall be void and of no effect, and the vacancy caused thereby shall be filled in the same manner and under the condition prescribed in the first instance.

Commissioners thus appointed by the citizens' board to fill vacancies on the board of commissioners shall, before entering upon the discharge of their duties, take the oath required of other officers of the city, but they shall not be required to give any official bond; and they shall hold their said offices only until their successors shall have been elected and qualified as prescribed in section fifty-four of this act.

Secs. 56 to 59, inclusive.

[Provide for absence of any officer; prohibit any commissioner or city officer from holding any other office; and direct purchase of supplies at lowest price possible.]

ARTICLE XI.

POLICE JUDGE AND OTHER OFFICERS.

Sec. 60.

[Fixes the powers of the police judge and provides for extension of authority of police officers.]

ARTICLE XII.

VOTE ON FRANCHISES, ORDINANCES, OFFICERS, ETC.

Sec. 61.

No franchise or ordinance shall be passed, and no contract shall be awarded nor any money appropriated for any one purpose in a greater sum than twenty-five dollars, and no appointment of any officer shall be made, nor any vacancy in office declared, without the affirmative vote of at least three members of the board of commissioners.

Sec. 62.

When any franchise shall have passed the board of commissioners it shall not become effective until after the next regular meeting time of the citizens' board, or a special meeting time of said body called to act on such franchise, and not then if said citizens' board at such meeting time expresses its veto to said franchise, as provided in section thirteen of this act.

Sec. 63.

If any ordinance passes the board of commissioners it shall become and remain effective as therein prescribed unless vetoed by the citizens' board at its next regular meeting time, or special meeting time called to act on said ordinance.

Sec. 64.

Whenever the citizens' board shall express its veto of any franchise or ordinance passed by the board of commissioners, it shall, not later than the second day thereafter, cause such franchise or ordinance with its veto thereof and its written reasons therefor, addressed to the board of commissioners, to be transmitted to the city clerk, and the city clerk shall submit the same to the board of commissioners, at its next regular meeting, or special meeting called for that purpose, which shall be noted in the minutes of said meeting; but a failure to transmit such franchise or ordinance within said time shall not render such veto void. If the franchise or ordinance shall be changed and again passed by the board of commissioners it shall be treated as a new or original ordinance and subject to the veto power of the citizens' board.

Sec. 65.

If there shall be a tie vote on the passage of any franchise before the board of commissioners, the mayor shall at once transmit said franchise, with a written statement that the vote on the passage of the same before the board of commissioners was a tie, to the president of the citizens' board, who shall lay the same before said citizens' board at its next regular meeting time thereafter, or prior special meeting time called for that purpose. If upon consideration of said franchise by the citizens' board a majority of all the members elected to said citizens' board shall vote for the passage of said franchise as transmitted from the board of commissioners, it shall be considered passed and adopted and shall become effective as prescribed by the terms thereof.

The citizens' board, through its president or otherwise, after the expiration of the time for the consideration of said franchise, shall at once transmit the same with the action of the citizens' board, if any, addressed to the board of commissioners, to the city clerk, who shall call the same to the attention of the board of commissioners at their next regular meeting, or special meeting called for the purpose, at which shall be noted in the minutes the action of the citizens' board on said franchise.

Sec. 66.

Publications of notice to present franchise and other preliminaries prescribed by the laws of the state relating thereto, shall be had in the manner prescribed by state laws before the board of commissioners shall act on any such franchise, but the passage of any franchise shall be *prima facie* proof that such notice was given as prescribed by law.

The word "franchise" whenever used in this act shall include every special privilege in, under and over the streets, highways and public grounds of the city which does not belong to the citizens generally by common right.

Sec. 67.

The style of any ordinance enacted by the board of commissioners shall be: *"Be it ordained by the Board of Commissioners of the City of Huntington."*

ARTICLE XIII.

LICENSES.

Secs. 68 to 71, inclusive.

[Establish the various trades for which a city license is required; empower the commissioners to remove all nuisances, and to construct sidewalks and curbs.]

ARTICLE XIV.

TAXES, LEVIES, ASSESSMENTS, ETC.

Secs. 72 to 88, inclusive.

[Empower the commissioners to levy and collect taxes; ordain that taxes assessed on real estate shall remain a lien thereon from the time the same are so assessed; that no taxes shall be collected for maintenance of public works, etc., for any year in which the city shall at its own expense provide for its own poor and keep its own roads, etc., in order; tax of $2 annually from each male adult to go into street and wharf fund; city treasurer to deposit city funds in some bank paying at least two per cent. interest; commissioners empowered to control condition of streets, etc., and required to let all contracts for improvements to the lowest bidder; authorized to issue and sell bonds at six per cent.; payment to be made by landowners on each side of improved street in proportion as the frontage in feet of his abutting land bears to the total frontage of all the land so abutting on the street; method of payment by commissioners for improvements; commissioners authorized to have a street improved on petition of property-owners; method of sewerage; assessments; liens provided for street improvements to constitute tax liens on the real estate against which they are assessed; city authorized to sell its bonds to pay its part of the construction of sewers, pavements, etc., but issuance of said bonds shall first be submitted to a vote of the people; cost of any improvement contemplated to include cost of making the assessments, surveys, printing, etc.; rule of description of lands; notice of assessment against abutting property to be published.]

ARTICLE XV.

CIVIL SERVICE BOARD.

Sec. 89.

For the purpose of making examinations of persons for offices or positions in the police and fire department, including the chiefs thereof, and the office of cemetery sexton, and prescribing rules for their conduct, the members of the board of commissioners shall act and be known as a "CIVIL SERVICE BOARD," the mayor being the presiding officer, and the city clerk *ex officio* clerk, of said board.

The civil service board shall adopt rules for its own government, and cause the minutes of its meetings to be recorded in a book especially for that purpose, which shall be kept by the city clerk at his office and open to public inspection. The civil service board shall, at least once a year and oftener if it deems it necessary, after ten days' notice to the public, published in two daily newspapers of opposite politics, giving the time and place of meeting, hold examinations for the purpose of determining the fitness and qualifications of applicants for offices and positions in the police department and fire department, and position as cemetery sexton, which examinations shall be practical and shall fairly test the fitness of the persons examined to discharge the duties of the position to which they seek appointment; and such examinations, and the declaration of the result thereof, shall be made with the aim to secure and maintain an honest and efficient police force, fire department force, and cemetery sexton, free from partisan distinction or control. Said board shall at once after each of such examinations place to record, in the journal of the civil service board, the result of said examination, giving the names of applicants and the position sought by them, and their respective percentage based on one hundred. In making such examinations the size, health, physical appearance, habits and moral surroundings shall be taken into consideration.

Secs. 90 to 104, inclusive.

[Provide for examinations for police and fire department positions; successful candidates to hold their positions during good behavior—method of hearing charges; code of laws for the city to be printed; city to have non-partisan administration; serving notice—sufficient if executed by officer of police department; commissioners held to be successors of former city officials; officers of Central City to continue till the commissioners of Huntington shall have qualified; former officials of Huntington to continue until their successors shall have qualified; city to be divided into election districts—canvassing board constituted for first election, and thereafter the commissioners thus to act; former ordinances of Central City and Huntington to remain in force except where inconsistent with the present charter; city clerk to be custodian of records and papers pertaining to both cities; town of Guyandotte to remain a part of Huntington upon adoption of this act; all other acts inconsistent with present charter to be re- pealed; act to take effect March 1, 1909.]

CHARTER OF LYNN, MASS.

"AN ACT TO REVISE THE CHARTER OF THE CITY OF LYNN."

(CHAPTER 602, LAWS OF 1910.)

Be it enacted, etc., as follows:

PART I.

Section 1.

The inhabitants of the city of Lynn shall continue to be a municipal corporation, under the name of the City of Lynn, and as such shall have, exercise and enjoy all the rights, immunities, powers, and privileges, and shall be subject to all the duties, liabilities and obligations provided for herein, or otherwise pertaining to or incumbent upon said city as a municipal corporation. In addition to the powers above enumerated it shall have the power to establish, buy, erect, maintain, own, lease and regulate wharves and docks, and charge wharfage and dockage.

Sec. 2.

The territory of the city shall continue to be divided into seven wards, which shall retain their present boundaries until the same shall be changed under the general law relating thereto in any year fixed by law for a new division of wards in cities, by vote of the municipal council at or prior to the making of such division; but the number of wards shall never be less than seven.

Sec. 3.

The government of the city and the general management and control of all its affairs shall be vested in a municipal council, which shall be elected and shall exercise its powers in the manner hereinafter set forth; except, however, that the general management and control of the public schools of the city and of the property pertaining thereto, shall be vested in a school committee.

Sec. 4.

The municipal council shall consist of five members, to wit, a mayor, who shall be the commissioner of public safety; a commissioner of finance, a commissioner of streets and highways, a commissioner of water and water works and a commissioner of public property. The school committee shall consist of the mayor and four other members. All the above officers shall be elected at large by and from the registered voters for terms of two years, unless it is otherwise provided in this act.

ELECTION.

Sec. 5.

The municipal election shall take place annually on the second Tuesday of December; and the municipal year shall begin at ten o'clock in the forenoon of the first Monday in January, and shall continue until ten o'clock in the forenoon of the first Monday of the following January. Every special election shall be held on a Tuesday.

Sec. 6.

In the year nineteen hundred and ten and in every second year thereafter there shall be elected at the annual city election of said city, the mayor, the commissioner of finance, the commissioner of streets and highways, and two members of the school committee, for the term of the two municipal years next following said election. There shall also be elected at said annual city election in the year nineteen hundred and ten the commissioner of water and water works, the commissioner of public property and two members of the school committee for the municipal year next following said election. In the year nineteen hundred and eleven and in every second year thereafter there shall be elected at the annual city election the commissioner of water and water works, the commissioner of public property and two members of the school committee, each for the term of the two municipal years next following his election. Except as aforesaid and as otherwise provided in this act, no city officers shall be elected at any city election. The above officers shall be elected by and from the registered voters of the city and may be residents of any part thereof.

Sec. 7.

On the third Tuesday preceding every annual or special city election at which any officer mentioned in section four is to be elected, there shall be held a preliminary election for the purpose of nominating candidates for such offices as under the provisions of this act or of any act in amendment thereof are to be filled at such annual or special city election. The notice calling for the said preliminary election shall be issued at least forty days before the date of the city election. No special election for mayor or a commissioner shall be held until after the expiration of forty days from the calling of the preliminary election, which under the provisions of this act is to be held on the third Tuesday preceding such special election.

Sec. 8.

At every preliminary election the polls shall be opened at six o'clock in the forenoon and shall not be closed before four o'clock in the afternoon, and except as is otherwise provided in this act every such preliminary election shall be called by the same officers and held in the same manner as an annual city election. The polling places shall be designated, provided and furnished, and official ballots, special ballots, ballot boxes, voting lists, specimen ballots, blank forms, apparatus and supplies shall be provided for every such preliminary election, of the same number and kind and in the same manner as at an annual city election, and the same election officers shall officiate as at an annual city election.

Sec. 9.

Except as provided in section sixty-three there shall not be printed on the official ballots to be used at any annual or special city election of said city the name of any person as a candidate for mayor, commissioner or member of the school committee, unless such person shall have been nominated for such office at a preliminary election held as provided in this act. There shall not be printed on the official ballots to be used at a preliminary election the name of any person as a candidate for nomination unless such person shall have filed within the time set forth in section ten of this act the statement of the candidate and also the petition described in section ten. Beginning with the current year political committees in the city of Lynn shall be elected at the state primaries instead of at the municipal primaries.

Sec. 10.

Any person eligible for any elective office for which provision is made herein may have his name printed as a candidate for such office on the official ballots to be used at a preliminary election, provided that he shall, at least ten days before such preliminary election, file with the city clerk a statement in writing of his candidacy, in substantially the following form:

I, ..., on oath declare that I reside at No........ street, in the city of Lynn; that I am a voter in said city registered to vote for a candidate for the office hereinafter named; that I am a candidate for nomination for the office of..........for the term of.........years, to be voted for at the preliminary election to be held on Tuesday, the.......... day of.........19...; and I request that my name be printed as a candidate for such office on the official ballots to be used at such preliminary election.

(Signed)

COMMONWEALTH OF MASSACHUSETTS.

Essex, ss.

Subscribed and sworn to this.........day of..........19..., before me,..........................Justice of the Peace.
(or Notary Public.)

and provided that he shall at the same time file therewith a petition of at least twenty-five voters of the city registered to vote for a candidate for said office, which petition shall be in substantially the following form:

Whereas,....................is a candidate for nomination for the office of..............................for the term of ....years, we, the undersigned voters of the City of Lynn, duly registered to vote for a candidate for said office, do hereby request that the name of said.............. be printed on the official ballots to be used at the preliminary election to be held on the..................Tuesday of ....19....

We further state that we believe him to be of good moral character, and qualified to perform the duties of the office.
Name of voters. Street No..........Street,.......... if any.

No acceptance by a candidate for nomination named in such petition shall be necessary for its validity or for its filing, and the petition need not be sworn to.

Sec. 11.

Women who are qualified to vote for members of the school committee may be candidates for nomination for that office at any preliminary election at which candidates for nomination for that office are to be voted for; and at such preliminary election they may vote for candidates for nomination for that office. They shall file the hereinbefore described statement and petition in all cases where the same are herein required to be filed by male candidates for that office.

Sec. 12.

On the first day, not being Sunday or a legal holiday, following the expiration of the time for filing the above described statements and petitions, the city clerk shall cause to be published in one or more daily newspapers of said city, the names and residences of the candidates for nomination who have duly filed the above mentioned statements and petitions, and the offices and terms for which they are candidates, as they are to appear on the official ballots at the preliminary election. Thereupon the city clerk shall prepare and cause to be printed the ballots to be used at such preliminary election; and the ballots so prepared shall be the official ballots and the only ballots that may be used at such preliminary election. They shall be substantially as outlined below:

OFFICIAL PRELIMINARY BALLOT.

Municipal Council.

For mayor.
For commissioner of finance.
For commissioner of streets and highways.
For commissioner of water and water works.
For commissioner of public property.

School Committee.

Sec. 13.

The name of every person who has filed a statement and petition as aforesaid, and his residence and the title and term of the office for which he is a candidate, shall be printed on said ballots, and the names of no other candidates shall be printed thereon. Ballots for use at the said election and for use by women qualified to vote for members of the school committee shall be prepared and furnished in the manner now provided by law.

PARTY DESIGNATIONS ABOLISHED.

Sec. 14.

No ballots used at any annual or special city election, or at any preliminary election shall have printed thereon any party or political designation or mark; and there shall not be appended to the name of any candidate any party or political designation or mark, or anything showing how he was nominated, or indicating his views or opinions. On all ballots to be used at annual or special city elections, or at preliminary elections, blank spaces shall be left at the end of each list of candidates for the different offices equal to the number to be elected thereto, in which the voter may insert the name of any person not printed on the ballot for whom he desires to vote for such office, provided that such person is eligible for such office.

Sec. 15.

The qualifications for voting at a preliminary election and at a city election shall be the same.

Sec. 16.

The election officers shall immediately upon the closing of the polls at preliminary elections count the ballots and ascertain the number of votes cast in the polling places where they respectively officiate for each person for nomination for the office for which he was a candidate; and they shall forthwith make returns thereof to the city clerk upon blank forms to be furnished to them as in city elections.

Sec. 17.

On the first day, not being Sunday or a legal holiday, following such preliminary election, the city clerk shall canvass said returns so received from the election officers, shall forthwith determine the results of said canvass, and shall forthwith cause the same to be published in one or more daily newspapers of said city.

NOMINATIONS.

Sec. 18.

The two persons receiving at a preliminary election the highest and second highest number of votes, respectively, for any office shall be the candidates whose names shall be printed on the official ballots to be used at the annual or special city election for which such preliminary election was held; except that in case two or more persons receive the same number of votes and more votes than any other person for the same office, then said persons shall be the candidates as aforesaid whose names shall be printed on said official ballots. If two or more persons are to be elected to the same office at such annual or special city election, the several persons to a number equal to twice the number so to be elected to such office receiving at said preliminary election the highest number of votes, the second highest number of votes, and so on to the number to be nominated, shall be the candidates whose names shall be printed on the official ballots to be used at such annual or special city election. If, in order to obtain the requisite number of candidates for any office, it becomes necessary to take one of two or more persons having the same number of votes for the same office, then the names of all the aforesaid persons having the same number of votes for such office shall be printed on the official ballot to be used at such annual or special city election, together with the names of all persons, if any, receiving a higher number of votes for such office, even though it makes the number of candidates more than twice the number to be chosen to such office. No names of candidates shall be printed on said official ballots except as provided in this section and in section sixty-three.

Sec. 19.

No acceptance of a nomination made at a preliminary election shall be necessary for the validity of such nomination.

ELECTIONS.

Sec. 20.

At a city election other than the above described preliminary election, the person receiving the highest number of votes for an office shall be deemed and declared elected to such office; and if two or more persons are to be elected to the same office the several persons receiving, respectively, the highest number of votes, the second highest, and so on to the number to be chosen to such office, shall be deemed and declared to be elected; but persons receiving the same number of votes shall not be deemed to be elected if thereby a greater number would be elected than are by law to be chosen.

Sec. 21.

The laws of the commonwealth relating to annual city elections, special elections of city officers, special elections in cities, election officers, voting places for elections, election apparatus and blanks, calling and conduct of elections, manner of voting at elections, counting and recounting of votes at elections, corrupt practices and penalties shall apply to all elections under this act, including preliminary elections, except as is otherwise provided herein.

GENERAL MEETINGS OF VOTERS.

Sec. 22.

General meetings of the registered voters of the city shall be called by the municipal council upon petition of at least five hundred of the said voters, which petition shall state the purpose or purposes of the meeting. Such meeting shall be held not later than three weeks after the filing of the petition; and notice thereof shall be given by the municipal council on the front page of at least one daily newspaper of the city, not less than three times within two weeks after the filing of said petition. A presiding officer shall be chosen for said meeting from those present; and the city clerk shall act as the clerk thereof and shall keep complete records of the proceedings. If so requested in said petition, or demanded at said meeting, any city officer or officers shall attend such meeting, and if called upon so to do shall place before the meeting any facts, documents, or other information relative to the subject-matter of said petition.

The city clerk or a justice of the peace shall administer an oath to any person or persons called upon to testify before said meeting, as aforesaid, including any city officer or officers, whose presence has been requested or demanded, and any person so placed under oath who shall willfully give false testimony before said meeting upon any point material to the matter of inquiry shall be guilty of perjury, and shall be subject to the provisions of chapter two hundred and ten of the Revised Laws and any amendment thereof. But no person shall be required to give testimony tending to incriminate himself.

The provisions of sections eight and nine of chapter one hundred and seventy-five of the Revised Laws, and any amendments thereof, shall be applicable to the conduct and procedure at said hearing. If for any reason any officer or officers are unable to attend said meeting, or if it be impossible to produce at said meeting the facts, documents, or other information requested as aforesaid, the meeting may be adjourned until such time as said officer or officers can attend, or said facts, documents or other information can be furnished. A copy of the records of said meeting and of any adjournment thereof shall be transmitted by the city clerk to the municipal council at its next meeting.

ABOLISHMENT OF PRESENT GOVERNMENT.

Sec. 23.

At ten o'clock in the forenoon of the first Monday of January, in the year nineteen hundred and eleven, the city council, board of mayor and aldermen, board of aldermen and common council, board of public works and public water board shall be abolished; the terms of office which the present mayor, aldermen, common councilmen, members of the board of public works, school committee and public water board are now serving shall terminate; and, except as is otherwise provided in this act, all the present powers and duties, under any general or special acts, of the mayor, board of mayor and aldermen, board of aldermen, city council, common council, board of public works and public water board shall devolve upon and be exercised and performed by the municipal council. At the aforesaid time the board of assessors shall become an appointive board, and shall be subject to all the provisions of this act relative to appointive boards. The municipal council shall be the judge of the election of its own members.

Sec. 24.

The municipal council elected as aforesaid shall meet at ten o'clock in the forenoon on the first Monday of January in each year; and the members of said municipal council, whose terms of office then begin shall severally make oath before the city clerk, or a justice of the peace, to perform faithfully the duties of their respective offices. The municipal council shall thereupon be organized by the choice of a president, who shall be called the president of the municipal council and shall hold his office during its pleasure. The president of the municipal council shall be some member thereof other than the mayor. The organization of the municipal council shall take place as aforesaid, notwithstanding the absence, death, refusal to serve, or non-election of the mayor, or one or more of the four other members: *provided,* that at least three of the persons entitled to be members of the municipal council are present and make oath as aforesaid. Any person entitled to make the aforesaid oath, who was not present at the time fixed therefor, may make oath at any time thereafter.

MEETINGS OF MUNICIPAL COUNCIL.

Sec. 25.

The municipal council shall fix suitable times for its regular meetings. The mayor, the president of the municipal council, or any two members thereof, may, at any time, call a special meeting, by causing a written notice, stating the time of holding such meeting and signed by the person or persons calling the same, to be delivered in hand to each member, or left at his usual dwelling place, at least six hours before the time of such meeting. Meetings of the municipal council may also be held at any time when all the members are present and consent thereto.

Sec. 26.

A majority of the members of the municipal council shall constitute a quorum; its meetings shall be public, and the mayor, if present, shall preside and shall have the right to vote. In the absence of the mayor, the president of the municipal council shall preside, and in the absence of both, a chairman pro tempore shall be chosen. The city clerk shall be, ex officio, clerk of the municipal council, and shall keep records of its proceedings; but in case of his temporary absence, or in case of a vacancy in the office, the municipal council may elect by ballot a temporary clerk who shall be sworn to the faithful discharge of his duties and may act as clerk of the municipal council until a city clerk is chosen and qualified. All final votes of the municipal council involving the expenditure of fifty dollars or over shall be by yeas and nays and shall be entered on the records. It shall vote by yeas and nays when that is practicable, and on the request of one member any vote shall be by yeas and nays and shall be entered upon the records. The affirmative vote oi at least three members shall be necessary for the passage of any order, ordinance, resolution or vote.

POWERS OF THE MUNICIPAL COUNCIL.

Sec. 27.

The municipal council shall have the power to do, except as is otherwise provided in this act, without the approval of the mayor, all things which the city council, board of aldermen, common council and public water board or board of public works can now do with such approval. The municipal council shall determine the policies to be pursued and the work to be undertaken in each department, but each commissioner shall have full power to carry out the policies or have the work performed in his department, as directed by the municipal council. Any notes, bonds or scrip which said city is authorized to issue shall be signed by its treasurer and countersigned by a majority of the municipal council.

Sec. 28.

The municipal council shall have full supervision of the erection, alteration and repair of all public buildings, including school buildings, except repairs and alterations of school buildings for which provision is made in the annual appropriation, and except as is otherwise provided in chapter one hundred and seventy-eight of the acts of the year nineteen hundred and nine. No department of the city and no corporation or person, shall at any time, open, dig up or otherwise obstruct any way or sidewalk, without the consent of the municipal council in writing previously obtained, except in case of an emergency.

Sec. 29.

The public library of the city shall be under the exclusive management and control of the municipal council, which shall have the power to name the trustees and to remove them for cause. The municipal council may increase or diminish the number of trustees and make such rules and regulations concerning the public library as it may deem expedient.

PUBLICITY FOR CONTRACTS.

Sec. 30.

Neither the municipal council nor the school committee shall make or pass any order, resolution, or vote appropriating money in excess of five hundred dollars, or making or authorizing the making of any contract involving a liability on the part of the city in excess of five hundred dollars, unless the same is proposed in writing and notice is given by the city clerk in at least one daily newspaper of the city, not less than one week before its passage, except an order, resolution or vote for the immediate preservation of the public peace, health or safety, which contains a statement of its urgency and is passed by a four fifths vote; and such notice shall be given as aforesaid upon the request of said municipal council or of the school committee.

Sec. 31.

When the municipal council shall pass any measure or an amendment or repeal of any measure, such measure, amendment or repeal so passed shall, except as is otherwise provided in this act, take effect at the expiration of ten days from its passage; *provided, however,* that if there be a time therein specified when it shall take effect, and such time be more than ten days after its passage, such measure, amendment or repeal shall, except as is otherwise provided in this act, take effect at the time so specified therein.

Sec. 32.

No measure passed by the municipal council or by the voters, as provided in this act, shall require the approval of any court or of the attorney-general, or shall be required to be published in order to become effective, unless otherwise provided in this act.

Sec. 33.

Upon vote of the municipal council the mayor shall sign, seal, execute and deliver in behalf of the city deeds and leases of land sold or leased by the city, and other deeds, agreements, contracts, leases, indentures, assurances, and instruments on behalf of the city, except as is otherwise provided herein. No part of the common shall be let or sold.

Sec. 34.

The mayor shall have no power of veto, and no measure which the municipal council shall make or pass shall be presented to him for, or shall require, his approval in order to be effective.

Sec. 35.

Each of the five commissioners provided for in section four of this act shall annually submit to the municipal council in the month of January detailed estimates of the amounts deemed necessary for his respective department for the financial year, which shall begin on the first day of January. No sum appropriated for a specific purpose shall be expended for any other purpose, and no expenditure shall be made or liability incurred by or in behalf of the city until the municipal council has duly voted an appropriation sufficient to meet such expenditure or liability, together with all prior unpaid liabilities which are payable therefrom, except that after the expiration of the financial year and before the fifteenth day of March, upon vote of the municipal council, liabilities payable out of the regular appropriation may be incurred to an amount not exceeding one fifth of the total appropriation made for similar purposes in the preceding year. At any time the unexpended balance of any sum appropriated for a specific purpose and not further required for such purpose may be transferred to another account by vote of the municipal council, but no money raised by loan shall be transferred to any appropriation from income or taxes. Nothing herein contained shall be taken to prohibit the payment at any time of executions against the city. This section shall not apply to appropriations and expenditures of the school committee, which shall continue to be governed by chapter one hundred and seventy-eight of the acts of the year nineteen hundred and nine.

Sec. 36.

No officer of said city, except in case of extreme emergency involving the health or safety of the people or their property, shall expend intentionally, in any fiscal year, any sum in excess of the appropriation therefor duly made in accordance with law, and any officer who shall violate this provision shall be punished by a fine not exceeding one thousand dollars, or by imprisonment for not more than one year, or by both such fine and imprisonment.

Sec. 37.

All loans issued by the city after the passage of this act shall be made payable in annual instalments in the manner authorized by section thirteen of chapter twenty-seven of the Revised Laws, as amended by section one of chapter three hundred and forty-one of the acts of the year nineteen hundred and eight. All bonds shall be offered for sale in such a manner that the effect of the premiums, if any, shall be to reduce the total amount of bonds issued.

MONTHLY STATEMENTS TO BE PUBLISHED.

Sec. 38.

The commissioner of finance shall each month have printed in pamphlet form a detailed itemized statement of all cash receipts and expenditures of the city during the preceding month and of all bills and accounts owed by the city at the end of the preceding month, in such a manner as to show the gross monthly revenue and expense of each department, and shall furnish copies thereof to the public library, to the daily newspapers published in said city, and to persons who shall apply therefor at the office of the city clerk. At the end of the municipal year he shall cause a complete examination of all books and accounts of the city to be made by competent accountants, and shall publish the result of such examination in the manner above provided for the publication of monthly statements. The provisions of this section shall apply to the school department of the city, and the school committee shall furnish the commissioner of finance with such information, facts, figures and data as may be necessary to carry out the provisions of this section so far as it applies to the school department.

CRIMINAL OFFENSE TO PARTICIPATE IN CONTRACTS.

Sec. 39.

It shall be unlawful for a member of the municipal council or school committee or for any officer or employee of the city directly or indirectly to make a contract with the city, or to receive any commission, discount, bonus, gift, contribution or reward from, or any share in the profits of, any person or corporation making or performing such a contract, unless such member, officer, or employee immediately upon learning of the existence of such contract or that such contract is proposed shall notify in writing the municipal council or school committee of such contract and shall abstain from doing any official act on behalf of the city in reference thereto. In case such interest exists on the part of an officer whose duty it is to make such a contract on behalf of the city, the contract may be made by another officer of the city, duly authorized thereto by the mayor, or if the mayor has such interest, by the commissioner of finance; except, however, that when a contractor with the city is a corporation or voluntary association, the ownership of less than five per cent. of the stock or shares actually issued shall not be considered as being an interest in the contract within the meaning of this act, and such ownership shall not affect the validity of the contract unless the owner of such stock or shares is also an officer or agent of the corporation or association or solicits or takes part in the making of the contract. A violation of any provision of this section shall render the contract in respect to which such violation occurs voidable at the option of the city. Any person violating the provisions of this section shall be punished by a fine of not more than one thousand dollars, or by imprisonment for not more than one year, or by both such fine and imprisonment.

ADMINISTRATIVE OFFICERS.

Sec. 40.

There shall be the following administrative officers, who shall perform the duties prescribed by law for them, respectively, and such further duties, not inconsistent with the nature of their respective offices and with general law, as the municipal council may prescribe, except as is otherwise provided herein: a city clerk, a city treasurer, a collector of taxes, a city auditor, a purchasing agent, a board of overseers of the poor consisting of six persons, a city engineer, a city physician, a board of health consisting of three persons of whom the city physician shall be one, a city solicitor, a board of park commissioners consisting of five persons, a board of sinking fund commissioners consisting of three persons, a board of assessors consisting of three persons, seven assistant assessors and a board of trustees of the public library consisting of seven persons. The mayor shall be, ex officio, chairman and a member of the board of the overseers of the poor.

DEPARTMENTS.

Sec. 41.

The administration of all affairs of the city shall be divided into five departments, to wit:—Department of public safety, department of finance, department of streets and highways, department of water and water works, and department of public property; and said departments are defined as follows:—

The department of public safety shall include the following sub-departments and all boards and offices connected therewith, to wit: police, fire, electrical, health, poor, legal, claims, weights and measures and license commission.

The department of finance shall include the following sub-departments and all boards and offices connected therewith, to wit: treasury, auditing, purchasing, assessing, sinking funds, tax collection, registration of voters and city clerk.

The department of streets and highways shall include the following sub-departments and all boards and offices connected therewith, to wit: highways and other ways, street lighting, street watering, sewers and drains and engineering. The commissioner of streets and highways, except as is herein otherwise provided, shall have exclusively the powers of, and be subject to the liabilities and penalties imposed by law on, surveyors of highways.

The department of water and water works shall include all boards and offices connected with the water supply of the city.

The department of public property shall include the following sub-departments and all boards and offices connected therewith, to wit: buildings, parks, public grounds and cemeteries.

Every official or board having to do with the affairs of the city, with the exception of such as pertain to the school committee, shall be included in one of the above five departments, and if the assignment to a department is not made hereunder, the municipal council shall by ordinance assign such office, offices, board or boards to the department best adapted to include the same.

Sec. 42.

The municipal council, subject to the provisions of section forty-four, shall have the power to appoint, suspend or remove the following officers, to wit: the city clerk, city treasurer, collector of taxes, city auditor, city solicitor, purchasing agent, assessors, sinking fund commissioners, and trustees of the public library.

Sec. 43.

The commissioner of public safety, commissioner of finance, commissioner of streets and highways, commissioner of water and water works, and commissioner of public property shall be administrative heads of their respective departments, and, except as is otherwise provided herein, shall have the power to appoint, suspend or remove any officer, officers, board or boards in their respective departments, subject to the provisions of section forty-four and the laws of the commonwealth.

Sec. 44.

Appointments to any office, offices, board or boards established by this act or by city ordinance, except foremen and day laborers and such offices as pertain to the school committee, shall be subject to the following provisions, to wit:— Two weeks preceding the appointment to any such office, offices, board or boards a statement of the position or positions to be filled shall be published in at least one daily newspaper of the city under the signature or signatures of the commissioner or commissioners empowered to appoint, and he or they shall therein request any candidate or candidates for said position or positions to submit his or their candidacy in writing to the commissioner or commissioners aforesaid. Not less than two nor more than four days prior to said appointment the said commissioner or commissioners shall cause to be published on the front page of at least one daily newspaper of the city a list of the names of all candidates who have made written application as aforesaid; but nothing herein contained shall prevent a commissioner from appointing to office a person who has not submitted his candidacy in writing as aforesaid. All removals from appointive offices shall be accompanied by a statement of the reason or reasons therefor under the signature of the commissioner removing the officer or officers, and a copy of said statement shall be filed in the office of the city clerk. This section shall not apply to officers or employees now classified under civil service laws.

Sec. 45.

All officers, whether heretofore elected or appointed, or appointed hereunder, shall, except as is otherwise provided herein, continue in office until their successors are appointed and qualified. Except as is otherwise provided herein the term of office of any officer, officers, board or boards for which provision is herein made shall not be fixed, but shall continue indefinitely, subject to the provisions of this act regarding appointments, suspensions and removals.

RECORD OF EMPLOYEES.

Sec. 46.

The commissioner in charge of each department shall cause to be kept in his department a record, subject to public inspection, of all persons appointed and employed therein and of all persons suspended or removed, and, in case of suspension or removal, of the grounds therefor.

PROVISION FOR CHANGES.

Sec. 47.

The municipal council may from time to time, subject to the provisions of this act and in accordance with general laws, establish additional offices and boards, assign them to the proper departments, and determine the number and duties of the incumbents thereof; and for such purposes it may delegate to such offices and boards any part of the administrative powers given by this charter to the commissioners hereinbefore mentioned. The municipal council may also from time to time consolidate appointive offices and boards, separate and distribute the powers and duties of such as have already been established, increase or diminish the number of persons who shall perform the duties of any appointive office or board, or abolish any appointive office or board subject to the provisions of this act and in accordance with general laws.

Sec. 48.

All administrative officers shall be sworn to the faithful discharge of their respective duties, and certificates of their oaths shall be made and kept in the office of the city clerk. All administrative boards and officers shall keep a record of their official transactions, and such records shall be open to public inspection.

BONDS.

Sec. 49.

The municipal council shall require the city treasurer, the collector of taxes, the city auditor and the purchasing agent to give bonds, with such surety or sureties as it shall deem proper, for the faithful discharge of their respective duties, and may require any other municipal officer intrusted with the receipt, care or disbursement of money to give such bond. No city money shall be deposited in any bank or trust company of which any member of the board of sinking fund commissioners or the treasurer of said city is an officer, director or agent.

Sec. 50.

Every administrative board, through its chairman or a member designated by the board, and every officer in charge of a department, may appear before the municipal council, and at the request of said municipal council shall appear before it, and give information in relation to anything connected with the discharge of the duties of such board or office; and the officer who appears shall have the right to speak upon all matters under consideration relating to his department.

PURCHASING DEPARTMENT.

Sec. 51.

The purchasing department shall consist of a purchasing agent and such assistants as the municipal council may from time to time deem necessary. The purchasing agent shall purchase all supplies for the city, except in case of an emergency; but all purchases or contracts for purchase exceeding twenty-five dollars in amount shall be based upon competition, and no purchases or contracts for purchase shall be made involving the expenditure of more than twenty-five dollars for any one class of supplies in any month, except by competition. The purchasing agent shall purchase all supplies for the school department in accordance with instructions given to him by the school committee. A record shall be kept by this department of the prices paid for all supplies, which shall be open to the inspection of any citizen. The salaries in this department shall be fixed by the municipal council.

SALARIES.

Sec. 52.

The salary of the mayor shall be thirty-five hundred dollars per annum, and the salary of each of the remaining four members of the municipal council shall be three thousand dollars per annum. These salaries shall be payable in equal monthly installments.

Sec. 53.

No member of the municipal council shall during the term for which he was chosen hold any other office the salary of which is payable by the city.

Sec. 54.

The municipal council shall establish by ordinance the salary or compensation of every appointive officer; but after the first municipal year succeeding the acceptance of this act no ordinance changing any such salary or compensation shall take effect until the municipal year succeeding that in which the ordinance is passed.

SCHOOLS.

Sec. 55.

The management and control of the public schools of the city shall be vested in the school committee, consisting of the mayor ex officio and four other members elected in accordance with the provisions of this act. Three of its members shall constitute a quorum. The mayor, when present, shall preside, and its meetings shall be public. All final votes of the school committee involving the expenditure of fifty dollars or over shall be by yeas and nays and shall be entered on the records. The committee shall vote by yeas and nays, when that is practicable, and on request of one member any vote shall be by yeas and nays, and shall be entered upon the records. The affirmative vote of at least three members shall be necessary for the passage of any order, resolution or vote.

Sec. 56.

The school committee shall meet for organization on the Tuesday next after the first Monday in January in each year. The committee shall be the judge of the election and qualifications of its members and shall determine the rules for its proceedings, unless it is otherwise provided herein. The members of the school committee shall be sworn to the faithful discharge of their duties.

Sec. 57.

The school committee may elect a superintendent of schools and may appoint such other subordinate officers and assistants, including janitors of school buildings, as it may deem necessary for the proper discharge of its duties and the conduct of its business; it shall define their terms of service and their duties and shall fix their compensation, and may suspend or remove them at pleasure. No member of the school committee, except the mayor, shall, during the term for which he is elected, hold any other office or position the salary or compensation for which is payable out of the city treasury.

Sec. 58.

The school committee, in addition to the powers and duties pertaining by law to school committees, shall have power to provide, when they are necessary, temporary accommodations for school purposes, and shall have the control of all school buildings and of the grounds connected therewith, and the power to make all repairs, the expenditures for which are made from the regular appropriation for the school department, except as is otherwise provided herein.

Sec. 59.

No site for a school building shall be acquired by said city unless the approval of the site by the school committee is first obtained. No plans for the construction of or alterations in a school building shall be accepted, and no work shall be begun on the construction or alteration of a school building, unless the approval of the school committee therefor is first obtained. Nothing herein contained shall require such approval for the making of ordinary repairs.

VACANCIES.

Sec. 60.

If there be a vacancy, by failure to elect or otherwise, in the municipal council, the council shall, by its remaining members, call a special city election to fill the vacancy or vacancies for the unexpired term or terms; except that if such vacancy or vacancies occur less than four months prior to the annual city election, the municipal council shall, by its remaining members, fill such vacancy or vacancies for the unexpired term or terms respectively. A person elected to fill any such vacancy shall, before entering upon the duties of his office, take oath before the city clerk or a justice of the peace faithfully to perform the same.

Sec. 61.

Upon the death, resignation or absence of the mayor, or upon his inability to perform the duties of his office, the president of the municipal council shall perform them, and if he also is absent, or unable from any cause to perform said duties, they shall be performed by such member of the municipal council as it may, from time to time, elect, until the mayor or president of the municipal council is able to attend to said duties, or until the vacancy is filled, as hereinbefore provided. The person upon whom such duties devolve shall be called "Acting Mayor," and, except as is otherwise provided in this act, shall possess the powers of mayor, but only in matters not admitting of delay.

Sec. 62.

If there is a vacancy in the school committee, by failure to elect or otherwise, the mayor shall call a joint convention of the municipal council and the school committee, at which the mayor, if present, shall preside, and the vacancy shall, by vote of a majority of all the members of the two bodies, be filled by the election of a member to serve for the remainder of the municipal year. At the next annual municipal election thereafter a member shall be elected by the qualified voters of the city, to serve for the remainder of the unexpired term of the member whose office is vacant.

RECALL.

Sec. 63.

The holder of any elective office may be removed at any time by the voters qualified to vote at city elections, and the procedure to effect his removal shall be as follows:

A petition signed by a number of such voters equal to at least twenty-five per cent. of the aggregate number of votes cast for candidates for mayor at the last preceding annual election at which a mayor was elected, demanding an election of a successor to the person sought to be removed, shall be filed in the office of the city clerk. Such petition shall contain a general statement of the grounds upon which the removal is sought. It need not be on one paper, but may consist of several distinct papers, each containing the said demand and substantially upon the same grounds, and all papers containing the said demand and statement which, in any one day, shall be filed at the office of the city clerk, shall be deemed parts of the same petition. Every signer shall add to his signature his place of residence, giving the street and street number, if any. One signer of every such paper shall make oath upon his information and belief, before a notary public, or a justice of the peace, that the statements therein made are true, and that each signature to such paper is the genuine signature of the person whose name it purports to be. Within ten days after the date of the filing of such petition, the city clerk, with the assistance of the registrars of voters, shall examine the petition to ascertain whether or not it is signed by the requisite number of voters, as above prescribed, and shall attach to said petition his certificate, showing the result of his examination. If, from the city clerk's certificate the petition appears not to be signed by the requisite number of voters, it may be supplemented, within ten days after the date of such certificate, by other papers, signed and sworn to as aforesaid, and all other papers containing a like demand and statement, and signed and sworn to as aforesaid, shall be deemed supplemental to the original petition. The city clerk shall within ten days after the expiration of the time allowed for filing the supplementary petition make a like examination of such petition, if any is filed, and shall attach thereto a new certificate, and, if it appears from such new certificate that the petition is still insufficient as to the number of signers as aforesaid it shall be returned to the person or persons filing the same, without prejudice, however, to the filing of a new petition to the same effect. If the petition, as originally filed or as supplemented, shall be certified by the city clerk to be sufficient, he shall present the same to the municipal council without delay, and the municipal council shall call the election so demanded, and shall fix a date for holding the same, which shall be not less than sixty nor more than seventy days after the date when the petition was presented by the city clerk to the municipal council. The municipal council shall make or cause to be made all arrangements for holding such election, and the same shall be held and conducted, returns thereof made and the results thereof declared in all respects as in the case of other city elections. The successor of any person removed shall hold office during the unexpired term of his predecessor.

Any person sought to be removed may be a candidate at such election, and unless he requests otherwise in writing the city clerk shall place his name on the official ballots without nomination. The person receiving the highest number of votes shall be declared elected. If some person other than the incumbent receives the highest number of votes, the incumbent shall thereupon be deemed to be removed from office. In case a person, other than the incumbent, receiving the highest number of votes shall fail to make oath before the city clerk or a justice of the peace, within thirty days after his election, faithfully to perform the duties of the office, the office shall be deemed vacant. If the incumbent receives the highest number of votes, he shall continue in office until the end of the term which he was serving at the time of such election, unless sooner removed therefrom by new and like proceedings. The name of no candidate other than the person sought to be removed shall be printed on the official ballots to be used at such election, unless such candidates be nominated as hereinbefore provided at a preliminary election.

INITIATIVE.

Sec. 64.

If a petition, signed by a number of the voters of said city, qualified to vote at city elections, equal to at least twenty-five per cent. of the aggregate number of votes cast for the candidates for mayor at the last preceding annual city election at which a mayor was elected, and requesting the municipal council to pass any measure therein set forth or referred to, shall be filed in the office of the city clerk, the municipal council, provided said measure be one which it has a legal right to pass, shall,

(a) Pass said measure without alteration, within twenty days after the attachment of the city clerk's certificate of sufficiency to such petition, or

(b) Forthwith, after the expiration of twenty days after the attachment of the said certificate of sufficiency to the petition, call a special election, unless an annual city election is held within ninety days after the attachment of the certificate of sufficiency; and at such special election, or annual city election, if one is so to be held, submit said measure without alteration to the voters of the city qualified as aforesaid. The date of said election shall be fixed as provided by section sixty-three.

If, however, a petition like the above described petition, and signed by a number of qualified voters equal to at least ten per cent. but less than twenty-five per cent. of the aggregate number of votes cast as aforesaid, is filed as aforesaid the municipal council shall

(c) Pass the measure therein set forth or referred to, without alteration, within twenty days after such attachment of the certificate of sufficiency, or

(d) Submit the same to the qualified voters of the city at the next annual city election.

The votes upon the said measure at an annual city election or at a special election shall be taken by ballot in answer to the question, "Shall the measure (stating the nature of the same) be passed?" which shall be printed on the ballots after the list of candidates, if there be any. If a majority of the qualified voters voting on the proposed measure shall vote in favor thereof, it shall thereupon become a valid and binding measure of the city, and no such measure passed as aforesaid by the municipal council, upon petition as aforesaid, or which shall be adopted as aforesaid at any such annual city election or special election, shall be repealed or amended except by the qualified voters of the city at an annual city election or special election. Any number of measures requested by petition, as aforesaid, may be voted upon at the same election, in accordance with the provisions of this section. The municipal council may submit a proposition for the repeal of any such measure, or for amendment thereof, to be voted upon at any succeeding annual city election; and should such proposition as submitted receive a majority of the votes cast thereon at such election, the measure shall thereby be repealed or amended accordingly. The vote upon such repeal or amendment at the annual city election shall be taken by ballot in answer to the question, "Shall the measure (stating the nature of the same) be repealed or amended (stating the nature of the amendment)?" which shall be printed on the ballots after the list of candidates, if there be any. Whenever any such measure or proposition is required by this act to be submitted at any election as aforesaid, the city clerk shall cause the same to be published once in each of the daily newspapers published in said city; such publication to be not more than twenty nor less than five days before the submission of the measure or proposition to be voted on. Petitions under the provisions of this section may consist of one or more distinct papers. In each of such papers the measure, the passage of which is requested, shall be set forth or referred to, and all such papers filed in any one day in the office of the city clerk shall be deemed to be parts of the same petition. Such petitions shall be signed, sworn to as to signatures, examined, re-examined, presented to the municipal council, shall have the city clerk's certificate of sufficiency or insufficiency attached thereto, and may be supplemented, in the same manner as petitions filed under section sixty-three. Any measure, passed under the provisions of this section by the municipal council, or by the voters, may prescribe such penalty for its violation as the municipal council, after this act takes effect, shall have a right to affix to a like measure for a breach thereof.

REFERENDUM.

Sec. 65.

If, during the ten days next following the passage of any measure by the municipal council, a petition, signed by a number of voters of said city, registered to vote at city elections, equal to at least twenty-five per cent. of the aggregate number of votes cast for candidates for mayor at the last preceding annual city election at which a mayor was elected, and protesting against the passage of such measure shall be filed in the office of the city clerk, such measure shall be suspended from going into operation, and it shall be the duty of the municipal council to reconsider the same, and if it is not entirely repealed the municipal council shall submit it, as is provided in sub-division (b) of section sixty-four to the registered voters of the city, and the said measure shall not go into effect or become operative unless a majority of the voters, qualified as aforesaid, voting on the same shall vote in favor thereof. The vote upon such a measure at an annual city election or special election shall be taken by ballot in answer to the question, "Shall the measure (stating the nature of the same) take effect?" which shall be printed on the ballot after the list of candidates, if there be any. Petitions under the provisions of this section may consist of one or more distinct papers. In each of such papers the measure, the passage of which is protested, shall be set forth or referred to, and all such papers filed in any one day shall be deemed to be parts of the same petition. Such petitions shall be signed, sworn to as to signatures, examined, re-examined, presented to the municipal council, shall have the city clerk's certificate of sufficiency or insufficiency attached thereto, and may be supplemented in the same manner as petitions filed under section sixty-three.

Sec. 66.

It shall not be necessary for the validity of any petition or statement provided for or required by the provisions of this act that any signer thereof add to his signature any residence other than the name of the street, and street number, if there be any, at which he resides at the time of signing.

Sec. 67.

All acts and parts of acts inconsistent herewith are hereby repealed: *provided, however*, that this repeal shall not affect any act done, or any right accruing or accrued or established, or any suit or proceeding begun in any civil case before the time when such appeal takes effect, and that no offences committed and no penalties or forfeitures incurred under the acts or parts of acts hereby repealed shall be affected by such repeal; and *provided, also*, that all persons who, at the time when said repeal takes effect shall hold any office under said acts shall continue to hold the same, except as is otherwise provided herein, and *provided, also*, that all by-laws and ordinances of the city of Lynn in force at the time when said repeal takes effect, and not inconsistent with the provisions of this act, shall continue in force until the same are repealed or amended, and all officers elected under such by-laws and ordinances shall continue in office, except as is otherwise provided herein.

ACCEPTANCE BY VOTERS.

Sec. 68.

If Part I. of this act be accepted, it shall take effect upon its acceptance for the annual city election to be held on the second Tuesday of December in the year nineteen hundred and ten, for the preliminary election for nominations, to be held, under the provisions of this Part, on the third Tuesday preceding the aforesaid annual city election, for the statements of candidates and petitions accompanying statements of candidates to be filed by persons whose names are to be printed on the official ballots to be used at such preliminary election, and for all things which appertain and relate to said annual city election, preliminary election, statements of candidates and petitions accompanying statements of candidates; and, it shall take effect for all other purposes at ten o'clock in the forenoon on the first Monday of January, in the year nineteen hundred and eleven.

PART II.

[This portion of the Act proposed an alternative form which was rejected by the voters in favor of the proposals contained in Part I.]

PART III.

Section 1.

This act shall be submitted to the registered male voters of the city of Lynn at a special election to be held for that purpose on the second Tuesday in October in the year nineteen hundred and ten. The provisions relative to marking the ballots, directions for voting and endorsement of ballot set forth in section two hundred and thirty-one of chapter five hundred and sixty of the acts of nineteen hundred and seven and acts in amendment thereof shall apply to said special election. At said special election the voters shall be entitled to vote primarily on the following question: "Shall the present charter be repealed?" and secondarily on the following question: If the present charter of the city of Lynn is repealed, shall the new charter of said city be:

"Plan 1: A commission to consist of five members",

or

"Plan 2: A mayor, and a city council of eleven members."

If on a majority of the ballots cast at said special election, the votes shall be for a repeal of the present charter of the city of Lynn, the plan receiving the larger number of votes on the secondary question shall be adopted as the charter for the city of Lynn. Plan 1 shall include all of the provisions of Part I of this act and if said Plan 1 is adopted, rt II of this act shall be inoperative. Plan 2 shall include of the provisions of Part II of this act and if said Plan 2 adopted, Part I of this act shall be inoperative. If on any llot, the voter shall vote for both Plan 1 and Plan 2, so ich of said ballot as refers to the secondary question shall t be counted.

c. 2.

So much of this act as provides for the holding of the special election as set forth in the above section shall take effect upon its passage. If at said special election the vote is for a repeal of the present charter of the city of Lynn, the provisions of said alternative plan (so) adopted for holding the city election shall then take effect and said alternative plan so adopted shall be in full force and effect upon the first Monday in January, nineteen hundred and eleven.

[Approved June 10, 1910.]

Texts of Proposed Charters

CHARTER OF BIRMINGHAM, ALABAMA*

(AN ACT TO PROVIDE AND CREATE A COMMISSION FORM OF MUNICIPAL GOVERNMENT AND TO ESTABLISH SAME IN ALL THE CITIES OF ALABAMA WHICH NOW HAVE OR WHICH MAY HEREAFTER HAVE A POPULATION OF AS MUCH AS ONE HUNDRED THOUSAND PEOPLE, ACCORDING TO THE LAST FEDERAL CENSUS.)

Be it enacted by the Legislature of Alabama:

Sec. 1.

All cities of the State of Alabama which have a population of as much as one hundred thousand people, according to the last Federal census, or which hereafter shall have such population according to any such census that may be taken hereafter, shall become organized under the commission form of government according to the terms of this Act.

Sec. 2.

In all cities of the State of Alabama which have such population, according to the last Federal census, a commission form of government shall be established according to the terms of this act within thirty days from its passage. Two persons shall be appointed by the Governor to hold office as Commissioners of each of said cities, one of said Commissioners to hold office for a term of three years and until the first Monday in November, 1914, and until his successor shall be elected and shall qualify as hereinafter provided, the other of said Commissioners to hold office for a term of four years and until the first Monday in November, 1915, and until his successor shall be elected and shall qualify as hereinafter provided. The Mayor or chief executive of every such city at the time this act shall be approved shall be and become, as soon as the other Commissioners take office as provided herein, the President of the Board of Commissioners of such city and one of such Commissioners, with the authority and duties hereinafter set forth, holding office for a term of two years and until the first Monday in November, 1913, and until his successor shall be elected and shall qualify as hereinafter provided.

Sec. 3.

In all cities not now having but which shall have a population of as much as one hundred thousand people, according to any Federal census that may be taken hereafter, a commission form of government shall be established according to the terms of this act within thirty days after the result of the taking of said census, showing such population, shall have been announced. Two persons shall be appointed by the Governor to hold office as Commissioners of each such city, one for a term of three years and until the first Monday in November thereafter and until his successor shall be elected and shall qualify as hereinafter provided, and the other for a term of four years and until the first Monday in November thereafter and until his successor shall be elected and shall qualify as hereinafter provided. The Mayor or chief executive of every such city at the time the results of the taking of said census shall be announced shall be and become President of the Board and one of the Commissioners of such city, as soon as the other Commissioners take office, for a term of two years and until the first Monday in November thereafter, and until his successor shall be elected and shall qualify as hereinafter provided.

Sec. 4.

The President and Commissioners provided for in Sections 2 and 3 above shall be known collectively as the Board of Commissioners of the city of .... (the name of said city to be inserted), and shall have the powers and duties hereinafter provided. The two Commissioners first appointed shall qualify for office in the manner prescribed in Section 12 of this Act, hereinafter set forth, on or before the first Monday of the month following the date of their respective appointments as soon as they shall have qualified for office in any city, then such city shall at that time and thereby be and become organized under the commission form of government provided by this act, and all three of said Commissioners shall forthwith take office and enter upon their duties.

Sec. 5.

The President of the Board of Commissioners and Commissioners of said city, to be known as the Board of Commissioners of said city, as provided, shall be municipal officers only, and shall have, possess and exercise only the municipal powers, legislative, executive and judicial, possessed and exercised by the Mayor and Board of Aldermen and Board of Police Commissioners, and any and all other boards, commissions and officers of such city of any and of every sort whatsoever except whatsoever power they may possess expressly or impliedly as State officers; and all such boards, commissions and officers except those provided for by this Act shall then and thereby be abolished, and the terms of office of any and all such officers or officials shall then and thereby cease. Said Board of Commissioners shall not have, possess or exercise any legislative, executive, judicial or administrative powers of the State or county, nor shall the offices held by them be State offices; provided, however, that the office of Commissioner, the term of which under the provisions of this Act expires on the first Monday in November, 1915, is and shall be a judicial office, and the Commissioner appointed thereto, and hereafter elected thereto, is clothed with full and ample power to administer justice under the ordinances of said city only, and to administer judicially the ordinances of said city only, and the legislative and executive powers hereinabove conferred upon the Commissioner whose term of office expires as aforesaid shall be an incident merely to said judicial office, and shall be confined only to municipal matters. Such city shall continue its existence as a body corporate under the name of "city of .... (inserting the name of said city). It shall continue to be subject to all the duties and obligations then pertaining to or incumbent upon it as a municipal corporation not inconsistent with the provisions of this Act, and shall continue to enjoy all the rights, immunities, powers, privileges and franchises then

* This law is, in form, a general one, applicable to all cities of over one hundred thousand inhabitants. Birmingham, however, is the only city in the state of this size.

enjoyed by it, as well as those that may thereafter be granted to it, not inconsistent with the provisions of this Act. All laws governing such city and not inconsistent with the provisions of this Act shall apply to and govern said city after it shall become organized under the commission form of government provided by this Act. All by-laws, ordinances and resolutions lawfully passed and in force in any such city under its former organizations not inconsistent with the provisions of this act shall remain in force until altered or repealed according to the provisions of this Act. The territorial limits of such city shall remain the same as under its former organization, and all rights and property of every description which were vested in it shall vest in it under the organization herein provided for as though there had been no change in the organization of said city; and no right or liability, either in favor of or against it, and no suit or prosecution of any kind shall be affected by such change unless otherwise expressly provided for by the terms of this Act. All employes of said city and all officials except those whose terms of office are abolished by this Act shall continue in office until otherwise provided by the said Board of Commissioners of said city. Provided, however, that Boards of Education existing in such cities shall not be affected by the provisions of this Act, except that where the members of the Boards of Education of such city had previously been elected by the Board of Aldermen of such cities, such Boards shall after this Act becomes effective be elected by the Board of Commissioners of such city.

Sec. 6.

Every city organized under the form of government provided for by this Act shall be governed and managed by the Board of Commissioners provided for herein. Each and every officer and employe of said city, except health officer and such persons as may be employed by him to enforce quarantine, other than the said President and Commissioners, shall be selected and employed by the said Board, or under its direction, and all salaries and wages paid by said city, except as otherwise provided by the terms of this Act, shall be fixed by said Board. The Commissioners shall prescribe and may at any time change the powers, duties and titles of all subordinate officers and employes of said city, except the title of city health officer, all of whom shall hold office and be removable at the pleasure of the Board of Commissioners. The powers and duties in such cities shall be distributed into and among three departments, as follows: (1) Department of public justice; (2) department of streets, parks, city and public property, and city and public improvements; (3) department of accounts, finances and public affairs. The powers and duties pertaining to each of said departments shall be fixed by the said Board of Commissioners, and altered from time to time as they may deem best, and one of the members of said Board shall be so assigned to take charge of each such department, and shall as head of such department exercise the duties and powers so provided by said Board, and said assignment may be changed at any time by a majority of said Board. Provided, however, that the Commissioner appointed to fill the office of Commissioner the term of which expires on the first Monday of November, 1915, and hereafter elected to said office the term of which expires as aforesaid, shall during his term of office exercise at all times the duties required by the Department of Public Justice.

Sec. 6½.

Health and quarantine matters shall be administered in accordance with the established public health system of the State and such health laws as are now in force, or may hereafter be enacted, and also in accordance with such ordinances as are now in force or may be hereafter legally enacted by the Commissioners.

Sec. 7.

Said Board of Commissioners shall hold regular meetings on Tuesday of each and every week at some regular hour to be fixed by said Board from time to time and publicly announced by it; and it may hold such adjourned, called and other meetings as may be necessary or convenient. The President of the Board when present shall preside at the meetings of said Board, but shall have no veto power. Two members of said Board shall constitute a quorum for the transaction of any and every business to be done by said Board, and for the exercise of any and every power conferred upon it, and the affirmative vote of two members of said Board shall be necessary and sufficient for the passage of any resolution, by-laws or ordinance, or the transaction of any business of any sort by said Board, or the exercise of any of the powers conferred upon it by the terms of this Act, or that may hereafter be conferred upon it. This provision shall not be construed, however, so as to prevent the said Board from delegating or assigning to one or more of its members, or to such boards, commissions, officers or employes as may be created or selected by it, the performance of such executive and judicial duties and powers as may be necessary or convenient providing the same is done by resolution, by-law or ordinance duly enacted according to the terms of this Act. All meetings of said Board at which any person not a city officer is present shall be open to the public. No resolution, by-law or ordinance granting any franchise, appropriating any money for any purpose, providing for any public improvements enacting any regulation concerning the public comfort, the public safety or public health or of any other general or permanent nature except a proclamation of quarantine shall be enacted except at a regular or adjourned public meeting of said Board. Every motion, resolution or ordinance introduced at any and every such meeting shall be reduced to writing and read before any vote thereon shall be taken, and the yeas and nays thereon shall be recorded. A record of the proceedings of every such meeting shall be kept in a well bound book, and every resolution or ordinance passed by the Board of Commissioners must be recorded in such book, and the record of the proceedings of the meeting be signed by at least two of the Commissioners before the action taken shall be effective. Such record shall be kept available for inspection by all citizens of each city at all reasonable times.

Sec. 8.

No resolution, by-law or ordinance granting to any person firm or corporation any franchise, lease or right to use the streets, public highways, thoroughfares or public property o[f] any city organized under the provisions of this Act, either in under, upon, along, through or over same shall take effect an[d] be enforced until thirty days after the final enactment o[f] same by the Board of Commissioners and publication of said resolution, by-law or ordinance in full once a week for three consecutive weeks in some daily newspaper published in said city, which publication shall be made at the expense of the persons, firm or corporation applying for said grant. Pending the passage of any such resolution, by-law or ordinance, or during the time intervening between its final passage and the expiration of the thirty days during which publication shall be made as above provided, the legally qualified voters of said city may, by written petition or petitions addressed to said Board of Commissioners, object to such grant, and if during said period such written petition or petitions signed by at least a thousand legally qualified voters of such city shall be filed with said Board of Commissioners, said Board shall forthwith order an election, at which election the legally qualified voters of said city shall vote for or against the proposed grant as set forth in the said by-law, resolution or ordinance. In the call for said election the said resolution, by-law or ordinance making said grant shall be published at length and in full at the expense of the city in at least two newspapers published in said city by one publication. If at such election the majority of the votes cast shall be in favor of said ordinance and the making of said proposed grant the same shall thereupon become effective; but if a majority of the votes so cast shall be against the passage of the said resolution, by-law or ordinance, and against the making of said grant, said by-law, resolution or ordinance shall not become effective, nor shall it confer any rights, powers or privileges of any kind, and it shall be the duty of the said Board of Commissioners after such result of said election shall be determined to pass a resolution or ordinance to that effect. No grant of any franchise or lease or right of user, or any other right in, under, upon, along, through or over the streets, public highways, thoroughfares or public highways property of any such city shall be made or given, nor shall any such rights of any kind whatever be conferred upon any person, firm or corporation, except by resolution or ordinance, duly passed by the Board of Commissioners at some regular or adjourned public meeting and published as above provided for in this section; nor shall any extension or enlargement of any such rights or powers previously granted be made or given except in the manner and subject to all the conditions herein provided for as to the original grant of same. It is expressly provided, however, that the provisions of this section shall not apply to the grant of sidetrack or switching privileges to any railroad or street car company for the purpose of reaching and affording railway connections and switch privileges to the owners or users of any industrial plant, store or warehouse; provided, further, that said sidetrack or switch shall not extend for a greater distance than one thousand three hundred and twenty (1,320) feet.

Sec. 9.

In every city which shall become organized according to the provisions of this Act an election shall be held on the third Monday in September after the expiration of two years after it shall have become so organized and on the same date of every succeeding year for the election of the President or other members of the Board of Commissioners whose term shall expire in that year, the President or Commissioner, as the case may be, then elected shall hold office for a term of three years from the first Monday in November of said year and until his successor shall be elected and shall qualify for office. Any person desiring to become a candidate at any election, except those by the Commission, which may be held according to the terms of this Act, for the office of President of the Board or other Commissioner to be elected may become such candidate by filing in the office of the Judge of Probate of the county in which said city is situated a statement of such candidacy accompanied by affidavit taken and certified by said Judge of Probate or by a notary public that such person is duly qualified to hold the office for which he desires to become a candidate. Such statement shall be filed at least twenty-one days before the day set for such election, and shall be substantially in the following form: "State of Alabama, ..., County. I, the undersigned, being first duly sworn, depose and say that I am a citizen of the city of ...., in said State and reside at .... in said city; that I desire to become a candidate for the office of .... in said city for the term of .... years at the election for said office, to be held on the .... day of September next; that I am duly qualified to hold said office if elected thereto, and I hereby request that my name be printed upon the official ballot at said election. (Signed) .... Subscribed and sworn to before me by said .... on this ... day of ...., 19.., and filed in this office for record on said day. .... Judge of Probate." Said statement shall be accompanied by a petition signed by at least five hundred persons who shall be qualified to vote at said coming election, requesting that such person become a candidate for said office at said election. The signers to said petition shall set forth their names in full and their residence addresses, and said petition shall be substantially like the following form: "We, the undersigned, duly qualified electors of the city of ...., and residing at the places set opposite our respective names, do hereby request that the name of .... be placed upon the official ballot as a candidate for the office of .... in said city for the term of .... years at the election to be held in this city on the .... day of September next. We further state that we know said .... to possess the qualifications necessary for said office (and to be, in our judgment, a fit and proper person to hold said office). Witness our hands on this the .... day of ...., 19..." At every such election all ballots to be used by the voters shall be printed and prepared by the said city and at its expense, and shall contain the names of all candidates placed in alphabetical order, directly underneath the words, "For President of the Board of Commissioners," "For Commissioner for the Term of .... Years," as the case may be. No name shall appear upon said ballot as a candidate for election except the names of such persons as have become candidates according to the provisions as above set forth, and no ballot shall be used at any such election except the official ballot prepared by the city. Whenever it shall happen that more than one Commissioner is to be elected at any election the candidate shall specify in the statement filed as above provided whether he is a candidate for the long or short term, and this shall be shown on the ballots prepared for such election.

Sec. 10.

At every election each voter shall vote for only one candidate for each office, and the candidate receiving the highest number of votes for such office shall be elected thereto, provided he receive a majority of all the votes cast for such office. In case no one of such candidates shall receive a majority of all such votes cast for the office for which he is a candidate another election shall be held on the same day of the following week for said office, at which the two candidates receiving the highest number of votes for said office shall be voted for. The candidate receiving the highest number of votes at such election shall be declared elected.

Sec. 11.

The President and other Commissioners provided for by this Act shall be not less than twenty-five years of age at the time of their election and shall be duly qualified electors of such city at the time of their election and they shall be elected by the vote of the legally qualified voters of such city. In case any person after he shall have been elected and duly qualified as such President of the Board or other Commissioner shall be declared ineligible to hold such office, a successor shall be chosen, as in case of vacancy caused by death, resignation or any other such cause.

Sec. 12.

Every person who shall be elected or appointed to the office of President of the Board or other Commissioner in any city organized according to the provisions of this Act shall on or before the first Monday of the month succeeding his election or appointment qualify by making oath that he is eligible for said office and will execute the duties of same according to the best of his knowledge and ability. Said oath shall be administered by the retiring Mayor or President of the Board of Commissioners of such city or a notary public. The term of office of every such President of the Board and of the other Commissioners shall begin on the first Monday of November succeeding the election, except as may be otherwise expressly provided by this Act.

Sec. 13.

The qualified voters of any city organized according to the terms of this Act may at any time file with the Board of Commissioners of such city at any regular meeting of said Board a petition or petitions asking for the resignation of the President of the Board or of any Commissioner of said city. Such petitions shall contain a general statement of the grounds upon which the removal of said official is requested, and each signer shall add to his signature, and opposite thereto, his residence address. In case such petitions shall be signed by at least three thousand voters duly qualified to vote for successor to said officer, and said officer shall not, on or before the next regular meeting of said Board, resign from office, then said Board at such meeting shall order an election to be held not less than thirty days nor more than forty days from the date of said meeting, at which election a successor to such officer to hold office for his unexpired term shall be voted for. At such election the person sought to be removed from office shall be a candidate to succeed himself, and his name shall be placed upon the official ballot without any affirmative action on his part; notice of such election shall be given by publication once a week for three successive weeks in some newspaper published in said city. The person who shall be elected to such office shall hold same for the unexpired term thereof, and if the person so elected be the incumbent whose removal has been requested, then he shall continue in office as though such petition had not been filed or such election held. Should no candidate at such election receive a majority of the entire votes cast under the provisions of this section another election shall be held on the same day of the following week for such office, at which the two candidates receiving the highest number of votes for said office shall be voted for. The candidate receiving the highest number of votes at such election shall be declared elected. Should the provisions as to the recall of Commissioners contained in Section 13 of this Act or should any other section or provision of this Act be held to be void or unconstitutional it shall not affect or destroy the validity of any other section or provision hereof which is not itself void or unconstitutional.

Sec. 14.

Whenever any vacancies shall occur in the office of President of the Board or other Commissioner of any city organized under the terms of this Act then his successor shall be elected by the two remaining members of the Board of Commissioners of such city. Every person who shall be elected to the office of President of the Board or other Commissioner of any such city under the provisions of this section or of the preceding section shall qualify for office as soon as practicable after such election, and shall be clothed with the duties and responsibilities and powers of such office immediately upon such qualification. He shall hold office for the unexpired term of his predecessor.

Sec. 15.

Each member of the Board of Commissioners of cities organized under the terms of this Act shall receive a salary of seven thousand dollars ($7,000.00) per annum, and at that rate for every fraction of a year during which he shall hold office. Such salary shall be paid in monthly installments at the end of every calendar month during which he shall hold office, said installments to be in payment for the portion of the month during which he shall hold office at the rate thus provided.

Sec. 16.

The employes of cities organized under this Act shall be selected by the Commissioners solely on account of their fitness and without regard to their political affiliations. It shall be unlawful to hold party caucuses or primaries for the purpose of nominating any employe to be selected by such Commissioners, and any person who shall solicit or accept a party nomination for any office to be filled by said Commissioners shall be thereby rendered ineligible for such office or for any other office under said city for a period of one year thereafter.

Sec. 17.

It shall be unlawful for any candidate for office, or any officer in such city, directly or indirectly, to give or promise any person or persons any office, position, employment, benefit or anything of value, for the purpose of influencing or obtaining the political support, aid or vote of any person or persons. Every Commissioner elected by popular vote in any such city shall within thirty days after qualifying file with the Judge of Probate of the county, and the same shall be published at least once in a newspaper of general circulation in such city, his sworn itemized statement of all his election and campaign expenses, and by whom such funds were contributed. Any violation of the provisions of this section shall be a misdemeanor punishable by fine of not more than three hundred dollars and be a ground for removal from office.

Sec. 18.
No officer or employe elected or appointed in any such city shall be interested, directly or indirectly, in any contract for work or material, or the profits thereof, or services to be furnished or performed for the city; and no such officer or employe shall be interested, directly or indirectly, in any contract for work or materials, or the profits thereof, or services to be furnished or performed for any person, firm or corporation operating interurben railway, street railway, gas works, electric light or power plant, heating plant, telegraph line or telephone exchange within the territorial limits of said city. No such Commissioner or other official of such city shall be interested in or any employe or attorney of any corporation operating any public service utility within said city. No such officer or employe shall accept or receive, directly or indirectly, from any person, firm or corporation operating within the territorial limits of said city any interurban railway, railway, street railway, gas works, water works, electric light or power plant, heating plant, telegraph line or telephone exchange, or any other business using or operating under a public franchise any frank, free pass, free ticket, or free service, or accept or receive, directly or indirectly, from any such person, firm or corporation any gift or other thing of value, or any service upon terms more favorable than are granted to the public generally. Any violation of the provisions of this section shall be a misdemeanor, and upon conviction thereof the guilty person shall be punished by a fine of not less than one hundred nor more than three hundred dollars, and may be imprisoned in the county jail for not more than ninety days. Every such contract or agreement shall be void. Such prohibition of free transportation shall not apply to policemen or firemen in uniform, nor to policemen in the discharge of their duty, nor shall any free service to city officials heretofore provided by any franchise or ordinance be affected by this section. Any officer or employe of such city, who, by solicitation or otherwise, shall exert his influence, directly or indirectly, to influence other officers or employes of such city to favor any particular person or candidate for office as President of the Board of Commissioners, or Commissioner of said city, or who shall in any manner contribute money, labor or other valuable thing to aid in the election of any person as President of the Board or Commissioner of said city, shall be guilty of a misdemeanor, and upon conviction shall be punished by a fine not exceeding three hundred dollars, and may also be imprisoned in the county jail for a term not exceeding thirty days.

Sec. 19.
The Commission shall each month print in pamphlet form a detailed statement of all receipts and expenses of the city and a summary of its proceedings during the preceding month, and furnish printed copies thereof to the daily newspapers of the city and to persons who apply therefor. At the end of each year the Commission shall cause a full and complete examination of all the books and accounts of the city to be made by competent accountants, and shall publish the result of such examination in the manner above provided for publication of statements of monthly expenditures. And the Governor is authorized at any time to have all the books and accounts of such city examined by a State examiner of public accounts, the cost of such examination to be paid by such city upon the presentation to the President of the Board of Commissioners of such city of a duly verified statement of such expenses made by such examiner of public accounts, approved by the Governor.

Sec. 20.
Any person offering to give a bribe either in money or other consideration to any voter for the purpose of influencing his vote at any election provided in this Act, or any voter entitled to vote at any such election receiving and accepting such bribe or other consideration, any person making false answer to any of the provisions of this Act relative to his qualifications to vote at said election, any person wilfully voting or offering to vote at such election who has not been a resident of this State for two years next preceding said election, or who is not twenty-one years of age, or is not a citizen of the United States, or knowing himself not to be a qualified voter of such precinct where he offers to vote, any person knowingly procuring, aiding or abetting any violation hereof shall be deemed guilty of a misdemeanor, and upon conviction shall be fined a sum of not less than one hundred dollars nor more than five hundred dollars, and may be imprisoned in the county jail for not less than ten nor more than ninety days.

Sec. 21.
Any employe of any such city who solicits support for any candidate for Commissioner, or any such employe who shall endeavor to influence any voter to vote for or against any candidate for Commissioner, shall be deemed guilty of a misdemeanor, and on conviction shall be fined not less than ten nor more than fifty dollars, and may also be imprisoned in the county jail for not more than ten days. Justices of the peace and judges of the inferior courts shall within their respective territories have jurisdiction of this offense.

Sec. 22.
All general laws of this State regulating and prescribing the conduct of municipal elections and the qualifications and registration of voters thereat shall apply to elections hereunder, except so far as expressly modified herein.

Sec. 23.
The Judge of the Probate Court of the county in which are located the cities covered by this Act shall record in a well bound book kept for that purpose all papers required to be filed with him under the terms of this Act, and shall receive therefor the compensation allowed by law for recording deeds.

Sec. 24.
It shall be unlawful for any candidate for Commissioner or for President of the Board, or for any other person in his behalf, to hire or pay, or agree to pay, any person to solicit votes at the polls in election, and unlawful for any person to

accept such hire or make such contract to pay, to solicit votes for the President of the Board or other Commissioner; and any person violating this section shall be guilty of a misdemeanor, and may be punished by fine not to exceed five hundred dollars for each offense, and the candidate violating this section shall thereby be disqualified for and rendered ineligible to the office sought.

Sec. 25.

No candidate for the office of President of the Board or other Commissioner can lawfully expend more than three thousand dollars ($3,000.00) of his own funds and the funds contributed by others in aiding his candidacy in any one election, a run off to be treated as a separate election. Any person violating the provisions of this section shall thereby be disqualified from holding said office, if successful, and his election may be contested on that ground.

Sec. 26.

The petitions provided by this Act may be by a number of separate instruments as well as by one instrument. No person but a qualified voter shall sign any petition provided for by this Act, and no person shall sign the name of another to any such petition, whether with or without authority; and no person shall sign more than one separate instrument as a petition for any single purpose herein provided. Each person signing such petition shall make affidavit thereon truthfully stating that he is a qualified voter under the laws of Alabama, and in said affidavit shall truthfully state his age, color, address, and whether or not he has paid all of the poll taxes required to be paid under the laws of Alabama to entitle him to vote at such time. Any violation of foregoing provisions of this section shall constitute a misdemeanor punishable by fine not to exceed three hundred dollars. No qualified voter who has signed any petition provided for herein can withdraw his signature. All petitions provided for herein must bear the certificate of the Judge of Probate of the county in which such city is situated that it has the number of signatures required by law of qualified voters, and it shall be the duty said Probate Judge to hear and determine all questions as the genuineness of signatures and the qualifications of vote signing such petition before giving such certificate; and su certificate of the Probate Judge shall be final and conclusiv Should said Probate Judge decide that any such petition w not signed by the required number of qualified voters it sha be his duty to return said petition with the written stateme of the details of its insufficiency to the persons presenti such petition, and such persons shall have ten days thereaft to have said petition signed as required by law, at the end which time they shall again present such petition to t Probate Judge for re-examination. For his services in passi on any such petition the Probate Judge shall receive from t person presenting such petition for his examination the co of the clerical work incident thereto and twenty per cent. such amount. Security for the payment of such costs mu be given at the time of the presentation of such petition.

Sec. 27.

Should vacancies exist simultaneously from any cause her inbefore provided for in two commissionerships so as to lea no quorum of said Board to fill same, an election to fill sa vacancies shall be called by the remaining Commissioner, be held not less than twenty nor more than thirty days fro the occurrence of the second vacancy. Notice of said electi and of the time of holding same shall be given by one pu lication at least fifteen days in advance of same in two more newspapers published in said city, at the expense said city. The Commissioners chosen at said election sh qualify as speedily as possible thereafter.

Sec. 28.

All laws and parts of laws, both local and general, in co flict with the provisions of this Act, are expressly repeal This Act shall take effect immediately upon its approval.

[Approved March 31, 1911.]

CHARTER OF SACRAMENTO, CALIFORNIA

(IN PART.)

(See pp. 38019-20)

ARTICLE XXII.

BOARD OF EDUCATION.

Sec. 221.

The Commissioners of the City of Sacramento shall be, ex-officio, members of and shall constitute the Board of Education, and shall hold office for a term of five years from and after the first day of July next succeeding their election; subject, however, to recall and removal from office, as specified herein and by general laws; provided, further, that their tenure of office as members of the Board of Education shall be concurrent with their respective terms as Commissioners of said City.

The Board of Education shall have full charge and control of all matters pertaining to the conduct of all public schools within said city, and shall exercise such powers, and perform such duties, with respect thereto as may be conferred or imposed upon them by law or by ordinance of the city.

The Board shall organize on the first Monday of July after this charter takes effect. It shall elect, from among its members, a President and a Vice-President, and during the absence or disability of the President the Vice-President shall perform his duties and exercise his functions, except as otherwise in this charter expressly provided.

The President shall preside over all meetings thereof and exercise such other powers, and perform such other duties, with respect to the business of the School Department of the city, as are conferred or imposed upon the President of the Board of Education by law or by any ordinance of the city.

The Board shall make, establish and enforce all necessary and proper rules and regulations for the government and progress of the public schools of the city, for the investigation of charges against any person in the employ of the department, and for carrying into effect all laws and ordinances pertaining to the public schools; and shall adopt and enforce an efficiency system and shall make all rules and regulations necessary to carry the same into effect.

The Board shall hold regular meetings at least once in each month and at such times as shall be determined by its rules. Special meetings may be called at any time by the President or by any three members of the Board; provided, however, that notice of such special meetings shall be personally served upon each member of the Board, unless he be absent from the city, not less than twelve hours prior to such meetings. Three members of the Board shall constitute a quorum for the transaction of business, but the affirmative vote of three members shall be necessary to pass or adopt any measure or to transact any other business affecting the public schools of the city.

The Board shall determine the rules of its proceedings; provided, however, that the yeas and nays shall be taken on all questions and entered on the records of the Board.

All meetings of the Board shall be open to the public and its records shall be open to public inspection.

Sec. 222.

Any member or officer of the Board of Education, who shall, while in office, unlawfully or corruptly accept any donation or gratuity in money or of any valuable thing, either directly or indirectly, from or in behalf of any teacher or candidate, or applicant for a position as teacher, upon any pretense whatever, shall be guilty of malfeasance.

Any member of the Board of Education, officer, or other person connected with the School Department, or drawing a salary from the Board of Education, who shall unlawfully or corruptly gain any advantage or benefit from any contract, payments under which are to be made, in whole or in part, from the Public School Fund, or from moneys raised by taxation or otherwise for the support of the public schools, shall be guilty of malfeasance.

Sec. 223.

In case of disaster from fire, flood, wind, riot, earthquake, or public enemy, the Board of Education may incur extraordinary expenditures in excess of the annual limit provided by law and in this charter for the repair, construction, and furnishing of school houses; and the City Commission may, by ordinance, cause to be transferred to the School Fund, from any moneys in any other fund not otherwise appropriated, sufficient moneys to liquidate such extraordinary expenditure.

Sec. 224.

As soon as may be practicable after organization, the Board of Education shall elect a Superintendent of Schools and such other assistants, clerks and employes as may be necessary, prescribe their duties and fix and order paid their compensation.

Sec. 225.

For the first two years of their service in the School Department of the city, teachers shall be subject to annual election. After two years' service, they may be elected for a term of three years. In the event that the Board of Education shall determine not to re-elect any teacher employed in the public schools of this city, the Board must, not later than two months prior to the expiration of the term for which such teacher was employed, serve, or cause to be served, upon such teacher, personally, a notice in writing directed to such teacher and informing such teacher of the intent to dispense with the services of such teacher at the expiration of said term of employment. A record of such service shall be kept in the office of the Board of Education, showing the date when, the place where, and the person by whom such notice was served. In the event that the Board of Education shall fail or neglect to serve such notice as hereinabove provided within the time herein limited, such teacher shall be deemed elected for, and shall serve another year in the same position in the School Department of the city.

ARTICLE XXVII.

RECALL OF ELECTIVE OFFICERS.

Sec. 275.

(1). Every incumbent of an elective office, whether elected by popular vote or appointed to fill a vacancy, shall be subject to removal from office by recall, but no affidavit of intention to circulate a petition for the recall of any incumbent, as hereinafter provided, shall be filed until such incumbent has actually held office under said election or appointment for at least six months. The procedure to effect such removal from office shall be as follows:

(2). A petition signed by qualified electors equal to ten (10) per centum of the total number of electors registered at the last municipal election at which a Commissioner was elected, requesting the calling of an election to determine whether or not the said incumbent of an elective office sought to be removed from office shall be removed from office by recall, shall be addressed to the Commission and presented to the City Clerk. The petition may request that such election shall be held at a special municipal election or at the next general municipal election.

(3). The petition for recall and removal from office shall be substantially as follows:

[Form of Certificate.]

(4). Each certificate must be on a separate sheet of paper and must contain the name of but one signer, who must make oath before a notary public or a verification deputy as to the truth and correctness of the statements made in such certificate.

These certificates shall be fastened together, as provided herein for petitions of nomination, except that they shall be bound as near as may be in lots of two hundred and fifty (250) certificates.

Immediately upon the receipt of such petition, the City Clerk shall endorse thereon the time at which said petition was received by him. The City Clerk shall thereupon immediately begin to examine said petition to ascertain whether or not it conforms to all the requirements of this charter.

Within ten days after such presentation he must finally determine whether or not it so conforms, and shall forthwith attach to said petition his certificate showing the result of his examination, and forthwith send by registered mail a copy of said certificate to the person named as the person to whom said petition shall be returned in accordance with this section. If the petition be found not to conform to the requirements of this charter, such certificate of the City Clerk shall designate as to the petition and as to each individual certificate included therein and found to be defective, the defect therein. If by said certificate of the City Clerk the petition is shown to be insufficient, it may be amended by the presentation within fifteen days after the date of mailing of said certificate by the City Clerk, of an additional recall petition containing additional recall certificates. The City Clerk shall within seven days after the presentation of such additional recall petition make like examination, and determination of the amended petition and attach to it a like certificate and mail a copy as aforesaid, and if his certificate shall show the amended petition to be insufficient, or if no additional recall petition shall have been presented, the petition shall be returned to the person named as the person to whom the petition is to be returned, and all proceedings and petitions under said affidavit of intention to circulate a petition for the recall of any incumbent, as provided in this section, shall be null and void.

If the City Clerk shall find the said petition or amended petition to conform to the requirements of this charter, he shall indorse his finding upon the said petition or amended petition and immediately file and present the same to the City Commission.

(5). Any signer of a petition for the recall may file with the City Clerk a certified revocation of his signature to such petition. In case said revocation is filed with the City Clerk before the said petition is filed by him, he shall cancel the said signer's signature on said petition.

(6). Before any petition for the recall of an officer is circulated for signatures thereto, an affidavit in triplicate by or on behalf of the person or persons proposing such recall shall be filed with the City Clerk, who shall at once deliver one of the said affidavits to the office of said officer sought to be recalled, and send one by registered mail to the residence of such officer. Said affidavit shall contain: a statement of the intention to circulate a petition for the recall of said officer; a statement in not more than two hundred (200) words giving the grounds for such recall; and the address of the party making the affidavit. Said officer sought to be recalled shall have five (5) days after the filing of such affidavit in which to formulate and send by registered mail to the address of the party making such affidavit a statement in not more than two hundred (200) words justifying said officer's course in office. These reasons for and against the recall of said officer shall be printed as a part of each individual certificate forming a part of the petition.

No original petition for the recall of any officer upon the grounds set forth in such affidavit shall be presented to the City Clerk later than forty (40) days after the filing of such affidavit.

(7). If the officer sought to be removed by recall shall not resign from office within five days after the petition is filed by the City Clerk, and if the petition requests a special election, the City Commission shall after due notice cause a special election to be held within not less than fifty (50) nor more than sixty (60) days after the filing of said petition, to determine whether the electors will recall said officer, or, if a general or a special municipal election is to occur within sixty (60) days after the filing of said petition, the City Commission may in its discretion postpone the holding of such election to such general municipal election.

(8). If the City Clerk or any member of the City Commission shall wilfully fail or neglect to do or perform any act or duty, in this article prescribed or directed to be by him or any of them done or performed, then and in that event the said City Clerk or such member of the City Commission shall not draw or receive any salary during his further continuance in office and the Auditor shall not audit or allow any claim therefor.

If any question of recall, for which a petition has been filed, in accordance with the provisions of this charter, be not submitted to the voters at or within the time elsewhere specified in this charter, such petition shall remain in force until such question has been submitted to the voters.

(9). Upon both the sample and official ballots there shall be printed in not more than two hundred (200) words a statement of the reasons for demanding the recall of the officer as set forth in the recall petition, and the statement, if any, in not more than two hundred (200) words, made by the officer justifying his course in office as set forth in the recall petition.

(10). At such recall election, the ballots shall read:

"Shall............(naming the officer) be recalled? Yes."
"Shall............(naming the officer) be recalled? No."

If a majority of the electors voting on the recall of the officer sought to be removed, shall vote in favor of such recall, said officer shall thereupon be deemed removed from office and his incumbency thereof shall terminate upon the declaration of the result of said election by the canvassing board thereof. In the published call for said election the Clerk shall name three disinterested electors who shall act as a canvassing board to canvass the returns of said election and to declare the result thereof in the same manner and with the same force and effect as otherwise herein provided for the canvassing boards of general municipal elections.

(11). The City Commission shall appoint a successor to the officer removed, who shall hold until the next general municipal election, at which time a successor to the officer removed shall be elected by the people in the manner provided for in this charter.

(12). In the event that a majority of the City Commissioners shall be simultaneously recalled, the City Clerk shall appoint successors of the Commissioners who have been recalled, to serve until other Commissioners have been elected, as hereinafter provided.

Within three days after the canvass of the vote of the election at which such Commissioners are removed, the Clerk shall issue a call for an election for the purpose of electing the successors of the officers so removed. Said election shall be held upon notice of not less than twenty and not more than twenty-five days, and said election shall be held within thirty days from the date of the canvass of the vote of the recall election. Nominations shall be made in the manner provided in Section 261 relating to the nomination of the City Commissioners, except that petitions for nominations shall be filed in the office of the City Clerk at least ten days prior to the date of the holding of said election, and shall contain the requisite number of signatures when filed, without power of amendment. The Clerk shall forthwith determine the sufficiency as to the number and genuineness of signatures of the petition. If the same be insufficient in these particulars, it shall be rejected, and if sufficient, the name of the person nominated therein shall be placed upon the official ballot as a candidate for the office for which he was nominated.

(13). The provisions of Article XXIV shall, except as hereinabove modified, apply to and govern all such elections.

(14). No person recalled under the provisions of this section shall be eligible for election or appointment to any office in the city for a period of one year from and after the date of his recall.

(15). Every person elected to fill a vacancy caused by the recall of an elective officer, as in this section provided, shall within four days from the declaration of the result of the election at which he was elected, qualify and assume the powers and duties of the office to which he was elected.

(16). If, at a recall election, a majority shall vote against recalling the officer sought to be removed, it shall require a petition signed by qualified electors equal to twenty per cent. of the total registered vote at the last municipal election at which a Commissioner was elected to initiate a subsequent recall election against such officer during the term for which he was elected.

(17). The City Commission shall, by ordinance, make such further regulations as may be necessary to carry out the provisions of this article, and to adapt the provisions of Article XXIV thereto.

CHARTER OF SPRINGFIELD, OHIO

[The charter of Springfield, O., is included here as being one of the most typical as well as one of the best drawn of the charters which provide the city manager plan. The population of the city (about 40,000) justifies its classification as one of medium size.

The charter is drawn in accordance with the municipal home-rule provisions of the Ohio constitution, which gives to the cities wide latitude in the exercise of municipal powers.]—ED.

We, the people of the City of Springfield, Ohio, in order to obtain the benefits of local self-government, to encourage more direct and business-like methods in the transaction of our municipal affairs, and otherwise to promote our common welfare, do adopt the following Charter of our city.

POWERS OF THE CITY

Sec. 1. The inhabitants of the City of Springfield, Ohio, as its limits now are or hereafter may be established, shall continue to be a body politic and corporate, to be known and designated as "The City of Springfield, Ohio," and as such shall have perpetual succession. It shall have and may exercise all powers which now or hereafter it would be competent for this charter specifically to enumerate, as fully and completely as though said powers were specifically enumerated herein; and no enumeration of particular powers by this charter shall be held to be exclusive.

THE CITY COMMISSION

Sec. 2. Creation and Powers. There is hereby created a City Commission to consist of five electors of the city elected at large, who shall hold office for a term of four years beginning January first after their election, excepting that the two members elected at the first election by the lowest vote shall hold office for the term of two years only.

All the powers of the city, except such as are vested in the Board of Education and in the Judge of the Police Court, and except as otherwise provided by this charter or by the constitution of the state, are hereby vested in the city commission; and, except as otherwise prescribed by this Charter or by the constitution of the state, the city commission may by ordinance or resolution prescribe the manner in which any power of the city shall be exercised. In the absence of such provision as to any power, such power shall be exercised in the manner now or hereafter prescribed by the general laws of the state applicable to municipalities.

Sec. 3. Qualifications of Members. Each member of the city commission, for at least five years immediately prior to his election shall have been, and during his term of office shall continue to be, a resident of the City of Springfield, Ohio, and shall have the qualifications of an elector therein. He shall not hold any other public office or employment except that of Notary Public or member of the state militia.

No candidate for the office of city commissioner shall make any personal canvass among the voters to secure his nomination or election, or the nomination or election by any other candidate at the same election, whether for municipal, county, state or other office. He may cause notice of his candidacy to be published in the newspapers, and may procure the circulation of a petition for his nomination; but he shall not personally circulate such petition, nor by writing or otherwise solicit any one to support him or vote for him. He shall not expend or promise any money, office, employment or other thing of value to secure a nomination or election; but he may answer such inquiries as may be put to him and may declare his position publicly upon matters of public interest, either by addressing public meetings or by making written statements for newspaper publication or general circulation. A violation of these provisions, or any of them, shall disqualify him from holding the office, if elected; and the person receiving the next highest number of votes, who has observed the foregoing conditions, shall be entitled to the office.

Sec. 4. Vacancies. Any vacancy in the city commission, except as otherwise provided in this charter, shall be filled by the remaining members by the vote of at least three. If the term of the office so filled does not expire for two years or more after the next regular municipal election following such vacancy, and such vacancy occurs in time to permit it, an additional commissioner shall then be elected; and, of those commissioners elected at such election the one having the lowest vote shall succeed such appointee and serve the unexpired term. In the event of more than one vacancy to be so filled by election, the same provisions shall apply.

If, by reason of resignations, deaths, failure to elect, or other circumstance, three or more vacancies exist or occur at the same time in said city commission, or if said commission fails to fill any vacancy within ten days after the samo occurs, then the trustees of the sinking fund and the members of the civil service commission shall convene in joint session, and by a majority vote of the members of the joint board forthwith make such number of appointments as may be necessary to constitute a city commission of three qualified members, which three members shall at once proceed to fill the remaining vacancies as hereinbefore provided. The clerk of the trustees of the sinking fund shall act as the clerk of the two boards in joint session, and shall cause his certificate of their action to be entered on the journal of the city commission.

Sec. 5. Salary and Bonds. Each member of the city commission shall receive, except as hereinafter provided, a salary of five hundred dollars a year payable in equal monthly installments; and shall give bond in the sum of ten thousand dollars with some bonding company regularly accredited to do business in the State of Ohio as surety thereof, to the approval of the sinking fund trustees; and the premium of each such bond shall be paid by the city.

Sec. 6. President. The city commission shall at the time of organizing elect one of its members as president and another as vice-president for terms of two years. In case the members of the city commission, within five days after the time herein fixed for their organization meeting, are unable to agree upon a president or a vice-president of such commission, then a president, or a vice-president, or both, as the occasion may require, shall be selected from all the members of such commission by lot conducted by the city solicitor; who shall certify the result of such lot upon the journal of the commission.

The president shall preside at all meetings of the commission and perform such other duties consistent with his office as may be imposed by it; and he shall have a voice and vote in its proceedings, but no veto. He may use the title of mayor in any case in which the execution of legal instruments of writing or other necessity arising from the general law of the state so requires; but this shall not be construed as conferring upon him the administrative or judicial functions of a mayor under the general laws of the state.

The president of the city commission shall be recognized as the official head of the city by the courts for the purpose of serving civil process, by the Governor for the purpose of military law, and for all ceremonial purposes. He may take command of the police and govern the city by proclamation during times of public danger or emergency, and he shall himself be the judge of what constitutes such public danger or emergency. The powers and duties of the president shall be such as are conferred upon him by this charter, together with such others as are conferred by the city commission in pursuance of the provisions of this charter, and no others.

If the president be temporarily absent from the city, or become temporarily disabled from any cause, his duties shall be performed during such absence or disability by the vice-president. In the absence of both president and vice-president the other members of the city commission shall select one of their number to perform the duties of president.

Sec. 7. Clerk and Employes. The city commission shall appoint a clerk who shall be known as the Clerk of the City Commission, and who shall keep records and perform such other duties as may be prescribed by this charter or by the commission. It may also appoint and employ such other officers and employes of its body as are necessary.

Sec. 8. Time of Meeting. At eight o'clock P.M. on the second day of January following a regular municipal election, or if such day be Sunday, on the day following, the city commission shall meet at the usual place for holding the meetings of the legislative body of the city, at which time the newly elected commissioners shall assume the duties of their office. Thereafter the city commission shall meet at such times as may be prescribed by ordinance or resolution, except that it shall meet regularly not less than one evening each week. The president, any two members of the commission, or the city manager, may call special meetings of the commission upon at least twelve hours written notice to each member, served personally or left at his usual place of residence. All meetings of the city commission shall be public and any citizen shall have access to the minutes and records thereof at all reasonable times. The commission shall determine its own rules and order of business and shall keep a journal of its proceedings.

Sec. 9. Penalty for Absence. For each absence of a city commission from a regular meeting of the commission, there shall be deducted a sum equal to two per cent of the annual salary of such member. Absence from five consecutive regular meetings shall operate to vacate the seat of a member unless the absence is excused by the commission by resolution setting forth such excuse and entered upon the journal.

Sec. 10. Legislative Procedure. A majority of all the members elected to the city commission shall be a quorum to do business, but a less number may adjourn from day to day and compel the attendance of absent members in such manner and under such penalties as may be prescribed by ordinance. The affirmative vote of at least three of the members shall be necessary to adopt any ordinance or resolution; and the vote upon the passage of all ordinances and resolutions shall be taken by "yeas" and "nays" and entered upon the journal.

Sec. 11. Ordinance Enactment. Each proposed ordinance or resolution shall be introduced in written or printed form, and shall not contain more than one subject which shall be clearly stated in the title; but general appropriation ordinances may contain the various subjects and accounts for which moneys are to be appropriated. The enacting clause of all ordinances passed by the city commission shall be, "Be it ordained by the City Commission of the City of Springfield, Ohio." The enacting clause of all ordinances submitted to popular election by the initiative shall be: "Be it ordained by the people of the City of Springfield, Ohio."

No ordinance unless it be an emergency measure, shall be passed until it has been read at two regular meetings not less than one week apart, or the requirement of such reading has been dispensed with by an affirmative vote of four of the members of the commission. No ordinance or resolution or section thereof shall be revised or amended, unless the new ordinance or resolution contain the entire ordinance or resolution or section revised or amended; and the original ordinance, resolution, section or sections so amended shall be repealed.

Sec. 12. Emergency Measures. All ordinances and resolutions passed by the city commission shall be in effect from and after thirty days from the date of their passage, except that the city commission may, by an affirmative vote of four of its members, pass emergency measures to take effect at the time indicated therein.

An emergency measure is an ordinance or resolution for the immediate preservation of the public peace, property, health, or safety, or providing for the usual daily operation of a municipal department, in which the emergency is set forth and defined in a preamble thereto. Ordinances appropriating money may be passed as emergency measures, but no measure making a grant, renewal or extension of a franchise or other special privilege, or regulating the rate to be charged for its service by any public utility, shall ever be so passed.

Sec. 13. Record and Publication. Every ordinance or resolution upon its final passage shall be recorded in a book kept for that purpose, and shall be authenticated by the signatures of the presiding officer and the clerk of the commission. Every ordinance of a general or permanent nature shall be published once within ten days after its final passage in the manner hereinafter provided.

Resolutions and ordinances providing for public improvements, to pay the cost of which special assessments are to be made, need not be published; but within ten days after the passage of each a notice shall be published as follows, the same being in addition to the notice required by law to be served on the property owners.

As to the resolution declaring the necessity of the proposed improvement, a notice shall be published headed "Notice of Public Improvement," stating when the same was adopted by the city commission, and setting forth the general nature and the extent of such improvement, including any change of street grade that is to be made, what part of the cost thereof is to be assessed against the property to be especially benefited thereby, and when water, gas or other street connection must be made.

As to the ordinance determining to proceed with the improvement, a notice shall be published headed "Notice of Determination to Proceed with Public Improvement," stating when the city commission adopted the same, describing the character and extent of the improvement in general terms, and setting forth within what time assessments on property specially benefited may be paid in cash, and for what period and at what interest bonds will be issued for that portion of the assessment not so paid.

In regard to the ordinance to provide for the issue of bonds, a notice shall be published headed "Notice of Bond Issue for Public Improvement," stating when the city commission adopted the same, describing the improvement in general terms, and stating the total amount of bonds to be issued, in what denomination, when maturing, how to be dated and numbered, the rate of interest, when and where payable, and the lowest price at which any portion of such bonds not taken by the sinking fund of the city, or of the city school district, will be offered at public sale. Wherever practicable notices of the same character required to be published regarding separate improvements shall be combined into one notice under a single heading.

No resolution declaring it necessary to proceed with any public improvement shall be adopted until complete plans, specifications, profiles and estimates have been submitted to the city commission and been approved by it; and the same, or a copy thereof, shall thereafter remain on file in the office of the city engineer subject to inspection by the public.

Sec. 14. Price and Mode of Publication. All of the above mentioned publications, as well as all other newspaper publications made by the city, shall be published in a newspaper or newspapers of general circulation in the municipality, in the body type of the paper and under head lines in eighteen point type, specifying the nature of the publication; and where legally permissible, such publication shall be made but once and in one newspaper only.

The newspaper carrying such publication shall be paid a price per inch of space used and the lowest and best rate offered, not exceeding that which it receives from regular commercial display advertisers for the quantity of space used. Whenever it may appear to the city commission that the rates offered by such newspapers are unfair, such other means of securing due publicity may be employed, in lieu of newspaper advertising, as the commission may by resolution determine.

CITY MANAGER

Sec. 15. Appointment. The city commission shall appoint a city manager who shall be the administrative head of the municipal government under the direction and supervision of the city commission, and who shall hold office at the pleasure of the city commission. He shall be appointed without regard to his political beliefs and need not be a resident of the city at the time of his appointment. During the absence or disability of the city manager the city commission may designate some properly qualified person to execute the functions of the office.

Sec. 16. Powers and Duties. The powers and duties of the city manager shall be:

(a) To see that the laws and ordinances are enforced.

(b) Except as herein provided, to appoint and remove all heads of departments, and all subordinate officers and employes of the city; all appointments to be upon merit and fitness alone, and in the classified service all appointments and removals to be subject to the civil service provisions of this charter.

(c) To exercise control over all departments and divisions created herein or that hereafter ma ybe created by the commission.

(d) To see that all terms and conditions imposed in favor of the city or its inhabitants in any public utility franchise are faithfully kept and performed; and upon knowledge of any violation thereof to call the same to the attention of the city solicitor, who is hereby required to take such steps as are necessary to enforce the same.

(e) To attend all meetings of the commission, with the right to take part in the discussions but having no vote.

(f) To recommend to the commission for adoption such measures as he may deem necessary or expedient.

(g) To act as budget commissioner and to keep the city commission fully advised as to the financial condition and needs of the city; and

(h) To perform such other duties as may be prescribed by this charter or be required of him by ordinance or resolution of the commission.

Sec. 17. Head of Departments. Excepting the departments of city solicitor, auditor, treasurer, sinking fund and civil service, and until otherwise provided by the city commission, any existing department now under the control of a special board, such as library, hospital and park, the city manager shall be the acting head of each and every department of the city until otherwise directed by the commission; but with the consent and approval of the commission, he may appoint a deputy or chief clerk to represent him in any department of which he is the acting head. No member of the city commission shall directly interfere with the conduct of any department, except at the express direction of the commission.

Sec. 18. Platting Commissioner. The city manager shall also be the platting commissioner of the city and he shall exercise the authority and discharge the duties of that office under the provisions of the general law of the state applicable thereto, except as the same may be modified by the city commission.

ADMINISTRATIVE OFFICERS AND DEPARTMENTS

Sec. 19. City Solicitor. The city commission shall appoint a city solicitor who shall hold office at the pleasure of the commission. The city solicitor shall act as the legal adviser to, and attorney and counsel for, the municipality and all its officers in matters relating to their official duties. He shall prepare all contracts, bonds and other instruments in writing in which the municipality is concerned, and shall endorse on each his approval of the form and correctness thereof; and no contract with such municipality shall take effect until his approval is endorsed thereon. He or his assistants shall be the prosecutor or prosecutors in any police or municipal court, and shall perform such other duties and have such assistants and clerks as the city commission may authorize. In addition to such duties he shall perform such other duties as may be required of him by the city commission, as well as such as may be required of city solicitors by the general laws of the state applicable to municipalities and not inconsistent with this charter or with any ordinance or resolution that may be passed by the city commission.

Sec. 20. City Auditor. The city commission shall appoint a city auditor who shall hold office at the pleasure of the commission. The city auditor shall issue all warrants for payments of money by the city. He shall keep an accurate account of all taxes and assessments, of all money due to, and all receipts and disbursements by, the municipality, of all its assets and liabilities, and of all appropriations made by the city commission. At the end of each fiscal year, and oftener if required by the city commission, he shall audit the accounts of the several departments and officers, and shall audit all other accounts in which the municipality is interested. He may prescribe the form of reports to be rendered to his department, and the method of keeping accounts by all other departments, and he shall require daily reports to be made to him by each department showing the receipt of all moneys by such department and the disposition thereof. Upon the death, resignation, removal, or expiration of the term of any officer, the city auditor shall audit the accounts of such officer, and if such officer shall be found indebted to the municipality he shall immediately give notice thereof to the city commission, and the city solicitor; and the latter shall forthwith proceed to collect the same.

In addition to such duties the city auditor shall perform such other duties as may be required of him by the city commission, as well as such as may be required of city auditors by the general laws of the state applicable to municipalities and not inconsistent with this charter or with any ordinance or resolution that may be passed by the city commission.

Sec. 21. City Treasurer. The city commission shall appoint a city treasurer who shall hold office at the pleasure of the city commission. The office of city treasurer may be combined with that of clerk of the city commission or with any other office not inconsistent therewith. The city treasurer shall be the custodian of all moneys of the municipality, and shall keep and preserve the same in such manner and in such place or places as shall be determined by the city commission. He shall pay out money only on warrants issued by the city auditor.

In addition to such duties he shall perform such other duties as may be required of him by the city commission as well as such as may be required of city treasurers by the general laws of the state applicable to municipalities and not inconsistent with this charter or with any ordinance or resolution that may be passed by the city commission.

Sec. 22. Purchasing Agent. The city commission shall designate some officer of the city, other than the auditor or treasurer, to act as its purchasing agent, by whom all purchases of supplies for the city shall be made, and who shall approve all vouchers for the payment of the same. Such purchasing agent shall also conduct all sales of personal property which the commission may authorize to be sold as having become unnecessary or unfit for the city's use.

All purchases and sales shall conform to such regulations as the commission may from time to time prescribe; but in either case, if an amount in excess of five hundred dollars is involved, opportunity for competition shall be given. Where purchases or sales are made on joint account of separate departments, the purchasing agent shall apportion the charge or credit to each department. He shall see to the delivery of supplies to each department, and take and retain the receipt of each department therefor. Until the city commission shall otherwise provide, the city manager of the city shall act as such purchasing agent.

Sec. 23. Trustees of the Sinking Fund. The board of trustees of the sinking fund as now organized and existing shall continue, and such board and all matters pertaining thereto shall be governed by the general laws of the state in effect January 1st, 1914, or thereafter enacted and applicable thereto; excepting that the members of said board shall serve without pecuniary compensation. The present members of said board shall continue to serve for their unexpired terms; but their successors shall be appointed, and vacancies in said board shall be filled, by the president of the city commission, with the consent of said commission entered upon its journal.

Sec. 24. Civil Service. The civil service commission as now organized and existing shall continue; and the civil service of the city, and such commission, and all matters pertaining thereto, shall be governed by the general laws of the state in effect January 1st, 1914, or thereafter enacted, which are applicable thereto. The present members of said board shall continue to serve for their unexpired terms; but successors to present members shall be appointed and vacancies in said board shall be filled by the city commission, and the members of the civil service commission shall serve without pecuniary compensation.

Sec. 25. Other Boards and Departments. All other administrative departments in existence January 1st, 1914, shall continue until otherwise provided by the city commission, and all administrative boards in charge of any administrative department of the city shall continue in office, and their successors shall be appointed as heretofore, excepting as other provision is made in this charter, or may hereafter be made by the city commission.

Excepting the officers, boards, commissions and departments hereinbefore specially mentioned and provided for, the city commission shall have power to establish, create, combine or abolish offices, boards, departments or divisions when in its opinion the proper administration of the business of the city so requires.

Sec. 26. Advisory Boards. The city commission at any time may appoint an advisory board or boards composed of citizens qualified to act in an advisory capacity to the city commission, the city manager or the head of any department, with respect to the conduct and management of any property, institution or public function of the city. The members of any such board shall serve without compensation for a time fixed in their appointment, or at the pleasure of the commission; and their duty shall be to consult and advise with such municipal officers and make written recommendations which shall become part of the records of the city.

Sec. 27. Salaries and Bonds. The city commission shall fix by ordinance the salary or rate of compensation of all officers and employes of the city entitled to compensation, other than their own; and may require any officer or employe to give a bond for the faithful performance of his duty, in such an amount as it may determine, and it may provide that the premium thereof shall be paid by the city.

Sec. 28. General Disqualifications. No member of the city commission, the city manager or any other officer or employe of the city, shall directly or indirectly be interested in any contract, job, work or service with or for the city; nor in the profits or emoluments thereof, nor in the expenditure of any money on the part of the city other than his fixed compensation; and any contract with the city in which any such officer or employe is, or becomes, interested may be declared void by the city commission.

No member of the city commission, the city manager or other officer or employe of the city shall knowingly accept any gift, frank, free ticket, pass, reduced price or reduced rate of service from any person, firm or corporation operating
a public utility or engaged in business of a public
within the city, or from any person known to him t
or to be endeavoring to secure, a contract with the cit
the provisions of this section shall not apply to the
portation of policemen or firemen in uniform or wearin
official badges, when the same is, or may be, provi
ordinance.

Sec. 29. Political Activity. Neither the city manag
any person in the employ of the city under him sha
any active part in securing, or contribute any money t
the nomination or election of any candidate or can
for the office of city commissioner, excepting to answ
questions as may be put to him and as he may de
answer.

Sec. 30. Penalties. The provisions of the two la
ceding sections shall not be considered exclusive, bu
addition to any other provisions of the general law
state applicable to the case; and a violation of an
visions of either of such sections shall subject the o
to removal from his office or employment, and to
ment by a fine of not exceeding one hundred dollars.

APPROPRIATIONS

Sec. 31. The Estimate. The fiscal year of the cit
begin on the first day of January. On or before t
day of November of each year the city manager sha
mit to the city commission an estimate of the expen
and revenues of the city departments for the ensuin
This estimate shall be compiled from detailed infor
obtained from the several departments on uniform
to be furnished by the city manager. The classifica
the estimate of expenditures shall be as nearly unif
possible for the main functional divisions of all depar
and shall give in parallel columns the following infor

(a) A detailed estimate of the expense of con
each department as submitted by the department.

(b) Expenditures for corresponding items for t
two fiscal years.

(c) Expenditures for corresponding items for the
fiscal year, including adjustments due to transfers b
appropriations plus an estimate of expenditures neces
complete the current fiscal year.

(d) Amount of supplies and material on hand at t
of the preparation of the invoice.

(e) Increase or decrease of requests compared w
corresponding appropriations for the current year.

(f) Such other information as is required by t
commission or that the city manager may deem advis
submit.

(g) The recommendation of the city manager as
amounts to be appropriated with reasons therefor
detail as the city commission may direct.

Sufficient copies of such estimate shall be prepar
submitted, that there may be copies on file in the c
the city commission for inspection by the public.

Sec. 32. Appropriation Ordinance. Upon receipt
estimate the city commission shall prepare an appro
ordinance but before finally acting upon such tentat
propriation the city commission shall fix a time an
for holding a public hearing upon the tentative approp
and shall give public notice of such hearing. The ci
mission shall not pass the appropriation ordinance u
days after such public hearing.

Sec. 33. Transfer of Funds. Upon request of t
manager the city commission may transfer any par
unencumbered balance of an appropriation to a pur
object for which the appropriation for the current y
proved insufficient, or may authorize a transfer to b
between items appropriated to the same office or depa

Sec. 34. Unencumbered Balances. At the close
fiscal year the unencumbered balance of each appro
shall revert to the respective fund from which it

propriated and shall be subject to future appropriation. Any accruing revenue of the city, not appropriated as hereinbefore provided, and any balances at any time remaining after the purposes of the appropriation shall have been satisfied or abandoned, may from time to time be appropriated by the city commission to such uses as will not conflict with any uses for which specifically such revenues accrued. No money shall be drawn from the treasury of the city, nor shall any obligation for the expenditure of money be incurred, except pursuant to the appropriations made by the city commission, but nothing in this or the preceding section shall be construed to authorize the application of revenue derived from a public utility of the city to any other purpose than that of the utility from which the same was derived.

PAYMENTS—REPORTS

Sec. 35. Payment of Claims. No warrant for the payment of any claim shall be issued by the city auditor until such claim shall have been approved by the head of the department for which the indebtedness was incurred and by the city manager, and such officers and their sureties shall be liable to the municipality for all loss or damage sustained by the municipality by reason of the corrupt approval of any such claim against the municipality. Whenever any claim shall be presented to the city auditor he shall have power to require evidence that the amount claimed is justly due and is in conformity to law and ordinance, and for that purpose he may summon before him any officer, agent, or employe, of any department of the municipality, or any other person, and examine him upon oath or affirmation relative thereto.

Sec. 36. Certification of Funds. No contract, agreement or other obligation involving the expenditure of money shall be entered into, nor shall any ordinance, resolution or order for the expenditure of money be passed by the city commission, or be authorized by any officer of the city, unless the city auditor shall first certify to the city commission or to the proper officer, as the case may be, that the money required for such contract, agreement, obligation or expenditure, is in the treasury, to the credit of the fund from which it is to be drawn, and not appropriated for any other purpose, which certificate shall be filed and immediately recorded. The sum so certified shall not thereafter be considered unappropriated until the city is discharged from the contract, agreement or obligation. The provisions of this section shall not apply to contracts or proceedings relating to improvements any part of the cost of which is to be paid by special assessments.

Sec. 37. Money in the Fund. All moneys actually in the treasury to the credit of the fund from which they are to be drawn, and all moneys applicable to the payment of the obligation or appropriation involved that are anticipated to come into the treasury before the maturity of such contract, agreement, or obligation, from taxes, assessments, or license fees, or from sales of services, products or by-products of any city undertaking, and moneys to be derived from lawfully authorized bonds sold and in process of delivery, for the purposes of such certificate shall be deemed in the treasury to the credit of the appropriate fund and shall be subject to such certification.

Sec. 38. Financial Reports. The city commission shall have furnished them a monthly balance showing in detail all receipts and expenditures of the city for the preceding month; and the aggregate receipts and expenditures of each department shall be published by the city commission in such manner as to provide full publicity. At the end of each year the city commission shall have printed an annual report, in pamphlet form, giving a classified statement of all receipts, expenditures, assets and liabilities of the city; a detailed comparison of such receipts and expenditures with those of the year preceding; a summary of the city commission proceedings and summary of the operations of the administrative departments for the previous twelve months. A copy of this report shall be furnished the state bureau of accounting, the public library and to any citizen of the city who may apply therefor at the office of the clerk of the city commission.

IMPROVEMENTS—CONTRACTS

Sec. 39. Limitation of Assessments. In levying special assessments to pay any part of the cost of any public work or improvement, the city commission shall not exceed any limitation as to the amount thereof which may be prescribed by the general laws of the state applicable to municipalities and in force at the time it is determined by the city commission that any such work shall be done or improvement made. Unless for special reasons which shall be stated in the ordinance levying an assessment or providing for the issue of bonds to pay any part of the cost of any such improvemnet to be made pursuant to contract, no such ordinance shall be passed, or assessment levied or money borrowed, until bids for the labor and material have been received and the approximate cost of the improvement accurately determined.

Sec. 40. Improvements by Direct Labor. Nothing in the preceding section shall be construed to prohibit the city commission from doing any public work or making any public improvement by the direct employment of the necessary labor and the purchase of the necessary supplies and materials, with separate accounting as to each improvement so made, but the city commission may upon so declaring by ordinance or resolution cause any public work or improvement to be done or made in such manner.

Sec. 41. Sewer, Water and Gas Connections. Before paving or otherwise surfacing or resurfacing any street or alley of the city the city commission shall determine the time within which sewer, water, gas or other connections shall be constructed, and shall give notice thereof to the persons or corporations required to make the same, and if a person or corporation fails to make any such connection when so required no permission to make the same shall thereafter be granted within five years from the completion of any such street improvement unless with the consent of four of the commissioners expressed by resolution adopted at a regular meeting of the commission and stating the reasons therefor. Nothing herein shall be construed to prohibit the city commission from providing that such connections may be made by the city and the cost thereof assessed against the lots and lands specially benefited thereby.

Sec. 42. Expenditures in Excess of $1000. When an expenditure, other than the compensation of persons employed by the city, exceeds one thousand dollars, such expenditure shall first be authorized and directed by ordinance of the city commission, and no contract involving an expenditure in excess of such sum shall be made or awarded except upon the approval of the city manager and the city commission.

Sec. 43. Time of Making Contracts. The city commission shall not enter into any contract which is not to go into full operation during the term for which all the members of such city commission are elected.

Sec. 44. Modification of Contracts. When it becomes necessary in the opinion of the city manager, in the prosecution of any work or improvement under contract, to make alterations or modifications in such contract, such alterations or modifications, if made, shall be of no effect until the price to be paid for the work and material, or both, under the altered or modified contract, has been agreed upon in writing and signed by the contractor and by the city manager and approved by the city commission.

Sec. 45. Bids in Excess of Estimate. In no instance shall contracts be let either as a whole, or in aggregate if bids for parts of the work are taken, which exceed the estimate for the improvement contemplated.

Sec. 46. Contracts—When Void. All contracts, agreements or other obligations entered into and all ordinances passed, or resolutions and orders adopted, contrary to the provisions of the preceding sections, shall be void.

ELECTIONS

Sec. 47. **Time of Holding Elections.** Regular municipal elections shall be held on the first Tuesday after the first Monday in November in the odd numbered years. Primary elections shall be held at the time provided by the general election laws of the state. Any matter which by the terms of the charter may be submitted to the electors of the city at any special election may be submitted at a primary election or at a regular municipal election.

Sec. 48. **Ballots.** The ballots used in all elections provided for in this charter shall be without party marks or designations. The whole number of ballots to be printed for any primary or regular election for the nomination or election of candidates for the office of city commissioner shall be divided by the number of such candidates, and the quotient so obtained shall be the number of ballots in each series of ballots to be printed. The names of the candidates shall be arranged in alphabetical order and the first series of ballots printed. The first name shall then be placed last and the next series of ballots printed, and this process shall be repeated until each name shall have been first. These ballots shall then be combined into tablets with no two of the same order of names together. The ballots shall in all other respects conform as nearly as may be to the ballots prescribed by the general election laws of the state.

Sec. 49. **Petitions for Place on Primary Ballot.** Candidates for the office of city commissioner shall be nominated only by a non-partisan primary election. The name of any elector of the city shall be printed upon the primary ballot if there is filed with the election authorities a petition in accordance with the following provisions, to-wit:

(a) Such petitions shall state the name and place of residence of each person whose name is presented for a place upon the ballot and that he is a candidate for the office of City Commissioner for the City of Springfield, Ohio.

(b) Such petitions shall be signed by electors of the municipality equal in number to two per cent of the total number of registered voters in the city.

(c) Such petitions shall contain a provision that each signer thereto thereby pledges himself to support and vote for the candidate or candidates whose names are therein presented for a place upon the ballot, and each elector signing a petition shall add to his signature his place of residence, with street and number, voting precinct, and date of signing, and may subscribe to one nomination for each of the places to be filled and no more. All signatures shall be made with ink or indelible pencil.

(d) The signatures of all the petitioners need not be appended to one paper, but to each separate paper there shall be attached an affidavit of the circulator thereof stating the number of signers thereto, that each person signed in his presence on the date mentioned, and that the signature is that of the person whose name it purports to be.

(e) Such petitions shall not be signed by any elector more than fifty days prior to the day of such primary election and such petition shall be filed with the election authorities not less than thirty days previous to the day of such election.

Sec. 50. **Acceptance.** Any person whose name has been submitted for candidacy by any such petition shall file his acceptance of such candidacy with the election authorities not later than twenty-five days previous to such election; otherwise his name shall not appear upon the ballot.

Sec. 51. **Election.** The candidates for nomination to the office of city commissioner who shall receive the greatest vote in such primary election shall be placed on the ballot at the next regular municipal election in number not to exceed twice the number of vacancies in the city commission to be filled, and the candidates at the regular municipal election, equal in number to the places to be filled, who shall receive the highest number of votes at such regular municipal election, shall be declared elected. A tie between two or more candidates for the office of city commissioner shall be decided by lot under the direction of the election author
as provided by the general electicn laws of the state.

Sec. 52. **General Laws to Apply.** All elections sha
conducted, and the results canvassed and certified, by
election authorities prescribed by general election laws,
except as otherwise provided by this charter or by ordina
or resolutions of the city commission hereafter enacted
general election laws shall control in all such elections.

THE INITIATIVE

Sec. 53. **Proposed Petition.** Any proposed ordina
including ordinances for the repeal or amendment of an o
ance then in effect, may be submitted to the city commi
by petition signed by at least five per cent of the total n
ber of registered voters in the municipality. All peti
circulated with respect to any proposed ordinance sha
uniform in character, shall contain the proposed ordin
in full, and shall have printed or written thereon the n
and addresses of at least five electors who shall be offi
regarded as filing the petition and shall constitute a
mittee of the petitioners for the purpose hereinafter na

Each signer of a petition shall sign his name in ink o
delible pencil and shall place on the petition, opposit
name, the date of his signature and his place of resid
by voting precinct and by street and number. The signa
to any such petition need not all be appended to one p
but to each such paper there shall be attached an affi
by the circulator thereof, stating the number of signe
such part of the petition and that each signature appe
to the paper is the genuine signature of the person w
name it purports to be, and that it was made in the pres
of the affiant and on the date indicated.

Sec. 54. **Time of Filing.** All papers comprising a pet
shall be assembled and filed with the clerk of the city
mission as one instrument, within one hundred and tw
days from the date of the first signature thereon, and
so filed, the clerk shall submit the same to the city
mission at its next regular meeting and provision sha
made for public hearings upon the proposed ordinance.

Sec. 55. **Petition for Election.** The city commission
at once proceed to consider such petition and shall
final action thereon within thirty days from the dat
submission. If the city commission rejects the pro
ordinance, or passes it in a different form from that set
in the petition, or fails to act finally upon it within the
stated, the committee of the petitioners, by written de
filed with the clerk of the city commission not later
twenty days after final action or inaction by the city
mission, may require that the proposed ordinance be
mitted to a vote of the electors in its original form, if, wi
prior to such demand, a petition for such election, s
after the final action or inaction of the city commissi
filed with such clerk bearing additional signatures of fiv
cent of the electors of the city, none of whom were si
of the first petition. Such clerk shall forthwith cause n
of the filing of such demand and petition to be publish
some newspaper of general circulation in the city, and
also within five days certify to the officers having cont
elections the proposed ordinance, stating whether or n
special election is demanded in the petitions, the perce
of registered voters who signed the two petitions in th
gregate, and the date on which he published the notic
mentioned.

Sec. 56. **Time of Holding Election.** If an election
be held not more than three months nor less than
days after the publication of such notice by the clerk,
proposed ordinance shall be submitted to a vote of the
tors at such election. If no election is to be held w
the time aforesaid, the election officers shall provide for
mitting the proposed ordinance to the electors at a s
election to be held not later than sixty days nor earlier
thirty days after the publication of such notice, if the

tion for such ordinance and the petition for such election so demand, and if the signers of the two petitions amount in the aggregate to at least twenty-five per cent of the registered voters of the city; otherwise the same shall be submitted at the next regular or special election. At least ten days before any such election the clerk of the city commission shall cause such proposed ordinance to be published.

Sec. 57. Ballots. The ballots used when voting upon any such proposed ordinance shall state the title of the ordinance to be voted on and below it the two propositions, "For the Ordinance" and "Against the Ordinance." Immediately at the left of each proposition there shall be a square in which by making a cross (X), the voter may vote for or against the proposed ordinance. If a majority of the electors voting on any such proposed ordinance shall vote in favor thereof, it shall thereupon become an ordinance of the city.

Sec. 58. Duty of City Solicitor. Before any ordinance so proposed shall be submitted to the city commission, it shall first be approved as to its form by the city solicitor, whose duty it shall be to draft such proposed ordinance in proper legal language, and to render such other service to persons desiring to propose such ordinance as shall be necessary to make the same proper for consideration by the city commission.

Sec. 59. Amendments and Repeals. No ordinance adopted by an electoral vote can be repealed or amended except by an electoral vote. But an ordinance to repeal or amend any such ordinance may, by resolution of the city commission, be submitted to an electoral vote at any regular election, or at any special municipal election called for some other purpose, provided notice of the intention so to do be published by the city commission not more than sixty nor less than thirty days prior to such election, in the manner required for the publication of ordinances. If an amendment is so proposed, such notice shall contain the proposed amendment in full. Such submission shall be in the same manner, and the vote shall have the same effect, as in cases of ordinances submitted to an election by popular petition.

THE REFERENDUM

Sec. 60. Petition for Referendum. No ordinance passed by the city commission, unless it be an emergency measure or the annual appropriation ordinance, shall go into effect until thirty days after its final passage. If, at any time within said thirty days, a petition signed by fifteen per cent of the total number of registered voters in the municipality be filed with the clerk of the city commission, requesting that any such ordinance be repealed or amended as stated in the petition, it shall not become operative until the steps indicated herein have been taken. Such petition shall have stated therein the names and addresses of at least five electors as a committee to represent the petitioners.

Referendum petitions need not contain the text of the ordinance or ordinances the repeal of which is sought; but shall contain the proposed amendment, if an amendment is demanded, and shall be subject in all other respects to the requirements for petitions submitting proposed ordinances to the city commission. Ballots used in referendum elections shall conform in all respects to those provided for in section fifty-seven of this charter.

Sec. 61. Proceedings Thereunder. The clerk of the city commission shall, at its next meeting, present the petition to the city commission, which shall proceed to reconsider the ordinance. If, within thirty days after the filing of such petition, the ordinance be not repealed or amended as requested, the city commission shall provide for submitting the proposed repeal or amendment to a vote of the electors, provided a majority of the committee named in the petition to represent the petitioners shall, by writing filed with the clerk of the city commission within twenty days after the expiration of the said thirty days, so require. In so doing the city commission shall be governed by the provisions of section fifty-six hereof respecting the time of submission and the manner of voting on ordinances proposed to the city commission by petition; excepting that the question of calling a special election for such purpose shall be determined by the demand and number of signers of the petition requesting the repeal or amendment of such ordinance, which number shall be twenty-five per cent of registered voters; and excepting further that the city commission may call, and fix the time for, a special election for such purpose, if in its judgment the public interest will be prejudiced by delay.

If, when submitted to a vote of the electors, such repeal or amendment be approved by a majority of those voting thereon, it shall thereupon go into effect as an ordinance of the city; but if any such amendment is clearly separable from the remainder of the ordinance and does not materially affect the other provisions of such ordinance, all sections of the ordinance except that sought to be amended and those dependent thereon shall take effect as though no referendum of any portion of the ordinance had been demanded.

Sec. 62. Referendum on Initiated Ordinances—Conflict. Ordinances submitted to the city commission by initiative petition and passed by the city commission without change, or passed in an amended form and not required to be submitted to a vote of the electors by the committee of the petitions, shall be subject to the referendum in the same manner as other ordinances. If the provisions of two or more ordinances adopted or approved at the same election conflict, the ordinance receiving the highest affirmative vote shall prevail.

Sec. 63. Emergency Measures. Ordinances passed as emergency measures shall be subject to referendum in like manner as other ordinances, except that they shall go into effect at the time indicated in such ordinances. If, when submitted to a vote of the electors, an emergency measure be not approved by a majority of those voting thereon it shall be considered repealed as regards any further action thereunder; but such measure so repealed shall be deemed sufficient authority for payment in accordance with the ordinance of any expense incurred previous to the referendum vote thereon.

Sec. 64. Preliminary Action. In case a petition be filed requiring that a measure passed by the city commission providing for an expenditure of money a bond issue or a public improvement be submitted to a vote of the electors, all steps preliminary to such actual expenditure, actual issuance of bonds, or actual execution of a contract for such improvement, may be taken prior to the election.

THE RECALL

Sec. 65. Recall Petition. Any or all members of the city commission may be removed from office by the electors by the following procedure.

A petition for the recall of the commissioner or commissioners designated, signed by at least five hundred of the electors of the city, and containing a statement in not more than two hundred words of the grounds of the recall, shall be filed with the city auditor, who shall forthwith notify the commissioner or commissioners sought to be removed, and he or they, within five days after such notice, may file with such auditor a defensive statement in not exceeding two hundred words. The city auditor shall at once upon the expiration of said five days cause sufficient printed or typewritten copies of such petition, without the signatures, to be made, and to each of them he shall attach a printed or typewritten copy of such defensive statement, if one is furnished him within the time provided. He shall cause one copy of such petition to be placed on file in his office, and provide facilities for there signing the same, and he shall also cause one copy to be placed in each of the several fire engine houses of the city, where the same shall be in the custody of the captain of the house, who shall provide facilities for there signing the same. The city auditor shall immediately cause notice to be published in some newspaper of general circulation in the city of the placing of such copies of such petition.

Such copies of such petition shall remain on file in the several places designated for the period of thirty days, during which time any of them may be signed by any elector of the city in person; but not by agent or attorney. Each signer of any of such copies shall sign his name in ink or indelible pencil, and shall place thereafter his residence by voting precinct, and by street and number.

Sec. 66. Notice. At the expiration of said period of thirty days the city auditor shall assemble all of said copies in his office as one instrument, and shall examine the same and ascertain and certify thereon whether the signatures thereto amount to at least fifteen per cent of the registered voters of the city. If such signatures do amount to such percent, he shall at once serve notice of that fact upon the commissioner or commissioners designated in the petition, and also deliver to the election authorities a copy of the original petition with his certificate as to the percentage of registered voters who signed the same, and a certificate as to the date of his last mentioned notice to the commissioner or commissioners designated in the petition.

Sec. 67. **Recall Election.** If the commissioner or commissioners, or any of them, designated in the petition, file with the clerk of the city commission within five days after the last mentioned notice from the city solicitor, his or their written resignation, the clerk of the city commission shall at once notify the election authorities of that fact; and such resignation shall be irrevocable, and the city commission shall proceed to fill the vacancy. In the absence of any such resignation the election authorities shall forthwith order and fix a day for holding a recall election for the removal of those not resigning. Any such election shall be held not less than thirty nor more than sixty days after the expiration of the period of five days last mentioned, and at the same time as any other general or special election held within such period; but if no such election be held within such period the election authorities shall call a special recall election to be held within the period aforesaid.

Sec. 68. **Ballots.** The ballots at such recall election shall conform to the following requirements. With respect to each person whose removal is sought, the question shall be submitted: "Shall (name of person) be removed from the office of City Commissioner by recall?" Immediately following each such question there shall be printed on the ballots the two propositions in the order here set forth:

"For the recall of (name of person)."
'Against the recall of (name of person)."

Immediately to the left of each of the propositions shall be placed a square in which the electors, by making a cross mark (X), may vote for either of such propositions.

Sec. 69. **Filling of Vacancies.** In any such election, if a majority of the votes cast on the question of removal of any commissioner are affirmative, the person whose removal is sought shall thereupon be deemed removed from office upon the announcement of the official canvass of that election, and the vacancy caused by such recall shall be filled by the remainder of the city commission according to the provisions of section four of this charter.

If, however, an election is held for the recall of more than two commissioners, candidates to succeed them for their unexpired terms shall be voted upon at the same election, and shall be nominated without primary election, by petitions signed, dated and verified in the manner required for petitions presenting names of candidates for nomination at a primary election, and similar in form to such petitions, but signed by electors equal in number to at least five per cent of the registered voters of the city, and filed with the election authorities at least thirty days prior to such recall election. But no such nominating petition shall be signed or circulated until after the time has expired for signing the copies of the petition for the recall, and any signatures thereon antedating such time shall not be counted.

Sec. 70. **Counting the Vote.** Candidates shall not be
nominated to succeed any particular commissione
one commissioner is removed at such election, t
at such election receiving the highest number c
be declared elected to fill the vacancy; and if m
commissioner is removed at such election, suc
equal in number to the number of commissior
shall be declared elected to fill the vacancies; ar
successful candidates, those receiving the great
votes shall be declared elected for the longer t
of ties, and all other matters not herein speci
for, shall be determined by the rules govern
generally.

Sec. 71. **Effect of Resignations.** No procee
recall of all of the members of the city comm
same election shall be defeated in whole or in
resignation of any or all of them, but upon the
any of them the city commission shall have pov
vacancy until a successor is elected, and the pr
the recall and the election of successors shall
have the same effect as though there had been n

Sec. 72. **Miscellaneous Provisions.** Except as
wise provided, no petition to recall any commissi
filed within six months after he takes office. N
moved by recall shall be eligible to be elected
upon or for a period of two years after the dat
call. The city auditor shall preserve in his offi
comprising or connected with a petition for a
period of one year after the same were filed.
of removal herein provided is in addition to such
ods as are, or may be, provided by general law.

Sec. 73. **Offenses Relating to Petitions.** No
falsely impersonate another, or purposely write
residence falsely, in the signing of any petition
referendum or recall, or forge any name theretc
such paper with knowledge that he is not a qu
of the city. No person shall sign, or knowingly
signed, any petition for recall at any place othe
the places hereinbefore designated for the sig
petitions. Nor shall any person employ or pa
accept employment or payment, for circulating
or referendum petition upon the basis of the n
natures procured thereto. Any person violatin
provisions of this section shall be deemed guilt
meanor and shall, upon conviction, be fined in
to exceed one hundred dollars and the costs o
The foregoing provisions shall not be held to be
but in addition to, all laws of the state prescri
for the same offenses or for other offenses re
same matter.

FRANCHISES

Sec. 74. **Grants Limited.** No grant, or renew
construct and operate a public utility in the str
lic grounds of the city shall be made by the cit
to any individual, company or corporation in vi
of the limitations contained in this charter.

Sec. 75. **Period of Grants.** No such grant
clusive, nor shall it be made for a longer perio
years. No such grant shall be renewed earlier t
prior to its expiration unless the city commis
a vote of at least four of its members first de
nance its intention of considering a renewal
grants of the right to make extensions of any
shall be subject as far as practicable to the
original grant and shall expire therewith.

Sec. 76. **Assignment.** No such grant shall
signed or otherwise alienated except with the e
of the city commission.

Sec. 77. **Right of Purchase.** All such grants
to the city the right to purchase or lease all th
the utility used in or useful for the operation
at a price either fixed in the ordinance making

ı terms reserved or not, to n of space in, over, under ıblic grounds occupied by in the opinion of the city 'equires, such fixtures may ocated, altered or discon-nes have the power to pass such utilities which in the required in the interest of nodation.

:tion shall be instituted or y the grantee of any such ditors, to set aside or have any such grant, the whole rfeited and annulled at the ›e expressed by ordinance. ɔn for the declaration of a for the violation by the f.

Every person or corpora-ıin the city limits, whether after obtained, shall keep the city suitable and com-detail the assets, financial fits and all the operations ıown by a complete system

within sixty days after the s the city commission shall › city commission a report ing the gross revenue, the ›etterments and additions, paid for interest and dis-, and such other informa-›n from time to time may hall prescribe the form for hall be made in the form ıch commission.

h person or corporation to supplementary or special commission may demand; rized representative, shall ve access to all the books, ›very such person or cor-:opies of same or any part

ıy be specifically enforced ınd in addition, each such to comply with the pro-ble to the City of Spring-'e dollars per day for each ›d in a civil action in the

o not apply to any utility communities not properly l, Ohio; but the city com-the same, or any part f any such utility operated

ıon of the state.

MISCELLANEOUS PROVISIONS

Sec. 84. General Laws to Apply. All general la state applicable to municipal corporations, now or enacted, and which are not in conflict with the p of this charter, or with ordinances or resolutions enacted by the city commission, shall be applicabl city; provided, however, that nothing contained in t ter shall be construed as limiting the power of the c mission to enact any ordinance or resolution not in with the constitution of the state or with the exp visions of this charter.

Sec. 85. Ordinances Continued in Force. All o and resolutions in force at the time of the taking this charter, not inconsistent with its provisions, s tinue in full force and effect until amended or repea

Sec. 86. Continuance of Present Officers. All per cept the members of the Board of Education and t Judge, holding office at the time this charter is adop continue in office and in the performance of the until provision shall have been otherwise made in ac with this charter for the performance or discontin the duties of any such office. When such provision s been made the term of any such officer shall expire office be deemed abolished. The powers which are c and the duties which are imposed upon any officer, department of the city under the laws of the state, any city ordinance or contract in force at the tim taking effect of this act shall, if such office or de is abolished by this charter, be thereafter exercised charged by the commission, officer, board or departm whom are imposed corresponding functions, powers a by this charter or by any ordinance or resolution of hereafter enacted.

Sec. 87. Continuance of Contracts and Vested Rig vested rights of the city shall continue to be vested not in any manner be affected by the adoption of t ter; nor shall any right or liability, or pending suit or tion, either in behalf of or against the city, be in a ner affected by the adoption of this charter, unless o herein expressly provided to the contrary. All entered into by the city or for its benefit prior to th effect of this charter shall continue in full force an All public work begun prior to the taking effect of t ter shall be continued and perfected hereunder. P provements for which legislative steps shall have be under laws in force at the time this charter takes ef be carried to completion in accordance with the p of such laws.

Sec. 88. Investigations. The city commission, or mittee thereof, the city manager and any advisory b pointed by the commission for such purpose, shall ha at any time to cause the affairs of any departmen conduct of any officer or employe to be investigated; such purpose shall have power to compel the at of witnesses and the production of books, papers a evidence; and for that purpose may issue subpoenas or attachments which shall be signed by the president or chairman of the body or by the officer making the investigation, and shall be served by any officer authorized by law to serve such process. The authority making such investigation shall also have power to cause the testimony to be given under oath to be administered by some officer authorized by general law to administer oaths; and shall also have power to punish as for contempt any person refusing to testify to any fact within his knowledge, or to produce any books, or papers under his control, relating to the matter under investigation.

Sec. 89. Oath of Office. All officers before taking office shall take the oath of office prescribed by law; but the oath of office of city commissioner shall be in writing and be filed with the city auditor and shall contain the assertion that in his candidacy for nomination and election he has not violated any provision of section three of this charter.

Sec. 90. Hours of Labor. Except in cases of extraordinary emergency, not to exceed eight hours shall constitute a day's work and not to exceed forty-eight hours a week's work, for workmen engaged on any public work carried on or aided by the city, whether done by contract or otherwise; and it shall be unlawful for any person, corporation or association, whose duty it shall be to employ or to direct and control the services of such workmen to require or permit any of them to labor more than eight hours in any calendar day or more than forty-eight hours in any week, except in cases of extraordinary emergency. Any person who shall violate any of the provisions of this section shall be deemed guilty of a misdemeanor and upon conviction be fined not to exceed five hundred dollars or be imprisoned not more than six months or both. This section shall not be construed to include policemen or firemen nor shall it be held to apply to any contract made prior to the taking effect of this charter.

Sec. 91. First Election. In order that the provisions of this charter may be put into full force and effect from and after January 1, 1914, five city commissioners shall be elected on the fourth day of November, 1913. Candidates for the city commission shall, at such election, be nominated by petition, and there shall be no primary. Such petitions shall contain the name of the candidate or candidates, and shall specify as to each candidate that he is nominated for the office of City Commissioner for the City of Springfield, Ohio, and shall state his place of residence, with street and number thereon, if any. Such petitions shall be signed for each candidate by qualified electors of the city not less in number than five per cent of the total registered voters of the city.

Signers of such petitions shall insert in them the names and addresses of such persons as they desire to the number of five as a committee who may fill vacancies caused by death or withdrawal.

Such petitions shall contain a provision that each signer thereto thereby pledges himself to support and vote for the candidate or candidates whose nominations are therein requested, and each elector signing a petition shall add to his signature his place of residence and may subscribe to one nomination for each of the five places to be filled and no more.

One of the signers to each such separate paper shall swear that the statements therein are true to the best of his knowledge and belief and the certificate of such oath shall be annexed.

Such petitions shall be filed with the Board of Deputy State Supervisors of Elections of Clark County, Ohio, not less than sixty days previous to the day of said election.

Any person whose name has been submitted for candidacy by any such petition shall file with the secretary or any member of such election board, before September 15, 1913, his written acceptance of such candidacy, which acceptance shall state that if elected he will qualify for and serve in such office during the term for which he is elected. It shall be the duty of the secretary or member of such election board with whom such acceptance is filed forthwith to make and deliver to such candidate a written certificate acknowledging the receipt of such acceptance and stating the date of its filing. If any candidate fails to file such acceptance his name shall not appear upon the ballot.

In the event of failure to elect commissioners at such election, the vacancies due thereto shall be filled under the provisions of section four of this charter at any time after November 15th, 1913; and the three members selected by the joint board shall have the four-year terms.

Sec. 92. Amendment of Charter. Amendments to this charter may be submitted to the electors of the city by a two-thirds vote of the city commission, and, upon petition signed by ten per cent of the electors of the city setting forth any such proposed amendment, shall be submitted by such city commission. The ordinance providing for the submission of any such amendment shall require that it be submitted to the electors at the next regular municipal election if one shall occur not less than sixty nor more than one hundred and twenty days after its passage; otherwise it shall provide for the submission of the amendment at a special election to be called and held within the time aforesaid. Not less than thirty days prior to such election the clerk of the city commission shall mail a copy of the proposed amendment to each elector whose name appears upon the poll or registration books of the last regular municipal or general election. If such proposed amendment is approved by a majority of the electors voting thereon it shall become a part of the charter at the time fixed therein.

Sec. 93. Saving Clause. If any section or part of a section of this charter proves to be invalid or unconstitutional, the same shall not be held to invalidate or impair the validity, force or effect of any other section or part of a section of this charter, unless it clearly appear that such other section or part of a section is wholly or necessarily dependent for its operation upon the section or part of a section so held unconstitutional or invalid.

Sec. 94. When Charter Takes Effect. For the purpose of nominating and electing officers and all purposes connected therewith and for the purpose of exercising the powers of the city as provided herein, this charter shall take effect from the time of its approval by the electors of the city. For the purpose of establishing departments, divisions and officers, and distributing the functions thereof, and for all other purposes it shall take effect on the first day of January 1914.

We, the undersigned members of the Charter Commission of the City of Springfield, Ohio, elected at a special election held on the 10th day of June, 1913, have framed and hereby propose the foregoing as a charter for the City of Springfield Ohio.

Done in duplicate in the City of Springfield, Ohio, this 18th day of July, A. D. 1913.

THE CHARTER COMMISSION

STEWART L. TATUM, President.
JAMES H. AUGUSTUS.
J. E. BOWMAN.
CHARLES G. HECKERT.
WILLIAM C. HEWITT.
T. J. KIRKPATRICK.
FRANCIS C. LINK.
ROBERT I. NETTS.
WILLIS M. WISE.
CHARLES BAUER.
JOHN W. GARNIER.
JOHN J. HOPPES.
HARRY S. KISSELL.
J. HOWARD LITTLETON.
W. S. THOMAS.
GEORGE L. RINKLIFF, Secretary.
GLENN M. WHITESELL, Assistant Secretary.

THE LOCKPORT PLAN

(Replacing original pages of same number)

[The so-called "Lockport plan" was embodied in a bill introduced in the New York legislature in 1911, but never passed. In form it is a general enabling act applicable to any city of the third class (that is, one having a population of less than 50,000) upon adoption by local referendum, and would have supplemented the special city charter. Many of the sections of the measure have to do with conditions local to New York state and, hence, are only included here by number and title. As the sections dealing with elections and general corporate powers of the city do not belong distinctively to the city manager plan, they are also omitted. This bill has been used as a model for practically all the subsequent city manager charters.—ED.]

The people of the State of New York, represented in Senate and Assembly, do enact as follows:

ARTICLE I.

GENERAL PROVISIONS.

Sec. 1. Short Title. This act shall be known as "The Optional Third Class Cities Law."

Sec. 2. The Term City. The term city as used in this act shall apply only to such cities of the third class as shall adopt or shall seek to adopt this act.

Sec. 3. Corporate Powers. The corporate powers of the city as defined in the charter are hereby confirmed.

Sec. 4. Application of This Act. The provisions of this act shall apply to all cities of the third class which shall adopt the same, as a whole, and shall file such notices of the adoption of the same as are herein provided, with the County Clerk of the county in which the city is situated.

ARTICLE II.

ADOPTION OF THIS ACT.

Secs. 5 to 9, Inclusive. [Provisions for submission of the question of adoption by the city to popular vote, record of result of vote, etc.]

ARTICLE III.

REORGANIZATION UNDER THIS ACT.

Sec. 10. First Election under this Act.
Sec. 11. Term of First City Council.
Sec. 12. The Period of Reorganization.
Sec. 13. Redistribution of Corporate Functions.
Sec. 14. Restrictions on Such Redistributions.
Sec. 15. Succession of Functions.
Sec. 16. No New Corporate Power.
Sec. 17. Organization within Departments.
Sec. 18. Special Authority to Borrow.

ARTICLE IV.

ELECTIONS AND RECALL OF OFFICERS.

[The text of **Secs. 19 to 23, inclusive,** follow closely the charter of Berkeley, California (q. v.).]

Sec. 24. Nomination by Deposit. (1) In lieu of a petition of nomination a deposit of fifty dollars in legal tender may be made by any candidate for the office of alderman and his name shall be entered upon the official ballot in all respects as if a petition had been filed and accepted. The city clerk shall give to such candidate a receipt for such deposit, which shall, in every case, be sufficient evidence of the payment therein mentioned.

(2) The sum so deposited by any candidate shall be returned to him in the event of his obtaining a number of votes at least equal to fifteen per centum of the number of votes cast for any candidate elected. Otherwise such sum shall belong to the city for its public uses.

(3) The sum so deposited shall, in the case of the death of any candidate after being nominated and before the election, be returned to the legal representative of such candidate.

ARTICLE V.

THE CITY COUNCIL.

Sec. 25. Legislative Power Vested. The legislative and general regulative powers of the city shall be vested in a city council which shall consist of five aldermen elected at large. There shall be no other elective officers of the city.

Sec. 26. Term of Aldermen. The term of alderman shall be four years, subject to recall by the voters of the city, as hereinbefore provided by this act.

Sec. 27. Resignations. Any alderman may resign at any time and his office shall be filled by the remaining members.

Sec. 28. Qualifications. The qualifications of alderman shall be the highest non-professional or non-technical qualifications specified for any officer under the charter.

Sec. 29. Compensation. Aldermen shall receive such salary, if any, as is granted by the charter. But the city council may determine upon an amount which they may consider a just and adequate compensation for their public services and may submit a proposition to the qualified electors of the city, at any regular or special election, to fix their compensation in that amount. Such proposition shall be submitted in the following form: "Shall the compensation of aldermen be fixed at (insert amount)?" If a majority of the electors voting shall vote affirmatively on such proposition, the salaries shall be fixed accordingly, to take effect on the first day of the calendar month next succeeding the official canvass of the vote and shall not be refixed except by the same process.

Sec. 30. Eligibility for Other Offices. No aldermen shall be eligible for any other municipal office during the term for which he shall have been elected, except in such ex-officio capacities as are provided for in this act, for which he shall receive no additional compensation. The acceptance of any other public office shall operate to vacate his membership in the city council.

Sec. 31. Meetings of City Council. (1) The city council shall meet for special purposes at all such times as are fixed therefor by the charter.

(2) An ordinance shall be passed, before this act shall be declared to be in full operation, providing a schedule of regular sessions to occur not less frequently than is fixed by the charter, and for the special sessions at which the city council shall act in the capacity of Board of Estimate and Apportionment and as the ex-officio governing board of any

corporate bodies within the municipality as hereinafter provided.

(3) Any two members may call a meeting.

(4) All meetings shall be public.

(5) Any citizen may have access to the minutes upon application to the city clerk.

CITIZEN'S MOTION.

(6) Any citizen may appear before the city council at any of its regular meetings and may present a printed motion. Said motion shall be acted upon by the city council, in the regular course of business, within fifteen days.

Sec. 32. **Quorum.** Three members shall constitute a quorum to transact business, but a smaller number may adjourn from day to day and compel the attendance of absent members.

Sec. 33. **Passage of Measures.** Three votes shall be required to pass any measure involving the expenditure of money, confirming appointments or removals, granting a franchise, or authorizing a bond issue. A simple majority shall suffice for the passage of any other measure. The signature of the mayor shall not be required in any case.

Sec. 34. **No Member Excused.** No member shall be excused from voting except on matters involving the consideration of his own official conduct. In all other cases a failure to vote shall be entered on the minutes as a negative vote.

Sec. 35. **Mayor to Preside.** The mayor shall preside at all sessions and shall have two votes in case of a tie.

Sec. 36. **Succession of Functions.** The city council shall succeed, severally and collectively, to all such powers, duties and penalties for non-performance or malfeasance, as are conferred, imposed or inflicted upon common councils and aldermen and councilmen in cities of the third class by the general laws of the state and the charter, and are not inconsistent with the provisions of this act. They shall likewise succeed to all the powers heretofore exercised by the several officers and boards of the city government, except as specifically granted to other bodies by the provisions of this act. But, in the case of such succession, the powers exercised shall not be executive or administrative except as hereinafter specified. And it is further provided that the limitations laid down in the charter and in the general laws of the state with regard to the exercise of powers and duties by the several administrative officers and boards, shall be applicable to the exercise of the said powers and duties by the city council, when said city council shall succeed to the said powers and duties, in so far as said limitations are not in conflict with the provisions of this act.

Sec. 37. **Powers and Duties of City Council; enumerated.**

Sec. 38. **Control Over Administrative Departments.** (1) The city council shall have power and it shall be their duty to issue general and special orders, by resolution, to the city manager, giving him authority to carry out, in accordance with law, the administrative powers and duties conferred and imposed upon the city.

(2) They shall require the city manager to present, once a year, a complete report, financial and otherwise, of the activities of the several departments of the city government, and special reports at any time.

(3) In cities where the charter provides for a Board of Estimate and Apportionment, that body shall consist of the city council meeting in special session, public notice whereof shall have been given as provided by Sec. 31 of this article. At such special session the city council may compel the attendance of all heads of administrative departments, and shall exercise the functions designated to the Board of Estimate and Apportionment by the charter.

(4) The city council may provide for a board of audit, or a special auditor, to be directly subject to their control, and independent of the city manager. Such board or officer shall have access to all vouchers and other public records within the several administrative departments at all times and shall have such powers consistent with the law as the city council may confer. But all claims arising from injury to pe property shall be audited and disposed of by the city

(5) The city council shall have power to validate a ful act performed by any administrative officer of t without its previous authority.

(6) In cities which are independent highway distr city council shall be ex-officio commissioners of high

Sec. 39. **Agents of the State Government.** Whene city council shall, in pursuance of the provisions of t assume the functions of boards which are essentia local agents of the state administration, they shall be able to the central administrative officer or body to extent of the powers granted and the duties imposed operation of this act.

Sec. 40. **Effect of Enumeration.** The enumeration power or powers herein granted the city council shall construed so as to exclude any others which may be by any other law applicable to the city and not inco with this act. The exercise of powers by the city shall be subject to the provisions of Article XI.

ARTICLE VI.

THE MAYOR.

Sec. 41. **How Chosen.** The mayor shall be that r of the city council who, at the regular election of office have received the highest number of votes. In ca candidates receive the same number of votes, one c shall be chosen mayor by the remaining three m elected to the city council. In the event of the mayor' nation or recall, the remaining members of the city shall choose his successor for the unexpired term, fro own number.

Sec. 42. **General Powers and Duties.** The powe duties of the mayor shall be such as are conferred up by this act, together with such others as are conferred city council in pursuance of the provisions of this act, others.

Sec. 43. **President of City Council.** He shall be pı of the city council and shall exercise all the powers co and perform all the duties imposed upon the presiding of the common council by the charter which are not sistent with this act. He shall appoint all standi special committees of the city council. He shall be nized as the official head of the city by the courts purpose of serving civil processes, by the Governor purposes of the military law, and for all ceremonial pı

Sec. 44. **Police and Military Powers.** His power command of the police and to govern the city by procla during times of great public danger shall not be abri abrogated.

Sec. 45. **Designation to Judicial Vacancies.** Dur disability of any municipal judge or justice of the pe mayor shall designate some properly qualified person during such disability.

Sec. 46. **Magisterial Powers.** He shall have power minister oaths and take affidavits.

Sec. 47. **Commissioner of Charities in Certain Cit** cities where the mayor is authorized by charter to the supervisors as a commissioner of charities, he sh tinue so to act.

Sec. 48. **Removal by Governor.** The power of th ernor to remove the mayor shall not be abridged.

Sec. 49. **No Judicial Powers; Mayor's Courts Ab** The mayor shall have no judicial power. The mayor' of Special Sessions and all other mayor's courts are abolished. The jurisdiction of the same shall be co by the city council upon some other municipal court.

Sec. 50. **Non-enumerated Functions...** Such functic enumerated in this act, as are conferred upon the m the city by charter or by the general laws of the state exercised by the city manager unless some other p shall be made by the city council.

Sec. 51. **Salary**...The salary of the mayor shall be twice the salary, if any, received by any other member of the city council.

Sec. 52. **Acting Mayor.** During the disability of the mayor, the functions of his office shall devolve upon some member of the city council designated by that body, who shall receive during such incumbency a pro rata of the excess over the alderman's salary which is allowed to the mayor under this act.

ARTICLE VII.

THE CITY MANAGER.

Sec. 53. **Administrative Head of Government.** There shall be chosen by the city council an officer to be known as the city manager, who shall be the administrative head of the city government.

Sec. 54. **Official Oath and Bond.** Before entering upon the duties of his office the city manager shall take the official oath required by law and shall execute a bond in favor of the city for the faithful performance of his duties in such sum as shall be determined upon by the city council.

Sec. 55. **Tenure of Office.** The tenure of the city manager shall be at the pleasure of the city council.

Sec. 56. **Not to Be Interested.** The city manager shall not be personally interested in any contracts to which the city is a party, for supplying the city with materials of any kind.

Sec. 57. **Duties; General.** It shall be the duty of the city manager to see that within the city the laws of this state and the ordinances, resolutions and by-laws of the city council shall be faithfully executed. In addition to such functions as are enumerated in this act he shall exercise all other powers and perform all other duties conferred and imposed upon mayors of cities, unless other designation shall be made by this act or by act of the city council.

Sec. 58. **Recommendations and Reports.** It shall be his duty to attend all meetings of, and to recommend to, the city council, from time to time, such measures as he shall deem necessary or expedient for it to adopt. He shall prepare business, and draw up resolutions and ordinances for adoption by the city council, and furnish them with any necessary information respecting any of the departments under his control.

He shall, at such times as the city council shall so require, present reports from the several departments, and shall draw up an annual report which shall consolidate the special reports of the several departments. He shall be a member of the Board of Estimate and Apportionment and shall present to that body, annually, an itemized estimate of the financial needs of the several departments for the ensuing year.

Sec. 59. **Appointments.** He shall appoint persons to fill all offices for which no other mode of appointment is provided. And no such appointment to or removal from such office shall be made without his consent.

Sec. 60. **Relation to Department Heads.** He shall transmit to the heads of the several departments written notice of all acts of the city council relating to the duties of their departments, and he shall make designations of officers to perform duties ordered to be performed by the city council.

Sec. 61. **Signs Certain Documents.** He shall sign such contracts, licenses and other public documents, on behalf of the city, as the city council may authorize and require.

Sec. 62. **Access to Public Records.** He shall have access at all times to the books, vouchers and papers of any officer or employee of the city and shall have power to examine, under oath, any person connected therewith. It shall be his duty, either in person or by the aid of a competent expert, to know the manner in which the accounts of the city and the various boards are kept.

Sec. 63. **Signs Warrants of Arrest.** He shall have power to sign warrants of arrest and to cause arrests for infraction, within the city, of the laws of the state and ordinances and other regulations of the city. He shall have general power to administer oaths and take affidavits.

Sec. 64. **May Revoke Licenses.** He shall have power to revoke licenses pending the action of the city council.

Sec. 65. **Office Consolidated with City Clerk's in Certain Cities.** In cities having a population of less than twenty thousand, according to the last preceding state enumeration, the office of city manager may be consolidated with that of city clerk, or other officer of similar functions.

Sec. 66. **Disability.** During the disability of the city manager the city council shall designate some properly qualified person to execute the functions of the office.

ARTICLE VIII.

[Secs. 67 to 74 contain special provisions to obviate possible conflicts of the act with provisions of the special city charters.]

ARTICLE IX.

[Secs. 75 to 82 relate to certain special matters of local significance in regard to appointments.]

ARTICLE X.

THE DEPARTMENT OF EDUCATION.

[By Secs. 83 to 94 the board of education is divested of its corporate character, and, so far as conditions permit, made a department of the general administration of the city. The board is appointed by the council.]

ARTICLE XI.

THE INITIATIVE AND REFERENDUM.

[The provisions of this article Secs. 95 to 99 are adapted from the charter of Berkeley, California (q. v.).]

ARTICLE XII.

[Miscellaneous provisions (Secs. 100 to 106)].

provisions of this act. But, in the case of such succession, the powers exercised shall not be executive or administrative except as hereinafter specified. And it is further provided that the limitations laid down in the charter and in the general laws of the State with regard to the exercise of powers and duties by the several administrative officers and boards, shall be applicable to the exercise of the said powers and duties by the City Council, when said City Council shall succeed to the said powers and duties, in so far as said limitations are not in conflict with the provisions of this act.

Sec. 37. Powers and duties of City Council; enumerated.

The City Council shall have power and it shall be their duty, subject to the positive grants of power to other bodies contained in this act:

(1) To exercise all the corporate functions of the city in relation to finance, including the power to borrow money, issue bonds, levy taxes and assessments and make appropriations.

(2) To buy, sell, lease, rent or condemn real estate and buildings. But the power of the tax-collecting officer to take any lawful action for the collection of delinquent taxes and assessments shall not be abrogated or abridged.

(3) To exercise the corporate powers in relation to contracts.

(4) To exercise such control over public utility plants, including the power to fix rates at which public utilities shall be furnished to consumers, as is vested in the city by the charter, or by the general laws of the State.

(5) To receive gifts of money, real estate and buildings, except those made for the uses of the Board of Education, and to control the disposition of the same.

(6) To grant and revoke licenses for the conduct of lawful forms of business and to pass ordinances governing their granting and revocation.

(7) To make all such readjustments and redistribution of the functions of administrative departments as are provided for in Article VIII.

(8) To confirm and reject appointments and removals as provided for in Article IX.

(9) To fix the compensation of appointive officers, boards and employees. But the salaries of officers and boards appointed for a fixed period shall not be lowered during their term. Nor shall any fees, fixed by act of the legislature, be altered.

Sec. 38. Control over Administrative Departments.

(1) The City Council shall have power and it shall be their duty to issue general and special orders, by resolution, to the City Manager, giving him authority to carry out, in accordance with law, the administrative powers and duties conferred and imposed upon the city.

(2) They shall require the City Manager to present, once a year, a complete report, financial and otherwise, of the activities of the several departments of the city government, and special reports at any time.

(3) In cities where the charter provides for a Board of Estimate and Apportionment, that body shall consist of the City Council meeting in special session, public notice whereof shall have been given as provided by Section 31 of this article. At such special session the City Council may compel the attendance of all heads of administrative departments, and shall exercise the functions designated to the Board of Estimate and Apportionment by the charter.

(4) The City Council may provide for a board of audit, or a special auditor, to be directly subject to their control, and independent of the City Manager. Such board or officer shall have access to all vouchers and other public records within the several administrative departments at all times and shall have such powers consistent with the law as the City Council may confer. But all claims arising from injury to person or property shall be audited and disposed of by the City Council.

(5) The City Council shall have power to validate any lawful act performed by any administrative officer of the city without its previous authority.

(6) In cities which are independent highway districts the City Council shall be ex-officio commissioners of highways.

Sec. 39. Agents of the State Government.

Whenever the City Council shall, in pursuance of the provisions of this act, assume the functions of boards which are essentially the local agents of the state administration, they shall be amenable to the central administrative officer or body to the full extent of the powers granted and the duties imposed by the operation of this act.

Sec. 40. Effect of enumeration.

The enumeration of any power or powers herein granted the City Council shall not be construed so as to exclude any others which may be granted by any other law applicable to the city and not inconsistent with this act. The exercise of powers by the City Council shall be subject to the provisions of Article XI.

ARTICLE VI.

THE MAYOR.

Sec. 41. How chosen.

The Mayor shall be that member of the City Council who, at regular election of officers, shall have received the highest number of votes. In case two candidates receive the same number of votes, one of them shall be chosen Mayor by the remaining three members elected to the City Council. In the event of the Mayor's resignation or recall, the remaining members of the City Council shall choose his successor for the unexpired term, from their own number.

Sec. 42. General Powers and Duties.

The powers and duties of the Mayor shall be such as are conferred upon him by this act, together with such others as are conferred by the City Council in pursuance of the provisions of this act, and no others.

Sec. 43. President of City Council.

He shall be president of the City Council and shall exercise all the powers conferred and perform all the duties imposed upon the presiding officer of the Common Council by the charter which are not inconsistent with this act. He shall appoint all standing and special committees of the City Council. He shall be recognized as the official head of the city by the courts for the purpose of serving civil processes, by the Governor for the purposes of the military law, and for all ceremonial purposes.

Sec. 44. Police and Military Powers.

His power to take command of the police and to govern the city by proclamation during times of great public danger shall not be abridged or abrogated.

Sec. 45. Designation to judicial vacancies.

During the disability of any municipal judge or justice of the peace the Mayor shall designate some properly qualified person to act during such disability.

Sec. 46. Magisterial Powers.

He shall have power to administer oaths and take affidavits.

Sec. 47. Commissioner of Charities in certain cities.

In cities where the Mayor is authorized by charter to sit with the supervisors as a Commissioner of Charities, he shall continue so to act.

Sec. 48. Removal by Governor.

The power of the Governor to remove the Mayor shall not be abridged.

Sec. 49. No judicial powers; Mayor's Courts abolished.

The Mayor shall have no judicial power. The Mayor's Court of Special Sessions and all other Mayor's Courts are hereby abolished. The jurisdiction of the same shall be conferred by the City Council upon some other municipal court.

Sec. 50. Non-enumerated functions.

Such functions, not enumerated in this act, as are conferred upon the Mayor of the city by charter or by the general laws of the State shall be exercised by the City Manager unless some other provision shall be made by the City Council.

Sec. 51. Salary.

The salary of the Mayor shall be twice the salary, if any, received by any other member of the City Council.

Sec. 52. Acting Mayor.

During the disability of the Mayor, the functions of his office shall devolve upon some member of the City Council designated by that body, who shall receive during such incumbency a pro rata of the excess over the alderman's salary which is allowed to the Mayor under this act.

ARTICLE VII.

THE CITY MANAGER.

Sec. 53. Administrative Head of Government.

There shall be chosen by the City Council an officer to be known as the City Manager, who shall be the administrative head of the city government.

Sec. 54. Official oath and bond.

Before entering upon the duties of his office the City Manager shall take the official oath required by law and shall execute a bond in favor of the city for the faithful performance of his duties in such sum as shall be determined upon by the City Council.

Sec. 55. Term.

The term of the City Manager shall be at the pleasure of the City Council.

Sec. 56. Not to be interested.

The City Manager shall not be personally interested in any contracts to which the city is a party, for supplying the city with materials of any kind.

Sec. 57. Duties; general.

It shall be the duty of the City Manager to see that within the city the laws of this state and the ordinances, resolutions and by-laws of the City Council shall be faithfully executed. In addition to such functions as are enumerated in this act he shall exercise all other powers and perform all other duties conferred and imposed upon mayors of cities except other designation shall be made by this act or by act of the City Council.

Sec. 58. Recommendations and Reports.

It shall be his duty to attend all meetings of, and to recommend to, the City Council, from time to time, such measures as he shall deem necessary or expedient for it to adopt. He shall prepare business, and draw up resolutions and ordinances for adoption by the City Council, and furnish them with any necessary information respecting any of the departments under his control.

He shall, at such times as the City Council shall so require, present reports from the several departments, and shall draw up an annual report which shall consolidate the special reports of the several departments. He shall be a member of the Board of Estimate and Apportionment and shall present to that body, annually, an itemized estimate of the financial needs of the several departments for the ensuing year.

Sec. 59. Appointments.

He shall appoint persons to fill all offices for which no other mode of appointment is provided. And no such appointment to or removal from such office shall be made without his consent.

Sec. 60. Relation to Department Heads.

He shall transmit to the heads of the several departments written notice of all acts of the City Council relating to the duties of their departments, and he shall make designations of officers to perform duties ordered to be performed by the City Council.

Sec. 61. Signs certain documents.

He shall sign such contracts, licenses and other public documents, on behalf of the city, as the City Council may authorize and require.

Sec. 62. Access to public records.

He shall have access at all times to the books, vouchers and papers of any officer or employee of the city and shall have power to examine, under oath, any person connected therewith. It shall be his duty, either in person or by the aid of a competent expert, to know the manner in which the accounts of the city and the various boards are kept.

Sec. 63. Signs warrants of arrest.

He shall have power to sign warrants of arrest and to cause arrests for infraction, within the city, of the laws of the State and ordinances and other regulations of the city. He shall have general power to administer oaths and take affidavits.

Sec. 64. May revoke licenses.

He shall have power to revoke licenses pending the action of the City Council.

Sec. 65. Office consolidated with City Clerk's in certain cities.

In cities having a population of less than twenty thousand, according to the last preceding state enumeration, the office of City Manager may be consolidated with that of City Clerk, or other officer of similar functions.

Sec. 66. Disability.

During the disability of the City Manager the City Council shall designate some properly qualified person to execute the functions of the office.

ARTICLE VIII.

ADMINISTRATIVE DEPARTMENTS.

Sec. 67. Duties of Departmental Heads.

The heads of departments shall perform, or delegate the performance of, all duties imposed upon them by the City Manager in pursuance of the general regulations of the City Council. They shall, of their own initiative, or upon his order, at any time, submit to him statements of the needs of their several departments and propose any measures, with or without specifications, which they may deem necessary or advisable for the welfare of the city. They shall prepare reports and make estimates of the probable financial requirements of their departments, in such form and at such times as he shall require. They shall sit with the City Council as advisory members of the Board of Estimate and Apportionment. They shall assemble upon the call of the City Manager for general consideration of the affairs of the city. They shall recommend the appointment and dismissal of subordinate officers and employees in their several departments.

Sec. 68. Prohibitions and limitations.

The powers of all administrative officers and boards shall be administrative and advisory only, with such exceptions as are hereinafter noted, and shall not extend to the enactment of general regulations, except for the purpose of controlling the organization within their several departments. No administrative officer or board shall buy, rent, lease, sell or condemn any real estate, buildings, public utility plants. Nor, except as specially provided in Article X, shall any such officer or board enter into any contracts, or borrow money on the credit of the city, or levy taxes or assessments, or receive gifts on behalf of the city, except for school purposes, of money, real estate or buildings, or grant franchises, or fix rates at which water, gas, electricity or any other commodity may be furnished to consumers.

Sec. 69. Authority for expenditures.

The administrative officers of the city other than the Board of Education shall not make any expenditures except upon the authority of a resolution of the City Council. But the City Council may at its discretion set aside for any department a fund for emergency expenses, and enact rules governing the same.

Sec. 70. Special provisions.

(1) Nothing in this article shall so be construed as to limit the tax-collecting officer in the exercise of the powers and duties granted by the general laws of the State and the charter of the city to take action for the collection of delinquent taxes and assessments.

(2) The Corporation Counsel or City Attorney shall not compromise any suit to which the city is a party, without the consent of the City Council.

(3) The Board or Commissioner of Health, or the officers exercising the powers of Boards or Commissioner of Public Safety, may take any action, not of general application, to prevent disease, fire, violence or any other menace to public health or safety, which shall have been granted by law before the adoption of this act, or which shall be granted. And for these purposes they may command the assistance of the police. The said Board or Commissioner of Health shall have power to draw up a Health Code which the City Council may adopt and incorporate in the ordinances of the city, or reject, but not amend.

Sec. 71. Certain duties of Treasurer.

The Treasurer of the city shall act as the fiscal officer of the Board of Education and shall be subject to its orders.

Sec. 72. Art Commissioners.

Art Commissioners, if any, shall have power to receive gifts, and shall be unrestricted in the use of the funds at their disposal by any other officers in the purchase of works of art. Their functions shall not be consolidated with those of any other department, but members of other departments may act ex-officio on such board.

Sec. 73. Administration of Special Funds.

In all cases where the administration of special funds, not essential to the ordinary functions of the city government, is entrusted by the charter to a definitely constituted body, they shall continue to be so administered. The City Council shall have power, within its corporate capacity, to create special funds and to fix rules for their administration.

Sec. 74. Officers as agents of State.

In so far as the departments of the city government are agents of the state government they shall be responsible for that part of the performance of any specific duty imposed by a central administrative agency as is consistent with the distribution of powers in this act and the acts of the Council supplementary thereto. That is to say: bodies entrusted with powers of general regulation shall be so far responsible; and bodies or officers upon whom specific performance is imposed shall be held responsible for the same by the central administrative agency. In such portions of the administrative side of the city government as are under the control of the City Manager, that officer shall be jointly responsible with his subordinates.

ARTICLE IX.

APPOINTMENTS AND REMOVALS.

Sec. 75. Direct Appointments by City Council.

The City Manager, Assessors, Art Commissioners, if any, Civil Service Commissioners, if any, such judges of the several courts, justices of the peace, constables, and commissioners of deeds, as are provided for by law, shall be appointed by a vote of a majority of the City Council, upon the nomination of any alderman. The term of all judges, justices of the peace, and constables shall be four years. The term of Commissioners of Deeds shall be two years; of Art Commissioners, Civil Service Commissioners and Assessors three years.

Sec. 76. Appointments by Department Heads.

(1) With the consent of the City Council, the heads of departments may appoint one or more persons who shall act as their personal assistants. They may also appoint, with such consent, other persons, to serve temporarily on a per diem compensation.

(2) The Corporation Counsel or City Attorney, with the consent of the City Council, may appoint his legal assistants.

Sec. 77. Appointments by City Manager.

The appointment of all other officers and employees shall be made by the City Manager, subject to confirmation or rejection by the City Council.

Sec. 78. Exceptions to Sections above.

But nothing in this act shall derogate from or alter the effect of, the laws applicable to the city in so far as they relate to appointments under the direction of Civil Service Commissioners. The Commissioners of Art may appoint curators and other special assistants.

Sec. 79. Term of officers of unfixed tenure.

The term of all officers and employees of unfixed tenure shall be at the pleasure of the appointing officer or body. No officer or appointee appointed by the City Manager shall be removed without the consent of the latter. Any officer of unfixed tenure may be removed without a hearing, but when so removed may demand of the appointing body a written statement of the cause for such removal, signed by all the members voting for the same. A failure on the part of the appointing body to issue such statement within two weeks after the receipt of such demand shall constitute a breach of the official oath of office.

Sec. 80. Removal of officers of fixed tenure.

Officers whose tenure is fixed by this act, may be removed by a majority of all members elected to the City Council after notice of at least one week, and a public trial upon specific charges. The salaries of such officers shall not be lowered during the term for which they were appointed.

Sec. 81. Disciplinary power of Police and Fire Departments.

The heads of the police and fire departments shall have power to suspend any of their subordinate officers in the interests of discipline. But any officer suspended for a period longer than three days may appeal to the City Council at any of its regular sessions, and they shall review his case and make any restitution, within the law, which they may deem advisable.

Sec. 82. Saving clause.

Nothing in this article shall apply to the Board of Education, its officers, and employees.

ARTICLE X.

THE DEPARTMENT OF EDUCATION.

Sections 83 to 94 inclusive.

[The Board of Education is divested of its corporate character, and, so far as conditions permit, made a department of the general administration of the city. The Board is appointed by the Council.]

ARTICLE XI.

THE INITIATIVE AND REFERENDUM.

Sections 95 to 99.

[The provisions of this article are adapted from the Charter of Berkeley, California (*q. v.*).]

ARTICLE XII.

MISCELLANEOUS PROVISIONS.

Sec. 100. Definitions.

The term "charter," as used herein, shall be deemed to refer to the charter of such city together with all the acts amendatory thereto. Whenever an officer or board is referred to, unless some other designation is made, it shall be deemed to refer to such officer or board as exercises the functions of the officer or board mentioned.

Sec. 101. Construction.

Sec. 102. Supervisors.

This act shall not apply to supervisors except as hereinafter provided. The following proposition may be submitted to the qualified electors of the city in conformity with Article XI of this act: "Shall the provisions of Article IV of The Optional Third Class Cities Law be applied to the election of the supervisors in the city of.............(insert name)?" If a majority of the electors voting at such election shall vote affirmatively on such proposition, the next succeeding regular election of supervisors shall be conducted in conformity with the aforesaid Article IV, if a sufficient interval of time shall have elapsed between the canvass of the vote on the aforesaid proposition and the succeeding regular election of supervisors to permit of the provisions of the said Article IV being applied. If such interval is too short to permit of such application of said article then such application shall be made at the election next succeeding the aforesaid regular election at which supervisors are to be elected.

Sec. 103. Public Corporations Dissolved.

All public corporations which exercise by the provisions of this act the functions of departments of the city government are hereby dissolved. The titles to their personal and real property is vested in the city.

Sec. 104. Saving clause.

Nothing contained in this act shall be construed to repeal any statute of the state or ordinance of the city or rule or regulation of the Board of Health, not inconsistent with the provisions of this act, and the same shall remain in full force and effect, when not inconsistent with the provisions of this act, to be construed and operated in harmony with its provisions. The powers which are conferred and the duties which are imposed upon any officer or department of the city under any statute of the state, or any city ordinance which is in force at the time of the taking effect of this act shall, if such office or department be abolished in pursuance of the provisions of this act, be therefore exercised and discharged by the officer, board or department upon whom is imposed corresponding or like functions, powers and duties under the provisions of this act. Where any contract has been entered into by the city prior to the time of the taking effect of this act, or any bond or undertaking has been given to or in favor of the city, which contains provisions that the same may be enforced by some officer, board or department therein named, but by the operation of this act such office, board or department is abolished, such contracts shall not in any manner be impaired, but shall continue in full force, and the powers conferred and the duties imposed with reference to the same upon the officer, board or department which has been abolished, shall thereafter be exercised and discharged by the officer, board or department upon whom is conferred or imposed like powers, functions or duties under the provisions of this act.

Sec. 105. Reversion to the charter.

Any city which shall have operated for more than six years under the provisions of this act may abandon such organization hereunder and may resume its charter by proceeding as follows:

Upon the petition of not less than 25 per centum of the electors of such city, a special election shall be called, at which the following proposition shall be submitted: "Shall the city of (name of city) abandon its organization under The Optional Third Class Cities Law and resume its charter?"

If a majority of the votes cast at such special election be in favor of such proposition, the officers elected at the next succeeding regular municipal election shall be those prescribed by the charter, and upon the qualification of such officers, such city shall become a city under the charter, but such change shall not in any manner or degree effect the property, right or liability of any nature of such city, but shall merely extend to such change in its form of government.

The sufficiency of such petition shall be determined, the election ordered and conducted and the results declared generally as provided by Article IV. of this act in so far as the provisions thereof are applicable.

Sec. 106. Act to take effect immediately.

This act shall take effect immediately.

Copies of the full text of this proposal are obtainable on request from the Lockport Board of Trade, Lockport, N. Y.

[illegible]

[illegible]

[illegible]

[illegible]

[illegible]

[illegible]

Reports from the Short Ballot Cities.

In the larger cities where the "Commission" plan has been in operation long enough to permit of a fair comparison with old conditions, The Short Ballot Organization secured a special paid correspondent who was requested to present the truth regarding the workings of the plan in his city, as he saw it. The letters from these men are believed to be thoroughly reliable accounts of the local conditions which they describe. Reports from other cities and authenticated information from other sources will be presented in later editions of the Digest.

COMMISSION GOVERNMENT IN HAVERHILL

REPORT BY SPECIAL CORRESPONDENT.

HAVERHILL, MASS, Dec. 21, 1910.

Haverhill, Mass., has just completed two years under its new form of municipal government; that the idea has worked out successfully and that a small city council is much better than two branches, is now admitted by those who opposed as well as those who advocated the change.

The municipal election of December 6, 1910, the third under the new method, has, however, demonstrated one fault, which is that the real principles of commission government were not embodied by those who changed the city charter; there is already talk of an appeal to the next Massachusetts legislature to remedy this defect.

The voters of Haverhill have for years past shown that they are peculiar in their likes and dislikes, and uncertainty prevails as to whether they would sanction any further changes in the method of electing city fathers; yet, unless a change is made, it is freely predicted that the municipal council will within a short time become as notorious as its old predecessor consisting of two boards.

The history of municipal politics in Haverhill teems with party strife. The city was instituted in 1870, and before the Australian ballot was adopted bosses were prevalent. There were straight and split tickets, the latter being printed just on the eve of elections with some of the straight nominees eliminated, and those whom the bosses wanted substituted. The population of the city, now being 44,000, is very cosmopolitan in character, which may be one reason for the varying success of the different parties, including the Socialists, whose influence during the latter history of the city has been alternately rising and falling.

Many older residents of the city recall that they were often fooled by the apparent straight ticket that was handed to them as they were about to cast their ballot, and a sharp eye was necessary to avoid being duped by the political tricksters.

These sharp practices were, however, eliminated by the Australian ballot, which is prepared by the city. Yet the party bosses continued to hold sway, but, state contests becoming mixed up with municipal fights, the voters revolted, and for the past fifteen years individual control of any number of voters in that city has been impossible.

The trouble over municipal politics began about twenty years ago, when it was charged that the Republicans "sold out," and since then the Republicans—as a straight party—have never regained control. Factions were created at that time, and the wounds have never been healed; meanwhile the voters have assumed more and more of an independent spirit.

It was in 1897 that the Socialists first gained their foothold in Haverhill, and for two years they elected a mayor as well as three aldermen. Their actual strength was about 700, and it was the sympathetic vote that landed their candidates in office. They, however, passed away almost as quickly as they arose, a concerted anti-socialistic movement being inaugurated.

The Socialists, however, got back into power in 1903, when their mayor was declared elected in a controversy over disputed ballots; but he served only one term, as the Republicans rallied and with the aid of Democratic voters placed Roswell L. Wood into the mayor's office.

In the state election caucuses previous to that time, the Republicans attempted to restrict the voters at the primaries to their own party, but it failed, as the bars were let down; and this tendency increased so that no question was raised about any voter who attended either the state or municipal primaries.

Though Mr. Wood was elected to a second term, he was bitterly opposed when he sought a third. He was, however, successful, and he also secured a fourth as well as a fifth term—an unprecedented vindication. It was under his administration that a new high school was started and—although nothing was ever proved—there were numerous rumors of graft.

It was after he secured a fifth term that the movement to change the form of government was advocated, and, following an address by President-Emeritus Eliot of Harvard, an association was formed for the purpose of launching the movement. A charter was drafted and submitted to the legislature, and after its passage there, accepted at a special election by the people.

The old form of government consisted of a mayor, one alderman elected at large from each of the seven wards, and two councilmen from each ward elected in each. Clashes were frequent between both branches over important measures, politics and the needs of constituents seeming to play an important part in guiding their voting.

Edwin H. Moulton was picked by the amended city charter advocates as their choice for mayor, and ex-Mayor Wood, who opposed the new form of government, ran again. After one of the bitterest and liveliest campaigns ever waged in Haverhill, the charter advocates were successful, Wood being defeated by 86 votes in a total of 7,499. The election was the signal for the disbandment of the civic association which had done so much when there was a deficit of about $80,000.

It was while Mayor Moulton was in office, in 1897, that he insisted upon department heads living within their appropriations, and one of his chief traits for the past two years has been watching the moneys and seeing whether the city could afford a thing or not before committing himself. He has never hesitated to protest, no matter how urgent the cause might be, if the money were not in sight to provide for it.

Previous to the change in the form of government, the municipal departments had been running behind yearly. This was naturally the case when the members of the city council paid but little heed to finances as long as their constituents obtained improvements, and this condition continued until the end of 1908, when there was a deficit of about $80,000.

Mayor Moulton promised that if elected he would run the city within its income of $12 per $1,000 of taxation for current expenses; and he has fulfilled his pledge, the financial statement showing that there was a surplus in 1909 of $36,511, while this year it is estimated that there will be a surplus of about $30,000.

The members of the municipal council were no sooner elected in 1908 than they began planning for the change in the administrative policy. A civil engineer who had served as city engineer was placed in charge of the street department, where in the past two years more work has been done than ever before known, the sum of $80,892 having been expended in 1909 and $136,479 this year. A former bank cashier was given charge of finances; a practical builder and contractor has had charge of public property, and a shoe worker has been supervisor of the public safety departments.

Aldermen Killam and Bean were first elected for one year and in 1909 were elected to serve two years, this being now the tenure for the mayor and aldermen. During the first year there were hardly any differences among the members of the municipal council, but the second election was no sooner over than it was intimated that Alderman Bean would oppose the re-election of the mayor.

The members of the municipal council incurred the enmity of some of their staunchest supporters on minor as well as important matters, so that jealousies cropped out even among people who had been ardent supporters of the amended city charter, just as had occurred under the old form of government.

One of the principal causes of this lack of harmony was a gas controversy that had existed for ten years. When the Socialists were in power in 1889, the gas plant was sold for about $500,000, and the new owners floated a like amount of bonds forming a holding company. As the company was only capitalized for $75,000—its earnings having been used in the development of the plant—the Socialists protested and asked for a reduction in the price of gas.

The state commission granted the petition, ordering an 80-cent rate instead of $1 net, but the company appealed and the case was taken to the courts, where it rested until a year ago, the issue being then forced by the municipal council which declared for municipal ownership. The company again changed hands last year, and the new owners agreed to reduce the price to 90 cents providing litigation was dropped.

The bonds that were floated ten years ago were bought up and a new company was formed, but it is as yet incomplete, and an agreement was made with the new company by which rebates were paid on the 90-cent basis dating from July 1, 1909, the rebates aggregating $20,000.

There is also a proviso that the rate will later be reduced to 85 and eventually to 80 cents. Alderman Bean protested against this action, but his colleagues accepted the offer, and their action was one of the main arguments advanced in the recent campaign against the re-election of Mayor Moulton and Aldermen Desmond and Harris.

The municipal ownership of the Haverhill electric plant was also included by the municipal council, which, being submitted to the voters, was rejected by an overwhelming vote, business men having pointed out that it would cost $1,000,000 to buy the plant and that the city would lose about $60,000 yearly in running the business.

The new owners of the gas company have already begun to spend about $500,000 in rebuilding its plant, and though it is admitted that the city would have had to pay $1,000,000 for it, this was not thought of by many voters, who only seemed to realize that they had not secured 80-cent gas and who believed they ought to have had a rebate since 1900.

The municipal campaign no sooner opened this year than Alderman Bean jumped into the fight against

Mayor Moulton. The latter and his colleagues made no campaign whatever, relying upon their records to win out, though their opponents in the ten days previous to the city election held street rallies nightly, Alderman Bean attacking the administration of which he had been a part.

The fact that they had not been allowed to vote upon the question of municipal ownership of the gas plant was the main issue of the election discussed by the working people, who comprise the majority of the voting strength of the city, and it was the constant attacks of ex-Mayor Wood that changed the sentiment, landing him in a two-year aldermanic berth at a salary of $1,800, and nearly defeating Mayor Moulton.

When Alderman Bean became a mayoralty candidate, he presented his resignation to the municipal council, to take effect January 1. It was accepted, whereupon he asked that his successor be chosen at the regular election. Such action was declared illegal as it would be impossible to fill a vacancy before it existed.

It was pointed out that if he resigned at once the municipal council would fill the vacancy and not the voters, as the amended city charter provides that if a vacancy occurs four months previous to a regular election, the power of filling it rests with the council.

Out of that fact the friends of Alderman Bean tried to make an issue, for a special election would cost $1,400, but it fell flat, many even predicting that he had no intention of resigning. The election was no sooner over than he was besieged to remain in office by people who had supported him, and he has since withdrawn his resignation, serving the remaining year of his two-year term.

The issue in the recent city election was directly between Mayor Moulton and Alderman Bean, but in the aldermanic contest there were four candidates, with the voters allowed to suport two. It is here, say those who advocated the new form of government, a mistake was made, and they are now advocating a change so that the lines will be more clearly defined.

It is now argued that the commission form of government ought to have been adopted, as in that case there would be only two men running for each of the five positions and "bullets" in voting for only one of the four aldermanic candidates as at present would be impossible. The peculiar features of the commission plan have at least been given a trial; the Socialists having attempted to use the recall, but failed through inability to obtain the necessary percentage (25) of the voters. The initiative has been taken up once, and the council considered the matter favorably.

That the new form of municipal government has been a success is conceded on all sides, as the stormy and midnight sessions that characterized the two-branch board have for the past two years been a thing of the past, business having been transacted quietly and like that of a business corporation.

Important questions have been discussed at conferences before the open sessions of the board and it is this lack of publicity that appealed to many. In his campaign speeches ex-Mayor Wood won much support by proclaiming for an open door policy at city hall and declaring that if elected he would see that everything was made public. But it is a question whether he will be able to accomplish this, for some of the city fathers are rather averse to publicity and prefer to transact business quietly rather than pose in the spotlight.

COMMISSION GOVERNMENT IN LYNN, MASS.

REPORT OF SPECIAL CORRESPONDENT

LYNN, MASS., May 1, 1912.

In no other city of substantially the same size in the entire country, perhaps, is there a local board of government more generally acceptable to the people than at Lynn, Massachusetts, a municipality of approximately 90,000 inhabitants, situated 14 miles northeast of Boston, where a council of five commissioners and a school committee of five, including the mayor, who is also commissioner of public safety, are in absolute control of affairs.

The administration of the city's business is nearly equally distributed among the nine individuals who are chosen at the polls and there has been no serious fault-finding, sustained by the facts, with any of their doings. Of course there is an occasional clamor from the disappointed politicians and once in a while criticism emanates from business interests that have been made to suffer by the newly introduced general system of competition, but upon the whole it can be truthfully said that commission government, in a little more than one year's honest trial, has been proven to be, to say the least, a vast improvement over the old dual system.

Direct responsibility of department heads has been a large factor in bringing order out of chaos, inspiring well-meaning city officials with new courage to perform their duties faithfully, and causing those who were regarded in the nature of mill-stones around the city's neck to be banished to the background. No longer does the spoilsman prevail in that community. Heads do not come off on each succeeding election day and there is none of the old-time hustling for patronage or trafficking in offices, even to the lowly degree of dog-catcher.

Higher wages are paid to city laborers, the policemen and firemen have received a general increase of about 10 per cent., and there have been rises in the salaries of about a dozen city officials. The laborers work but eight hours a day, and in only one other New England city is the compensation greater than in Lynn. For years there had been an agitation for more pay and shorter hours for the men who work with their hands, but the appeals were in vain until the inauguration of the new form of government.

Lynn's experience since January 2, 1911, when commission government went into effect, has been that with the right men at the helm, the small, compact governing board is so far superior to the old-fashioned, clamorous, double-headed City Council that there is no room for doubt as to the mental attitude of the electorate toward the two propositions.

Eleven aldermen and twenty-five councilmen, nearly every one of whom invariably had a pet project of a purely sectional nature of his own to promote, formerly held sway, and their noisy sessions, devoid of actual accomplishment along constructive lines, had become intolerable. With the abolition of the dual system, the secret meetings of sub-committees also went out of existence never to return, it is hoped.

Suggestions for improvement in handling municipal affairs are encouraged. Hearings, occupying several hours upon some occasions, are given without formal requests being filed, as was required under the old regime, and they are never closed until all of the interested parties have had ample opportunity to tell their side of the story.

Competitive bids are obtained upon every public improvement involving contracts when the expenditure exceeds a couple of hundred dollars, and the proposals, which are invariably sealed, are always opened at a regular session in the presence of the five commissioners and newspaper men. A purchasing department has been established, through which practically everything needed by the various departments is obtained, and there has already been a saving of several thousand dollars. The salary of the purchasing agent has been fixed at $1,800 per annum, and he has two women clerks. One of the first acts of the Municipal Council was to abolish the office of city messenger by whom a large part of the materials and supplies were bought under the old form. The city messenger's salary was $1,000 per year.

Another office that went out of existence with the incoming city government was that of mayor's clerk, and clerk of committees. An ordinance was adopted creating the office of mayor's private secretary, and this is now held by a young woman who also acts as clerk for the finance commissioner.

For many years it was an open secret that the police department was in a more or less demoralized condition. Its conduct was governed by a committee composed of the mayor and two aldermen who were more often than otherwise disagreed concerning the policy to be pursued in divers directions, and in seeking to obey the conflicting mandates of their superiors at City Hall, policemen succeeded only in bringing down wrath upon their own heads.

Whether there was any truth in the assertions has never been proven beyond a doubt, and yet no vigorous denial was ever heard to have been made to the current rumors that the police department was an instrument for the protection of law violators who happened to be "in right" with the ruling powers. Under commission government, the mayor has sole charge of the police. In the parlance of the day, he has the power "to hire and fire" with no other restriction than is imposed by the Civil Service.

Some of the bitterest opponents of the new charter raised the cry that it vested too much power in one man and predicted that the police department could be wielded as a political club, the undesirable effects of which would be far-reaching, but up to the present day there have been no developments tending to support that contention.

On the contrary, in fact, this one-man jurisdiction over the police can properly be regarded as almost a blessing. This is due in the largest measure, it should be said, to the personality of the man whom the people of Lynn saw fit to elect mayor. When Hon. William P. Connery, after four unsuccessful attempts for the mayoralty, was swept into the office upon a tidal wave of reform, he found Lynn infested with gambling joints and other illegal places, the existence of which, according to common rumor, was well known to the police. One resort, generally referred to as "The House of Darkness," located in the heart of the business district, had never been molested, although it had been in operation for at least a decade.

Within twenty-four hours after he had taken the oath of office, Mayor Connery issued a public statement in which he said in substance: "I want the citizens to understand that under the new charter the mayor is the administrative head of the police department and if things do not go right there, then I am the one to blame. The entire responsibility for the enforcement of law and order rests upon me, and if I don't get results I should not be allowed to remain in office."

Some of the traffickers in vice needed no further warning. They moved elsewhere. But these who took flight were the few. The others, most of them powerful through former political intrigues, remained until their establishments were driven to the wall by the unwonted activities of the police.

Acting under instructions direct from the mayor, the "Connery coppers," so-called, scoured the city night and day for promoters of policy games into whose hands daily went hundreds of dollars from the pockets of factory employees, and in less than two months there were so many police court convictions that this form of gambling has practically disappeared from Lynn. For five years the city has been no-license and the chief executive is an enthusiastic advocate of prohibition. Consequently there has been, under his administration, a more rigid enforcement of the liquor laws than ever before. Privileges to clubs have been withdrawn, and the Municipal Council has even refused to grant "pony express licenses," under which intoxicating liquors could be transported within the city limits.

An investigation by a special commission disclosed that the accounts of the Board of Public Works had not been properly kept for several years, and thereupon there was more trouble, the climax of which was the abolition of the board with the introduction of the commission charter. Under the administration of the one commissioner, there has not been one breath of discord in the department of streets and highways. George H. McPhetres, who was elected to that office, resigned a position as a foreman of a street paving concern to take up his new duties. In his first year as a public servant more street paving, sidewalks and sewers were laid than during any similar period since Lynn's incorporation as a city. This year the smooth paving will be done by street department employees. Hitherto this class of work has been given out to contractors.

A finance committee of five members formerly held the city's purse strings, and that their grip was none too secure became apparent to all too frequently, when, in winding up fiscal years it was necessary to float deficiency loans. In justice to the last mayor under the dual system it should be explained that he made an heroic effort to check departmental waste, but although he succeeded in making a far better showing than many of his predecessors, no denial can be made of the fact that financially, as well as morally, the city of Lynn was never so well off as it is to-day.

Frank A. Turnbull, the youngest member of the commission, who has charge of the department of finance, is the only one of the five commissioners who has, in recent years, had any experience in the City Council. At the polls he was the only successful candidate who had a narrow escape from defeat. And yet, despite the antagonisms arising out of his stand for a charter which proposed a single governing board of eleven aldermen, he has probably contributed more toward justifying the institution of commission government than any other city official.

Upon his election, he cast aside his overalls and jumper in the pressroom of a local newspaper, and has assiduously devoted himself to the solution of the many dollar problems which have confronted the city for years. Having kept closely in touch with about every essential detail of the ordinary and extraordinary undertakings handled and mishandled by the City Council in the previous half dozen years, he was in a position to be of invaluable aid in the reconstruction period, and by unswerving loyalty to the city's interests, he has already outlived, apparently, what disadvantages he may have suffered from a political-personal standpoint, because of former allegiances.

Among the officials under the jurisdiction of the finance commissioner are the assessors, who were previously elected at the polls. Being answerable to no superior officer at City Hall, the assessors distributed the tax burdens arbitrarily and there was much dissatisfaction on the ground of alleged favoritism. Developed tracts of land with apartment houses thereon were, it is claimed, assessed at no higher rate than if they were woodland, and it was further asserted that the small home-owners were taxed to the full value of their holdings while the more pretentious realties of the wealthy were allowed to escape for what might be considered but a fractional part of an equitable assessment.

These complaints have been investigated by the finance commissioner with the result that the valuation of the city was increased more than $7,000,000 the first year and nearly $4,000,000 of this came from two of the largest manufacturing concerns. About $1,000,000 more represented increased valuation of residence property in the fashionable district, and the remaining $2,000,000 was from new buildings.

From $20 per $1,000, where it had been for four years, the tax rate has dropped to $19.40 per $1,000, and another decrease is anticipated this year. Commissioner Turnbull, explaining this phase of the situation, says: "I know of no reason why Lynn cannot have an $18 tax rate within a few years providing we make progress toward settling the heritages of the past at the same rate as has prevailed up to this time. While it is not our intention to discourage manufacturing enterprises, we must get the taxes they owe us. The big and little in point of influence must share the burdens of a twentieth century municipal service alike. On this issue I am willing to stand or fall."

Land damage cases, which have been on court calendars for a dozen years or more, have been taken up by the Municipal Council and settled out of current expense funds. Deficiencies in the sinking funds aggregating approximately $300,000 due to the failure to provide funds to meet requirements in years gone by, are being taken care of by a serial arrangement, and projects which the old City Council howled over but never actually initiated are under way.

Since 1896 the old City Council had annually agitated the erection of a union municipal stable but, like in all other things, they succeeded only in starting talkfests. The building department obtained plans which were subjected to the harshest kind of criticism, and there was the usual difference of opinion concerning the site. Last May the Municipal Council first gave its attention to the municipal stable project, and without any long-distance word punishment the commissioners came to the conclusion that there should be two stables, one for the street department in the eastern section of the city and the other for all other departments to be located in West Lynn.

In 1909 the Massachusetts Legislature gave the city of Lynn permission to borrow $100,000 outside of the debt limit for the construction of a schoolhouse in the southeastern section. Immediately there was a hub-bub over where the school should be placed. Cliques were formed among the residents of half a dozen neighborhoods and strings were pulled upon various aldermen and councilmen until the subject became so disagreeable that the city officials by common consent failed to discuss it any further.

When the same tactics as to sectional preference were tried upon them, the commissioners listened patiently, and, after carefully sifting the evidence, voted to seize by right of eminent domain several parcels of land for the acquirement of which there had been but little agitation. The building contracts were then awarded and the schoolhouse will be ready for occupancy in September.

Financially, Lynn has always been in sounder condition than most other Massachusetts cities, but even though this is so, there was ample opportunity to improve upon the methods in vogue prior to the introduction of commission government, and this has been done. One of the flaws in the system, which was immediately corrected, was the practice of issuing indeterminate notes, payment upon which were made only when it was convenient to do so. Sinking fund requirements were neglected, until it was suddenly discovered in 1909 that there was a shortage of $300,000. Last year $26,000 was set aside toward offsetting the delinquency, and this year approximately $30,000 is being applied toward the same end.

Under the new charter all loans are made payable in annual installments, and the serial bonds thus floated are sold upon such terms that the effect of the premiums reduce the total amount of bonds issued in this way, as will be readily seen, the sinking fund element of the city's financial affairs will eventually be wiped out of existence and in its place will be substituted a situation approaching the pay-as-you-go plan.

Another innovation which is having a salutary effect is the provision that no city official, except in cases of extreme emergency involving the health or safety of the people or their property, shall expend intentionally in any fiscal year, any sum in excess of appropriations under penalty of a fine not exceeding $1,000 or one year imprisonment or both.

Monthly financial statements were issued under the old form of government, but they were of such a complicated character as to reveal nothing which department heads might desire to conceal. Unpaid bills were held back for months and even carried over from one year to another.

In the reorganization of the finance department this evil has been reduced to a minimum if not completely eliminated. No extraordinary expenditure is now made by any department chief unless the order is given through the purchasing agent, or by vote of the Municipal Council, and it is required that all bills shall be in the hands of the city auditor within thirty days after the article purchased has been received and approved as to the quality. Two financial statements are now published monthly. One of these shows in a general way the appropriations, estimated receipts for the year, the actual receipts to the date of issuance, the credits, transfers, monthly and total expenditures, transfers to and from various accounts, unexpended balances, loans, cash in banks, valuation of city property, net bonded indebtedness and gross assets and liabilities.

The other statement discloses itemized receipts and expenditures. From this pamphlet one can learn the whereabouts of almost every dollar, except the money disbursed upon payrolls. Since 1910, the net bonded indebtedness of Lynn has increased nearly $200,000, but this is due principally to the fact that $175,000 has been borrowed for the extension of the water supply system and $100,000 for the schoolhouse to which reference has already been made. This year also, a $35,000 annex to the Shepard Grammar School and a $1,500 fire station will be built out of the proceeds of serial bonds. Funds have, moreover, been provided in the same manner for the renovation of an insanitary police station, the installation of an eight-circuit police signal service, and the construction of a tuberculosis hospital to accommodate 100 patients.

By concerted action, the Municipal Council, aided by a citizens' committee, carried a fight for the abolition of Boston & Maine grade crossings by depression, to the Legislature, where the proposition was defeated by a tie vote in the Senate, after the House had by an overwhelming majority declared itself in favor, despite the fact that the previous city government had acquiesced to elevation and more than $1,000,000 worth of the work had already been done.

The commission charter is so framed that the Municipal Council and school committee are continuing bodies. At the first election, the mayor, commissioners of finance and streets and two members of the school committee were chosen for two years and the commissioners of water and public property and two members of the school committee for one year. In December, 1911, the men elected for the short terms were returned to office for two years by such marked majorities as to emphasize the claim concerning the popularity of commission government.

One warning note should be sounded, however, to which cities having a view toward commission government should hearken. Lynn and other commission cities are governed more by individuals than by law, and it is imperative that there should be a thoroughly aroused civic consciousness in any community where the dual system is made to disappear in favor of say a governing board of five commissioners.

Publicity—last degree publicity—is absolutely essential to the success of commission government.

The short ballot puts a self-defensive weapon into the hands of the electorate, which can be most effectively used, when occasion requires, under commission government.

COMMISSION GOVERNMENT IN DES MOINES

REPORT OF SPECIAL CORRESPONDENT.

DES MOINES, IOWA, Dec. 21, 1910.

When Des Moines abandoned the old aldermanic system of government and abolished the ward lines and party designation at the head of the ticket, the people's interest in municipal affairs underwent a marked change.

In 1900, a total of 13,434 votes were cast for Mayor. The vote in 1902 was 13,039. In 1904 only 10,852 voters went to the polls. The great falling off was due to the fact that the Mayor elected in 1902, after a disastrous administration, left the executive office to "tend" bar in a local saloon. He had received his nomination at the hands of the Republicans, and was elected easily over a better man, the Democratic nominee. In 1906, a slight increase of interest is noticeable in the vote for Mayor, the total being 11,627. Still, at that time, fully 18,000 Des Moines men were eligible to vote for Mayor. In fact, the vote then, as in previous years, was generally to be measured by the activity of the politicians, rather than commensurate with the civic interest.

In 1908 the first Des Moines Plan election was held, and immediately the voters showed signs of life. They accepted their first opportunity to vote for men of their own selection, rather than the products of partisan primaries. In 1908, 14,067 votes were polled for Mayor. In 1910 these figures were increased to 15,034.

A higher degree of efficiency in the transaction of the business of the city became evident immediately upon the change from the old to the new. The prohibition of rewards or promise of rewards for political services eliminated many undesirable applicants for minor positions, who, under the old method of "free and easy" political bargaining, would have worked their way to the pie-counter. If the council of the first administration made any such appointments, it dexterously concealed its motives for such selections. Once it was charged that the first chief of police, who received his appointment by three votes out of five, was favored because of his alleged activity in the interests of the men electing him. This charge was strenuously denied, and, in fact, never definitely established. But so many people believed that he was appointed for political reasons, and there was so much gossip and newspaper scandal that before his first year ended a way of displacing him was found and the scandal subsided. The humor of this situation did not escape everybody; because only the year previous the office of chief of police, with all the other good plums, was given to the men who did the work of the candidates. No attention was paid to the consideration of fitness, and the practice was regarded as an institution and was not held in disrespect. The people were a long time in finding out that the practice was becoming the ruin of their government.

It is true that in the second administration there are more signs of small politics than in the first. These indications are with reference to appointments. No councilman has ever been charged with grafting or with any of the American customs with reference to distributing or withholding patronage in the form of contracts, etc.; but, at the present time, the demands of the liberal element would be adequately satisfied if a certain public official could realize his desires. This element finds its essence in the Consolidation Club, which is an organization of rather uncertain means of support, but with definite and public aims. Although the present administration has not gone so far as to re-establish the "red light" district, abolished by its predecessor, it has, however, shown a leniency to the keepers of cheap restaurants and chop-houses where immoral women congregate and drink beer, as well as to cigar dealers, druggists and others, who operate candy raffles and small games of chance. An interesting fact is the reduction of the former chief of police to the ranks of a patrolman. He had been instrumental in closing the houses of ill-fame and driving out the inmates. First he was dropped only a notch in rank, but there were later notches, and now he is swinging a club on a beat. The administration did this in the face of strong public sentiment and against the advice of two influential daily newspapers, indicating either that it is not in close touch with public sentiment or that its head is not unwilling to return to private citizenship.

Early in the administration of the previous Mayor, when he began putting on the lid, the liberal element (the Consolidation Club being not then in existence) circulated a petition for his recall. The petition was not a success. Nobody but the circulator, who afterwards became president of the Consolidation Club, knew how near it reached the mark of "25% of the voters." But it was the nucleus for a campaign that defeated the Mayor for re-election. He had so compromised himself with all the conditions that needed or seemed to need reforming, that he was snowed under. And now the people are just as much dissatisfied with his successor—the other extreme.

The Des Moines Plan did bring from his seclusion a big local figure, John MacVicar. Mr. MacVicar is probably the best known authority upon municipal subjects. He is secretary of the League of American Municipalities, and is the life of that organization. Fifteen or eighteen years ago he came into local prominence by leading a fight against the water company. He has been regarded as the people's hope in their dealing with the public service corporations, and is now conceded to be the backbone of the city council, and the man most to be relied upon when the people's rights are in jeopardy. He has charge of the important department of streets and public improvements, and under his supervision comes all the work out of which grafting was so easily possible under the old form of government. He has a decided aversion to favoritism, poor inspection, and inefficiency in the matter of city work, and, despite the existence of a Mayor, who is supposed to supervise, is the point around which most of the business of the city gravitates.

There is always trouble in the Des Moines city council, due, according to the belief of many, to the nature of the government. The commissioners meet three times a week in the daytime. Surrounded by reporters, the character, inclinations, ambitions, and prejudices of the five men soon become clearly understood by the newspaper men, and their observations are reflected in their reports of the proceedings. The editors take their cues from the news stories, and through this route comes the impressions of the public. The councilmen consequently set themselves up for constant study by the newspaper readers, and it influences their dispositions. For one thing, it makes them assertive. Knowing the value of public opinion, they strive to make a picture of a public official doing good service. Sometimes it would seem that there is something of affectation in these pictures, but nevertheless it operates to the improvement of the government. There being no committee rooms, there is no fighting behind closed doors. It is in the open, and everybody sees it. Little differences grow, and it is a poor day for business when two or more members of the Des Moines council do not quarrel and furnish a spicy newspaper story. There is, however, some good in it, Des Moines people know, because it keeps all eyes on the city hall.

Only one question has been referred to a vote of the people, this being the question of establishing a market house, decided in the affirmative.

There has been a decrease in the tax levy. In 1900 the levy for city purposes was 40.3 mills on the dollar upon 25% of the actual valuation. The levy for 1908 was only 36.4 mills, and for 1909, 37.1 mills. At the end of the first year under the Des Moines Plan there was a balance of $120,000 in the city treasury. At the end of the last year under the old plan there was a deficit of $180,000, which the new council met by a bond issuance. The reason for the increase in the tax levy for the second year under the Des Moines Plan is due to extraordinary expenses made necessary by laying and paving abutting government property, and by a city bond, not subject to taxation. The per capita cost of operating the government in 1906 was 10.21; in 1908, 9.56; in 1909, 9.71. Supervision of all matters of accounts and finance by a councilman designated for that purpose has brought favorable results throughout the entire government. Closer supervision has improved the work and possibilities of the free public library, and has drawn the professional bond shark out of the police court.

The establishment of the new form of government has encouraged business methods and has been marvelous in the development of public concern. Members of the council and subordinates are under constant scrutiny. Especially is the council always in the spotlight. The strength and weakness of each councilman is magnified as if by magic, and there is no "unknown" in the city council.

The people are satisfied with their new form of government and probably not five per cent. of them would vote for a return to the old system.

COMMISSION GOVERNMENT IN DES MOINES

LETTER FROM THE MAYOR

[In pursuance of the aim of the Editor and Publishers to present the truth concerning the working of the Commission plan in different cities, the following letter is given space here.]

DES MOINES, IOWA, March 29, 1911.

To The Short Ballot Organization,
New York.

In your Digest of Short Ballot Charters, page 74301, there is what purports to be a report of a special correspondent concerning commission government in Des Moines. Certain inaccuracies therein give a very wrong view of the situation in Des Moines and some others give a very erroneous view of my own attitude on questions of city government, both moral and political.

For example, paragraph 6 tells a story which is in a large measure true, but which did not apply to the Mayor at all, but instead of that did apply to the head of the department of public safety, who alone was responsible for the clean-up in the last administration, and who was defeated just as your article says. The former Mayor, however, had the solid support of this club in his campaign and I myself was elected in the face of the solid opposition of the same organization.

The matter of opinion which you express at the end of paragraph 7 is, of course, a matter of opinion to which anybody is entitled if the facts seem to him to warrant it.

Paragraph 5 certainly does a great injustice to the city of Des Moines in its statement as to the attitude of the present administration towards morality. Des Moines has for nearly three years now been doing its best to eradicate entirely, not only the "Red Light District," but the whole social evil. Without giving you my own personal statement as to our conditions, I should like to cite you to the report of the committee from Minneapolis sent here to investigate this matter and to report the facts to the Mayor and city council. This committee consisted of Mr. Stiles P. Jones and the Mayor's secretary, Mr. Williams. Some parts of their reports were made public through the press in Minneapolis, some of the papers there garbling this report and others giving briefly the true situation here. I asked this committee in particular to go everywhere about our city and find out everything possible, and gave them every privilege and assistance to do this. Mr. Jones wrote me at some length as to what they found and to the effect that conditions were well in hand and certainly as good as could possibly be hoped for.

The "Red Light District" is entirely out of existence, no such thing as an open house of prostitution exists in Des Moines and no prostitute is allowed to remain in this city longer than to establish a case of prostitution against her. Of course, there are lewd women in the city from time to time. It takes some time to discover their whereabouts and to establish cases against them. They do not, however, await a second prosecution, for, although upon the first proven offense they can only be fined, yet a second successful prosecution sends them to the penitentiary. The consequence is that we have no permanent denizens of the underworld here and certainly have prostitution reduced to a very desirable minimum. We are doing our best to eradicate this cardinal evil and are certainly having such success as to warrant the encouragement of everybody who believes in public morality as I asume your publication does, and I do not believe that your publication would knowingly do either our city or the cause of morality the wrong that your article inflicts.

Very truly yours,
JAS. R. HANNA, *Mayor.*

COMMISSION GOVERNMENT IN DES MOINES

THE ELECTION OF THE THIRD COMMISSION.

[During April, 1912, a regular biennial city election was held in Des Moines, and three of the commissioners, Messrs. Ash, Schramm and MacVicar, all of whom had held office under the two preceding administrations, were retired. Mr. John MacVicar had been identified with the Commission plan not only in Des Moines, but in its progress throughout the country. He had been considered, in fact, one of the chief exponents of the idea.

These facts were widely heralded in the press as indicating a change of heart on the part of Des Moines toward the Commission plan. This attitude was reflected in the headlines which appeared in various newspapers such as "Commission City Backslides," "The Des Moines Relapse," "Civic Interest in Des Moines Flags." It has seemed important, therefore, that a statement be made as to what actually happened at this election, and the editor has made a number of inquiries in Des Moines, in the hope of properly interpreting the results of the election.

In August 1911 the city experienced a street railway strike, involving delicate questions of police administration. Mr. Zell Roe, at the time the head of the department of public safety, is said to have conducted himself with reference to the striking employees, so as to win their unanimous approval. Almost simultaneously with the street car trouble, Mr. MacVicar initiated an ordinance changing the distribution of the departments whereby Mr. Roe was transferred to the department of streets and Mr. MacVicar himself became the head of the department of public safety. Since this change in the department, Mr. MacVicar had adopted a policy of vigorous enforcement of the laws, especially those relating to vice. In the recent election there were combined against him the union labor people who believed that the change in departments had been instituted as a result of the labor troubles, and the so-called "Liberal" element, who favored a less strict enforcement of the laws, also not a few voters outside these classes, who censured Mr. MacVicar's course in making the change in departments in the absence of Mayor Hanna and Mr. Roe. No one of these three classes of voters was sufficiently large to carry the election, but the combination of minorities was sufficient to overwhelmingly defeat Mr. MacVicar and the two other members of the old commission who voted for the change.

Out of these results two facts are evident.

In the first place, the city of Des Moines has not reverted to a wide-open-town policy. This is shown by the fact that Mr. Zell Roe, who is known as an exponent of the "Liberal" idea, and is conscious of the fact, refused to take the commissionership of public safety. It is further and more convincingly illustrated by the fact that Mayor Hanna, elected two years ago as an opponent of the open-town policy, was re-elected on his record by a majority over an avowed open-town candidate of 5,463, the largest majority yet given any candidate under the commission plan—a majority larger by 5,447 than he received two years ago. That the council is with the mayor in his enforcement policy is shown by the fact that on the nomination of Councilman Needham, head of the public safety department, the new council chose as its chief of police a Mr. Jenny, ex-truant officer and a radical temperance reformer, under whose vigorous administration the gamblers have been driven to cover, the dance halls have been placed under strict regulation and the saloons are keeping within the law.

Secondly, Des Moines is not tired of the Commission plan. Nowhere in Des Moines have we been able to find a disposition, owing to the recent events, to criticise the plan itself. On the contrary, the election was a most striking demonstration of the principles which distinguish the Des Moines plan. The voters knew where each candidate stood on the live questions presented at the election. The individual candidates stood upon their public records and were compelled to defend them in the pre-election campaign. The vote was the largest ever cast in any city election, evincing the growing interest of voters in city affairs under the new plan.—*Ed.*]

COMMISSION GOVERNMENT IN TOPEKA

REPORT OF SPECIAL CORRESPONDENT

TOPEKA, KANS., Mar. 8, 1911.

Commission government went into operation in Topeka by the election and installation of a Mayor and four commissioners in April, 1910. The Mayor is chairman of the commission and has immediate charge of the fire and police departments. Another commissioner has charge of the two public utilities owned by the city, the water works and street lighting plant. A third commissioner has the care of the streets and the engineering department. A fourth has the public parks and sanitation. The fifth member of the commission has the finances.

The only serious opposition to the adoption of the new method of conducting the city government based itself on the generally accepted fact that the city was decently governed, that its municipal affairs were free from scandal, that there was reasonable economy of management, and that there was no complaint of politics controlling either the Mayor or council.

The then Mayor advocated the change, nevertheless, on the ground that it provided a more businesslike system. Although the election came in the midst of the term for which he had been elected, he advised the change. He himself was a candidate for Mayor under the commission plan, after a vote had been taken and the city by a good majority in a large vote determined to try the new system.

The then Mayor had been a Democrat, but was nominated as a Citizen's candidate at the time of his first candidacy for Mayor, having served two terms acceptably as a non-partisan member of the city council. Opposed to him in the primary for nomination for Mayor under the commission plan were two other candidates, a Democrat who had repeatedly been a candidate of his party, and a leading flour miller of no fixed party affiliation. At the primary the sitting Mayor and the miller, J. B. Billard, received the largest number of votes and thus became the opposing candidates for Mayor at the election a week later.

At the election Mr. Billard was elected by a considerable majority. It is rather remarkable that he had been one of those most strongly opposed to commission government. After a year's service as Mayor he is now one of the strongest defenders of the commission system, on business grounds.

For the four commissionerships other than Mayor there were 28 candidates at the primaries. These candidates were not running for any particular department, but on their general merits. At the primaries eight nominees are made, two for each commissionership. At the election the four nominees receiving the largest vote are elected as the four commissioners. After their installation into office, the entire commission determine among themselves their selection of departments.

As the result of the election the city found itself with a miller and leading business man for Mayor, a barber in charge of the public utilities, a young man who had managed a small iron works and foundry as commissioner of finance, a merchant in charge of parks and sanitation, and a house mover, with two years' experience in the city council, as commissioner of streets and engineering. Every man was well known to the community.

An objection to the commission plan that had been urged upon workingmen was that the Third Ward, the residence of the wealthy part of the city and of the city's leading citizens, would dominate the city. It turned out that the Third Ward had no member of the commission. The two workingmen's wards had three of the five members, including the Mayor. The only ward getting two commissioners was the First, which, being separated from the other five wards of the city by the river, feared it would be left "outside the breastworks." Sentiment in that ward was overwhelming against commission government. Two of its residents were elected, and one the Mayor.

Party emblems and nominations are forbidden by the commission statute. The names of candidates at the primary are printed on one ballot in alphabetical order, with no party designation. Every voter votes for one nominee for Mayor and four for commissioners. At the ensuing election a week later every voter again votes for one candidate for Mayor and four for commissioners. It is simply a filtering process. The voters get two chances to pick their choice.

The former system comprised a Mayor and twelve councilmen, two from each of the six wards. Their salaries were $2,000 to the Mayor and $200 each to the councilmen, the aggregate being $4,400. Present salaries are $2,500 to the Mayor and $1,800 to each of the four commissioners, aggregating $9,700.

Among the last acts of the expiring administration was the substantial increase of the salaries of the police, fire, street, engineering and every other department of the city. This handicap of the new government largely accounts for the absence of criticism of the showing of no saving in the cost of the city government. The expiring administration, further, drew and paid out $35,000 from the levy made for the ensuing year, which began with April. The new commissioners were, therefore, $35,000 short of their levy and had a larger budget to sustain, owing to the general increase of salary lists. The city has been conducted, nevertheless, without borrowing funds. The financial showing is therefore regarded as good.

The commission system, advertised as a wonderful business plan, has not reduced taxes in the year it has been under operation. For the first time, however, a finance commissioner has regularly, every three months, printed in the newspapers an itemized report of the cost of the city government, classified by departments, with comparisons with the year just preceding. Notwithstanding that these reports show no reduction in expense in any of the departments, no criticism of the commissioners or of the system is heard. It is in the business methods of the conduct of the city's affairs that the new system generally approves itself, so that to all appearances opinion seems to be settled on all sides in its favor. Council meetings under the old plan had been held monthly, with special meetings once or twice during every month. The system was one of debate and reference to committee. Some times the committees could be got together to consider the matters so referred to them. Sometimes they could not and matters were deferred. Persons having business with the city were directed by the Mayor and council to the committee; the committee was slow to meet and slow to act when it did meet. The policy of debate and discussion prevailed all through the system, rather than a policy of action.

Under the new system there are no committees, no debating sessions, but regular meetings twice a week for business, which is transacted on the spot. Persons having business with a department go to its head, who is personally responsible, who has a fixed office in the city building, and who gives the most of his time in his office every day to the work of the city. Matters wholly within his department are determined and action taken by him. Matters involving more than one department are brought by him to the general meeting,where they are determined. Persons having business with the city, therefore, find that their business is done, instead of being interminably

tion of a combine or "machine" composed of the administration. There are some symptoms of a tendency of the men in office to stand by one another, but so far as this is in evidence at all it is the natural effect of the policy of opposing candidates to avoid picking out in advance any particular department. The "outs" make their campaign against the "ins" generally. If one commissioner happens to be particularly weak in one locality, or among a certain element, opposing candidates privately state to the enemies of that commissioner that they are seeking his particular job. In another part of the city or with another element, they are candidates for another commissioner's place. The evolution of this plan of campaign naturally induces sitting members to work more or less in concert. Otherwise there is no "administration" organization.

It is perhaps of interest to note what effect municipal suffrage for women has upon the city elections. Full suffrage has been enjoyed by women in city elections for a quarter of a century in Kansas. As a rule the women have taken no active part in city contests, except on occasions when some candidate particularly obnoxious to the prohibtion element has come forward. Organization among the women centers in the Federation of Women's Clubs, which has a large membership in all parts of the city. This Federation took a positive stand against the adoption of commission government, on the ground that it threatened a backward step on the saloon question. But the strong support of the new system among the temperance element of the men somewhat reassured many of the women on this point, and their opposition to the change by the time the vote was taken had disintegrated. But in the first primaries and commission election there was a marked falling off in the women's registration, and their vote was light. This spring the revival of the saloon question in the mayoralty contest has brought out a heavy women registration, and they promise to be an important factor. It is worth noting that during the long period of woman suffrage in Topeka no woman has ever been a candidate either for Mayor, member of the city council, nor in the last two years, for commissioner. But in all contests, when the male vote was fairly equal on the "wet" and "dry" issue, the women have been a decisive factor.

On the whole, the commission plan, during the brief period of its operation, has met reasonable expectations. There are no respects in which it has "fallen down" in comparison with the former system, while its general operation is more efficient. Party politics has been entirely divorced from it, and the double choice of primary and general election satisfies the popular desire for a popular, representative government.

The initiative, referendum and recall are available, but have not been used, nor has there been any demand for them. They are regarded, however, as desirable reserved powers and as valuable in their moral effect.

Candidates opposed to the re-election of the present commissioners, other than Mayor, have been slow to announce themselves this spring. There were, however, early two announced candidates against the Mayor's renomination. A third candidate, representing the temperance element, who have been very much dissatisfied, not with the Mayor's enforcement of the prohibition law, but with his continual public declarations in interviews and addresses against the policy of prohibition and in favor of resubmission of the constitutional provision, was "drafted" into the race by a meeting of prominent temperance leaders. It is admitted by the opponents of the Mayor that he has given the city, so far as his departments are concerned, a business administration. In defence of his position the Mayor declares that he has enforced the law, that the city is "dry," and that so long as prohibition is in the Constitution of the State it is the duty of the executives to enforce it. Opposition to his re-election is on the ground that he does not represent the prevailing sentiment of the city, and that his public appearances and interviews are injurious to the policy that the city by a large majority approves. Besides the Mayor and the temperance candidate opposing him, two other candidates are seeking the Mayor nomination, both claiming to favor strict enforcement of the prohibitory law, but opposed to the "wet" and "dry" issue as a determining factor in municipal elections.

The four other commissioners are candidates for re-election, and seven other candidates are in the race, making eleven candidates, from whom eight are to be nominated at the primaries, and four elected at the final poll. As against twenty-eight candidates for commissioner and three for Mayor a year ago, there are therefore eleven candidates at this time for commissioner and four for Mayor. Except as regards the temperance question in the mayoralty contest, the issues in the election are personal, the contest turning entirely on the relative merits of the candidates. Party politics is so fully eliminated that the party affiliations of the candidates have not been mentioned. There are no organizations behind any of the candidates. Every candidate has called his friends into consultation in meetings at which his personal organization has been perfected for conducting his campaign. The individual candidate and his friends solicit votes for him, ward meetings are held in behalf of every candidate, at which speeches are made by him and his friends urge his individual claims for nomination. But no meeting has been held at which more than one candidate speaks, or at which more than one candidat is favored. The contest, in short, is strictly a persona affair, "slates" or machine methods being, so far, car fully avoided by the candidates.

COMMISSION GOVERNMENT IN LEAVENWORTH

REPORT OF SPECIAL CORRESPONDENT

Leavenworth, Kan., Mar. 27, 1911.

Leavenworth, the first City in Kansas to adopt the Commission form of Government, has, after three years trial, decided that it is far superior to the old political ward system. The concentration of responsibility in the hands of a few men, elected at large, in a non-political election, has been found to result in more efficiency and less extravagance. The laborious processes of the old Council system are eliminated and the Mayor and four Commisioners, sitting about a directors' table one night a week, transact more business in one hour than the old City Council used to transact in four meetings lasting three hours each.

When the Commission form of Government was proposed for Leavenworth, the City was in dire straits. The state authorities had just closed 185 saloons, two gambling houses and numerous other resorts in the City, and thus shut off a revenue of about $90,000 a year which the proprietors used to pay the City in the form of forfeited bonds, police court fines and other subterfuges for evading the law. The politicans in office, after finding that the law really was to be enforced and that there was absolutely no way to allow law violations and collect the illegal revenue without being ousted from office, declared that the city faced ruin and in order to impress on the public, the fact that closing the joints was going to bring disaster on the city, the administration started its campaign of economy by cutting off all street lights, sanitary measures and street sweeping forces.

After about a week of darkness and with disease threatening from the unsanitary condition of the city, the business men, most of them men who had never before taken enought interest in city affairs to vote at a primary election, began to look into the matter. Their first decision, and it is unanimous, was "If we cannot get revenue from the saloons, we don't want saloons." But the political administration took no steps toward purifying the moral atmosphere of the city. Next, some of th leading business men took enough interest to investigat the claims of a local newspaper to the effect that th $90,000 a year revenue collected from joints and brothel had not paved a foot of street or paid off a penny of th City debt. The business men, to their surprise, dis covered that the claim was correct and a meeting wa called and an organization, the Greater Leavenwort Club, perfected, and a petition circulated, asking th city administration to call an election on the propositio to substitute the commission form of government for th political system. Two petitions were rejected on technic alities by the unfriendly administration and the inter est became so keen throughout the city that the thir petition was accepted and the election followed. Th politicians designated polling places adjacent to saloon under brothels and in other locations where ladies woul not be likely to go to vote. The business men, thoroughl aroused by such indignities, personally conducted th campaign and stood guard all day at the polls that thei wives and mothers might not be insulted. The Commi sion Plan carried by an overwhelming majority. S great was the victory, in fact, that a ticket composed o five leading business men and manufacturers, who agree to serve without salary, was elected without opposition.

E. W. Crancer, a wholesale hardware dealer, w elected Mayor, and he immediately took steps to put th City finances in such condition that some knowledge the City's debts and resources might be available at an time. As a result of his efforts a splendid accountin system is now in operation and the exact financial stan ing of the city is as easily ascertainable any day as that of any well conducted bank or other institutio The police force was cleaned out and men selected b cause of their fitness for the work regardless of the political alliances. A small army of aged street sweepe gave way to two modern street flushing tanks with acti young attendants. The fire department was re-organiz and every department of the city gone over carefully. On his first day as Mayor, Mr. Crancer surprised the jailors and inmates at the City Jail by sitting down to dinner with the prisoners. But he didn't eat, instead he cancelled the contract for supplying the prisoners with food and went out and bought the inmates the first good meal they had enjoyed in the prison.

The Mayor and Commissioners were working without salary and they had absolutely no political ambitions and they set aside all political traditions, policies and practices, and, from the howl that went up from the politicians and the men thrown out of fat City jobs, together with their friends and the friends of those who sought in vain, jobs for which they were not qualified, it was really feared by the friends of the commission government that a successful attempt would be made to throw the City into the hands of politicians again.

The attempt was made at the end of the first year and a strong political ticket was put in the field in the Spring of 1909, to oppose the Greater Leavenworth Club ticket, which comprised three of the original five commissioners and two new men. Mr. Crancer, the first Mayor, taking a nomination as commissioner and Mr. Omar Abernathy, a millionarie furniture manufacturer accepting the nomination as Mayor. To the chagrin of the politicians and the surprise of the business men, the Greater Leavenworth Club ticket won again by an overwhelming majority, forever, it is believed, putting an end to political attempts to get control of the City. It was found that the heaviest support the business men's ticket got was in the working men's wards, the very precincts which the political bosses predicted would be against the "silk stocking" candidates, giving them big majorities. The "Silent Vote," unheard of in days of the ward system, puzzled the politicians and gratified the best interests of the city for it demonstrated that although the general public is quick to criticize and slow to show approval, it will if given the proper chance, indorse a clean, business administration of public affairs at the polls every time. At this writing another election is pending and while several independent candidates, all desirable business men, are candidates, the political organizations are taking no part in the campaign and there is every reason to believe that the ticket selected by the Greater Leavenworth Club will be nominated and elected.

When the first Mayor and Commissioners took charge of Leavenworth's affairs they found a chaotic state of affairs at the City Hall. The City was practically without revenue, the taxes for the year having been requisitioned from the County Treasurer in advance and the City employees unpaid for three months and a small fortune in floating debts pressing for payment. By a skillful rearranging of the funds and a vigorous prosecution of lawbreakers with a resulting harvest of perfectly legal fines, the City Commissioners not only cleared the moral aspect of the town, but managed to restore the city's credit. Expenses were cut to the minmum, and sentiment and political policy cut no figure with the officials when they wielded the axe.

The total debt of the City on April 13, 1908, when the new form of government went into effect, was $666,-882.14. consisting of general and special improvement bonds and refunding bonds, $472,769.24, of the debt being the latter. In three years the Mayor and Commissioners have paved 8.34 miles of street, laid 18.44 miles of curb and 4.06 miles of sewer, at a total cost of $295,-666.68 and the total net increase in the public debt in that time is only $15,960.06. At the same time the city has paid off nearly $150,000 of its share of the county debt. The tax rate for city and county purposes is now less than $1.90 on the $100 valuation whereas it was $3.12 on the $100 previously.

The City is more sanitary, better lighted, has better police and fire protection and best of all, the people are united in anything and everything that makes for a Greater Leavenworth. Two large factories, one a furniture factory covering two blocks and five stories high, costing nearly $200,000 and another nearly as large which will cost almost as much, each employing hundreds of men, are a direct result of the adoption of the commission form of government and the purifying of the moral atmosphere of the City. Mr. Helmers, head of the first factory mentioned, stated publicly, when the question of the adoption of the new form of government was being put before the voters, that if it failed to carry, he would not build in Leavenworth. He gave as his reason the statement that without ideal labor conditions the town would be unfit for factories and that with a political government and the domination of the lawless element, there could be no labor conditions satisfactory to the manufacturer.

The improvements made by the city in the past three years, outstrip the accomplishments of any ten consecutive years previously and not one foot of paving was laid without a majority petition of the property owners. Private individuals and local corporations followed the progressive lead set by the city and building boom followed. Buildings which had stood empty and neglected because of their proximity to joints or gambling houses, were renovated and quickly rented; factories made extensive improvements, the telegraph and telephone companies were forced to put their wires underground: hundreds of old-fashioned wooden awnings were condemned and torn down, defective side walks were replaced, under protest in many instances, with walks of concrete, and many other steps which made for public betterment if not for political power, were taken. Even the City printing, always the bone of contention in a town of 25,000 people, was for the first time let by contract to the lowest bidder. In three years the city has saved over $12,000 on the printing alone by taking this step. Although the efficiency has not been impaired, but rather improved, the departmental expenses have been decreased nearly a half, from $17,000 a month to less then $10,000.

"Centralization of power" which was the warning of the politicians when the new form of government was proposed, has failed to exhibit itself so far, but "Centralization of Responsibility" has come and with it better government. Simplicity dominates in every department. "Efficiency" is all that is demanded of any city employee and since the commission form of government went into effect no policeman or other city employee has ever had to answer to the City Officials for any part he has taken in political campaigns, unless he has allowed politics to interfere with the performance of his duties.

Under the new Kansas Commission Charter Act, the right of recall is granted and the elections are strictly non-political, no political designation being allowed on the ballots and the names of the nominees being arranged in alphabetical order on the ticket. No franchise can be granted without submitting the proposition to the voters and any commissioner who warrants in excess of the funds of his department, can be immediately ousted from office.

Although the women vote on municipal matters in Kansas, it is a matter of pride to the Greater Leavenworth Club that every election under commission so far has been carried for the business administration by a majority of the male vote. The women almost invariably vote for the business ticket.

LEAVENWORTH, Kan., Apr. 19, 1911.

In the election just closed, the commission government received another indorsement from the people of Leavenworth. Albert Doege, a commissioner for two terms under the commission form of government, was elected mayor and four business and professional men of high standing in the community elected commissioners. No attempt was made by any political organization to get control of the city and three business men who were given nominations withdrew before election in order to avoid a contest which would have resulted in establishing factions. Their names were left on the ballots as they could not lawfully be removed, but they announced that inasmuch as the support was stronger for other candidates, they would not cause a contest by asking the support of their friends. The result was a friendly election.

Mayor Doege and his four commissioners, upon taking office, reappointed practically all the appointees holding office, thus carrying out the commission policy of rewarding efficiency with reappointment. It was feared by the friends of the commission government that the new administration might be inclined to fill appointive offices with new men and the action of the mayor and commissioners settled a very important point, for a precedent has now been established which will undoubtedly be adhered to.

Albert Doege, the new mayor, is a wealthy soap manufacturer. The four commissioners are Harry Dolde, cigar manufacturer; Dr. R. E. Nelson, dentist; Anton Swoboda, Standard Oil agent; Charles Cox, printer. Organized labor put two candidates in the field, Charles Cox and Wm. Shaughnessy, both printers. Cox, who is an employing printer as well as a member of the union, and a popular citizen, received the support of the business element in addition to the support of the unions and was easily elected. Shaughnessy received a comparatively small vote.

COMMISSION GOVERNMENT IN WICHITA

REPORT OF SPECIAL CORRESPONDENT.

WICHITA, Kan., May 8, 1911.

Following an agitation of three years' duration for a more efficient city government, the voters of Wichita, Kansas, on February 2, 1909, adopted the Commission Form as authorized by the State Legislature two years before. This plan provides for conduct of the city's affairs by a mayor and four commissioners, who are expected to give all their time to the duties of their respective offices.

Its adoption was not the result of political tactics. On the other hand it was delayed nearly two years in order to to usher it in under favorable auspices. The anti-saloon wave which swept over Kansas in 1907 placed in power a mayor inexperienced in civic affairs and with little knowledge of politics. His enemies claimed that he became the tool of a political gang. In order to halter his authority it was proposed soon after his election to adopt the commission plan of government. Men who had the interest of the city more at heart than the success of their political plans prevented such action.

The first campaign, as Wichita's city campaigns always have been, was bitterly waged. The fight centered upon the mayor. It seemed that before the time for filing of nomination papers closed every man out of a job would be a candidate for commissioner. The eliminating process as provided for in the primary ten days before the city election left a representative of each of the two great factions for mayor. The eight men nominated for commissioners were representative business men. Combinations were made and the factions battled fiercely. Each side used a newspaper. Thousands of dollars were spent to get the voters lined up and advertising matter was scattered all over the city. The result overthrew the men in power the two years previous and placed in power men who started out with many promises.

Wichita was fortunate in that the first mayor elected under the new plan took an active part in framing the bill passed by the legislature. He was thoroughly acquainted with its phraseology and intent, and sought during his two years in office to follow the spirit of the law. He was an ardent church worker, a heavy property owner, and of fine qualities, thoroughly polished, and a gentleman. No question was ever raised as to his honesty.

The personnel of the first commission was complex. One of the commissioners was a retired farmer and a heavy property owner. He was inclined to be lax in meeting an issue, slow to act, and subject to personal influence. But no question was ever raised as to his honesty.

Another commissioner was a born fighter for justness and right, but not a politician. He had made a fortune by careful management and strict business principles. His stand on many public questions when consumers and public service corporations were battling made him immensely popular. He alone of the four commissioners was re-elected and by the largest vote given any candidate at the second election under the commission form of government.

The other two commissioners were assailed from all sides owing to their tactics and votes upon certain issues in which the people and public service corporations were lined on opposite sides. One of these two belonged to an old school of politics. He was a pioneer settler and many times an office holder. He stood for re-election upon his record and was hopelessly beaten at the primary. The other was charged with manipulations in an official capacity for his own private gain. An investigation of his department was demanded and an attempt was made to expose his official acts. Backed by powerful influences he blocked these investigations.

A little over a year of commission rule and the battle against graft was begun. It has not ended. Men have been sentenced to prison and others dishonored. A stigma was placed on the city and enemies to commission government became active. Graft in the police department, coupled with a protective system to criminals in return for an agreement upon their part not to operate in Wichita, caused a shake up in the police forces. The mayor was criticised for appointing the men who were exposed. A secret room in the basement of the City Hall, where alleged immoral acts were committed, was traced to the fire and police departments. Its discovery and the "whitewashed" investigation which followed, had nearly as much to do with the unpopularity of the first commission as did the uncovering of "treating with criminals in the police department."

The new government inherited a deficit of $300,000

and a run down condition in all departments. It organized a city administration upon a big scale, increased taxation and made public most of its actions. Wichita at this time began an era of upbuilding. The population increased by leaps and bounds. The bank clearings reached the $2,500,000 mark, then the $3,000,000 mark, and on up to within a few dollars of $4,000,000 weekly. New buildings constructed in Wichita in 1909 amounted to $3,629,660. The city doubled its paving and sidewalks.

But so filled with personal interest in erecting their homes, putting up tall business blocks and reaching out for business were the people that they gave little heed to the city government. And while the city was swelling its commerce and battling down trade opposition, graft crept in, clutched some of the municipal departments and threatened ruin to the commission.

Hampered as the city was with such persons forming a majority of the first commission, and by the conditions under which it went into office and those which developed later, results were obtained that could not have been brought about under the mayor and council system.

The people wanted a zoo for their park. The commissioner of parks started a public subscription. The people responded and the city now has a small but fine collection of animals.

Somebody suggested that the city should have two ostriches. As no funds were available to make the purchase in the name of the city, the commissioner of parks went to officials of a gas and electric company, which had purchased ground to construct an enormous power plant. On the site for the power house were several old houses. The park commissioner asked for and was given one of these buildings. He sold the house and started an ostrich fund. A public spirited citizen donated the city an old automobile. The park commissioner sold the machine and with the receipts from the sale of the house bought two ostriches and several other animals.

Under the old system of city government these deals would have required months to close. The park commissioner made the transaction within a month.

Wichita sold few of its bonds to its own citizens until the commission got in power. One day the commissioner of finance was struck with the idea that Wichita residents should be drawing interest paid by Wichita. He placed $40,000 worth of bonds in his pockets and called upon an ex-saloon keeper. He left the former saloon man holding the bonds while he had a check for $40,000.

Through a little personal work by the commissioner and the city auditor Wichita now has a fair bond market at home.

Under the former plan of government no one, other than eastern bond companies, ever thought about buying bonds. There was but one man to look after these details, the mayor, and he was too busy on other matters which required all his attention to hastily look after.

In the first report made by the mayor under the new plan, he said:

"In these reports which I hope our citizens will read carefully, we have a history of our city during the first nine months of its existence under the Commission form of Government. Our system is in an experimental stage. There are many changes which should be made in the plan. These will be made more apparent to the people and those connected with the administration of the city's affairs by longer and riper experience."

The above expressions came from the mayor, who as a member of the State Legislature, helped frame the bill making a city governed by a commission possible, yet who saw defects in the plan as provided in this State.

A year later, after stormy scenes, during which the people would not have been surprised to have found out most anything about the men they had elected to office, the mayor in his annual report said:

"The success of this new form of government in the judgment of the citizens of Wichita will be largely determined by the accomplishments of this commission. During the last two years the city of Wichita has grown rapidly in population, value of property and improvements. In the year of 1910 the building permits exceeded in amount those of any other year, amounting to $4,372,401.00. The records show that the population increased more during the year 1910 than in any other year in Wichita's history. Business has been reported as being exceptionally good and the railroads report more cars hauled in and out of Wichita during the past year than in any other year.

"This prosperity, which is healthy and permanent, may have come to Wichita under some other form of government but the truth is that it came in greater proportions under the commission plan than it did under the old plan."

The second city campaign under the commission form has passed. It demonstrated that opposition to the commission is right in some respects. A powerful political combination can manipulate a primary so that it can win with its candidate against the wishes of two-thirds of the voters. It takes an enormous slush fund to do it. It was done in Wichita during the recent campaign.

The story of how it was done shows one weakness of the commission form of city government in Kansas. It is a weakness that must be remedied to retain the support of its warmest friends.

The faction overthrown two years ago abided its time. Powerful influences were at work continuously. Attacks were planned, wire pulled and money raised. Five can didates for mayor appeared on the primary ticket. One was a Socialist, one a representative of a combination of interests, and the other three made their fight without organizations and without campaign contributions. The uncovering of deplorable conditions in the police and fire departments made the first mayor unpopular. He was not a candidate for reelection.

The "Interests" candidate took poll after poll of the city, watching the campaign carefully. Ward heelers were put to work. The three independent candidates refrained from attacking each other, but centered their forces against the so-called machine man. The Socialist candidate was not considered a factor.

One of the many unfortunate events during the campaign was the government's part in one of the exposes of city affairs. A former city official was pardoned by the President after pleading guilty to being a partner in crime with safeblowers. He turned state's evidence under the promise of immunity. The safeblowers were sent to prison. This event, coupled with dissatisfaction at the condition of the city primary, increased the Socialist vote from 2,300 to 3,600.

The Special Interests hired teams and automobiles and got out their vote. They had the only hired workers at the polls. Many of them voted for the Socialist, figuring that by so doing it would place the Socialist on the ticket with their man. This resulted in a big surprise. The Socialist was high man. The Special Interests' candidate nosed out two of his opponents by a few hundred votes. The combined vote of the three anti-political and independent candidates was more than that of the Socialist and Special Interests.

A great wave of resentment swept over the city. Hundreds of influential business men declared their intention of supporting the Socialist candidates.

Very little attention had been given to the candidates for commissioners. Two members of the first commission alone sought re-election. One was elected, receiving the highest number of votes of any of the candidates. When the voters went to the polls they had to select either Socialists or an unpopular candidate for mayor and four independent candidates for commissioner. The Socialists had stood together and pulled through the primary with their entire slate.

Following the wave of resentment at the political trick that had been played at the polls a majority of the voters swallowed their "bitter pill" and defeated the entire Socialist ticket. In defense of their campaign the so-called Special Interests claim that the "end justified the means."

The second commission has assumed control under unfavorable conditions. Each of the four commissioners received over a thousand more votes than the mayor; one who had been a public favorite under the first commission received nearly 1,500 more votes than the mayor.

Already there is an agitation for a recall of the mayor. He is charged with violating not only his campaign promises in regard to civil service, in all departments, but has violated the law relating to civil service in the police department by causing to be discharged competent officers and substituting ward healers and political lieutenants. Among the present mayor's bitterest opponents is a feeling that a campaign for a recall so soon after an election would be a violation of the spirit of the commission law, as it is claimed that a man should be given an opportunity to "make good" at least.

This argument is anwered by the most active agitators for a recall who claim that he was mayor previous to the commission form and left the first commission a $300,000 deficit as an inheritance.

These are the arguments one will hear in discussing with the average voter the present conditions in Wichita. Brushing aside party differences and personalities, the commission form of government as applied a little over two years in Wichita would table something like this:

POINTS AGAINST THE NEW FORM.

1.—*Destruction of moral influence of city voters upon political parties.*

(a) Special interests may cause men to form combinations, thereby making friends of moral and immoral elements which in a measure prevents parting of ways in county and State campaigns.

2.—*Increased expenditures.*

(a) Mayor and Commissioners receive $9,600 yearly, while mayor and council received approximately $7,000 less.

(b) Increase in salaries of appointive officers. (This increase amounted to thousands of dollars and the city is about evenly divided upon the justness of it.)

(c) More appointive offices were created — partly due to the public will to have a better accounting system, better parks and more public improvements.

3.—*Faulty primary and election procedures.*

(a) Anyone who gets a few names to a petition can be a candidate regardless of qualifications.

(b) A political party that puts out one candidate for mayor and four candidates for commissioners can pull them through the primary by sticking together if there is not more than one other combination in the field.

(c) Unpopular candidates may be forced upon the voters because there is no way to bring out an independent candidate after the primary.

(d) Strong organization backed with a slush fund can defeat the will of the majority by getting out its votes when the opposition conducts it campaign according to the spirit of the commission law.

(e) Too much interest centered upon candidates for mayor, who under the plan operative in Wichita has no more power than one of the commissioners.

4.—*Lack of executive head.*

(a) Inability of mayor to execute authority over other departments when commission is opposed even though such authority should be executed.

(b) No way to remove inefficient or dishonest officers without majority of commission consenting.

(c) No method of procedure to investigate a commissioner or the mayor without endless litigation.

(d) Lack of opportunity to secure evidence to show reasons for recall.

5.—*Men elected to office not representative.*

(a) No representative of labor has had voice in two commission governments — men elected were rich, had no trades, and never did any work, with possibly two exceptions.

(b) Cry being made that city is being ruled by plutocrats, whereas under old system men of all walks in life had seats in council.

It has been suggested that one way to prevent "boss rule" would be for each voter to designate at the primary his first, second and third choices for mayor and possibly commissioners.

By adding each candidate's totals of choice ballots the one most acceptable to the majority would be a candidate at the regular election opposed to the second choice candidate.

This remedy probably will be suggested to the legislature for legislative purposes.

POINTS IN FAVOR OF NEW FORM.

1.—*Better candidates and cleaner campaigns.*

(a) Loyalty to party does not force voter to support one in whom he has no confidence as "bolting party ticket" is unknown.

(b) Candidate who has not "made good" on individual record cannot get confidence of voters.

(c) An unpopular candidate cannot be pulled through by party combination as there are no straight ballots.

(d) Combinations are harder to form as no limit can be placed on number of candidates.

2.—*More simple and business like.*

(a) Commissioners in giving all their time to city affairs have been able to get at the bottom of propositions very promptly.

(b) No trouble for citizen to take up urgent business and get action without delay.

(c) Decrease in number of elective officers — there are fewer political debts to pay.

(d) Ward interests practically eliminated as commissioners are elected from city at large.

(e) Less fear upon the part of elective officers at result of turning down unattractive propositions.

(f) Better accounting system.

(g) More publicity on handling of finances and less likelihood of juggling of finances.

(h) Application of civil service in proper manner gives city better appointive officers.

(i) Proper regulation of public service corporations more easily obtained.

One of the most talked of criticisms against the commission form of selecting candidates for the final election is the length of the primary ballots. Voters have supported personal friends against their wishes, thereby making it easier for the combinations to pull through with their men.

But the first primary campaign taught many politicians to keep out of the race unless they had individual records to back them. The second primary ticket contained a dozen less candidates and some of these received a woefully small vote. If precedent can be used in forecasting, the next primary ticket will contain fewer names than the second. And so it would seem the lesson of one primary will simplify the succeeding primaries until the minimum of useless timber will be before the voters.

Lack of interest in the primary election is not marked in Wichita. For instance, in the recent city campaign, about 12,000 votes were cast at the primary for candidates for mayor. At the regular election, ten days afterwards, but a little over a thousand more votes were cast for mayor out of a total registration of 21,000. More votes were cast at the first primary and first election under the commission form than during the second campaign. Unfavorable weather conditions cut a figure in the last regular election.

Should Wichita desire to return to the mayor and council plan, it cannot do so until 1913. Such was the wording of the charter adopted by the city when it took what it thought was a forward step in municipal affairs by adopting the Kansas idea of commission government.

Checked up to the voters to-day, Wichita might reject the present system and elect to return to the old. If it did it probably would be for a political reason.

The people realize that the fault is not with the system, but with the men who have administered the system.

COMMISSION GOVERNMENT IN KANSAS CITY, KAN.

REPORT OF SPECIAL CORRESPONDENT

Kansas City, Kansas, October 15, 1911.

Commission government has improved—greatly improved—conditions in Kansas City, Kansas. One of the most visible evidences of this is the undisputed fact that the new government has partially removed and greatly improved politics.

Partially? Yes, for while commission government promised to evaporate the political mist that has cursed cities since their history and left them to throw off a stifling strength after each election, it has not entirely done so here. Yet it has cleared the atmosphere so that even the near-sighted may see beyond—a distance which it will take only until another election to reach—and behold a progressive city overshadowed by sky, clear of political shadows.

It is not surprising that politics has not been entirely eliminated when it is taken into consideration that Kansas City, Kansas, made up of several fair sized cities which have been annexed from time to time, was besmeared with political mire to the very hub when the government was changed. The cities that are now united in forming Kansas City, Kansas, were governed by politicians, many of the lowest grade if they can be graded. It was only natural that there was a rush of the bosses of each to gain control of the greater city. In foiling their desires commission government has been the salvation and yet there is a species of revolution in the workings of commission government; there are conditions which exist in this city which are disappointing to those who had indulged in sanguine expectations, and looking around for a scrapegoat the one within easy reach is politics.

There is no doubt that politics is having a disturbing influence on the government, for whatever interferes with the smooth operation of events must be held accountable for every consequence of such interruption, regardless of the need or desirability of the interference.

Obviously the motives of the commissioners are frequently selfish and in themselves scarcely commendable; but it appears to be a natural law that the selfishness of the individual shall bring about great good to the many and so it will probably prove in the government of this city.

Then the disappointing state of conditions also is attributed to the fear of the recall. The commissioners themselves will confess that the recall places a damper on the greater advances which are suggested to their minds. They claim that much can be done, yet in the doing of great things—things which would materially change certain conditions—one makes enemies and that when it is considered that so much trouble can be caused a commissioner by only 25 per cent. of the voters at the former election signing a petition for a recall, there is much hesitancy in exciting that enmity. The recall brings out the yellow in a commissioner's makeup, yet it is generally regarded as essential to commission government in this city. It is the safeguard and while it might dampen the more radical movements of the officials it does not hinder them in their more commonplace matters. Without it one commissioner might work untold damage to the community and one needs only to reflect on the extent of the power of a commissioner and opportunity for graft and corruption should he be so disposed, to join the number already in the larger majority in this city standing firm for the continuance of the recall clause.

It is even suspected that there may be politics of some sort in the inner working of the commission at the present time since the discovery was made that the commissioners have allowed for to great a deterioration in the city's inventory during the last administration. Had they made a rosy estimate there would presumably be no reflection on their conduct. They might, perhaps, have been commended for contributing to those elements that make for business cheer.

Mayor-Commissioner James E. Porter and Commissioners Henry Dean, Otto Anderson, James E. Cable and James E. Caton, comprise the Commission. All except Commissioner Caton have been in office since commission government was inaugurated in this city in April, 1910. Caton was elected at the last spring election to fill the vacancy of Charles Green, who, after serving for the first year refused to run for re-election. Green was a big man, and it is without contradiction that had he desired to be re-elected, as did the others, he would have been successful.

The first year of commission rule was accepted by the people as better than the old form; the vote at the spring election this year in re-electing all the old commissioners gave the stamp of the voter's approval. There were those who expected greater things, but they were broad-minded enough to realize that in the changing of a government there were many drawbacks and were willing to give the old commissioners more time—which was obviously necessary, in perfecting the new government. Green flatly refused to run again, and Caton was selected by the voters to fill his place. The last election occurred the second week in April and the commissioners took charge a week later, each for a term of two years.

Before taking up the work that has been accomplished it is well to refer personally to the men clothed with the authority to do business for the city. Mayor James E. Porter, a Democrat, has been in public life for years; he is often referred to as the policeman-mayor. In starting on his career in this city years ago he patroled the streets in the garb of a policeman. He made a good officer. He was advanced to captain and was regarded as a clean-cut officer, one above the ordinary. A few years later he was elected Sheriff of Wyandotte county and in that office is credited with having done his duty. We find him in such offices until the voters decided to have commission government.

When this decision was reached the old officers, Mayor U. S. Guyer, a Republican, and thirteen aldermen had a year yet to serve. Guyer had had much trouble with his councilmen and had fought them on many important questions until the council was divided and all their time was taken up in the carrying out of personal matters and little attention was paid to the city's benefits, in fact so strong was the oposing sides that it was difficult to get any legislation passed. The voters realized this and the new government came with a welcome. Mayor Guyer favored the commission government, and worked hard for it. He was a candidate for mayor-commissioner. He was opposed by Porter and defeated, although he argued that he deserved the election by gracefully submitting to the change of government, the inauguration of which cut his term of office short one year.

Mayor Porter is a good man, clean of heart, conscientious, with a trace of stubborness in his make-up that enables him to say no to his friends when mindful that they are seeking some action for only personal gain. He is strong morally, yet weak in educational and other matters which are essential to the mayorship under commission government. It can truthfully be said that he is hardly big enough for the place. He has been favored by having the good will of the commissioners, without which he would have been possibly an utter failure. While the commission charter vests in him the great things, and while it would be unfair to say that he has been a failure, yet, even his closest friends, freely admit that he is not the man, when measured from an educational and business experience career, for so high an office should great difficulties confront him. He has not had the experience of governing large business firms or corporations, and has not the education and ability to step forward in civic bodies or enterprises and take the initiative steps, so necessary. His life work has been a public officer—a policeman—and in his high moral conduct alone has he been successful. In the moral uplift of the city he has governed his police department with a steady hand until it is undisputed that Kansas City, Kansas, a city of 100,000 population, is the cleanest of any of the entire United States. The city—dry as are all cities in Kansas—has not been overrun by liquor dives and lawless sales of intoxicants, and even the private houses where a case or two of beer have been delivered for disbursement to a few, have been so guarded that few if any now exist. The gamblers and their dives which found room under the old government have practically all been looted to other ports and it is safe to say that not a single gambling house or house of immorality remains. In Mayor Porter's appointment of Henry Zimmer to the office of chief of police, he has a man of sterling qualities and ever willing and ready to carry out the mayor's bidding regarding all lawlessness. Zimmer has long been in politics, was once elected a representative on the Democratic ticket, and has served as chief of police under councilmanic rule when debauchery was tolerated. He is a man of his word, however, and while he is said to have permitted gambling under the old rule he has stood by the mayor who last apointed him, and has been unusually active in carrying out the mayor's orders. Old gamblers or law violators of any kind respect his stand and know that his word is law and that none can gain recognition as a friend of his if they seek to continue their former lawless activities. Chief Zimmer is the man for the place and in fulfilling the mayor's desires is true to his trust. Instructions are so regarded by him and his knowledge of former gamblers only makes him more proficient in his destruction of them.

So, while Mayor Porter may be lacking in some things, he has been most successful in the carrying out of his idealistic city idea—that of a clean city. In this regard alone commission government has been of untold worth in the hands of the present mayor.

Mayor Porter gets a salary of $4,000 per year. He

earns it, but it is very doubtful if he could earn that much as manager or superintendent of any firm or corporation. In fact he is not the man who would be placed in such an office if only his ability was considered. He has saved considerable from the salaries of his public offices and when his present term expires there is no probability that he would seek such an office.

Henry Dean, commissioner of parks and public buildings, is credited, and rightly so, with being the biggest man of the commission. He is the dictator, and, while the other commissioners would wince at the intimation, it is nevertheless true, and so regarded by the general public. He is, or was, a Republican, and it is Dean who has taken the most decided stand to eliminate politics from city government. His declaration in open meetings to "get away from politics" has been frequently heard by those who have attended. Dean was a lawyer before being elected to commissioner, one of the shrewdest in the city. His shrewdness has stood him well and it is seldom that his will is not carried out by the vote of the majority of the commission when he so desires. He is large enough not to fight over minor matters, leaving the jangling in these instances to the others, but on the greater matters he soars on a higher plane than the rest and, when once making a declaration, fights for it with a determination that is seldom overcome. He is an orator. It is he who fills the mayor's place in addresses of welcome, etc., to conventional bodies and at civic meetings. When fighting to gain his end he appears neither friend or foe, often taking the floor and, in loud expressions, lays down the law in loud and rather boisterous declarations, his hands clinched often raps on the desk, to aid to the decisiveness of his words. He is seldom openly crossed by the others and in his shrewdness weaves the web that generally holds three or more of the votes—the majority—when the vote is taken. He is fearless and is regarded as fearful to the others, although they would stand up any time and any place and deny it. It is the sort of influence that is unable to be seen, yet is in evidence. Good commissioner? Yes. It is his fearlessness that makes him so. He is a good man to have at the head of any city and, although a politician, has got away further perhaps than any other from party lines. Five men like him as commissioners would be the city government and all party lines would be abolished; their pride, if nothing else, would not permit dictation from any person. Dean's initiative steps have been the result of advancement along broader lines. He has fathered more new ordinances than any other commissioner and, while some have been very hard—such as the muzzling of dogs the entire year—they have been regarded as good ones.

Otto Anderson, a Republican, Commissioner of Streets, was elected by the largest vote of any commissioner. He is a Swede, and is a self-made man. His first work in the city was on the street and soon he engaged in the grocery business. He is far from being a politician, but his square dealings and his honest business methods have won for him the esteem of the community. He has worked hard as a commissioner as he would work for himself or wherever employed. What is lacking in the way of education is made up in his fairmindedness for those who placed him in office. He is a man seldom credited with any great or the more initiative steps, yet is liked for his willingness to take a hand in all matters that have come to his attention. He is a good man for the position, and has accomplished much in the betterment of things in his department. He is slow to act, but, when once his mind is made up, he is just as slow to change it. He is a vote-getter, not by scheming or being a politician, but by having the confidence of the people. He has been mentioned as the next candidate for mayor. Whether he entertains this idea or not it is the general opinion that should he run he would be defeated, as many of his warmest friends who supported him for commissioner, would not regard him as a man big enough for mayor. He is known as the frank Swede, and anyone can get an audience with him, and they will be treated fairly and openly. Association of graft or unfairness with his name is like trying to make people believe that water is not wet. They simply smile and forget it the next moment. He is a good, conservative business man, possibly too conscientious to please all to be of the greatest good.

James E. Cable, a Democrat, Commissioner of Water and Light, is also a conscientious man, having the interests of his work at heart. His duty, considering the fact that the city has its own water plant and is to have its own electric light plant, is one of the most anxious of any. Under his department have occurred the most important business deals of the city government, and, while a more practical man might be desired, he has done his duty to the best of his ability, and he has endeavored to give the city the best for the money.

James E. Caton, a Republican, the newly elected commissioner, is the head of the finance department is so slow that he is burdensome on the progress of a city. He was formerly city auditor, and is claimed and acknowledged to be an expert accountant, and on this he was elected to fill the vacancy caused by Mr. Green. He is adept at figures, and, when that is said, it is all said. It is well that a man at the head of this department, one of the most important in the city government, should be careful. The commission laws are very rigid regarding the expenditure of moneys and the transfer of sums from one fund to another, but there needs to be a man who can grasp the situation and apply it at once. In this Caton fails. He reads the statutes over and over again and interprets the law too forcefully to make a good financier. There have been cases where the city would have saved money by the employment of a man in a certain department, but Caton has referred to the law and has taken no pains to avoid a technicality whether it interferes with the good of the city financially or not. A good business man at the head of a corporation would grasp these by-ways which lead to a greater success. Why should not the finance man at the head of the city? It would mean a saving of money and a lowering of taxes. No harm could come, and why let a technicality of law obstruct? Why follow the law so closely as to make it a detriment instead of a help? The laws are made for protection and are rigid, but when a city and her residents are to be benefited by a slight dodge to the right or to the left, why not do so? It would be only carrying out the desire of the people who made the laws and help the city and her people. Caton, it can be truthfully said, has fallen short of the expectations. He is honest, yet too much afraid to make a stand. He is rather an anchor on the shoulders of those at the head of the other departments. Caton should do his pondering at home nights, and come to his office read to act.

During the first year of commission government there was little attempted in the way of improvements and there was little criticism of the officials. The voters waited to let the commissioners get righted. After the last election there were greater things expected. Immediately afterward there was some criticism because the appointments were referred from meeting to meeting. Caton's seeming desire to step in and name the employees of the City Clerk, City Treasurer and City Auditing offices offhand seemed to grate against the other commissioners. The first hitch occurred when Caton presented the name of a real estate man for City Treasurer named William Blodgett. Blodgett had been in the race for Commissioner and had run next to the lowest successful man on the ticket. There was dissatisfaction expressed that the men receiving the largest votes at the election should be so closely allied and it was claimed that if Blodgett, who is regarded as a straightforward and honest young man, should be appointed it would combine the votes at the next election and that the new form of government would revert back to the ways of the old government. Blodgett's name was presented by Caton, however, but it failed to be indorsed by the other commissioners. A woman had held the office before, and there were those who favored the appointing of another woman. The controversy was talked while many meetings passed and finally the name of Miss Kate Daniels was presented by Caton unexpectedly. She was indorsed by every commissioner. Mayor Porter delayed the appointing of a police judge for several weeks and finally presented the name of Jay Carlisle and he was indorsed. The other appointments were much the same as was made during the former year, with the exception of the City Clerk, Gerard Little, assistant the former year, being appointed.

A few weeks later the first intimation of graft was given public notice. The commissioners had been several weeks in letting a contract for the engineering work of a new municipal lighting plant, made possible by the voters favoring a special bond issue. Many executive sessions were held by the commissioners and the city hall was overrun by engineers and their representatives in arguing for the contract. The contract was finally let one afternoon and the next day an attorney for one of the unsuccessful bidders appeared at the city hall and talked to Caton, telling him that some of the commissioners had intimated that his firm could have had the contract had they been willing to pay enough for it. Commissioner Caton (this is also evidenced by the depositions) told the attorney to place the information in writing. This was done and the petitions charging Dean, Cable and Anderson with attempted bribery were delivered to Caton. Dean openly demanded a hearing and was backed by Cable and Anderson. This resulted in several persons being called to testify, suit finally being brought in the courts against the engineering firm that had intimated the attempted bribery. This case is still pending, but is scheduled to come up for hearing soon.

This publicity had an undesirable effect and has not yet been entirely lived down. Caton was scored by the other commissioners for the method which he employed in keeping the matter secret for a day or more, and the feeling creeps out in some ways since.

Since then the commissioners have been gusy. The municipal water plant is self-supporting and furnishing the best of water to the consumers. New machinery has but recently been installed and the revenues derived will pay all expense and provide a sinking fund.

A few weeks ago contracts were let for a new municipal lighting plant and this will be rushed to completion. It will be operated in connection with the water plant, the engines and boilers being operated in connection so as to run both plants at a less expense. The city will doubtless be benefited, and the new plant as well as the old one is expected to be self-sustaining.

There has been a rapid benefit in the park and boulevard system. Nearly seven miles of boulevards are now completed, and a system is being carried out to connect every part of the city. This work is a credit to Park and Boulevard Commissioner Dean, and when his term of office expires he will be able to point with pride to his work which will be substantial enough for a monument. Under Dean the city parks have been greatly improved. Nearly all of the $150,000 appropriated for parks has been expended together with the one-half mill levy. Over 100 acres of land is now city property for parks and playground purposes and many parks have already been improved. The heretofore barren places are now provided with swimming pools, swings, base ball diamonds, tennis courts and benches and children and older people flood these parks afternoons and evenings and enjoy their conveniences. Trees and flowers were used in beautifying and now the park system is being favored by almost everyone. The parks are scattered in various parts of the city and provide, in this manner convenience to the largest number. Some of the improved plots have so increased the value of adjoining property that it is beginning to dawn on property owners that they should have them even if they must donate the land to be improved.

Many miles of streets have been paved under the direction of Dean. Sidewalks have been built, repaired, and made over. Contractors who have paved some of the streets under the old rule were called and made to repair defective parts which was provided for by the contracts and overlooked by former aldermen. Each contractor was assured that he must comply with the contract and although some of the pavements had been laid seven or eight years ago, they had to be repaired, as the guarantee clause was found to provide for the caring of the work for a period of ten years. This work cost the city absolutely nothing. It remained for some one having direct charge of this part of the city government to get after the contractors. It is safe to say that contractors will be more careful in the quality of material used in the future.

There is more satisfaction expressed in the manner in which the people's affairs are looked after. A person wishing to make a complaint of any sort now makes it direct to the commissioner at the head of the department. If they don't know under whose head it comes they tell it to one of the commissioners and it is referred to the right officials. The people have some knowledge who to hold responsible and if the complaint is not looked after, which does not often happen, where one man must take the blame, he can go to the commissioners' meeting and point his finger directly to the neglectful person and demand some consideration.

The health of the city is much improved. A pure milk campaign has just ended. Two months ago when it was started the recently appointed city chemist, which is a newly created office, took several samples of milk and analyzed them. There was not a one up to the standard, some showing but one per cent. butter fat. Arrests were made, and the milkmen charged with selling impure milk were brought before the municipal judge. Fines were assessed—not fines which would permit milkmen selling water and paying the fines and still make more money than they would selling good milk—but fines of from $25 to $100. The campaign was carried on in earnest. It was necessary to fine some milkmen two and three times before they realized the cheapest way—that of giving the milk consumers value for their money. They learned their lesson eventually, and ten days ago, when the city chemist took twenty different samples and tested them, there was not one below the standard, and many one per cent. above it. It was commission government that made such a campaign so successful.

Recently the commissioners created the office of a city Building Material Inspector. His duties will be many, and material in all public buildings will have to stand his approval. A City Electric Inspector is also a new addition, and the electric contractors doing work in the city will have to have all the wiring inspected. It costs the residents nothing, yet it insures first-class work.

The fire protection has been greatly improved. Two new stations have been built in the outlying districts. These are equipped with motor fire apparatus and well manned. The buildings are substantially built of concrete and attention is given the convenience and comfort of the firemen. The buildings will remain long after the commissioners are out of office as a monument of credit to them.

A new city hall is fast nearing completion. It will be a modern up-to-date structure, and when completed will serve the needs of the city for years.

All contract work is let to competitive bidders, and thus the lowest possible price is secured. The aim of the commissioners has been and still prevails to make all their work substantial, and while the expense is greater, it is cheaper in the long run and gives the city a distinctive, enterprising spirit. It welcomes home seekers.

The question of the city debt is thought for some misgivings. Since the commission government has been installed the city has been on a paying basis. Not so under the old system, and we are still suffering from the debts accumulated under the old system. It was the practice under the former rule to pay only what debts were necessary and to create a bonded indebtedness against the city whenever possible. The result was that when the commission government was installed some provision had to be made for the taking up of the old debts. This year's tax levy was increased from 86½ cents on a $100 valuation to 91½ cents to take care of bonds which will fall due as late as 1913. These bonds were all accumulated under the old system and have kept piling up year after year until they have reached enormous proportions. It is the plan to provide for the taking up of these bonds as they fall due, and if this is practiced for a few years and accomplished without creating any new debts it can readily be seen that within a few years this city will be out of debt, and the tax levies will then be greatly lowered and yet all expenses will be met annually.

The rise of taxes has given the anti-commission followers something to howl about, but the course pursued is the course any corporation would follow in meeting old debts and finally placing said business on a strict cash basis, which is recognized as the only right way.

There was not a candidate for commissioner who was elected at last election who made a campaign on the strength of lowering the taxes. Those who knew how the city was in debt made no such claim, as it would be impossible to do so. The debts have been made and must be paid off, and when the yearly output in interest on these old debts is discontinued the city will reap the reward in lower taxes. It must come sooner or later if the present course is followed, as it will be if commission government is continued, as there is every evidence that it will be.

The commissioners are taking interest in learning why some of the taxes have been unpaid. The county commissioners are asked to make a report to the city commissioners if the amounts of all back taxes, those paid, those unpaid and those compromised. An attorney representing the county commissioners made a statement only a few days ago to the effect that at least $50,000 in back taxes would be collected this year. This will be turned over to the city. Heretofore no report has been made to the city by the county commissioner. The city accepted only the amount turned over to them and no knowledge of who had not paid or of the compromise were furnished. With the activity of the city commissioners along this line there is sure to be a larger yearly return to the city treasury. The city is simply assuming a business attitude toward the county and expects a settlement in full or a due explanation why it is not made.

Commission government is good. A report two years hence will reveal it in Kansas City, Kansas, with a reality that cannot be disputed. Commission government needs big men, yet the restrictions on them are sufficient to warrant their best services regardless of their personal desires, whether good or bad.

Who will be the next commissioners? They will be men elected by the people and made to answer to the people. They will not be elected by ward politicians and made to answer to the same individuals who soar under and are really proud of that name.

Have we the necessary men? We have men who are honest and capable in a way. We will pick the best we have and we have as good as any other city in the United States. Municipal affairs are regarded with more importance under the commission rule. Men will school themselves on municipal affairs now with the incentive of commission government before them. The demand for men of ability to run city affairs has always been here, but there has been no incentive to men of brains to enter such a course of study before commission government was inaugurated. Only the grafters and less capable men, men who could not make a living in any other vocation except by playing politics, have been open for the aldermanic positions.

The present commissioners hold offices until April, 1913.

COMMISSION GOVERNMENT IN KANSAS

(CITIES OF THE SECOND CLASS)

REPORT OF SPECIAL CORRESPONDENT.

EMPORIA, Kan., Nov. 9, 1911.

The commission form of government in the second-class cities of Kansas has gained a sturdy hold in the past two or three years, and is growing. Five years ago the commission idea was new. Now twenty-five Kansas cities are operating under the commission plan, and twenty of these are cities of the second class. Starting as an experiment in most towns, the commission form of government in the smaller cities has developed into an unqualified success. The experience of several towns, picked at random, will serve to prove this.

PITTSBURG.

Take Pittsburg, for example, a city of 14,755 inhabitants in the southeast corner of the state. Last April it finished its first year of rule under the commission form. During this year it prospered without the aid of saloons, or the revenues of the saloon tax that it depended upon for many years. At the end of the year there was plenty of money in the treasury and a clear way ahead for more funds. In its first year of the new rule Pittsburg paid all expenses—payrolls, electric light bills, everything—without the monthly $2,000 that came from the saloons and dives. At the close of business when the new year began, there was $190,000 in available cash on hand in the city treasury, distributed among the various funds.

How this was accomplished is told by some of the business men and commissioners. One of these, William Lanyon, Jr., the first commissioner of finance, and for many years a councilman under the aldermanic system, said in an interview: "The first thing we did was to lay out a rigid line of economy and then stay by that line. We did that to allow Pittsburg to pay its bills without the saloon revenue. The commissioners worked for a meager salary that the city some day might have something of which it would be proud. We reduced every expense as much as possible and soon we began to see where we would be able to make things move. Then came tax time and with the taxes we soon had money in the treasury at the close of every week. Pittsburg was placed on a solid foundation by its first board of commissioners. The people all are satisfied with the new idea of government and none would willingly return to the old system."

Mr. Lanyon is a banker. He says there has been a material increase in business in the town since the new form of city rule began. Many improvements are noticeable throughout the city. Many thousands of dollars have been expended in building new streets and sidewalks. The city has just finished the construction of an immense sewer at a saving of several hundred dollars. The people are interested in civic affairs, and assist the commissioners in running the business of the city.

"There are not two hundred persons in Pittsburg who would return to the old system," said Fred B. Wheeler, president of the Pittsburg Commercial Club.

Pittsburg's new board of commissioners, which assumed its duties in April, is hewing closely to the line of economy laid down by the first board. Dr. Asbury C. Graves, the new mayor-commissioner, has dispensed with useless officials wherever practicable, and has reduced the salary of certain officials whose whole time is not required in their work.

PARSONS.

Parsons, in Labette county, is a busy railroad center. Eighteen months ago it went under the commission form of government. At that time the city was issuing warrants which were stamped "unpaid for lack of funds," and the city was bankrupt, to all practical purposes. Under the commission, the city now is operating on a cash basis, has more than $40,000 in the treasury, and has liquidated $12,000 in warrant indebtedness incurred in previous administrations.

Parsons was fortunate in securing a first-class mayor, which the friends of the commission give as the main reason for the signal success of the commission. O. H. Stewart is the man, and he was re-elected to a second term without opposition. He is a banker by profession, and he applied business methods to the affairs of the city. He instituted a retrenchment policy when he first came into office, cutting down expenses all along the line, but not at the expense of public safety or good government. He demanded that the city police department give the city protection, as well as prevent the violation of the prohibitory law. Under his lead, as actual chief of police, he has pumped new life into this department. When he stepped into office bootleggers and jointists were operating flagrantly, with almost no interference from the police. Half a hundred bootleggers and dozens of joints and drug stores were engaged in the unlawful sale of liquor. Now the dives are gone; there are no bars in the rear rooms of drug stores, and a handful of bootleggers skate on thin ice every time they peddle their wares in the back streets and alleys. Stewart is not a politician; he is a business man applying business methods to the management of a city's affairs.

While the force of the mayor dominated the prosperity of Parsons in its start in commission government, the personnel of the commission is a peculiarly fortunate combination of talents. With a banker at the head, the commission consists further of a railroad machinist, a real estate man, a contractor and a lumberman. These men have applied their judgment to the needs of the city with singular smoothness and have worked in harmony. As a whole, the people of Parsons are highly satisfied with their new government.

John Madden, a hard-headed lawyer, the general attorney of Kansas for the Missouri, Kansas & Texas Railroad Company, pays Mr. Stewart a high tribute, saying: "He has been successful along financial lines. and I consider the city fortunate in being able to secure his services. He is a man of splendid character and has done much to build up the city. I presume there are some violations of the moral code in Parsons, but I am satisfied that an effort has been made by the mayor and members of the commission to make Parsons a moral town, and they have succeeded admirably." Parsons has 12,463 inhabitants.

ABILENE.

The jump from Parsons to Abilene is a long one across country, and a long one in type of town. Parsons is a noisy, bustling railroad center; Abilene a conservative country community in the heart of the wheat belt. But Abilene has done something original, and has elected two young men on its commission—both of whom are graduates of the State University. Arthur Hurd, the mayor, is a stripling of thirty years, with a fresh sheepskin from the University Law School. When the commission wave inundated Abilene last spring, the younger voters settled on Hurd, ran him through a hot campaign, and landed him in the mayor's chair. "Too many old fogy ideas in this burg," said the youngsters; "we want some young blood"—and they got it. The conservative citizens of the town—the men who have wrested small-sized fortunes from the soil through drouths and grasshoppers and floods and bugs and blight—shook their heads sadly over the calamity of this election. But Hurd has surprised them. His university training has not pulled him off the ground, and he sailed into the job of mayor with a liking. He first instituted a paving campaign, and Abilene has had more paving the past summer than in all its previous history. Hurd did not stop with the streets, but he caused the alleys in the business section to be paved, and he was not above spending his time on the job with the workmen to get the best results. His legal training has given him a capacity for detail, and he has lined up the affairs of the city systematically.

Mattison, the other university graduate, has the advantage of Hurd in years, and received an excellent experience by a four years' term in the county treasurer's office. He is shrewd and conscientious. Forney, the father of the Belle Springs Creamery Company, which is one of the leading industries of the cream and butter fat trade of the state, gives the commission poise, and his calm judgment balances the enthusiasm of the younger men.

B. D. Whitehead, owner of one of the largest dry goods houses in the town, has noticed the attitude of the commission toward the business men, and said to a correspondent: "When I go to the city building on business, these commissioners show pleasure in meeting me, and seem glad to get the ideas of the merchants. While they do not approve of everything we have to say, there seems to be a feeling of public spiritedness, which means results in the best interests of the city at all times. Without a doubt the commission form is a success in Abilene."

IOLA.

Iola, with 9,032 inhabitants, has met with this experience: For the first time in years the general expenses have been kept within the general revenue. On April 30, 1911, the total balance in all funds was $66.-199.06, showing an increase, after paying off several thousand dollars of floating indebtedness incurred by previous administrations, of $24,381.19 for the year. The schedule of expenditures by departments compared to that of the previous year show how the Iola commissioners are able to make this splendid balance:

Departments:	Year ending April 30, 1911.	Year ending April 30, 1910.
General administration	$ 1,466.60	$ 9,683.37
Police department	4,033.71	6,933.82
Fire Department	2,995.23	3,295.35
Engineering department	539.25	1,786.65
Department of Health and Sanitation	2,352.35	2,472.01
Street and Alley Department	3,180.53	10,932.00
Cemetery	1,261.61	1,389.96
Park	467.90	1,331.57
Public Library	1,721.56	....
Water and Light Bond Coupons paid	4,002.19	4,000.00
Refunding Bond Coupons paid	2,300.00	2,300.00
Railroad Bond Coupons paid	1,040.00	1,040.00
Internal Improvement Bonds paid	34,993.24	34,293.63
Internal Improvement Coupons paid	13,860.38	14,119.37
Time Warrants paid	25,960.63	33,336.38
Gas Department	66,838.81	82,598.49
Water Department	14,162.14	14,744.92
Electric Department	10,096.04	12,280.65
Total	$191,272.17	$236,438.17

A few items through the departments are enlightening. In 1910, under the council form, the city attorney's "salary and expenses" were $1,061.68; in 1911, $734.60. Election expenses, drawn from the general fund, were $711.14 in 1910; in 1911, $263.58. An elastic category of "miscellaneous" in the general fund shrank amazingly in 1911, being $468.47 against $7,950.60 for the previous year. The salary account for police patrol dropped in the twelve-month from $4,161.46 to $2,062.38, and the salary of the police judge from $900 to $300. Labor in the engineering department cost only $466.34 in 1911, while in 1910 it was $1,418.02, and the pay of the garbage man fell off from $1,007.76 to $885.60—the result of contract under the competitive bid plan. And so on, for the big showing in the totals.

Charles F. Scott, of Iola, formerly congressman from Kansas, and editor of the Iola Daily Register, said, in referring to the commission form: "The plan has been in operation nearly two years here, and has worked satisfactorily. Good men have been elected to office, and they have worked in harmony. Iola always has been well and honestly governed, so there was no room for spectacular stunts by the commission. I think it is generally agreed, however, that there has been improvement rather than deterioration under the commission plan. It all depends on the men. We have been fortunate in getting good ones."

EMPORIA.

Emporia, with 9,050 people, adopted the commission form a year ago in April. At the election, the new government carried five to one, the women's votes helping materially in the victory. The first commission was a peculiar combination of men. Frank McCain, a plasterer who had lived in the town many years, was elected mayor, while the commissioners were William Corbett, a Welsh stone mason, and William Lawler, a real estate and insurance man. Corbett assumed charge of the streets and public utilities and Lawler of the financial department. The commission worked mainly in harmony, though McCain and Lawler were the members at cross-purposes, and wherever Corbett stood decided questions during the opening year. At the first annual election, McCain was succeeded by Edgar Fessenden, a grocer.

With office assistants and superintendents of departments there is not enough work to keep the three men busy. Usually, however, one of them is on hand every hour of the day for the manifold complaints which gravitate to a city building. This, indeed, is a significant phase of the new government, as it appears in this town. There is a responsible officer for every detail. If Mrs. B. in the First Ward wants ten wagonloads of dirt from the paving excavation, which is twice as many as Mrs. C., in the next block, is getting, Commissioner Corbett walks out to the house, looks over the situation, and makes a decision. If he offends the feelings of one of the women, as usually is the case, he is a living object at which complaints may be cast. Strange to say, this is a point in favor of the commission. In its last analysis, it means that the commissioner is on the job to bear the burden for its every phase. Which is exactly what every business man does.

The Emporia commission has conducted a strenuous campaign in collections, and the returns this year are $4,000 larger than they were the last year under the council. Bonds to the amount of $13,000 have been paid off, and there is $3,300 in the sinking fund. At that, the income of the city has been decreased by loss of receipts from the electric plant, which has been leased to a corporation in return for street cars.

An era of improvements has been under way. In a year and a half, the commission has added forty-seven blocks of paving to the town, making a total of more than ten miles, and has passed petitions for twenty-seven blocks more next year. It has built one and one-half miles of sanitary sewer, and one-half mile of storm sewer. The system of arc lights for street lighting has been superseded by the Tungsten system, which allows a light on every street corner within the city limits. Current for each arc light was an expense of $72 per year, while for the Tungstens it is $14 each annually. The main street is now illuminated by a White Way, and the city pays one-half the light bill for this improvement while the merchants pay the other half. The commission has improved the municipal water system by building a subsidiary pipe line from the pumping station to the reservoirs, at a cost of $14,000, and by the installation of electric turbine pumps at the pumping station, an expense of $16,000. The new pumping equipment is considered a forward step, while the city is assured greater fire protection. The commission also is investigating the possibility of supplying the city with water from wells, instead of from the Neosho river.

An up-to-date bookkeeping system is now in use at the city offices. The daily balances, which now are taken, were unthought of under the council system. A city matron, established by the commission, looks after the poor, and assists the mayor in his dispensations of charity. The town band gets $600 annually, by order of the commission, for its services in training young boys to become skillful musicians. The parks get generous encouragement from the commission, the last levy for the purpose being $2,000, which is four times as much as any council ever devoted. Recently, the mayor wiped out an unsightly spot by enclosing the town garbage dump with high board fences. It was an ugly place, offensive both to passersby and to neighboring residents, but no city official ever had given it his attention. The mayor sold the space on the fences to business firms for advertising purposes, using the proceeds to pay for the lumber, and the improvement did not cost the city a cent. The dump now is under personal supervision of the garbage collector, and irresponsible dumping has been stopped. A small thing, but enough to prove the value of a man on the job. Countless small items in the city's business are handled satisfactorily for this reason.

THE REFERENDUM INVOKED.

Emporia tried out the referendum and found it good. The greatest single issue that the town had faced in its history came up last year when the project of leasing the municipal electric plant to a Dayton, Ohio, firm for a period of twenty years, in exchange for a street-car line, came up. It precipitated a great agitation. The discussion split the town into highly partisan factions, but the referendum election, which carried in favor of street cars 1,563 to 1,063, settled it. The people had spoken on a question of grave public concern; there were no recriminations, no cries of a bribed city council. The public voice had decided the matter once for all, and cars now are running up and down the streets, with all citizens satisfied that the will of the majority is ruling.

NEWTON.

Newton has felt the benefits of the commission form of government principally in its water system. The mayor, Jerry Dunkleberger, has made himself independently wealthy through shrewd investments in real estate from the income of a locomotive engineer. His experience has made him intensely practical and peculiarly fitted for the mayor's position. In addition to the duties of his office he has assumed management of the water department. Newton has an especially pure quality of water, pumped from wells located seven miles from the town. The water, for quantity and quality, has made Newton famous, but the plant was poorly managed under the council. In eighteen months, Mr. Dunkleberger has caused $25,000 to be expended in improving the equipment and adding to the well supply, while the expenses of operation have been cut down by fifty per cent. A. E. Hurford, a successful merchant, is commissioner of finance, and Dr. Ocran Roff, a practising physician, commissioner of utilities. Dr. Roff has arranged his practise in order to give a large part of his time to the affairs of the city. The commission works harmoniously and has the loyal support of the citizens. Col. P. M. Hoisington, secretary of a building and loan association, said: "The streets and alleys of Newton show no improvement under the commission form, for all available money has been applied to the water system, which is our chief pride. But we like the commission better for the secure sense it gives us of practical application in all affairs. While the city is conducted more economically, the commission has not cut down taxes. Instead we are putting our extra money into sinking funds to pay off our debts." Indeed, Mr. Hoisington's observation is true of most towns under the commission plan. The commissions of Kansas have not reached the point where they can make a showing by lowering the taxes. As long as sinking funds are receiving more attention than ever now, the tax reduction seems bound to come. Newton has a population of 7,862.

PRATT.

Pratt, one of the smaller towns with the commission, has a characteristic body. A former councilman is mayor and a banker and retired farmer are commissioners of finance and utilities respectively. The city government is systematized and expeditious, and the town, which has 3,302 people, is planning large improvements. Pratt has had the commission only six months, but the change of government was supported by a large majority at the election; and the new form has the full respect of the community.

CHANUTE.

The commission idea is growing in the second-class cities of the state. Chanute, a town of 9,272 inhabitants, is the latest to adopt the commission, and the election, which was held November 7, carried by a majority of 306. Every precinct in the town, five in number, gave a majority to the commission.

There is the "other side" to the commission plan, and this has not been sounded in Kansas with greater force than by Walt Mason, the noted poet-philosopher and editorial writer of Emporia. Recently, he said in a letter to a friend: "It would take too much space to go into details. It is sufficient to say that the commissioners, who are ignorant and narrow-minded men, seem to take an unholy delight in queering every project that promises to benefit the town. Emporia has but one manufacturing industry that amounts to anything. This factory, a growing and prosperous concern, wanted a switch across a business street. There was no earthly reason why it should not have a dozen switches, but the commissioners would not grant it until the business men of town went out and got up a petition that couldn't be turned down. Meanwhile Wichita, sizing up the situation, made a bid for the factory in question, and probably will get it. (The factory still is in Emporia and negotiations to move it are dead.) The town is sore over the incident and several minor ones showing the bullheadedness of the commissioners, who sit brooding at the city hall, like three owls in an ivy-mantled tower, thinking up new ways to show their hostility to the business interests of the town."

"These three commissioners would kill any town; they are prejudiced, hide-bound individuals, without business experience, and the owner of a prosperous peanut stand would not entrust it to them. There is no probability that better men will succeed them, for first-class men won't give all their time and energies to the city for such salaries as are prescribed for a town of Emporia's size. The best the defenders of the commission can say is that it would be a good thing if good men were elected. Any system would be admirable under such conditions. Where city government is given over to three men, the election of one chump is a calamity; the election of two chumps is a disaster; the election of three is chaos."

To which William Allen White has replied: "On the other hand, Mr. Mason should not overbear us with his argument. For nothing but a benevolent despotism will automatically insure good government. It is enough for any system that it will work if good men are elected by the people. The council system will not work even with good men, for divided responsibility shifts the blame and makes it impossible for voters to locate the trouble. Under the commission form of government, the people may not only elect good men, but they may see just exactly which good man has gone wrong, and so elect another in his place. In the first-class cities in Kansas, the recall expedites matters."

COMMISSION GOVERNMENT IN SOUTH DAKOTA*

REPORT OF SPECIAL CORRESPONDENT.

SIOUX FALLS, S. D., Mar. 13, 1911.

Sioux Falls, with a population of 15,000, was the first South Dakota city to adopt the commission plan of government for cities. This was two years ago. Since then her example has been followed by Huron, Yankton, Canton, Dell Rapids, Chamberlain, Pierre, the capital, Rapid City, Vermillion, where the State university is located, and Aberdeen—ten in all. The plan is growing in popularity in South Dakota, and this year will see many more towns and cities in the State adopt it. The last legislature passed a new law permitting cities, by a majority vote, to adopt the "three-man plan"—a Mayor and two commissioners. In cities of the first class, the salary of the Mayor under this plan is put at $2,000 annually, and of the commissioners at $1,500. A vote can be had on the change of plan on petition of 15 per cent. of the voters, and it is certain that Sioux Falls at least will vote upon the change from five commissioners to three.

In the last two years the city has paid debts to the aggregate of $100,000—about equally divided between the school board and the city commission—both under the same plan. The floating debt is being reduced, and a sinking fund accumulated for debt payment in the future. Those who expected that the commission could wield a magic wand and abolish taxes, or through some legerdemain, create assets and wipe out liabilities are, of course, disappointed; but those who welcome taxes high enough to stop the accumulation of debt, and to head the city towards a program of debt payment, and wise economy of administration, are more than satisfied. Should a vote be taken to return to the old plan, the proposal would not muster 10 per cent. of the voters. Sioux Falls is growing fast. She has a city water plant into which all the profits are being put for necessary extensions, and there is constant pressure for new school buildings, new city buildings, and much grading and paving and sewerage. All these things mean a snugly heavy tax, but the citizens are happy in the belief that they have at last discovered the best machinery for good results and the plan is increasingly popular in Sioux Falls.

George W. Burnside is the Mayor. He is a man of strong personality and seems always to control enough of any civic body of which he is a member to get his way. It is unfortunate that he does not enjoy the reputation of being a good business man. This is the only trouble which Sioux Falls has experienced with her commission plan. Under the commission law as first adopted, there was no provision for a primary. The result was that there were three candidates for Mayor, and Mayor Burnside was elected, being a minority selection. His choice for commissioner was elected in a similar way last spring. One of the holdover commissioners is a great admirer of the Mayor, and hence Mayor Burnside can now get through the commission about anything he favors. The last legislature passed the "three-man plan" bill and also attached the primary feature to the old law, so that in the election which comes this spring, the commissioner elected must be the choice of the majority. This, it is believed, will solve the problem of Sioux Falls, as meeting the only trouble it has experienced with the plan. In Sioux Falls, politics, both party and factional, have been entirely eliminated from city affairs, and the man who endorses a candidate for places on the commission because of party or factional adantage soon finds himself doing an unpopular thing.

Huron

In Huron a petition has been filed for the recall of the Mayor and all of the commissioners after a year in office. No misconduct is charged, but the taxpayers object that too high a tax levy was made for purposes of debt payment. Huron became deeply involved financially through her struggles to get the State capitol. Up to a year ago no attempt had been made to provide for the payment of the outstanding debt. Sinking fund levies were made, but the funds so realized were illegally used for current expenses. When the new commission took office, it found the city's books in frightful shape. No one knew how much the city owed, nor when it was due. Though levies for a sinking fund had been repeatedly made, the commission found but $504.33 in the sinking fund. It at once made a levy of $25,000 for sinking fund account—the levy being especially large because of past neglect. Huron is a small place—5,791 by the last census

* The South Dakota laws on the Initiative and Referendum are distinctive in the fact that they provide for the submission of questions to a popular vote on a five per cent. petition, which is lower than that provided for in any other general state law. The writer of this report deals at length with the workings of these laws. While the material herein refers to the operation of the general law, the principles involved are presumably applicable to cities.

—and the levy was a heavy burden. It was this act which has resulted in the impending recall. The election has not yet been held, but the general impression is that the commission will be sustained. It is worth noting that when the commission took charge it set an accountant at work to find out about things and discovered $811 in a bank in New York to the credit of the city, which had been previously overlooked by the city council.

Rapid City

In Rapid City, the wide-open element fought the adoption of the plan, but it carried by a close vote. In December this writer visited Rapid City, after the plan had been in force the better part of a year, and found the citizens there more united than they have been in many years. One of those who opposed the plan candidly confessed that he was mistaken and that he had tried to defeat what had proved to be a good thing for Rapid City.

The Initiative and Referendum

South Dakota has been laughed at, from one end of the Union to the other, because of the "freak ballot" which it submitted to the voters of this State at the election last November. This ballot has been on exhibition in many places, and has attracted as much attention as the man-eating hyena at the circus, or the six-legged calf in the side show. The ballot was 77 inches long (six and one-half feet), and was 10 inches wide. It was printed in nonpareil type, and diligent but unavailing search has been made for some one who read it all through, except the proofreaders and the campaign orators. In addition to this, at the same election, another ballot, 22 inches long, carrying the proposed amendments to the constitution, was submitted, so that the total of proposed laws voted on, as shown by the two ballots, reached the impressive display of 99 inches, or eight and one-fourth feet of laws, printed in the finest of type, with the hope that the average voter would carefully digest the same, compare the proposed measures with other States, judicially contemplate the matter from all sides, and reach a wise and intelligent conclusion! This is the initiative and referendum stripped of theory, and in actual practice.

HOW SOUTH DAKOTA GOT IT

It was in 1896, at the end of a period of hard times, that the issue of the free and unlimited coinage of silver at the ratio of 16 to 1, was sprung upon the country. On that issue a combination of Democrats and Populists carried the previously steadfast Republican State of South Dakota. The legislature which followed was controlled by Populist leaders, and among the things submitted was the Initiative and Referendum. This was a proposed amendment to the constitution, and it provided that five per cent. of the voters could, on petition, demand a vote upon a measure, before it could become a law, "except such laws as may be necessary for the immediate preservation of the public peace, health or safety, support of the State institutions, and its existing institutions." There was no discussion of the proposed amendment in the newspapers, or from the platform, not one voter in one hundred understood it, ignorance and indifference carried it in the election which followed, and put it in the constitution, where it now remains—a solace to special interests and a menace to the real welfare of the State.

OUR FIRST TASTE

For several years the Initiative and Referendum remained unused, and we were content to have something fancy that at the same time was causing no discomfort. Then a scandal arose over the divorce laws of the State. We had a three months residence in South Dakota that was not established with any thought of facilitating divorce, but was the time acceptable in a new country like South Dakota. North Dakota had the same residence provision. This began to attract the attention of the matrimonial misfits from New York and other eastern States, and before South Dakota realized it, several cities were enjoying a "divorce colony," which brought thousands of dollars into the pockets of lawyers, hotel keepers and merchants. The moral sense of the State revolted and the time of residence was changed to six months, with the idea that this would put an end to the business. This reform was led by Bishop William H. Hare, Episcopal bishop for South Dakota, who died last year, beloved by all South Dakotans. This change in the law drove the business to North Dakota. That State then raised the time of residence to a year. The colony came back to South Dakota in increasing numbers and undiminished affront. The best sentiment of the State again protested, and the next legislature, almost by unanimous vote, raised the time of residence to one year. It was then that South Dakota got its first taste of the Referendum. The lawyers, hotel men, jewelers, liverymen, and merchants, who enjoyed the business, caused it to be invoked on the new law. There was no hope that it could be defeated in the election. In fact no campaign was made for it, in the election which followed, two years later. The sentiment of the people was aroused and was overwhelming, but the Referendum was invoked because it gave two years more of the business. Thus the first use of the Referendum in South Dakota was in behalf of the special interest to defeat the moral sentiment of the State through two years' delay in a moral reform which was almost unanimously desired. When the election was held the law was vindicated, and the divorce business was sent to Reno, Nevada, which is now the western clearing house for the matrimonial misfits of the east.

THE FREAK BALLOT

This had given the minority a taste of what might be done through this convenient system, and this brought to the State the "freak ballot" of last November. That ballot carried twelve different propositions. Among them was a proposal to establish the system of county option. The anti-county option people started an educational campaign. They plastered the State with "Vote No" signs. They bought advertising space in the newspapers, and in their advertising matter urged the voters to "Vote No." The "Vote No" signs stared from the bill boards in cities, from the elevators in the country, from telephone poles and from barns and fences. Those who favored county option saw the drift of this dangerous campaign and started out, too late, with a "Vote Yes" propoganda. The result was that every measure submitted was defeated, with one exception, and that was a measure so strongly favored by everybody that even the "Vote No" sentiment could not quite overtake it, though it had a close call.

Below is given the returns on the special submission on the freak ballot:

	Yes.	No.
Renting Lands	48,152	44,220
Salary, Attorney-General	35,932	52,397
Equal Suffrage	35,289	57,709
Debt Limitation	32,612	52,233
Revenue Amendment	29,830	52,043
New Institutions	36,128	47,625
County Option	42,416	55,372
Electric Headlights	37,914	48,938
"Czar" Law	32,160	52,152
Embalmers Law	34,560	49,546
Congressional Districts	26,918	47,893
Militia	17,852	57,440

WAS VOTING INTELLIGENT?

The mere statement that eleven of the twelve submissions were defeated does not prove lack of discrimination on the part of the voters. All of the eleven measures might have been bad. It will be noted, however, in looking over these returns that the range in the "Yes" column, is 30,300, while in the "No" column it is only 13,489. The militia law was defeated by 39,588 majority while equal suffrage, against which more votes were cast, was defeated by only 22,420 majority. In other words, the "Vote No" campaign carried the negative voters clear through the list, so that they would be sure to "get" what they were after, while the "Vote Yes" faction, having waged a less diligent campaign, failed to arouse the same activity and land the "Yes" vote down the list. The militia law was last on the ballot and the "Yes" voters got tired before they reached it!

In this list was a law requiring the railroads to equip their engines with electric headlights. This was one of the reform measures. The railroads invoked the referendum upon it, with no thought of beating it, but merely to get two years' delay. No one was more surprised than the railroads when they learned that the law was defeated by the sovereign voice of the people of South Dakota! So certain were the legislators that the defeat of the measure did not reflect the will of the people that the legislature, which has just adjourned, re-enacted the measure, and it will again be submitted to the referendum, so that there will be no electric headlights for two years more, and not then if there should happen to be another "Vote No" campaign.

Another of the measures was one forbidding the State legislature to establish any new State institutions without a vote of the people. South Dakota, with less than 600,000 population, has four normal schools, which are maintained at great expense, and the constitutional amendment was desired to stop the establishment of any more expensive and useless State institutions. It was so worthy a measure that there should not have been 1,000 votes against it. No one thought it was in the slightest danger of being defeated. It lost by 11,497 majority. The militia law was passed by a practically unanimous vote in the legislature. The Referendum on it was invoked by a few Socialists in the Black Hills, who are opposed to any military organization. The proposed law merely adopted the form of military organization outlined by the war department, and was in no respect revolutionary or objectionable. It was defeated by nearly 40,000 majority.

The revenue amendment was the *piece de resistance* of the reform movement in this State. It was their joy and pride. It was intended to put the express companies in a position where they would have to pay taxes on their income, instead of on visible property. It was slaughtered by 22,193 majority, in spite of the heroic efforts made to rescue it from the "Vote No" snowslide, and once more the special interests triumphed by reason of the Referendum.

The vote on county option was perhaps the only one which really reflected the sentiment of the voters on the special submissions. Without doubt it caused the defeat of all the others. Governor Vessey was so strongly of this opinion that he tried to get the last legislature to re-enact the "czar law," which had been defeated by 20,000 majority, on the ground that the voters did not know what they were doing when they voted it down. This was a measure giving the power of removal to the Governor of local officers who failed or refused to enforce the law. The equal suffrage people also contended that their measure had been buried because of the "Vote No" campaign, and all but induced the legislature to submit it again.

The plain fact is that the voters went at the ballot blind. "I haven't read the ballot and don't intend to," the voters would say, "but I am going to vote against everything until a stop is put to a ballot which it is not possible for me to understand." This writer started out to poll the first twenty-five men he met as to what they intended to do with the "freak ballot." This was three weeks before election. Not one of the twenty-five had read the ballot, and all but six of them declared they were going to "vote against everything."

REFERENDUM REFORMERS ALARMED

It cost the taxpayers about $150,000 to print the legal notice of the election in the newspapers. This aroused a great hue and cry against the cost of the system. The newspapers urged the legislature to reduce the number of publications from four times to two times, and to submit an amendment raising the percentage required to invoke the referendum to 15 or 20 per cent. The demand for the increase in the percentage came from the friends of the Referendum who were thoroughly alarmed by the report that a company was being organized which would agree to supply, for a fixed fee, the required number of signers to invoke the Referendum on any law to which the Referendum was applicable. Nothing was done by the legislature towards raising the percentage. To change it would require a vote of the people, and it is by no means certain that with the sullen attitude of the people against the whole business, even a measure to end the farce, could pass. The legislature did pass a measure for the publication on the ballot of only the title to the law, as is done in Oregon, and limiting publicity to a pamphlet put out by the State, so that in the future voters will have less chance to post themselves than they have had in the past. The newspapers are angry at this invasion of their legitimate business field, and the present prospect is that the free publicity expected from them will not be forthcoming. The legislature also attached the "emergency clause" to every measure which could muster a two-thirds vote. This was done under an old decision of the supreme court that the legislature is the sole judge of "an emergency" which, stated in another form, means that the legislature, by a two-thirds vote, has the power to repeal a constitutional provision. No one thinks that the supreme court, as now constituted, would hold this good law, and the State is searched in vain for a good lawyer who thinks that the legislature can so deny the right of Referendum. There is now likelihood of a test case and should this be brought forward, and the decision be as expected, no one knows to what extent the Referendum business would be carried in the election in November, 1912. Were it not for this old decision, it is certain that twenty or thirty measures would have to run the gauntlet of the Referendum —and perhaps more. A good roads law—the first ever passed in this State, and a sane and wise measure—is certain to be among those on which the Referendum will be invoked next year. It failed to get over the "emergency" deadline. So general was the "emergency" attached that a protest went up and public sentiment forced the legislature, in its dying days, to refuse to attach the "emergency" clause to a number of debatable measures, while several worthy bills were killed because of an attempt to saddle this clause upon it.

THE 'RICHARDS" MEASURE

One of the measures to be voted upon at the election in November, 1912, is the "Richards Primary Law." This is a measure drawn by R. O. Richards, of Huron, one of the leading "progressives" of the State. He has drawn a primary law to take the place of the one now in force, under which nominations for minor offices are made largely through the accident of a name and to restore in some form the State convention idea. The measure is 22 pages long, and no one as yet pretends to understand it. The legislature turned it down, but Mr. Richards has secured names enough to submit it to the people under the initiative. The measure may be the finest one yet devised, but the members of the legislature voted it down without discussion. The theory of the Initiative and Referendum is that the poor, beleagured, humble busy voter will master this long and complicated proposal, compare it with the present law, judge it by the enactments of other States, and render an intelligent judgment upon it. We leave it to good guessers as to whether or not they are likely to do this.

COMMISSION GOVERNMENT IN GALVESTON

REPORT OF SPECIAL CORRESPONDENT.

GALVESTON, Texas, Dec. 23, 1910.

The city of Galveston, Texas, has played the scale of city government, and after ten years' experience has reached the definite conclusion that it has at least partially solved the problem with its commission plan. The smaller in proportion to population in Galveston than smallest in proportion to population in Galveston than any other city in the country. There are a large number of laborers here; one-fourth of these are negroes and a large number of the remainder are foreign born. There are a large number of saloons, and saloons usually participate in politics; and yet under these conditions the commission plan is a success here.

The general election laws of Texas provide for nominations for city offices by political parties, as well as for independent candidates. Any citizen can become a candidate and upon securing a petition signed by five per cent. of the number voting at the previous city election, can have his name placed on the official ballot. Provision is made by law for the printing of the names of candidates in columns under the names of the respective political parties or in the independent column in alphabetical order.

The history of city government in Galveston prior to the adoption of the commission plan would be but a repetition of the history of city government in other cities—good, bad and indifferent. The annual budgets during the last few years under the aldermanic system exceeded the income and produced an annual deficit of $100,000. Every two years the legislature was asked for authority to issue $200,000 in floating indebtedness bonds to meet this over-expenditure. Galveston was proud of its record for never having suffered with a dishonest mayor in its seventy and more years of aldermanic government. And yet the city's greatest trouble has been with its board of aldermen, their political jugglery, their caucuses, and their speechmaking. When the great storm struck Galveston on September 8, 1900, the city was practically bankrupt. It had defaulted in the payment of interest on its bonded indebtedness. Scrip saleable only at a big discount was being issued to meet current bills. The city hall, fire engine houses, waterworks, and electric lighting station were in ruins, the public buildings badly damaged, and wooden block street paving in a deplorable condition. According to the city auditor's report, the floating debt of the city on January 1, 1901, was $204,974.54. Civic life was at stake. Prominent business men and taxpayers decided that there was an imperative necessity that the city charter be overhauled; that a new charter be adopted to bring municipal government down or rather up to a business basis. Suffice to say that, after a bitter fight in which the professional politicians and other politicians fought hard against a reform system, the legislature granted a new city charter and the commission plan was inaugurated.

With the exception of the present mayor-president, all of the commissioners have served from the inauguration of the system, having been returned to office at each election, every two years. The Mayor-President, Judge Lewis Fisher, is a lawyer and has served as county attorney, county judge, and district judge, resigning from the district judgeship to accept the presidency of the commission board. Mr. Kempner, Commissioner of Finance and Revenue, is president of the Texas Bank and Trust Company, president also of the Board of Trade, and identified with many other institutions in the city. Mr. Lange, Commissioner of Waterworks and Sewerage, is the head of a large wholesale commission and grocery house. Mr. Austin, Commissioner of Streets and Public Property, is in the real estate business; and Mr. Norman, Commissioner of the Fire and Police Departments, is engaged in the fire-insurance and bond business.

The mayor-president receives a salary of $2,000 per annum and each of the four Commissioners $1,200. The city attorney and city engineer are the only employees receiving fees. The city's system of bookkeeping and accounting is in keeping with the commission plan itself. The city hall is a business office and not a loafing place for politicians. The press of the city publishes in detail all that transpires at the weekly meetings of the city board.

Outside of the bonds issued for grade-raising purposes since the advent of the commission government, the city has issued and is about to issue only the following: For building and repairing school buildings under the direction of the school board, $50,000; for a duplicate water-main across Galveston Bay, $100,000 (the city's fresh water supply is piped from artesian wells fourteen miles up on the mainland); for additional brick street paving, drainage, shell roads, and additional filling for the streets, $300,000. The issuance of these bonds was authorized by popular vote.

The city owns its own waterworks, costing more than $1,500,000. Also its own sewer plant as well as electric light plant. All three give general satisfaction. The city also maintains a very efficient and well equipped fire department.

The recall feature, as viewed by those who have given the subject study as applied in Texas, does not meet with favor, especially where the percentage is low, and there is a cosmopolitan population. It is charged here that this feature is a two-edged sword and subject to improper use, and is more an injury to the commission plan than a benefit. This was proved in the city of Fort Worth, Texas, where an attempt was made through petition to force the police commissioner to stand for re-election by an element that he had offended through the performance of his sworn duty. The state statute contains ample provision for the removal of incompetent or corrupt public officials. The recall is not necessary and only tends to complicate. Business men will not hold public office where they are liable to be called upon to go through one or more campaigns during a single term of two years. It is very difficult at best to induce competent business men to run for office.

What the city commission has accomplished for Galveston, under the most adverse circumstances, has indeed been wonderful. The total floating debt of the city—$204,974—has been paid. The commissioners secured and paid for the services of a board of eminent engineers which resulted in devising plans for the great sea wall and raising the grade of the city, which has been completed at a total cost to the city and county jointly of more than $4,000,000; rebuilt the city hall and the water works and pumping station and electric light station; extended the water system; built three new fire company houses; remodeled and repaired others after the storm had damaged them; repaved with brick the streets throughout the entire business section at a cost of over $225,000; built rock and shell roads at a cost of more than $195,000; provided a large amount of drainage at a cost of $265,780; extended the sewer system and adjusted the question of interest on the bonded debt by obtaining a reduction in the rate for a period of five years. Altogether $650,000 has been expended out of the general fund for paving shell roads and drains, with the exception of $48,088.07, which was obtained from sale of bonds. The city has also paid off a number of old judgments, inherited from former administrations, aggregating $28,026, and retired $475,000 of the bonded debt; has purchased new fire engines and other equipment. The city employees have been paid promptly in cash and the summer seasons passed through without borrowing a dollar. All this has been accomplished without a bond issue or a dollar of increased taxation, except the bonds issued for protective purposes.

The city collects interest on bank balances from bonded depositories; collects a special vehicle tax, which goes to the street improvement fund, and enforces sewer connections. The city has metered its water service; has cleared the sidewalks of fruit-stands and other obstructions, which had occupied them for years, has prosecuted to a finish all outstanding lawsuits; collects taxes promptly; has destroyed the policy evil and gambling, and adopted an ordinance driving the saloons from the residence district of the city.

Board of Commisisoners of the City of Galveston. Under the commission plan the mismanagement of a department is promptly laid at the door of the neglectful commissioner, not only by the general public but by the mayor-president and the other members of the board. This knowledge of personal responsibility and watchfulness causes each commissioner to take a personal interest and to feel a special pride in the proper management of his department, realizing as he must that the merits as well as the defects are easily recognized by his associates, as well as by the public generally. The mayor and commissioners are directors in the proper sense of the term. The detail work is done by the superintendents, heads of departments and clerks.

The city charter requires that the board shall meet in regular session at least once every week. These meetings take place every Thursday afternoon at six o'clock, and rarely last more than an hour and a half. The meetings are conducted in a dignified, business-like manner, and are free from dispute and confusion. The commissioners sit around a directors' table, the mayor presiding. The city attorney and the heads of the various departments are required by the city charter to attend all meetings of the board. But little speech-making is indulged in, and the presence of idle spectators is an exception rather than the rule. Business is transacted promptly, but without any undue haste. All important matters are discussed and differences adjusted in conference. The city attorney has great influence with the commissioners, and his advice is freely sought.

The laboring class has had several candidates in the field for positions on the board of city commissioners, but their own people failed to unite on them and in each principle or labor question is involved, the laboring class —at least so the experience in Galveston has been—

seldom vote as a unit in any political contest. This is due to the number of political hirelings in their ranks, and they are in evidence at every election. And though these so called "labor leaders" make some noise, they inspire but little confidence and possess but little real influence. The negroes number about one-fourth of Galveston's population; while the majority can be influenced by whiskey, money, and prejudice, there are some very good citizens among them here.

"Too many cooks spoil the broth," is an old saying, which can well be applied to a board of twelve or more aldermen. In Galveston it has been clearly proved, after ten years' experience, that four commissioners and a mayor or president can transact the business of sixteen aldermen and a mayor—and do it better, more expeditiously, and with the greatest harmony.

COMMISSION GOVERNMENT IN HOUSTON

REPORT BY SPECIAL CORRESPONDENT.

Houston, Tex., Jan. 25, 1911.

In Houston the Mayor, H. Baldwin Rice, is the whole thing. While for the most part this is due to the fact that the City Commission Charter vests in him plenary powers in the conduct of the City's affairs, to a great extent it is due to the man.

If it is a bridge that the citizens desire shall be built, or a street that they desire paved, it is to the Mayor they present their petitions; not to that Commissioner who has charge of matters pertaining to streets and bridges.

It is the same with relation to the Fire Department, the Police Department, the Water Department—throughout the whole of the ramifications of the municipal government. So much so have the people come to look upon the Mayor as the all powerful, the Do-it-all, that if it is desired a certain ditch shall be cleaned, they call upon him, and their petitions are for the most part oral and presented in person.

If there is a labor dispute, the disputants on each side of the controversy present their case to the Mayor and request that he act as mediator. If there is a church to be built the congregation straightway sends a delegation to interview the Mayor and secure his subscription as a header for the list. If there is a sick man who desires assistance to the end that he may reach a western clime in quest of relief, it is upon the Mayor that he calls in person and presents his petition.

If a subscriber of the telephone company feels that the service rendered is not what it should be and that he should make complaint, it is to the Mayor nine times out of ten he makes complaint instead of complaining to the officials of the 'phone company. If the car service is not just what the patron believes it should be, he complains to the Mayor.

The Mayor is held responsible for everything, almost, in the town of Houston. It is he that is abused because of the shortcomings of the public service corporations; he is censured because of the town's moral conditions. He is alternately abused and praised. The very people who abuse him on one occasion, praise him on other occasions.

He is the most democratic Mayor in the country. His office is open at all times to all callers, yet he is called the Czar. He meets all comers. To some he says yes; to others he says no. He can say yes to the most humble citizen within the town's borders, and he can say no to the City's most influential. He can say yes to his personal and political enemies, and he can say no to his most intimate personal, political and business friends. It depends upon what it is, not upon who it is.

He has been Mayor for five years, having been installed with the inauguration of the Commission form of government. During that period Houston has grown rapidly—phenomenally. Not a public service corporation in the City has been able to keep its equipment up to the demand for service. The demand of one year has been such as to render useless, almost, the equipment installed during the year preceding. The officials of these corporations were not able to anticipate. Yet, though the City had a floating debt of more than $400,000 when the Commission form was installed, within a short time it was placed on a cash basis and has been kept on a cash basis ever since.

The Houston Commission Charter has been closely perused by municipal officials all over the country—by people who, having noted its success in Houston desired to acquaint themselves with its provisions. But the Charter does not disclose the talisman back of the accomplishments in Houston under the Commission form, lest business men may recognize in that Charter the fact that it clothes a business man with the authority to do business, just about as the working plan of any large corporation clothes its officials with the authority to conduct the business in a business way.

During the first couple of years of the Commission form of government, when the City was recovering from her weight of debt and placing herself on a cash basis, little was attempted in the way of improvements. Streets, bridges and fire protection were improved as far as it was possible, while school buildings were repaired and patched as best could be. Then the City officials got busy. Since then five modern school buildings have been erected entire, each costing $50,000; an extension of the Central High School building has just been completed at a cost of $75,000, and extensions to other buildings have been made to the extent of $50,000.

The City has purchased three plots of ground for park purposes; one of seven acres for $7,000; one of fifty-five acres for $50,000, and one of twenty-six acres with improvements upon it that can be utilized, for $18,000. In addition, through the management of the officials, there have been donations along a winding stream by citizens for a four hundred foot driveway which will eventually connect the City's three parks, forming them into a circular chain, the driveway circling ten miles. The value of the donations for this purpose on a conservative basis at the time of the donations was $100,000. Every bit of the property purchased, as well as the donations, has increased in value three fold since the City acquired title.

For years the people of Houston had recognized the need of an auditorium. The newspapers had urged upon capitalists the building of an auditorium as an investment and the commercial clubs had discussed the question year in and year out, hoping to interest capital in the enterprise. Mayor Rice was invited to attend one of these meetings about eighteen months ago that he might give his views as a business man. His remarks were very few, but to the point. He quietly informed those at the meeting that the City of Houston, out of the general revenues, would erect the auditorium.

The auditorium, covering a space 250x125, seating 7,500, costing, ground and all, $400,000, has just been completed and turned over to a Board of Trustees to manage.

It is such acts as this that forces the Mayor's individuality upon the people. He had not even consulted the other four members of the Commission prior to making the announcement—sensational announcement under the circumstances—that the municipal government would erect the auditorium. Those attending the meeting knew that he had not consulted his colleagues. Yet they knew the Mayor would make good; they knew that his colleagues would back him up, and they did back him up, and if any of them ever felt resentment over the fact that he had not conferred with them and secured their advice prior to making the announcement nothing ever transpired to disclose such feeling of resentment in any of them.

That is one of the reasons why he is called the Czar. Another reason that they call him the Czar is that when an influential man calls upon him seeking some special privilege that he is not entitled to the Mayor can bring his clenched fist down on his desk with a resounding thud, accompanied by a thunderous "No!" He has done this to his most intimate friends, and they have liked it, though they have called him the Czar.

Mayor Rice owns a launch—an expensive launch. It is anchored on the Buffalo bayou, a stream which the people of Houston have been endeavoring to have the government convert into a canal for sea-going vessels for twenty-five years. The Mayor has been saturated with the ship canal idea. He has talked it upon every occasion as Houston's most valuable asset. Congress, just prior to his installation had appropriated $400,000 for the improvement of the stream, and the money was being spent as government money for waterway improvements is most often spent—in a leisurely, listless way.

The Mayor got busy with his launch. He invited capitalists to Houston and took them for a trip down the stream and out into the bay. He entertained them in a princely manner and in his impressing way convinced them of the advantages of the Houston ship canal (Buffalo bayou). They went away saturated with the ship canal idea. He took Congressmen from wide sections of the country on such trips; members of the National Rivers and Harbors Committee were taken on such trips; army engineers were taken on such trips.

There have been results. Every Congress has made appropriations and the work of the government dredges has been of a more businesslike kind. Some months ago, the people of Houston, becoming saturated with the ship canal idea, determined that it should no longer be a theory or a dream, so a Committee was sent to Washington to propose to Congress that the people of Houston would bond themselves to the extent of $1,250,000 if Congress would appropriate a sum equal. Canal contractors had estimated that the canal could be completed a twenty-five foot depth with two and a half million dollars. Congress made a provisional appropriation of the sum asked. Recently the people voted to bond themselves for the other half, and the completion work will be under way in a short time.

This all cost the Mayor money—money out of his own pocket. His salary of $4,000 per annum, with a fund of $1,000 per annum for incidentals to his office, would not pay for the gasoline and lubricants used on his boat. In fact, during the five years that he has been in the office it has cost him the total sum of more than $100,000.

The money was handed out to churches, to charitable institutions, to beggars—but the greater portion of it was spent in entertaining on his boat and forcing upon the attention of the people at home as well as upon the members of Congress and upon capitalists of the country, the importance of Buffalo bayou as a ship way.

There has not been with the Mayor on the Board of Commissioners a strictly business man. There have been some good men, some capable men, but none of them had had real business training.

The first Board was composed of the Mayor—Rice—and James A. Thompson, James B. Marmion, James Appleby and J. Z. Gaston.

These men were simply elected by the people as Commissioners—Aldermen. It devolved upon the Mayor to designate the duties of each, by nominating each as the Chairman of a Committee.

James A. Thompson was a printer. He had been a member of the old Council for years and was considered an expert in municipal affairs, and honest. He was made Chairman of Sewers, of Health, of Engineering, of Lights. A year later, when the City by a bond issue purchased the water system, that was added to the duties of Thompson, his title being Chairman of Water, Lights, Health, Scavenger, Engineering and Sewers.

Thompson handled the ramifications of his various duties in a remarkable manner. He was the superintendent over all of them. When the water system management was added to his duties he took over the clerical forces of the old company. The old company's superintendent was not taken. The old company had been paying a high salary to a president, a high salary to a secretary, a high salary to a manager, and a high salary to a superintendent. Thompson embraced all of these official positions within himself, minus the salaries. He put the plant on a business basis and began making extensions of mains, something that the old company could never be forced to do, notwithstanding there had been a controversy extending through the State and Federal courts, and he continued as the head of the other divisions of his Committee, economy being the slogan throughout. Mr. Thompson had a small desk at which he sat all day, smoking black cigars and thinking, giving occasional instructions or handling complaints made by patrons of the Water Department or other divisions. His desk contained a dozen pigeon holes in which there were neatly arranged a few papers—a very few. He has a deformed middle finger.

No matter what question anyone asked him concerning some particular operation of some particular division of his work, whether it was as to the water plant, the sewer plant or the Health Department, he could drop that deformed finger on a paper in one of the pigeon holes and bring forth facts stated in figures. He did not consider that it was remarkable. He said that he had put a little printing office system into the thing.

Thompson was not a politician. He, notwithstanding he had been a Councilman for years, had never attended a political meeting, had never urged his candidacy. He was not a man of policy. He was rather gruff at times to those who went to his office with complaints. Not that anyone who ever came in contact with him could or would say that he was not on the square, but his lack of diplomacy sometimes made them angry. He would talk just as gruff to the wealthiest and most influential as to the little fellow who peddles on the street. As a matter of fact, he showed less patience with the big fellow than with the little fellow. He gave as his reason that the big fellow as in a position to know better and should have had more sense than the little fellow. The influential fellow, however, finally worked up a sufficient sentiment among the voters to defeat Thompson two years ago.

Gaston had also been a member of the old Council. It was he who during the old Council, when the thing was not popular with the other Councilmen, presented the resolution favoring the Commission form of government, and he, with the aid of Thompson, fought it through until it carried, aided by the strong public sentiment. And for that reason Gaston has been called the father of the Commission form.

In his younger days he was a machinist, and later, during the time he was a member of the old Councils, operated a small general Ward store, Aldermen in those days not being required to give their full time to their municipal duties.

Gaston was chosen as a member of the Commission principally because he was considered the father of the thing. He, though, a politician in a quiet way of the Ward stripe, was a valuable man. He was made Chairman of the Finance Committee and Chairman of the Board of Appraisement, the Board which fixes the assessable value of property, and Chairman of Parks and Public Buildings. As Chairman of the Finance Committee he affixes his signature to documents bearing upon the City's finances, but the financier is, and has been from the beginning, the Mayor. As Chairman of the Committee on Parks, he simply went out and looked over the ground in a formal way just before the Mayor closed the deal for the park lands. As Chairman of Public Buildings, he hastened to second the Mayor when he learned that the Mayor had announced to the Business League that the City would build the auditorium. On the Board of Appraisement his work has been of a delicate nature, and he has handled it in a creditable manner. He was twice re-elected.

James Appleby had never had experience in municipal affairs. He had been an auditor for one of the railways entering Houston, and having held such a position with a railway it was taken for granted that he was a business man. The people supposed that only a man of business ability was capable of holding such a position for a railway. He was chosen Chairman of Fire and Police Committee, and his work was to look after the details of handling the Police and Fire Departments. He did not exhibit much business acumen during the two terms he held the office and did not offer for the third term.

James Marmion had been a blacksmith. He was considered about the best horseshoer in Houston. He was an amateur ball player and became a member of most of the fraternal lodges. He was shy on schooling. He had not gone through the High School; he was busy and energetic and made friends fast, and they elected him to the office of Justice of the Peace. Later the young attorneys who had been practicing in his Court urged his election to the office of City Recorder, and elected him.

Later, when the Commission ticket was being made up and it was realized that strength was needed to beat the former Anti-Commission forces, who had brought out a ticket to capture the Commission after it was decided the City should be governed on a Commission basis, Marmion was considered as the man who could help the Commission ticket to win. He was put on the ticket and won with the rest of it.

Marmion served out the short term and was re-elected. The only reason he was placed on the ticket the second time was that it was desired the entire first ticket should be returned, just for the effect of the thing on the outside world.

Marmion, however, could never harmonize with the Mayor. From the first there had been friction. He is sincere, and no one will question his honesty, but he has a way of listening to the opposition and taking advice from them. He listened to the discomfits, and when they told him that the Mayor was a Czar and cited some iron-handed acts to him, straightway he felt that the Mayor was a Czar and that he was usurping the prerogatives of each of the Commissioners. Marmion decided that the Mayor should not usurp the prerogatives of his office, and thus there was friction. He was made the Chairman of the Street and Bridge Committee and had charge of the improvements and repairs naturally coming under these heads. When the Mayor, without consulting him, decided to pave a given street and prepared to pave it Marmion threw obstacles in his way, presenting motions in the Council changing the street to some other. He was always voted down, for only himself voted to sustain himself. Finally the friction had grown until relations became very strained. Meantime the appropriation for the upkeep of streets and bridges was used and the streets and bridges had not been kept up. This caused the Mayor to relieve Marmion of his duties as Chairman of the Street and Bridge Committee. The Council backed the Mayor and a Superintendent of Streets and Bridges was appointed, and all that was left for Marmion to do was draw his salary each month. He was at his desk every day, however, and attended every Council meeting, for he still was a Commissioner elected by the people and had a Council vote, and had the right to introduce resolutions and offer motions. He did both often, and just as often his motions and resolutions were antagonistic to the existing order of things, and just as often they were voted down by the other three Commissioners.

After serving his second term as Commissioner he ran against Rice for the office of Mayor, and he was given a fair vote. All the discomfits from the old days rallied to his support. It was not for love of Marmion so far as they were concerned, but hatred of Rice and the other members of the Commission.

This was in 1908. In that municipal campaign James A. Thompson was defeated. His defeat was due to his apathy for things savoring placation. One of the powers in the City as a vote manipulator—a very strong man in business circles—felt that he had a grievance at Thompson because his water bill was large. Thompson refused to scale it down, and this man threw all his influence into the City campaign, and as a result Thompson, one of the best men in the Commission, was defeated by a narrow margin.

Appleby did not offer for re-election in this campaign. Thus, with Marmion out, with Appleby and Thompson out, three new men were elected. Jack Kennedy, a railway contractor and bridge builder of long years of experience, and who had, under the old regime, been connected with the municipality in street and bridge work, was elected as an administration candidate; W. J. Kohlhauff, a printer, and who had been a member of the Council just prior to the inauguration of the Commission form, and who had fought the Commission resolution when presented to the Council by Gaston, and who later fought the enactment of the new Charter before the Legislature, and later, after the Charter had become a law, was a candidate in opposition to the citizens' Commission ticket, was this time elected as an administration candidate. He found that the friends of Commission were too strong to oppose, and he became a friend of the Commission form and of the administration conducting it. Robert L. Jones, also a member of the old Council prior to the enactment of the Commission form and who had fought the resolution, was elected as an anti-administrationist, he having fallen heir to the break caused by the defeat of Thompson.

Kennedy was made Street and Bridge Commissioner, the place held by Marmion; Kohlhauff was made Fire Commissioner, while the Police Commissioner part of the duties that had devolved upon Appleby were reserved by the Mayor for his own management, he feeling that the position of Fire Commissioner was heavy enough for Kohlhauff. Jones was made Water Commissioner, while the duties of looking after the lights, health, engineer and sewers, as looked after by Thompson, were reserved by the Mayor as part of his own duties in connection with the duties devolving on the Police Commissionership.

And thus, with the beginning of the management of the City two years ago, three new men were in the Council, one of them an avowed anti-administrationist —elected as such—one lukewarm administrationist and one administrationist, giving the balance of power to the Mayor, with Gaston and Kennedy to be counted on for sure.

There was but little friction during the two years. Kohlhauff was too much of a politician to openly oppose any move made by the Mayor, while Jones, though he was in an opposition attitude most of the time, was too weak to prevent the enactment of any law urged by the Mayor.

This brings the Commission form of government up to February 1, 1911, with a campaign on—with Rice without a ticket, trying for re-election, and with two other candidates in the field, one of them representing the remnant of Anti-Commissionists still in existence, and with all the present members of the Council as candidates for re-election and half a dozen more candidates for these places, some of them avowed Commission men and some of them avowed Anti-Commissionists.

Now, for a brief resume of the things that the Commission had accomplished. The foregoing will disclose that from the beginning, aside from the aid given by Thompson, the Commission has been a one-man government from the beginning.

When the Commission was installed the City had a floating debt of more than $400,000. Merchants of the City were not anxious for the City's business for the reason that they had had no assurance as to the payment of the bills the City owed them.

Something like $100,000 was due the City in back taxes. A number of suits had been pending in tax matters and one of them, a test, had been carried to the higher courts. The City won. That forced a payment of all taxes due, and the $100,000 helped much. There was retrenchment, and the City's working forces were scaled down to a minimum, while but little was done in the way of improvement. In fact, no improvements were made the first year—just a few repairs here and there.

With the bringing in of the first year's taxes the authorities got busy and began paving streets and building bridges. Three modern brick school houses were erected at a total cost of $150,000. Meantime the Water Department had been taken charge of, a bond issue for its purchase having carried. A bond issue was later voted for $700,000, for extension and improvement of water mains, for extension of sanitary sewers, for construction of a thirteen-foot mile and a half long storm sewer, needed to lift the swampy portion of the City out of the mud, and for the construction of ship slips, wharfs and terminals at the Houston ship turning basin.

The tax rate was first reduced from $2 on the $100 valuation to $1.90; it was next reduced to $1.80, and still later to $1.70. The charge for street lights made by the electric company was reduced from $90 per annum to $70.

During the five years from the installation of the Commission form to January 1, 1911, more than ten miles of streets were paved with brick, fully sixty miles were paved with shell. In the matter of shell, the City purchased her own dredge, which was stationed in Trinity Bay, fifty miles distant, where the shell supply is practically inexhaustible, and where the dredge is operated by the City's own forces. Contracts were made with barging companies to deliver the shell in the City for 50 cents per cubic yard. By this management, figuring the cost of digging the shell at 15 cents per yard, the cost of barging at 50 cents, and the cost of hauling by wagon from the wharf and spreading on street at 75 cents, the shell is placed for vehicles to run on at a total of $1.40 per cubic yard. Placed on the streets six inches in thickness, this gives eighteen square feet of paved street for that cost.

The City later erected three more school buildings, one for colored children and two for whites, and made an extension to the High School.

The auditorium above referred to is now complete. The cost of erection was made from the general revenues. The City will erect a viaduct connecting the north section with the south in the heart of town, and costing $500,000. This is a bond issue recently voted.

When the Commission was installed the saloons were open day and night, Sunday and holidays; gambling houses occupied almost every upper floor on the main thoroughfare, while a racing pool room was in full blast and a couple of bucket shops, and there were two dirty variety theaters. There was a delectable quarter almost in the heart of town, within half a block of a leading church. It had been the notorious tenderloin district for years, and shady characters were domiciled in many different sections of the City. There were dozens of policy and lottery wheels in operation.

At once the variety theaters were closed and the gambling houses, bucketshops and pool rooms put out of business. It simply needed the demand of the Mayor. Those in control of these places knew the man and knew that it would be worse than useless to oppose him; so they closed without an effort at resistance. It was the same relative to the policy wheels.

An ordinance was adopted closing the saloons at 1 in the morning and prohibiting them from opening before 5. And they were prohibited from opening from midnight Saturday until 5 o'clock Monday morning. This was before the State Legislature enacted the midnight closing law in Texas. Houston was operating under her own law for more than a year before the state acted. And the law was enforced strictly to the letter. In fact, very few attempts were made to sell clandestinely.

Then the question of looking after the under world was taken up. There were many churchmen who were of the opinion that the habitues of the tenderloin should be run out of the City; that the gamblers should be forced to seek pastures new forthwith. Very zealous people they were, and seeing what the Mayor and his aids were accomplishing they were desirous of acting the part of advisers, almost dictators. When these people were informed by the Mayor that the City intended to segregate the lewd women and force all in the City to domicile in one district, there was much complaint, much denunciation, some of it from the pulpit, and committees of the righteous were appointed to call upon the Mayor and make demands. The Mayor met these committees thus:

"I am the Mayor of all the people of Houston, the good and the bad; the Mayor of the gambler as well as the Mayor of the Preacher and his flock. Houston has these people in her midst. We have no right to force them to leave and thus dump them on other Cities; you church people have not been able to reform them; none of you church people desire that any of them shall reside near you; we cannot annihilate them. Then, if you do not desire that they shall reside near you, if we cannot reform nor annihilate them, and since it would be unjust to other communities to run these people to them, we will select a place and segregate them—a place where they will be out of sight of your daughters."

None of the zealots attempted to answer the argument and the old district was cleaned out and all the women of the underworld forced to take up their residence in a district which, as far as possible, removes them from the residents of the City, and there they have been forced to stay.

As for the gamblers, those who sought honest employment were encouraged; those who refused to seek employment were arrested as vagrants and put to work on the streets.

For years in Houston two blocks on one side of the main thoroughfare had been in full possession of the gamblers, who stood on the sidewalks in crowds. Ladies had not walked on those two blocks for years. The corner occupied by the racing pool room on the ground floor and a large gambling room on the upper floors, and which for years and years had been the congregating place for all sorts of criminals, confidence men, pickpockets and the like, is now occupied on the ground floor by a leading bank, while the upper floors are occupied as offices.

During the municipal campaigns for years prior to the installation of the Commission form there had been purity candidates in the field for positions of Mayor and Aldermen. Each time they were defeated. They made their campaigns on the promise that they would rid the City of the gamblers. They were opposed not altogether by the gambling and saloon element. Many of the business element, the property owners, opposed them. These assumed to believe that if the town was made a "closed" town it would kill business. They wanted the town run wide open.

The five-year period closing January 1, 1911, witnessed a phenomenal growth in Houston. During that period the population increased fully thirty-five per cent., which shows that there is nothing in the wide-open-town theory. Many of the men who had for years lived as gamblers are now in business, and are successful. The man who operated the big pool room has been quite successful as a real estate promoter. He would not have a return to the old way, nor would the men who were once professional card dealers in charge of the games who are still here working in legitimate lines. Those who could not reconcile themselves to the change left the City.

Now, the question that will occur is: "What did the Commission form have to do with all this?"

Save that the Commission form gives the power to a powerful man who is powerful for the right, it had nothing to do with it. A powerful man, powerful for the wrong, could, under the Commission form, go just as far in the opposite direction.

One of the arguments—the main argument—put forth by friends of the Commission form during the campaign for it was that the elimination of Ward lines—by the election of Aldermen at large from the City instead of from Wards—would raise the standard of the Aldermen, that while a man might be able to control the voters in a single Ward and place himself in the Council, he could not control votes enough at large. This is proven to be a fallacy by the fact that the men now occupying places as Aldermen have been connected with the City for years, two of them having been looked upon as Ward politicians, and who had bitterly opposed the Commission form.

It simply goes to show that such a thing as lifting municipal government from the level of politics is an irridescent dream.

To the point: The office of Commissioner pays $200 per month. Not a man now holding down the job of Commissioner could earn that salary in any other walk in life. The office of Mayor pays $4,000 per annum. The present Mayor, for his business qualifications, could command a salary of $25,000.

In the natural order of things, under such conditions, Houston has been managed municipally by a one-man authority, and because this one man had been a power for the right, a power of business foresight, a shrewd financier, Houston has leaped forward and the success of her Commission form of government has attracted world-wide attention.

Are there other men in the City aside from Rice capable of having conducted the City's affairs so successfully? Yes, scores of them.

But how many business men—men now at the head of big affairs—could be brought to feel that they could afford to devote their full time for a period of two years, neglecting their own affairs meantime and paying money out of their own pockets? Just about as many, perhaps, as could be found in any other City in the country the size of Houston. They are very few. Up to this time, none that have heretofore been successful in managing large affairs have offered themselves as Mayor. Rather, the business people of Houston have year after year, despite his desire to retire, forced Rice to offer for re-election.

Much of the work that has been done during his encumbency has been of the foundation order, the working out of large systems of improvement and beginning at the foundation. And because of the foundation character of his work, and his desire that the work shall be carried out along the lines laid down, he has felt impelled to remain, feeling that it would be a risk to trust the work in the hands of the men who have up to this time offered themselves as Mayor.

In the numeration of the things done during the Commission the matter of school management was overlooked. The schools had been in the hands of the politicians for years. The new Charter provides that the Council shall place the management of the schools in the hands of trustees. Rice did the placing, his nominations being endorsed by the Council.

On the School Board there is one Republican, though Houston is almost wholly Democratic; there is one Hebrew, though the Jews are not as a rule recognized by the social or political world. There are five members. All are business men. They have the full conduct of the schools, the City making appropriations of funds for their conduct. The City simply supplies the money and furnishes the buildings and the School Board handles the schools, selecting a business agent, the superintendent and the principals and allowing the superintendent and principals to select the teachers, and the plan has proven successful.

The campaign for new municipal officers is now (Jan. 25, 1910) on. The election occurs April 10. The indications are at this time that Rice will be returned. It is a free for all race, and the indications are that there will be many changes so far as the Aldermen are concerned.

COMMISSION GOVERNMENT IN DALLAS, TEXAS

REPORT BY SPECIAL CORRESPONDENT.

Dallas, Texas, July 3, 1911.

Commission government in Dallas is four years old. It is just embarking on its fifth year now. Up to the present time it may be said to have been a success, not, perhaps, an unequivocal success, but so much better than the old councilmanic form that the people are content to retain it until a better form is developed.

Its great strength has been that it has given Dallas a businesslike administration. Its weakness, in the eyes of the people at large, is that it tends toward autocracy and that it gives large interests and business interests more favors than it does the common people. This has given rise to a slight suspicion on the part of the people.

But a summary of the four years under the commission in Dallas shows that more has been accomplished in the way of civic improvement, public works, regulation of trade and traffic, establishment of governmental economies than in 20 years before under the uncertain rule of politically-made councils of aldermen.

The history of the commission in Dallas up to the present time is the history of one set of men. The original mayor and four commissioners were re-elected after their first two years in office and served until May of this year. The men who have succeeded them are just learning the ropes and are as yet nearly untried.

To tell the history of the creation of the commission is to relate the history of the Citizens' Association. It is responsible for the election of the first commission, for the re-election of these same men, and for the election of their successors. It is a quasi-political organization. It maintains its general alignment from year to year and has been so successful since the commission form was established, that it has been stronger than the city Democratic party and indeed, all other political parties put together.

After the Dallas commission charter, modelled upon the Galveston plan, was granted by the legislature, the Citizens' Association sprang into existence. Years of councilmanic misrule had been irksome to the business element of the city. The main street of the business section was a mudhole, and that was typical of the condition of public works throughout the city. The progressive element, made up largely of young business men who were making large fortunes in the rapidly-growing city, demanded an administration that would keep pace civically with the progress they were making commercially.

Henry D. Lindsley, a young, energetic man at the head of a large insurance company, sprang to the fore. By his leadership he crystallized this unexpressed sentiment of the business men and in a short time he had them organized. This was the Citizens' Association. All the business men, with the other elements of the population they controlled, or which were favorable to a business administration, were enrolled in the Association's membership.

It became a popular movement. The city was enthusiastic for a change and this was what the Citizens' Association offered.

The search for candidates began. They were not hard to find. So high had the ideals been placed that business men were willing to leave their desks and sacrifice their business for the sake of "lifting Dallas out of the mud," as the campaign slogan voiced it. So the Citizens' Association was able to put before the voters as candidates, a set of men highly qualified for the new work.

Stephen J. Hay was the man they put up for mayor. He was a comparatively young man, 43 years old. He was just on the crest of a successful business career. He had started without a cent as a young boy, had worked his way, educated himself and risen to sufficient esteem in the community to be elected president of the board of education. He was serving his fourth term in this capacity when nominated for mayor.

For commissioner of finance and revenue, the Citizens' Association selected another high class man, Charles B. Gillespie. He had gained valuable experience during several terms as county tax collector and was engaged in a lucrative real estate business when nominated. He was highly honored as a citizen and respected as a business man and was noted for his honesty. This latter quality had won for him the sobriquet "Honest Charley."

Dan F. Sullivan, a good-natured and intelligent Irishman, whom the Citizens' Association selected as their candidate for commissioner of waterworks and sewerage, was the only man on their ticket who had ever held down a city hall job before. Sullivan had been police commissioner by appointment and was later superintendent of the water department. At the time of his nomination he was conducting a large and profitable plumbing business. Sullivan had plenty of political strength and he was put on the ticket to draw a vote that otherwise might have gone against the "Cits."

The two remaining candidates were snatched entirely from private life. They had not been in the public service before. Harry L. Seay, 35, a rising young lawyer, with a highly respected family behind him, was selected for fire and police commissioner. William Doran, a retired capitalist, who had made his start in Texas on the cattle ranges and his fortune in Dallas in the packing business, was named for commissioner of streets and public property.

In the field against the Citizens' Association ticket were several independent candidates. Curtis P. Smith, the incumbent mayor, ran for re-election. But the people of Dallas were tired of ring-made government, and the victory of the Citizens' candidates was decisive and crushing.

This, then, was the auspicious start of the commission form of government in Dallas. The selection of men for the first commission proved to be exceptionally fortunate. Hay proved to be a constructive mayor, though conservative. His great service to the board was his ability to keep his colleagues free from factional differences and harmony prevailed in the commission until the very end of its second term.

Doran quickly showed strong characteristics. He virtually dominated the board. He openly expressed his intention of favoring all reasonable privileges for big business interests in Dallas. He was for doing everything that would make for the commercial progress of the city. He was sometimes referred to as the "Joe Cannon of the commission." But he showed himself to be a driving force in all departments of his work and street paving under his regime went forward with a bound. The first thing he did was to pave Main street from beginning to end of the business district and the "shame of the city," as this muddy thoroughfare had been called, was removed.

Gillespie proved a wonderful expert on finances. He had an infinite capacity for detail. The tax department was revolutionized under his intelligent management and he started with great success the work of collecting delinquent taxes that administration after administration preceding had passed up as hopeless.

In the same businesslike manner, Sullivan and Seay took up the work of their departments. It was not long before the water department had under way a project to build an immense impounding reservoir to meet the rapidly increasing needs of the growing city. A new jail was built to replace an ancient and inadequate calaboose, a relic of the town constable days, and the unmetropolitan system of part-pay policemen was abolished and a department organized on modern lines.

It was generally supposed that when the new commission went into the city hall, all the old political jobholders would go out the back door. But the new rulers had a surprise in store for them. Less than half a dozen city employes were fired. The commision took the men they found at the desks in the city hall, told them that as long as they did their work satisfactorily their jobs would be safe and went along without the slightest upheaval. The plan worked. The fellows who had been in the habit of sitting around doing nothing all day and drawing their salaries at the end of the month got busy. In a short time the city hall was as industrious and as systematically occupied as the most modern office establishment. The secret was that the commissioner in charge of each department saw that the men under him had enough work to keep them busy.

The people as a whole were much pleased with their new government. They saw public works begin to spring up in every part of the city. They found they could go to the city hall and make requests and file petitions and get a respectful hearing from the powers in authority. They learned that action on their demands was taken quickly and decisively. They learned they could deal with the commissioners as they would deal with their merchants or their lawyers and that it was not necessary to curry favor with influential politicians to get results.

It was generally conceded at the end of the first year that the new officers had earned their salaries and a little more. The mayor, under the charter, receives $4,000 per year, the commissioners $3,000 each. In the twelve months vast improvements had been made.

In addition to the work in the tax department and police departments already alluded to, the commission had purchased sites for two new fire engine houses, had ordered built a new waterworks pumping station to replace the old one which was submerged every time the Trinity River flooded, had paved many important downtown streets, authorized the investment of $17,000 in park lands, created the office of city chemist, authorized inspection of dairies and foods dispensed in Dallas, and reorganized practically all departments to increase their efficiency.

The commissioners started in office with an overdraft in the general fund of $129,575. At the end of their first year they had reduced this to $49,373. Receipts during the year from all sources in the general fund had amounted to $472,157. Disbursements for the same period amounted to only $399,657, making a saving of $27,500 for the first year of the commission. This was applied on the overdraft and helped reduce it.

Flushed with the success of their first year and backed by a liberal support on the part of the citizenship, the commissioners entered upon their second year with the determination to double the results of their first eleven months in office.

One of the most important acts was their reduction of the rate for city arc lights from $73 to $60 per year per light. This was accomplished largely through Commissioner Doran's efforts. Doran also continued to push the street paving work. It was extended into the residence sections, and streets that property owners had been ready to pave for months, were finally permanently improved.

Commissioner Sullivan, in the water department, had started the year with an overdraft of $47,521. He was able to report at the end of the year a cash balance in his fund of $5,708. The overdraft had been absorbed.

The same was true of the general fund. It had started with an overdraft of $49,373 on May 1, 1908. When May 1, 1909, rolled around, the general fund was found with a credit balance of $10,290. The commissioners had not only taken up nearly $50,000 of debt, but had earned for the city over $10,000 additional.

These accomplishments had their effect on the citizens. They saw that the men in the city hall were going at city municipal problems as business men go at commercial problems.

What was the result? Long before the time came for a new election, long before the customary time for nominations, the Citizens' Association quietly circulated a petition and one day some of the leaders appeared at the city hall with this petition signed by over 5,000 voters, asking the mayor and commissioners to stand for election again.

Mayor Hay and his associates complied and were again overwhelmingly elected. In fact, the Democratic party opposition this time was wrecked on the shoals before election day. Pat O'Keefe, a former alderman and a city hall job-holder under the commission was so loyal to his new leaders that he managed to split the city Democratic executive committee into two factions, his side opposing nominations by the party, the other putting out a ticket. The controversy was carried into the courts and O'Keefe's faction won. The commissioners had no opposition, except the nominees of the Socialist party.

The next two years were an an era of growth and steady development in Dallas. The businesslike character of the board was further demonstrated by the results the members accomplished. In finances the mayor was able to report at the end of the next fiscal year, May 1, 1910, cash balances in all funds aggregating $879,492 and only the general school fund overdrawn to the extent of $2,000.

A new problem arose in a shape of a drouth which scaled the city's water supply down to the minimum and called for stringent regulations. Sprinkling and use of city water for any but sanitary and ordinary household purposes was prohibited and Commissioner Sullivan, backed by the board, began to take every emergency means to keep up a sufficient supply.

This situation ultimately led to the severest criticism the board received during its four-year administration. A large faction of the citizens demanded the boring of artesian wells, others called for more dams in the river, others supported the commission in its efforts to rush the White Rock reservoir to completion.

In spite of everything that could be done, the water supply dwindled through the persistent dry weather, until in December, 1910, the amount on hand was sufficient only for fire protection purposes and the insurance companies demanded that the domestic supply be shut off. It was. The once popular commissioners were thus placed in an unpopular position with the general populace and were soon the targets for much condemnation. The water remained shut off about three months, during which time the city delivered from sprinkling carts and water wagons, water by the tubful from door to door. Rain finally partly relieved the drouth conditions in the spring of 1911 and the domestic supply was resumed.

In spite of the seriousness of the water situation and the demands it made upon the commissioners, they were able to report a large amount of public works. Bearing directly on the water question, they had negotiated the sale of $500,00 in waterworks improvement bonds voted at the previous election and with the money derived therefrom were rapidly closing deals for many tracts of land for the big reservoir, and building the White Rock dam. Five new artesian wells to augment the surface water system were also bored.

For new parks and playgrounds (the latter were unheard of in Dallas until the commission form was established) the board spent over $50,000.

Trouble between the city and the Barber Asphalt Paving Company had resulted in the serious disrepair of several downtown streets. The commissioners effected a cash settlement with the paving company by which the equivalent of $57,000 was paid to the city in lieu of repairs the company had failed to make. The two remaining principal streets of the business section were paved with creosoted wood blocks and the improvement of Main street, which Commissioner Doran had paved first, was extended a mile further out.

In the fire department, two new fire stations were built at a cost of about $30,000 and five pieces of automobile apparatus purchased.

An emergency hospital was established, an inspectorship of weights and measures created, much new territory annexed to the city, and the houses renumbered on the century system at the expense of the city.

The confidence of the public, so far as the commissioners' expenditures were concerned, was thus commented upon by the mayor:

"The desire on the part of the public to place at our disposal large sums of money for public improvements is an evidence of confidence on the part of the citizens which we greatly appreciate. In fact, our citizens have shown a disposition to vote larger issues of bonds for various kinds of improvements than the Board of Commissioners has been willing to recommend."

During the incumbency of the Hay commission the following bonds were voted by the people and issued by the commissioners:

Public schools	$50,000
Street improvements	100,000
Waterworks improvements	500,000
Waterworks permanent imp.	500,000
Public schools	200,000
Sanitary sewers	100,000
Public schools	100,000
Waterworks improvements	100,000
Street improvements	350,000
Total	$2,100,000

The following bonds were voted by the people, but have not yet been issued:

Reformatory	$25,000
Hospital	100,000
Sewage disposal plant	550,000
Public schools	250,000
Total	$925,000

The bonded debt of Dallas at the present time is $4,116,250. The bond limit as fixed by the charter is $5,000,000. The commissioners will present to the next legislature a charter amendment raising the limit to $7,000,000.

When the Hay commission went out of office in May of this year it was able to report the following accomplishments as the result of the first four years of commission government in Dallas:

Practical completion of reservoir for permanent water supply at cost of $750,000.

Erection of new pumping stations at two original reservoirs.

Drilling ten artesian wells.

Establishing the meter system for measuring water consumption.

Laying of 65 miles of water mains at cost of $267,000.

Laying of 36 miles of permanent paving including all downtown streets at cost of $966,000.

Putting city on cash basis, the only overdraft being $122,000 in the water department fund due to the drouth emergency.

Employment of City Plan Expert George B. Kessler of Kansas City, Mo., to evolve a plan of beautification for Dallas:

Purchasing four new parks.

Establishing an emergency hospital.

Selling the city hall with the purpose of erecting a larger and finer building.

Reducing the cost of street lighting to $60 per light per year.

Securing natural gas at a cost of 50 cents per thousand to replace artifical gas at $1.35 per thousand.

Installing street signs and new house numbers.

Erecting two fire stations and purchasing automobile apparatus.

Erecting city jail and establishing Gamewell and Bertillon systems.

When campaign time came round again (1911), the mayor and the four commissioners announced that they would not be candidates for re-election and the Citizens' Association again got busy. This time the opposition was more determined. The bad water situation gave the opponents of the "Cits" an opportunity. Two factions sprang up, the Jeffersonian Democrats, a relic of the old city Democratic party, and the Progressives, a sort of non-partisan organization.

The Citizens' Association nominated W. M. Holland, a lawyer, formerly judge of the county court at law; W. T. Henderson, the incumbent city auditor; R. R. Nelms, the incumbent secretary and collector of the water department; F. W. Bartlett, a lawyer, and J. Early Lee, an insurance man.

These candidates were not as strong as their predecessors. In the face of the determined opposition, it took a second election to put them in office. The confidence of the public has been a little shaken by the fierce campaign and there is not the general and wholesome support of these new commissioners that the original board enjoyed.

But they are showing themselves able men. They have devoted practically all the time since they took their oaths to dealing with the water situation, and to their credit it may be said that Dallas has conquered a serious menace and probably has a water supply now that will be adequate for years to come.

The general utility of the commission seems to have been proved beyond a reasonable doubt in Dallas. It is possible under the system to accomplish more in a given time than could be done in twice or thrice the time under the preceding form. The commission holds regular meetings, open to the public on the afternoons of Monday, Wednesday and Friday each week. Between times each commissioner is at liberty to attend to the details of his own departments. The commissioners debate and discuss many things among themselves, so that the regular meetings of the board really represent finished business. The tangles have been untied beforehand.

Under the Hay regime, during the negotiations for natural gas, when the rate was under discussion, the board held one or two meetings behind closed doors with the gas promoters. So great was the public outcry that such proceedings have not been repeated.

The Dallas charter, modelled in general on the Galveston plan, contains provisions for the initiative and referendum and the recall. The initative and the recall have been tried. Both have been sustained in the highest courts of the state.

THE INITIATIVE AND RECALL INVOKED.

The initiative was invoked by the people in an effort to regulate telephone rates. The people desired to pay their telephone bills *after* the service was rendered, instead of in advance, and to be allowed 10 per cent. reduction for prompt payment within a period of ten days after the bills became due. An initiative ordinance was passed to this effect. The telephone company fought it, the case was carried to the highest court of appeal and an opinion rendered sustaining the principle of the initiative, but denying the people the right to regulate public utility rates of private corporations.

The recall has been twice invoked. Both times it has been resorted to in connection with school affairs.

In the face of popular disapproval and for alleged political reasons, the school trustees removed Joseph Morgan, a beloved principal of the high school, and Charles D. Tomkies, a well-liked teacher of English. No charges were stated against them at the time of their removal. The public demanded a reason and a public hearing for the two favorites. Two members of the board voted against a public hearing and this was the coal that started a fire of public indignation. The fire burned into the form of a recall movement and these two trustees, Messrs. John W. George and John C. Mann, were removed and replaced by J. B. McCraw and J. D. Carter.

In the campaign charges of misconduct and incompetency had been made against Superintendent of Schools Arthur Lefevre and as soon as the recall election was over, the public demanded not only a public hearing for Morgan and Tomkies, but an investigation of Lefevre's administration of the schools.

Carter and McCraw were in a hopeless minority against the old members of the board. The investigation started, the old members blocked every attempt to produce any evidence damaging to Lefevre and the inquiry was made a farce. Again public wrath flamed into an invocation of the recall. This time the movement demanded the ousting of all the old board except one man who had gained his place by appointment to fill a vacancy.

Again the recall worked. The new men went in and their first act was to remove Superintendent Lefevre and fill his place with a man of their own selection. They also reinstated Morgan and Tomkies.

Lefevre, backed by one of the ousted trustees, went to the courts for an injunction to restrain the new men taking office. On this issue a test case was made and carried through the courts to the state supreme court. The court unequivocally sustained the recall. In the opinion, written by Chief Justice Brown, this language is used:

"The policy of reserving to the people such power as the recall, the initiative and the referendum, is a question for the people themselves in framing the government, or for the legislature in the creation of municipal governments. It is not for the courts to decide that question. We are unable to see from our viewpoint how it can be that a larger measure of sovereignty committed to the people by this method of government and a more certain means of securing a proper representation in any way militates against its character as a republican form of government and that it is thereby rendered in any sense obnoxious to the provisions of the Constitution of the United States."

It can be said, then, as a whole, that the people of Dallas have found their commission form of government, as organized under the present charter, a succes So long as they hold these checks upon their electi officers, they feel they can control public affairs prett well.

The short ballot, the initiative and referendum an the recall make a combination that seems to fill the bi pretty well.

COMMISSION GOVERNMENT IN COLORADO SPRINGS

REPORT BY SPECIAL CORRESPONDENT

Colorado Springs, Dec. 28, 1910.

After eighteen months of government under the commission plan Colorado Springs has decided that the experiment is well worth its cost in time, trouble and money. Like most things worth having, good government was secured only after a struggle, and although the experience thus far has not produced perfect results it nevertheless has been as satisfactory as anybody had a right to expect.

Like nearly every other city, big and little, Colorado Springs had suffered from misgovernment. It was never a question of graft or dishonesty, but always of inefficiency caused by getting the wrong men in office. Square pegs were fitted into round holes, with the usual result—loose joints in the governmental machinery. The intelligent, progressive element of the citizenship who wanted greater efficiency in public affairs did not know how to go about getting it, or else was too busy or too indifferent to make the effort. The business of nominating and electing candidates was left to the professional politicians, and then the officials elected paid obligations by giving responsible appointive positions to men whose only qualification was their ability to swing the vote in their own precincts.

Up to this point the political history of Colorado Springs does not differ essentially from that of a hundred cities east and west. But in 1906 one of the newspapers began an agitation for the adoption of the commission plan, holding that no permanent improvement could be made as long as the old system of government was maintained. The Colorado Constitution authorizes cities of the first and second classes to adopt their own charters, and govern themselves independent of the statutes which apply to cities not under charter government. In the November election a proposal to hold a "charter convention" for the purpose of framing a charter was defeated because of the injection of extraneous matters. Under the law the question could not again be submitted for two years, but in November, 1908, it was put before the people a second time and the proposal carried by a majority of about twelve to one. This remarkable change in public feeling was due mostly to an added accumulation of governmental ills in the intervening period.

A charter convention of twenty-one representative citizens was elected January 19, 1909. The list included seven lawyers, seven merchants, one college professor, one physician, one printer, one real estate operator, one contractor, and two men who, because of their varied interests, can best be ticketed as capitalists. The convention produced a fundamental law for Colorado Springs which was adopted almost without opposition at a special election. A point that deserves more than passing notice is that while the charter convention was almost entirely dominated by its legal members, and especially by the "corporation" lawyers, the result of its labors was an instrument which contains the initiative and referendum, the recall, and model provisons for insuring non-partisan elections. The two or three lawyers who really ran the convention are engaged extensively in the practice of public service corporations, mining companies, and other great corporate concerns, and it is doubtful whether they were really in sympathy with the radical measures which they put into the charter. But they recognized the popular demand for such measures, and not only put them there but took pains to frame them in such a way as to insure their effectiveness.

The charter provisions governing elections entirely abolish conventions, the party label on the ballot and other schemes calculated to give partisan advantage. On the petition of twenty-five qualified electors any citizen can have his name placed on the ballot as a candidate for one of the five elective offices. But he must make affidavit "that he has not become a candidate as the nominee or representative of, or because of any promised support from, any political party or any committee or convention representing or acting for any political party." The ballot is simplicity itself. The voter simply places a cross mark in a circle opposite the name of the candidate for whom he desires to vote. All distinguishing marks are forbidden, and make the ballot void.

Provision is made for a first, or primary election, which, however, may be final as to any office if one candidate happens to get a majority of all the votes cast for that office. But if no candidate gets a majority this election is considered merely as a primary, and another election is held two weeks later at which only the names of the two high candidates for each office appear on the ballot. This insures the election of every official by an actual majority vote.

This untrammeled condition brought into the field a large crop of candidates at the first election. There were five candidates for mayor and twenty-seven for the four councilmanic positions. The total vote for mayor was 5,256, of which the high man got 2,127 and the low man 71. The latter individual was a Socialist and depended on the Socialist party for his support, though of course he could not get his party name on the ballot. The highest vote cast for any candidate for the council was 2,561, and the lowest was 59, also for a Socialist.

The primary eliminated all but ten candidates, two for each position, and at the second election two weeks later a mayor was chosen by a majority of 1,484, receiving 3,989 votes as against 2,505 for his opponent. Of the four councilmen chosen the two with the highest votes will hold office four years and the two low men a little less than two years, or until the regular municipal election in April, 1911.

These were the only elections that have been held in Colorado Springs under the commission form of government. The interest aroused, as shown by the size of the vote, was greater than under the old form. The campaigns were fought principally through the newspapers, for the ordinary party machinery was rendered ineffective by the strict charter provision against corrupt practices, the use of carriages on election day, and in general eliminating partisan politics.

Normally, Colorado Springs is Republican in municipal affairs by from 1,000 to 1,200 majority, but the mayor elected under the commission plan is a Democrat, and so is one of the councilmen. Of course each of the regular party organizations worked, in so far as it could, to elect its own men. In the mayoralty contest the fight was essentially political. The Republican strength was divided between two candidates and became so bitter that when one of them was eliminated in the primary his supporters threw their strength to the Democrat and elected him to "get even" with the other faction. But the contest over the four councilmanic positions was fought wholly without regard to politics. Apparently it did not occur to anybody to inquire whether any one candidate was a Republican or a Democrat, and each man made his campaign entirely on the issue of personal fitness.

The victorious candidate for mayor was an insurance agent, fairly successful in his private business, of irreproachable character, unidentified with public affairs, and not especially well known to the community at large. People who knew him well accounted him a hard-headed business man who would give the city a good administration principally because of his insistence on efficiency. They did not expect a brilliant administration, for he is by no means a man of unusual attainments; but he is honest, sincere and effective within his limitations.

The Mayor is Commissioner of Water Works, and each of the other councilmen is at the head of a department—Finance, Public Works and Property, Public Health and Sanitation, and Public Safety. The four commissioners are men of only average ability, but with plenty of honesty and common sense. Finding after a time that the mayor's temperamental peculiarities operated as a bar to harmonious action they have adopted a course of opposition to him in which they are unquestionably supported by the community. It should not be assumed, however, that the mayor's attitude has seriously impaired the efficiency of the administration; it has only acted as a brake or drag. After all, obstinacy and conceit are not cardinal sins, and if one mayor has too much backbone of the wrong kind the people can find some consolation in the reflection that there have been executives in the past who did not have enough backbone of any kind.

Under the charter Colorado Springs has only five elective officials, all others being classed as employees and appointed by the mayor, except the clerk and attorney, who are appointed by the council. Severe criticism has been made of certain of the mayor's appointments as being essentially political, but he has made others which are far above the level of former days. He refused to reappoint the fire chief whom he found in office at the beginning of his administration and named instead a man who had just been removed from his position as chief of the Pueblo Fire Department for political reasons. The appointee had an excellent record, both in Pueblo and in a large eastern city, and the character of his work in Colorado Springs has abundantly justified the choice. But the politicians were fairly stunned when they found the mayor actually sending to another city for a fire chief, despite the abundance of "good material" at home. The general public, however, regarded the innovation with complete satisfaction as an application of sound business principles to public affairs.

Mayor Avery announced in the beginning that his appointments would be non-partisan, in accord with the spirit of the new order and likewise in recognition of the part played by Republicans in his own election. Of course this procedure has been entirely unsatisfactory to two elements of the population—the Democratic partisans who contend that inasmuch as the mayor is a Democrat he should appoint no Republicans, and the Republican partisans who think he has given the best plums to

Democrats. This sort of criticism needs no answer. The appointments, as a whole, have been as satisfactory to the community as political appointments ever are, and the character of service rendered by the appointees has been above the average of other days.

A notable instance of this is the case of the city engineer. The salary of this position is nominal and in the past considerable difficulty has been experienced in getting thoroughly capable men to stand for election. It was not altogether a matter of insufficient compensation, but of politics as well, for good engineers are seldom politicians and dislike to enter political contests. The problem was easier under the appointive system. Mayor Avery chanced to find the right man, Thomas L. Waggener, en engineer of distinction, who ten years ago built the Short Line Railroad to Cripple Creek, one of the marvels of modern railway engineering of the West. Mr. Waggener accepted the appointment and his service has been of a high character, especially in the preliminary work of street paving.

The initiative and referendum and recall provisions of the charter have thus far been useful only as a sort of legal sword of Damocles over the heads of the council. Fortunately the charter convention surrounded these provisions with effective safeguards against their abuse, but it did not swathe them in red tape in such a way as to destroy their usefulness. They are in the charter, and everybody knows it, most of all the officials against whom they could be invoked. Unquestionably the effect has been more circumspect conduct in the council. There are plenty of people who would like to recall the mayor, but he has done nothing on which the procedure could be legally justified and it is certain that any attempt to put the machinery of the recall in motion would fall flat.

In considering the case of Colorado Springs two factors demand attention, which, it might reasonably be assumed, would have tended under any form of administration to give the city better government. These are the distinctive quality of the city's population, and the institution of woman's suffrage. Colorado Springs is by no means a typical Western city; indeed, it is the very antithesis of the average city of its size. It is a "made-to-order" town, founded forty years ago by General William J. Palmer, a well-known railroad builder, who remained until his death, two years ago, its lavish benefactor. General Palmer as owner of the town site company inserted a clause in each deed providing that if liquor was ever made or sold on the premises the property should revert to the original owner. This famous "liquor clause" has stood the test of the United States Supreme Court and been declared valid, and it has been effective in entirely excluding saloons from Colorado Springs.

Thus the first and most difficult of the problems that used to confront Western border towns—the control of the disorderly element—was solved. This element had no use for a temperance town and gave it a wide berth, and at the same time there was attracted from the East a superior class of people who came to enjoy the remarkable climatic advantages of the place, to avail themselves of the educational facilities offered by Colorado College (also founded by General Palmer), and to bring up their children amid the good influences created by the "liquor clause."

Thus it happens that Colorado Springs is today a city of wealth and culture. This element of the Colorado Springs population, together with the element which is more conspicuous by reason of its quiet refinement than its wealth or social activity, has always been restive under local governmental abuses. But strangely enough it did nothing to correct them. It did as such people do the country over—refused to soil its hands with politics and submitted to abuses rather than take the trouble of ending them.

To just what extent, if any, woman suffrage has been responsible for either good or bad conditions in municipal government in Colorado Springs will always be a hotly debated question. As a rule the final decision depends, in individual cases, on the state of mind in which the question is approached. But it would be very difficult, perhaps impossible, to point to a single distinct triumph which can fairly be said to have been attained through woman suffrage. It is true that the Woman's Club as an organization, and the large majority of the representative women as individuals, heartily supported the movement to obtain a charter for Colorado Springs and institute the commission form of government. But in so doing they merely acted in accord with the feeling of the best element of the community as a whole, and it is certain that the same result would have been attained without equal suffrage. Public opinion was ripe for the change and it is doubtful whether any form of opposition could even have delayed, much less prevented it.

However, since the adoption of the charter some good work has been done by an organization of women, the Civic Club, in stimulating public interest in civic matters, especially such matters as street and park improvement, children's playgrounds, the public schools, and the proposed creation of a "civic center." The business of the club has been conducted with unusual tact and intelligence, and its influence seems likely to become an important factor in the city's development along the lines of its activities.

On the whole, Colorado Springs is well satisfied with the first eighteen months of commission government. It has accomplished many things worth while and it has failed to accomplish other things that are equally desirable, but it is working steadily toward a higher plane. It is getting results for which it struggled in vain under the old complicated and inefficient system of administration. Figured in dollars and cents the expense of government has been appreciably reduced, for although the amount of money raised by taxation and disbursed is as great as ever, the city is getting greater value for every dollar. The efficiency of the departments has been increased to such an extent that the city clerk, a capable and reliable official, estimates that there has been a thirty per cent. gain in economy. If there is anybody that wants to go back to the old plan of government he has not stood up to be counted.

COMMISSION GOVERNMENT IN BERKELEY

REPORT BY SPECIAL CORRESPONDENT.

Berkeley, Cal., Dec. 21, 1910.

When the new Berkeley charter went into effect a little over a year ago, the commissioners increased the tax rate of the city to the limit fixed by the charter, 99 cents on the $100. This increased the revenues of the city about $62,000. During the year the number of electric lights was about doubled, the police force was restored to its full quota—which under the previous administration had been a financial impossibility—and similar treatment was given the fire department. Numerous improvements were made in the fire and police alarm system. Additional expenditures over the previous year were made in repairing streets and in furnishing the new city hall. The engineer's office had been changed by the new charter from a fee to a salaried office, so that this expense was new. In addition, the council was now paid salaries, whereas the previous board of trustees had served free.

These increased expenditures, counting in the most part for better service on municipal lines, amounted in all to $57,438.33. The surplus on hand at the close of the first fiscal year was $32,876.44, making a total apparent increase of $90,314.77. The increased revenue had amounted to $62,987.87, so that the amount on hand, at the end of the first fiscal year under the new charter, in excess of the increase of revenue, was $27,326.90.

A comparative statement of the total receipts and expenditures for the two fiscal years, the one preceding and the other following the adoption of the commission form of government, is given below:

Fiscal year ending June 30, 1909:

Balance on hand July 1st, 1908	$ 17,029.49
Total receipts during year	222,693.21
Total resources for year 1908-9	239,722.70
Total expenditures, including amounts transferred to special funds	227,867.91
Balance on hand June 30, 1909	$ 11,854.79

Fiscal year ending June 30, 1910:

Balance on hand July 1st, 1909	$ 11,854.79
Total receipts during year, 1909-10	290,855.00
Total resources	$302,709.79
Total expenditures, including amounts transferred to special funds	269,833.35
Balance on hand June 30, 1910	$ 32,876.44

It is to be noted in the above that, although the table shows a balance on hand at the beginning of the second year tabulated of $11,854.79, there was outstanding against this an indebtedness of $15,000, which had been contracted for the payment of an incinerator site. This subsequently compromised for $5,000. Heretofore, also, the proceeds of sales for delinquent taxes have been added to the general receipts, but under the new charter all property on which taxes are delinquent must be sold to the city. This decreased the revenue and surplus for the year in the sum of $3,577.38, which would come in subsequently.

In his annual report at the end of the first fiscal year of the new administration the mayor advised a reduction of the tax rate by five or six cents, believing that such reduction might safely be made in view of the increased economy of the commission plan as operated here. This reduction was actually made, so that the tax rate of the city is now 93 cents on the $100, putting the city among the lowest in the state in this regard.

The council holds a meeting regularly every Tuesday morning. There was some objection to this on the part of a few residents who desired, according to their statements, to attend the meetings but were not able to do so as long as daytime sessions were held. The council thereupon planned to hold one night meeting a month for the transaction of such business as specially interested the residents; as, for instance, protests against street openings, the specification of assessment districts and other matters. At the first of these night meetings the lobby contained two persons, besides the janitor. At the second meeting, although the class of subjects under discussion was as outlined above, there were but three present in the lobby, not including the janitor. The council thereupon abandoned night meetings.

At its first election under the new commission plan of government, Berkeley elected its four commissioners and a mayor chiefly from a class that had never before taken part actively in the affairs of the municipal government. With two exceptions, none of them had ever before been in politics in this or any other city. The mayor is an attorney, his chief commissions having been from the Western Union Telegraph Company, though he has also had a considerable practice from other sources. It was with much real difficulty that he was persuaded to run for office, the final method used to get him to run being an appeal to his desire to see the new charter properly put in action, he having been a member of the freeholder board which drafted it. His salary has been $2,400 a year. He declares the monetary loss to him because of the necessity of abandoning his practice in part has been considerably greater than this. His prestige throughout the state, however, as head of one of the cities where the commission is in vogue, has greatly increased, and this is expected ultimately to bring about a more than compensating reimbursement for his present loss. He was recently elected president of the California League of Municipalities for the term of 1910-1911. The man who was chosen commissioner of finance and revenue is a real estate dealer of considerable success in Berkeley and a graduate of the University of California. His own business before he became commissioner was in a prosperous condition and so remains, he finding sufficient time outside his official duties to attend to it. The commissioner of supplies is the retired president of one of the city's banks. The commissioners of public works and of public health and safety have both been business men of standing in the community and have both previously held positions in the municipal government. The commissioner of public works was city engineer under the preceding administration.

The board of education, also elective, consists of the commissioner of finance and revenue above noted; one woman, who had been quite prominent in club work in the city and president of the federated mothers' clubs; a professor of the University of California; a physician, and a real estate dealer. The auditor, the only other elected officer, had served in the same position in the city government for several terms.

In the year and a half of the present administration the recall has neither been used nor even suggested.

Three or four initiative petitions have been circulated, but none of them has ever come to a vote, being abandoned by their proposers for one reason or another, but in only one case because the council took cognizance, in adopting ordinances, of provisions required by the petitioners. There was a most noticeable willingness on the part of the citizens to sign petitions during the first year of the new government, apparently attributable to a desire to watch the workings of this new and unusual mode of government. At least, that there was such willingness was proved by the requests of many, after petitions were presented, for the withdrawal of their names, the reason usually stated being that the signers had not "understood the purport of the petition."

"It is to be hoped," the mayor wrote in his first annual report, "that some more satisfactory method may be devised for initiating proceedings than by the present system of petitions which, owing to the well known thoughtless practice and accommodating habit of signing petitions of whatever nature, but too often represent only the hopes and desires of the promoters of the proceeding, rather than the well considered judgment of the great body of signers."

With this object in view, the city council subsequently passed an ordinance requesting the stating by signers of petitions of their reasons for so signing, and making some other regulations of the petitioning power. The adoption of the ordinance aroused immediate opposition, the claim being made that the ordinance limited rights granted the people by the charter. Referendum proceedings were instituted and the final enforcement of the ordinance prevented. The referendum will be voted upon by the people at the next city election, April, 1911.

So far as service rendered is concerned, there seems to be a general satisfaction with the officials elected to initiate the commission plan of government in this city. There has been a sort of underbreath of dissatisfaction emanating chiefly from that portion of the citizens which was politically opposed to the administration at its election. Not so much recently, however, as immediately following the election, has this been apparent, and it seems to have been due rather to chagrin than to real opposition either to the men chosen or the instrument by which they have operated. At the beginning of 1911, with the second elections under the charter in prospect four months away, there seems little activity among the members of the faction which opposed the present administration at the polls, while on every hand there is a demand that many, if not all, of the present officials succeed themselves. Yet there has been no apparent apathy among the citizens. Daytime meetings of the council have been well attended. Questions before the council have been repeatedly discussed by semi-official bodies. Administrative matters are, in fact, more widely discussed on the streets than ever before. The first election under the new charter brought out a vote of 5,100 in a registration of 8,200. A subsequent state election, in which both state and county fights were fiercely contested, brought to the polls only 200 more.

The idea of old-line political divisions, which always dominated the city, seems entirely to have disappeared so far as municipal affairs are concerned. There are, for instance, two Democrats among the five commissioners, despite the fact that at the last primary the city registered ten Republicans to every Democrat.

COMMISSION GOVERNMENT IN TACOMA

REPORT OF SPECIAL CORRESPONDENT.

TACOMA, WASH, April 12, 1911.

It was just one year ago today that Tacoma's commission form charter took effect and the first mayor and commissioners provided by that charter, took office. If judgment is to be passed on the eventualities that one year's trial of the commission form have developed, it can in truth be said that the commission form has been a complete failure in Tacoma.

Not that material civic progress has been lacking, for, in view of the depressed financial and general business conditions prevailing throughout the Far Northwest the past twelve months, Tacoma has never enjoyed a more progressive year. A municipal hydro-electric power plant that will cost completed, in excess of $2,500,000, will develop 32,000 horse power and will enable Tacoma to retail the cheapest electric power for both domestic and industrial consumption west of the Rocky Mountains has been started. A gravity water system that, if completed on schedule time—August 1, 1912—will give Tacoma unlimited quantities of absolutely pure mountain water, has been started of construction and will cost $2,000,000 before its supply is delivered in the city. The Tacoma unit of the Stone & Webster public service utility syndicate of Boston, has been successfully blocked in an attempt to increase street car fares to suburban districts beyond the five-cent limit. Bonds for two vertical lift bridges to cost together $630,000 have been floated and sold and working plans for the structures are under way. Bonds for a municipal dock to cost $125,000 have been floated and sold and a temporary dock opened to care for an immense marine passenger traffic that had for years previously been handled over a wretchedly small and dangerous dock. Two handsome concrete bridges, costing together $85,000 have been thrown across one of Tacoma's five deep gulches within a block of each other, one to care for street car and heavy team traffic, and the other for automobile and pedestrian traffic. Street paving and grading operations, sidewalk construction and sewer and water main extensions, aggregating an outlay of more than $1,000,000 have either been completed or are now under way.

But few of these municipal attainments, which are additional to private development enterprises that have aggregated an outlay of over $5,000,000 can be credited to the commission form of government, nor to the five men in whom the task of running the city has been vested. The initial steps were taken and the basic foundations for each achievement outlined, laid by the old ward system council, which was notorious for its petty bickerings and petty grafts and to banish which the commission charter was finally adopted after two years of agitation by the improvement clubs of the city, which number some twenty.

Each of these undertakings has been carried forward by the municipal commission because the commissioners realized that each was favored by a public sentiment which it would be suicidal to ignore. Individually the commissioners were each one opposed to one or another of the undertakings. Instead of burying their personal views and beliefs and going forward efficiently with the work the citizens demanded done, they allowed their own ideas to stand uppermost constantly with the result that the commission has been in a foment among itself during its entire official existence. So called "chewing matches" that would have put the old ward system council to blush have characterized legislative session after legislative session of the commission. Their lack of harmony has naturally extended to the men under the commissioners, until at the present writing all departments of the municipality are in a state of unrest, and personal partisanship that works for anything but efficiency has returned to vogue—the element of city hall politics, at whose eradication the commission charter was primarily aimed.

The prime provisions of the charter—publication of monthly reports of each department; operation of the civil service in all branches and departments; a limit of $500 on the campaign expenditures of any one candidate at any one election—have been persistently and completely ignored. Such acts, accompanied by an increase of $105,000 in the current operating expenses of the city over the expenses for the last twelve months under the ward council system, when it was confidently believed the commission form would reduce city expenses, and the enactment of the so-called "freak legislation" that has placed Tacoma up to the ridicule of the entire country, combined in invoking operation of the charter's recall provision against the entire municipal commission. This recall, will necessitate four elections, which will in themselves cost the city $12,000.

Members of the committee of 15 freeholders, who framed the commission charter, differ as to the primary cause of the so apparently complete failure of the commission form during its first year's trial in Tacoma. In the last analysis, however, the failure may be attributed to the fact that the salary of $400 a month the mayor gets, and $350 a month for each commissioner, were not attractive enough to encourage men competent to handle the affairs of a $70,000,000 corporation like the city of Tacoma, to enter the field as candidates. At the time of the first election, the fact that success depended on the election of men such as a private corporation of large interests would employ to run its affairs, was not realized. There were 52 aspirants for the five places on the commmission and not one of them, save the man who was elected mayor, had ever commanded as great a salary in private life as offered him in case of election. The mayor had been successful as a dealer in agricultural implements and had amassed a fortune of about $100,000, but none of the other aspirants had ever been more than business men of small or moderate incomes, and none, save eight, had had previous experience in city affairs. It is realized now that if the bad start the city has made under the commission form is to be overcome, men of demonstrated ability must be placed in office, and to that end W. W. Seymour, a former New York banker and philanthropist, who during 20 years of residence in the Northwest has rebuilt and rejuvenated 20 or more run-down public service corporations such as gas, telephone and street railway companies, and whose hobby is public playgrounds, parks and social settlement work, has been persuaded to sacrifice his personal business affairs and make the run for Mayor against A. V. Fawcett, the commission form mayor against whom the recall has been invoked.

This necessity for a second election has brought out a weakness of the commission charter for whose eradication sentiment is gathering. At the recall primary, Mr. Seymour received 8,500 votes; Mayor Fawcett 7,200, and Barth, Socialist candidate (despite the charter provision prohibiting party lines), 3,200 votes. Seymour had a clear plurality of 1,300 votes over Fawcett, but lacked 1,900 of a majority over all votes cast. It is conceded by supporters of all three men that the vote indicated clearly the popular choice and that two additional weeks of campaign turmoil, and the expenditure of $3,000 more for another election, are made uselessly necessary by the charter wording. The best informed students of the commission form, including members of the committee which framed the charter, now assert that the principle of securing popular choice by use of the primary election would be in no wise jeopardized by substitution of the words "plurality shall elect" for "must receive a majority of all votes cast."

As may have been inferred, the commission which the Citizens Welfare League is now endeavoring to recall, is sadly rent and torn by partisanship.

Mayor A. V. Fawcett has been a candidate for some office, either municipal or state, at every election since 1892. As elections occur every two years, this means that he has stood for election 20 times. He has succeeded three times—once as county commissioner of Pierce County, once before, in 1900, as mayor, and again in 1910 as mayor. Three times he ran as a Democrat, four times as a Republican, twice as a Populist and the remaining times as a fusion candidate or independent. In other words, A. V. Fawcett is a professional politician, proudly acclaims the fact, and asserts with good reason that "they are all afraid of the old man." When he announced his candidacy for mayor under the commission plan, he accompanied his announcement with the assertion that he "was ferninst the commission form." A man noted for his personal charities, however, he had a strong following that was not reckoned with, and he was elected by an overwhelming majority.

This was before the franchise was granted Washington women. Just how Fawcett "plays" the political game is well illustrated by two incidents. In the last 20 years he has loaned over $20,000 in small amounts of from $5 to $100 to acquaintances who have come to him "down and out," and asked his assistance. These loans have been made almost entirely on no better security than "I. O. U.'s" yet every cent, save about $500, has been repaid. During several Christmas seasons in the "lean" years that now and then visit the Far Northwest, Mr. Fawcett has purchased turkeys by the carload and distributed them among poor and needy families, for which charity he is popularly known as "Turkey Fawcett." Of necessity a man who does such things has a large following which cannot readily be broken. Mr. Fawcett is not a man of any polish or culture, but has a knack of being a "hale fellow well met" among the class of voters who are known in Tacoma as "Third warders" —men who live in lodging houses and work at odd jobs here and there, yet are qualified citizens. Mr. Fawcett makes it a point to know these men individually by name and when he walks the street it is interesting to hear his "Hello Bill" and "Hello Harry" to his admirers. Until the recall primary Fawcett had the vote of the Third Ward, wherein is the "redlight district" and the greater number of the city's saloons, in the hollow of his hand. He still has this following, although it has been weakened to some extent by what is known as the "Fawcett anti-treating ordinance." Although Fawcett has always been an "open town" man, and made his campaigns for municipal suffrage on that platform, he asserted six months after his last election that he had had a "change of heart." He said he intended alleviating the sufferings of the poor by curbing the saloons and to this end he introduced and had passed his anti-treating ordinance. Under this ordinance it is a misdemeanor, on the part of the bar tender, punishable by fine and by revocation of the saloon's license, to sell a man a drink of any kind, or to sell a drink in a cafe, unless that drink is consumed by the man who pays for it. For example. Bill Smith may go into a saloon and order and pay for a dozen beers. If Bill Smith drinks that dozen beers, no misdemeanor has been committed. But if Bill Smith calls John Jones to the bar and gives John one of the beers and John drinks it, a misdemeanor has been committed. Nor has it been committed by either Bill Smith or John Jones. The bar tender is guilty and liable to punishment. Undoubtedly Mayor Fawcett intended the ordinance to prevent the 11,000 or more men who work in Tacoma's saw mills and factories at $1.50 a day and upwards, from stopping in saloons on their way home with their week's pay Saturday night, and squandering the greater part of their earning in treating any and all who chance to be in the saloon. The anti-treating ordinance went to a referendum vote and the church element of the city, failing to realize the mayor's political purpose, voted solidly for it and it carried. Although the mayor does not have control of the police force, he set about immediately to enforce the ordinance which was promptly violated by the ruse of having adequate supplies of small change in saloons, so that the man who wants to treat can get the exact change to pay for the drink; hand the man he wants to treat the price of the drink and let the latter pay for it, thereby saving the bar tender from a misdemeanor, but at the same time getting effectively around the ordinance. Lacking ability to use the police force, and being "at outs" with the commissioner of public safety who is the head of the police department, Mayor Fawcett employed a large force of detectives at his own personal expense to obtain evidence and convict saloon keepers who violated the law. In the meantime it had been discovered that a five-story building which the mayor and his brother own jointly, at South C and 15th Streets, contained two saloons—one a wholesale establishment with a government license, and the other an ordinary "Third ward" saloon, with a city license. The mayor's enemies at once began to make recall campaign capital out of this seeming inconsistency and it nettled the mayor. Seeking to make himself "strong" with the church people who had voted for the ordinance, the mayor had his detectives watch the city license saloon in his own building—a saloon that pays him and his brother $450 per month rental. The detective obtained evidence of violation all right, and the mayor saw to it that the very first conviction under his ordinance was the conviction of the saloon keeper in his own building. The saloon keeper was fined $50 and costs. The mayor's "gallery play," as his loving (?) contemporaries on the commission termed it, was too palpable for the general public to endure, and the mayor was condemned by both press and pulpit. Two weeks after the ordinance went into effect the mayor withdrew his force of private detectives and the ordinance, at this writing, with election one week away, is being violated in practically every saloon in the city. In his campaign for the ordinance, Mayor Fawcett issued propaganda in which he pictured a husband drinking up his week's wages at a bar, himself standing at the side of the bar, holding up a "big stick" labeled "anti-treating ordinance," and on the reverse of the page a poor woman sitting beside a fireless fireplace, nursing a babe and trying to comfort three other children on the floor around her. There was just one caption over this propaganda. It read: "Is Kate Getting a Square Deal?" Mayor Fawcett's present wife's name (he has been married and divorced twice and is the father of 14 children) is Kate. His use of her name in this connection gave his opponents the tip to look into the Mayor's personal record, and a perusal of the court records revealed a wretched story of domestic infelicity, suffering and infidelity which is being used against the mayor.

The anti-treating ordinance, however, has had the effect of throwing the saloon element and the church element together, and Mayor Fawcett is counting on capturing the Socialist vote at the second election which was cast for the eliminated Socialist candidate at the first election. The situation is especially peculiar, but it is believed that the female vote will go strongly against Mr. Fawcett, largely on account of his personal family record.

The troubles and bickerings in the municipal commission began with its very first executive session. Under the charter, the commissioner of public safety has complete control of the police and fire departments. The incumbent, Lester W. Roys, was for 15 years city clerk of Tacoma under the ward council system, but he also was opposed to the commission form, and was elected largely on his previous record in a routine city position.

Ignoring the civil service provision of the charter,

Mayor Fawcett at the first meeting of the commission presented Mr. Roys a list of names of men who had aided his (Fawcett's) election, with the request to Mr. Roys to "Put them on the force." "But we have no civil service commission yet, and there is no eligible list," replied Mr. Roys. "The charter specifically provides civil service for all city employes, and although I do not believe in the commission form, I shall follow the law. If these friends of yours can pass the examinations, I will be glad to appoint them. Otherwise there will be nothing doing." Mayor Fawcett had worked diligently for the election of Mr. Roys and was angry when the latter refused his request. "To h—— with civil service" was one of the expressions he used, and right there started a breach between the mayor and the commissioner of public safety, which has widened until it is now beyond bridging. When agitation for closing the restricted district and preventing gambling and boxing contests, which had been countenanced for a year, was started by the Welfare League, Mayor Fawcett plead helplessness, saying that he had no control of the police department and it was up to Mr. Roys. Mr. Roys favors a properly conducted restricted district and refused to close the town. Then Mayor Fawcett prevailed on Commissioner of Finance Ray Freeland to introduce a resolution closing the city and calling on the commissioner of public safety to act. The resolution carried and the town was closed, and on the day that the largest boxing match ever arranged in Tacoma was to have been staged. The promoters of this match, being assured that no interference would be made if no decision was rendered and the state law against prize fighting therefore not violated, had spent over $2,000 in preparations for the event, Tommy Burns being the main promoter. One hundred and ten members of the Washington legislature, which was in session at Olympia at the time, came over to Tacoma to witness the affair only to find that the lid had been clamped down. While the church people approved the closing of the town, their sense of fair play objected to the way it had been accomplished, and they were free to say that Fawcett had used a "pliable member of the commission" to achieve the end in order to discredit Commissioner Roys.

Shortly after this occurrence bonds for two bridges, as previously related, were authorized and sold. Instead of opening a regular competition for designs, however, Mayor Fawcett, who had seen a vertical lift bridge in operation at Portland, Oregon, announced that Tacoma would build two vertical lift bridges. He refused absolutely to allow designers of bascule or trunnion pivot bridges to bid on the work. He was told that the vertical lift bridge had proved a failure everywhere tried in the United States, except at Portland. Civic organizations wired the chief engineers of practically all railroads in the United States, asking their opinions on bridges. They condemned the vertical lift and urged that the greatest care be exercised in selecting a type. The civic bodies sent committees to wait on the mayor, but he refused to receive them.

"To h—— with the civic bodies," he said. "I'm running this town." This despite the fact that bridge construction, under the charter, is solely a matter for the commissioner of public works to work out, subject to the approval of the commission. Commissioner of Public Works Owen Woods favored a vertical lift bridge, and Mayor Fawcett persuaded Finance Commissioner Ray Freeland, the "pliable" member of the commission, to vote with Woods and himself for a vertical lift bridge. Then, despite the protests that flooded him from citizens generally, the mayor had a contract for designing the two bridges drawn up with a Kansas City engineering firm, which holds a monopoly on all vertical lift bridge patents. This contract specifies that the engineers shall receive their pay—$24,000—before the bridges are entirely completed and accepted by the city, and is said by corporation attorneys who have examined it to be the loosest contract of the kind they have ever seen. While improvement clubs and civic bodies continued sending their protests, Mayor Fawcett signed the contract and the engineers are now at work on their plans.

In the mean time, Commissioner of Light and Water Nicholas Lawson was going ahead calling for bids for the $2,500,000 hydro-electric power plant and $2,000,000 gravity water system with the mayor dictating every detail. Commissioner Woods and Roys objected to the loose methods that they said characterized this work and voted against every item. The mayor, however, succeeded in keeping Lawson and Freeland with him and the contracts have been let. The projects will be paid for by warrants secured by the city's light and water fund, the contractors agreeing to take their chances on disposing of the warrants. Protests from the civic bodies and improvement clubs were ignored in regard to these projects, as they had been ignored in the case of the bridge contracts.

It has been stated that Commissioner of Public Safety Roys refused to ignore the civil service. He is the only member of the commission who has done so. Commissioner of Light and Water Lawson arbitrarily discharged an electrical engineer of recognized ability, who had been employed by the old ward council to carry through the hydro-electric project, because that engineer, Frank

C. Kelsey, drew $500 a month salary. "I won't have a man under me who gets more pay than I do," said Mr. Lawson. And so saying he gave Kelsey the blue envelope and placed an entirely inexperienced man in the position at $250 a month. Commissioner Lawson had had some experience in small hydraulic mining projects in Alaska, but is an uneducated Scandinavian and a man who will listen to no one save Mayor Fawcett. Commissioner of Finance Ray Freeland, the youngest member of the commission, graduated from the Tacoma High School ten years ago and entered the city treasurer's office as a clerk. He proved a most efficient detail routine man and advanced rapidly, until he was finally elected city treasurer. Not one doubt of Freeland's honesty has ever been expressed, and until he came to work with Mayor Fawcett he was possibly the most popular city official in Tacoma. But Mayor Fawcett seemed to have a hypnotic influence over Freeland, and the latter has done whatever Fawcett has demanded him to do. Freeland's "lack of backbone" as it has come to be known, will more than likely defeat him at the coming recall election on the commission. Commissioner Roys, while he has come nearest to obeying the charter of any of the five, is fully as much of a "bullhead" once he makes up his mind, as is Mayor Fawcett. Mr. Roys will not stoop to the means to accomplish his ends, however, that Fawcett will, but has not proved a satisfactory official on account of his continual "fights" with the mayor.

Commissioner Owen Woods, of the Department of Public Works, comes nearest to being a satisfactory official of any. Woods was commissioner of public works during one administration under the old ward council plan and did very satisfactory work. He has mapped out more material development and construction enterprises during his incumbency under the commission plan than any other member of the commission, and stands a good show of being reelected.

The failure of the commission form of government in Tacoma then, if it has been a failure, is attributable to the men whom the people elected. They are men of inferior abilities; men whose personal records are clouded; men who are not "big" enough to bury personal differences in the sake of the common good. One year has sufficed to show Tacoma that she is on the right track but has merely allowed herself to wander off on by paths. A strong man, one whose abilities and whose personal cleanliness cannot be assailed, stands to be the next mayor. Thus far 30 aspirants have filed their candidacies for the four commissionerships. They are in the main men of much better standing, calibre and reputation than those who aspired for election a year ago. The stigma that the year's failures have brought; the ridicule that Tacoma has been subjected to in the world at large as a result of "freak legislation" and petty bickerings among her officials, has stung her to the quick. The officials of the Welfare League assert that, given another twelve months, Tacoma will be showing the same happy result under the commission plan as have Des Moines and Galveston. The shortcomings of the charter thus far found will be corrected they say. And Tacoma will prove that municipal government "of the people, for the people and by the people" can yet be had in the Far Northwest.

[*The Mayor and two other members of the City Council were recalled after the above was written.—Ed.*]

COMMISSION GOVERNMENT IN SPOKANE

REPORT OF SPECIAL CORRESPONDENT

SPOKANE, WASH., May 1, 1912.

Commission government has been in operation in Spokane since March 14, 1911, under a charter prepared by a board of fifteen freeholders and adopted at a special election held December 28, 1910. The charter was drafted as a result of a thorough investigation by an advisory committee and board of freeholders who proposed to embody in the charter the most advanced principles of this form of city government.

A year's trial is scarcely sufficient to form a basis for judgment as to the success or failure of any system of government which necessitates a radical departure from old methods and practices. Considering the magnitude of the problems confronting the five newly elected commissioners and the difficulties involved in the reorganization of a municipal corporation affecting the interests of more than 100,000 people, with a heritage of conditions due to years of inefficient council government passed on to them, it seems scarcely possible to form a definite opinion regarding the advantages or disadvantages of the new form of city government.

From one standpoint the new government has precious little to offer a public promised great and substantial improvements. It is maintained that while operating expenses have increased to a marked degree, construction outlays, which measure actual improvement for the city, have been materially reduced. In short, the city commission is charged with spending more money and doing less work for the city than was done under the old council form. It is claimed that the commissioners lack energy, ability and initiative; that they are dominated by the labor forces of the town and are enamored with fads and fancies, such as the municipal ownership of telephones, the single tax idea, and socialism; that the departments are not working in harmony; and that although the commissioners are personally honest their administration of the city government is inefficient and wasteful. There is undoubtedly a strong sentiment of dissatisfaction and disapproval of what the commissioners are doing. On the part of a small group, at least, this dissatisfaction has crystallized in the form of a series of amendments to the charter intending to return to a modified form of council government and a series of recall petitions directed against each of the present commissioners. Financially and in almost every other respect the new government, it is asserted, has proved to be a dismal failure.

To the above criticisms the city commissioners and their supporters reply that the high operating expenses are due to conditions inherited from the old administration which it was impossible to change without a serious loss to the city. As against increased operating expenses, it is maintained, that in the actual cost of public improvements (an item not shown in the expense accounts of the city) there has been a saving of more than 10 per cent. to the property owners. They point to the elimination of graft and the sinister methods of the lobby about the city hall; to the straightforward and business-like management of all the departments; to the financing of the water department debt and assured lower rates for all consumers of water; to reorganized and more efficient police, fire, health and inspection departments; to the directness and simplicity of handling public business in comparison with the cumbersome and slow method of the old form. They ask simply for fair treatment and more time to demonstrate the unquestioned superiority of the commission form of government under the new charter.

Between the enthusiastic supporters who can see nothing but a long list of benefactions due solely to the change in government and the extreme opponents, who find no words suitable to express their sentiment of scorn and disgust with the feeble efforts of the commission, the great majority of the people of Spokane appear to be pleased with the change in their form of government. The prefer to reserve judgment, however, and await developments before arriving at a conclusion regarding the success or failure of their new administration. To the people of Spokane, then, and to those outside of the city watching with interest the developments under the new charter, it must be apparent that the new government is still on trial and has yet to demonstrate its efficiency and superiority over the government which it replaced.

The first election under the preferential system of voting as provided by the charter does not indicate very much regarding the success of this new type of ballot. Under the simple method of qualification for candidates (twenty-five signatures only being required) ninety-six filed papers and ninety-two names were finally printed on the somewhat formidable looking "short" ballot. According to the election provisions of the charter any candidate receiving a majority of first choice votes is declared elected. For those not receiving a majority of first choices the second choices are added. Any candidate receiving a majority of first and second choices combined is elected. If the required number are not elected by first and second choice votes additional choices are then counted and those receiving the highest total votes are elected. Only one commissioner, Robert Fairley, was elected by first choice votes, receiving 12,779 out of a total 22,058. For the remaining members of the commission, it was necessary to take the sum of the second and additional choices and the members were elected by total votes ranging from 9,896 to 7,394. The contest was very close, as may be seen by the fact that no less than six candidates had a total vote of from 6,000 to 8,000, with several men running but a small number of votes behind the winning candidates. The figures indicate that the major portion of the vote was divided among about twenty of the list of candidates, thirty-four receiving less than 1,000 each. The nine highest candidates by first choice preferences were:

		First Choice	Total
1.	Robert Fairley	12,779	15,418
2.	William J. Hindley	7,513	9,896
3.	C. M. Fassett	6,284	8,558
4.	David C. Coates	6,272	7,525
5.	S. A. Anderson	4,661	7,012
6.	N. W. Durham	4,604	6,650
7.	M. J. Luby	4,304	7,299
8.	Zora E. Hayden	4,260	7,394
9.	Leonard Funk	4,007	6,094

The final count of votes resulted in the election of the first four candidates in the order named above, second and additional choices raising only one candidate, Zora E. Hayden, from the eighth on the list to fifth, thus assuring his election as above Anderson, Durham and Luby. As Hayden, Funk, Luby, Durham and Anderson seemed to be backed largely by the same organizations in the city, particularly the public service corporations and other special business interests, the character of the commission was but slightly changed by means of additional preferences. The preferential ballot is held to have been partially responsible for breaking the old-time city ring composed of the public service corporations, contractors and vice elements. Whereas the opponents of the system claim that it merely added confusion to the system of voting without any compensating advantages.*

It seems to be the general opinion that the five commissioners elected were among the best and most capable men in the long list of candidates, and that if the city failed to get a first-class type of men, it was because such men did not qualify and enter the contest for commissioner. That a Congregational minister received the second highest vote and a Socialist ran fourth on the list was due in all probability to personal popularity and active campaigning rather than to the preferential ballot. One more election, at least, will be required to show whether the form of ballot will have any marked effect upon the politics of the city.

*As this system of voting is comparatively new in the United States the form of the ballot is given:

GENERAL MUNICIPAL ELECTION

City of Spokane, March 7th, 1911

INSTRUCTIONS.

To vote for any person, mark a cross (X) in a square ( ) to the right of the name.

VOTE FIRST CHOICE FOR FIVE candidates, or ballot will be void. Second and Third choice is NOT COMPULSORY.

Vote only FIVE FIRST CHOICES, and only FIVE SECOND CHOICES.

Vote as many Third choices as you wish.

Vote your FIRST CHOICES in the first column.

Vote your SECOND CHOICES in the second column.

Vote in the THIRD COLUMN for all the OTHER CANDIDATES whom you WISH TO SUPPORT.

DO NOT VOTE MORE THAN ONE CHOICE FOR ANY ONE CANDIDATE, as only the one choice will count.

All distinguishing marks make the ballot void.

If your wrongly mark, tear, or deface this ballot, return it and obtain another from the election officers.

FIVE COMMISSIONERS TO BE ELECTED.

CITY COMMISSIONERS	First Choice	Second Choice	Additional Choices
John Doe		X	
Richard Roe	X		
William Brown			X

The men elected commissioners were well known throughout the city, although only one of them had held public office before. W. H. Hindley, who was selected as Mayor and Commissioner of Public Affairs, was a Congregational minister who resigned his pulpit to enter the campaign. He was one of the most noted and popular preachers of the city. He is a man of liberal religious views and is known to favor the single tax and other economic reforms. His only distinct public service prior to his election was on a Citizens' Committee which secured a bond issue to develop and maintain an excellent park system for the city. Robert Fairley, Commissioner of Finance, is a Scotchman who came to Spokane in the early 70's, worked as a day laborer, carpenter and molder. He still holds a card in the carpenters' union and is proud to be identified with the laboring class. He has held office continuously for more than ten years, serving for three terms of three years each as City Comptroller. For his work in this office he earned the title "watchdog of the treasury." He is very well known throughout the city and his election as the only commissioner chosen by first choice votes attests to his popularity.

D. C. Coates, the Commissioner of Public Works, was lieutenant-governor of Colorado and took an active part in the labor disturbances of that state. He has lived in Spokane only a few years, where he soon became an active leader of the labor unions, gaining notoriety by leading a big procession of laboring men to the city hall to demand a wage scale of three dollars a day for work on public improvements. He was a member of the Committee of Fifteen who drafted the charter. Coates is a Socialist and was endorsed by the labor unions and the Socialist party, although he has since been repudiated by the state organization of his party for refusing to furnish an undated resignation as required by party rules. The Socialist local organization of the city sustained him in his action, and under his leadership a new organization known as the Social Democratic party has been formed.

Zora E. Hayden, Commissioner of Public Safety, was engaged in the lumber business, serving as a representative of several large lumber companies. He is a prominent member of the Manitou Park Improvement Club, from whose members an organization was formed to support his candidacy. His election was largely due to the active work of the Hayden Clubs and the support of large business and financial organizations. He is regarded as the special representative of the business interests of the city. C. M. Fassett, Commissioner of Public Utilities, was proprietor of one of the oldest and largest assaying firms west of Chicago. He was President of the Chamber of Commerce and resigned the position to go on a trip. While away from the city, he was nominated and elected to the City Commission. He was a member of the Committee of Fifteen who drafted the charter and is a strong advocate of the single tax.

It seemed a disappointment to many that able business and professional men were not attracted by the salary and special opportunities afforded under the new charter, for although the men elected constitute a strong and capable commission, only two of the successful candidates had demonstrated exceptional ability in the management of public affairs or private business.

Three separate reports have been made covering the financial operations of the new government during six months, nine months and twelve months respectively. In the first place the State Bureau of Inspection and Supervision of Public Offices went over the books and prepared a statement of the finances from April to September 1911, with the corresponding months of the previous year. The following comparisons are presented:

	1910	1911
Total Operating Expenses..	$811,173.54	$953,519.80
Total Betterments	788,173.26	532,295.60
Total Expenditures ...	$1,599,346.80	$1,485,815.40
Total Operating Increase..................		$142,346.26
Total Betterment Decrease.................		255,877.66

The state accountants noted that an increase in the police department was authorized by the old administration; that a paving plant entailing an expenditure of more than $28,000 was a new enterprise; that the increase in the street department was due chiefly to the cost of maintaining additional paved streets, but that after making these allowances there was a big net increase of about $110,000 in the departments to a net decrease of less than $20,000.

Another statement prepared by an accountant for the contractors' association covers nine months under the new administration. In the summary of this statement it appears that the total operating expenses were $472,017.77 for 1910 and $666,388.99 for 1911, with an increase of $194,371.22. $56,676.80 of this amount is then deducted as representing permanent improvements, leaving a total increase in operating expenses for nine months of $137,694.42. As a result of an examination of the books for the first nine months the astounding comparison is offered that whereas nearly $2,000,000 worth more of local improvements were under process of construction during 1910 than in 1911, yet the cost of administration under the Commission form has increased over $15,000 per month. A report submitted to the Spokane *Chronicle* covering a period of twelve months, though not so unfavorable in its conclusions, indicates the same general tendency—a marked increase in operating expenses with a corresponding decrease in construction work.

As against this record of increasing cost for operation the commissioners offer the following accomplishments in a summary of the achievement of their first year's administration. Commissioner Fassett, for the department of public utilities, has funded the $1,000,000 water department debt so that it is now placed on a basis of 5 per cent. instead of 6 per cent., as was the case formerly, and the expense in connection with water extensions has been reduced so that the commissioner has assured the public that lower water rates will soon be granted to all consumers. To demonstrate the economic management of the water department the commissioner states that for the month of February there were 1,200 more services in 1912 than in 1911, but that for the month 43,467,920 gallons less have been pumped and the revenue has increased $2,287.28. A large part of this increase in revenue has been due to the installation of meters.

The most important work of this department, however, had to do with the regulation of the gas and electric companies. Commissioner Fassett drew up a set of rules and regulations for these companies, but as they are under state control the matter was taken up directly with the state public service commission and the rules as formulated by Commissioner Fassett were adopted and promulgated as the regulations of the state commission. The result not only testifies to the ability and efficiency of the city commissioner, but also has brought about the saving of at least $50,000 to the people in the matter of gas alone.

The most spectacular work of the new commission and that which is subjected to the severest criticism is in the department of Public Works under the direction of the energetic Socialist commissioner, David C. Coates. It is the work of this department which has antagonized the contractors' association of the city, has led to several hearings in which the management of the department has been under fire, and has been responsible primarily for the circulation of recall petitions. This department makes the greatest claims for economy in behalf of the new administration. The adoption of a day labor policy in competition with the contractors of the city is held to have resulted in a saving of no less than 10 per cent. in the price property holders have had to pay for improvements since the inauguration of commission government. This reduction along with a lowering of the estimates of the city engineers on all contracts has meant a net decrease of more than 20 per cent. on cost to property owners of all improvement work. As a result of these reductions it is estimated that no less than $30,000 were saved to the property owners of the city for each month of commission government. The very vigorous opposition to the new government by contractors indicates that they have suffered rather rough treatment at the hands of the commissioners.

The Public Works department not only offers a record of a big decrease in construction contracts, but the most marked success of the department is shown in the management of street cleaning, where the cost of the repairs to asphalt pavements was reduced 50 per cent., and 44 miles of paved streets were cleaned at a monthly expense of $6,250, as against $5,250 to clean 14.47 miles during the previous year. The department of Public Works under its very active leader is looked upon by many as the real, live and progressive department of the government.

In the other departments the following changes and improvements have been accomplished. Saloons have been slightly reduced in number, are now more carefully inspected, and stricter rules for their control have been formulated. The police and fire departments have been reorganized in the direction of greater efficiency. Instead of supporting the plan for a segregated vice district or permitting open and flagrant violation of the law against prostitution, the City Commission has adopted the policy of suppression and there seems to be no doubt that conditions have been very decidedly improved by this action. The firm and effective enforcement of the law against this evil may easily be ranked as one of the greatest improvements due to the change in form of government.

Under the mayor, as director of the department of public affairs, the health department has instituted a rigorous system of inspection of markets, restaurants and dairies. But the most notable accomplishment of this department is the organization of a municipal charity commission. The municipal commission was established by ordinance, the members being appointed by the mayor, and the body as a whole being under the supervision of the city commissioners. The ordinance provides that any person soliciting charity (other than the authorized representatives of the Associated Charities, the Y. M. C. A., the Y. W. C. A. and church charities) must have a license from the commission. As a condition of granting this license or permit, the commission investigates the charity concerned, to determine whether or not it is worthy and necessary. The penalty for soliciting without a license or without credentials is not more than thirty days in jail and a fine not to exceed $100, or both. The commission has no employees, and for that reason the Associated Charities often makes investigations at its request. This commission has charge of the apportionment of funds among charitable institutions of the city and is at work upon a comprehensive scheme of charity to be administered by the city with a view of eliminating the present plan of more or less haphazard relief by private boards or societies.

Between this list of accomplishments and the complaint that city expenses have increased without any compensating advantages, it is very difficult to strike an average which represents the actual status and results of commission government in Spokane. The thirteen mill tax of a year ago was continued without an increase largely, it is claimed, because of the fear of objections against the extravagance of commission government. In spite of an increase in valuation of about fifty millions of dollars, the present revenues are not sufficient to meet expenditures, so that the city is carrying a deficit to date, according to the estimate of the Commissioner of Finances, of, at least, $100,000. This means that next year an advance in the tax levy will be required to cover the regular expenses of running the government—a not very pleasant situation to face by those who rather vociferously urged commission government because of anticipated decreases in the budget and tax levies. Petty bickerings among the members of the commission and a lack of energy and initiative in the development of a constructive policy for city improvements militate against that public support which the new government might reasonably expect.

An undercurrent of opposition has crystallized in a series of amendments to the charter and a recall petition for each of the commissioners. The charter amendments are clearly intended to effect a return to the old form of council government. The elective officers are to include ten councilmen, a mayor, treasurer, and comptroller to be elected under the ward system for a term of two years. All office holders are to be property holders (a provision directed especially against Socialists) and are to receive salaries varying from $900 for council to $3,000 for mayor. Three members of the council are to have charge of each department. Reports are circulated that a large number of the required list of signatures for both amendment and recall petitions have been secured, but keen political observers are not anticipating an early recall election. The fact that one of the most active leaders in the recall movement was forced to close a moving picture gallery because of publicity due to an investigation by the city commission regarding a violation of city ordinances is not likely to add prestige to the opposition, nor is it a great advantage to have the very active support of a group of contractors who are no longer profiting as richly from the city treasury. The forces behind the recall petitions represent thus far too exclusively a disgruntled minority who have in some form or other suffered at the hands of the new government. When the chief opponents may be characterized as belonging to a group of contractors, agents of public service corporations, and the vice element, it appears that the city commissioners have reason to feel complimented at the enemies they have made. In the words of one of Spokane's prominent business men, the opponents of commission government so far have furnished no real ground for opposition; they belong either to the special interests that have suffered because of the change or they manifest the conservative business man's tendency to oppose all change and reform. On the part of reliable business men of the city there is a disposition to say that the new government has meant an improvement, that although the commissioners are not as strong a type of men as ought to be secured to manage city affairs, they nevertheless are personally honest and are giving the city a cleaner, more vigorous and straightforward administration than was possible under the former council system.

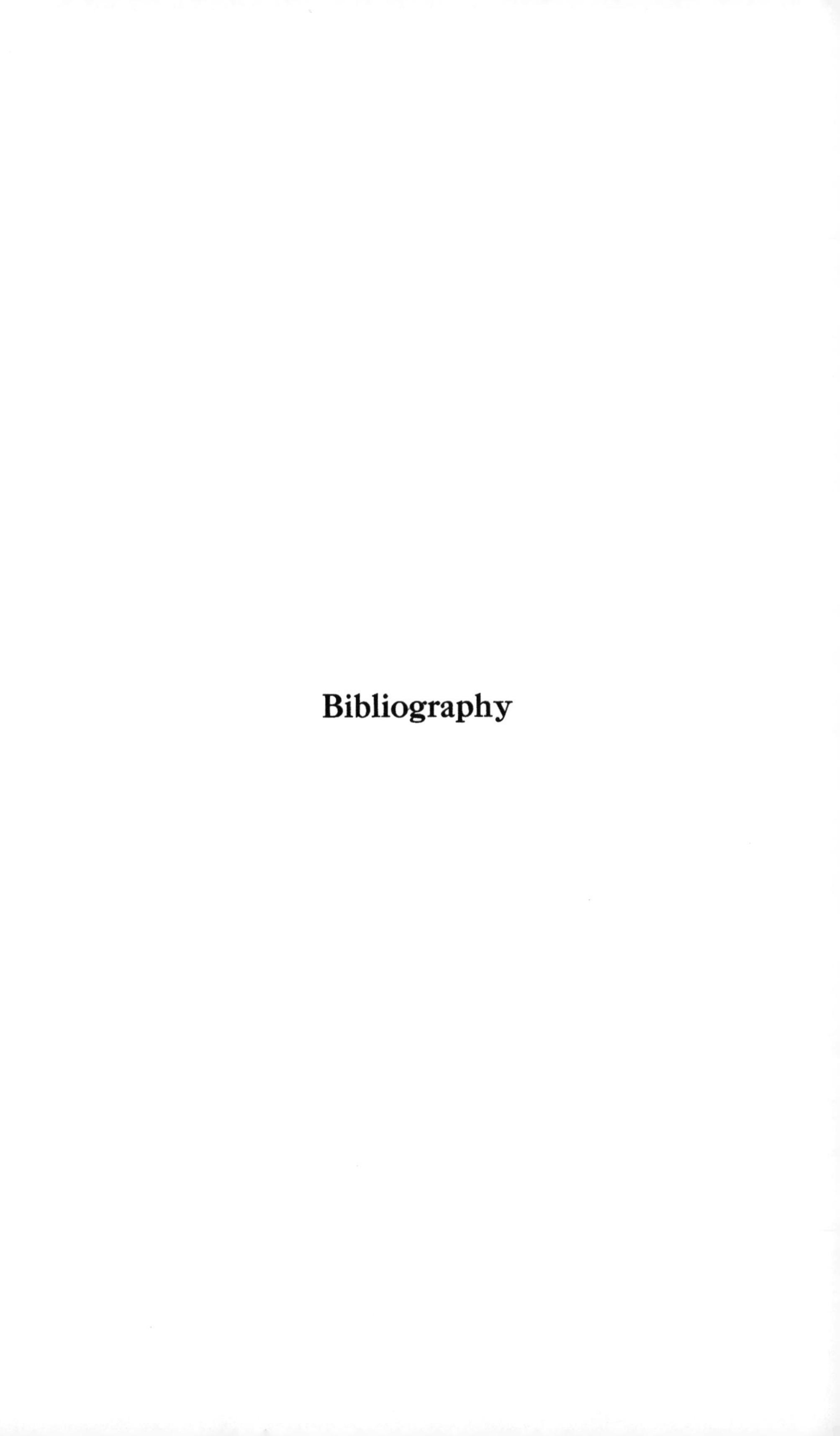

Bibliography

I.

CITY GOVERNMENT—GENERAL

(Select List.)

Books.

DEMING, H. E.—Government of American Cities: a program of democracy. Putnam, 1909, $1.25.

FAIRLIE, J. A.—Essays in Municipal Administration. MacMillan Co., 1908, $2.50.

FULLER, R. H.—Government by the People. MacMillan Co., 1908, $1.00.

GOODNOW, F. J.—Municipal Government. Century Company, 1909, $3.00.

——Municipal Problems. MacMillan Company, 1908, $1.50.

HOWE, F. C.—The City, the Hope of the Democracy. Scribner's Sons, 1906, $1.35.

MUNRO, W. B.—Government of European Cities. MacMillan Company, 1908, $2.50.

ROWE, L. S.—Problems of City Government. Appleton & Co., 1908, $1.50.

SHAW, ALBERT.—Municipal Government in Great Britain. MacMillan Co., $2.00.

TEN EYCK, JOHN.—Government for the People. Moffat Yard & Co., 1907, $.60.

WILCOX, D. F.—Great Cities in America. MacMillan & Co., 1910, $1.25.

WILCOX, D. F.—Study of City Government. MacMillan Co., $1.50.

WILSON, W.—Civic Problems. Civic League, 1909.

ZUEBLIN, CHAS.—A Decade of Civic Development. University of Chicago Press, 1905, $1.25.

Magazine Articles.

ALLEN, W. H.—How to Keep Government Efficient. World's Work, 14: 9255-9359, Aug., 1907.

CRANE, G.—A Cure for Municipal Bribery. Arena, 36: 289-292, Sept., 1906.

ELIOT, C. W.—Municipal Government. New England Magazine, 40: 393-397, Jan., 1909.

FLOWER, B. O.—Democracy and Municipal Government. Arena, 32: 377-391, Oct., 1904.

FORD, H. J.—Municipal Corruption. Political Science Quarterly, 19: 673-686, Dec., 1904.

FORD, H. J.—Cause of Political Corruption. Scribner's, Jan., 1911.

GARVIN, L. F. C.—Better City Government. Arena, 41: 38-41, Jan., 1909.

MACGREGOR, F. H.—City Government: Address before League of Wisconsin Municipalities. Municipality, Sept., 1909.

WOODRUFF, C. R.—Forces Moulding the City of the Future. Charities, 17: 235-237, Nov. 3, 1906.

II.

COMMISSION GOVERNMENT—GENERAL

[This bibliography contains such references as are likely to be available in well equipped public libraries. In addition to the sources mentioned here, is a great mass of newspaper comment, a reference to part of which may be found in Ford H. MacGregor's "City Government by Commission" (*infra*). A few of the cities furnish reports from time to time of the doings of the commissions and the general progress of the city. These may be had by writing to the mayors of the several cities, especially those of Berkeley, Cal., Houston, Texas, Des Moines, Ia., and Keokuk, Ia.

The National Short Ballot Organization keeps a close watch on the development of the movement and is glad to furnish special information at any time in so far as available. An up-to-date list of the cities adopting Commission government appears in the *Short Ballot Bulletin* as a regular feature. This may be had on application to the publishers.

Articles on Commission government will be found from time to time in the *American City*, the *National Municipal Review*, published by the National Municipal League; in the *Municipal Journal and Engineer* (New York) and in the *City Hall* (Des Moines).]

Books

The principal books on Commission Government are as follows:

"Dethronement of the City Boss."—John J. Hamilton. Funk & Wagnalls, 1910, $1.20. This was the first book on the subject and is an interesting account by a newspaper man, formerly a resident of Des Moines, who is thoroughly conversant at first hand with the practical aspects of his theme.

"Commission Government in American Cities."—Ernest S. Bradford. Macmillan & Co., 1911, $1.25. A careful, complete analysis of every phase of organization of Commission governed cities, with some attention to the practical workings of the plan in various cities.

"Government by Commission."—Edited by Clinton Rogers Woodruff, Secretary of the National Municipal League. Appleton & Co., 1911, $1.50. This contains a number of papers delivered from time to time before the annual conferences of the National Municipal League.

"Commission Government in American Cities."—Constitutes the November, 1911, issue of the Annals of the American Academy of Political and Social Science (Philadelphia). Treats the theoretical and practical phases of Commission government comprehensively. The several articles are written by experts in their particular fields.

"Commission Government."—Ford MacGregor, of the University of Wisconsin. University of Wisconsin Bulletins, No. 423 is a scholarly work by a western man. It contains an excellent bibliography up to the time of publication.

During the summer of 1912 the Bureau of Municipal Research (New York) will issue through Appleton & Co. "Progressive City Government." This will consist of a study and analysis of the administrative methods of ten commission cities, with constructive suggestions with reference to budget-making, accounting, purchasing, health work, public works and city planning, by Henry Bruere, Director, Bureau of Municipal Research. William Shepherdson, member of the staff of the Bureau of Municipal Research, collaborator in the collection and compilation of material. D. Appleton & Co., $1.50.

Magazine Articles and Pamphlets

ARNDT, W. T.—Municipal Government by Commission. *Nation*, 83: 322, Oct. 18, 1906.

BATES, F. G. (Comp.)—Commission Plan of City Government. Bulletin Extension Division, University of Kansas, March, 1910.

BEALE, J. H., JR.—City Government by Commission. Address before Economic Club of Boston, Jan. 21, 1908.

BERRYHILL, J. G.—Des Moines Plan of Municipal Government. Address before Iowa State Bar Association, July, 1908, at Waterloo.

BRADFORD, E. S.—Commission Plan: What it Means. *Citizens' Bulletin* (Cincinnati), 7: 1-2, July 3, 1909.

BRADFORD, E. S.—Comparison of the Forms of Commission Government to date. Read at Buffalo meeting of the National Municipal League, 1910.

CAMPBELL, R. A.—Des Moines Plan of Municipal Government. *American Political Science Review*, Aug., 1907.

——Des Moines Plan of Municipal Government. *Am. Pol. Sci. Rev.*, 2: 571-574.

CHEESEBOROUGH, E. R.—Commission Plan. *Citizens' Bulletin* (Cincinnati), April 18, 1908.

CHILDS, R. S.—Story of the Short Ballot Cities. The National Short Ballot Organization, New York, 1912.

CITY COUNCIL needed no less than a Mayor. Based on Prof. F. I. Herriott's Compilations. *Plain Talk* (Des Moines), Jan. 9, 1907.

CITY GOVERNMENT BY COMMISSION.—*Nation*, 92: 496-7, May 18, 1911.

COCHRANE, C. H.—Should New York be Governed by a Commission? *Broadway Magazine*, 17: 547-552, Feb., 1907. "How western municipalities handle the business of the people and what advantages this method would have for New York."

COMMISSION GOVERNMENT.—A Brief. *Dartmouth College Speaker*, Sept., 1908.

DALY, WM., JR.—Watch Commission Government Grow. *Everybody's*, 25: 548-50, Oct., 1911.

DEHONEY, C.—Breaking Down Ward Lines in Cities. *World To-day*, 18: 487-490, May, 1910.

DES MOINES PLAN.—Affirmative, H. E. Sampson; Negative, W. W. Wise. *Midwestern* (Des Moines), June, 1909.

DES MOINES PLAN, followed by questions and answers. *City Hall* (Des Moines), 10: 357-359, April, 1909.

DILLON, SIDNEY J.—City Government by Commission. Address before Economic Club of Boston, Jan. 21, 1908.

DORBY, R. C.—Danger of Electing Wrong Men. *City Hall*, 10: 405, June, 1909. Answer by Commissioner MacVicar.

DURAND, E. D.—Council Government vs. Mayor Government. *Political Science Quarterly*, 15: 426-451, 675-709, Sept., Oct., 1900.

ELIOT, CHAS. W.—City Government by Commission. Address before Economic Club of Boston, Jan. 11, 1907.

——City Government by Fewer Men. *World's Work*, 14: 9419-9426, Oct., 1907.

——Municipal Government. *New England Magazine*, n. s. 70: 393-397, June, 1909.

——Municipal Government by Commission. *South Atlantic Quarterly*, 8: 174-183, April, 1909.

EXPERTS DISCUSS DES MOINES PLAN.—*City Hall*, 10: 408-413, June, 1909.

FULLER, O. M.—Municipal Government by Commission. Address before Chamber of Commerce of Erie, Pa., April 15, 1909.

GILBERTSON, H. S.—Short Ballot in American Cities. *Review of Reviews*, Jan., 1912.

GEMUENDER, MARTIN A.—Commission Government. *National Municipal Review*, April, 1912.

GROWTH OF COMMISSION GOVERNMENT.—*World's Work*, 23: 262-3, Jan., 1912.

GROWTH OF GOVERNMENT BY COMMISSION.—*Ind.*, 71: 1221-2, Nov. 30, 1911.

HASKEL, H. J.—Texas Idea. *Outlook*, 85: 834-835, April 13, 1907.

HEAD, JAMES M.—City Government by Commission. Address before Economic Club of Boston, Jan. 11, 1907.

HERRIOTT, F. I.—Defects of Commission Plan. Delivered before Prairie Club, Des Moines, Jan. 12, 1907.

HUSTON, CHAS. D. (Commission of Cedar Rapids).—Municipal Government. *City Hall* (Des Moines), 10: 252-257, Jan., 1909.

ILLINOIS SENATE. Commission Government of Galveston, Houston and Dallas. Report made to the Senate of Illinois by the special sub-committee appointed to investigate. Address Secretary of State, Springfield, Ill.

IOWA, UNIVERSITY OF.—Commission Plan. Address before the Forensic League, $1.00.

IVINS, WM. M.—City Government by Commission. An Address by Chairman of Committee on the Revised Charter of New York before Economic Club of Boston, Jan. 21, 1908.

MACFARLAND, H. B. F.—Address on the Commission Form of Government. Published by Board of Commissioners, Washington.

MACVICAR, JOHN (Commission of Des Moines).—City Government by Commission. *City Hall* (Des Moines), 10: 316-319, March, 1909.

MOORHEAD, F. G.—Bringing Dead Cities to Life. *Technical World,* 12: 621-628, Feb., 1910.

MOWRY, DON E.—Governing Cities by Commission. *La Follette's Weekly Magazine,* 1: 7, March 27, 1909.

MUNICIPAL GOVERNMENT BY COMMISSION.—*Broadway Magazine,* 17: 547-552, Feb., 1907.

MUNRO, W. B.—Galveston Plan. *Chautauquan,* 51: 110-124, June, 1908.

MUNRO, W. B.—Galveston Plan. Proceedings of Providence Conference for Good City Government, 1907. (*Address before the National Municipal League, Philadelphia.*)

NATIONAL VIEW OF DES MOINES PLAN.—*City Hall* (Des Moines), May, 1909.

ORGANIZED LABOR OPPOSES COMMISSION PLAN.—*Iowa Unionist* (Des Moines), April 12, 1907.

PEARSON, P. M., *ed.*—Intercollegiate debates, being briefs and reports of many intercollegiate debates. New York: Hinds, Noble & Eldredge, 1909, pp. 507. "The Commission System of Municipal Government" (with bibliographical references), pp. 461-477.

PEORIA.—City Government by Commission. Report of a Committee of the Commercial Club of Peoria, Ill., on Commission Government as operated in Des Moines. *The Municipal Economist,* 1909.

RECENT DEVELOPMENTS IN COMMISSION GOVERNMENT.—*Outlook,* 97: 710, April 1, 1911.

REMAKING OF CITY GOVERNMENT.—*Nation,* 93: 594-5, Dec. 21, 1911.

REVOLUTIONARY MOVEMENT IN CITY GOVERNMENT.—*New England Magazine,* n. s. 45: 253-7, Nov., 1911.

RUSSELL, CHARLES E.—Sanity and Democracy in American Cities. *Everybody's,* 22: 435-447.

RYAN, OSWALD.—The Commission Plan of City Government. *American Pol. Sci. Rev.,* Feb., 1911.

SAMPSON, H E.—Des Moines Plan of City Government. *Century,* 74: 970, Oct., 1907.

SHAMBAUGH, B. F.—Des Moines Plan of City Government. American Political Science Association Proceedings, 4: 189-192, 1907.

SIX MONTHS OF GOVERNMENT BY COMMISSION.—*Midland Municipalities,* 16: 77-83, Dec., 1908.

SLOSSON, W. B.—Government by Commission in Texas. *Independent,* 63: 195-200, July 25, 1907.

THREE GREAT EXPERIMENTS.—*Independent,* 64: 1409-1410, June 18, 1908.

TOPEKA CITY CLUB.—City Commission Charter—a Representative City Government.

TURNER, GEO. KIBBE.—City Government by Commission. Address before Economic Club of Boston, Jan. 11, 1907.

——New American City Government. *McClure's,* 35: 97-108, March, 1910.

UNGUARDED COMMISSION GOVERNMENT.—*Arena,* 38: 431-432, Oct., 1907.

WHITLOCK, BRAND.—Spread of Galveston Plan. *Circle,* 2: 289-290, Nov., 1907.

WILLIAMS, C. ARTHUR.—Government of Municipalities by Board of Commissioners. *Gunton's Magazine,* 27: 559-570, Dec., 1904.

WISE, W. W.—Des Moines Plan. *Midwestern* (Des Moines), 3: 35-36, June, 1909.

WOODRUFF, C. R.—Forces Moulding the City of the Future. *Charities,* 17: 235-237, Nov. 3, 1906.

——Simplified City Government. *Yale Review,* n. s. 1: 206-20, Jan., 1912.

Negative References

BEALE, J. H., JR.—City Government by Commission. Economic Club of Boston, Jan. 21, 1908.

CARPENTER, D. F.—Some Defects of Commission Government. *Ann. of Amer. Acad.*, Nov., 1911, p. 192.

CHADWICK, F. E. (REAR AD.).—Newport R. I.) Charter. Amer. Pol. Science Assn. Proceedings, 1906, 3: 58-66.

CHADWICK, F. E. (J. M. HEAD AND OTHERS).—Municipal Government by Board (or Commission) vs. Mayor and Council. Bulletin, League of American Municipalities, 8: 108-121, Oct., 1907.

CHADWICK, F. E.—Newport Plan. Proceedings of the Providence Conference for Good City Government, 1907, pp. 166-77. (National Mun. League.)

* CITY HALL.—Municipal Government by Commission. 10: 258-61, Jan., 1909.

——Experts Discuss Des Moines Plan. 10: 408-13.

——Summary of an Article by Miss Agnes Thurman. 11: 251-252, Feb., 1910.

COOPER, W. G.—Objections to Commission Government. *Ann. of Amer. Acad.*, Nov., 1911, p. 183.

GARVIN, LUCIUS F. C.—Better City Government. *Arena*, 41: 38-41, Jan., 1909.

GEMUENDER, M. A.—Commission Government. *National Municipal Review*, April, 1912.

HERRIOTT, F. I.—Defects of Commission Plan. Prairie Club, Des Moines, Jan. 12, 1907.

IOWA UNIONIST (Des Moines).—Organized Labor Opposes Commission Plan. April 12, 1907.

IVINS, W. H.—Address before Economic Club of Boston.

PETERSON, SAMUEL.—Some Fundamental Principles Applied to Municipal Government. Bulletin of the University of Texas, June 1, 1905.

PLAIN TALK (Des Moines).—Jan. 9, 1907. City Council Needed no less than Mayor.

——Jan. 16, 1907. Some Facts and Figures.—W. N. Jordan.

——Jan. 19, 1907. Municipal Reforms Needed.

——Jan. 26, 1907. Galveston Plan Hostile to Business Efficiency.—F. I. Herriott.

——Feb. 2, 1907 Dominant Mayor Essential in Good City Government.

——Feb. 16, 1907. Commission System and Non-Partisan Government.

SIKES, GEO. C.—How Chicago is Winning Good Government. Proceedings of the Providence Conference for Good City Government, 1907. (National Mun. League.)

STARZINGER, VINCENT.—Superior Legislation. Commission: Not a Superior Legislative Body. City: Not a Business Corporation. (Published in H. W. Wilson's Handbook Series, Commission Plan of Municipal Government.)

WISE, W. W.—Des Moines Plan. *Midwestern* (Des Moines), 3. 35-6, June, 1909.

WEBSTER, W. A.—Problem of City Government. (Address 6 Beacon Street, Boston, Mass.)

---

*Organ of the League of American Municipalities.

III.

GOVERNMENT OF INDIVIDUAL CITIES.

NOTE: References to "*Digest*" are to the section of this book entitled "Reports from Short Ballot Cities." References to *Ann. Am. Acad.*, unless otherwise stated, are to the Nov., 1912, issue.

ALABAMA

Birmingham

BIRMINGHAM UNDER THE COMMISSION PLAN.—Hon. Walker Percy. *Annals of American Academy of Political and Social Science*, Nov., 1911, p. 259.

CALIFORNIA

Berkelely

MODEL MUNICIPAL CHARTER.—W. C. Jones. *Ind.*, 71: 575-8, Sept., 1911.

BERKELEY, CALIFORNIA, UNDER COMMISSION FORM OF GOVERNMENT.—W. C. Jones. *Ann. Am. Acad.*, Nov., 1911, p. 265.
Digest, pp. 78001-03.

San Diego

WHAT HAS BEEN ACCOMPLISHED IN 100 DAYS UNDER COMMISSION GOVERNMENT.—By Grant Conard (Mayor). *City Hall*, 11: 91-93, Sept., 1909.

COLORADO

Colorado Springs

GOVERNMENT BY COMMISSION IN COLORADO SPRINGS.—*Survey*, 23: 502-504, Jan. 6, 1910.

DEFECTS OF COMMISSION GOVERNMENT.—Dunbar F. Carpenter. *Ann. Am. Acad.*, 192.
Digest, pp. 77001-04.

IOWA

Cedar Rapids.

PROCEEDINGS OF THE CITY COUNCIL OF CEDAR RAPIDS UNDER THE COMMISSION PLAN OF GOVERNMENT.—1908-1909. *Cedar Rapids Monthly.*

Des Moines

WHAT GOVERNMENT BY COMMISSION HAS ACCOMPLISHED IN DES MOINES.—J. J. Hamilton. *Ann. of American Academy of Social and Political Science*, Nov., 1911, p. 238.
Digest, pp. 74301-303.

SOLVING MUNICIPAL PROBLEMS IN DES MOINES.—Neal Jones. *Circle*, July, 1909.

EIGHTEEN MONTHS' TRIAL OF THE DES MOINES PLAN.—A. J. Mathis. Oct. 25 (1909), *City Hall*, 11: 166-173, Nov., 1909.

THE DES MOINES PLAN OF CITY GOVERNMENT.—Annual Report of the City of Des Moines, Des Moines, 1909. 1908-1909, pp. 11-23.

COMMISSION PLAN.—*Cur. Lit.*, 50: 477-8, May, 1911.

ORIGINATOR OF THE DES MOINES PLAN.—*Hampton's*, 26: 248-50. Feb., 1911.

RECENT DEVELOPMENTS IN COMMISSION GOVERNMENT.—*Outlook*, 97: 710, April 1, 1911.

KANSAS

Abilene

Digest, p. 74520.

Chanute

Digest, p. 74523.

Emporia

RESULTS OF COMMISSION GOVERNMENT IN EMPORIA.—*Ann. Am. Acad.*, pp. 252 *et seq.*
Digest, p. 74521.

Iola

Digest, pp. 74520-21.

Kansas City

RESULTS OF COMMISSION GOVERNMENT IN KANSAS CITY, KANS.—*Ann. Am. Acad.*, p. 247.
Digest, pp. 74513-18.

Leavenworth

Digest, pp. 74504-06.

Newton

Digest, p. 74522.

Parsons

Digest, p. 74519.

Pittsburg

Digest, p. 74519.

Pratt

Digest, p. 74522.

Topeka

Digest, pp. 74501-04.

Wichita

Digest, pp. 74507-11.

MASSACHUSETTS

Haverhill

EXAMPLE OF HAVERHILL.—DeMont Goodyear. *Ind.*, 66: 194-195, Jan. 28, 1909.

Digest, pp. 71001-03.

Lynn

Digest, p. 71005.

NORTH DAKOTA

Minot

COMMISSION GOVERNMENT IN THE WEST.—*Ann. Amer. Acad.*, p. 66.

NEW JERSEY

THE COMMISSION STATUTE OF NEW JERSEY.—John M. Mathews, *Ann. Amer. Acad.*, p. 103.

ADOPTIONS AND REJECTIONS UNDER THE COMMISSION STATUTE OF NEW JERSEY.—J. A. Dear. *Ann. Amer. Acad.*, p. 108.

SOUTH DAKOTA

Huron

Digest, p. 75501.

Rapid City

Digest, p. 75502.

Sioux Falls

Digest, p. 75501.

TEXAS

Austin

THE COMMISSION AS IT OPERATES IN AUSTIN, TEXAS.—A. P. Wooldridge. *Ann. Amer. Acad.*, p. 236, Nov., 1911.

Dallas

Digest, pp. 76021-26.

Galveston

GALVESTON'S COMMISSION PLAN OF CITY GOVERNMENT.—E. R. Cheeseborough. *Ann. Amer. Acad.*, Nov., 1911, p. 221.

Digest, pp. 76001-03.

A BUSINESS CORPORATION.—G. K. Turner. *McClure's*, 27: 610-620, Oct., 1906.

NEW GALVESTON.—C. A. Williams. *World To-day*, 7: 1462, Nov., 1909.

NEW GALVESTON.—W. B. Slosson. *Ind.*, 56: 1382, Jan. 16, 1904.

GALVESTON'S PLAN OF GOVERNMENT.—E. C. Barker. *Nation*, 93: 163, Aug. 24, 1911.

Houston

RESULTS IN COMMISSION GOVERNMENT IN HOUSTON, TEXAS.—J. H. Farbar. *Ann. Amer. Acad.*, Nov., 1911, p. 231.

Digest, pp. 76011-18.

COMMISSION GOVERNMENT.—E. C. Rice. Brief Synopsis of the Commission Plan of City Government. *Municipal Journal and Engineer*, 28: 118-119, Jan. 26, 1910.

ANNUAL MESSAGE OF MAYOR AND ANNUAL REPORTS OF THE OFFICIALS, 1905-1906 TO DATE.

HOUSTON AND ITS CITY COMMISSION.—G. W. James. *Arena*, 38: 144-149, Aug., 1907.

COMMISSION GOVERNMENT IN HOUSTON.—E. S. Bradford. *Municipal Journal and Engineer*, 25: 174-175, Aug. 5, 1908.

CONCENTRATION OF POWER IN THE HANDS OF THE MAYOR AT HOUSTON.—*Outlook*, 82: 5, Jan. 6, 1906.

WASHINGTON

Spokane

SPOKANE'S NEW CHARTER.—*Amer. City*, pp. 259-63, Nov., 1911.

Digest, p. 78307.

Tacoma

Digest, pp. 78301-05.

WEST VIRGINIA

Huntington

RESULTS OF COMMISSION GOVERNMENT IN HUNTINGTON, W. Va.—G. I. Neal. *Ann. Amer. Acad.*, Nov., 1911, p. 255.

WISCONSIN

COMMISSION GOVERNMENT IN THE WEST.—F. H. MacGregor. *Ann. Amer. Acad.*, Nov., 1911, p. 61.

IV.

SPECIAL PHASES OF CITY GOVERNMENT.

Civil Service, Public Utilities, School Boards, Short Ballot, Initiative, Referendum, and Recall, Municipal Accounting.

CLEVELAND, F. A.—Chapters on Municipal Administration and Accounting. Longmans, Green & Co., 1909, $2.00.

EWART, J. A., et al.—Civil Service Manual. Home Correspondence School, 1908, $2.50.

FLEMING, W. H.—Civil Service, Tariff, and other speeches. Caldwell, 1909, $2.50.

BEARD, C. A.—The Ballot's Burden. Political Science Quarterly, 24: 589-614, Dec., 1909.

BRANNAN, R. O.—Control of Public Utilities by States. City Hall, 10: 273, Jan., 1909.

BRIDGMAN, R. L.—Civic Righteousness via Percentages. Atlantic, 102: 797-802, Dec., 1908.

CAMPBELL, H. M.—Representative Government vs. Initiative and Primary Nominations. North American Review, 190, 222-230, Aug., 1909.

CHILDS, R. S.—A Real Democracy.

——The Short Ballot.

——Politics without Politicians.

——Story of the Short Ballot Cities.

(Mr. Childs' pamphlets are obtaininble on request, of The Short Ballot Organization, 381 Fourth Ave., New York City.)

COMMONS, J. R.—Referendum and Initiative in City Government. Political Science Quarterly, 17: 609-630, Dec., 1902.

DIRECT LEGISLATION through Initiative and Referendum. Arena, 37: 672-630, June, 1907.

HARRIS, S. H.—The Will of the People. Westminster, 168: 675-690, Dec., 1907.

HORN, P. W.—City Schools under Commission Government. Educational Review, 37: 362-374, April, 1909.

MEYERS, B. H.—Public Utilities Control in Wisconsin. Citizens' Bulletin, 4: 1, Dec., 1908.

MOWRY, D. E.—Saving the City's Money. World Today, 17: 1215-1216, Nov., 1909.

THE REFERENDUM, Victory in Municipal Government. Arena, 33: 549-550, May, 1905.

REFORMING MUNICIPAL ACCOUNTING.—Nation, 80: 86-87, Feb. 2, 1905.

REVISING CHICAGO'S CIVIL SERVICE SYSTEM.—Charities, 21: 775-775, Feb. 8, 1909.

THATCHER, G. A.—Initiative and Referendum. Independent, 64: 1191-1195, May 28, 1908.

UNRECOGNIZED REFERENDUM.—Nation, 83: 550-551, Dec. 27, 1906.

WHAT ARE MUNICIPAL BONDS?—Independent, 65: 59, July 2, 1908.

V.

GENERAL AND MISCELLANEOUS.

FAIRLIE, J. A.—Local Government in Counties, Towns, and Cities. Century Co., 1906, $1.25.

SHAFFNER, M. A.—Municipal Home Rule Charters. Madison, Wisconsin: Free Library Commission, 1909, 25 cents.

LOWELL, A. L.—Permanent Officials in City Government. National Conference for City Government, 1908: 215-222.

PETERSON, SAMUEL.—Some Fundamental Political Principles Applied to Municipal Government. Bulletin of the University of Texas, June 1, 1905.

WHEN PUBLICITY Plays Detective on Municipal Accounting. Review of Reviews, 39: 94-95, Jan., 1909.

WOODRUFF, C. R.—Charter Making in America. Atlantic. 103: 628-639, May, 1909.

BIBLIOGRAPHY

Magazine Articles

AMERICAN CITY—"The Lockport Proposal;" A city that wants to improve commission government (June, 1911). "How a Little City is Progressing under a City Commissioner" (July, 1913).

ANNALS OF THE AMERICAN ACADEMY OF POLITICAL AND SOCIAL SCIENCE—The Lockport Proposal, by F. D. Silvernail (November, 1911).

CALIFORNIA OUTLOOK—"The Commission Form and the City Manager Plan," by E. M. Wilder, Commissioner, Sacramento, Calif. (Oct. 25, 1913).

COLLIER'S WEEKLY—"Showing the Job-Holder to the Door" (May 17, 1913).

ENGINEERING NEWS—"The City Manager Plan" (May 13, 1913).

LITERARY DIGEST—"Dayton's Unique Charter" (August 30, 1913).

THE MUNICIPAL JOURNAL AND ENGINEER—"Dayton's New Government" (August 21, 1913). "Springfield's New Government" (September 18, 1913).

NATIONAL MUNICIPAL REVIEW—"The Theory of the New Controlled Executive Plan," by Richard S. Childs (January, 1913). "The City Manager Plan," by L. D. Upson (October, 1913). "The Vital Points in Charter Making from a Socialist Point of View," by Carl D. Thompson (July, 1913). "The Coming of the City Manager Plan," by Richard S. Childs, the report of the Committee of the National Municipal League on Commission Government (January, 1914). [The *Review* contains each month a department entitled "Notes and Events," under which all the new developments in city charter-making are recorded.]

THE OUTLOOK—"The Practical Short Ballot" (May 10, 1913). "The City Manager Plan" (August 23, 1913).

THE PUBLIC—"The Municipal Business Manager" (June 27, 1913).

REVIEW OF REVIEWS—"Public Administration: A New Profession," by H. S. Gilbertson (May, 1913).

THE SHORT BALLOT BULLETIN—[The bi-monthly organ of The National Short Ballot Organization notes the progress of the City Manager plan in each issue.]

TOWN DEVELOPMENT—"The Sumter City Manager Plan" (June, 1913). "The Commission-Manager Plan in Dayton" (July, 1913).

WORLD'S WORK—"Progress of Simplified Municipal Government" (June, 1913).

(*Appendix*)

Miscellaneous Documents

CHARTER OF BOSTON, MASS.

AN ACT RELATING TO THE ADMINISTRATION OF THE CITY OF BOSTON AND TO AMEND THE CHARTER OF SAID CITY.

[CHAPTER 486, LAWS OF 1909.]

Section 1.

[Relates to terms of office of mayor, etc., under old laws.]

Sec. 2.

The mayor from time to time may make to the city council in the form of an ordinance or loan order filed with the city clerk such recommendations other than for school purposes as he may deem to be for the welfare of the city. The city council shall consider each ordinance or loan order presented by the mayor and shall either adopt or reject the same within sixty days after the date when it is filed as aforesaid. If the said ordinance or loan order is not rejected within said sixty days it shall be in force as if adopted by the city council unless previously withdrawn by the mayor. Nothing herein shall prevent the mayor from again presenting an ordinance or loan order which has been rejected or withdrawn. The city council may originate an ordinance or loan order and may reduce or reject any item in any loan and, subject to the approval of the mayor, may amend an ordinance. All sales of land other than school lands, all appropriations for the purchase of land other than for school purposes, and all loans voted by the city council shall require a vote of two-thirds of all the members of the city council; and shall be passed only after two separate readings and by two separate votes, the second of said readings and votes to be had not less than fourteen days after the first. No amendment increasing the amount of land to be sold or the amount to be paid for the purchase of land, or the amount of loans, or altering the disposition of purchase money or of the proceeds of loans shall be made at the time of the second reading and vote.

Sec. 3.

All appropriations, other than for school purposes, to be met from taxes, revenue, or any source other than loans, shall originate with the mayor, who within thirty days after the beginning of the fiscal year shall submit to the city council the annual budget of the current expenses of the city and county, and may submit thereafter supplementary budgets until such time as the tax rate for the year shall have been fixed. The city council may reduce or reject any item, but without the approval of the mayor shall not increase any item in, nor the total of a budget, nor add any item thereto, nor shall it originate a budget. It shall be the duty of the city and county officials, when requested by the mayor, to submit forthwith in such detail as he may require estimates for the next fiscal year of the expenditures of the department or office under their charge, which estimates shall be transmitted to the city council.

The city auditor may, with the approval in each instance of the mayor, at any time make transfers from the appropriation for current expenses of one division of a department to the appropriation for current expenses of any other division of the same department, and from the reserve fund to any appropriation for the current expenses of a department; and may also, with the approval of the mayor, at any time between December first and February first, make transfers from any appropriation to any other appropriation, provided, however, that no money raised by loan shall be transferred to any appropriation from income or taxes. He may also with such approval apply any of the income and taxes not disposed of in closing the accounts for the financial year in such manner as he may determine.

Sec. 4.

Every appropriation, ordinance, order, resolution and vote of the city council, except votes relating to its own internal affairs, shall be presented to the mayor, who shall make or cause to be made a written record of the time and place of presentation, and it shall be in force if he approves the same within fifteen days after it shall have been presented to him, or if the same is not returned by him with his objections thereto in writing within said period of fifteen days. If within said period said appropriation, ordinance, order, resolution, or vote is returned by the mayor to the city council by filing the same with the city clerk with his objections thereto the same shall be void. If the same involves the expenditure of money, the mayor may approve some of the items in whole or in part and disapprove other of the items in whole or in part; and such items or parts of items as he approves shall be in force, and such items or parts of items as he disapproves shall be void.

Sec. 5.

Except as otherwise provided in this act, the organization, powers, and duties of the executive departments of the city shall remain as constituted at the time when this section takes effect; but the mayor and city council at any time may by ordinance reorganize, consolidate, or abolish departments in whole or in part; transfer the duties, powers, and appropriations of one department to another in whole or in part; and establish new departments; and may increase, reduce, establish or abolish salaries of heads of departments, or members of boards. Nothing in this act shall authorize the abolition or the taking away of any of the powers or duties as established by law of the assessing department, building department, board of appeal, children's institutions department, election department, fire department, Franklin Foundation, hospital department, library department, overseers of the poor, schoolhouse department, school committee, or any department in charge of an official or officials appointed by the governor, nor the abolition of the health department.

Sec. 6.

No contract for lighting the public streets, parks, or alleys, or for the collection, removal, or disposal of refuse, extending over a period of more than one year from the date thereof, shall be valid without the approval of the mayor and the city council after a public hearing held by the city council, of which at least seven days' notice shall have been given in the City Record.

Sec. 7.

The city council at any time may request from the mayor specific information on any municipal matter within its jurisdiction, and may request his presence to answer written questions relating thereto at a meeting to be held not earlier than one week from the date of the receipt of said questions, in which case the mayor shall personally, or through a head of a department or a member of a board, attend such meeting and publicly answer all such questions. The person so attending shall not be obliged to answer questions relating to any other matter. The mayor at any time may attend and address the city council in person or through the head of a department, or a member of a board, upon such subject as he may desire.

Sec. 8.

[No officer of the city may be interested in contracts to which the city is a party, etc.]

THE EXECUTIVE DEPARTMENT.

Sec. 9.

All heads of departments and members of municipal boards, including the board of street commissioners, as their present terms of office expire (but excluding the school committee and those officials by law appointed by the governor), shall be appointed by the mayor without confirmation by the city council. They shall be recognized experts in such work as may devolve upon the incumbents of said offices, or persons specially fitted by education, training or experience to perform the same, and (except the election commissioners, who shall remain subject to the provisions of existing laws) shall be appointed without regard to party affiliation or to residence at the time of appointment except as hereinafter provided.

Sec. 10.

In making such appointments the mayor shall sign a certificate in the following form:

CERTIFICATE OF APPOINTMENT.

I appoint (Name of Appointee) to the position of (Name of Office) and I certify that in my opinion he is a recognized expert in the work which will devolve upon him, and that I make the appointment solely in the interest of the city.

——————— Mayor.

Or in the following form, as the case may be:

CERTIFICATE OF APPOINTMENT.

I appoint (Name of Appointee) to the position of (Name of Office) and I certify that in my opinion he is a person specially fitted by education, training, or experience to perform the duties of said office, and that I make the appintment solely in the interest of the city.

——————— Mayor.

The certificate shall be filed with the city clerk, who shall thereupon forward a certified copy to the civil service commission. The commission shall immediately make a careful inquiry into the qualifications of the nominee under such rules as they may, with the consent of the governor and council, establish, and, if they conclude that he is a competent person with the requisite qualifications, they shall file with the city clerk a certificate signed by at least a majority of the commission that they have made a careful inquiry into the qualifications of the appointee, and that in their opinion he is a recognized expert, or that he is qualified by education, training or experience for said office, as the case may be, and that they approve the appointment. Upon the filing of this certificate the appointment shall become operative, subject however to all provisions of law or ordinance in regard to acceptance of office, oath of office, and the filing of bonds. If the commission does not within thirty days after the receipt of such notice file said certificate with the city clerk the appointment shall be void.

Sec. 11.

[Expenses of civil service commission to be paid by commonwealth, which shall be reimbursed by city.]

Sec. 12.

A vacancy in any office to which the provisions of section nine of this act apply shall be filled by the mayor under the provisions of said section and pending a permanent appointment he shall designate some other head of a department or member of a board to discharge the duties of the office temporarily.

Sec. 13.

Members of boards shall be appointed for the terms established by law or by ordinance. Heads of departments shall be appointed for terms of four years beginning with the first day of May of the year in which they are appointed and shall continue thereafter to hold office during the pleasure of the mayor.

Sec. 14.

The mayor may remove any head of a department or member of a board (other than the election commissioners, who shall remain subject to the provisions of existing laws) by filing a written statement with the city clerk setting forth in detail the specific reasons for such removal, a copy of which shall be delivered or mailed to the person thus removed, who may make a reply in writing, which, if he desires, may be filed with the city clerk; but such reply shall not affect the action taken unless the mayor so determines. The provisions of this section shall not apply to the school committee or to any official by law appointed by the governor.

Sec. 15.

The positions of assistants and secretary authorized by section twenty of chapter four hundred and forty-nine of the acts of the year eighteen hundred and ninety-five, except those in the election department, are hereby abolished, and except as aforesaid the said section is hereby repealed.

The civil service laws shall not apply to the appointment of the mayor's secretaries, nor of the stenographers, clerks, telephone operators and messengers connected with his office, and the mayor may remove such appointees without a hearing and without making a statement of the cause for their removal.

Sec. 16.

[No official to expend sums in excess of appropriations.]

THE FINANCE COMMISSION.

Sec. 17.

Within sixty days after the passage of this act the governor with the advice and consent of the council shall appoint a finance commission to consist of five persons, inhabitants of and qualified voters in the city of Boston, who shall have been such for at least three years prior to the date of their appointment, one for the term of five years, one for four years, one for three years, one for two years, and one for one year, and thereafter as the terms of office expire in each year one member for a term of five years. Vacancies in the commission shall be filled for the unexpired term by the governor with the advice and consent of the council. The members of said commission may be removed by the governor with the advice and consent of the council for such cause as he shall deem sufficient. The chairman shall be designated by the governor. His annual salary shall be five thousand dollars, which shall be paid in monthly instalments by the city of Boston. The other members shall serve without pay.

Sec. 18.

It shall be the duty of the finance commission from time to time to investigate any and all matters relating to appropriations, loans, expenditures, accounts, and methods of administration affecting the city of Boston or the county of Suffolk, or any department thereof, that may appear to the commission to require investigation, and to report thereon from time to time to the mayor, the city council, the governor, or the general court. The commission shall make an annual report in January of each year to the general court.

Sec. 19.

Whenever any pay roll, bill, or other claim against the city is presented to the mayor, city auditor, or the city treasurer, he shall, if the same seems to him to be of doubtful validity, excessive in amount, or otherwise contrary to the city's interest, refer it to the finance commission, which shall immediately investigate the facts and report thereon; and pending said report payment shall be withheld.

Sec. 20.

[The commission authorized to employ experts, etc., and to incur certain expenses.]

Sec. 21.

[Reference to the full statement of power granted to commission in Chapter 562, Laws of 1908.]

Sec. 22.

[Powers and duties of city clerk defined.]

Sec. 23.

[Powers and duties of city auditor defined.]

Sec. 24.

[Relates to manner of letting contracts.]

Sec. 25.

[Certain duties of an auditor defined.]

Sec. 26.

[Relating to manner of issuing loans.]

Sec. 27.

[Heads of departments to furnish lists of employees to auditor.]

Sec. 28.

The jurisdiction now exercised by the board of aldermen concerning the naming of streets, the planting and removal of trees in the public ways, the issue of permits or licenses for coasting, the storage of gasoline, oil, and other inflammable substances or explosive compounds, and the use of the public ways for any permanent or temporary obstruction or projection in, under, or over the same, including the location of conduits, poles and posts for telephone, telegraph, street railway, or illuminating purposes, is hereby vested in the board of street commissioners, to be exercised by said board with the approval in writing of the mayor; and the mayor and city council shall have authority to fix by ordinance the terms by way of cash payment, rent, or otherwise, upon which permits or licenses for the storage of gasoline or oil, or other inflammable substances or explosive.

Sec. 29.

[Provision for publication of "City Record."]

Sec. 30.

Every officer or board in charge of a department in said city, when authorized to erect a new building or to make structural changes in an existing building, shall make contracts therefor, not exceeding five, each contract to be subject to the approval of the mayor; and when about to do any work or to make any purchase, the estimated cost of which alone, or in conjunction with other similar work or purchase which might properly be included in the same contract, amounts to or exceeds one thousand dollars, shall, unless the mayor gives written authority to do otherwise, invite proposals therfor by advertisement in the City Record. Such advertisement shall state the time and place for opening the proposals in answer to said advertisement, and shall reserve the right to the officer or board to reject any or all proposals. No authority to dispense with advertising shall be given by the mayor unless the said officer or board furnishes him with a signed statement which shall be published in the City Record giving in detail the reasons for not inviting bids by advertisement.

Sec. 31.

[Relates to condemnation of land.]

Sec. 32.

[Time of first municipal election.]

Sec. 33.

[The fiscal year.]

Sec. 34.

In Boston beginning with the current year political committees shall be elected at the state primaries instead of at the municipal primaries.

CHARTER AMENDMENTS.

Sec. 35.

At the state election on November second, nineteen hundred and nine, the then registered male voters of the city of Boston shall be entitled to vote upon the following plans, which shall be printed upon the official ballot in the following form. The voter shall make a cross in the space at the right of the plan which he desires to have adopted. No ballot shall be counted upon which the voter has made a cross in both spaces.

Plan No. 1. The term of mayor to be two years; the city council to consist of one member from each ward (except wards twenty and twenty-four, which shall have two each) nominated in primaries and elected for two-year terms, and nine members elected at large for three-year terms; nominations for school committee, mayor, and councilmen-at-large to be made by independent nominations and by delegates elected by the voters in the primaries.

Plan No. 2. The term of mayor to be four years, subject to recall after two years by not less than a majority of all the voters in the city; the city council to consist of nine members elected at large for three-year terms; all nominations for a municipal election to be made by petition of not less than five thousand voters, without party designations on the ballot.

Sec. 36.

If a majority of the votes cast under the provisions of section thirty-five of this act are in favor of the first plan, then sections thirty-seven to forty-three of this act, both inclusive, shall take effect and sections forty-five to sixty-one, both inclusive, shall be inoperative.

THE MAYOR.

Sec. 37-43.

[Details Plan No. 1, which was rejected at the subsequent charter election.]

ALTERNATIVE CHARTER AMENDMENTS.

The remaining sections of the act were accepted by the voters.

Sec. 44.

If a majority of the votes cast under the provisions of section thirty-five of this act are in favor of the second or alternative plan, then sections forty-five to sixty-one of this act, both inclusive, shall take effect and sections thirty-seven to forty-three, both inclusive, shall be inoperative.

THE MAYOR.

Sec. 45.

The mayor of the city of Boston shall be elected at large to hold office for the term of four years from the first Monday in February following his election and until his successor is chosen and qualified, except as hereinafter provided.

Sec. 46.

The secretary of the commonwealth (unless notified as hereinafter provided) shall cause to be printed at the end of the official ballot to be used in the city of Boston at the state election in the second year of the mayor's term the following question: Shall there be an election for mayor at the next municipal election? with the words Yes and No at the right of the question and sufficient squares in which each voter may designate by a cross his answer to such question. If a majority of the qualified voters registered in said city for said state election shall vote in the affirmative on said question, there shall be an election for mayor in said city at the municipal election held in January next following said state election, and the same shall be conducted, and the result thereof declared in all respects as are other city elections for mayor, except that the board of election commissioners shall place on the official ballot for said election without nomination the name of the person then holding the office of mayor (other than an acting mayor), unless in writing he shall request otherwise. The mayor then elected shall hold office for four years, subject to recall at the end of two years as provided in this section. If said question is not answered in the affirmative by the vote aforesaid no election for mayor shall be held and the mayor shall continue to hold office for his unexpired term. If prior to October first in the said second year of his term, the mayor shall file with the secretary of the commonwealth a written notice that he does not desire said question to appear upon the ballot at said state election it shall be omitted; his term of office shall expire on the first Monday of February following; and there shall be an election for mayor in said city at the municipal election held in January next following said state election, and at such municipal election the mayor's name shall not be placed on the official ballot unless he is nominated in the manner provided in section fifty-three of this act.

Sec. 47.

If a vacancy occurs in the office of mayor within two months prior to a regular municipal election other than an election for mayor, or within four months after any regular municipal election, the city council shall forthwith order a special election for a mayor to serve for the unexpired term, subject if the vacancy occurs in the first or second year of the mayor's term to recall under the provisions of the preceding section. If such vacancy occurs at any other time there shall be an election for mayor at the municipal election held in January next following, for the term of four years, subject to recall as aforesaid. In the case of the decease, inability, absence or resignation of the mayor, and whenever there is a vacancy in the office from any cause, the president of the city council while said cause continues or until a mayor is elected shall perform the duties of mayor. If he is also absent or unable from any cause to perform such duties they shall be performed until the mayor or president of the city countil returns or is able to attend to said duties by such member of the city council as that body may elect, and until such election by the city clerk. The person upon whom such duties shall devolve shall be called "acting mayor" and he shall possess the powers of mayor only in matters not admitting of delay, but shall have no power to make permanent appointments except on the decease of the mayor.

THE CITY COUNCIL.

Sec. 48.

There shall be elected at large in said city a city council consisting of nine members. At the first election under this act there shall be elected nine members of said city council. No voter shall vote for more than nine. The three candidates receiving the largest number of votes at said election shall hold office for three years, the three receiving the next largest number of votes shall hold office for two years, the three receiving the next largest number of votes shall hold office for one year. In case two or more persons elected should receive an equal number of votes those who are the seniors by age shall for the division into classes hereby required be classified as if they had received the larger number of votes in the order of ages. Therafter at each annual municipal election there shall be chosen at large three members of the city council to hold office for a term of three years. No voter shall vote for more than three. All said terms shall begin with the first Monday of February following the election.

Sec. 49.

Each member of the city council shall be paid an annual salary of fifteen hundred dollars; and no other sum shall be paid from the city treasury for or on account of any personal expenses directly or indirectly incurred by or in behalf of any member of said council.

Sec. 50.

The city council shall be the judge of the election and qualifications of its members; shall elect from its members by vote of a majority of all the members a president who when present shall preside at the meetings thereof; shall from time to time establish rules for its proceedings, and shall, when a vacancy occurs in the office of any member, elect by vote of a majority of all the members a registered voter of said city to fill the vacancy for the remainder of the municipal year. The vacancy for the remainder of the unexpired term shall be filled at the next annual municipal election, unless the vacancy occurs within two months prior to such municipal election, in which event the city council shall forthwith order a special election to fill the vacancy for the unexpired term. The member eldest in years shall preside until the president is chosen and in case of the absence of the president, until a presiding officer is chosen.

Sec. 51.

All elections by the city council under any provision of law shall be made by a viva voce vote, each member who is present answering to his name when it is called by the clerk or other proper officer, and stating the name of the person for whom he votes, or declining to vote as the case may be; and the clerk or other proper officer shall record every such vote. No such election shall be valid unless it is made as aforesaid.

Sec. 52.

No primary election or caucus for municipal offices shall be held hereafter in the city of Boston, and all laws relating to primary elections and caucuses for such offices in said city are hereby repealed.

Sec. 53.

Any male qualified registered voter in said city may be nominated for any municipal elective office in said city, and his name as such candidate shall be printed on the official ballot to be used at the municipal election: provided, that at or before five o'clock P. M. of the twenty-fifth day prior to such election nomination papers prepared and issued by the election commissioners, signed in person by at least five thousand registered voters in said city qualified to vote for such candidate at said election, shall be filed with said election commissioners, and the signatures on the same to the number required to make a nomination are subsequently certified by the election commissioners as hereinafter provided. Said nomination papers shall be in substantially the following form:

COMMONWEALTH OF MASSACHUSETTS
CITY OF BOSTON

NOMINATION PAPER.

The undersigned, registered voters of the City of Boston qualified to vote for a candidate for the office named below, in accordance with law, make the following nomination of candidates to be voted for at the election to be held in the City of Boston on January 19 .

NAME OF CANDIDATE. (Give first or middle name in full).	OFFICE FOR WHICH NOMINATED.	RESIDENCE. Street and Number, if any.

SIGNATURES AND RESIDENCES OF NOMINATORS.

We certify that we have not subscribed to more nominations of candidates for this office than there are persons to be elected thereto. In case of the death, withdrawal or incapacity of any of the above nominees, after written acceptance filed with the board of election commissioners, we authorize (names of a committee of not less than five persons) or a majority thereof as our representatives to fill the vacancy in the manner prescribed by law.

SIGNATURES OF NOMINATORS. To be made in person.	RESIDENCE MAY 1, OR, AS THE CASE MAY BE, APRIL 1.	WARD.	PREC.	PRESENT RESIDENCE.

ACCEPTANCE OF NOMINATION.

We accept the above nominations.

(Signature of Nominees.)

COMMONWEALTH OF MASSACHUSETTS.

Suffolk, ss.: Boston, 19

Then personally appeared who, I am satisfied, is one of the signers of the within nomination paper, and made oath that the statements therein contained are true to the best of his knowledge and belief, and that his post-office address is ——————

Before me,

—————— Justice of the Peace.

Sec. 54.

If a candidate nominated as aforesaid dies before the day of election, or withdraws his name from nomination, or is found to be ineligible, the vacancy may be filled by a committee of not less than five persons, or a majority thereof, if such committee be named, and so authorized in the nomination papers. Nomination papers shall not include candidates for more than one office except that not more than three or nine, as the case may be, candidates for city council may be included in one nomination paper, and not more than two candidates for school committee may be included in one nomination paper. Every voter may sign as many nomination papers for each office to be filled as there are persons to be elected thereto and no more. Nomination papers in each year shall be issued by the board of election commissioners on and after but not before the day next following the state election.

Sec. 55.

Women who are qualified to vote for a member of the school committee may be nominated as and sign nomination papers for candidates for that office in the manner and under the same provisions of law as men.

Sec. 56.

Sec. 56. The names of candidates appearing on nomination papers shall when filed be a matter of public record; but the nomination papers shall not be open to public inspection until after certification. After such nomination papers have been filed, the election commissioners shall certify thereon the number of signatures which are the names of registered voters in the city qualified to sign the same. They need not certify a greater number of names than are required to make a nomination, with one-fifth of such number added thereto. All such papers found not to contain a number of names so certified equivalent to the number required to make a nomination shall be invalid. The election commissioners shall complete such certification on or before five o'clock P. M. on the sixteenth day preceding the city election. Such certification shall not preclude any voter from filing objections as to the validity of the nomination. All withdrawals and objections to such nominations shall be filed with the election commissioners on or before five o'clock P. M. on the fourteenth day preceding the city election. All substitutions to fill vacancies caused by withdrawal or ineligibility shall be filed with the election commissioners on or before five o'clock P. M. on the twelfth day preceding the city election.

Sec. 57.

The name of each person who is nominated in compliance with law, together with his residence and the title and term of the office for which he is a candidate shall be printed on the official ballots at the municipal election, and the names of no other candidates shall be printed thereon. The names of candidates for the same office shall be printed upon the official ballot in the order in which they may be drawn by the board of election commissioners, whose duty it shall be to make such drawing and to give each candidate an opportunity to be present thereat personally or by one representative.

Sec. 58.

No ballot used at any annual or special municipal election shall have printed thereon any party or political designation or mark, and there shall not be appended to the name of any candidate any such party or political designation or mark, or anything showing how he was nominated or indicating his views or opinions.

Sec. 59.

On ballots to be used at annual or special municipal elections blank spaces shall be left at the end of each list of candidates for the different offices, equal to the number to be elected thereto, in which the voter may insert the name of any person not printed on the ballot for whom he desires to vote for such office.

Sec. 60.

All laws not inconsistent with the provisions of this act, governing nomination papers and nominations for, and elections of municipal officers in the city of Boston, shall so far as they may be applicable, govern the nomination papers, nominations and elections provided for in this act. The board of election commissioners shall be subject to the same penalties and shall have the same powers and duties, where not inconsistent with the provisions of this act, in relation to nomination papers, preparing and printing ballots, preparing for and conducting elections and counting, tabulating and determining the votes cast under the provisions of this act, as they have now in relation to municipal elections in said city.

Sec. 61.

The provisions of this act shall apply to any special municipal election held after the year nineteen hundred and nine in the city of Boston, except that nomination papers for offices to be filled at such elections shall be issued by the election commissioners on and after the day following the calling of said special election. Every special municipal election shall be held on a Tuesday not less than sixty days nor more than ninety days after the date of the order calling such special election.

Sec. 62.

All acts and parts of acts so far as inconsistent with this act are hereby repealed; all ordinances and parts of ordinances so far as inconsistent with this act are hereby annulled; and all acts and parts of acts affecting the city of Boston not inconsistent with the provisions of this act are continued in force; provided, however, that the provisions of chapter four hundred and forty of the acts of the year nineteen hundred and nine shall not apply to any election held hereunder prior to the first day of April in the year nineteen hundred and ten.

Sec. 63.

Sections one to fourteen, both inclusive, and sections twenty-seven, twenty-eight and thirty-one of this act shall take effect on the first Monday of February, in the year nineteen hundred and ten, excepting that so much of section one as is included in the first two sentences thereof, to and including the word "respectively," shall take effect upon the passage of this act; sections sixteen and twenty-three of this act shall take effect thirty days after the passage of the same; section thirty shall take effect ninety days after the passage of this act; and sections fifteen, seventeen to twenty-two, both inclusive, twenty-four to twenty-six, both inclusive, twenty-nine, thirty-two to thirty-six, both inclusive, forty-four, and sixty-two shall take effect upon the passage of this act.

[Approved June 11, 1909.]

CONSTITUTION OF OKLAHOMA

PORTION OF ARTICLE XVIII.

INITIATIVE AND REFERENDUM.

Sec. 4 (a).

The powers of the initiative and referendum, reserved by this Constitution to the people of the State and the respective Counties and Districts therein, are hereby reserved to the people of every municipal corporation now existing or which shall hereafter be created within this State, with reference to all legislative authority which it may exercise, and amendments to charters for its own government in accordance with the provisions of this Constitution.

Sec. 4 (b).

Every petition for either the initiative or referendum in the government of a municipal corporation shall be signed by a number of qualified electors residing within the territorial limits of such municipal corporation, equal to 25 per centum of the total number of votes cast at the next preceding election, and every such petition shall be filed with the chief executive officer of such municipal corporation.

Sec. 4 (c).

When such petition demands the enactment of an ordinance or other legal act other than the grant, extension or renewal of a franchise, the chief executive officer shall present the same to the legislative body of such corporation at its next meeting, and unless the said petition shall be granted more than thirty days before the next election at which any city officers are to be elected, the chief executive officer shall submit the said ordinance or act so petitioned for to the qualified electors at said election; and if a majority of said electors voting thereon shall vote for the same, it shall thereupon become in full force and effect.

Sec. 4 (d).

When such petition demands a referendum vote upon any ordinance or any other legal act other than the grant, extension, or renewal of a franchise, the chief executive officer shall submit said ordinance or act to the qualified electors of said corporation at the next succeeding general municipal election, and if, at said election, majority of the electors voting thereon shall not vote for the same, it shall thereupon stand repealed.

Sec. 4 (e).

When such petition demands an amendment to a charter, the chief executive officer shall submit such amendment to the qualified electors of said municipal corporation at the next election of any officers of said corporation, and if, at said election, a majority of said electors voting thereon shall vote for such amendment, the same shall thereupon become an amendment to and a part of said charter, when approved by the Governor and filed in the same manner and form as an original charter is required by the provisions of this article to be approved and filed.

Lightning Source UK Ltd.
Milton Keynes UK
UKHW020812130219
337247UK00012B/678/P